KW-409-386

Radical Politics
in South Asia

Edited by
Paul R. Brass
and
Marcus F. Franda

Contributors
Paul R. Brass
Marcus F. Franda
Robert L. Hardgrave, Jr.
Robert N. Kearney
Talukder Maniruzzaman
Mohan Ram

The MIT Press Cambridge, Massachusetts, and London, England

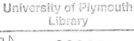

University of Plymouth
Library

Item N   900636137X

Shelfmark
320·954 RAD

MIT Press

0262020998

BRASS
RAD POL SOUTH ASIA

Copyright © 1973 by
The Massachusetts Institute of Technology

All rights reserved. No part of this book may be reproduced in any form or by any means, electronic or mechanical, including photocopying, recording, or by any information storage and retrieval system, without permission in writing from the publisher.

This book was designed by The MIT Press Design Department.
It was set in Monotype Times Roman
by Wolf Composition Company, Inc.
printed on Warren's Old Style Offset
by The Maple Press Company
and bound in G.S.B. "Winterset"
by The Maple Press Company
in the United States of America.

Library of Congress Cataloging in Publication Data

Brass, Paul R
    Radical politics in South Asia.

    (Studies in communism, revisionism, and revolution 19)
    Includes bibliographical references.
    1. Political parties—India—Addresses, essays, lectures. 2. Political parties—Bangladesh—Addresses, essays, lectures. 3. Radicalism—India—Addresses, essays, lectures. 4. Communism—India—Addresses, essays, lectures. I. Franda, Marcus F., joint author. II. Title. III. Series.
JQ298.A1B73   320.9′54′05   73-402
ISBN 0-262-02099-8

90 0636137 X

Radical Polit
in South Asia

University of Plymouth Library

Subject to status this item may be renewed
via your Voyager account

http://voyager.plymouth.ac.uk

Exeter tel: (01392) 475049
Exmouth tel: (01395) 255331
Plymouth tel: (01752) 232323

WITHDRAWN
FROM
UNIVERSITY OF PLYMOUTH
LIBRARY SERVICES

Center for International Studies,
Massachusetts Institute of Technology

Studies in Communism, Revisionism, and Revolution
(formerly *Studies in International Communism*)
William E. Griffith, general editor

To the People of Bangladesh

Contents

Illustrations

Maps

Figures

Tables

Contributors

Paul R. Brass is Associate Professor of Political Science and Asian Studies at the University of Washington. He received his B.A. from Harvard College and his M.A. and Ph.D. from the University of Chicago. He has visited South Asia three times since 1961 for field research and travel. He has published articles and contributions on Indian politics in various journals and books and is the author of *Factional Politics in an Indian State: The Congress Party in Uttar Pradesh.*

Marcus F. Franda is an Associate of the American Universities Field Staff, stationed in New Delhi. He received his B.A. from Beloit College and his M.A. and Ph.D. from the University of Chicago. He visited South Asia for field research twice before joining AUFS in December 1971 to report on India and Bangladesh. He has written numerous articles and contributions on Indian and Bengal politics, has translated several Bengali novels and short stories, and is the author of *Radical Politics in West Bengal* and *West Bengal and the Federalizing Process in India.*

Robert L. Hardgrave, Jr., is an Associate Professor of Government at the University of Texas at Austin. He received his B.A. from the University of Texas and his M.A. and Ph.D. from the University of Chicago. He has visited South Asia for field research twice since 1964, specializing in South Indian politics. He has written many articles and three books on India including *India: Government and Politics in a Developing Nation, The Nadars of Tamilnad: The Political Culture of a Community in Change,* and *The Dravidian Movement.*

Talukder Maniruzzaman is Associate Professor and Head of the Department of Political Science, Rajshahi University, Bangladesh. He received his B.A.(Hons.) and M.A. from the University of Dacca, Bangladesh, and his Ph.D. from Queen's University, Canada. He was in Bangladesh during the recent successful independence movement. He has published articles on politics, political parties, and political development in Pakistan and Bangladesh for various journals and is the author of *The Politics of Development: The Case of Pakistan (1947–1958).*

Mohan Ram is a journalist and scholar of Indian Communist politics. He was a university teacher before he turned to professional journalism in 1961. Among his books are: *Indian Communism: Split Within a Split* (1969), *Maoism in India* (1971), and *The Politics of Sino-Indian Confrontation* (forthcoming).

Robert N. Kearney is a Professor of Political Science at Syracuse University. He received his B.A. and M.A. degrees from the University of Iowa, studied at the School of Oriental and African Studies of the University of London, and received his Ph.D. from the University of California,

Los Angeles. He has visited Ceylon six times for field research since 1961. He has written numerous articles and contributions on politics in Ceylon in journals and books and is the author of three books, *Trade Unions and Politics in Ceylon, Communalism and Language in the Politics of Ceylon,* and *The Politics of Ceylon: Participation and Competition in Sri Lanka* (forthcoming).

Preface

This volume, based entirely on original research by the contributors, is the first book-length comparative study of regional radical movements in the major centers of radical political strength in the South Asian countries of India, Bangladesh, and Ceylon. In it, we have discussed the leading political parties, groups, and revolutionary activities of both the Communist and democratic Socialist movements. The main concern of the volume is how the radical Left parties have adapted to their local environments and have succeeded or failed in building political strength. The focus is on the indigenous roots of South Asian radicalism rather than on the international ties of the radical parties.

The regional studies concentrate upon the leading movements in the strongest centers of radical politics in South Asia—in the Indian states of Kerala, West Bengal, and Andhra, which have been the primary sources of Communist strength in India; in Bihar, which has been a stronghold of the radical Socialist movement and of the CPI; in Bangladesh; and in Ceylon. The introductory essay attempts both to draw together and compare the information provided by the contributors on their regions and also to discuss more broadly the development of radical politics in the entire South Asian region, building upon previous research and writing by other scholars.

As we worked on and wrote the contributions to this volume, dramatic changes affected all three countries. In Ceylon, a revolution led by young people burst forth in April 1971 against the government and was quelled only with difficulty and with foreign support. In December 1971, Bangladesh emerged out of rebellion and war between India and Pakistan as a new nation and the first successful secessionist movement in the postcolonial era. In India, Mrs. Gandhi consolidated her power over the Congress, and the Congress returned to a dominant position in Indian politics at the center and in the states in parliamentary elections in 1971 and legislative assembly elections in 1972. The radical Left has both influenced and been influenced by these momentous changes in recent years. Insofar as it has been possible to do so in the face of events so close to us in time, we have attempted to assess their importance for the future of radicalism in South Asian politics.

This volume represents collaborative research across both ideological and international boundaries. Four of the contributors are political scientists from universities in the United States; one has been both a scholar of Indian Communist movements and a participant in them; and one of our contributors is head of the political science department at the University of Rajshahi in Bangladesh. The contributions reflect our different backgrounds and perspectives; but the volume has, we hope, an underlying coherence of subject matter and theme.

The project was begun in November 1967 with the sponsorship of William E. Griffith and the encouragement of Myron Weiner, both of the Center for International Studies at M.I.T. The research for and the writing and editing of the volume were carried out with grants provided by the Center for International Studies at M.I.T. from Ford Foundation funds, from the Research Council of Colgate University, and from the South Asia Committee in the Institute for Comparative and Foreign Area Studies of the University of Washington. The editors express their appreciation to Professors Weiner and Griffith for their unfailing support and guidance at critical moments in the development of the project and of the present volume.

The editors are also grateful to several people who read and commented on drafts of the various contributions to the volume: Harry Blair, Linda Brass, Biplab Dasgupta, Kenneth M. Dolbeare, Carolyn Elliott, John Osgood Field, Vonnie Franda, Joel Gandelman, Pavle Jevremovic, W. H. Morris-Jones, Soman Mukherjee, M. Rasheeduzzaman, James R. Townsend, and the members of the South Asia seminar at the University of Washington. Excellent secretarial assistance was provided at various stages in the preparation of this volume by Ms. Roberta Nelson and Mrs. Rose Shablak.

Paul R. Brass
Marcus F. Franda
19 April 1972

Abbreviations

AICC	All-India Congress Committee
AICCCR	All-India Coordination Committee of Communist Revolutionaries
AID	Agency for International Development
AIKS	All-India Kisan Sabha
AISF	All-India Students Federation
AITUC	All-India Trade Union Congress
AL	Awami League
APCCCR	Andhra Pradesh Coordination Committee of Communist Revolutionaries
APPWA	All-Pakistan Progressive Writers Association
ASC	Asian Socialist Conference
BKD	Bharatiya Kranti Dal
CBI	Central Bureau of Intelligence
CCCR	Coordination Committee of Communist Revolutionaries
CCP	Ceylon Communist Party
CEC	Central Executive Committee
CENTO	Central Treaty Organization
CIA	Central Intelligence Agency
CITU	Centre of Indian Trade Unions
CMPO	Calcutta Metropolitan Planning Organization
CMU	Ceylon Mercantile Union
COP	Combined Opposition Parties
CP	Communist Party
CPC	Communist Party of China
CPGB	Communist Party of Great Britain
CPI	Communist Party of India
CPM	Communist Party of India (Marxist)
CPML	Communist Party of India (Marxist-Leninist)
CPP	Communist Party of Pakistan
CPSU	Communist Party of the Soviet Union
CRP	Communist Revolutionary Party
CRP	Central Reserve Police
CSP	Congress Socialist Party
CTUF	Ceylon Trade Union Federation
DMK	Dravida Munetra Kazhagham
EBCP	East Bengal Communist Party
EBR	East Bengal Regiment
EBSL	East Bengal Students League
EBWM	East Bengal Workers Movement

EMS	E. M. S. Namboodiripad
EPAL	East Pakistan Awami League
EPCP	East Pakistan Communist Party
EPCPML	East Pakistan Communist Party (Marxist-Leninist)
EPNAP	East Pakistan National Awami Party
EPR	East Pakistan Rifles
EPSU	East Pakistan Students Union
FB	Forward Bloc
FBM	Forward Bloc (Marxist)
FBR	Forward Bloc (Ruikar)
GL	Gurkha League
HMS	Hind Mazdoor Sabha
IAS	Indian Administrative Service
ICS	Indian Civil Service
ILO	International Labor Organization
INA	Indian National Army
INDF	Indian National Democratic Front
INTUC	Indian National Trade Union Congress
ISP	Indian Socialist Party
JCTUO	Joint Committee of Trade Union Organizations
JKD	Jana Kranti Dal
JVP	Janatha Vimukthi Peramuna
KLP	Krishikar Lok Party
KMPP	Kisan Mazdoor Praja Party
KPCC	Kerala Pradesh Congress Committee
KPR	K.P.R. Gopalan
KSP	Kerala Socialist Party
KTP	Karshaka Thozhilai Party
LCD	Loktantric Congress Dal
LSS	Lok Sevak Sangh
LSSP	Lanka Sama Samaja Party
LSSP(R)	Lanka Sama Samaja Party (Revolutionary)
MEP	Mahajana Eksath Peramuna
ML	Muslim League
MLA	Member of the Legislative Assembly
MNA	Member of the National Assembly
MP	Member of Parliament
MPA	Member of the Provincial Assembly
NAP	National Awami Party
NEFA	Northeast Frontier Agency

NWFP	Northwest Frontier Province
PCC	Pradesh Congress Committee
PDF	People's Democratic Front
PDM	Pakistan Democratic Movement
PIA	Pakistan International Airlines
PRI	Party Realism Index
PSP	Praja Socialist Party
PVD	Progressive Vidhayak Dal
RCC	Revolutionary Communist Committee
RCPI	Revolutionary Communist Party of India
RPI	Republican Party of India
RRP	Ram Rajya Parishad
RSP	Revolutionary Socialist Party
SAC	Students Action Committee
SCF	Scheduled Caste Federation
SDC	Srikakulam District Committee
SEATO	Southeast Asia Treaty Organization
SLFP	Sri Lanka Freedom Party
SNDP	Sri Narayana Dharma Paripalana Yogam
SP	Socialist Party
SSP	Samyukta Socialist Party
SUC	Socialist Unity Centre
SVD	Samyukta Vidhayak Dal
UF	United Front
ULDF	United Left Democratic Front
ULF	United Left Front
UNP	United National Party
UP	Uttar Pradesh
VLSSP	Viplavakari Lanka Sama Samaja Party
WPI	Worker's Party of India

South Asia

Bangladesh

Bihar

West Bengal

Andhra
Pradesh

Kerala

Ceylon

South Asia

1
Political Parties of the Radical Left in South Asian Politics

Paul R. Brass

Parties of the radical Left in South Asia have not received the attention they deserve from political scientists concerned with South Asian politics. Two book-length scholarly studies of Indian Communism were published by political scientists more than a decade ago.[1] Myron Weiner's *Party Politics in India*[2] surveyed the history of the Socialist parties in India up through the early 1950s but was concerned primarily with only one aspect of Socialist and party politics in India, the phenomenon of frequent party splits and mergers. There have been a few scholarly articles and portions of books devoted to the South Asian Communist and Socialist parties from time to time, but a decade passed after 1959 without a single book-length study of leftist politics in South Asia written by an academic political scientist. Only in the last few years has major attention been paid to the analysis of leftist politics in this region. A history of the Lanka Sama Samaja Party (LSSP) in Ceylon was published in 1968, and a history of the splits in the Communist movement in India was published in 1969.[3] Marcus Franda's *Radical Politics in West Bengal,* published in 1971, was the first major academic study of a regional leftist movement in India *ever* published.[4] The present volume is the first book-length comparative study of regional radical movements in the major centers of radical political strength in the South Asian countries of India, Bangladesh, and Ceylon.

There are some fairly obvious reasons for this neglect of radical politics in South Asia. One is that the Indian National Congress has so dominated Indian political life that many political scientists have been more attracted to explaining its success than in examining its less successful rivals. Second, the most successful challenges to Congress dominance and the most dramatic political movements in South Asia have been movements based upon regional languages, religions, and cultures. These too have

---

[1] John H. Kautsky, *Moscow and the Communist Party of India: A Study in the Postwar Evolution of International Communist Strategy* (New York: Technology Press of M.I.T. and Wiley, 1956); and Gene D. Overstreet and Marshall Windmiller, *Communism in India* (Berkeley: University of California Press, 1959).
[2] Myron Weiner, *Party Politics in India: The Development of a Multi-Party System* (Princeton, N.J.: Princeton University Press, 1957).
[3] George Jan Lerski, *Origins of Trotskyism in Ceylon: A Documentary History of the Lanka Sama Samaja Party 1935–1942* (Stanford, Calif.: Hoover Institution on War, Revolution and Peace, 1968) and Mohan Ram, *Indian Communism: Split Within a Split* (Delhi: Vikas Publications, 1969).
[4] Marcus F. Franda, *Radical Politics in West Bengal* (Cambridge, Mass.: M.I.T. Press, 1971).

absorbed the attention of the few academic political scientists concerned with South Asian affairs. Third, the subject of radical politics has been a sensitive one, especially for American scholars in India and more so in the military-dominated regime of Pakistan. Fourth, many young scholars have simply not wanted to touch a subject so tainted by Cold War ideology and so often lacking in any other kind of analytical perspective.

Many of these reasons for the past neglect of radical politics in South Asia are no longer valid. Although Mrs. Gandhi's Indian National Congress has been restored to a dominant position both at the center and in most of the Indian states by the 1971 elections to the Lok Sabha and by the 1972 legislative assembly elections, many non-Congress parties have also held power in the last five years. After the 1967 General Elections, non-Congress governments came to power in more than half the Indian states. In Kerala, West Bengal, Bihar, Uttar Pradesh, and Punjab, parties of the radical Left were major components of those non-Congress governments. In Kerala and West Bengal, the Communist Party of India (Marxist) has been the leading party in electoral support, if not always in number of seats won. Consequently, Congress dominance has lately been challenged in the Indian states and not only by parties based upon regional sentiment. Punjab and Tamil Nadu have been dominated by regionally oriented political parties expert in the manipulation of cultural symbols, but Kerala and West Bengal have been more influenced by leftist-oriented political parties, whose leaders speak the language and use the symbols of Marxism.

The subject of radical politics remains a sensitive one in South Asia, but Cold War ideology and propaganda have lately been replaced by more detached and analytical perspectives. Social scientists have been using more of the tools of their disciplines in comparing radical movements in different areas of the world and attempting to define the conditions for the success or failure of such movements rather than simply operating on the tired assumptions of Cold War propagandists. Area specialists have also altered the perspective on radical movements by their greater concern for the indigenous roots and aspects of radical politics rather than with the international aspects. While each of the contributors to this volume has his own ideological point of view, we have all at least attempted to approach our subject with detachment and with the tools and perspectives of political scientists and South Asian area specialists.

The questions and topics that have concerned us in this volume reflect those perspectives. We have focused upon the major parties of the radical Left in South Asia, that is, upon those parties that seek in their long-term ideological goals a fundamental transformation of their societies in the

direction of socialism and communism, including goals of social ownership of the means of production in their societies, equality, and mass
political participation. We have concentrated our attention upon those
regions of South Asia where such parties have been strongest—Kerala,
West Bengal, and Andhra for the Communist parties; Bihar for the Communist Party of India (CPI) and the radical Socialists; Ceylon for the
Communist, Trotskyite, and Marxist parties; and Bangladesh for the Communist parties and the National Awami Party. Although we have touched
upon the question of the international ties of the radical parties, the main
concern in this volume is not how the Communist and other parties relate
to Peking or Moscow but how they have adapted and succeeded or not
succeeded in building political strength in their local environments.

The emphasis in this volume is upon organized political parties whose
commitments to one or another version of socialism or communism are
explicit in their names and party constitutions. Much of the research
and analysis reported here deals with the electoral and parliamentary
activities of the leftist parties, but the contributors have also given attention to the agitational, extraparliamentary activities of these parties and
to the recent adoption of violent revolutionary tactics by the Marxist-
Leninist and Maoist groups. The relative emphasis given to the electoral
and parliamentary activities of the parties of the radical Left in this volume does not reflect only the easier availability of information on such activities in South Asia, but it also reflects the importance given to them
by most of the radical parties themselves in this region of the world.

The term "socialism" is common currency in the South Asian political
arena. More parties in South Asia claim to be "socialist" than anything
else. It is a word comparable to "democratic" or "liberal" in Europe and
North America in its frequency of usage and vagueness of content. Consequently, not every party that claims to be "socialist" is necessarily a
party of the radical Left in fact. The Indian National Congress, for example, adopted a socialist orientation in its party conference at Nagpur
in 1954, and it has been adopting a leftist posture under the leadership
of Mrs. Gandhi in recent years. Moreover, many Congressmen have
been more committed to radical change than many members of the more
explicitly "socialist" parties. Yet, the Indian National Congress has not
been included as a party of the radical Left in this volume for two
reasons. First, its social composition and its ideology are more inclusive
than those of any other major, organized party in India. It still includes
classes, groups, and individuals whose political orientations cover a
spectrum from far Right to far Left. Second, whatever its pretensions,
the Congress has clearly been the Center party in Indian politics in

fact—not only in ideology and social composition, but as the leading party in government. Its Center position has been partly a function of the attitudes taken towards it by other parties, which fall broadly into three groups—those representing cultural or regional or ethnic interests that claim that Congress policies are discriminating against such particular interests; those that claim that Congress politics are promoting too radical social change; and those that claim that Congress politics are not sufficiently progressive or are not really implementing socialism in practice. A more precise definition of the scope of this volume for India then is that the emphasis is upon the parties and movements of the radical Left whose commitments to one or another version of socialism or communism are explicit *and* whose self-definition places them to the left of Congress on social and economic issues.

In Ceylon, there have been two Center parties. One, the United National Party (UNP) has been clearly Center-Right; the other, the Sri Lanka Freedom Party (SLFP) has been Center-Left. Consequently, the scope of the coverage of Ceylon parties in this volume includes parties that define themselves to the left of the SLFP. For Bangladesh, the Awami League is the Center party and our coverage includes parties to its left. Thus, the theme of this entire volume may be seen as the prospects for radical change in a direction to the left of the existing political centers in South Asia.

How far the self-definition of the parties of the radical Left conforms to reality is another moot question. It will be seen that the ideologies and organization of radical Left parties in South Asia differ greatly and that, by other kinds of criteria than those used here, one or another political party might have been excluded from the analysis. Keeping this problem in mind, one can only caution the reader to note that the grounds for inclusion and exclusion used here have been self-definition to the left of the existing political center.

Two main sets of questions run through this volume. One set relates to the conditions for the success or failure of parties of the radical Left in developing societies. What kinds of leadership have developed in these parties? To what extent, if at all, have the radical parties succeeded in recruiting to leadership positions members of the classes and castes whose interests they seek to defend and represent? How successful have the radical parties been in building stable and effective organizations? To what extent have the radical parties succeeded in relating Marxist-derived ideologies to South Asian conditions? From which regions, classes, and groups do the radical parties derive their main support?

The second set of questions relates to the functioning of radical and revolutionary parties in a parliamentary system. What happens to revolutionary parties when they have access to power like other parties in a parliamentary system? Do they seek to subvert and monopolize the institutions of government to which they have access or do they tend to become domesticated and reformist? Finally, can radical social and economic change be institutionalized in a parliamentary system in which Communist and other radical parties play a significant role?

Not all the contributors to this volume have addressed themselves to all these questions, in part because not all these questions are relevant in every region of South Asia. However, these themes and questions are recurrent throughout the various contributions. I have tried in this introductory essay to draw these questions together in a systematic manner by presenting both an overview of radical politics in the South Asian countries and a comparative analysis of the regional strength of the radical movements. In doing so, I have drawn upon the data and arguments of my colleagues who have contributed to this volume and upon the broader research and literature on radical politics in the South Asian countries.

The basic argument of this introductory essay comprises four interrelated propositions. The first is that indigenous factors have been more important than international influences in the development of both the Communist and Socialist movements in the South Asian countries. The second is that the requirements of political adjustment to national, regional, and local environments have been more important influences upon the strategies and tactics of the parties of the radical Left than ideological beliefs. The third proposition is that political adjustment among the older and best-organized radical parties of the Left in South Asia, outside of Bangladesh, has led them increasingly in the direction of reformism rather than revolution. Finally, the tendency toward reformism has become so marked among the older radical parties that new political formations have been developing in recent years that have attempted to reintroduce revolutionary aspirations and actions into South Asian politics.

Origins and Development

The Communist and Socialist parties of South Asia have their origins in the 1920s and 1930s. In the early 1920s, scattered groups of Communists working in India and abroad were linked together and to the Communist International by M. N. Roy. However, Roy's influence as a link among Indian Communists and with Moscow soon declined and was replaced by the Communist Party of Great Britain, whose emissaries played an important role in the officially recognized founding of the Communist Party of India (CPI) in 1925.[5] Until the 1930s, the CPI in India consisted of a number of widely scattered semiconspiratorial groups operating largely independently of, and in opposition to, the main nationalist forces in the subcontinent. In contrast, the contemporary Socialist parties of India can trace their origins more precisely to a specific founding conference in Patna in May 1934, when the Congress Socialist Party was founded as an organized group within the main nationalist organization, the Indian National Congress.

At first, the Communist and Socialist groups were antagonistic to each other and worked separately. However, in 1936, the Communists adopted united-front tactics and succeeded in gaining admission into the Congress Socialist Party (CSP). In the period between their admission into the CSP in January 1936 and their expulsion from it in March 1940, Communists succeeded in gaining control over the state units of the CSP in south India—particularly in Andhra, Tamil Nadu, and Kerala.[6]

The Second World War had a profound impact upon the development of both major segments of the radical Left in India, both of which acted independently of the predominant leadership of the Indian National Congress. At first, the Communists, along with other nationalists, opposed India's participation in the British war effort. However, the transformation of the war into a People's War, with the entry of the Soviet Union into it in 1941, turned the CPI line around to one of support for the British war effort. In July 1942 the CPI was legalized.[7] During the war years, the CPI built its party organization and mass organizations so that, by the end of the war and at Independence, the CPI was a major organized force in Indian politics. On the other hand, the CPI support for the British war effort and then, later, its alliance with the Muslim

[5] Overstreet and Windmiller, *Communism in India*, pp. 43, 80–81; S. G. Sardesai, *Why Communists?* (Bombay: Popular Prakashan, [1966]), pp. 7–10; *Proceedings of the Seventh Congress of the Communist Party of India, Bombay, 13–23 December 1964: Documents* (New Delhi: CPI, 1965), p. 195 (hereafter cited as *Seventh Congress Documents*).

[6] On CPI-CSP relations in this period, see, among other sources, Weiner, *Party Politics in India*, pp. 26–27; Hari Kishore Singh, *A History of the Praja Socialist Party (1934–59)* (Lucknow: Narendra Prakashan, 1959), pp. 51, 55, 61, 63–64, 66–68; Overstreet and Windmiller, *Communism in India*, pp. 166–167, 179; and Madhu Limaye, *Why Samyukta Socialist?* (Bombay: Popular Prakashan, [1966]), p. 9.

[7] Overstreet and Windmiller, *Communism in India*, p. 206.

League, which also supported the British during the war years, caused the estrangement of the Communists from the mainstream of Indian nationalist sentiment.[8] However, even this disadvantage of Communist activities during the Second World War was felt less in the south where the CPI's support for regional language movements mattered more than its alienation from the Indian National Congress and where the problems of Hindu-Muslim relations and of Pakistan were less keenly felt. In the north, in contrast, CPI support for both the war effort and the Muslim League is still remembered by many Hindu nationalists with resentment.

The Socialist movement also departed from official Congress policies during the Second World War, but with different consequences. The older Congress leaders had ambivalent feelings concerning the British war effort. They opposed the way in which India had been drawn into the war without consultation, but their sympathies were with the British and they were reluctant to launch a major civil disobedience campaign. In any case, the British authorities wasted no time in arresting and jailing the entire older leadership of the Congress. Consequently, during the war, leadership of the major anti-British campaign, known as the Quit India movement, fell to the hands of the younger, more radical, and more militant Congress Socialists.[9] The August 1942 Quit India movement was a movement led predominantly by the Congress Socialists and was most successful in the north Indian states of Bihar and Uttar Pradesh. Although the Quit India movement departed from official Congress policy in the deliberate and extensive use of violence by the Socialists, it was a movement in the mainstream of Indian nationalism, carried out within the broad goals of Congress policy of the time. It is largely for this reason that the Socialist parties of north India retain a nationalist respectability that the Communists lost at that time. The combination of Socialist dominance of the 1942 movement and Communist support for the war effort and the Muslim League in this period also largely explains the greater strength of the contemporary Socialist parties and the relative weakness of the Communist parties in the northern Hindi-speaking states.

After the war and Independence, the Communist and Socialist movements continued to follow entirely different paths. The CPI in the early postwar years adopted a line of violent struggle, which led to its suppression by the government of India. The party reverted to a peaceful

---

[8] Ibid., pp. 215, 218–219.
[9] Hari Kishore Singh, *History of the PSP*, pp. 79–81.

line in time for the 1952 General Elections, when the party demonstrated its strength in the southern states, particularly Kerala (then Travancore-Cochin) and Andhra (Hyderabad), although it also showed strength in West Bengal and Punjab. In the northern, Hindi-speaking states, the CPI had almost no strength in the First General Elections.

The CPI, unlike the Socialist parties, retained its unity long into the post-Independence period until 1964, when the first major split in the Communist movement occurred, leading to the formation of a second party, the Communist Party of India (Marxist) or CPM. In 1967, a second split occurred, this time from the CPM, leading to the formation of the Communist Party of India (Marxist-Leninist) or CPML. The causes and consequences of these party splits will be discussed in detail below.

The Socialist movement in post-Independence India was fed from two different original sources. The first source was the Congress Socialist Party, which formally seceded from the Congress and took the name Socialist Party (SP) in 1948.[10] The second source consisted largely of non-Socialist factional leaders who had been defeated at the all-India level and in several of the states in struggles for power in the Congress and who defected from the Congress to contest the 1951 General Elections as the Kisan Mazdoor Praja Party (KMPP).[11] After the 1951 elections, these two organizations merged into the Praja Socialist Party (PSP).[12] The more militant, anti-Congress members of the PSP split off in 1955 to re-form the Socialist Party.[13] The two Socialist parties retained a separate existence until June 1964, when they merged into a new entity called the Samyukta Socialist Party (SSP). In January 1965, however, some dissatisfied PSP members split off and revived the PSP, leaving the bulk of Socialist members in the new SSP. In August 1971, the SSP and PSP leaderships merged the two parties once again into a united Socialist Party (SP). Although some discontented elements in the PSP retained the old name and continued to function separately, the SP was the only Socialist group with significant national strength in India in 1972.

The Left movements in East Bengal and in Ceylon have also been divided into two segments, but with historical experiences quite different

[10] Weiner, *Party Politics in India*, chap. 3; and Hari Kishore Singh, *History of the PSP*, chaps. 4 and 5.
[11] Weiner, *Party Politics in India*, chap. 4; and Hari Kishore Singh, *History of the PSP*, pp. 128–129.
[12] Weiner, *Party Politics in India*, chap. 5; Hari Kishore Singh, *History of the PSP*, chap. 7; Limaye, *Why Samyukta Socialist?*, p. 11.
[13] Limaye, *Why Samyukta Socialist?*, pp. 11–13.

from those of the Indian movements. The East Pakistan Communist Party (EPCP) was part of the Bengal CPI until partition. After partition, the EPCP suffered severe handicaps that inhibited its development.[14] Most of the EPCP members were Hindus, who were not able to organize the Muslim masses of East Bengal, but rather suffered from communal antagonisms of the post-Independence period. Most EPCP members in fact migrated to West Bengal at the time of the communal violence in Bengal in 1950. In addition, the East Bengal party suffered even more than the West Bengal party from the consequences of the militant strategy pursued between 1947 and 1951. Finally, the opportunities for political organization were far more severely restricted under the military regime in Pakistan from 1958 until 1969. In recent years, a host of new Communist political formations and factions have been formed within and outside of the former EPCP. They are described in detail in Maniruzzaman's contribution to this volume.

The non-Communist Left in East Bengal does not have a very long history. It is represented primarily by the two wings of the National Awami Party,[15] which was first founded in 1957 by Maulana Abdul Hamid Khan Bhashani as a splinter from the Awami League. Before the military regime was established, the NAP was an important party in Pakistan politics. After 1962, it joined in the developing opposition to Ayub Khan and his regime, supporting Miss Fatimah Jinnah against him in the 1965 presidential election. The party has been severely weakened since 1967 by a split, out of which developed two National Awami parties, one led by Muzaffar Ahmad and the other by Maulana Bhasani. The NAP(B) of Maulana Bhasani has been the stronger of the two parties in East Bengal, but it took an ambivalent position concerning participation in the 1970 elections and won no seats. Since the breakup of Pakistan in 1971, the Bangladesh, or Muzaffar, wing of NAP(W) has come to be known as NAP(M).

The history of the radical Left as an organized political force in Ceylon goes back to December 1935, when the founding conference of the Lanka Sama Samaja Party (Ceylon Socialist Party) or LSSP was held.[16]

[14] This analysis is derived from Marcus F. Franda, "Communism and Regional Politics in East Pakistan," *Asian Survey* 10, no. 7 (July 1970), 588–606.
[15] This account is based upon M. Rashiduzzaman, "The National Awami Party of Pakistan: Leftist Politics in Crisis," *Pacific Affairs* 43, no. 3 (Fall 1970), 394–409; see also Craig Baxter, "Pakistan Votes—1970," *Asian Survey* 11, no. 3 (March 1971), 207–208.
[16] Robert N. Kearney, "The Communist Parties of Ceylon: Rivalry and Alliance," in Robert A. Scalapino, ed., *The Communist Revolution in Asia: Tactics, Goals, and Achievements*, 2d ed. (Englewood Cliffs, N.J.: Prentice-Hall, 1969), p. 392.

The Ceylon Socialist movement has been noteworthy for its ideological and formal organizational connections with Trotskyism and the Trotskyite Fourth International.[17] During the Second World War, the non-Trotskyites in the LSSP broke away to support the war effort and to form the Ceylon Communist Party (CCP). For a time after Independence, these parties were the leading opposition parties against the dominant United National Party (UNP).[18] The rise of the Sri Lanka Freedom Party (SLFP) as the main party of opposition to the UNP, and lately the stronger of the two, has placed the radical Left parties in the position of desired and often essential coalition partners in SLFP-dominated governments. Both wings of the radical Left have suffered from splits in the last two decades. Two Communist and three Socialist parties were in existence by 1958.[19] The rightist Ceylon Communist Party and the predominant wing of the old Lanka Sama Samaja Party have, since 1964, worked in alliance with the SLFP, while the more revolutionary elements from both parties have withdrawn to form splinter organizations. The Lanka Sama Samaja Party has been expelled from the Fourth International for its participation in SLFP governments.[20]

This brief outline of the origins and development of radical Left parties in South Asia reveals the following common features. In all three countries, leftist politics and political organizations have had a long history, going back to the 1920s in India and Pakistan and to the 1930s in Ceylon. Also, in all three countries, two wings of the radical Left have developed—one Communist, the other Socialist—each of which has in turn splintered into two or more parties. The period just before and during the Second World War was the period of the break of all organizational connections between Communist and Socialist parties in South Asia. Only in East Bengal has there remained some interpenetration of Communist party and National Awami Party cadres. The period since Independence has seen many splits of old Left parties and the formation of new ones in both major segments of the radical Left. The process of development of old parties, of splintering from them, and of the formation of new parties has produced a rich variety of leftist groups in South Asia. The remainder of this essay will be devoted to examining similarities and differences among them in leadership, organization, ideology,

---

[17] See Lerski, *Origins of Trotskyism in Ceylon.*
[18] Kearney, "Communist Parties of Ceylon," pp. 392–393.
[19] Ibid. and Kearney's chapter in this volume.
[20] George J. Lerski, "The Twilight of Ceylonese Trotskyism," *Pacific Affairs* 43, no. 3 (Fall 1970), 384.

and popular support and to an assessment of their impact upon radical political change in South Asia.

Leadership and Organization

Leadership Composition

It hardly needs stressing that communism and socialism are supposed to represent preeminently the interests of the working class, which is also supposed to act as the vanguard of revolution and provide leadership for it. Working class representation has, in fact, often been strong in the Communist and some Socialist parties in the Soviet Union and Western Europe. Elsewhere, however, it is now widely recognized that the leadership of radical Left parties has been drawn from other than proletarian sources. Burks has emphasized the nonproletarian character of Communist party leadership in the countries of Eastern Europe, where the leadership has been "dominated by bourgeois elements, primarily professional," with only "minority representation" from the urban proletariat.[21] Ninety percent of a sample of Greek activist Communist leaders were found to have come "from families of substance."[22] The typical Greek Communist leader in this sample was a rural-born member of such a family who had moved from his birthplace into a professional occupation in the city.[23] Asian Communist and Socialist party leaders also have rarely come from proletarian or even poor peasant origins. Robert A. Scalapino and most of the contributors to his volume on Asian Communism have emphasized that Communist party leaders in most Asian countries have tended to be of elite status and to come from high-income families.[24]

Scalapino has also remarked upon the different kinds and styles of leadership that have developed in Asian Communist parties. He has argued that Asian Communist parties have tended to be dominated in their early stages of development by "ideologues," men who have been attracted to communism for intellectual reasons and who have little skill in mass politics. In the second stage of growth in Asian Communist parties, when they begin to contest seriously for power, the leadership comes to be dominated by "activist" leaders with organizational skills and an

[21] R. V. Burks, *The Dynamics of Communism in Eastern Europe* (Princeton, N.J.: Princeton University Press, 1961), p. 22.
[22] Ibid., p. 29.
[23] Ibid., p. 27.
[24] Robert A. Scalapino, "Communism in Asia: Toward a Comparative Analysis," in Scalapino, *Communist Revolution in Asia*, pp. 14–15, 33.

orientation to action. When Communist parties become consolidated and offer attractive inducements to their members, a "careerist" leadership emerges, attracted to the party as a vehicle for "personal advancement." Scalapino argues that activist leadership predominates in most contemporary Asian Communist parties but that the South Asian Communist parties are only beginning to develop an activist segment in otherwise ideologue-dominated parties.[25]

Although there are important differences among the parties of the radical Left in South Asia and also between regions in both the socioeconomic composition and type of leadership, the range of variation is not very broad. Most South Asian parties of the Left have been dominated by middle and upper class leaders of elite caste status, but some of the parties in some regions have integrated into leadership positions men of lower class and caste status. Also, most of the Left parties have been founded and dominated in their early stages by intellectual leaders, but most of the stronger parties contain activist and populist leaders also, with organizational skills and mass appeal. For example, it is apparent from Hardgrave's account of the Kerala Communist leaders that many of them are well read in Communist and Socialist literature. E. M. S. Namboodiripad is a prolific author of theoretical books and pamphlets. Yet, Hardgrave has stressed that the Kerala Communist leaders tend to have a "'practical" rather than an intellectual orientation and that leaders of low-caste origins have come into leadership positions in the Communist parties there. Franda has emphasized the elitist and intellectual character of Bengali communism and the failure of the party to integrate low-caste men into leadership positions in the party, but the West Bengal CPM also has had skillful organizational direction, particularly from the party secretary Pramode Dasgupta. Some of the Andhra Communist leaders have been intellectual leaders, but most have been mass leaders. In Bihar, the two leading radical Left parties have not differed greatly in the socioeconomic background of their leaderships on the whole, but the most prominent leaders of the two parties have come from different class backgrounds and take distinct kinds of approaches to politics. The CPI has had an elitist, intellectual, and organizationally oriented leadership; whereas the SSP leaders have come from low-caste or low-income families, have been more populist than intellectual, and have been skilled in mass politics more than in building organizations. Not surprisingly, therefore, the SSP

[25] Ibid., pp. 7, 13–16.

has had the greater popular support in Bihar, while the CPI has had the stronger organizational apparatus. The Ceylon and East Bengal Marxist parties have recruited their leaderships from upper and middle class and elite status groups. Both the LSSP and CP leaders have come for the most part from "upper-middle class professionals and intellectuals, often from prominent and wealthy families," with only a few lower-level leaders from white-collar or industrial occupations.[26] Similarly, the party leaders of both segments of the East Pakistan National Awami Party have come from middle-class backgrounds.

Clearly, like the East European and most Asian Communist parties, the radical Left parties in South Asia tend to draw their leaderships from nonproletarian classes, primarily from urban professional and intellectual groups and from rural families of wealth and social prominence. Intellectual leadership also tends to be prominent, if not dominant, in most South Asian radical parties. Nor is an elitist-intellectual leadership necessarily a hindrance to success, as the West Bengal Communist parties have shown. Still, it does seem true more often than not that the more successful Left parties in South Asia have been infused with low-caste and lower-class leadership elements and have developed prominent leaders with either organizational skills or a flair for mass politics.

In most of South Asia, however, the development of new leadership elements and skills in the radical Left parties has just begun. Leaders from working-class and peasant origins are a minority of the leadership of all radical Left parties in South Asia, though the Kerala CPM and the Bihar SSP have had more such leaders than most radical Left parties in the area. There is, however, one distinction between the leaderships of the Communist and democratic Socialist parties that is fairly uniform throughout South Asia, namely, the relative prominence of whole-time workers in the party who have never had any vocation other than politics. Such people have overwhelmingly dominated both the CPI and the CPM, much more so than either the SSP or the PSP. Fifty percent of Bihar CPI leaders compared to only 10 percent of SSP leaders have been party professionals (see table 6.10). Among the delegates to the Seventh Congress of the CPI in 1964, 443 were whole-timers and only 64 had other vocations than politics.[27] In the Fourth Lok Sabha, 80 percent of the CPM MPs and 73.7 percent of the CPI MPs, but only 42.1 percent

[26] Citation from Kearney's contribution to this volume, p. 420.
[27] *Proceedings of the Seventh Congress of the Communist Party of India, Bombay, 13–23 December 1964, Vol. 3: Discussions* (New Delhi: CPI, 1965), pp. 72–76 (hereafter cited as *Seventh Congress Discussions*).

of the SSP MPs and 15.4 percent of the PSP MPs were party professionals.[28] The CPI and the CPM have combined intellectual and organizational leadership elements, whereas the SSP has emphasized populist leadership and has been weaker in both intellectual and organizational skills. The PSP has emphasized intellectual leadership above all and has had fewer mass leaders or leaders with organizational skills than other parties of the radical Left in South Asia.

Organization

CHARACTERISTICS

Parties of the radical Left in South Asia have developed different types of organizational structures and modes of operation with regard to common problems of party organization. The parties differ in the location of their strategic decision-making units, in the role of leadership in the party and the relationship between leaders and rank-and-file party members, in attitudes toward organizational growth, and in the importance attached to mass and front organizations. The different organizational structures and styles adopted by the radical Left parties have had different consequences for the growth and development of the parties.

Two basic problems of party organization in South Asia, which are common in federal and parliamentary systems generally, concern the locus of decision-making authority as between various levels of the party organization and as between the organizational and electoral wings of the party. The radical Left parties differ both in the location of the strategic decision-making units and in the degree of diffusion of decision-making authority. Generally speaking, the locus of decision-making authority in the Communist parties of India has been in the state units. The central units of the party—the all-India Party Congress, the National Council, the Central Executive Committee, and the secretariat—either meet too infrequently to be effective; are divided on personal, factional, or regional grounds; or are neglected by the elected members. Communist party documents over the years have frequently bemoaned the fact that the duly-elected Politburo or secretariat members who are supposed to provide central direction to party activities have been too busy with the affairs of their own provinces even "to come and work at the Centre." [29]

[28] Ratna Dutta, "The Party Representative in Fourth Lok Sabha," *Economic and Political Weekly* 4, nos. 1 and 2 (January 1969), 180.
[29] "Review Report of the PB (1953)," in *Indian Communist Party Documents, 1930–1956* (Bombay: The Democratic Research Service, 1957), p. 169 (hereafter cited as *ICPD*).

State party organizations have not sent "regular reports" to the party headquarters and have not replied to communications from the center.[30] Those central party leaders who have been concerned with all-India party matters have not coordinated affairs between provinces but have confined their work to functional spheres of party activity such as trade unions or peasant organization. The consequence for the central party organization has been absence of central control over provincial activities and fragmentation of decision-making authority at the center itself.[31] In contrast, the state party organizational leaderships in the Communist parties have generally maintained their independence from central direction, their control over district and local committees, and their authority over elected members to the legislative assembly.[32] The distribution of authority in the Communist parties is reflected in the distribution of party dues in the CPI constitution—10 percent for the national council; 40 percent for the state council; and the remaining 50 percent distributed among district, branch, and local committees " in such proportion as decided by the state executive committee concerned." [33] With regard to the Communist and Awami parties in East Bengal, of course, the question of central party control hardly arose. Even before the secessionist movement, connections between west and east wing parties were never more than formal.

There is no difficulty in asserting with confidence that the state units of both Communist parties (particularly the CPM) in India are the most strategic decision-making units in the parties and that this distribution of authority is unlikely to change in the future. It is less easy to assert

[30] Ibid., p. 170.

[31] These and other failings of the central CPI organization are noted in ibid., pp. 163–165, 168–171, 174–177; "Report to the Party Congress (1956)," in *ICPD*, pp. 252–254, 260–261; "Organisational Methods and Practices of Party Centre (1956)," in *ICPD*, 304–321; Ajoy Ghosh, "New Situation and Our Tasks," *New Age* 10, no. 5 (May 1961), 40; "Organisational Report," in *Seventh Congress Documents*, pp. 122–129; and Overstreet and Windmiller, *Communism in India*, pp. 347–348.

[32] The supremacy of the state party units of the Communist parties has been noted in Franda, *Radical Politics in West Bengal*, chap. 3; in Ralph Retzlaff, "Revisionists and Sectarians: India's Two Communist Parties," in Scalapino, *Communist Revolution in Asia*, p. 330; and in Overstreet and Windmiller, *Communism in India*, p. 544. Maintaining control over the district and local committees has, however, sometimes been difficult. See, for example, the complaint concerning the loss of authority of the Assam state executive of the CPI over its district and local units in "Report on the General Elections in Assam," *New Age* 11, no. 5 (May 1962), 27.

[33] "Constitution of Communist Party of India," in *Documents Adopted by Eighth Congress of the Communist Party of India*, Karyanandnagar, Patna, 7–15 February 1968 (New Delhi: CPI, 1968), art. 10, p. 377 (hereafter cited as *Eighth Congress Documents*).

with any confidence that the present continued dominance of the organizational over the parliamentary/electoral wings of the bigger state parties will continue indefinitely. Conflict between organizational leaders and electoralists has long been endemic in the West Bengal Communist parties. Hardgrave has pointed out in his contribution to this volume that E. M. S. Namboodiripad has placed his weight in the Kerala party on the side of freedom of the party-in-the-government from control by the party organization. The problem of party-government relations is likely to become an increasingly important kind of division in the states where the Communist parties are contestants for "partial political power." [34]

In contrast to the Communist parties, decision-making authority in the Socialist parties in India is distributed differently. It is, first of all, distributed more diffusely. Central party leaders maintain frequent contact with state party leaders and problems. There is more traveling back and forth between state capitals and New Delhi of both state and central party leaders. Second, the state party organizational leadership tends to be less important than state Communist party leadership in relation to both national and local party units on such issues as selection of party candidates to contest elections. [35] The distribution of party membership fees in the SSP, for example, reflected the greater diffusion of authority and the equality among units. Party membership fees were divided equally among all units in the party organization. [36] Third, the parliamentary party leadership has tended to be independent of or dominant over the organizational apparatus of the party. Finally, authority in the party has been exercised in a more informal manner through consultations among groups of leaders, whatever their formal positions, than is the case in the more formally structured Communist parties.

The role of leadership and the character of leader-follower relationships in the Communist and Socialist parties of India has also been different. The Communist parties have never had any all-India leaders who have commanded the respect of party members throughout the country. [37] Even

---

[34] The phrase "partial political power" comes from Franda, *Radical Politics in West Bengal*, chap. 7.

[35] Hari Kishore Singh, *History of the PSP*, p. 159.

[36] Samyukta Socialist Party, *Constitution*, as adopted at the Second National Conference at Kota (Rajasthan), 3–6 April 1966 (New Delhi: SSP [1966]), rule 11, p. 15.

[37] This fact is acknowledged in the CPI "Organisational Report," in *Seventh Congress Documents*, p. 133, where the problem of the "cult of personality" is discussed and is considered more of a regional than a national problem for the party: "It is true the leadership as a whole or sections of it did not command that much confidence from the ranks throughout the country. But individual leaders are demigods for sections of Party members in their respective areas."

in the states, with the exception of E. M. S. Namboodiripad in Kerala, the party leaders have tended not to be dynamic, charismatic figures. The Socialist parties, particularly the SSP, have had a greater emphasis on personalized leadership by towering personalities. Dr. Rammanohar Lohia, the *de facto* leader of the SSP until his premature death in 1967, was the most colorful of the all-India Socialist leaders. In the states also, the SSP leaders have tended to be more populist than the intellectual and organizational leadership of the CPI.

Not surprisingly, therefore, leadership conflicts and leader-follower relations have tended to be different in the Communist and Socialist parties. All parties of the radical Left in South Asia have suffered from leadership conflicts and factional divisions, but such conflicts in the Socialist parties have tended to be more personalized and more open than in the Communist parties, where conflicts have usually been phrased in ideological terms and kept out of public view as far as possible. Some of the Socialist parties in South Asia, particularly the SSP in India and the Lanka Sama Samaja Party in Ceylon have taken pride in the vigor of their inner-party controversies, whereas the Communist parties emphasize discipline and prohibit inner-party groupings in principle. In practice, however, inner-party debate has been often as vigorous, if less open, in the Communist parties.[38] Documents of the CPI have recognized this fact and deplored "the disorganized state of our Party—the indiscipline, alien class habits and methods and wrong style of work that have struck deep roots into our organization." [39] Moreover, even though inner-party groupings or factions are not supposed to be formed in the CPI, factional divisions within the party have been intense and long-lasting.[40] For a time, the CPI gave the appearance of greater cohesion than other Indian political parties and seemed, until 1964, to be immune from "organized defection." [41] Since 1964, clearly, the Communist parties have also suffered from party splits. Still, indiscipline and factionalism leading to defections from the radical Left parties have been more serious in their consequences for the Socialist than for the Communist parties in India.[42] In the period between 1957 and 1967 the Socialist parties lost 107 legislators to other parties by defection and gained 6, whereas the Communist

---

[38] See, for example, the comments in Overstreet and Windmiller, *Communism in India*, pp. 348–350.
[39] "Organisational Report," in *Seventh Congress Documents*, pp. 110–111.
[40] Overstreet and Windmiller, *Communism in India*, p. 531.
[41] Ibid., p. 354.
[42] Compare Weiner's comments on defection and indiscipline in the Socialist parties in *Party Politics in India*, pp. 38–39, with those of Overstreet and Windmiller just cited.

parties lost only 10 and gained none. In 1967–1968 the Socialist parties lost by defection 26 out of 206 legislators or 13 percent whereas the Communist parties lost only 2 out of 249 elected, less than 1 percent.[43]

Factionalism in the South Asian Communist and Socialist parties has had many different kinds of bases and has found expression in diverse ways. Pure leader-follower groupings exist in the radical Left parties, particularly at the local level, as they do in the Congress and other parties in Indian politics. Leadership conflicts at higher levels between strong personalities have also existed. Divisions in the Communist parties have been based on differences in strategy and tactics, on different functional interests, on regional differences, on differences between generations, and on differences between persons recruited into the party from different socioeconomic and political backgrounds.[44] The consequences of factionalism for both Communist and Socialist parties have been continuing indiscipline, which tends to lead both to defections and to organizational deficiencies. Although "organized defection" has never been as common from the Communist parties as from the Socialist parties and the Communist movement did not split formally until 1964, Communist Party organization suffered severely from the pervasive factionalism that for long preceded the split. Communist Party documents of the early post-Independence period referred to the deterioration of the party organization as a result of the "long period of inner-Party struggle and confusion" that occurred in the years between 1947 and 1951.[45] In the 1950s, other party documents clearly indicate that the central organization of the CPI was virtually paralyzed and that the entire party was divided "from top to bottom" as a consequence of inner-party conflict.[46] Thus, the major differences between the Communist and Socialist parties with regard to factionalism have been not its existence but the attitude taken by the parties toward inner-party controversy and the consequences of factionalism. Factional conflicts in the Socialist party have been more open and

---

[43] The figures on the number of defectors by party come from Subhash C. Kashyap, *The Politics of Defection: A Study of State Politics in India* (Delhi: National Publishing House, 1969), p. 8.

[44] On the various bases of factionalism in the Communist parties, see Overstreet and Windmiller, *Communism in India*, pp. 4, 349–350, 532; *ICPD*, xvii–xix; and Franda, *Radical Politics in West Bengal*, chaps. 2, 3 and 9.

[45] "Revew Report of the PB (1953)," in *ICPD*, p. 161.

[46] See especially the "Report to the Party Congress (1956)," in *ICPD*, pp. 225–226, 252–254, 272–275, 303 and "Organisational Methods and Practices of Party Centre (1956)," in *ICPD*, pp. 304–306, 308–313, 319–320.

have more frequently led to "organized defection." Such conflicts in the Communist parties have been concealed as far as possible and have been more likely to cause internal paralysis of party organization than defection.

The Communist and Socialist parties in India have also differed in their attitudes toward the enrollment of members. The Communist parties have tended toward more restricted enrollments than the Socialist parties, whose enrollment has been relatively more open. Tables 1.1 and 1.2 give the available membership figures for the CPI and the PSP. Although membership figures for both parties have fluctuated over time in relation to the various internal and external crises faced by the parties, PSP membership has been generally higher than CPI membership in comparable periods. The difference between the two parties is less great, however, when membership figures are compared against party votes polled in the general elections. The ratio of party members to party votes polled for the CPI was 1:152 in 1952; 1:91 in 1957; 1:115 in 1962; and 1:34 in 1967 (using 1966 membership figures). The available ratios for the PSP are 1:84 in 1957 and 1:94 in 1962. The only radical left party in India that has striven to achieve a large mass membership is the SSP, which claimed an enrollment of 476,266 in 1966–1967,[47] which works out to a member:voter ratio of 1:18 (using the 1967 election results for the comparison figure). The CPM claimed a membership of 82, 670 in 1967 and 76,425 in 1968.[48] Both figures were less than half the claimed membership of the CPI in 1966. In Ceylon, until recently, neither the LSSP nor the CPI has enrolled large memberships. Throughout most of its history, the LSSP has been deliberately elitist in its attitude toward recruitment of members.

If the Indian Socialist parties have been more concerned with mass membership, the Communist parties in India and the LSSP in Ceylon have placed more emphasis on building mass organizations and party fronts—trade unions, peasant organizations, student organizations, and the like. The CPI gained control over all the leading mass organizations of workers, peasants, and students during the Second World War. However, Communist control over the mass organizations has declined since then as other parties have competed with the Communists in this area,

[47] Samyukta Socialist Party, *Tratiya Rashtriya Sammelan, 28, 29, 30, 31 December '67 wa 1 January '68, Pradhanamantri ki Report* (New Delhi: SSP, [1967]), pp. 58–59.
[48] *Political-Organisational Report of the Central Committee to the Eighth Congress of the Communist Party of India (Marxist)* (Calcutta: CPM 1969), app., table 1.

Table 1.1 CPI Membership, 1934–1970

Year	Members	Year	Members
1934	150	1952	30,000
1942	5,000	1954	75,000
1943	15,563	1957	125,000
1944	25,000	1958	218,532
1945	30,000	1959	178,718
1946	53,000	1962	107,762
1947	60,000	1965	101,034
1948	89,263	1966	172,902
1950	20,000	1970	243,238

Sources: 1934–1957 from Overstreet and Windmiller, *Communism in India*, p. 357, originally published by the University of California Press and reprinted by permission of The Regents of the University of California; 1958, 1959, and 1962 from "Organisational Report," in *Seventh Congress Documents*, pp. 109 and 120; 1965 and 1966 from "Organisational Report," in *Eighth Congress Documents*, p. 172; 1970 from *New Age*, 17 May 1970, p. 10.

Table 1.2 PSP Membership, 1949–1950 to 1964

Year	Members	Year	Members
1949–1950	129,447	1958–1959	274,752
1952–1953	264,391	1959–1960	251,092
1954–1955	189,339	1960–1961	340,992
1955–1956	280,825	1961–1962	N.A.
1956–1957	141,651	1963[a]	94,440
1957–1958	95,677	1964	197,317

Sources: Figures for 1949–1950 to 1960–1961 are from *Report of the Sixth National Conference of the Praja Socialist Party, Bhopal, June 8–10, 1963* (New Delhi: PSP, n.d.), p. 84. Later figures are from Phulgenda Sinha, "The Praja Socialist Party of India," unpublished Ph.D. dissertation, American University, 1968, p. 233.

[a]Phulgenda Sinha attributes the low membership figure in this year to a change in the membership year of the party from "July 1 to June 30" to "January 1 to December 31," in consequence of which, presumably, only six months' membership enrollment was included in 1963.

as a consequence of the "adventurist" line pursued by the party in the early postwar years, and as a result of the split in the CPI in 1964.[49]

There is no way of determining with any degree of accuracy the current position of the various radical Left parties among trade union, peasant, and student organizations.[50] However, the general impression conveyed by available documents and secondary sources is that the trade union movement in Inda is badly divided among trade union federations allied with the Congress, both Communist parties, and the Socialists, but that the leading parties in trade union organizations are the Congress and the Communist parties. AITUC, the Communist-affiliated federation of trade unions, had a verified membership of 433,564 in 808 affiliated unions in 1966. This figure represented a considerable decline from the peak verified figure 758,314 in 736 unions in 1951 and 1952 and from the claimed 1947 figure of 796,174 in 601 unions (table 1.3). In contrast, the Congress-dominated INTUC federation, which claimed a membership of only 412,193 in 227 unions in 1947, had a verified membership of 1,417,553 in 1,305 unions in 1966 and a claimed membership of 1,982,116 in 2,023 unions in 1969. The Socialist-dominated trade union federation, the HMS, had a membership of 697,287 in 419 unions in 1949 and a peak membership of 804,494 in 574 unions in 1952, but its verified membership was only 436,977 members in 258 unions in 1966.

In recent years, the primary struggles for influence and support in the Indian trade union movement have taken place between INTUC and the Communist-influenced trade unions, on the one hand, and between CPI- and CPM-influenced unions, on the other hand. For six years after the split in the CPI in 1964, the two Communist parties struggled for dominance in the AITUC, but the CPI leadership group led by S. A. Dange maintained its control over the national organization throughout. In May 1970 at Calcutta, the CPM trade union leadership established a new all-India trade union federation, the Centre of Indian Trade Unions (CITU). It claimed a founding membership of 804,637,[51] which compares with the claimed AITUC membership of 1,862,371. Both figures are surely inflated. Certainly, AITUC has greater strength than CITU

[49] Overstreet and Windmiller, *Communism in India*, p. 404.
[50] For some past figures on enrollment and other general descriptions, see Overstreet and Windmiller, *Communism in India*, chap. 16; Phulgenda Sinha, "The Praja Socialist Party of India," unpublished Ph.D. dissertation, American University, 1968, pp. 331–343; and Hari Kishore Singh, *History of the PSP*, pp. 106–114.
[51] *People's Democracy* 6, no. 23 (7 June 1970), 5.

Table 1.3 Membership of and Number of Unions Affiliated to the Leading Indian Trade Union Federations, 1947–1970

Year	INTUC		AITUC		HMS	
	Number of Affiliated Trade Unions	Membership	Number of Affiliated Trade Unions	Membership	Number of Affiliated Trade Unions	Membership
1947	227	412,193	601	796,174		
1948	498	1,033,614	N.A.	N.A.		
1949	847*	1,023,117*	754*	741,035*	419*	679,287*
1950	1,043*	1,431,878*	722*	730,636*	460*	698,720*
1951	1,232*	1,548,568*	736*	758,314*	517*	804,337*
1952	913*	1,268,606*	736*	758,314*	574*	804,494*
1953	587*	919,258*	334*	210,914*	220*	373,459*
1954	606*	888,291*	925*	655,940	331*	492,362*
1955	604*	930,968*	481*	306,693*	157*	211,315*
1956	617*	971,740*	558*	422,851*	119*	203,798*
1957	672*	934,385*	N.A.	N.A.	138*	233,990*
1958	727*	910,221*	807*	537,567*	151*	192,948*
1959	886*	1,023,371*	814*	507,654*	185*	241,636*
1960	860*	1,053,386*	886*	508,962*	190*	286,202*
1961	1,520	1,663,893	N.A.	N.A.	N.A.	N.A.
1962	1,403	1,736,458	N.A.	N.A.	N.A.	N.A.
1963	1,219*	1,268,339*	952*	500,967*	253*	329,851*
1966	1,305*	1,417,553*	808*	433,564*	258*	436,977*
1968	1,911	1,904,449	1,971	1,515,186	N.A.	770,405
1969	2,023	1,982,116	N.A.	N.A.	N.A.	N.A.
1970	N.A.	N.A.	2,878	1,862,371	N.A.	N.A.

Sources: Shiva Chandra Jha, *The Indian Trade Union Movement: An Account and an Interpretation* (Calcutta: Firma K. L. Mukhopadhyay, 1970), pp. 193, 198, 202; Government of India, Ministry of Information and Broadcasting, *India: A Reference Annual, 1964* (Delhi: Ministry of Information and Broadcasting, 1964), p. 342; ibid., *1961*, p. 381; ibid., *1958*, p. 416; ibid, *1955*, p. 438; ibid., *1954*, p. 305; ibid., *1953*, p. 299; *New Age*, 8 February 1970, p. 7; *Trade Union Record* 26, no. 13 (5 July 1969), 7; Government of India, Department of Labour and Employment, Labour Bureau, *Pocket Book of Labour Statistics, 1969* (Delhi: Manager of Publications, 1970), pp. 51–52; Indian National Trade Union Congress (Rashtriya Mazdoor Congress), *Report (May 1968 to April 1969)* (New Delhi: Indian National Trade Union Congress, 1969), app., pp. 34–35 and *Report (December 1965 to April 1968)* (New Delhi: Indian National Trade Union Congress, 1968), p. 194; K. N. Vaid, *Trade Unions in India* (New Delhi: Shri Ram Centre for Industrial Relations, 1965), pp. 6–19.
* Figures verified by the government of India. Other figures are those claimed by the federations and are usually inflated.

in Bombay and is probably also stronger in West Bengal and Kerala. On an all-India basis, INTUC is still stronger than either of the two Communist federations or the Socialist-dominated HMS.

At the founding conference of CITU, B. T. Ranadive was elected president. He has argued for the necessity of developing a more militant and more politically oriented trade unionism in India, in contrast with the allegedly more conciliatory, economic-interest-oriented, and "class-collaborationist" trade union activities of INTUC, AITUC, and HMS. In fact, he has insisted in classical Leninist rhetoric that "the fundamental problems of society . . . cannot be solved unless the working class aided by its allies captures political power in an open class combat and vanquishes the oppressors, that they cannot be solved through elections within the framework of the Constitution." Rather, the trade union movement must move "out of its narrow economic groove" and join forces "with the wider political movement to lead an assault on the citadels of political power." [52]

Outside the trade union movement, none of the parties appear either to be dominant or to have very considerable strength. The state of the mass organizations in 1964 was described with some irony in the CPI organizational report as follows:

The leaders of the rival party [CPM] have started earnestly to split the AITUC because it is the only live [mass] organisation. . . . With regard to the other mass organisations, there is nothing to split at present because they are virtually defunct.[53]

Only the Communist parties in India have made serious efforts to organize associations of peasants and agricultural laborers. The organizational reports of both the CPI and the CPM since the split have complained about the sorry state of organization in the rural areas and have urged party members to pay more attention to the work of organizing poor peasants and agricultural laborers. As in the trade union movement, the two Communist parties struggled to gain control over the All-India Kisan Sabha (AIKS), the leading peasant association in India. Each Communist party now has its own AIKS, but the CPM Kisan Sabha has been the more vigorous of the two in recent years. Neither peasant association, however, has acquired a vigor or a membership enrollment comparable to what exists in the trade union movement. All the parties of the radical Left continue to compete with each other and with other parties in building

[52] Ibid., no. 21 (24 May 1970), 6–7.
[53] "Organisational Report," in Seventh Congress Documents, p. 144.

and gaining control over mass organizations, but the primary efforts of all parties continue to be devoted to the electoral arena and the mass organizations continue to suffer from both inattention and the splitting activities of rival parties.

The differences between the Communist and Socialist parties in organization can be summarized as follows. Authority in the Communist parties tends to be concentrated at the state level and in the organizational apparatus of the party, whereas authority in the Socialist parties is more diffusely distributed and weighted more in favor of the parliamentary leaders. Although all radical Left parties have suffered from factionalism and indiscipline, the Communist parties have emphasized the need for discipline more than the Socialist parties and the LSSP, which place a higher value on inner-party controversy. The Communist parties have also had greater success in imposing discipline insofar as they have lost fewer legislators by defection. The Communist parties and the LSSP have tended to place greater restrictions on enrollment than the Socialist parties, but only the SSP has attempted to build a broad mass-membership party. Finally, the Communist parties have placed relatively greater emphasis on building and controlling mass organizations of workers, peasants, and students, but the primary organizational efforts of all radical Left parties have increasingly been devoted to electoral politics.

PARTY SPLITS

Factionalism and inner-party controversies are endemic and pervasive in South Asian political parties and party splits are inevitable consequences of them. There are very few political parties in South Asia that have not either fragmented or developed out of a party split. Many parties in South Asia, all along the ideological spectrum, have multiplied like cells, creating near-duplicates of each other—often with the same name, except for the addition of a specific identifying marker to distinguish a party from its counterparts. Occasionally, the splinters and fragments will merge into a new combination with a new name, only to begin the process of division anew.

The Communist and Socialist parties in South Asia exemplify this process in characteristic fashion. Three Communist parties with all-India pretensions and several smaller regional Communist parties have been formed in this way in the Indian states. There have been two major Socialist parties in India in recent times and innumerable regional Socialist parties, which have split and merged and split again. There have been two Communist and two Trotskyite parties in Ceylon; three Communist parties and two left-wing versions of the National Awami Party in East Bengal.

Although the splits in the Communist parties in South Asia have had some relationship to international events, in most cases of party splits and mergers in these countries, the important causal factors have been indigenous ones. The point needs stressing in connection with the splits in the Communist parties of South Asia because of the persistence of old myths concerning the structure of the international Communist movement, which have been only modified in recent scholarly treatments of the subject. The matter is also complicated in South Asia by the tendency of rival parties to discredit each other by identifying their opponents as agents of a foreign power. As far as the Indian Communist parties are concerned, however, even the qualified statement that the Sino-Soviet dispute "created splits in the [Asian Communist] parties or widened splits that were already existent" [54] exaggerates the influence of the Sino-Soviet conflict on indigenous Indian Communist affairs. As the Chinese themselves have recognized, events in India, and particularly the unwillingness of the Soviet Union to support China in its conflicts with India, were more of a factor in the Sino-Soviet dispute than vice versa.[55]

There have been two major splits in the Indian Communist movement, in 1964 and in 1969. In 1964, the CPI split into the two leading constitutionally oriented Communist parties—the Communist Party of India (CPI) and the Communist Party of India (Marxist) or CPM. The CPI interpretation of the split is that it "was inspired and facilitated by the factionalist intervention of the Chinese Communist leaders who, failing to make our Party toe their dogmatist and chauvinist line, slandered our Party as 'revisionist,' 'Dange clique' and 'agents of the bourgeoisie' and gave an open call to split it." According to this version, factionalism in the party originated during the Sino-Indian border dispute and "reached a decisive stage with the Chinese aggression in October 1962 when the National Council adapted the line of national defence against the Chinese aggression." [56]

In fact, the split in the CPI may be more meaningfully viewed as the logical culmination of internal divisions in the party that developed in

[54] Scalapino, "Communism in Asia" p. 48.
[55] Chalmers Johnson, "Building a Communist Nation in China," in Scalapino, *Communist Revolution in Asia*, pp. 77–78.
[56] "Organisational Report," in *Seventh Congress Documents*, pp. 99–110; citations from pp. 99–100.

the early years after Independence concerning the appropriate strategy to be followed towards the Congress party and government. The pro-Congress stance of the right wing of the party, which also tended to be pro-Soviet on international affairs, was reflected very strongly during the developing Sino-Indian conflict from 1959 onwards, which precipitated a "stampede to the Right" in the CPI especially at the time of the Chinese invasion in October, 1962.[57] During the Sino-Indian and Sino-Soviet dispute periods from 1959 to 1964, there were actually three major groupings in the CPI—the Right group, a Left group, and a centrist group. While there were some in the Left group with pro-Chinese inclinations, the centrist group, which included such key figures as E. M. S. Namboodiripad of Kerala and Jyoti Basu of Bengal, was not pro-Chinese. If anything, E. M. S. Namboodiripad's inclinations in the Sino-Soviet dispute favored the Soviet side. The Left and centrist groups did not, in any case, support the Chinese position at this time, either in the Sino-Soviet or Sino-Indian dispute, but rather objected to the extreme anti-Chinese and pro-Nehru position of the Right faction. For its part, the Congress government used the occasion of the Chinese invasion and the alleged pro-Chinese position of the Left and centrist groups as a pretext to arrest all the prominent Left and centrist leaders. While the Left and centrist Communists were in jail, the Right faction consolidated its position in the national and state party organizations. The split in 1964 occurred when the jailed comrades were released and found their rivals entrenched in key positions in the party organization. The split in 1964, then, related to power in the party and to long-standing issues concerning strategy and tactics on which there had long been two lines. The series of events surrounding the Sino-Indian and Sino-Soviet disputes were precipitating factors in rather than causes for the split at that time.

The 1964 split also had a strong regional basis. The militant anti-Congress sentiment in the old CPI was concentrated, naturally, in areas where the CPI was a strong contender for power against the Congress—particularly in the party strongholds of Kerala, West Bengal, and Andhra. It has been in these three states also that the CPM has been strongest—particularly in Kerala and West Bengal. However, both parties—the CPI and the CPM—have maintained strong organisations with subregional bases of strength in the three leading Communist strongholds. Elsewhere

---

[57] The best analysis of the 1964 CPI split is by John B. Wood, "Observations on the Indian Communist Party Split," *Pacific Affairs* 38, no. 1 (Spring 1965), 46–63. See also Franda, *Radical Politics in West Bengal*, chap. 4; and Retzlaff, "Revisionists and Sectarians," pp. 338–351.

in India, with the exception of Tamil Nadu where the CPM is the stronger of the two parties, either the CPI has emerged as the dominant party or neither party has had significant strength. In Ceylon, where a split occurred in 1964 also and where the Sino-Soviet dispute seems to have had a greater impact,[58] the older, rightist and pro-Soviet leadership has emerged strongest.

A second split in the Communist movement in India occurred in 1969, when a faction of the CPM in Bengal, which had been leading a violent agitation in the Naxalbari subdivision of a North Bengal district, split from the party to form the Communist Party of India (Marxist-Leninist) or CPML.[59] Unlike the CPI and the CPM, the CPML is strictly a revolutionary organization, which has not participated in electoral politics. It has received the blessings of the Communist Party of China but has had wholly indigenous origins. The immediate impact of this split has by no means been as severe as the earlier split for either of the two larger Communist parties. The CPML has caused embarrassment to the CPM in Bengal and has intensified the already severe divisions in the Communist movement in Andhra, where several new regional Communist organizations coexist with the older Communist formations. The CPML has also fostered the development of a new revolutionary romanticism in India, especially among students and young people, which in turn has increased the pressures for militancy, particularly in the CPM.

However, the latest wave of revolutionary violence in India has been less successful than the Communist revolutionary movement in the early post-Independence period.[60] Although Naxalite activities have been prominent in certain rural pockets in West Bengal, Bihar, and Andhra, the Naxalite revolutionaries do not have a permanent base anywhere in India. There are no "liberated" areas in India. The failure of the Naxalite revolutionaries to establish a permanent base is reflected in their several tactical shifts in the past few years.[61] In 1969, the Naxalbari tactic of establishing a base for a guerrilla movement was extended to Midnapore district in West Bengal. The failure of the CPML in Midnapore was followed by a shift to the tactics of individual terrorism in the rural areas. At the end of 1969 and early 1970, Naxalite activists engaged in "urban guerrilla

---

[58] Kearney, "Communist Parties of Ceylon," pp. 405–411.
[59] See Marcus F. Franda, "India's Third Communist Party," *Asian Survey* 9, no. 11 (November 1969), 797–817.
[60] On this point, see Mohit Sen, "The Naxalites and Naxialism," *Economic and Political Weekly* 6, nos. 3, 4 and 5 (January 1971), 195.
[61] Mohan Ram, "Shift in Naxalite Tactics," *Economic and Political Weekly* 6, no. 34 (21 August 1971), 1793–1794.

activity," but this movement too has petered out in the face of government repression. It was reported in August 1971 that some 2,400 CPML cadres were in jail, that the party was divided again on tactics, and that a tactical shift back to a rural strategy was again being considered.[62]

Although the CPML of Charu Mazumdar has been the leading Maoist party in India during the past few years, it has been faced with internal divisions, with competition from a proliferation of new Maoist formations, and lately with an apparent loss of favor in relation to the Communist Party of China (CPC). In Andhra, the Andhra Pradesh Revolutionary Communist Committee has been the most prominent competitor of the CPML for supremacy, but there have developed a whole host of new Maoist groups and factions in Andhra and elsewhere. In July 1971, it was reported that there were seven Naxalite parties in Kerala alone.[63] The CPML has recently also suffered from a loss of favor with the CPC because of the CPC support for the Pakistan government against the secessionist movement in Bangladesh, which was supported by some CPML cadres.[64]

The Communist movement in East Bengal has also split into a number of fragments in recent years. The first major split occurred in 1966 when a group that took the name East Pakistan Communist Party (Marxist-Leninist) (EPCPML) split from the East Pakistan Communist Party (EPCP). The EPCPML has, like the CPML in India, favored a peasant-based revolution in Pakistan. In addition to these two parties, Maniruzzaman has identified three other organized Communist groups in East Bengal. Although he has divided them into pro-Soviet and pro-Peking groups, it is apparent that they have differed in the past primarily with respect to strategies for achieving power and for promoting Bengali aspirations for regional autonomy. Moreover, Franda has pointed out elsewhere that neither the Soviet Union nor China has shown much interest in the domestic Communist parties in East Bengal.[65]

The history of splits and mergers in the Socialist movement is far more complicated than in the Communist movement. The early post-Independence history of the formation of the Praja Socialist Party out of the Socialist Party and the Kisan Mazdoor Praja Party after the 1952 elections

[62] Ibid.

[63] Mohit Sen, "The Stage of the South," *Economic and Political Weekly* 6, no. 30–32 (July 1971), 1511.

[64] Mohan Ram, "Polycentric Maoism," *Economic and Political Weekly* 6, no. 26 (26 June 1971), 1277–1278 and Sumanta Banerjee, "Maoists: Doing without China?" ibid. 6, no. 27 (3 July 1971), 1321–1322.

[65] Franda, "Communism and Regional Politics in East Pakistan," p. 599.

has been fully documented elsewhere.[66] Since the formation of the PSP in 1952, there have been two major party splits. The first split was led by Dr. Rammanohar Lohia and Madhu Limaye in 1955. It was precipitated by two events that had as their common focus the same question that has plagued the Communist movement, namely, whether to cooperate with or oppose the Congress. The first event was the formation of a Congress-supported PSP government in Kerala in 1954 and a police firing that occurred while that government was in power.[67] Dr. Lohia and Madhu Limaye both condemned the police firing and opposed the whole idea of a PSP government depending upon the Congress for support. The second event was the reaction of followers of Ashok Mehta in the party, particularly in Bombay, to the Awadi declaration of the Congress party, which set forth the establishment of socialism in India as the party's objective.[68] The followers of Ashok Mehta in the party saw this declaration as providing a new basis for cooperation with the Congress, whereas Dr. Lohia and Madhu Limaye, supported particularly by the Uttar Pradesh wing of the party, were opposed to any such cooperation with the Congress. The climax to these disputes was reached in 1955 with an open split in the PSP and the formation of the Socialist Party. The new Socialist Party had its main strength in UP, Madhya Pradesh, and Andhra.[69] Elsewhere, the split had little impact upon the PSP.

If the PSP emerged strongest after the split in 1955, it was nearly destroyed by the merger with the SP in 1964 and the subsequent split of January 1965. After the 1962 General Elections, in which the Congress once again emerged victorious throughout the country and in which the Socialist parties performed dismally, three lines of thought were evident in Socialist attitudes towards the Congress. One was the Ashok Mehta line that now saw continued opposition to the Congress as futile and that finally culminated in the movement of Ashok Mehta and many of his followers into the Congress party in 1963–1964. The second line of thought, centered in the PSP, favored the continued existence of an independent Socialist movement strengthened by unity with the SP. The third line of thought, centered in the SP, favored a renewal of militant opposition to the Congress in alliance with any and all opposition parties. The last two tendencies led to a temporary merger of the PSP and the SP into a new party, the Samyukta Socialist Party (SSP), in June 1964.

---

[66] Weiner, *Party Politics in India*, chaps. 2, 5.
[67] Hari Kishore Singh, *History of the PSP*, pp. 200–206.
[68] Ibid., pp. 207–215 and Limaye, *Why Samyukta Socialist?*, p. 12.
[69] Hari Kishore Singh, *History of the PSP*, pp. 229ff.

However, the new party was soon divided on a whole series of issues, including interpersonal relations and decorum in the party, the leadership of Dr. Lohia, the question of the quantum of representation in the new party to which the PSP was entitled after the defection to the Congress of the followers of Ashok Mehta, and the question of alliances with other parties, particularly the Jan Sangh and the CPI.[70] The more moderate PSP members, opposed to the leadership of Dr. Lohia and to the policy of alliances with the Jan Sangh and the CPI, left the party in January 1965 and revived the PSP. However, many old PSP members refused to go with the splitters. Consequently, this series of events in 1964 and 1965 left the PSP very seriously weakened and left the new SSP as the leading party of socialism in India, particularly in the Socialist strongholds of Bihar and Uttar Pradesh. The disastrous results of the 1971 Lok Sabha elections for the Socialist parties precipitated new merger negotiations, which culminated in the reunification of the bulk of the leadership cadres of the SSP and the PSP into the new Socialist Party (SP) in August 1971. Some PSP cadres in several states refused to join the new party and retained the old PSP organization, but the SP was by far the most important democratic Socialist party in India in 1972 and the PSP was reduced to insignificance as a political force in the legislative assembly elections in nearly every state.

Alliance policy has also been a critical factor in the splits in the Communist Party of Ceylon and in the LSSP. The predominant segments of both the CCP and the LSSP have opted for a strategy of cooperation and coalition with the SLFP, whereas the Left CP and the revolutionary LSSP(R) have opposed such alliances.

Clearly, throughout all the splits and mergers in both the Communist and Socialist movements in South Asia, one theme is dominant, namely, the question of the strategy and tactics to be followed toward the parties, authorities, and classes in power. This question has everywhere been the crucial one for parties of the radical Left out of power. How this question has been answered in South Asia by the predominant elements in the radical movements of India, Bangladesh, and Ceylon is crucial not only for the future of those movements but for the civil order of their societies. Consequently, the answers given deserve more detailed discussion in the context of the general ideology and strategy of the radical Left parties, which are analyzed in the following section.

[70] S. M. Joshi, *The Split at Varanasi: Some Notes* (Bombay: Lokamat Prakashan [1965]).

Ideology, Strategy, and Tactics

The Importance of Ideology

All political parties combine appeals to leaders, members, and followers based upon both ideal and material benefits.[71] Parties do differ, however, in the extent to which ideal considerations or ideology matter, in the elaboration of their ideologies, in the functions which ideology performs for party maintenance and expansion, and, of course, in the content of their programs. Radical parties of the Left tend to emphasize ideal appeals and benefits. Nevertheless, they also differ significantly from one another in these four respects, namely, in the importance of ideology, in the degree of its elaboration, in the functions it performs, and in its content.

For some radical parties, adherence to the ideology of the party in a more than formal sense is a condition for membership. Communist parties especially stress the importance for party members of understanding the underlying ideological principles of the party and emphasize party education. Moreover, for many members of such parties, a commitment to the party, which is based on an ideological appeal, is a total one. Other radical parties are less concerned with underlying principles than with immediate policies and programs. A formal commitment to the broad principles of socialism, equality, and social justice is sufficient and is quickly translated into concrete policies that become more important in practice than the principles behind them. Members of such parties—particularly the democratic Socialist parties in South Asia—may feel less bound to the ideology of the party than do Communist party members. Appeals to members of the less ideologically oriented leftist parties are more contingent. In the more ideological parties, immediate policies may be less important than and may be sacrificed for long-term goals. In the less ideological parties, deviation from the concrete policies of the party may provide party members with grounds for defection.

Radical parties also differ in the degree of elaboration of their ideologies and principles. Marxist-Leninist parties naturally have elaborate ideological underpinnings, which are constantly undergoing evaluation and reevaluation. A proper Marxist-Leninist party is supposed to derive its bases of action and its specific policies only after the nature of the existing state structure has been specified, the stage and the movement of historical forces in the world are internally determined, the classes that constitute

71 Cf. Carl J. Friedrich's definition of party in *Constitutional Government and Democracy: Theory and Practice in Europe and America*, rev. ed. (Boston: Ginn, 1950), p. 419.

enemies and those that constitute allies of the working class identified, and the broad strategy and tactics appropriate to all these formulated. For such parties, there is a danger that they may move only in an ideal world of abstractions and that they may become paralyzed or inhibited from acting pragmatically because of a commitment to an "understanding" that has become irrelevant. Other radical parties have less elaborate ideological underpinnings. A broad world and historical view may be only implicit, while the party programs speak of general principles and specific policies designed to achieve them. The Marxist-Leninist party may want to achieve a classless society, but may have no specific policies designed to eliminate class inequalities because the time may not be right. The more pragmatic Socialist party will present specific policies to reduce class inequalities in the present.

Radical parties of the Left also differ in the functions performed by ideological and policy appeals for party maintenance and expansion. Marxist-Leninist parties in Asia generally and in South Asia particularly tend to have a strong leadership component of intellectuals for whom ideological discussion and debate are the essence of politics.[72] The more dominant such leadership in the party, the less active the party is likely to be. Moreover, the kinds of ideological appeals that draw intellectuals to the Marxist-Leninist parties are usually far removed from the concerns of the mass of the people. The problem for the leadership of the Marxist-Leninist parties is to find the means to translate ideological issues into bases for action and policies that will win mass support and to avoid the "tendency to dwell in an ideal word of ideological formulae." [73] The less ideologically oriented radical parties have less difficulty in this regard. Policies may be more easily selected in terms of their mass appeal on issues of immediate concern to the poor and the downtrodden. The SSP in India, for example, self-consciously resisted the radical Left tendency to separate "the abstract and the general from the concrete and particular" and insisted on specifying the meaning of abstract principles in terms of "immediate programmes." [74] The danger in this situation is one of opportunism, of departure from socialist principles for the sake of winning mass support and access to power.

The extent and character of ideological commitment in radical parties also affects their cohesion and unity. The more ideologically oriented par-

---

[72] See Scalapino, "Communism in Asia," p. 205.
[73] Overstreet and Windmiller argued that the CPI exceeded "nearly all other Communist parties" in this tendency; *Communism in India*, p. 352.
[74] Limaye, *Why Samyukta Socialist?*, pp. 14–15.

tics tend to be more cohesive in the short run than the radical parties with more contingent and specific appeals. However, ideology itself may also be divisive and provide either a cause or a pretext for factional division leading to splits in Marxist-Leninist parties.

Finally, parties of the radical Left in South Asia can be distinguished according to the content of their ideologies and their present or past ties to international movements. The basic line of division here is between the Marxist-Leninist parties and the Left parties that either are not explicitly Marxist-Leninist or whose Marxism has been heavily infused with indigenous ideologies.[75] In the former category are the various Communist parties in the South Asian countries, the Marxist Left parties in West Bengal, the Lanka Sama Samaja Party in Ceylon, and the like. In the second category are the broadly Socialist, Gandhian, and Islamic Socialist parties of South Asia—the SSP and the PSP in India and the National Awami Party in East Bengal. The Marxist-Leninist parties in turn can be distinguished by their relationship to the international Communist movement. On the one hand are the leading Communist parties that grew out of a once united and internationally linked Communist movement—the CPI, CPM, and CPML in India; the EPCP in East Bengal; and the two Communist parties in Ceylon. On the other hand, there are the small Marxist Left parties in Bengal, the tiny non-Communist revolutionary parties in Kerala, the Trotskyite LSSP in Ceylon, and the like.

The leaders of the various radical Left parties in South Asia have confronted a number of major questions of ideology, strategy, and tactics during the past two decades. The various radical parties have differed among themselves on such questions, and they have also divided internally on issues of strategy and tactics, not infrequently to the point of splitting, leading to the formation of new radical parties. Differences in the importance of ideology to the radical Left parties, in the content of their ideologies, and in the political structures in which they operate have influenced the choice of strategy and tactics. The important ideological issues have also varied among the different parties and in the differing contexts in South Asia, but several themes have been especially prominent in ideological debate in the radical Left in India, Pakistan, and Ceylon. They are questions concerning the strategy for achieving power, the tactics for achieving power, the attitude to be taken toward nationality issues and problems of regionalism, specific policies for economic development, and international ties and foreign policy.

[75] See, for example, Myron Weiner's comments on "the Indianization of socialism," in *Party Politics in India*, p. 30.

The Major Ideological Issues

COALITION STRATEGIES AND STATE POWER

THE COMMUNIST PARTIES In India, both the Marxist-Leninist and democratic Socialist segments of the radical Left have divided internally on the
question of the attitude to be taken toward the Indian National Congress,
which led the nationalist movement and has held an unbroken monopoly
of power in the central government since Independence. There have been
two tendencies within both segments of the radical Left—one favoring, in
varying degrees and forms, cooperation with the Congress or sections of it;
the other favoring militant opposition to the Congress. The terms of the
ideological debate on this issue have centered around differing assessments
of the class composition of the Congress party and government, of the progressive character of Congress domestic and foreign policies, and of the
strength and danger of the right reactionary and communal forces and
parties in Indian politics. In practice, however, the attitudes taken by
groups and parties toward the Congress have been profoundly influenced
by their perceptions of the vulnerability of the Congress, which in turn have
varied in the differing regional contexts of Indian politics.

The history of ideological debate on the strategy for achieving power
and the attitude to be taken toward the Congress in the Communist movement in post-Independence India can be divided into two periods. The
first period, between 1947 and 1951, was characterized by fundamental
cleavage on the nature of that government and on the proper strategy to
be used against it.[76] Three distinct lines developed in this period. One line,
dominant at Independence, was supported by P. C. Joshi and S. A. Dange
in India and by Rajani Palme Dutt, the British Communist friend of the
CPI. This line identified the Congress government as a government of the
big bourgeoisie in alliance with feudal elements, but it distinguished Pandit
Nehru from his own government as a progressive force who, with support
from the Left, could be persuaded to pursue progressive policies. This line
called for a nonviolent anti-imperialist strategy based on four classes (proletariat, peasantry, petty bourgeoisie, and middle bourgeoisie) in opposition to the proimperialist and reactionary tendencies in the Congress
government but in support of the anti-imperialist tendencies represented
by Nehru. The second line, associated with B. T. Ranadive in India and
supported until 1948 by the Yugoslav party outside India, [77] identified the

---

[76] This discussion is based upon Overstreet and Windmiller, *Communism in India*,
chaps. 12–13; and Kautsky, *Moscow and the Communist Party of India*, chaps. 1–5.
[77] On the position of the Yugoslav party on these issues before their 1948 expulsion
from the Cominform, see Overstreet and Windmiller, *Communism in India*, pp.
258–259, 268, 274.

Nehru government as a bourgeois-capitalist government, representing both the big and middle bourgeoisie, and called for a revolutionary, three-class (proletariat, peasantry, and petty bourgeoisie) anticapitalist strategy based upon urban violence and armed insurrection in the countryside. The third line, called the Andhra line, looked upon the Communist-led insurrection then in progress in Telengana as a model for the more general application in India of a Maoist strategy. The Andhra Communists characterized the Nehru government as still a colonial government dominated by the big bourgeoisie, and called for an anti-imperialist, antifeudal and national liberationist strategy uniting all classes except the big bourgeoisie and feudal landlords—but including the middle bourgeoisie and rich peasants—in a united front. The Andhra line advocated the extension of agrarian revolution throughout India, wherever possible.[78] Thus, three kinds of issues were in dispute in the period between 1947 and 1951, namely, whether the Congress government or Nehru deserved Left support, whether the basic class strategy was to be anticapitalist or anti-imperialist, and whether or not armed struggle was to be used to achieve power. The international Communist movement was then divided on similar issues; so no coherent guidance from it was forthcoming.

In the second period of ideological debate on the issue of the attitude to be taken toward the Congress party and government, a consensus developed in the CPI on a nonviolent anti-imperialist strategy (sometimes called "peaceful neo-Maoism").[79] Three sets of events occurred to bring about this shift. The first was the failure of violent and insurrectionist tactics in the cities and in Telengana against the armed might of the government of India and the discrediting of both violence as the primary form of struggle and the anti-capitalist strategy as a guide for the struggle. Since 1951, no major group of Indian Communists has seriously promoted the adoption of a thoroughgoing anticapitalist strategy for the Indian revolution, although violent tactics have again become prominent among certain groups since 1967. The second set of events was the emergence of a consensus in the international Communist movement, after the expulsion of the Yugoslav party, on a neo-Maoist, anti-imperialist strategy in which the use of armed struggle was not universally prescribed. The third set of events was the series of shifts in international politics by which India's policy of nonalignment became acceptable to the Soviet Union and by which Indo-Soviet relations became increasingly cordial. It therefore became possible for the pro-Nehru elements in the CPI to adopt a more

[78] For a 1950 statement of the Andhra line, see "Statement of the Editorial Board of 'Communist' on L. P. P. D. Article," in *ICPD*, pp. 49–60.
[79] Kautsky, *Moscow and the Communist Party of India*, chap. 5.

consistent and coherent anti-imperialist strategy combined with a line favoring support for the Congress government.

The emergence of a consensus on an anti-imperialist, antifeudal strategy within the CPI barely concealed a continuing basic difference between groups in the Communist movement that preferred a more or less favorable policy towards the Congress and groups that preferred more or less militant opposition to the Congress. At the Third Party Congress of the CPI in 1953 in Madurai, a consensus was reached on the strategy of "peaceful neo-Maoism," that is, an anti-imperialist, all-class strategy (including rich peasants), in which "all forms of struggle" were to be used, but partisan warfare was not to be an immediate tactic.[80] On the issue of support for or opposition to the Nehru government and related questions, however, the party reached only an "uneasy compromise," choosing "to oppose the government, but to support specific acts."[81] At Palghat in 1956, the party moved closer toward support for progressive Congress policies and toward advocating alliances with progressive sections of the Congress but rejected an even more strongly rightist proposal for a Congress-CPI united front.[82] At Amritsar in 1958, the perennial issue of the proper attitude toward the Congress was partly submerged in the more momentous shift of the CPI toward "constitutional communism" and a firm commitment toward a peaceful transition to socialism.[83] The old issue emerged once again more strongly than ever prior to the Sixth Party Congress at Vijayawada in 1961. Before the Seventh Party Congress in 1964, the party finally split.

Although the difference between the groups in the CPI in this period was a tactical one, tortuous efforts were made by both sides to elaborate a convincing ideological superstructure from which the desired tactics

[80] Many of the important documents pertaining to the Madurai Congress are contained in *ICPD*, pp. 71–194. For interpretations of these documents and the issues at Madurai, see Kautsky, *Moscow and the Communist Party of India*, chap. 6; Overstreet and Windmiller, *Communism in India*, chap. 4; and Mohan Ram, *Indian Communism*, chap. 2.

[81] Overstreet and Windmiller, *Communism in India*, p. 312.

[82] See the documents pertaining to the Palghat Congress in *ICPD*, pp. 195–345; Mohan Ram, *Indian Communism*, pp. 71–72. The shift toward a stronger pro-Congress orientation at Palghat is evident in formulations that prescribed for the CPI the role of demanding "consistent application of the principles which the Government itself has accepted" and offering "constructive criticism" of the government rather than "denunciation and condemnation." These citations are from the "Report to the Party Congress" submitted by the Central Committee of the party at Palghat, in *ICPD*, pp. 239 and 251.

[83] Mohan Ram, *Indian Communism*, pp. 73–76.

could be derived. Thus, debate centered around the extent of differentiation within the national bourgeoisie between its monopolist and non-monopolist segments; the extent of dominance by the bourgeoisie, particularly its monopolist segments, in the Congress government; the extent to which Congress agrarian policies had promoted capitalist land relations; and the extent to which the Congress government followed anti-feudal, anti-imperialist policies at home and in foreign policy.[84] Although there never existed two completely consistent alternative ideological positions on these questions during this period of ideological debate, the tendency of the pro-Congress elements in the CPI was to argue that the Nehru government was a government of the entire bourgeoisie in which the monopolist segments were *not* dominant; that the national bourgeoisie was engaged in completing the national democratic revolution against the feudal-landlord remnants in Indian society and that Communist policy should support this tendency, which included policies of industrialization and agrarian reform; that Congress agrarian policies were benefiting all segments of rural society, not simply the developing capitalist landlord class;[85] and that the foreign policy of the Congress government, despite occasional deviations, was essentially a policy of peace and nonalignment. Therefore, the pro-Congress or Right tendency in the CPI favored a four-class, anti-imperialist strategy of support for the progressive policies of the Congress to keep the Congress on the correct path. To this end, the rightist elements in the CPI favored unity of Left and democratic forces, *including* progressive sections of the Congress. Thus, the rightist CPI tendency was toward united front from above with non-Congress Left forces and united front from below with the masses supporting the Congress, with the goal of creating a national democratic front including progressive segments of the Congress.

The anti-Congress or Left tendency in the CPI in this period was to argue that the Congress government was a government of the bourgeoisie in which the monopolist sections were increasingly dominant and were willing to compromise even with landlord and feudal elements and with foreign monopoly capital; that the government, far from completing the national democratic revolution, was becoming increasingly repressive of

[84] The major documents in which these ideological issues were debated in this period can be found in *ICPD*. Other documents and important theoretical articles are found in the old monthly *New Age*. See especially the competing draft programs prepared for the Sixth Party Congress in *New Age* 10, no. 4 (April 1961).
[85] See, for example, K. Satyanarayana, "Developments in Agriculture in the Andhra Region," *New Age* 10, no. 1 (January 1961), 50–55.

civil liberties and was adopting increasingly exploitative industrial policies and ineffective agrarian reforms; that Congress agrarian policies had already established capitalist land relations in various parts of the country;[86] and that the foreign policy of the Congress government was deviating more and more from a policy of peace and nonalignment toward a vacillating and even proimperialist position. Consequently, the Left tendency in the CPI favored united-front-from-below tactics with non-Congress Left forces against the Congress, with the goal of moving toward a People's Democracy under the leadership of the working class and the Communist Party. Those groups in the CPI that adhered to this Left tendency ultimately split from the united Communist party in 1964 to form the CPM.

I have argued so far that the two elaborate ideological tendencies that have divided the Communist movement in India during the past two decades are largely ideological superstructures that have overlain an uncomplicated difference between groups that have favored support for the Congress and its progressive policies and groups that have favored more militant opposition to the Congress. This difference in turn derives from different strategies toward power in Indian politics, between those who have favored a national strategy and those who have favored building power in the states where the Communist movement has been strong. The strongest support for a national strategy has come from those national leaders of the CPI who have lacked a strong regional base and from those state Communist parties that have been relatively weak and remote from power or could conceive of exercising power only as minor partners in a united front. National leaders of the CPI who fit this description include, among others, P. C. Joshi, a man from a state with a weak Communist movement (Uttar Pradesh) who spent most of his party life at national headquarters; S. A. Dange, with strong roots in the Bombay trade unions, but also from a state (Maharashtra) with a weak Communist movement; and Z. A. Ahmad, a man from Sindh who became prominent in the Uttar Pradesh party organisation for a long period, then moved to central headquarters. Support for the rightist tendency and for the CPI has been strongest in the states—with the exception of Andhra—where the Communist movement has been weakest, for example, Assam, Bihar, Maharashtra, Orissa, and Uttar Pradesh.

The anti-Congress tendency in the Communist movement and the bulk of the support for the CPM, in contrast, have come from regionally en-

---

[86] See, for example, N. Prasada Rao, "Recent Developments in Agriculture in Andhra Region," *New Age* 9, no. 10 (October 1960), esp. 40, 44–45, 47; P. K. Tandon, "Changes in Landownership Pattern in U.P.," ibid. 10, no. 1 (January 1961), 34–49; and, by the same author, "Agricultural Development in Uttar Pradesh," ibid. 10, no. 2 (February 1961), 37–53.

trenched leaders and from states in which the Communists have been serious contenders for power. Although for some time some of the centrist leaders avoided taking a clear position on the ideological issues, the bulk of the support for the anti-Congress tendency in the Communist movement came from regional leaders like Jyoti Basu from Bengal, E. M. S. Namboodiripad from Kerala, P. Sundarraya from Andhra, and Harkishan Singh Surjeet from the Punjab. Moreover, the predominant strength of the CPM has been in the two states of Bengal and Kerala, where the party has for long seriously contended for power with the Congress and has lately been the leading political party in both states in electoral support.

The distinction between those leaders and groups in the Communist movement that have been oriented more toward achieving power at the center and those that have been oriented more toward regional power cannot explain entirely the ideological differences that have developed on the issues of class strategy and support for or opposition to the Congress. In all states, but particularly in Andhra or the Punjab, there have been intraregional, factional, and personal differences at the state level that have impelled some leaders and groups toward the CPI and others toward the CPM, though their ideological positions may not be fully in tune with that of their chosen party. The Andhra party, historically one of the three strongest parties in the Communist movement in India, provided important ideologists for both tendencies and divided equally between the CPI and the CPM after the split. The explanation here relates to the special history of the Andhra Communist movement, which has always been more intensely divided on issues of tactics as well as class strategy than any other state Communist movement in India, as the chapter by Mohan Ram in this volume so vividly reveals. Even in the states like Bengal, Kerala, and Bihar where one tendency has predominated, local personal and factional differences have left some representatives of the opposing tendency in each state. Nevertheless, it is a central argument of this essay that the single most important variable determining the attitudes of Communist groups and leaders toward the Congress is national-regional orientation toward political power.[87] The second important set of variables is the regional, factional, and personal relationships between groups and individuals, which operates in such a way that if a dominant regional group opts for an anti-Congress strategy, the rival group will choose a pro-Congress strategy. Thus, in Bengal and Kerala, the CPI has found it useful to ally with Congress (R) not only because its national leaders seek power

---

[87] It should be noted that the distinction being made here concerns an orientation towards political power and not toward nationalism or regionalism. A party may be oriented toward achieving power in a region of India without necessarily using regional sentiment to achieve power.

at the center but because its local leadership seeks to defeat the CPM and achieve power in those states.

The Communist movement in India has also been divided on the choice of coalition partners from among the existing array of political parties and groups in India. Both major wings of the Communist movement have perceived three types of political parties in India—the Congress, the parties of Right reaction and communalism, and the parties of the democratic Left. In principle, the Right Communist strategy in India has been oriented toward the goal of creating a national democratic front comprising progressive sections of the Congress and the parties of the democratic Left, by which are meant the CPI, the CPM, the SSP, the PSP, and the Republican Party. The parties of Right reaction and communalism, which include the Jan Sangh, Swatantra, and many regional parties such as the Muslim League in Kerala and the Akali Dal in Punjab, have generally been considered to be inappropriate coalition partners.

The nationally oriented CPI strategy of the national democratic front has encountered several obstacles over the years. In the first place, the persisting strength of the Congress at the center (while its regional units have, in many areas, broken into fragments) has constantly kept the CPI leaders in a dilemma as to how to implement the strategy of including the Congress masses and progressive sections of the Congress in the front without being swamped by the Congress. Second, Left and democratic unity has proved more often than not to be a chimera and has foundered upon the anti-Communism of the PSP and the anti-Congressism of the SSP. Third, the national strategy itself has produced persistent strains both with the Left tendency in the old CPI and the present CPM and with regional units of the present CPI. The problem here has frequently been that regional units of the party have found it impossible to work with "Left and democratic" local units of parties such as the PSP and the SSP but have often found the road to power to lie in coalition with regional communal parties, such as the Muslim League in Kerala and the Akali Dal in the Punjab.

The conflict in the old CPI between the rightist national strategy and the regionally oriented strategy is well illustrated by the changes in the party line that occurred between the Third and Fourth Party Congresses at Madurai in 1953 and at Palghat in 1956. In 1953, the Communist party was a serious contestant for political power in the southern states, particularly in the old states of Hyderabad, Travancore-Cochin, and Madras. The party congress at Madurai, therefore, adopted a slogan calling for the formation of a "Government of Democratic Unity" as an alternative to Congress rule where possible.[88] By the time of the Fourth Party Congress at Palghat, however, the political situation in India had been drastically altered. The CPI strategy of alternative government had failed, particularly in the Andhra elections of 1955.[89] In the meantime, the rightist elements in the CPI had been buoyed by the dramatic shifts in Indo-Soviet relations, climaxed by the visits of Khrushchev and Bulganin to India in 1955, which strengthened the rightist view of the progressive character of the Congress government and the need for a national strategy. Consequently, at Palghat, the rightist strategy emerged dominant, with a clear national focus and with an emphasis on certain points critical of the regional orientation. The Madurai line was criticized for lacking "a national-political approach," that is, for failing to see that the Congress government was now playing an anti-imperialist role.[90] The Travancore and Andhra party units were criticized for adopting a "sectarian" attitude towards the PSP,[91] which had proved to be an unreliable coalition partner in the politics of those states. At the same time, the Muslim League, with which the Travancore party had reached electoral understandings, was declared a communal party with which the CPI was not to have a united front.[92] Electoral understandings with such parties for local benefit were criticized as opportunist tactics that "discredit the Party all over the country."[93] The efforts of the CPI would be more productively spent in winning over "the democratic masses that follow the Congress" and in bringing together the parties of "the democratic opposition," that is, the SP, the PSP, and the CPI.[94] Moreover, the democratic front constructed in this way ought not to be conceived as "an anti-Congress front," but as a front including sections of the Congress organization where possible.[95]

From Palghat onward, the rightist, national strategy in the CPI became increasingly prominent at party congresses and in party publications. The Right strategy increasingly called for unity with the Congress against the

[88] "Draft Political Resolution," in *ICPD*, p. 111; "Review Report of the PB (1953)," in *ICPD*, pp. 129–134 and 154–159; Mohan Ram, *Indian Communism*, p. 64.
[89] "CC Resolution on Andhra Elections (1955)," in *ICPD*, pp. 216–222; "Report to the Party Congress (1956)," in *ICPD*, pp. 272–273.
[90] "Report to the Party Congress," in *ICPD*, pp. 257–258.
[91] Ibid., pp. 264–267.
[92] Ibid., p. 299.
[93] Ibid., p. 301.
[94] Ibid., p. 276.
[95] Ibid., pp. 297–298.

forces of Right reaction and communalism,[96] which were defined to include not only Swatantra and Jan Sangh but the regional parties—the Muslim League, the DMK, and the Akali Dal.[97] Since the split in the CPI in 1964, the CPI has continued to pursue the strategy of the national democratic front, which, at Bombay in 1964 and at Patna in 1968, was defined in terms of power at the center and Left and democratic unity, including the Congress masses and progressive sections of the Congress.[98] If one accepts the CPI strategy at face value as designed in fact to achieve power at the center and Left unity, then that strategy has suffered three massive setbacks since the 1967 General Elections. The first was the reassertion of the primacy of regional imperatives in the formation of the non-Congress coalition governments in the north in which the CPI participated with previously proscribed coalition partners such as Jan Sangh, Swatantra, and the Akali Dal.[99] The second has been the nearly complete disintegration of Left unity in recent years.[100] The third was the electoral understanding of the CPI in the 1971 elections with Congress (R) and the PSP and the electoral alliance between Congress (R) and the CPI in 1972, which contributed to the massive restoration of Congress dominance in both national and state politics. (See table 1.4 for the results of the 1971 Lok Sabha elections.)

If, however, the immediate purpose of the strategy has been to ally with the Congress not to achieve power but to defeat the CPM, then the strategy

[96] See, for example, the "Draft Programme of the Communist Party of India," prepared for the Sixth Party Congress by S. A. Dange, P. C. Joshi, and G. Adhikari, *New Age* 10, no. 4 (April 1961), esp. 22–39; the speech of Ajoy Ghosh, "New Situation and our Tasks," ibid. 10, no. 5 (May 1961), 55 and 60–68; and "Communique of the National Council of the Communist Party of India," ibid 11, no. 5 (May 1962). 2–4.

[97] "Communique of the National Council of the CPI," *New Age* 11, no. 5 (May 1962), 2; see also the postsplit CPI document, "The Programme of the Communist Party of India," in *Seventh Congress Documents*, p. 45 and *Seventh Congress Discussions*, pp. 39, 47, 50.

[98] *Seventh Congress Discussions*, pp. 43–45; "Political Resolution," in *Seventh Congress Discussions*, pp. 67–74; "Political Resolution," in *Eighth Congress Documents*, pp. 14–19 and 22 and "Political Report," in *Eighth Congress Documents*, pp. 25–27, 119, 139–140. The explicit description of "power at the centre" "as the crucial political question before the nation" is an Eighth Congress formulation.

[99] Paul R. Brass, "Coalition Politics in North India," *American Political Science Review* 62, no. 4 (December 1968); "Political Report," in *Eighth Congress Documents*, pp. 104–107. However, the CPI has insisted, somewhat defensively, that it will not countenance a coalition with Jan Sangh and Swatantra at the center; *Eighth Congress Documents*, p. 119.

[100] For some expressions of CPI frustration over the failures of the Left parties to unite, see "Political Report," *Eighth Congress Documents*, pp. 64, 67, 89, 91, 99–104, 110, 135–139.

has been more successful. Although the CPM did as well in the 1971 Lok Sabha elections as the CPI, it was roundly defeated in the 1972 state assembly elections. For the first time since the split, the CPI won more seats than the CPM in every state in which elections were held (table 1.7). The greatest blow to the CPM came in West Bengal where the Congress, riding on the wave of India's victory in Bangladesh, won 217 out of 280 seats, the CPI won 35 seats, and the CPM only 14.

Paradoxically, the main benefit of the CPI national strategy has gone to the party's regional units in Kerala where the alliance with Congress (R) in the Kerala midterm elections in September 1970 led to the defeat of the CPM and the formation of a government led by the CPI. However, the CPI success in Kerala also reveals again the importance of regional imperatives in coalition building, for the anti-CPM coalition included the Muslim League that had been redefined at Patna as a party with "a positive role to play in advancing the democratic movement in that state." [101]

The orientation of the Left Communists towards achieving power in the states, particularly in Kerala and Bengal, has involved a different conception of appropriate alliance partners. The Left strategy has been to build

Table 1.4   Seats Won by Political Parties in the Lok Sabha, 1971 Midterm Elections

Party	Seats Won
Congress (R)	350
CPM	25
CPI	23
DMK	23
Jan Sangh	22
Congress (O)	16
Telengana Praja Samithi	10
Swatantra	8
SSP	3
PSP	2
Other parties and independents	33
Total	515

Source: *Indian Recorder & Digest* 17, no. 4 (April 1971), 5.

[101] "Political Report," *Eighth Congress Documents*, p. 78. Compare this statement with the CPI's resolution on the 1965 Kerala elections when the party announced its refusal to have any "truck with reactionary communal groups such as the Muslim League and the Kerala Congress"; "Resolutions on Current Events," *Seventh Congress Documents*, pp. 182–185 on the "Kerala Elections."

coalitions not with the Congress but against the Congress in order to provide an alternative government. Since Jan Sangh and Swatantra are parties of no consequence in Kerala and Bengal, it has been easier for the CPM to follow in practice the principle, which it holds in common with the CPI, of avoiding association with these parties of Right reaction and communalism. However, the Left strategy has always been more receptive in both principle and practice towards coalition with regional parties such as the Muslim League in Kerala and the Akali Dal in the Punjab. Although the CPM favors Left and democratic unity also, in common with the CPI, it has had only partial success in forging Left unity at the regional level and none at the national level. In Kerala and Bengal, the CPM has in the past successfully led Left coalitions, but in both states in the most recent elections—in 1970 in Kerala and 1971 and 1972 in Bengal—the CPM was isolated from its major previous Left coalition partners.

The divergence in the Communist movement on strategies for achieving power has, therefore, been a divergence on three interrelated issues—on the attitude to be taken towards the Congress government at the center, on whether a national strategy or regionally oriented strategies for achieving power are more appropriate for Indian conditions, and on the choice of appropriate coalition partners. The divergence within the Communist movement on these issues became increasingly acute until finally the CPI split over these issues in 1964 into two separate parties. Since 1964, the two parties have increasingly become rivals for power, following not merely different but opposed strategies, particularly in the states of Kerala and Bengal where the CPM has been the leading party in opposition to the Congress and where the CPI has chosen to ally with the Congress (R) to defeat the rival Communist party.

Similar differences within the Communist movement in Pakistan and Bangladesh have existed on the question of the appropriate attitude to be taken towards the regime. In the early post-Independence period, the Ranadive line was pursued in Pakistan, as in India, and met with equally disastrous results. After 1951, the Communist parties divided both on issues of coalition strategy and on attitudes towards the Ayub Khan regime. Before the establishment of the Ayub Khan regime, the Communists in East Bengal divided between groups that wanted to work separately from other parties and groups that worked within the Awami League and the NAP. During the regime of Ayub Khan, the rightist and pro-Soviet Communist groups opposed Ayub Khan whereas the leftist Communist groups supported him. Since the downfall of Ayub Khan and the growth of the regional movement in East Bengal, the pressures on all political groups to pursue an antiregime and proautonomy, if not prosecessionist position, were enormous. However, the continued support of Peking for the Pakistan government complicated the position of those Communist groups that had identified with Peking in the past. During the secessionist movement, the pro-Peking groups were divided and confused whereas the pro-Moscow groups took an unequivocal prosecessionist stance. In the first successful "national liberation" movement in an Asian country outside of Indochina, the People's Republic of China was on the opposing side, and its position helped bring about the disintegration of the Maoist groups in Bangladesh.

In Ceylon, the issue for the Communist parties and the LSSP has been whether or not to ally with the SLFP and to participate in SLFP-dominated coalition governments. The predominant segments of both the Communist and former Trotskyite movements have opted for such a strategy, while the minority segments have moved toward militant opposition to all non-Marxist parties and away from participation in SLFP-dominated governments.

THE SOCIALIST PARTIES   Parallel differences within the democratic Socialist movement in India have existed on the issue of the strategy to be used to achieve power, although the differences have been argued with much less ideological elaboration. Parallel to the Right Communist tendency in the democratic socialist movement has been "the cooperationist approach" [102] towards the Congress, for which Ashok Mehta has been the chief ideological spokesman. Mehta presented his thesis on the "compulsions of the backward economy" at the Betul Convention of the PSP in 1953. He argued then that the efforts to develop the economy of India had aroused discontents that were being channeled through traditional mechanisms of caste, community, and region. The Socialist movement had a common interest with the Congress in economic development and in opposing such reactionary and parochial forms of protest. That is, the PSP had more in common with the Congress than with the forces opposed to the Congress. Consequently, the democratic parties should demarcate "areas of agreement" among them, possibly including a common program and participation in a broad-based government so that the extreme Communist and communalist opposition forces would be driven to the fringes of Indian politics.[103]

The "cooperationist" line of Ashok Mehta and the PSP actually contained within it two prescriptions that affected PSP attitudes towards potential coalition partners. One prescription was for cooperation with the

[102] This term is from Limaye, *Why Samyukta Socialist?*, p. 12.
[103] Hari Kishore Singh, *History of the PSP*, pp. 183–185.

Congress. The other prescription was that the PSP should avoid alliances with both Communist and communalist parties and should ally only with "like minded parties." The first prescription was followed through to a logical conclusion by Ashok Mehta and many of his followers in 1963–1964 when he accepted the position of minister of planning in the Congress government at the center and many of his followers joined the Congress party in the various states where the PSP had some strength, particularly in UP and Bihar. Those in the PSP who did not interpret cooperation with the Congress as implying formal merger into it on an organizational or individual basis found that the second prescription severely limited their potential coalition partners in both state and national politics. Until 1967, the PSP followed a largely isolationist posture with regard to electoral agreements and coalitions with other parties. The merger with the SP in 1964 was dissolved abruptly, partly on the issue of coalition strategies. The PSP also generally avoided agreements and cooperative agitations with either the Jan Sangh on the Right or either of the Communist parties on the Left. After 1967, the PSP, along with most other parties, participated in the all-party non-Congress governments that were formed especially in the north Indian states, but the party soon reverted to its policy of avoiding alliances with the extreme Left and the extreme Right. In the 1971 parliamentary elections, however, the PSP, along with the CPI, participated in electoral adjustments and agreements with the Congress (R). Thus, the cooperationist tendencies in both the Communist and democratic Socialist movements in India ultimately merged in a national understanding in 1971, from which the Congress (R) emerged dominant, the CPI relatively unscathed, but the PSP virtually eliminated as a serious national party (see table 1.4).

Parallel to the Left tendency in the Communist movement in India has been the democratic Socialist line of militant opposition to the Congress, represented particularly by the SP (later the SSP), whose chief ideological spokesmen have been Dr. Rammanohar Lohia and Madhu Limaye. Like the Left Communists, the SSP leaders argued that the Congress government, far from pursuing progressive or radical policies, was responsible for promoting increasing inequalities and injustice in India. The responsibility of the radical Left in these conditions was to build itself up "as an alternative to the Congress." [104] The SSP leaders recognized that such an alternative could not be built by a single Left party or even by the entire leftist movement in India. Moreover, unlike the CPM, the SSP was never a potential alternative dominant party to the Congress in any region of

[104] Limaye, *Why Samyukta Socialist?*, pp. 11–12.

India, with the possible exception of Bihar. Consequently, the SSP adopted an alliance strategy different from all other Left parties, namely, of open alliance or coalition with any party opposed to the ruling Congress party at the center. Since the CPI and the PSP had opted for understandings with Congress (R) and the CPM had been concerned to oppose Congress (R) only in the states and had not been interested in a national strategy, the SSP had to seek its coalition partners primarily on the Right. Thus, in the 1971 parliamentary elections, the SSP joined forces with Congress (O), Jan Sangh, and Swatantra against Congress (R). Not surprisingly, this national SSP strategy caused intense internal dispute in the party in the one region, Bihar, where the SSP had been a major force and where local conditions would suggest that an alliance with Congress (R) would be more promising to achieve power. The dismal failure of the national SSP strategy of opposing the Congress (R) eliminated the SSP also as a serious national party, which suggests that regional strategies are likely to be more important for the radical Socialists in the future as well.

In effect, therefore, the only Left party that has been able to pursue a national strategy *at all* without destroying itself has been the CPI. The PSP and the SSP national strategies have ended in disaster. The CPM emerged as the second largest opposition party in the national parliament in 1971 largely on the basis of its regional strength in Bengal, where it won 20 of its 25 seats.

The issues before the National Awami parties in East Bengal have been somewhat different. There was little disagreement in the NAP on opposition to the Ayub Khan regime. Nor has either segment of the NAP been an important potential alliance partner for the Awami League. The NAP(M) has been generally more favorable to alliances and to parliamentary politics than the NAP(B). However, both parties have been relegated to tiny minority positions in both national and regional politics in Pakistan and in East Bengal. As in Ceylon, Tamil Nadu, and the Punjab, all the leftist forces in East Bengal have played a secondary role to the dominant regional party, the Awami League.

THE NATIONALITY ISSUE, REGIONALISM, AND MINORITY RIGHTS
THE COMMUNIST PARTIES Although differences within the Communist movement in India over national and regional strategies for achieving power have been a major cause of division, these differences have not extended to any profound disagreement on nationality policy or on attitudes towards regionalism and minority rights between the Right and Left tendencies in the old CPI or between the present CPI and the CPM. In the pre-Independence period and beyond Independence until the early 1950s,

the predominant line in the party favored a thoroughgoing application of a Soviet and Stalinist nationality policy. From this perspective, India was seen as a multinational state containing many nationalities in varying stages of development. The principle of self-determination was considered applicable to the nationalities of India, including the Muslim population of the subcontinent. Consequently, the CPI in 1945 and 1946 not only accepted the idea of the creation of Pakistan but favored the granting of sovereignty to all the nationalities of India. The election manifesto of the CPI for the 1946 elections proposed that independent India be constituted into "a confederation of free nation-states." [105]

In the post-Independence period, this rather literal application of Soviet nationality policy to India faded out of Communist rhetoric, probably for three reasons.[106] First, the leading advocate of this extreme policy of support for separatism, P. C. Joshi, was replaced as general secretary of the party in 1948. Second, Soviet foreign policy shifted towards a pro-India and pro-Indian unity position. Third, in the aftermath of the bitterness associated with the partition of India in 1947 and the suppression of the Telengana uprising in 1951, it became clear to the CPI leadership that support for further separatism would be both an unpopular and an unsuccessful policy in Indian politics.

Consequently, since the early 1950s, the Communist parties have moved to a position of identification with the unity of India. It is true that the Right tendency in the CPI has been more unequivocal in this regard than the Left tendency and the CPM, but this difference itself is a reflection more of the different attitudes towards the Congress than of serious disagreements over the desirability of maintaining the unity of India. The rightists in the CPI have increasingly seen national unity and opposition to "communalism and casteism" as slogans for forging a united front with progressive Congressmen, whereas the leftists in the CPI and the CPM have preferred to accuse the Congress itself of promoting policies disruptive of Indian unity.

It is sometimes argued that Communists, especially in India, are particularly cynical and skillful in their manipulation and exploitation of

[105] Overstreet and Windmiller, *Communism in India*, p. 498; Selig S. Harrison, *India: The Most Dangerous Decades* (Princeton, N.J.: Princeton University Press, 1960), pp. 151–152.

[106] Cf. Franda, *Radical Politics in West Bengal*, chap. 9 and Harrison, *India: The Most Dangerous Decades*, pp. 171–174. For examples of the developing CPI emphasis on "national unity" and rejection of its earlier line, see "Ramamurthy's Letter to N. M. Jaisoorya and G. M. Shroff (1953)," in *ICPD*, p. 193 and Ajoy Ghosh, "New Situation and Our Tasks," pp. 53–56.

national differences and of their own nationality policy.[107] Selig Harrison argued a decade ago that the Communist Party has been successful in India primarily in those regions where it has based its power on "politically strategic regional castes" and on "the manipulation of regional patriotism." [108] In fact, both Communist parties have laid great stress on linguistic, regional, and minority group demands in the Indian states and in East Bengal. Both major wings of the Communist movement in India have supported the demands for the creation of linguistic states, for regional autonomy for tribal groups in states that contain large tribal populations, for protection of the rights of linguistic and religious minorities in the linguistic states, and for greater state autonomy in relation to the central government.[109] Like other secular political parties in India, the Communist parties have benefited when they could identify with powerful regional movements and suffered when they could not or when they have been caught between the demands of competing groups. It does not appear, however, that the Communist parties in general have been more successful in this regard than other secular parties in India. Communist strength in Kerala, Bengal, and Andhra no doubt is partly related to earlier and continuing Communist identification with regional sentiments in those states, but the Communist parties even there have not used prominently symbols of regional nationalism and elsewhere in India Communist success along these lines has not been great. The old CPI benefited from the formation of the Samyukta Maharashtra Samiti United Front,[110] which led the drive for the division of the old Bombay State, but the Communist movement remains weak in Maharashtra. In many other states, the Communist parties have been confronted with well-entrenched regional political organizations that have made linguistic or tribal group demands more effectively than the Communists have. For example, in Bihar, the Jhar-

---

[107] Harrison, *India: The Most Dangerous Decades*, esp. pp. 146–149, 169, 176–177, 264.

[108] Ibid., p. 181.

[109] For some examples of CPI views on these issues, see "Draft Political Resolution (1953)," in *ICPD*, p. 119; "Report to the Party Congress (1956)," in *ICPD*, p. 245; S. A. Dange, P. C. Joshi, and G. Adhikari, "Draft Programme of the Communist Party of India," *New Age* 10, no. 4 (April 1961), 17–18; Bhupesh Gupta and P. Ramamurti, "Draft Programme of the Communist Party of India," ibid. 10, no. 4 (April 1961), 13, 23, 25, 33; "The Programme of the Communist Party of India," *Seventh Congress Documents*, pp. 29–30, 49, 54; "Political Resolution," *Eighth Congress Documents*, pp. 69–76. See also the CPI and CPM manifestos for the 1967 General Elections in R. Chandidas et al., *India Votes: A Source Book on Indian Elections* (New York: Humanities Press, 1968), pp. 51, 68–69.

[110] Ajoy Ghosh, "New Situation and Our Tasks," pp. 37–38.

khand party has traditionally favored the creation of a separate state for the tribal areas of Chota Nagpur, whereas the CPI demand has been a more moderate one for "regional autonomy for the Adivasi people." [111] In Punjab, the Communist parties supported demands for linguistic reorganization and for the creation of Punjabi Suba, but they opposed the phrasing of the demands in religious communal terms and opposed both the Jan Sangh and the Akali Dal for doing so. [112] In Assam, the Communist parties have been hopelessly entangled in the web of communal conflicts among Bengalis and Assamese, Assamese and tribals, Hindus and Muslims, with little benefit to Communist strength. [113] In north India, both Communist parties have identified completely with Muslim minority grievances and demands[114] and have won some Muslim support, but Muslims are a small minority throughout most of north India and constitute an inadequate and unreliable base for continuing Communist strength.

Nor, finally, have either of the Communist parties benefited from the official language issue at the center. For a time in the early post-Independence period, the CPI was divided into pro- and anti-Hindi groups, but the CPI announced "qualified support" for encouragement of Hindi as an official language for interstate communication at the Madurai conference in 1953.[115] The position of both major Communist parties has remained more or less the same on this question ever since, that is, encouragement of Hindi, but with no imposition of Hindi on non-Hindi states and regions.[116]

The symbols of language, religion, region, tribe, and caste have had great popular appeal in post-Independence Indian politics. Powerful political movements have been built upon them, particularly in Tamil Nadu and the Punjab. Secular political parties face a dual dilemma in dealing with such symbols and with movements based upon them. If they do not sympathize or identify with such symbols and movements, they lose a potentially decisive support base, perhaps permanently. If they do identify with such symbols and movements, they may lose the support of opposed

111 Tarun Dutt, "The Problem of Bihar Tribals," *New Age* 9, no. 6 (June 1960), 30–37; citation from p. 36.

112 See Harkishan Singh Surjeet, "Language and Linguistic Reorganisation in Punjab," *New Age* 9, no. 7 (July 1960), 35–50; Bhupesh Gupta and P. Ramamurti, "Draft Programme," p. 33; Ajoy Ghosh, "New Situation and Our Tasks," pp. 38–39; "Political Report," in *Eighth Congress Documents*, pp. 82–83.

113 Ajoy Ghosh, "Assam," *New Age* 10, no. 7–8 (July–August 1961), 25–38.

114 See Z. A. Ahmad, "The Muslim Convention," *New Age* 10, 7–8 (July–August 1961), 65–78; Chandidas et al., *India Votes*, pp. 51 and 69.

115 Overstreet and Windmiller, *Communism in India*, pp. 501–505; see also Harrison, *India: The Most Dangerous Decades*, pp. 258–262, 264.

116 "Political Resolution," in *Eighth Congress Documents*, p. 19; "Political Report," in *Eighth Congress Documents*, p. 69; Chandidas et al., *India Votes*, pp. 51 and 68.

groups or of secular elements in society. In other words, there is no formula
for exploiting regional symbols and sentiments in India. Nor are Communist parties any better at doing so than other secular parties in Indian
politics.

The position of the Communist parties in East Bengal in relation to
Bengali regional aspirations has been similar to the position of the Communist parties in Punjab and Tamil Nadu. That is, although the Communists have often played important roles in movements on behalf of the
Bengali language and for greater autonomy for East Bengal, they have not
been able to capture regional symbols. As in Punjab and Tamil Nadu, a
non-Communist party, the Awami League, has provided the principal
forum for the expression of regional demands. It also succeeded in retaining control over the national liberation movement and formed the first
government of independent Bangladesh. The role of both the Communist
and Trotskyite parties in Ceylon has been even more marginal with regard
to linguistic and cultural group demands. The SLFP has completely
dominated the expression of Sinhalese national sentiment in politics,
whereas the Communist parties and the LSSP identified with Sinhalese
demands later than the SLFP and with reluctance.

THE SOCIALIST PARTIES Issues of language and caste have been more
divisive between parties in the democratic Socialist movement in India
than they have been among the Communist parties. The SSP deliberately
and militantly used appeals based on language and caste in a distinctive
way among the parties of the radical Left. In contrast to every other
radical party in India, the SSP proposed a policy of reservation of 60 percent of places in party organization and in government for representatives
of backward segments of society, defined to include backward and scheduled castes, Muslims, tribals, and women. The SSP was most successful in
using this broad-based appeal in Bihar, where it won some support among
rising backward and low caste groups. The SSP in Bihar was also in a
position to implement this policy in its own party organization and in the
United Front governments in that state. However, the experience of
the SSP in the first non-Congress government in Bihar, described in the
chapter on Bihar in this volume, has demonstrated that the party's caste
policy was a double-edged weapon that could be turned against the party
by discontented leaders and groups.

The SSP also distinguished itself in the radical Left by its militancy on
the issue of Hindi. It came forward with a vigorous demand for abolition
of English from public life in India and immediate replacement of English
by Hindi and other regional languages. In this way, the SSP, as a predominantly Hindi-region party, identified with powerful regional sentiments

in the north. However, the SSP's Hindi policy had some undesirable consequences for the development of party strength. First, it made it difficult for the SSP to build strength or to find allies outside the Hindi region itself. Second, its pro-Hindi position antagonized minority groups in the north, particularly Muslims who wish to see Urdu protected against the spread of Hindi.

The militancy of the SSP on caste and language contrasted with the PSP position on these issues, which was the most moderate of all parties on the Left. The PSP sometimes participated in or supported linguistic movements in Maharashtra and the Punjab, but its policies on language, caste, and regionalism have been the least distinctive of the parties of the Left. The PSP often opposed the use of linguistic, caste, and communal appeals and especially opposed the SSP use of such symbols, which it often claimed was a major obstacle to the unity of the two parties. Neither in its 1967 nor in its 1971 election manifesto did the PSP even refer to issues of language, caste, or minority rights except to express in a general way its opposition to untouchability.[117]

In East Bengal, both National Awami parties favored the movements for increased regional autonomy. The NAP(B) position on this issue before the 1971 elections was the same as that of the Awami League. During the liberation war, both National Awami parties supported the struggle and contributed fighting cadres to it.

THE QUESTION OF TACTICS: PARLIAMENTARISM OR REVOLUTION

THE COMMUNIST PARTIES Questions concerning appropriate tactics for carrying on revolutionary struggles and achieving power are never far from the surface of ideological discussion among parties of the radical Left. Within the Communist movement in India, such questions have been persistently discussed. There have been two periods since Independence in India that have been marked by especially intense debate and division within the Communist movement on issues of tactics—between 1947 and 1951 and from 1967 to the present.

In the period between 1947 and 1951, as was mentioned above, there were fundamental divisions within the CPI on both strategy and tactics. The nonviolent, pro-Congress tendency, dominant at Independence, was replaced for a time by the Ranadive revolutionary, anticapitalist strategy in theory and by the use of violent and insurrectionary tactics in Telengana

---

[117] See Chandidas et al., *India Votes*, pp. 79–85 for the PSP manifesto for the 1967 elections and *Handbook of Election Manifestos, 1971, Commerce* supplement of 20 February 1971 (Bombay: *Commerce*, 1971), pp. 87–101 for the 1971 PSP election manifesto.

and in Bengal in practice. The Ranadive line was opposed in theory from both the Right and the Left in the party. The Joshi-Dange group in the CPI opposed both the anticapitalist strategy and the use of violence. The Andhra Communists favored the extension of agrarian revolutionary violence but wanted to base it upon a Maoist four-class alliance. In the meantime, the insurrection in Telengana was suppressed by the Indian army, and the organizers of rural revolutionary violence in Bengal were arrested and the movement defeated. By 1951, therefore, the Ranadive line had been discredited in theory in the party debate and defeated in practice by state power.[118]

From the early 1950s onwards, a gradual consensus on strategy and tactics developed within the CPI, combining elements of both the Joshi-Dange and Andhra lines. That consensus involved, first, an agreement on an anti-imperialist, four-class strategy for achieving power and, second, a gradual de-emphasis on revolutionary tactics and an increasing concentration of party resources in the electoral-parliamentary arena. Until and through the Madurai Conference of the party in 1953, the CPI documents continued to refer in a qualified way to the use of armed violence as a means of revolutionary struggle. Thus, the formation of "people's liberation armies" was considered desirable, but only "when the necessary internal conditions allow for it." [119] Party documents emphasized that "all forms of struggle" were to be used in pursuing popular causes and in achieving power, from partisan warfare to electoral politics, to "partial struggles" for specific demands of the people, and to the provision of relief by party members to people in distress.[120] Increasingly, in practice, only electoral politics and nonviolent agitational methods were used by the CPI.

The adoption of a peaceful, parliamentary path of Socialist transition and the disavowal of violent tactics were firmly established by the CPI at the Fourth and Fifth party congresses at Palghat in 1956 and at Amritsar in 1958. The Palghat conference followed closely on the heels of the Twentieth Congress of the CPSU, at which Khrushchev announced the new line of the Soviet party of peaceful transition to Socialism as a viable path

---

[118] The ideological debate and the struggle for power between the contending groups in the CPI in this period are described in Overstreet and Windmiller, *Communism in India*, chaps. 12 and 13.
[119] "Statement of the Editorial Board of 'Communist' on L.P.P.D. Article," in *ICPD*, p. 52.
[120] Ibid., esp. p. 59; "Questions to and Answers by R. P. Dutt," in *ICPD*, pp. 61–70; "Tactical Line (1953)," in *ICPD*, pp. 71–85; "Review Report of the PB (1953)," in *ICPD*, pp. 166–167.

under certain conditions. At Palghat, the CPI indicated its intent to act as a parliamentary party of opposition within the constitutional system.[121] Between the Palghat conference in 1956 and the Amritsar conference in 1958, the achievement of power by the Kerala CPI in 1957 reinforced the movement towards "constitutional communism," which became, unequivocally, the party line at Amritsar.

It deserves stressing that though the Right and Left tendencies in the CPI at this time were divided on the attitude to be taken towards the Congress, they were not divided on the issue of tactics. In fact, it was the successes of the Kerala Communists as much as any other factor that strengthened the CPI movement towards parliamentarism. If anything, the Left tendency was even more emphatic than the Right in its adherence to parliamentary institutions and peaceful means. When the right and left wings of the CPI presented alternative draft programs for the Sixth Party Congress in 1961, there were no substantial differences between the Right program and the Left program on tactics. Both draft programs, in nearly identical terms, referred to the parliamentary system as "an advance for the people" and argued that India's "parliamentary and democratic institutions" should be strengthened and transformed from instruments of the bourgeoisie to instruments of the working people and that this should be done by the achievement of a stable majority by "the working class and its allies." Moreover, both draft programs presented the Communists as dedicated to the "further strengthening" of India's parliamentary institutions.[122]

From the Amritsar conference in 1958 until 1967, the primary issues of tactics in the Communist movement concerned the proper uses of parliamentary and electoral politics, not whether or not they should be used at all. The main issue, of course, was how vigorously those institutions should be used to oppose the Congress. In addition to this issue, which divided Right and Left, Communists in this period were concerned with how parliamentary institutions could be used effectively to advance the cause of Left and democratic forces and to achieve power without succumbing to reformist and opportunist tendencies. Since India's parliamentary institutions were under bourgeois control and the elections were "loaded against the toiling masses as the press and other means of propaganda are controlled by monopoly interests," it was argued that parliamentary politics must be used by Communists in conjunction with

[121] "Report of Ajoy Ghosh to the Fourth Congress of the CPI (1956)," in *ICPD*, esp. pp. 331, 333–335.
[122] S. A. Dange, P. C. Joshi, and G. Adhikari, "Draft Programme," pp. 21, 38–39; Bhupesh Gupta and P. Ramamurti, "Draft Programme," pp. 15–16, 20.

"extra-parliamentary mass struggles" in order to change "the course of parliamentary policies in favor of the masses."[123] Thus, in addition to participating in electoral politics, the Communist parties in the '50s and '60s led or participated in "struggles and campaigns" on particular issues. For example, a whole series of movements on the issues of food-grain prices and food scarcity was launched by the CPI in 1958 and 1959 in Uttar Pradesh, Bengal, Punjab, and Tamil Nadu. Other campaigns were launched on other issues—against the betterment levy in Punjab in February 1959; against increased taxes in Bihar in April 1959; on issues of land reform and land ceilings in Kerala, Tamil Nadu, Bihar, and West Bengal in 1960.[124] In 1963 and 1964, another major series of agitations was carried on by the CPI and its trade union and peasant auxiliaries—a Great Petition and March to Delhi on 13 September 1963, concerning, among other issues, the Compulsory Deposit Scheme and the Gold Control Order; an AITUC-led struggle in 1963–1964 over bonus and linking of dearness allowance with the cost of living index; a food-grain prices *satyagraha* in August 1964. The CPI also participated in the series of *bandhs* or general strikes that were carried on by Left parties in Kerala, Maharashtra, Gujarat, Uttar Pradesh, and West Bengal in this period.[125] In 1966 and 1967, the CPI led or participated in food movements in Bihar, West Bengal, and Uttar Pradesh; in trade union actions in Bombay, Amritsar, Coimbatore, and Delhi; and in peasant agitations for implementation of land ceiling laws and distribution of cultivable wastelands to landless and poor peasants in Bengal, Punjab, Andhra, and Uttar Pradesh.[126]

The Right and Left tendencies in the old CPI and the present CPI and CPM have never differed on the question of combining parliamentary and extraparliamentary tactics. The split in the CPI in 1964 centered on the question of whether or not both types of tactics were to be used to dislodge the Congress from power or whether they were to be used to unite with progressive elements in the Congress as well and to push the Congress more in a left direction. Since the split in 1964, both parties have continued to use both types of tactics in pursuit of their different strategies for achieving power. However, the CPM has insisted that its political-tactical line is to be distinguished from what it considers to be the revisionism of the CPI. Pamphlets of the CPM since the split have distinguished the "correct" line from the revisionist line on several points. The CPM argues that it "strives

---

[123] "The Programme of the Communist Party of India," in *Seventh Congress Documents*, pp. 27–28.
[124] Ajoy Ghosh, "New Situation and Our Tasks," pp. 26–37.
[125] "Organisational Report," in *Seventh Congress Documents*, pp. 115–117.
[126] "Political Report," in *Eighth Congress Documents*, pp. 97–98.

to achieve the revolution by peaceful means," but that a violent revolution will probably ultimately be forced upon the working class in self-defense against the violence of the ruling classes.[127] This does not, however, mean that the CPM is to be led into the trap into which they claim that contemporary Left-adventurists have fallen, namely, of being drawn "into unequal class battles" and being destroyed.[128] For the present, therefore, peaceful and parliamentary tactics are to be pursued. However, the CPM claims to place more emphasis on building mass organizations and mass struggles than the CPI. From the CPM theoretical point of view, the CPI places too much emphasis on parliamentarism and too little upon work with the masses, whereas the CPM claims to view the parliamentary struggle as secondary to the struggle to build mass unity and mass organization.[129] The CPM also argues that parliamentary democratic institutions in India are but a facade behind which the big bourgeoisie and feudal landlords pursue their antipeople policies.[130]

It is difficult, however, to see substantial differences in practice between the parliamentary and extraparliamentary activities of the CPI and the CPM. The CPI certainly does not rule out the possibility that violence may ultimately prove necessary, though it is more hopeful of a nonviolent way than the CPM in theory. Nor does the CPI dispute the need to build the unity and organization of the masses. The CPM argues that "the fatal blow to the existing regime will be delivered not in the parliamentary arena but in the arena of direct revolutionary mass struggle." [131] The CPI would probably not dispute this assertion, but there has been a difference of emphasis in the CPM and CPI lines in both their images of the nature of the present struggle and the utility of parliamentary institutions in promoting revolutionary change. In practice, however, the main efforts of both parties so far have been directed to the parliamentary arena and to nonviolent extraparliamentary mass movements.

Since 1967, however, the older issue of the appropriateness of parliamentary and nonviolent tactics for revolutionary parties has been raised once again in the Communist movement. This question has affected the CPM more than it has the CPI and it has developed most acutely in the states of Bengal, Andhra, and Kerala. The immediate precipitating factor in reviving the issue of violence or nonviolence in a major way for the

---

[127] *Letter to Andhra Comrades* (Calcutta: CPM, n.d.), p. 27.
[128] Ibid., p. 41.
[129] *Political-Organisational Report of the Central Committee to the Eighth Congress of the Communist Party of India (Marxist)* (Calcutta: CPM, 1969), p. 195.
[130] Ibid., p. 191.
[131] Ibid., p. 195.

Communist movement was the peasant agitation led by a faction of the CPM in the Naxalbari subdivision of Darjeeling District in north Bengal in the spring and summer of 1967, which focused on issues of distribution of uncultivated land held by tea estates to tribal cultivators. Although the Naxalbari agitation began in traditional nonviolent ways, a police firing in May precipitated a chain of violent clashes that continued through July until the United Front government of Bengal finally took determined action to suppress the developing revolt.[132]

Although the Naxalbari agitation was localized, in its violent aspects unplanned, and ultimately unsuccessful, it has become the symbol of revolutionary tactics in the contemporary Communist movement. Perhaps more important than the agitation itself was the fact that it took place in the context of a factional dispute within the CPM in Bengal on issues of tactics and that it was suppressed by a United Front government in which the CPM was the major party. Consequently, the Naxalbari agitation focused attention in the Communist movement very dramatically and very early after the 1967 elections on the question of the appropriateness of Communist parties exercising "partial power" in state coalition governments in a bourgeois-landlord dominated state structure.

On this question of "partial power," the two leading Communist parties have held similar views. The CPI has taken the view that the non-Congress coalition governments are "to be conceived as instruments of struggle for advancing the cause of the masses," and that mere participation in a coalition government does not absolve the Communists from continuing to promote mass actions outside the government.[133] In practice, Hardgrave has argued that the CPI has tended to opt for "efficient administration" rather than for "struggle" when in power in Kerala.[134] The CPM leaders in Bengal and Kerala have argued that their participation in coalition governments in those states is designed to lay the groundwork for future radical change and to "break the Constitution from within."[135] In Bengal, Andhra, and Kerala, however, there have been elements in the Communist movement that treat such arguments with disbelief and dismiss them as unrealistic and opportunistic.

In April 1969, the Bengal Naxalites who disapproved of the role of the

---

[132] The most thorough and impartial account of the original Naxalbari agitation and its consequences is contained in Franda, *Radical Politics in West Bengal*, chap. 6.

[133] "Political Report," in *Eighth Congress Documents*, pp. 114–115.

[134] Robert L. Hardgrave, Jr., "The Marxist Dilemma in Kerala: Administration and/or Struggle," *Asian Survey* 10, no. 11 (November 1970), 998; see also his contribution to this volume.

[135] *Hindu*, 8 July 1969, cited in Hardgrave's chapter in this volume.

CPM in Bengal politics formed India's third Communist party, the Communist Party of India (Marxist-Leninist) or CPML, with a leadership taken largely from the Left faction of the Bengal CPM, and with international support from the Communist Party of China.[136] The CPML has, since its formation, taken an uncompromising antiparliamentary position and has argued that only an armed revolution in the countryside can bring socialism to India and that India is ready for such a revolutionary upheaval. Similar developments have taken place in Andhra where violent tactics have been followed in Srikakulam district and in other parts of the state and where an organization called the Andhra Pradesh Revolutionary Communist Committee competes with the local CPML leadership in pursuing separate interpretations of Maoist revolutionary strategy. Pressure from "Naxalite" elements has also affected the cohesion of the CPM in Kerala.

Thus, the issue of revolutionary versus parliamentary tactics has once again assumed major proportions in the Communist movement in India in a way similar to the earlier period of ideological debate between 1947 and 1951. In both periods, localized violence and insurrection—in Telengana in 1947–1948 and in Naxalbari in 1967—became symbols of revolutionary struggle for elements discontented with the parliamentary path in the Communist movement. In both periods also, the sanction of the Chinese revolution and Maoism were invoked to legitimize the use of violent revolutionary strategies. There are two considerable differences, however, between the social and political contexts of these two periods. The earlier debate occurred in the context of a more united national and international Communist movement, which meant that the pressures were toward the evolution of an ideological consensus. The present debate is occurring in a context of an internally and externally divided Communist movement, which means that the restraints upon the most revolutionary groups and factions for independent political action are reduced. Second, the earlier debate took place at a time when the Indian National Congress completely dominated Indian political life and when the prospects of Communists achieving power in India, let alone by peaceful means, were remote. The present debate takes place at a time when Communists have been exercising "partial power" in the Indian states and when rival Communist parties have been competing with each other, as well as with the Congress, for power. In such a situation, opportunities exist for rival political groups to support revolutionary groups and strategies as a means of embarrassing each other. In general, therefore, the altered context of

[136] Franda, *Radical Politics in West Bengal*, chap. 7.

the revived debate on revolutionary or parliamentary tactics in the Communist movement suggests that the achievement of a new ideological consensus is unlikely and that pressure on the two parliamentary Communist parties to become more militant will increase.

In East Bengal, there have also been two periods of severe internal division within the Communist movement on the question of tactics. During the first period, 1947 to 1951, the issues in East Bengal were identical to those in India. Like the CPI, the EPCP adopted an "adventurist" policy at this time, which precipitated an even more severe repression of the party in East Bengal than in India. After 1951, when the Indian Communists moved more and more into the parliamentary-electoral arena, the East Bengal Communists also adopted more peaceful tactics. Since the restrictions on Communist political activity were greater in Pakistan than in India, Communists in East Bengal tended to work through other parties, first the Awami League, then the National Awami Party.

During the Martial Law regime and the early years of Ayub Khan's regime, there was very little opportunity for political party activity at all in Pakistan. When the restraints on party activity were loosened, the Communist and National Awami parties were divided on the issue of support for or opposition to the Ayub Khan government, but not on the question of tactics, which did not become a major issue again until the crumbling of the regime in 1969. From 1969 until the beginnings of the civil war in March 1971, the Communist movement was divided between a rightist Communist Party that favored a peaceful path and five other Communist parties and groups that favored different versions of Maoist revolutionary activity in East Bengal. After March 1971, of course, the West Pakistan army increased the pressures upon all political groups in East Bengal to advocate violent resistance to the West Pakistani troops. All the segments of the radical Left supported the liberation war, including the Maoist groups. Neither the Soviet Union nor China showed any inclination to support the transformation of the war in East Bengal into a revolutionary struggle. India's support was unequivocally placed behind the Awami League.

The pressures on the older radical Left parties for more revolutionary postures have been great in both West and East Bengal, but they reached astounding proportions in March and April 1971 in Ceylon where an organization called the Janatha Vimukthi Peramuna (JVP) or People's Liberation Front, led by educated unemployed graduates who had been building an organization underground since 1965, launched a major rebellion from strongholds of the established leftist parties against a coalition government in which the LSSP and the CP were participants.[137] As usual, charges have been leveled against the JVP that it is a foreign-inspired and foreign-led organization—in this case by the North Koreans! However, the available reports suggest that this revolt is also entirely indigenous in inspiration. The revolt has been quelled, but not entirely suppressed, by a Ceylon government containing a Communist and a Trotskyite party in the coalition with arms provided by the United States, the Soviet Union, Great Britain, India, Pakistan, and Yugoslavia. Such are the forces that are ranged against revolution in our time when the interests of a great power are not served by it. Both the East Bengal and Ceylon cases demonstrate unequivocally the absence of material foreign support in South Asia for revolutionary (as opposed to secessionist) movements.

THE SOCIALIST PARTIES   The Socialist movement in India has also undergone considerable debate and internal division on questions of tactics. In a sense, the Socialist movement has a more hallowed tradition of the use of revolutionary violence than the Communist movement in India. Communist violence in India has never amounted to more than isolated acts of terrorism in the pre-Independence period and to localized rebellions such as in Telengana and Naxalbari in the post-Independence period. The Socialist movement, however, used widespread armed violence throughout large parts of north India, especially, during the 1942 Quit India movement. The Quit India movement was the only major pre-Independence nationalist movement in which violence was used as a deliberate tactic. The movement was led predominantly by young Congressmen who had been active in the Congress Socialist Party. The deliberate decision by Congress Socialist leaders to pursue armed insurrectionary tactics in 1942 led to controversy and division among Socialists concerning the ethical issue of using violence, which most Congressmen and some Socialists could not condone.[138]

In the post-Independence period, there has been some antiparliamentary sentiment among a few Socialist leaders,[139] but no serious advocacy of the use of violence in either of the two leading Socialist parties. The main issues since Independence have concerned the kinds of nonviolent tactics that ought to be used and the degree of militancy that should be infused into them by Socialists. The Socialist movement has been broadly divided between "Lohiaites," predominantly in the SSP, who have emphasized the persistent and militant use of a wide variety of acts of civil disobedience,

[137] See Urmila Phadnis, "Insurgency in Ceylon: Hard Challenge and Grim Warning," *Economic and Political Weekly* 6, no. 19 (8 May 1971), 965–968.
[138] Hari Kishore Singh, *History of the PSP*, pp. 79–81.
[139] Ibid., p. 166.

and more moderate Socialists, predominantly in the PSP, who have tended to use less demonstrative and disruptive tactics and to place more emphasis on parliamentary conventions. The SSP, while eschewing violence, insisted that civil disobedience must be used "in a decisive way" in addition to electoral politics[140] and that India's parliamentary institutions ought to be used more demonstratively than British parliamentary traditions permit.[141] The PSP, in contrast, argued that civil disobedience movements should be used "sparingly and in a discriminating manner." [142]

POLICIES FOR ECONOMIC DEVELOPMENT

THE COMMUNIST PARTIES Communist parties in power have been associated traditionally with a characteristic combination of agricultural and industrial policies for economic development, namely, an emphasis on the development of heavy industry as an urgent priority and various forms of collectivization of agriculture to make possible large-scale mechanized farming.[143] In the period before achieving power, however, Communist parties do not usually advocate collectivization measures for agriculture, which are considered measures of socialist construction. In the non-Communist states of Asia generally and in India particularly, Communist party policies are designed to assist in the completion of the anti-imperialist and antifeudal democratic revolution. The CPI has argued that the policies it has supported, though they will not bring about socialism, will take India along a path of "noncapitalist development."

The policies of the CPI and the CPM do not differ substantially on most matters.[144] For industry, both parties have favored rapid industrialization, with the emphasis on heavy industry; limitations on the investment of foreign private capital in India's industrial development; and nationalization of key industries, foreign-owned industries, banks, and foreign and wholesale trade. These policies are not measures to promote socialism or

---

[140] Limaye, *Why Samyukta Socialist?*, p. 21.

[141] Ibid., pp. 26–29.

[142] N. G. Goray and Surendranath Dwivedy, *Why Praja Socialist?* (Bombay: Popular Prakashan [1966]), p. 45.

[143] In Asia, such policies have been adopted by the Chinese, Mongolian, North Korean, and North Vietnamese parties. See Chalmers Johnson, "Building a Communist Nation in China"; M. T. Haggard, "Mongolia: The First Communist State in Asia"; Chong-Sik Lee, "Stalinism in the East: Communism in North Korea"; and John C. Donnell and Melvin Gurtov, "North Vietnam: Left of Moscow, Right of Peking"; all in Scalapino, *Communist Revolution in Asia*, pp. 60–67, 100–103, 130–133, 159–162.

[144] Statements of them can be found throughout the various sources previously cited, particularly the following: *Seventh Congress Documents*; *Eighth Congress Documents*; Chandidas et al., *India Votes*; and *Handbook of Election Manifestos, 1971*.

social ownership, but to prevent imperialist and monopoly capitalist domination of the process of industrial development. Both Communist parties have emphasized that nationalization of industries, which are then placed under the control of bureaucratic managers, is state capitalism, not socialism. Consequently, they have also advocated policies for "effective democratic control over, and employee participation in the management of, nationalised sector[s] of the economy." [145] The two Communist parties in Ceylon also have similar programs for the industrial and commercial sectors of the economy, emphasizing nationalization of banks, the large estates, and the import-export trade.[146] The Communist parties in East Bengal have not had occasion in recent times to formulate specific policies since they have been prohibited from participating in parliamentary politics.

The agricultural policies advocated by the two leading Communist parties in India have emphasized measures to complete the antifeudal aspect of the democratic revolution, that is, to free the peasantry from the remaining feudal relations in agriculture and to break the power of the remaining feudal landlords and ex-princes. Consequently, both parties have supported measures directed against the big landlords—cancellation of the privy purses, ending of compensation to the former zamindars, and the imposition and effective implementation of land ceilings laws. The Communist parties have also supported measures to protect the interests of the peasants—conferring property rights on tenants who actually cultivate the land, distributing uncultivated land and land made surplus by land ceilings legislation to small peasants and the landless, and abolition of land revenue. However, the CPI and the CPM differ significantly in their orientation to particular rural classes and in their attitudes toward investment in the agricultural sector. Both parties claim to favor the unity of all peasant classes and agricultural laborers against the feudal and capitalist landlords, but the CPI strategy has emphasized an appeal to the middle and rich peasants whereas the CPM has been more strongly oriented toward the poor peasants and the landless laborers. Also, the CPI has favored increased mechanization of agriculture, including the more rapid development of tractor-based farming and the spread of "large-scale mechanized state agricultural farms," whereas the CPM has continued to emphasize provision of more modest agricultural inputs—seeds, fertilizers, and water—to

---

[145] *Handbook of Election Manifestos, 1971*, p. 145.
[146] Justus M. van der Kroef, "Ceylon's Political Left: Its Development and Aspirations," *Pacific Affairs* 40, nos. 3 and 4 (Fall and Winter 1967–1968), 267 and 273.

the poor and middle peasants.[147] In Ceylon, Justus M. van der Kroef has remarked that the "pro-Peking" Communist party has attempted "to raise the issue of 'feudal landlordism' among the peasantry, but with only indifferent success thus far" in a country where (outside of the estates), "only four percent of the holdings exceed five acres." The pro-Peking party has also called for "distribution of state-owned land to the landless." [148]

The two Communist parties in India have also held in common a set of policies on India's food problem, oriented toward the protection of the interests of the peasants and consumers against the black marketeers and hoarders. These policies have included: procurement of food grains in the open market—that is, not monopoly procurement by the state—at a fair price; regular supply of food grains to fair price shops; and the guarantee of a minimum price to peasants and a maximum price for consumers. The pro-Peking Communist party in Ceylon has also called for "an agricultural subsidy and price support plan." [149]

THE SOCIALIST PARTIES The specific policies of the Socialist parties in India[150] have had much in common with those of the Communist parties, with one major exception. Both the SSP and the PSP have favored nationalization of key industries and increased public sector activity in industrial development. The SSP, but not the PSP, also favored taking over of foreign assets in India. Both parties favored similar agricultural and food policies—land ceilings and land redistribution, abolition of land revenue, guaranteed prices for the peasants, food procurement, rationing, and "active State participation" in wholesale and foreign trade[151] to control prices of food and other commodities. The SSP opposed anything more than what it called a "rehabilitation compensation" for expropriated landholders,[152] princes, and other property owners. In these respects, the policies of the SSP and PSP were broadly similar to those of the CPI and the CPM.

---

[147] *Nineteenth Session of the All-India Kisan Sabha, Amravati, 10–12 January 1968: Proceedings and Resolutions* (New Delhi: All-India Kisan Sabha, 1968), p. 16. For a cogent statement of the CPM rural class appeal, see Communist Party of India (Marxist), Resolution of the Central Committee, *Tasks on the Kisan Front* (Calcutta: CPM, 1967).

[148] van der Kroef, "Ceylon's Political Left," pp. 273–274.

[149] Ibid., p. 273.

[150] For SSP and PSP policy statements, see Limaye, *Why Samyukta Socialist?*; Goray and Dwivedy, *Why Praja Socialist?*; Chandidas et al., *India Votes*; and *Handbook of Election Manifestos, 1971*.

[151] *Handbook of Election Manifestos, 1971*.

[152] Limaye, *Why Samyukta Socialist?*, p. 16.

In contrast to the Communist parties, however, the Socialist parties pay homage to Gandhian principles in their advocacy of measures of economic and political decentralization. Economic decentralization means support for small-scale and cottage industries. Political decentralization means that both Socialist parties have favored granting increased powers, especially financial powers, to local and district panchayats and increased democratization of local and district panchayats and councils through such means as direct, rather than indirect, elections.

Both Socialist parties also have advocated a distinctive income and expenditures policy, involving the restriction of incomes and expenditures in a ratio of 1:10 between the highest and lowest members of society, with a maximum ceiling on both income and expenditure for all.

The policies of the LSSP in Ceylon have been generally similar to the policies of other Left parties in India and Ceylon, involving nationalization of key industries and trade and an income ceiling. However, unlike the other major Left parties, the LSSP has advocated the "development of modern state collective farms along with cooperatives for smallholders." [153]

The National Awami parties in East Bengal have had fewer opportunities than the other Socialist parties in South Asia to articulate specific policies for economic development and social change. Among the specific policies associated with the NAPs, M. Rashiduzzaman has noted the following "vital demands on behalf of the peasants, . . . a fair price for jute, the abolition of land-holding and money-lending, the reduction of taxes, the establishment of proper irrigation systems, [and] nationalisation of the jute trade." [154] The NAP(M) has also "declared that feudalism in various forms should be abolished and that landlords' surplus land would be distributed among the peasants." [155]

INTERNATIONAL TIES AND FOREIGN POLICY

THE COMMUNIST PARTIES Conventional wisdom, supported by a good deal of scholarship on the question, has generally supported the view that nearly all Communist parties outside of the Soviet Union and China are agents of an international conspiracy, supported and directed from Moscow and/or Peking. As the differences between the Soviet Union and China became acute in the late 1950s and early 1960s, it became fashionable to speculate as to whether or not this or that Communist party in a particular country was allied with the CPSU or with the CPC. When the split between the Soviet and Chinese parties occurred and was paralleled

[153] van der Kroef, "Ceylon's Political Left," p. 258.
[154] Rashiduzzaman, "NAP of Pakistan," p. 398.
[155] Ibid., p. 401.

by splits in the Communist parties in other countries, it only remained to determine which fragment was pro-Soviet and which pro-Chinese. The basic assumption throughout, however, is that once the outside agent has been discovered, the actions of the internal Communist party can be predicted because it will follow the dictates of the external guiding power.

Although it has sometimes taken considerable imagination and a skill in tortuous argumentation that parallels that of Communist ideologists, this interpretation has been applied to the Indian Communist movement as well. From this perspective, the Communist movement in India has been seen as a foreign transplant that, throughout its early history, followed every twist and turn in Soviet foreign policy and in international Communist strategy.[156] Not only did the CPI adjust its foreign policy views to parallel those of the Soviet Union and later those of the Sino-Soviet alliance, but it adopted and shifted its internal strategies—"Left," "Right," or "neo-Maoist"—upon instructions from Moscow.[157] When the split in the international Communist movement occurred, the CPI also thereafter divided into two parties—one considered pro-Soviet and the other alleged to be pro-Chinese. Now, there is no doubt that the Communist movement in India, in its origin and development, has received foreign support and guidance and that internal shifts in the party line have frequently followed upon shifts in the line of the CPSU. Nevertheless, this approach to the Communist movement in India is oversimplified and concentrates attention only upon certain restricted dimensions of Communist politics and policies in India.

There are several difficulties with accepting this approach to the Communist movement in India. First, it tends to concentrate attention on the foreign and international dimensions of Communist politics, rather than upon the internal activities of the Communist parties. For example, a frequently-cited case of a CPI twist to conform to Soviet foreign policy interests was the 1941 shift in the CPI view of the Second World War from an imperialist war to a people's war after the German attack on the Soviet Union. It is often argued that this was a shift that estranged Indian Communism from Indian national sentiment at the time, which opposed cooperation with the British war effort. The argument is true, but it is also true that Communist agreement to cooperate in the British war effort in India gave the CPI legality and an opportunity to organize the party and its auxiliaries while the Congress organization was out of operation. If the

---

[156] See especially the "Introduction" to *ICPD*, pp. vi–xi.
[157] This is the thrust of the entire Kautsky book, *Moscow and the Communist Party of India*.

1941 CPI shift is viewed only as a slavish shift in internal policy at the dictate of a foreign power, then the internal advantages of the shift from the CPI point of view may be missed.

A second difficulty with the dependency view of communism in India is that it tends to give excessive importance to Communist rhetoric on issues of strategy. Analysts of the 1947 to 1951 period of intense ideological debate in the CPI have paid much attention to the arguments over strategy and tactics—whether the party should follow an anti-imperialist or anti-capitalist strategy, united front from above or united front from below, violence or nonviolence, and the like. Every shift in the internal debate has been sought to be traced to some directive or other from a Moscow theoretician. Not only does this kind of approach direct attention to the transmission of messages between the CPSU and the CPI and away from the internal conflicts within the CPI itself, but it attaches too much importance to the ideological issues themselves. In fact, as I have argued above, much of the debate concerning strategy and class analysis among Indian Communists constitutes an ideological superstructure built upon different perceptions toward the opportunities for achieving power in Indian politics rather than an attempt to fit national strategy to international strategy and then to derive specific tactics from the grand design to fit the Indian situation.

A third difficulty with the conventional view is that it looks upon the international Communist system as a transmission belt in which instructions are sent from the center to the periphery. In fact, even during the heyday of Stalin's dominance, this view was not accurate. It is more useful for our purposes to perceive the international Communist system as an arena in which factional groups at the center (whether in Moscow or Peking) contest for dominance and ideological supremacy and use the experience of Communist groups in the peripheries to support their positions, while Communist groups in the peripheries do the same and use the outcome of conflicts at the center to support their local positions. To take the 1947–1951 period in India once again, the resolution of the inner-party debate at that time in favor of a "neo-Maoist" peaceful anti-imperialist strategy has been perceived as a consequence of direction from Moscow. Yet, there were parallel conflicts within the CPSU, the Cominform, and the CPI within this period.[158] The "Right" strategy of P. C. Joshi and S. A. Dange in India was supported briefly by the Soviet theoretician Zhukov in the CPSU and by the British Communist Rajani Palme Dutt. The "Left" anticapitalist strategy of B. T. Ranadive in India was supported by the Soviet theoreticians Dyakov and Balabusevich, and by the Yugoslav

[158] See Overstreet and Windmiller, *Communism in India*, chaps. 12 and 13.

party. The "neo-Maoist" strategy of the Andhra Communists drew its inspiration from Mao and the Chinese revolution at a time when Soviet and Chinese theoreticians themselves were not in full agreement on the meaning of Maoist strategy and its applicability to other Asian countries. Ultimately, within the CPSU, the Cominform, and the CPI, an ideological consensus on a peaceful, neo-Maoist, four-class strategy was reached, but the path toward this consensus was ridden with internal conflicts within the CPSU, within the Cominform, and within the CPI. Finally, and most important, during the periods when consensus does not exist, conflicts within the peripheral parties may influence the outcome of conflicts at the centers; there will be times when center parties and periphery parties are out of phase, and there may be times when foreign advice is ignored or even rejected.[159]

These characteristics of the international Communist arena existed even in the era of Stalinist dominance, but they have become more pronounced as the Sino-Soviet dispute developed into a split in the international Communist movement. The relationship of India and the Indian Communist parties to the Sino-Soviet dispute brings out these characteristics of the international Communist arena very sharply. A conventional, dependency view of Indian Communism would suggest that the split in the CPI followed upon and was caused by the Sino-Soviet split, leading to the formation of a pro-Soviet CPI and a pro-Chinese CPM. In fact, it is now generally recognized that Sino-Indian relations themselves had a profound impact on the Sino-Soviet dispute and the divergence between the foreign policy interests of the Soviet Union and China. More important, the right wing of the CPI took a stronger pro-Nehru, anti-Chinese position on the issue of Sino-Indian relations than the Soviet Union was at first willing to take and stuck to it against advice from Moscow. On the other side, the left wing in the CPI never took a pro-China position, but objected strenuously to the adoption by the right wing of a position of complete identification with the Nehru government on foreign policy in general and specifically toward China. Thus, from the point of view of the Indian Communist movement, the Sino-Soviet split in no way caused the split in the CPI. Rather, the total commitment of the right wing of the CPI to the anti-Chinese foreign policy of the Nehru government constituted the last precipitating factor dividing the two wings of the CPI on the traditional question of support or opposition to the Congress.

[159] The Indian Communist tradition of disagreeing with foreign advice goes back as far as the 1920s and M. N. Roy's opposition to Lenin on the question of supporting "bourgeois nationalist movements" in colonial countries. See Overstreet and Windmiller, *Communism in India*, p. 30.

What then are the current international ties and orientations of the Communist parties of India? The CPI has taken a pronounced pro-Soviet, anti-Chinese position in the international Communist movement. More than that, it has contributed to the division by the stridency of its attacks on China. It has approved generally of the foreign policy of the government of India as "a policy of peace, nonalignment and anti-colonialism" [160] and has called for the strengthening of these tendencies and of tendencies toward "friendship and co-operation with the Soviet Union and other socialist countries." [161] The CPM has refused to take sides in the Sino-Soviet dispute. Although it has considered itself fully a part of the international Communist movement, it has identified with the more independent national Communist parties such as those of Romania, Cuba, North Vietnam, and North Korea. [162] The CPM has vehemently criticized the foreign policy of the Congress government, which, it argues, "repeatedly compromises with the reactionaries in her foreign policy." [163] As in other aspects of CPI-CPM differences, however, it is the attitude toward the Congress that is at issue, not the details of India's foreign policy. Both leading Communist parties favor recognition by India of the North Vietnamese, East German, and North Korean governments; support for the revolutionary forces in South Vietnam; improved relations with China and Pakistan; and general resistance to neocolonialist and U.S. imperialist pressures on Indian foreign policy. [164] The CPML is the only Indian Communist party that has had the support of the Chinese Communist Party. The CPML in turn patterns its internal revolutionary strategy upon the Chinese model of armed agrarian uprisings and identifies its external enemies as both U.S. and Soviet imperialism. [165]

The divisions in the Ceylon Communist movement have reflected more the divisions in the international Communist movement than has been the case in India and the differences between the two Ceylon Communist parties "have largely been argued in the vocabulary of the Sino-Soviet breach." [166] Unlike the CPM in India, the dissident CCP has not attempted to separate its ideological position from that of the Chinese Communist Party and has not been disavowed by it. Also unlike the CPM in India, the

160 "The Programme of the Communist Party of India," in *Seventh Congress Documents*, p. 32.

161 *Handbook of Election Manifestos, 1971*, p. 115.

162 Franda, *Radical Politics in West Bengal*, chap. 7.

163 *Handbook of Election Manifestos, 1971*, p. 141.

164 *Handbook of Election Manifestos, 1971*, pp. 115 and 141.

165 Franda, "India's Third Communist Party," pp. 805–806.

166 Kearney, "Communist Parties of Ceylon," p. 405.

pro-Peking CCP has played a definitely secondary role in Ceylon parliamentary politics, where it has been overshadowed by the pro-Moscow Communist party. Nevertheless, when the differences between the two Communist parties on strategy and tactics in Ceylon politics are examined, there are parallels with the split in India. Like the CPI, the pro-Moscow CCP has emphasized alliance with the dominant left-of-center party, the SLFP, more than the pro-Peking CCP has done. It has also been accused by the pro-Peking CCP of placing excessive emphasis on parliamentary politics. Finally, it has been suggested that both "conflicting personal ambitions and outlooks" and generational differences played an important role in the split in the Ceylon Communist movement.[167]

The leftist groups in East Bengal are also customarily divided into pro-Moscow and pro-Peking segments, but this division seems to have much less significance there than in Ceylon for three reasons. First of all, neither the Soviet Union nor China has shown much interest in or given much support to Bengali Communism.[168] Second, the number of Communist formations described by Maniruzzaman is so large that any simple division between pro-Moscow and pro-Peking groups is likely to obscure more than it reveals. As in India and Ceylon, the divisive issues in East Bengal have centered around the attitude to be taken toward the regime, toward parliamentary politics, and toward alliances with other parties. Third, the support of the People's Republic of China for the Yahya Khan regime in Pakistan left the indigenous East Bengali Maoists no choice but to set off on their own, which they did in adopting strategies of support for the Bangladesh liberation war.

THE SOCIALIST PARTIES International ties between the Socialist parties in India and foreign Socialist parties have always been looser than those between the Communist parties and the international Communist movement. Nor has there ever been any question of external guidance of the Indian Socialist movement by a foreign Socialist party. Indian Socialists played an important role in the First Asian Socialist Conference held in Rangoon in 1953 and in the Second Asian Socialist Conference at Bombay in 1956.[169] The Asian Socialist Conferences were attended by some Socialist parties that also were members of the Socialist International, but no formal linkage was established between the two international Socialist organizations. Pakistan was represented by a Socialist delegate at both Asian

[167] Ibid., p. 406.
[168] Franda, *Radical Politics in West Bengal*, chap. 9.
[169] Saul Rose, *Socialism in Southern Asia* (London: Oxford University Press, 1959), chaps. 2 and 13.

Socialist Conferences, but there was some difficulty in deciding upon the appropriate representation from Ceylon. There was no representation from Ceylon at Rangoon. The LSSP was invited to join the ASC provided it withdrew from the Fourth International. When the LSSP declined to do so, the Sri Lanka Freedom Party was invited instead.[170]

Since the Second Asian Socialist Conference, international ties between the Indian Socialist parties and foreign Socialist parties have amounted to little more than occasional international conferences attended by Indian Socialists and exchanges of fraternal greetings by Indian and foreign Socialist parties at national party conferences. The PSP also has been a "consultative member" of the Socialist International.[171] In general, however, links between the European-dominated Socialist International and South Asian Socialist parties have been loose, informal, and frequently characterized by differing perspectives on international issues.

The Socialist parties of India also have distinctive foreign policy orientations that separate them from the Communist parties. Both the PSP and the SSP emphasized their desire for an independent Indian foreign policy based firmly on India's national interests.[172] The PSP proposed to substitute the creation of "a third bloc of non-aligned and other nations" for "the negativist concept of non-alignment." [173] It urged preparation for an impending war with Pakistan and China along the entire northern frontier of India. That preparation should include the manufacture of nuclear weapons. The PSP opposed the Tashkent Declaration that restored the *status quo ante* between India and Pakistan after the 1965 war. It opposed any negotiations with China on the Sino-Indian border dispute, which it considered only an incidental aspect of Chinese aggressive designs against India. The SSP foreign policy differed in detail and deemphasized military means, but its goals were similar. It proposed that India's national will be oriented toward the recovery of "lost territories," [174] toward the restoration of Tibetan independence, and toward the protection of the interests of Indians overseas. Like the PSP, the SSP opposed the Tashkent Declaration and opposed compromise with China. It favored breaking diplomatic relations with China. The SSP differed from the PSP, however, on manufacturing a nuclear bomb, which it considered "futile talk." [175]

170 Ibid., pp. 245–247.
171 *Report of the Fifth National Conference of the Praja Socialist Party* (New Delhi: PSP, [1959]), p. 22.
172 See Limaye, *Why Samyukta Socialist?*, chap. 8 and Goray and Dwivedy, *Why Praja Socialist?*, chap. 8.
173 Goray and Dwivedy, *Why Praja Socialist?*, p. 10.
174 Limaye, *Why Samyukta Socialist?*, p. 52.
175 Ibid., p. 66.

The differences between the democratic Socialist parties and the Communist parties on issues of foreign policy are profound and obviously derive from entirely different premises concerning the nature of international politics. The Communist parties, whatever their inclinations in the Sino-Soviet dispute, begin with an orientation toward great power conflicts, that is, toward the conflict between the capitalist-imperialist and Socialist camps. They seek to define India's position within this global arena. The democratic Socialist parties, in contrast, seek to keep great power conflicts out of South Asia. They argue from the premise that an independent Indian foreign policy is possible, both in the world arena and in local conflicts with Pakistan and China. Thus, the Communist parties tend to be militantly anti-imperialist in their orientation in the global arena, but moderate in their orientation to local conflicts. The democratic Socialist parties tend to be moderate and independent in their attitudes toward global conflicts, but militant in their attitudes toward India's relations with Pakistan and China.

Opposition to the pro-Western policy of the Pakistan government and the desire for a more "independent foreign policy" were among the primary issues in the original formation of the NAP in 1957.[176] Since the division of the party in 1967, one segment has been considered pro-Moscow and the other pro-Peking in its inclinations, but both National Awami parties have been articulating foreign policy demands that reflect the East Bengal desire for a reduced emphasis in international politics on hostility to India and reduced reliance on the United States. These aspirations have fit Soviet foreign policy better than China's, which has favored alliance with the West Pakistan regime against India and has traded its support to Pakistan on Kashmir for Pakistan's support against India in connection with the Sino-Indian border dispute.

THE LSSP AND THE FOURTH INTERNATIONAL The clearest case in South Asia of the subordination of international ties to indigenous political considerations has been provided by the LSSP. The LSSP, which until 1964 was the strongest Trotskyite political party in the world, compromised its revolutionary ideology and sacrificed its formal tie with the Fourth International by joining in a coalition government with the SLFP in 1964.[177] The decision to join the government in 1964 led to its expulsion from the Fourth International and the recognition in its stead of the dissident LSSP(R). No doubt the consequences of a break with the Fourth International are less serious than the breaking of ties by a Communist party

[176] Rashiduzzaman, "NAP of Pakistan," p. 395.
[177] Lerski, "Twilight of Ceylonese Trotskyism," p. 384.

with Moscow or Peking, but the LSSP decision in 1964 does seem to be part of a more general pattern in South Asian radical politics toward political adjustment to domestic politics and toward decreasing concern for international recognition.

Regional Strength and Popular Support

Regional Strength

THE COMMUNIST PARTIES OF INDIA

There is a very great range of variation in the strength of the Communist parties of India both from state to state and within each state. The existence of wide variation in Communist strength in India makes it possible to consider some of the prominent explanations concerning the sources of support for the Communist movement in general and in India in particular. In this section, areas of Communist strength and weakness will first be identified, after which some of these explanations will be tested against the data. Measures of electoral performance (as opposed to party membership) will be used to compare the strength of the two leading Communist parties because electoral measures are more accurate and reliable than party membership figures which, in any event, have a high intercorrelation with measures of electoral performance in India. No quantitative measures are available to compare the strength of the nonelectoral revolutionary parties, whose areas of strength are revealed only when they engage in revolutionary actions and whose activities will be analyzed in the regional contributions to this volume.

Table 1.5 shows the percentages of votes polled by the Communist parties in state legislative assembly elections between 1952 and 1972 and the rank of the Communist party in each state compared to other parties contesting the elections. The election results for all states have been adjusted retroactively to conform to existing boundaries. The table brings out very clearly the high degree of regionalization of Communist strength in India. The Communist parties have consistently been a major force in the politics of only three states—Kerala, West Bengal, and Andhra. In those states, the total Communist vote has ranged from a low of 10.4 percent in West Bengal in 1952 to a high of 42.4 percent in West Bengal in 1971. The average total Communist vote in the three states for all elections is 28.9 percent for Kerala, 26.2 percent for West Bengal, and 19.0 percent for Andhra. In all three states, with the exception of Andhra in 1967, one of the Communist parties has been either the first or second party in its state in terms of popular electoral support. The table also shows the impact of the 1964 split of the Communist movement on the three leading parties. The consequences of the split seem to have been least damaging in West Bengal, where the combined strength of the Communist parties has remained as high as or higher than presplit levels; moderate in Kerala, where the combined Communist strength has never returned to the 1960 peak; and severe in Andhra where the two Communist parties have been equally divided and where their combined strength in 1967 declined to 15.4 percent and in 1972 sank to only 9.0 percent.

The remaining states can be divided into three groups according to the strength of their Communist parties. In one group are two states, Punjab and Tamil Nadu, where the Communist parties at one time showed promise or achieved a significant position in the politics of the state. The high point for the Punjab CPI was in 1957 when the party polled 17.7 percent of the votes and was second in the state in popular support. It deserves note, however, that this peak of strength was achieved at a time when the leading non-Congress party in Punjab, the Akali Dal, had merged temporarily with the Congress, leaving the CPI as the major organized opposition party. In Tamil Nadu, the CPI achieved its best vote in 1952 and maintained a similar level of strength through the next three elections but declined severely after the split. More generally, however, the position of the Communist parties in both these states has been seriously limited by the fact that the major non-Congress parties in both states have been well-entrenched regional parties oriented to regional nationalism.

A third group of states is constituted of Bihar, Assam, Orissa, and Maharashtra, where the level of support for the Communist movement has either remained fairly stable or has grown. In all these states also, the CPI has emerged as the dominant Communist party after the split. These are states in which the CPI generally wins a small number of seats (enough in Bihar to make it an important force in coalition politics) and where the party has some potential for growth and may acquire importance in the future.

The final group of states comprises the six states of Uttar Pradesh, Rajasthan, Mysore, Haryana, Madhya Pradesh, and Gujarat. In all these states, the average Communist vote is considerably below 5 percent and has not gone above 5 percent except in 1962 in Uttar Pradesh and Rajasthan. Moreover, in all these states, an already weak Communist movement has deteriorated after the split. One is tempted to suggest that these are states in which the Communist movement has no future. However, there are two kinds of political situations that make the future unpredictable in these states. Uttar Pradesh, Rajasthan, Haryana, and Madhya Pradesh

Table 1.5 Percentages of Valid Votes Polled by Communist Parties of India in State Legislative Assembly Elections, 1952–1972

Stateᵃ	1952 %	1952 Rankᵇ	1954 %	1954 Rank	1957 %	1957 Rank	1960–1962ᶜ %	1960–1962 Rank	1965 CPI %	1965 CPI Rank	CPM %	CPM Rank	1967 CPI %	1967 CPI Rank	CPM %	CPM Rank
Kerala	17.5ᶜ	(2)	17.3	(2)	35.4	(2)	39.1	(1)	8.3	(4)	19.7	(2)	8.6	(3)	23.5	(2)
West Bengal	10.4	(2)			18.3	(2)	25.0	(2)					6.5	(4)	18.1	(2)
Andhra Pradesh	21.8ᵍ	(2)			29.5ᵍ	(2)	19.5	(2)					7.8	(3)	7.6	(4)
Punjab	8.2ʰ	(3)			17.7	(2)	9.8	(3)					5.2	(4)	3.3	(6)
Bihar	1.1	(8)			4.9	(5)	6.2	(4)					6.9	(5)	1.3	(8)
Assam	2.8	(4)			8.1	(3)	6.4	(3)					5.1	(3)	2.0	(6)
Orissa	5.6	(4)			8.4	(4)	8.0	(4)					5.3	(5)	1.2	(7)
Maharashtra	3.4ᵍ	(5)			5.2	(5)	5.9	(4)					4.9	(5)	4.1	(4)
Tamil Nadu	7.9	(3)			7.3	(2)	7.7	(4)					1.8	(5)	1.3	(8)
Uttar Pradesh	0.9	(9)			3.8	(4)	5.1	(5)					3.2	(7)	1.2	(5)
Rajasthan	0.6	(7)			3.0	(4)	5.4	(4)					1.0	(6)	1.1	(6)
Mysore	1.5ˢ	(5)			1.9	(3)	2.3	(6)					0.5	(8)	1.1	(6)
Haryana	#ⁱ	(9)			6.7	(3)	2.5	(6)					0.9	(6)	0.5	(7)
Madhya Pradesh	0.6	(8)			1.6	(6)	2.0	(7)					1.1	(7)	0.2	(9)
Gujarat	0.5	(9)			0.0		0.2	(8)					0.0		0.0	
India	4.3				7.7		8.6						4.1		4.6	

Source: Craig Baxter, *District Voting Trends In India: A Research Tool* (New York: Columbia University Press, 1969).
ᵃ States have been ranked according to the percentage of votes polled by the CPI and CPM combined in the 1967 elections.
ᵇ The rank columns refer to the ranking of the Communist parties in their states in terms of percentage of votes polled in each election. Thus, e.g., the CPI in Kerala in 1952 polled the second highest percentage of votes in that state, whereas the Bihar CPI polled the eighth highest percentage in that state in the same year.
ᶜ All figures in this column, except for Kerala and Orissa, refer to the Third General Elections of 1962. The Kerala figure is for the 1960 midterm election, the Orissa figure for 1961.
ᵈ Midterm elections in Haryana in 1968, in the other states in February 1969.
ᵉ Kerala elections in September 1970, the others in March 1971.

| State | 1968–1969[d] | | | | 1970–1971[e] | | | | 1972[1] | | | | Average Combined Communist Vote % |
| | CPI | | CPM | | CPI | | CPM | | CPI | | CPM | | |
	%	Rank	%	Rank	%	Rank	%	Rank	%	Rank	%	Rank	
Kerala					9.3[J]	(3)	23.4[J]	(1)					28.9
West Bengal	7.0	(4)	20.0	(2)	8.6[k]	(3)	33.8[k]	(1)	8.4	(3)	27.5	(2)	26.2
Andhra Pradesh									6.0	(2)	3.0	(3)	19.0
Punjab	5.0	(4)	2.9	(5)					6.5	(3)	3.3	(5)	10.3
Bihar	10.1	(4)	1.2	(10)					7.0	(5)	1.6	(N.A.)	6.7
Assam									5.1	(3)	2.6	(4)	6.4
Orissa					4.2[k]	(6)	1.2[k]	(11)					6.8
Maharashtra									2.8	(N.A.)	0.8	(N.A.)	4.8
Tamil Nadu					2.5[k]	(4)	1.5[k]	(4)					6.6
Uttar Pradesh	3.1	(6)	0.5	(10)									2.8
Rajasthan									1.6	(5)	1.0	(7)	2.8
Mysore									1.0	(6)	1.0	(5)	1.9
Haryana	0.3	(9)	0.1	(10)					2.0	(N.A.)	0.4	(N.A.)	2.2
Madhya Pradesh									1.0	(4)	0.03	(N.A.)	1.3
Gujarat									0.5	(N.A.)	0.2	(N.A.)	0.3
India									4.2		4.5		7.6

[1] This figure comes from Ralph Retzlaff, "Revisionism and Dogmatism in the Communist Party of India," in Robert A. Scalapino, ed., The Communist Revolution in Asia: Tactics, Goals, and Achievements (Englewood Cliffs, N.J.: Prentice-Hall, 1965), p. 315.
g The figure here is for the CPI and the PDF.
h The figure here is for two Communist parties which existed in Punjab then—CPI and CP(L).
i Less than 0.05%.
J Figures from Overseas Hindustan Times, 26 September 1970.
k Figures from W. H. Morris-Jones, "India Elects for Change—and Stability," Asian Survey 11, no. 8 (August 1971), 732.
l Preliminary figures, from American Embassy paper entitled "State Assembly Elections—1972: Final Party Position, Seats and Popular Votes (Prelim.), All-India and By State."

are states in which the level of institutionalized support for all political parties has been low. Mysore and Gujarat are states where the Congress has been overwhelmingly dominant and the only institutionalized party since Independence. In all these states, any well-organized political force might build electoral support in the future. There is nothing to suggest, however, that the Communist parties in these states are particularly well situated to take advantage of these conditions.

The regional character of the Communist parties in India is revealed even more clearly in table 1.6, which shows the percentage of seats contested by the CPI and the CPM since 1952 in all states. In no state in India has either of the Communist parties ever contested all seats. This fact alone suggests two interrelated conclusions concerning Communist politics in India. First, it indicates that neither Communist party has anywhere in India been a contender for political dominance or hegemony. Second, it suggests that everywhere in India, the Communist parties have been dependent upon alliances with other parties to achieve power.

A comparison of tables 1.6 and 1.7 makes it possible to compare Communist party aspirations, achievements, and prospects. From this point of view, the four groups of states can be reduced to three broad groups in terms of Communist strength and future prospects—states where the Communist parties are or have been contenders for "partial power"; states where the Communist parties are or have been marginal political forces, where they have some strength but cannot play a decisive role; and states where the Communist parties are or have been of little or no consequence in the contest for political power.

In the first group again are the three states of Kerala, West Bengal, and Andhra. In these three states, in every election, one of the Communist parties has contested at least 20 percent of the seats. It deserves note, however, that the peak aspiration for the Communist parties in two of the three states occurred at least a decade ago—in 1962 in Kerala when the CPI contested 85.71 percent of the seats and in 1957 in Andhra when the CPI contested 76.67 percent of the seats.

What about the peak achievements of the Communist parties in these three states? If we use the relationship between the percentage of seats won and percentage of deposits lost to total seats contested by the Communist parties as a rough measure of their organizational capacities in elections (see table 1.7), we can determine the peak achievement for each party in each state. Using this rough measure as a guide, two significant conclusions can be reached. First, in all three states, the time of peak aspiration for the Communist parties has not been the time of peak achievement. Both Communist parties have usually done better—won more seats or lost fewer deposits or both—when they have contested a smaller number of seats, particularly when they have also made electoral adjustments or alliances with other parties. In Kerala, the CPM did its best in 1967 (P.R.I. of +88.14) when it contested considerably fewer than half (44.36 percent) of the seats in the state. In Bengal, both the CPI and the CPM did their best in 1969 in terms of *both* seats won and deposits lost (P.R.I. of +88.33 and +81.44, respectively) when the CPI contested only 12.86 percent of the seats and the CPM only 34.64 percent. Of course, on both occasions, the Communist parties benefited from electoral alliances with other parties, which suggests that a large portion of the organizational resources of the Communist parties must be devoted to building such alliances if they are to achieve "partial power." It is true that the CPM won more seats in West Bengal in 1971 (when it contested 85 percent of the seats practically without benefit of electoral alliances) than it did in 1969, but it also lost more deposits and it also lost its access to power in the state government after the election. In Andhra, the peak achievement of the CPI (P.R.I. of +62.04) occurred in 1952 when the party contested only 45.19 percent of the seats. The second important conclusion concerning Communist strength in these three states is that in only two of them has the organizational capacity of the Communist parties to win election contests increased over time, namely, in Kerala and West Bengal. The 1962 election was the last occasion when a Communist party in Andhra won more seats than it lost deposits. In contrast to Kerala and West Bengal, where *both* Communist parties have become institutionalized forces in the politics of their states, in Andhra, both Communist parties have been disintegrating as serious electoral parties. There is some question in fact whether the Andhra Communist parties at this stage ought not to be considered marginal political forces in their state's politics.

The second group of states, in which the Communist parties have been marginal political forces, includes Punjab, Bihar, Assam, Orissa, Maharashtra, and Tamil Nadu. The Communist parties in these states have had some success in winning electoral contests and, in Punjab and Bihar for a time, have even held "partial power," but their performance has been erratic. On two occasions, the CPI in Punjab (in 1957) and the CPI in Bihar (in 1969), they contested more than half the seats in their state assembly contests. However, for the most part, these are states in which the Communist parties usually contest no more than a third of the legislative assembly seats. Moreover, these are also states where the Communist parties generally perform indifferently in the seats they do contest. On occasion, in some of these states, the Communist parties have had limited successes in the electoral arena. The CPM in the Punjab in 1969 and in

Table 1.6 Number and Percentage of Seats Contested by Communist Parties of India in State Legislative Assembly Elections, 1952–1972

State	1952 No.	1952 %	1954 No.	1954 %	1957 No.	1957 %	1960–1962 No.	1960–1962 %	1965 CPI No.	1965 CPI %	1965 CPM No.	1965 CPM %	1967 CPI No.	1967 CPI %	1967 CPM No.	1967 CPM %	1968–1969 CPI No.	1968–1969 CPI %	1968–1969 CPM No.	1968–1969 CPM %
Kerala Cont.	N.A.	N.A.	33	30.84	100	79.37	108	85.71	78	58.65	73	54.89	22	16.54	59	44.36				
Kerala Total	128		107		126		126		133		133		133		133					
West Bengal Cont.	89	35.60			104	41.27	145	57.54					62	22.14	134	47.86	36	12.86	97	34.64
West Bengal Total	250				252		252						280		280		280		280	
Andhra Pradesh Cont.	108a	45.19			230ab	76.67	136	45.33					104	36.24	83	28.92				
Andhra Pradesh Total	239				300		300						287		287					
Punjab Cont.	35c	31.82			50	50.14	30	34.88					19	18.27	13	12.50	29	27.88	9	8.65
Punjab Total	110				86		86						104		104		104		104	
Bihar Cont.	22	6.92			60	18.87	84	26.42					98	30.82	31	9.75	163	51.26	29	9.12
Bihar Total	318				318		318						318		318		318		318	
Assam Cont.	18	17.14			22	20.95	31	29.52					22	17.46	14	11.11				
Assam Total	105				105		105						126		126					
Orissa Cont.	33	23.57			43	30.71	34	24.29					31	22.14	10	7.14				
Orissa Total	140				140		140						140		140					
Maharashtra Cont.	51a	16.94			32	12.12	56	21.21					41	15.19	11	4.07				
Maharashtra Total	301				264		264						270		270					
Tamil Nadu Cont.	52	25.74			54	26.34	68	33.01					32	13.68	22	9.40				
Tamil Nadu Total	202				205		206						234		234					
Uttar Pradesh Cont.	44	10.23			90	20.93	147	34.19					96	22.59	56	13.18	109	25.65	21	4.94
Uttar Pradesh Total	430				430		430						425		425		425		425	
Rajasthan Cont.	13	6.88			24	13.64	45	25.57					20	10.87	22	11.96				
Rajasthan Total	189				176		176						184		184					
Mysore Cont.	20a	9.48			20	9.62	31	14.90					6	2.78	10	4.63				
Mysore Total	211				208		208						216		216					
Haryana Cont.	1	1.64			14	25.45	12	22.22					12	14.81	8	9.88	3	3.70	1	1.23
Haryana Total	61				55		54						81		81		81		81	
Madhya Pradesh Cont.	22	6.51			25	8.68	42	14.58					33	11.15	9	3.04				
Madhya Pradesh Total	338				288		288						296		296					
Gujarat Cont.	8	5.06			0	0.00	1	0.65					0	0.00						
Gujarat Total	158				132		154						168							

State		1970–1971 CPI No.	%	CPM No.	%	1972 CPI No.	%	CPM No.	%
Kerala	Cont. Total	31 133	23.31	72 133	54.12				
West Bengal	Cont. Total	111 280	38.64	237 280	84.64				
Andhra Pradesh	Cont. Total					41 280	14.64	208 280	74.29
Punjab	Cont. Total					59 287	20.56	32 287	11.15
Bihar	Cont. Total					13 104	12.50	17 104	16.35
Assam	Cont. Total					53 318	16.67	52 318	16.35
Orissa	Cont. Total					28 114	24.56	19 114	16.67
Maharashtra	Cont. Total	27 140	19.23	11 140	7.86				
Tamil Nadu	Cont. Total					43 270	15.93	21 270	7.78
Uttar Pradesh	Cont. Total	10 234	4.27	37 234	15.81				
Rajasthan	Cont. Total					5 184	2.72	21 184	11.41
Mysore	Cont. Total					4 216	1.85	18 216	8.74
Haryana	Cont. Total					11 81	13.58	4 81	4.94
Madhya Pradesh	Cont. Total					6 296	2.03	4 296	1.35
Gujarat	Cont Total					13 168	7.74	0 168	0.00

Sources: Craig Baxter, District Voting Trends in India: A Research Tool (New York: Columbia University Press, 1969); 1970–1971 figures for Kerala from Overseas Hindustan Times, 26 September 1970 and for West Bengal, Orissa, and Tamil Nadu from Morris-Jones, "India Elects for Change—and Stability," p. 732; 1972 figures from American Embassy, "State Assembly Elections—1972."
a CPI + PDF.
b 1955 + 1957.
c CPI only; does not include CP(L).

Table 1.7 Seats Won and Deposits Lost by Communist Parties of India in State Legislative Assembly Elections, 1952–1972, Given as Numbers and Percentages of the Number of Seats Contested

State	1952 Cont. No.	Won No.	%	LD No.	%	1954 Cont. No.	Won No.	%	LD No.	%	1957 Cont. No.	Won No.	%	LD No.	%	1960–1962 Cont. No.	Won No.	%	LD No.	%
Kerala P.R.I.[a]	N.A.	25	N.A. N.A.	N.A.	N.A.	33	23	69.70 +69.70	0	0.00	100	60	60.00 +57.00	3	3.00	108	29	26.85 +26.85	0	0.00
West Bengal P.R.I.	89	28	31.46 +10.11	19	21.35						104	46	44.23 +41.35	3	2.88	145	50	34.48 +28.27	9	6.21
Andhra Pradesh P.R.I.	108[b]	77	71.30 +62.04	10	9.26						230[bc]	37	16.09 +5.22	25	10.87	136	51	37.50 +33.09	6	4.41
Punjab P.R.I.	35[d]	6	17.14 −28.57	16	45.71						50	3	6.00 −12.00	9	18.00	30	9	30.00 −10.00	12	40.00
Bihar P.R.I.	22	0	0.00 −68.18	15	68.18						60	7	11.67 −25.00	22	36.67	84	12	14.29 −30.95	38	45.24
Assam P R I	18	1	5.56 −61.11	12	66.67						22	4	18.18 +4.54	3	13.64	31	0	0.00 −38.71	12	38.71
Orissa P.R.I.	33	7	21.21 −21.21	14	42.42						43	9	20.93 −20.93	18	41.86	34	4	11.76 −14.71	9	26.47
Maharashtra P.R.I.	51	7	13.73 −19.60	17	33.33						32	13	40.63 +37.50	1	3.13	56	6	10.71 −12.50	13	23.21
Tamil Nadu P.R.I.	52	14	26.92 +7.69	10	19.23						54	4	7.41 −25.92	18	33.33	68	2	2.94 −35.30	26	38.24
Uttar Pradesh P.R.I.	44	0	0.00 −90.91	40	90.91						90	9	10.00 −44.56	50	55.56	147	14	9.52 −59.19	101	68.71
Rajasthan P.R.I.	13	0	0.00 −84.62	11	84.62						24	1	4.17 −54.16	14	58.33	45	5	11.11 −44.41	25	55.55
Mysore P.R.I.	20[b]	1	5.00 −65.00	14	70.00						20	1	5.00 −40.00	9	45.00	31	3	9.68 −61.29	22	70.97
Haryana P.R.I.	1	0	0.00 −100.00	1	100.00						14	2	14.29 −35.71	7	50.00	12	0	0.00 −75.00	9	75.00
Madhya Pradesh P.R.I.	22	0	0.00 −86.36	19	86.36						25	2	8.00 −40.00	12	48.00	42	1	2.38 −78.57	34	80.95
Gujarat P.R.I.	8	0	0.00 −62.50	5	62.50						—	—	—	—	—	1	0	0.00 0.00	0	0.00

State	1965 CPI					1965 CPM					1967 CPI					1967 CPM				
	Cont. No.	Won No.	%	LD No.	%	Cont. No.	Won No.	%	LD No.	%	Cont. No.	Won No.	%	LD No.	%	Cont. No.	Won No.	%	LD No.	%
Kerala P.R.I.[a]	78	3	3.85 −65.38	54	69.23	73	40	54.79 +42.46	9	12.33	22	19	86.36 +86.36	0	0.00	59	52	88.14 +88.14	0	0.00
West Bengal P.R.I.											62	16	25.81 −9.67	22	35.48	134	43	32.09 +19.40	17	12.69
Andhra Pradesh P.R.I.											62	7	11.29 −33.87	28	45.16	54	5	9.26 −20.37	16	29.63
Punjab P.R.I.											19	5	26.32 0.00	5	26.32	13	3	23.08 −15.38	5	38.46
Bihar P.R.I.											98	24	24.49 −23.47	47	47.96	31	4	12.90 −61.29	23	74.19
Assam P.R.I.											22	7	31.82 +9.09	5	22.73	14	0	0.00 −71.43	10	71.43
Orissa P.R.I.											31	7	22.58 −29.03	16	51.61	10	1	10.00 −40.00	5	50.00
Maharashtra P.R.I.											41	10	24.39 +7.32	7	17.07	11	1	9.09 −18.18	3	27.27
Tamil Nadu P.R.I.											32	2	6.25 −68.75	24	75.00	22	11	50.00 +40.91	2	9.09
Uttar Pradesh P.R.I.											96	13	13.54 −54.17	65	67.71	56	1	1.79 −80.35	46	82.14
Rajasthan P.R.I.											20	1	5.00 −80.00	17	85.00	22	0	0.00 −86.36	19	86.36
Mysore P.R.I.											6	1	16.67 −33.33	3	50.00	10	1	10.00 −30.00	4	40.00
Haryana P.R.I.											12	0	0.00 −100.00	12	100.00	8	0	0.00 −100.00	8	100.00
Madhya Pradesh P.R.I.											33	1	3.03 −87.88	30	90.91	9	0	0.00 −100.00	9	100.00
Gujarat P.R.I.											—	—	—	—	—	—	—	—	—	—

Sources: Compiled from Craig Baxter, *District Voting Trends in India: A Research Tool* (New York: Columbia University Press, 1969); 1970–1971 figures for Kerala and West Bengal from *Overseas Hindustan Times*, 26 September 1970 and *Amrita Bazar Patrika*, 22 March 1971, respectively; 1970–1971 figures for Orissa and Tamil Nadu from *On the General Election of March 1971: Resolutions and Review Report of the National Council of the Communist Party of India*, New Delhi, 23 to 28 April 1971 (New Delhi: CPI, 1971) p. 106; 1972 figures from American Embassy, "State Assembly Elections—1972."

Table 1.7 (continued)

State	1968 & 1969										1970 & 1971									
	Cont. No.	Won No.	%	CPI LD No.	%	Cont. No.	Won No.	%	CPM LD No.	%	Cont. No.	Won No.	%	CPI LD No.	%	Cont. No.	Won No.	%	CPM LD No.	%
Kerala P.R.I.	36	30	83.33 +83.33	0	0.00	97	80	82.47 +81.44	1	1.03	31	16	51.61 N.A.	N.A.		72	28	38.89 N.A.	N.A.	
West Bengal P.R.I.											111	13	11.71 −38.74	56	50.45	237	111	46.83 +36.28	25	10.55
Andhra Pradesh P.R.I.																				
Punjab P.R.I.	29	4	13.79 −48.28	18	62.07	9	2	22.22 +11.11	1	11.11										
Bihar P.R.I.	163	25	15.34 −41.10	92	56.44	29	3	10.34 −55.18	19	65.52										
Assam P.R.I.																				
Orissa P.R.I.											27	4	14.81 N.A.	N.A.		11	2	18.18 N.A.	N.A.	
Maharashtra P.R.I.																				
Tamil Nadu P.R.I.											10	8	80.00 N.A.	N.A.		37	0	0.00 N.A.	N.A.	
Uttar Pradesh P.R.I.	109	4	3.67 −69.72	80	73.39	21	1	4.76 −71.43	16	76.19										
Rajasthan P.R.I.																				
Mysore P.R.I.																				
Haryana P.R.I.	3	0	0.00 −100.00	3	100.00	1	0	0.00 −100.00	1	100.00										
Madhya Pradesh P.R.I.																				
Gujarat P.R.I.																				

State	1972 CPI					1972 CPM				
	Cont. No.	Won No.	%	LD No.	%	Cont. No.	Won No.	%	LD No.	%
Kerala										
P.R.I.										
West Bengal	41	35	85.37	N.A.		208	14	6.73	N.A.	N.A.
P.R.I.			N.A.					N.A.		
Andhra Pradesh	59	7	11.86	N.A.		32	1	3.13	N.A.	N.A.
P.R.I.			N.A.					N.A.		
Punjab	13	10	76.92	N.A.		17	1	5.88	N.A.	N.A.
P.R.I.			N.A.					N.A.		
Bihar	53	35	66.04	N.A.		52	0	0.00	N.A.	N.A.
P.R.I.			N.A.					N.A.		
Assam	28	3	10.71	N.A.		19	0	0.00	N.A.	N.A.
P.R.I.			N.A.					N.A.		
Orissa										
P.R.I.										
Maharashtra	43	2	4.65	N.A.		21	1	4.76	N.A.	N.A.
P.R.I.			N.A.					N.A.		
Tamil Nadu										
P.R.I.										
Uttar Pradesh										
P.R.I.										
Rajasthan	5	4	80.00	0	0.00	21	0	0.00	19	90.48
P.R.I.			+80.00					−90.48		
Mysore	4	3	75.00	N.A.		18	0	0.00	N.A.	N.A.
P.R.I.			N.A.					N.A.		
Haryana	11	0	0.00	N.A.		4	0	0.00	N.A.	N.A.
P.R.I.			N.A.					N.A.		
Madhya Pradesh	6	3	50.00	N.A.		4	0	0.00	3	75.00
P.R.I.			N.A.					−75.00		
Gujarat	13	1	7.69	N.A.		—	—	—	—	—
P.R.I.			N.A.					—		

a Party Realism Index, calculated by subtracting the smaller percentage from the larger percentage of seats won and deposits lost to total seats contested. A minus sign indicates that the percentage of deposits lost was greater than the percentage of seats won.
b CPI + PDF.
c 1955 + 1957.
d CPI only; does not include CP(L).

Tamil Nadu in 1967 and the CPI in Punjab and Bihar in 1972, in Orissa
in 1967, and in Maharashtra in 1957 won a respectable proportion of the
seats they contested while not losing an inordinately large number of security deposits. At all other elections in all these states, however, both Communist parties have lost more deposits than they have won seats.

The last group of states, in which the Communist parties have been of
little or no consequence in state politics, includes Uttar Pradesh, Rajasthan, Mysore, Haryana, Madhya Pradesh, and Gujarat. With the exception of Uttar Pradesh for a brief period in 1967, these are states in which
Communist parties have not had access to power in the state government.
With the exception again of Uttar Pradesh in 1962, the Communist parties
in these states have never contested more than 25 or 26 percent of the seats
in their states. Moreover, in the seats that they have contested, their performance has usually been dismal. In every election in every one of these
six states, except during the elections of 1972 when the CPI fought in
alliance with Congress (R), the proportion of lost deposits to seats contested has been higher than the proportion of seats won. On some occasions, a Communist party's candidates in one of these states have lost their
security deposits in every seat contested.

How can the differential strength and weakness of the Communist movement in the Indian states be explained? A variety of possible explanations
can be applied to the Indian data. At the most general level, one body of
theory has attempted to relate Communist strength in different parts of the
world to levels of modernization and economic development. Lipset, in
Political Man, suggested an inverse relationship between increasing
modernization and support for Communist parties in Europe and North
America.[178] A retest of Lipset's hypothesis by Marsh and Parish, using a
more nearly universal data base, found that Lipset's hypothesis of a linear
inverse relationship between modernization and Communism did not
hold.[179] However, Benjamin and Kautsky, in a 1968 article, argued that
there was a relationship between Communist party strength and level of
economic development but that the relationship was curvilinear. That is,
it was hypothesized and confirmed by the evidence "that Communist
party strength is lowest at the lowest stage of economic development, rises
gradually with economic development, crests at a fairly high level of such

---

[178] Seymour Martin Lipset, *Political Man: The Social Bases of Politics* (New York:
Anchor Books, 1963), chap. 2.
[179] Robert M. Marsh and William L. Parish, "Modernization and Communism: A
Re-Test of Lipset's Hypotheses," *American Sociological Review* 30 (December
1965), 934–942.

development, and declines sharply with the highest level." [180] Let us see how these broad hypotheses hold up in a comparative examination of the regional strength of the Communist parties in the Indian states.

Table 1.8 compares the Communist vote in the Indian states with a set of indicators of modernization and economic development similar to those used by Lipset, Marsh and Parish, and Benjamin and Kautsky, and shows the product-moment correlation coefficient (r) between the 1967 Communist vote and the various indicators. It is easier to test for the existence of a linear relationship between the Communist vote and measures of modernization and economic development with the Indian data than it is to test for the existence of a curvilinear relationship because our N is relatively small and the range of variation in the Indian states on the indicators used by Benjamin and Kautsky is much less than in their study, which covered a range from advanced industrial countries to the least modernized countries in the world. However, we can see if the three categories of states we have identified in terms of Communist electoral strength group in similar ways on any of the indicators.

The evidence in table 1.8 concerning the hypothesized relationships between Communist strength and modernization and economic development is mixed. Three specific indicators of economic development—per capita income, urbanization, and energy consumption per capita—show almost no relationship or very little relationship to the 1967 Communist vote. A composite indicator of economic development and modernization, percentage of population living in the top two categories of development districts as defined in the 1961 census, also shows only a slight positive association with the Communist vote. However, the indicator, percentage of working force in agriculture, which is comparable to the Benjamin and Kautsky indicator of agricultural population as percentage of population, shows a strong negative correlation. That is, the lower the work force in agriculture in an Indian state, the higher the Communist vote. Benjamin and Kautsky found the relationship between Communist party strength and their indicator to be curvilinear, such that countries with more than two-thirds and less than one-sixth of the population in agriculture had weak Communist parties whereas countries with agricultural populations between one-sixth and two-thirds of the total population had stronger Communist parties. The range of the work force in agriculture in the Indian states is between 46.8 percent and 82.0 percent, with only two states—Kerala and West Bengal—below two-thirds. In the range that is

[180] Roger W. Benjamin and John H. Kautsky, "Communism and Economic Development," *American Political Science Review* 62, no. 1 (March 1968), 111.

Table 1.8 Comparison of Communist Vote with Selected Indicators of Modernization and Economic Development in the Indian States

State	1967 Communist Vote %	Rank	1967 SSP-PSP Vote %	Rank	1952 Congress Vote %	Rank	Per Capita Income[a] Rs.	Rank	Urbanization %	Rank	Working Force in Agriculture %	Rank	Energy Consumption Per Capita[b] KWH	Rank	Literacy %	Rank	Circulation of Newspapers[c] %	Rank	Total Population Living in Upper Half Development Districts %	Rank
Kerala	32.1	(1)	8.6	(7)	35.8	(13)	393	(10)	15.1	(10)	46.8	(1)	38.7	(10)	46.9	(1)	10.1	(3)	89.5	(2)
West Bengal	24.6	(2)	4.0	(10)	38.3	(10)	498	(5)	24.5	(4)	57.8	(2)	98.6	(1)	29.3	(5)	6.6	(4)	62.1	(8)
Andhra Pradesh	15.4	(3)	0.4	(15)	31.7	(14)	438	(7)	17.4	(8)	73.3	(8)	25.3	(12)	21.2	(10)	1.6	(10)	55.7	(10)
Punjab	8.5	(4)	1.2	(14)	31.3	(15)	575	(1)	23.0	(5)	66.7d	(4.5)	84.3d	(3.5)	26.7	(7)	2.9	(7.5)	85.9d	(4.5)
Bihar	8.2	(5)	24.6	(1)	41.9	(7)	299	(15)	8.4	(13)	79.4	(13)	49.0	(8)	18.4	(12)	0.9	(14)	22.1	(14)
Assam	7.1	(6)	8.2	(8)	43.5	(6)	441	(6)	7.7	(14)	78.3	(12)	4.4	(15)	27.4	(6)	1.5	(11.5)	58.0	(9)
Orissa	6.5	(7)	13.7	(3)	38.1	(11)	347	(14)	6.3	(15)	76.2	(10)	57.0	(7)	21.7	(9)	0.7	(15)	4.3	(15)
Maharashtra	6.0	(8)	8.7	(6)	47.3	(4)	526	(2)	28.2	(1)	72.3	(7)	87.1	(2)	29.8	(4)	10.9	(2)	73.0	(6)
Tamil Nadu	5.9	(9)	1.4	(13)	37.9	(12)	434	(8)	26.7	(2)	63.5	(3)	63.5	(5)	31.4	(2)	11.4	(1)	100.0	(1)
Uttar Pradesh	4.5	(10)	14.1	(2)	47.9	(3)	374	(11)	12.9	(12)	76.9	(11)	19.3	(13)	17.7	(13)	2.4	(9)	40.7	(12)
Rajasthan	2.2	(11)	5.6	(9)	39.8	(9)	356	(13)	16.3	(9)	81.9	(14)	14.6	(14)	15.2	(15)	1.5	(11.5)	44.8	(11)
Mysore	1.6	(12)	11.4	(4)	0.4	(2)	420	(9)	22.3	(6)	75.0	(9)	44.1	(9)	25.4	(8)	3.3	(6)	65.3	(7)
Haryana	1.4	(13)	3.8	(11)	40.1	(8)	504	(4)	17.3	(7)	66.7d	(4.5)	84.3d	(3.5)	19.8	(11)	2.9	(7.5)	85.9d	(4.5)
Madhya Pradesh	1.3	(14)	10.0	(5)	46.6	(5)	373	(12)	14.3	(11)	82.0	(15)	26.3	(11)	17.1	(14)	1.0	(13)	33.0	(13)
Gujarat	0.0	(15)	3.7	(12)	56.1	(1)	523	(3)	25.8	(3)	72.0	(6)	61.6	(6)	30.5	(3)	4.4	(5)	87.7	(3)
India	8.7		8.6		42.2		418		18.0		N.A.		48.3		24.0		4.7		55.3	
r with 1967 Communist Vote	−0.10		−0.10		−0.55		0.01		−0.01		−0.77		0.10		0.66		0.41		0.17	
r with 1967 PSP-SSP Vote	−0.10				0.16		−0.72		−0.61		0.93		−0.37		−0.27		−0.32		−0.69	

Sources: Per capita income: *Reserve Bank of India Bulletin* 23, no. 9 (September 1969), 1447; urbanization: *Census of India, 1961,* Paper No. 1 of 1962, p. 325; literacy: ibid., vol. 2, part II-A(ii), p. xlvi; population in upper half development districts: ibid., vol. 1, Part I-A(i), p. 19; working force in agriculture: Kedarnath Prasad, *The Economics of a Backward Region in a Backward Economy (A Case Study of Bihar in Relation to Other States of India),* vol. 1 (Calcutta: Scientific Book Agency, 1967), pp. 72–73; energy consumption per capita: ibid., pp. 135–136; circulation of newspapers: Government of India, Ministry of Information and Broadcasting, *Press in India, 1965* (New Delhi, 1965), vol. 2, p. 38; urbanization and literacy for Haryana: Government of Haryana, Planning Department, *Draft Proposals: Fourth Five-Year Plan* (Chandigarh: Controller, Printing and Stationery, [1967]).

a 1964–1965.
b 1962–1963.
c 1964.
d Figures for Punjab and Haryana in these columns are for the Punjab before the 1966 reorganization and division of the state.

comparable to the Benjamin and Kautsky categories, the Indian data support their conclusion, namely, that areas with very high proportions of the population in agriculture have weak Communist movements, whereas strong Communist parties tend to be found in areas where a considerable portion of the work force is engaged in nonagricultural pursuits. However, the absence of an association between the Communist vote and other indicators of economic development argues against a general conclusion concerning the relationship between Communist strength and economic development. Rather, it suggests that the composition of the work force in the transition from an agricultural to a nonagricultural society may be a key factor. The Communist parties in the Indian states also generally perform better in urban than in rural areas. In 8 of the 12 states that have city constituencies, the combined Communist vote was higher in 1967 in the cities than in noncity constituencies (table 1.9).

The Communist vote also correlates more strongly with the two indicators of modernization—literacy and circulation of newspapers—than with the indicators of economic development. The correlation with literacy of .66 is fairly high, that with circulation of newspapers (.41) moderate for a sample of this size.

All these correlations, however, must be treated with considerable caution because of the wide discrepancy in the strength of the strongest Communist states, on the one hand, and the rest of the states, on the other hand. Moreover, there are profound differences in the whole basis of life in the two major centers of Communist strength. West Bengal combines a rural rice-growing economy and a massive urban-industrial complex. Kerala combines a rural rice-growing and cash-crop economy with plantation agriculture and food-processing industries. High correlations seem to occur between the various variables and the Communist vote when Kerala and West Bengal are close together in rank order, low correlations when Kerala and Bengal are farther apart. Yet, the support base for the Communist parties in these two states is entirely different, which raises the question of the ecological fallacy in the use of aggregate data here. The profound difference between the support bases of the Communist parties in West Bengal and Kerala is revealed clearly in table 1.10, which shows the correlation coefficients *by district* within each state for the CPI and CPM with indicators of income, urbanization, and literacy. Whereas correlations between the states show no relationship between income or urbanization and the Communist vote in 1967, the district correlations for West Bengal do show statistically significant correlations on both these measures, as well as on literacy, with the CPM vote.

Table 1.9 City and Noncity Vote Percentages for the Communist and Socialist Parties in the Indian States, 1967 General Elections

	CPI		CPM		CPI + CPM		PSP		SSP		PSP + SSP	
	Noncity Vote %	City Vote %	Noncity Vote %	City Vote %	Noncity Vote %	City Vote %	Noncity Vote %	City Vote %	Noncity Vote %	City Vote %	Noncity Vote %	City Vote %
Andhra Pradesh	7.1	14.4	7.7	4.2	14.8	18.6	0.2	—	0.2	3.4	0.4	3.4
Assam	5.3	—	1.8	—	7.1	—	7.1	—	3.1	—	10.2	—
Bihar	6.8	12.8	1.2	3.5	8.0	12.8	7.0	1.3	18.2	1.1	25.2	2.4
Gujarat	—	—	—	—	—	—	2.8	8.1	0.2	1.4	3.0	9.5
Haryana	1.0	—	0.4	—	1.4	—	0.2	—	3.5	—	3.7	—
Kerala	8.2	16.3	24.2	10.4	32.4	26.7	0.2	0.9	8.5	7.0	8.7	7.9
Madhya Pradesh	0.7	8.1	0.1	1.9	0.8	10.0	5.1	0.7	5.2	6.0	10.3	6.7
Maharashtra	4.5	13.1	1.0	—	5.5	13.1	3.6	6.5	4.3	2.7	7.9	9.2
Mysore	0.5	2.4	0.8	2.5	1.3	4.9	8.8	2.3	2.5	2.8	11.3	5.1
Orissa	5.3	—	1.2	—	6.5	—	12.1	—	1.5	—	13.6	—
Punjab	6.2	1.9	2.8	—	9.0	1.9	0.1	4.9	0.8	0.1	0.9	5.0
Rajasthan	0.9	1.3	1.2	0.5	2.1	1.8	0.6	3.9	5.0	—	5.6	3.9
Tamil Nadu	1.8	1.7	3.8	6.6	5.6	8.3	1.0	—	0.6	—	1.6	—
Uttar Pradesh	3.2	4.0	1.1	1.9	4.3	5.9	4.3	1.4	10.2	6.9	14.5	8.3
West Bengal	6.4	7.0	16.1	29.3	22.5	36.3	2.1	0.8	2.5	0.1	4.6	0.9
India	4.0	6.4	4.3	7.5	8.3	13.9	3.4	2.1	5.3	2.5	8.7	4.6

Source: Government of India, Ministry of Information and Broadcasting, Fourth General Elections: An Analysis (New Delhi: Registrar General, India, 1967).

Table 1.10 District-Level Correlation Coefficients for Selected Indicators of Modernization and Economic Development with the 1967 CPI and CPM Votes in Indian State Legislative Assembly Elections

State	Income		Urbanization		Literacy	
	CPI	CPM	CPI	CPM	CPI	CPM
Andhra	−0.04	−0.09	−0.18	−0.12	−0.04	0.03
Assam	N.A.	N.A.	−0.14	−0.01	0.39	0.31
Bihar	0.04	0.32*	−0.003	0.62*	−0.11	0.37
Haryana	0.28	−0.74	0.45	−0.52	0.06	−0.44
Kerala	0.28	−0.32	−0.51	0.12	0.55	−0.49
Madhya Pradesh	0.19	0.22	0.36*	0.39*	0.20	0.28
Maharashtra	−0.08	0.13	−0.13	0.08	−0.20	0.12
Mysore	0.26	−0.12	−0.09	0.03	0.05	0.09
Orissa	0.60*	−0.18	0.06	−0.06	0.54*	0.36
Punjab	−0.59	−0.41	0.17	0.06	0.32	−0.34
Rajasthan	−0.07	0.06	−0.01	0.13	0.16	0.36
Tamil Nadu	−0.08	−0.24	−0.15	−0.26	−0.06	0.09
Uttar Pradesh	−0.17	−0.26	−0.19	0.01	−0.01	0.04
West Bengal	0.07	0.65*	0.13	0.56*	0.14	0.67*

Source: Provided by the courtesy of W. H. Morris-Jones and B. Das Gupta.
* Indicates that the correlations are statistically significant at a 5% level of confidence.

Several observers of the Communist movement in India, including all the contributors to this volume, have noted that Communist strength is distributed unevenly within the states in which the Communist parties are strongest. The Calcutta-Durgarpur-Asansol subregion in Bengal[181] and Telengana in Andhra are examples of subregional areas of Communist strength within the Indian states, which have their counterparts in other states. Donald Zagoria has attempted to uncover common patterns in the highest support Communist districts *across* state boundaries and has identified 40 districts in India where the Communist vote was highest in the three general elections after 1957.[182] These districts are located in nine states and the union territory of Tripura (although 30 of the districts are in the three strongest Communist states of Kerala, West Bengal, and Andhra). In an ecological analysis of these 40 districts and in a correlation and regression analysis of the Communist vote with ecological variables in 285 districts throughout India, Zagoria has identified two variables that are frequently associated with rural Communist strength, namely, "landlessness in combination with high rural population density." [183] He hypothesizes that the combination of high rural density with landlessness produces a particularly "conflict-ridden relationship between the landowners and the landless" [184] that is conducive to Communist support in the countryside.

Zagoria's analysis of the ecology of Communist support districts is useful, but it brings out again the difficulties involved in applying a single explanation for Communist support in the whole of India. In fact, Zagoria himself found that the general pattern of association of Communist support with landlessness and high density did not hold in western India where "communism correlates with areas in which large landowners predominate." [185] In fact, the pattern of association with high density and landlessness seems really to hold up well only in the south. Zagoria's data, carefully scrutinized, reveal the regional diversity of Communism in India more than a common pattern. In Kerala and Andhra, where densities and landlessness are very high, there is bound to be an association between these two variables and Communist strength. In Bengal, however, the other great area of Communist support, Communist strength is concen-

[181] The importance of this subregion for Communist support in West Bengal has been emphasized by Marcus F. Franda.
[182] Donald Zagoria, "The Ecology of Peasant Communism in India," *American Political Science Review* 65, no. 1 (March 1971), 145.
[183] Ibid., p. 147.
[184] Ibid., p. 149.
[185] Ibid., p. 158.

trated in and around the great urban industrial belt surrounding and extending out from Calcutta. In the "Eastern Zone" in Zagoria's analysis, which includes Bengal, it is not surprising, therefore, that the variables, density and landlessness, explain no more than 25–30 percent of the variation in the Communist vote.

Another type of explanation of variations in Communist strength in Asia generally and in India particularly has placed greater emphasis on nationalism and regionalism than upon modernization and economic development. According to this view, Communist parties in Asia have been most successful where they have been "able to utilize effectively—and if possible, to capture—the nationalist movement." [186] The Indian National Congress, not the CPI, was the dominant nationalist force in India as a whole before Independence; but the Congress was not dominant everywhere, nor has national sentiment been equally strong everywhere in India. In fact, Selig Harrison has argued that the ability of the Communist movement to identify with regional, rather than national, sentiments in India is a critical variable in explaining differences in Communist strength. Harrison's argument was that the Communist parties have been strong in India where they have identified successfully with regional forces and politically strategic regional castes, weak where they have failed to do so.[187]

There is, in fact, a relationship between present areas of Communist strength and areas where Congress control of the nationalist movement was weakest. If we take the 1952 Congress vote as the closest measure of its strength in the nationalist period and correlate this with the 1967 Communist vote, we get a moderately strong negative correlation. The Communist parties were strongest in 1967 in areas where the Congress was weakest in 1952. However, it is far more difficult to develop a measure of the strength of regional forces than it is to develop a measure of the strength of national forces. Regional sentiment in the Indian states has taken a variety of forms and types of organization. There is no difficulty in classifying the Akali Dal and the DMK as regional forces in their respective states, but what about the Marxist Left in Bengal or the Swatantra Party in Orissa? In a sense, all non-Congress parties in India are "regional forces"; and all parties, including the Congress, must somehow relate to regional sentiments to succeed. All parties must also find some stable basis of support, particularly rural support, to succeed—whether that stable basis comes from a "politically strategic regional caste" or from a rural

[186] Scalapino, "Communism in Asia," p. 34.
[187] Harrison, *India: The Most Dangerous Decades*, chap. 6.

class. Therefore, to say that Communist strength "corresponds to the pattern of Communist identification with regional forces" is to say only that the Communist parties operate under the same constraints in India as all other parties. In Punjab and Tamil Nadu, regional parties have been particularly successful in manipulating regional symbols and have prevented the Communist parties and other non-Congress parties from acquiring significant strength. Elsewhere, as in Kerala and West Bengal, no single party has monopolized regional sentiment; rather, regional symbols have been used successfully by the Communist parties and other parties as well. It is, therefore, generally true that the Communist movement has been strongest where Congress control of nationalism has been weakest and where there are no well-entrenched non-Communist regional parties, but even where the Communist parties have been strongest, they have had to compete with other regional parties in the use of regional symbols.

It also deserves note that the Communist parties have been strongest in those areas where Communist cadres dominated the Socialist wing (Congress Socialist Party) of the Indian National Congress before Independence. Communists controlled or had a majority in the CSP before Independence in Andhra, Tamil Nadu, Kerala, Orissa, Bengal, and Punjab. Communists were in a minority in the CSP in Bombay city, Central Provinces (Madhya Pradesh), Maharashtra, UP, Mysore, Gujarat, and Bihar.[188] The correspondence between former areas of Communist strength in the CSP and present areas of Communist strength is very close. In a sense, this correspondence supports the general argument that Communists have been most successful where they have "been able to utilize effectively" the nationalist movement. That is, the Communist parties are now strongest in areas where the Congress was weak and where Communist members were an important force within the Congress before Independence.

The two broad types of explanations for the variations in Communist strength that we have considered so far are vastly different. The ecological approach tends to treat Communism as a dependent variable and to identify the kinds of socioeconomic contexts in which Communist parties achieve success. The explanations that focus on the relationship between nationalism and regionalism stress more the ability of the Communist parties to relate effectively to their regional environments. A related kind of explanation that can be brought to bear on this question focuses more directly on differences in the organizational skills of the Communist parties

---

[188] "Plan of Work," in *ICPD*, pp. 40–45; M. R. Masani, *The Communist Party of India: A Short History* (London: Derek Verschoyle, 1954), p. 69.

in relating to other social and political forces in their environments, that is to say, their abilities to apply in practice united-front tactics with other groups. Communists themselves consider this question of tactics to be of decisive importance. Here, however, we have to consider not only Communist strength as measured by percentage of votes won but Communist ability to win seats in the legislative assemblies.

We do not have enough data on Communist party alliance strategies for every state to compare Communist skills in this regard systematically, but the information available does suggest strongly that the ability of a Communist party to forge electoral alliances in an Indian state is a crucial factor in its success. Let us look again at the data in tables 1.6 and 1.7 and compare the best and poorest performances of the Communist parties in the high support states. The best performance of the CPM in Kerala occurred in 1967 when it won 52 out of 59 seats and lost no security deposits. The worst Communist performances occurred in 1960, when the undivided party contested 108 seats but won only 29, and in 1965, when the CPI contested 78 seats and won only 3. Yet in 1960 the CPI polled 39.1 percent of the vote and in 1967 the CPM polled only 23.5 percent of the vote. The difference clearly was that in 1967 the CPM led a seven-party United Front against the Congress, which was isolated in this election; whereas in 1960 it was the CPI that fought alone against an electoral alliance of the Congress, the PSP, and the Muslim League. The dismal performance of the CPI in 1965 also largely reflects its inability to forge electoral alliances; its only alliance partner in that election was the relatively inconsequential Revolutionary Socialist Party.[189]

Similarly, in West Bengal the best seat-winning performances of the CPI occurred in 1969 and in 1972; of the CPM in 1969. The worst performances were of the CPI in 1971 and the CPM in 1972. In 1969, the CPI and the CPM fought the elections together with 11 other parties in a massive non-Congress United Front. In 1971, there were two separate leftist fronts and the two Communist parties fought against each other.[190] In 1972, the CPI benefited from its alliance with Congress (R) whereas the CPM fought practically alone.

The peak seat-winning performance of the Andhra CPI occurred in 1952 when the party won 77 out of 108 seats contested and won 21.8 percent of the vote. In that election the CPI contested in alliance with the

[189] D. R. Mankekar, *The Red Riddle of Kerala* (Bombay: Manaktalas, 1965), chaps. 10 and 11; *Indian Recorder & Digest* 13, no. 1 (January 1967), 18; and ibid. 13, no. 2 (February 1967), 21.
[190] Franda, *Radical Politics in West Bengal*, chap. 5.

Socialist Party. The low points of Communist performance in Andhra occurred in 1967 and in 1972 when both the CPI and the CPM lost more security deposits than they won seats and polled a combined vote of only 15.4 percent and 9.0 percent, respectively. In 1969, the two Communist parties fought alone and fought each other. However, even the 1972 alliance between Congress (R) and the CPI failed to arrest the continuing and precipitous decline of both Communist parties in this state.

The regional studies in this volume all bring out clearly the importance of alliance strategies in Communist success. Although strength in the electorate and seat-winning capacity vary somewhat independently, it appears that the ability of the Communist parties to implement their united-front tactics in concrete electoral alliances with other parties is a decisive factor in Communist party electoral performance. A detailed state-by-state history of alliance patterns for each election would be necessary to confirm this hypothesis conclusively, but the available evidence is strongly suggestive.

What general conclusions, then, can be drawn about variations in Communist electoral strength in India? There is no strong general relationship between levels of economic development and modernization in the Indian states and Communist strength. The indicators of per capita income, urbanization, energy consumption per capita, and the composite indicator derived from the 1961 census of India do not show any significant associations with Communist support at the state level. However, the evidence does suggest that Communist parties tend to be most successful in regional environments where the composition of the working force has begun to change from a predominantly agricultural basis and where literacy rates and newspaper circulation are relatively higher. But, it must be kept in mind that the regional context of Communist party support varies considerably from state to state in India such that the support base for Communism in Bengal and in Kerala or other states may be significantly different. There is some association between Communist strength and areas of high density and landlessness, but this is more of a regional than an all-India pattern. With regard to nationalism and regionalism, the Communist parties in India have been strongest in areas where Congress dominance of the nationalist movement was weakest and where Communist party members were dominant in the Socialist wing of the Congress. Like all other parties in India, the Communist parties have done better when no other party has successfully captured regional symbols and when they have been able to relate to regional sentiments, but nowhere have the Communist parties themselves monopolized regional symbols. With regard to the capacities of the Communist parties to win seats, as contrasted with votes, the crucial variable has been the organizational skill of the parties in forging electoral alliances with other parties and avoiding direct conflicts with each other.

THE DEMOCRATIC SOCIALIST PARTIES OF INDIA

Table 1.11 shows the distribution of party vote percentages for the leading all-India Socialist parties from 1952 to 1972. The table does not reflect accurately the strength of the non-Communist Left in each state because the regional parties of the Left, which are not easy to classify, have not been included. Also, the 1957 figure and the average percentage for all elections are lower than they should be because of the fact that vote percentages are not available for the SP for 1957.

Keeping these limitations of the data in table 1.11 in mind, it is possible to compare the regional strength of the leading all-India Socialist parties with the Communist parties and with each other and to follow the changes in Socialist strength in the states. On the whole, there is an inverse relationship between Socialist strength and Communist strength in the Indian states. The overall correlation between the 1967 Communist vote and the 1967 Socialist vote is −.10 (see table 1.8). Moreover, it is clear that the main areas of Socialist strength are quite different from the main areas of Communist strength. The bastions of the democratic Socialist parties have been the two great north Indian states of Bihar and Uttar Pradesh. Kerala, West Bengal, and Andhra ranked 7th, 10th, and 15th, respectively, in terms of PSP-SSP support in 1967. There is also a considerable difference in the character of the dispersion of Socialist and Communist strength in the Indian states. There is a somewhat more even distribution of Socialist strength than of Communist strength in the states. The average vote of the Communist parties in Kerala, West Bengal, and Andhra is between two and three times that of the next strongest Communist support state, whereas there is no similar gap between the highest Socialist support states and other states. If Socialist strength is more evenly dispersed, however, Communist strength is greater than that of the Socialist parties in their respective regional strongholds. The Communist parties in Kerala and West Bengal are more powerful and better institutionalized parties than the Socialist parties in Bihar and Uttar Pradesh.

There have been considerable differences in the regional distribution of the strength of the two Socialist parties also. In 1967, in the two strongest Socialist support states of Bihar and Uttar Pradesh, the SSP was the leading party, as it was also in Madhya Pradesh, Maharashtra, Kerala, Rajasthan, West Bengal, Haryana, Punjab, and Andhra. The PSP was the

Table 1.11 Percentage of Valid Votes Polled by Socialist Parties[a] of India in State Legislative Assembly Elections, 1952–1972

State[b]	1952 SP		KMPP		1954 PSP		1957 PSP		1960–1962 PSP		SP		1965 PSP		SSP		1967 PSP		SSP	
	%	Rank	%	Rank	%	Rank	%	Rank	%	Rank	%	Rank	%	Rank	%	Rank	%	Rank	%	Rank
Bihar	18.8	(2)	2.9	(5)			16.0	(2)	14.2	(3)	5.2	(5)					7.0	(4)	17.6	(2)
Uttar Pradesh	12.0	(2)	5.7	(4)			14.5	(2)	11.5	(3)	8.2	(4)					4.1	(6)	10.0	(3)
Orissa	11.8	(3)	0.5	(5)			9.8	(3)	11.1	(3)	0.7	(6)					12.2	(4)	1.5	(6)
Mysore	7.2	(3)	13.1	(2)			14.1	(2)	14.2	(2)	0.9	(8)					8.9	(2)	2.5	(5)
Madhya Pradesh	8.8	(2)	6.0	(3)			13.2	(2)	10.7	(3)	4.7	(4)					4.7	(4)	5.3	(3)
Maharashtra	12.7	(2)	0.7	(9)			10.7	(2)	7.2	(3)	0.5	(7)					4.1	(7)	4.6	(6)
Kerala	14.3	(3)	4.5	(4)	16.7	(3)	10.4	(3)	14.3	(3)	—	—	0.4	(10)	8.1	(5)	0.2	(9)	8.4	(4)
Assam	13.3	(2)	6.0	(3)			12.7	(2)	12.7	(2)	1.5	(5)					6.9	(2)	3.3	(5)
Rajasthan	3.9	(5)	0.5	(8)			2.5	(5)	1.5	(7)	3.7	(5)					0.8	(7)	4.8	(4)
West Bengal	2.8	(6)	8.6	(3)			9.3	(3)	5.0	(3)	#	(14)					1.9	(7)	2.1	(6)
Haryana	5.9	(4)	0.2	(7)			1.8	(5)	1.1	(7)	3.8	(5)					0.2	(8)	3.6	(3)
Gujarat	8.6	(2)	7.4	(3)			4.9	(2)	7.7	(3)	#	(9)					3.3	(3)	0.4	(5)
Tamil Nadu	5.8	(4)	4.0	(5)			2.6	(3)	1.3	(6)	0.4	(10)					0.9	(6)	0.5	(7)
Punjab	3.0	(6)	0.4	(10)			0.9	(5)	0.7	(7)	#	(10)					0.5	(9)	0.7	(8)
Andhra Pradesh	8.4	(4)	9.9	(3)			5.6	(3)	0.3	(7)	0.6	(5)					0.2	(8)	0.4	(6)
India	9.7		5.1				10.1		7.0		2.7						3.4		5.2	

State	1968–1969 PSP		SSP		1970–1971 PSP		SSP		1972 SP		Average Combined Socialist Vote %
	%	Rank	%	Rank	%	Rank	%	Rank	%	Rank	
Bihar	5.7	(5)	13.7	(3)					16.1	(2)	19.5
Uttar Pradesh	1.7	(7)	7.8	(4)							15.1
Orissa					6.1	(5)	1.2	(9)			11.0
Mysore									1.7	(4)	12.5
Madhya Pradesh									6.3	(3)	11.9
Maharashtra									4.6	(N.A.)	9.0
Kerala					2.4	(10)	4.1	(7)			12.0
Assam									5.7	(2)	12.4
Rajasthan									2.4	(4)	4.0
West Bengal	1.3	(10)	1.9	(7)	0.8	(10)	0.7	(11)	0.9	(N.A.)	5.0
Haryana	0.1	(11)	0.9	(7)					0.3	(N.A.)	3.0
Gujarat									1.0	(5)	6.7
Tamil Nadu					1.0	(8)	0.3	(9)			3.4
Punjab	0.5	(11)	0.8	(9)					0.9	(N.A.)	1.4
Andhra Pradesh									0.4	(N.A.)	5.2
India									4.5		9.5

Sources: Compiled from Craig Baxter, *District Voting Trends in India: A Research Tool* (New York: Columbia University Press, 1969); Morris-Jones, "India Elects for Change —and Stability," p. 732; and American Embassy, "State Assembly Elections—1972."
a The table does not include exclusively regional Socialist parties.
b States have been ranked according to the percentage of votes polled by the PSP and SSP combined in the 1967 elections.

stronger of the two parties in 1967 in Orissa, Mysore, Gujarat, and Tamil Nadu. It deserves note that the SSP, which identified with Hindi sentiment in the north, was the stronger of the two parties in every state in the vast Hindi-speaking region of north and central India.

The most striking facts about both Socialist parties are the steady decline in their all-India strength and their increasing displacement as serious political parties in most of the states. In 1952, the combined Socialist vote in all states was 14.8 percent (compared to only 4.3 percent for the Communist parties), and one or both of the Socialist parties ranked second or third in popular support in 11 of the 15 states. In the 1960–1962 elections, the combined PSP-SP vote was down to 9.7 percent (compared to 8.6 percent for the Communist parties), and one or both of the Socialist parties ranked second or third in popular support in 10 of the 15 states. By 1967, however, the combined Socialist vote was down to 8.6 percent (compared to 8.7 percent for the Communist parties), and one or both Socialist parties ranked second or third in popular support in only 7 states. In 1972, the united SP polled only 4.5 percent of the all-India vote, and the SP ranked second or third in only 3 states.

Thus, a general comparison of the regional strength of the two leading Socialist parties with the two leading Communist parties indicates the following conclusions. Socialist strength has been more evenly dispersed, less regionally concentrated, than Communist strength. But, the Socialists do not have any regional bastions comparable to the Communist strongholds of Kerala and West Bengal. The Socialist parties, particularly the SSP, have been stronger than the Communist parties in the northern Hindi-speaking states, whereas the Communist parties have been strongest in the non-Hindi-speaking states of Kerala, West Bengal, Andhra, and Punjab. The Socialist parties have generally declined in all-India popular support and in the number of states in which they are important political forces. In terms of all-India popular support, the democratic Socialist and the Communist parties had equal strength in 1967, but in 1972 the combined Communist vote was nearly double that of the Socialists in the state elections.

The 1967 combined PSP-SSP vote correlates quite differently with the indicators of modernization and economic development than the 1967 Communist vote. Whereas the Communist vote correlates positively with most indicators of modernization and economic development, the democratic Socialist vote correlates negatively with all such indicators (table 1.8). Moreover, whereas most of the positive associations of the Communist vote with the various indicators are weak, several of the negative associations of the Socialist vote with the indicators are fairly strong. The strongest correlation is a remarkable .93 for the 1967 Socialist vote with the variable percentage of working force in agriculture (or −.93 with percentage of working force in nonagricultural occupations). All the other correlations are consistent— −.72 with per capita income, −.61 with urbanization, −.37 with energy consumption, −.69 with the composite indicator based on development districts, −.27 with literacy, and −.32 with circulation of newspapers. Clearly, and unambiguously, the PSP-SSP vote was highest in 1967 in the least economically developed and least modernized states of India. Moreover, both the PSP and the SSP tended relatively more than the CPI and the CPM to do better in noncity than in city constituencies (table 1.9). The least city-oriented party of the four from this point of view in 1967 was the SSP, which polled 5.3 percent of the noncity vote in all India and only 2.5 percent of the city vote. In 11 of the 15 states, the SSP did better in noncity than in city constituencies. The PSP also did better, on the whole, in noncity than in city constituencies on an all-India basis and in 10 of the 15 states.

Clearly, therefore, from all points of view, the distributions of the strength of the democratic Socialist and Communist parties in India have been quite different. The Communist parties of India have been strongest in areas where the Congress was weakest; in the non-Hindi-speaking states; and, on the whole, in the more economically developed and modernized states. The democratic Socialist parties have been strongest in areas where the Congress itself was strong (.16 correlation with 1952 Congress vote), in the Hindi-speaking states, and, overwhelmingly, in the less economically developed, less modernized states.

THE REGIONAL STRENGTH OF THE RADICAL LEFT IN PAKISTAN AND CEYLON

The distribution of support for the parties of the radical Left has been even more clearly demarcated regionally in Pakistan than has been the case in India. Moreover, the reasons for the differential distribution of radical Left party support in Pakistan can be more unambiguously related to a combination of historical and regional factors. Communism in Pakistan has, historically, been an East Bengali phenomenon. Moreover, it has been largely an extension of the sentiment for Communism among Hindu intellectuals in prepartition Bengal. Consequently, Communism in Muslim East Bengal, where regional nationalism has been the most potent political force, has had little appeal.

The National Awami parties of Pakistan have also had a clear regional distribution of support. The NAP(B) has been exclusively an East Bengal party, representing a combination of appeals to both leftist and regional sentiment, but it was completely overshadowed in the 1971 elections by the Awami League. The NAP(W) has been nearly exclusively a regional party, appealing to regional sentiment in two minority West Pakistan provinces—the Northwest Frontier Province and Baluchistan.[191] Consequently, it is apparent that leftism in Pakistan has been exclusively associated with regional forces in the west and with regional and minority sentiment in the east. It is also clear that the radical Left has not done well in East Bengal because the limited political activity that has been permitted has been dominated by the regionalist Awami League and that the NAP(W) has done well in West Pakistan only in areas where regional sentiment has been strong.

If regional sentiment has been more important in explaining the distribution of radical Left party support in Pakistan than in India, it has been less of a factor in Ceylon. The strength of the radical Left parties in Ceylon has been confined to the western and southern provinces of the island, close to Colombo, where these parties have historically concentrated their organizational resources and where there are large concentrations both of wage earners and of minority castes.[192] However, the radical Left parties in Ceylon have not profited at all from either the resurgence of Sinhalese nationalism, which has been monopolized politically by the SLFP, or from the organization of Tamil protest in the north, which has been the political preserve of Tamil parties, particularly the Federal Party.

In general, therefore, the regional distribution of Left party strength in Pakistan and Ceylon confirms the argument that was made above, on the basis of the evidence from India, concerning the importance of regional nationalism. That is, regional sentiment has been a powerful force in all three countries. All parties, including parties of the Left, have had to make some adjustments to regional nationalism where it has developed. In some parts of South Asia, particularly the Punjab, Tamil Nadu, East Bengal, and Ceylon, the leading political parties in recent years have been regionally oriented centrist parties. In those areas, parties of the radical Left have had to adjust to regional sentiment simply to survive. In other parts of South Asia, particularly in Kerala, West Bengal, and Andhra for the Com-

[191] In the 1971 elections the NAP(W) emerged as the leading party in both these provinces, winning 13 of 40 seats in the NWFP and 8 of 20 seats in Baluchistan in the provincial assembly contests; Craig Baxter, "Pakistan Votes—1970," *Asian Survey* 11, no. 3 (March 1971), 211.

[192] W. Howard Wriggins, *Ceylon: Dilemmas of a New Nation* (Princeton, N.J.: Princeton University Press, 1960), pp. 136–138; and Kearney "Communist Parties of Ceylon," p. 394.

munist parties and north India for the SSP, the radical Left parties have been more successful in using regional symbols and have also succeeded in bringing economic issues more to the forefront. However, in South Asia as a whole, it does not appear that the parties of the radical Left have been particularly skillful in making use of regional symbols for political purposes.

Popular Support

Parties of the radical Left in West European countries have traditionally been associated with and derived their support primarily from the industrial labor force, particularly the unionized labor force. In Eastern Europe, however, there has been no such association. Burks has argued that, in Eastern Europe, Communist party support developed in rural areas in Slavic countries and particularly among Slavic minorities with special attachments to Russia. In general, he found that ethnic factors were more important than class factors in explaining variations in Communist strength.[193] Successful Asian Communist parties have also tended to find mass support in rural areas among the peasantry, and in several countries, among particular ethnic minorities,[194] but most Asian Communist parties continue to have their main strength in large cities.

Radical parties of the Left in South Asia have all followed broad multi-class strategies in seeking popular support in both urban and rural areas, but there have been differences between parties and between regions in class emphasis and in the success of the parties in winning support from particular groups. All parties of the radical Left in South Asia have sought support from the working classes in urban industrial areas. In Ceylon, the strength of the Marxist parties has been concentrated in the urbanized, modernized areas of the country where literacy rates are high and where the nonagricultural work force is large. Marxist parties in Ceylon have had support particularly from clerical workers. They have not, however, had much strength in the rural areas.[195]

Communist support in East Bengal has been "confined almost entirely to the petty bourgeoisie or lower middle classes, and to students."[196] Older

---

[193] Burks, *Dynamics of Communism in Eastern Europe*, chaps. 2–4 and passim.
[194] For example, ethnic minority Chinese support for the Malayan Communist Party (ibid., pp. 180, 182; and Francis L. Starner, "Communism in Malaysia: A Multi-front Struggle," in Scalapino, *Communist Revolution in Asia*, p. 222) and tribal minority support for the Pathet Lao in Laos (Bernard B. Fall, "The Pathet Lao: A 'Liberation Party,' " in Scalapino, *Communist Revolution in Asia*, pp. 173–191).
[195] Kearney, "Communist Parties of Ceylon," pp. 379–381.
[196] Franda, "Communism and Regional Politics in East Pakistan," p. 596.

support bases in the trade unions and rural areas have been eroded as the strength of the movement has disintegrated.[197] Little is known about the support bases of the NAP in East Bengal, but party leaders have sought to build support among both peasants and workers.[198]

In India, the CPI has been the strongest of the radical Left parties in the trade unions in most urban industrial areas. The CPI has maintained its control over AITUC and, as Hardgrave points out, is stronger than the CPM in the Kerala trade unions. However, the urban industrial labor force does not constitute an adequate support base in an agricultural society for radical Left parties interested in winning power. Nor does the CPI or any other radical Left party have overwhelming dominance in the trade union movement, which continues to be divided and weak in most Indian cities.

All the stronger radical Left parties in the Indian states have won some kind of mass base in the countryside. If the opportunities are greater in the rural areas than in the cities for mobilizing popular support, however, the pitfalls are also greater. Although all the radical Left parties claim to be following multiclass strategies in the countryside, the nature of land distribution in most parts of India makes it difficult to implement such strategies in practice. If a party seeks support from the landless, the small and middle landholders will be antagonized, and vice versa. Communist party ideologists have long been aware of this dilemma. Moreover, the two leading Communist parties in India have developed different rural strategies with respect to the landless and the peasants. The CPI has tended to appeal more to all categories of peasants than to the landless, whereas the CPM appeals have been made more to the poor peasants and the landless. Franda and Hardgrave have shown that in the two leading Communist strongholds of Kerala and Bengal, the CPI has been stronger among the middle peasants whereas the CPM has been stronger among the landless and agricultural laborers. In Andhra, the class appeals of both Communist parties in the rural areas have been more mixed. Both parties have sought support from agricultural laborers and from poor, middle, and rich peasants as well, but Mohan Ram has emphasized the relationship of the Communist parties to the agricultural laborers.

The limited survey research and ecological data available confirm these assertions, and provide additional information on the support bases of radical Left parties in India. Sheth has used survey data from interviews with political party supporters in the 1967 elections to compare the support bases of the leading all-India parties in terms of age groups, level of

197 Ibid., p. 599.
198 Rashiduzzaman, "NAP of Pakistan," p. 399.

education, place of residence, occupation, caste, income, and size of land-holding.[199] Most of the data reported do not separate the support bases of the CPI and CPM or the SSP and the PSP, which are combined in two general categories of "Communist parties" and "Socialist parties." Nor has any regional breakup of the data been made available. The results nevertheless show significant differences in the support bases of the Communist and Socialist parties. In comparison with other all-India parties, the Communist and Socialist parties tend to find support more among younger voters, under age 35, than do other parties, with the Communists drawing 25 percent of their vote from the age group 21–25 and 35 percent from the age group 26–35, whereas the Socialist parties draw 16 percent of their vote from the youngest age group and 43 percent from the age group 26–35. In most other respects, however, the support bases of the two groups of parties are quite different. The Communist parties combine support from both illiterates and highly educated voters, whereas the Socialist parties combine support from both illiterates and the less educated, but proportionately less than the Communists from the highly educated. Communist party supporters are "proportionally distributed" (in relation to the sample distribution) in rural and urban areas, whereas the Socialist parties tend to be more heavily rural in their support bases. Between the two Socialist parties, the PSP has had some urban support, whereas the SSP has been nearly exclusively based in the rural areas. The Communist parties are strong among white-collar workers, professionals, and the working class; have "negligible" support in the business class; and tend to have less support than other parties among landowning cultivators. However, Sheth notes that the CPI "draws more support from the cultivating class whereas the [CPM] has more support among the workers, both industrial and agricultural." [200] The Socialist parties are strongest among landless agricultural laborers; draw "more or less proportionally from urban white-collar and business occupational categories"; but do not have much support among skilled factory workers.[201] The Communist parties draw heavy support from low castes, roughly proportional support from middle castes, and less than proportional support from upper castes, Harijans and tribals, and from Muslims in the sample. The Socialist parties draw more than proportional support from both low caste groups and from Harijans and tribals, roughly proportional support from upper

[199] D. L. Sheth, "Profiles of Party Support in 1967," *Economic and Political Weekly* 6, nos. 3, 4, and 5 (January 1971), 275–288.
[200] Ibid., p. 288.
[201] Ibid., p. 281.

castes, and less than proportional support from middle castes and Muslims. Between the two Socialist parties, "the PSP draws more support from upper castes whereas the SSP draws significantly more from the lower castes." [202] Surprisingly, the Communist parties draw less than proportional support from "lowest," "low," and "middle" income groups, but significantly greater support from high income groups; whereas the Socialist parties draw proportionately more support from the "lowest" and "low" income groups and proportionately less support from the "middle" and "high" income groups. Finally, the Communist parties draw their strongest support among landowners holding 5 to 10 acres; proportional support among landowners with less than 5 acres; and less than proportional support among landowners holding more than 10 acres. In contrast, the Socialist parties draw very strongly from peasants with less than 5 acres of land and do proportionately less well among the middle and rich peasants.

In general, the broad results confirm the images that these two groups of parties have. The parties of the radical Left have in common a capacity to draw support from the new and young voters, the illiterates, agricultural workers, and the low castes. The Communist parties draw more support from the highly educated, the middle-class professionals, the white-collar and industrial workers, and the high income groups. The Socialist parties draw more support (proportionally) than the Communists in the rural areas, particularly among small cultivators, Harijans, and tribals. In other words, the Communist parties tend more to combine both elite and mass, rural and urban, support bases whereas the Socialist parties, particularly the SSP, have tended more exclusively to "draw their main support from the poorest and the most deprived sections of rural society." [203]

More detailed information on the relationship between radical Left party support and the distribution of cultivators and agricultural laborers by district is available from the ecological analysis done by W. H. Morris-Jones and B. Das Gupta. Their data, shown in table 1.12, is broken up by state for each of the four leading radical Left parties. Table 1.12 shows that, in the Communist party strongholds of Kerala, West Bengal, and Andhra there are statistically significant correlations between the CPM vote and the percentage of agricultural laborers and the percentage of cultivators. In Kerala and Andhra, the CPM vote is associated positively with agricultural laborers, whereas in West Bengal, the CPM vote is associated

[202] Ibid., p. 288.
[203] Ibid., p. 285.

Table 1.12   District-Level Correlation Coefficients for Cultivators and Agricultural Laborers with Radical Left Party Votes, 1967 Indian State Legislative Assembly Elections

State	Cultivators				Agricultural Laborers			
	CPI	CPM	PSP	SSP	CPI	CPM	PSP	SSP
Andhra	−0.16	−0.08	−0.36	−0.39	0.33	0.45*	0.11	−0.63*
Assam	−0.32	−0.71*	−0.25	−0.31	−0.50	0.32	0.14	−0.55
Bihar	0.10	0.01	−0.38	−0.41	−0.07	−0.13	0.49	0.45
Gujarat	—	—	−0.08	0.14	—	—	0.09	−0.23
Haryana	−0.61	0.35	−0.67	0.65	0.31	−0.41	0.95	−0.38
Kerala	0.32	−0.08	−0.13	−0.39	−0.40	0.73*	−0.21	0.08
Madhya Pradesh	−0.25	−0.24	0.05	0.06	−0.19	−0.13	0.28	−0.09
Maharashtra	0.04	−0.18	0.16	0.21	0.18	0.05	−0.51*	−0.18
Mysore	−0.54*	−0.11	0.28	−0.11	0.40	0.03	−0.27	−0.11
Orissa	−0.49	−0.41	−0.59*	0.04	−0.14	−0.33	−0.27	0.12
Punjab	0.04	0.11	−0.15	0.47	0.06	0.10	0.09	−0.25
Rajasthan	−0.02	−0.09	−0.32	0.19	0.14	0.07	−0.32	−0.06
Tamil Nadu	0.05	−0.11	0.04	−0.09	0.37	0.18	0.19	−0.02
Uttar Pradesh	0.18	−0.14	−0.12	−0.08	0.07	0.29	−0.004	0.34
West Bengal	−0.01	−0.69*	0.14	0.01	0.03	−0.09	−0.13	−0.08

Source: By courtesy of W. H. Morris-Jones and B. Das Gupta.
* Statistically significant at 5% level.

negatively with the percentage of cultivators. These findings are consistent with the assertion that, in these states, the CPM seeks support more among the landless than among the peasants.

The remaining correlations in table 1.12 are more difficult and more risky to interpret, but there are some interesting patterns. First, there are no statistically significant positive associations between the vote for any radical Left party and the percentage of cultivators. The highest positive associations are .32 for the CPI in Kerala, .35 for the CPM in Haryana, .28 for the PSP in Mysore, and .65 for the SSP in Haryana. Although the correlation for the SSP in Haryana is relatively high, it is not statistically significant; nor does the SSP have much strength in this state. All the statistically significant correlations between radical Left party votes and the percentage of cultivators are negative. In contrast, all the radical Left parties except the SSP have more positive than negative associations with agricultural laborers. Even the SSP shows positive correlations with agricultural laborers in its two strongholds of Bihar and Uttar Pradesh. The leading conclusions from these general patterns are clear. First, areas where there are large numbers of agricultural laborers provide a more fertile ground for parties of the Left than areas where there are large numbers of cultivators. Second, there is no evidence that any Left party has established itself firmly in any state in peasant strongholds.

There do not appear to be any persistent patterns of support on the part of any religious minorities or caste groups for any of the radical Left parties. As we have noted, Selig Harrison has argued that the Communist movement has been strong where it has acquired support from politically strategic regional castes such as the Kammas in Andhra and the Ezhavas in Kerala. However, Mohan Ram's contribution to this volume and other studies of Andhra politics have shown that Communist support in Andhra is fairly diverse and that Kamma allegiances are divided. Hardgrave has argued that, although the Communist parties have been strong in Kerala among the Ezhava and untouchable communities, these castes have been internally divided in their political allegiances along class lines. Moreover, Communists in Kerala have won support from poor Nairs, Christians, and Muslims as well. Still, the strong support given to the CPM in Kerala by the Ezhava community has been a major factor in the persisting Communist strength in that state. Harrison's generalization, then, can be accepted if it is modified to suggest only that support from a politically strategic regional caste may be one kind of factor that contributes to Communist strength in India.

There is certainly no general pattern of association in the Indian states between the distribution of radical party strength and that of the scheduled castes and tribes or religious minorities. On the whole, with only minor and not easily explained exceptions, Morris-Jones and Das Gupta found the Communist vote share more often than not negatively associated with both scheduled castes and tribes and minorities in the 1957, 1962, and 1967 elections.[204] Over these three elections, the PSP and SSP showed 36 positive and 38 negative correlations with scheduled castes and tribes. However, the PSP and SSP correlations with religious minorities have been more persistently negative over time. In the three elections, only 19 correlations with religious minorities were positive, whereas 54 were negative, for these two parties.

In general, therefore, there is no single group and no single factor that can explain variations in radical party strength in India. The CPI is the strongest of the radical Left parties in the trade union movement, but the CPM is stronger in the great Calcutta-Durgapur-Asansol industrial region

[204] W. H. Morris-Jones and B. Das Gupta, "India's Political Areas: Interim Report on an Ecological Electoral Investigation," *Asian Survey* 9, no. 6 (June 1969), 411–413.

of Bengal. The CPM has developed strong bases of support among agricultural laborers in Kerala and in Andhra, but not elsewhere. No striking patterns emerge for either the PSP or the SSP, except for a negative association with religious minorities. The allegiances of the great mass of the peasantry, of the scheduled castes and tribes, and of the religious minorities are very widely distributed in India among both the radical Left and other parties. More detailed and more refined kinds of analyses are necessary to disaggregate these broad categories of the population and to uncover their political allegiances.

The Radical Left and the Restoration of Congress Dominance

Recently, it has been suggested that the whole basis of Indian electoral behavior has been undergoing a transformation from the old reliance upon "primordial" appeals and patron-client relationships to a new emphasis upon social and economic issues. The latter emphasis was detected in survey research on the 1967 elections and in Mrs. Gandhi's issue-oriented appeal in the 1971 elections.[205] Three questions arise in this connection. One is whether the results of the 1967, 1971, and 1972 elections do in fact support the contention that class and issue politics have lately been more important than ethnic and patronage politics. The second question is, If so, does this represent a shift over time or a difference in the appeals made at different levels or in different arenas in Indian politics? The third question is, How have the radical parties affected or been affected by these shifts or differences?

On the first question, there are two views. One argues that the 1967 elections showed "that the Indian voter is developing new secular identifications and commitments that cut across traditional primordial relationships, acquire a new political character, and provide new linkages with secular authority." [206] This assertion is based on the findings that, in the parliamentary elections, 82 percent of the electorate identified with a political party and that more than 80 percent of the electorate had views on broad social, economic, and political issues. At this point, it need only be pointed out that there is little relationship between the evidence used and the general assertion concerning "new secular identifications," since Indian voters continue to identify with both secular and nonsecular parties and have views on both secular and cultural-communal issues. Even more

[205] See especially Rajni Kothari, "Continuity and Change in India's Party System," *Asian Survey* 10, no. 11 (November 1970), 937–948 and W. H. Morris-Jones, "India Elects for Change—and Stability," *Asian Survey* 11, no. 8 (August 1971), 719–741.

[206] Kothari, "Continuity and Change in India's Party System," p. 940.

pertinent is the limited evidence from the 1971 parliamentary elections, which suggests that appeals to Muslims and scheduled castes may have had as much or more to do with the overwhelming victory of Congress (R) as appeals based upon broad social and economic issues such as bank nationalization.[207]

On the second question, I have argued elsewhere that in Uttar Pradesh voters have in the past behaved in terms of a hierarchy of values that permits them to vote locally in terms of personal and jati ties, in legislative assembly contests in terms of caste categories and religious affiliation, and in parliamentary contests in terms of religious affiliation and/or broad socioeconomic issues.[208] The results of the 1971 elections in the three states where parliamentary and legislative assembly elections were held simultaneously suggest that such a distinction between levels of the Indian political system continues to be relevant. In Tamil Nadu, the Congress left the legislative assembly arena to the DMK and divided the parliamentary seats by agreement, leaving most to the DMK. In Orissa, Congress did much better in the parliamentary than in the assembly contests. However, in Bengal, Congress and CPM fought each other equally hard in parliamentary and assembly contests and polled approximately the same vote at both levels. The results in Tamil Nadu suggest a willingness on the part of both the Congress (R) and DMK leadership to separate one arena from another, but they also recognized the superiority of the DMK in both arenas. The results in Orissa suggest that here, as in Uttar Pradesh, the voters themselves make distinctions between arenas. The results in Bengal, however, suggest a different conclusion, namely, that in a state where a strong regionally based party is entrenched it can resist the inroads of a strong national political organization. Moreover, it appears that the success of the CPM in Bengal in resisting the Congress landslide was based as much, if not more, on Bengali regional sentiment as it was on secular, national issues.[209] The same argument can be made in reverse concerning the failure of the CPM to resist the Congress landslide in 1972 in West Bengal, for it came in the aftermath of the victory of the Indian army in bringing independence to Bangladesh, for which Mrs. Gandhi received the credit. Finally, although the landslide victories of Congress (R) in the 1971 parliamentary elections and the 1972 assembly elections cannot be

[207] See, for example, Morris-Jones's comments on the Congress victories in Muslim and scheduled caste constituencies in UP, "India Elects for Change—and Stability," pp. 734–735.
[208] Paul R. Brass, "Caste and Hierarchy of Values in Uttar Pradesh Politics," mimeographed, 10 July 1965.
[209] Morris-Jones, "India Elects for Change—and Stability," p. 737.

gainsaid, they by no means eliminated the strength of the parties of regional or ethnic sentiment. In ten states in 1971, the parties that either successfully resisted Congress inroads or came in second place in popular vote were either regionally based parties or parties expressing regional sentiment—the Jan Sangh in Madhya Pradesh, Himachal Pradesh, Bihar, and Maharashtra; the Telengana Praja Samiti in Andhra; the Naga National Council in Nagaland; the Utkal Congress in Orissa; the Akali Dal in Punjab; the DMK in Tamil Nadu; and the BKD in Uttar Pradesh.[210] In 1972, however, the regional parties placed second in only six states—the Jan Sangh in Madhya Pradesh, Himachal Pradesh, and Kashmir; the Peasants and Workers Party in Maharashtra; the Akali Dal in Punjab; and the All Parties Hill Peoples Conference in Meghalaya.

On the third question concerning the relationship of the radical Left to the new style of politics, the evidence is also ambiguous. In no state in the 1971 Lok Sabha elections did a party of the non-Communist Left poll either first or second to the Congress in popular vote. However, in three states—West Bengal, Kerala, and Assam—one of the Communist parties did so. In West Bengal, the CPM won more votes and seats than Congress (R). In Kerala, the CPM won more votes but fewer seats than Congress (R). In Assam, the CPI polled a poor second. In 1972, the CPI polled second in popular support only in Andhra, the CPM only in West Bengal, and the Socialists only in Assam and Bihar. The results suggest that, in the national political arena, the new Congress appeal has completely overridden the appeals of the parties of the non-Communist Left and has encountered serious competition primarily from the regionally entrenched Communist parties and other parties of explicit or implicit regional appeal.

The results of the 1971 and 1972 elections are not encouraging to the prospects of the parties of the radical Left. A dynamic and more leftist Congress has been restored to a firmer dominance at the center of the political system, in most of the Indian states, and to the left of center of the ideological spectrum. Parties of regional and ethnic sentiment continue to be strong in several states. The CPI increased its seat-winning capacity in 1972 on the strength of its alliance with Congress (R), but the CPI strategy has done more to keep the CPM from power than it has done to bring the CPI closer to power. The CPM has been badly defeated by the Congress in Kerala and Bengal, but its electoral support base has not been destroyed. In the radical Left, the Socialist movement has been most weakened in recent years and the anti-Congress strategy of the SSP has proved ultimately to be a tilting at windmills.

The implications of the 1971 and 1972 election results, then, reinforce the emphasis given in this volume to the region as a focus in the study of the radical Left. The radical Left is simply not in serious competition for power at the center. It has survived only where it has either allied itself with a much more powerful national party, as in the case of the CPI in alliance with Congress (R), or where it has succeeded in building a regional base and in relating to regional sentiment. It is important to stress, however, that appeals to regional sentiment are not the special hallmark of the parties of the radical Left in India. These parties continue to operate in a political system where ethnic, cultural, and regional appeals matter profoundly, but where class appeals are also important, and possibly increasingly so. The successful radical Left parties are not simply parties of regional sentiment, but parties that have both a regional and class appeal and that relate effectively not only to symbols of regional nationalism but to the specific social structure of their region. It must be remembered that regional variations in social and economic structure in India are as important as the cultural variations between regions. It is a wholly different matter for a radical party in north India to attempt to draw support from the unorganized and socially fragmented rural mass of agricultural laborers and poor peasants than it is for the CPM to draw support from the organized, culturally conscious caste category of Ezhavas in Kerala. It is in this sense also that regional considerations matter in the success or failure of radical parties in South Asia.

Radical Party Performance: The Impact of Radical Politics on Political and Social Change in South Asia

Radical parties have exercised "partial power" in Ceylon and in the Indian states of Kerala, West Bengal, Bihar, Uttar Pradesh, and Punjab. Communist parties have been included in coalition governments in Ceylon and in these Indian states and have been the dominant party in such governments in Kerala and West Bengal. With the exception of Kerala, however, where radical parties have been in power for long periods from time to time since 1957, the governments in which Left parties have been in power have been unstable and short-lived. An assessment of radical party performance in power can only be tentative, therefore. However, such an assessment must be attempted because it raises a basic question that has never been answered satisfactorily anywhere else in the world, namely, whether radical social and economic change can be carried on peacefully in a parliamentary system in which Communist parties play a significant role.

The West European answer to this question during the two Cold War decades was no. It was argued particularly in France and Italy that the Communist parties were agents of a foreign power; that they would use the opportunity to exercise power to gain control of the institutions of the army and the police to impose totalitarian rule; and that it was necessary, therefore, for the non-Communist parties to band together in coalitions to defend republican institutions. Such arguments have not been absent from political rhetoric in South Asia. Anti-Communist coalitions have also been proposed and formed from time to time, particularly in Kerala. There have also been periods when the Communist parties have deliberately used violent rather than parliamentary methods, just as there have been periods when governments in South Asia have attempted to weaken the Communist parties by political repression, by imprisoning their entire leadership cadres.

On the whole, however, the milieu in which radical parties have operated in South Asia has been entirely different from that of Western Europe. The radical Left parties, including the Communist parties, have more often than not been free to participate in the electoral arena, to launch mass struggles and civil disobedience movements, and to participate in coalition governments with other parties when opportunities have been favorable. What use have they made of these opportunities, and what consequences have there been when radical parties have been in power?

Radical parties have had an impact both on legislation and on implementation of legislation. The impact of radical parties on legislation has been both direct and indirect. India is a country where socialist rhetoric and socialist ideology have dominated policy making and legislation but where conservative influence has dominated in the implementation of policy. Industries are nationalized and placed in the hands of upper class bureaucrat-managers. Landlords and princes are abolished, but generously compensated. Land ceiling laws are passed but not implemented. In this area of policy and legislation, radical parties have had their greatest direct and indirect impact. Out of power, they have pressed the Congress to enact legislation nationalizing industries and big banks, to abolish the privy purses of the princes, to impose land ceilings, to abolish land revenue, and to guarantee the security of tenants. Radical Left pressure may not have always been necessary to persuade the Congress to enact such laws, but they have reinforced the leftist pressure for these kinds of enactments. When they have been in power, the Communist and Socialist parties have themselves passed laws of this sort, particularly land ceiling and tenancy laws in Kerala and abolition of land revenue in north India. The non-Congress governments that came to power in Kerala, West Bengal, Bihar, Uttar Pradesh, and Punjab after the 1967 elections, and in which radical parties were prominent, passed a whole series of measures that fall in the category of temporary relief and protection for tenants, workers, salaried employees, and students.[211] However, no major new legislation involving bold new reforms has been enacted by the non-Congress governments during the past few years.

The impact of the radical Left on policy in Ceylon has been similar. Leftist economic reforms were first felt in Ceylon under the government of S. W. R. D. Bandaranaike, which came to power in 1956. Left-wing members of the SLFP and left-wing coalition partners in that government succeeded in achieving the nationalization of transport and of the port of Colombo and in providing some security of tenure to cultivators.[212] The SLFP-LSSP-CP coalition government took power in 1970 with an agreed program involving constitutional reform that will provide for greater popular participation in administration; economic changes that will include expanded public sector activities; and a return to "positive non-alignment." [213] The movement is definitely leftward, but radical changes were not anticipated. Moreover, the program clearly failed to inspire the more revolutionary Marxist groups that rose in revolt against the government in the spring of 1971.

The most controversial aspects of radical Left performance in power in recent years in India have occurred with respect to the implementation of laws previously enacted by the Congress regime, but not enforced. The most spectacular issues of this sort have arisen out of efforts to protect the rights of tenants and to enforce land ceiling legislation, particularly in Bihar and Bengal. It was out of these efforts, which began with the United Front governments of Bengal and Bihar after 1967, that the so-called land grab movement was launched. This movement originated in Bengal in the form of action by local units of the CPM, encouraged by the state government, to occupy lands illegally or allegedly improperly held by big landlords or their benami agents.[214] It later spread to Bihar and other parts

---

[211] See the CPI assessment of the performance of these governments in "Political Report," *Eighth Congress Documents*, pp. 111–116.

[212] S. Arasaratnam, *Ceylon* (Englewood Cliffs, N.J.: Prentice-Hall, 1964), pp. 31–32.

[213] A. Jayaratnam Wilson, "Ceylon: A New Government Takes Office," *Asian Survey* 11, no. 2 (February 1971), 177–184.

[214] Franda, *Radical Politics in West Bengal*, chap. 7.

of India. Two aspects of this "land grab" movement deserve stressing. One is that the image conjured up of large-scale Communist-encouraged theft of private land is highly exaggerated. The emphasis in these movements has been upon dramatizing the need for enforcement of land ceilings legislation already on the books and for eliminating loopholes in the law. Second, it is not at all clear that the movements have benefited the tenants. In Bihar, landlords have responded to such movements by evicting their tenants. In Bengal, the "land grab" movement has encouraged the formation of landlord associations and an intensification of class conflicts in the countryside.

In general, therefore, non-Congress governments in which the radical Left parties have participated in India and Ceylon have promoted essentially reformist measures in both legislation and in the administration of existing laws. No bold new radical programs have been introduced. On the other hand, where they have been in a position to do so, the radical Left parties have identified with and tried to assist disadvantaged groups and classes in the society—particularly tenants, the urban working class, students, and lower class and lower middle class salaried employees.

Besides the limited time in which radical Left-influenced governments have been in power, there are three other constraints that limit the ability of radical parties in India to effect radical social and economic changes. One is the nature of the Indian federal system, which gives many crucial powers of policy making and resource collection and distribution to the central government rather than to the states. As long as the Congress retains its dominance at the center, no really radical policies can succeed in a single state that do not meet the approval of the central government. Second, radical Left parties have nowhere—not even in Kerala and Bengal —been able to form coalitions that are exclusively Left in composition and legislative support. All non-Congress governments in post-Independence India have either included in the government or relied for critical support upon independents, centrist groups, and sometimes even right-wing parties. Moreover, it has been rare that even Left unity has been maintained in a state's politics for long. There is nowhere in India a unified radical Left alternative to the Congress. Finally, there exists the implied restraint of the threat of political repression. The central government has a considerable array of powers that it can, and sometimes does, bring to bear upon recalcitrant state governments. Instability can be fomented by political allies of the central government in a state as a pretext to remove a state government from office, suspend the legislature, and impose President's Rule, as was done in Kerala in 1959. Political opponents can then be arrested and imprisoned under preventive detention and similar laws and detained for years in jail, as was done to the entire leadership cadre of the left wing of the CPI from 1962 to 1964.

Clearly, therefore, the prospects for radical change in South Asia by conventional parliamentary means are severely limited. The radical Left parties in India and Ceylon do not have the necessary popular support or the necessary unity to force the pace of radical change. On balance, right-wing, centrist, and regional political forces are stronger in India than the forces of the radical Left. The radical Left parties, therefore, operate in the context of a severe political dilemma. If they attempt to move too rapidly, they face the constraints of India's federal system, of contemporary political alignments, and of the threat of repression. If they become too reformist and gradualist, they face the prospect of defection by more radical and revolutionary groups. In Ceylon, a full-scale rebellion has been launched by radical youths disaffected from or dissatisfied with the pace of change promoted by left-of-center governments. So far, however, it is apparent that the balance of force in Ceylon has rested with the established government. Similar force would be available to the government of India if it were faced with a major revolutionary or secessionist threat. The implications of these events for the future functioning of radical parties and politics are clear. Excessive gradualism and reformism by radical Left parties will produce disaffection on the part of radical cadres, students, and young people. However, if this disaffection takes the form of genuine revolutionary or secessionist movements, they will be repressed by armed force with the aid of external powers. The support of external powers, which has generally been necessary for the success of revolutionary movements elsewhere, is not readily available in South Asia because of the regional and great power stalemate in international politics in the South Asian region. The parties of the radical Left in South Asia are on their own. They must maintain a militant posture, promote mass movements, and keep up constant pressure for radical policies to maintain popular support and to promote social change, but their ultimate impact is likely to be only gradualist and reformist despite all the commotion.

Kerala

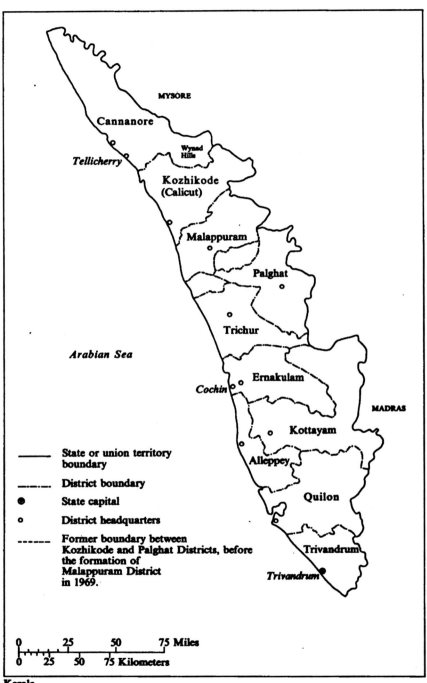

MYSORE

Cannanore

Wynad
Hills

Tellicherry

Kozhikode
(Calicut)

Malappuram

Palghat

Trichur

Arabian Sea

Ernakulam

Cochin

MADRAS

Kottayam

	State or union territory boundary
	District boundary
●	State capital
○	District headquarters

Alleppey

Quilon

Former boundary between
Kozhikode and Palghat Districts, before
the formation of
Malappuram District
in 1969.

Trivandrum

Trivandrum

| 0 | | 25 | | 50 | | 75 Miles |
| 0 | 25 | 50 | 75 Kilometers | | | |

Kerala

2

The Kerala Communists: Robert L. Hardgrave, Jr.
Contradictions of Power

Kerala is in many ways a miniature of India, with all of India's contradictions pushed to their extremes. Kerala is India's smallest state, with a higher birthrate and greater pressure on the land than any other area of India. Kerala abounds in agricultural wealth, but half of its food supply must be imported. International exports from Kerala bring in 25 percent of India's dollar earnings, and yet Kerala's per capita income is the lowest in India. Kerala has the highest literacy rate and the highest rate of unemployment in India, as well as the largest community of Christians and the highest Communist vote. Kerala is at once a bastion of orthodox Hinduism, with the most elaborate system of caste ranking in India, and, at the same time, a region deeply affected by rapidly accelerating processes of social mobilization and change. With many of the "prerequisites" of political modernization, Kerala is regarded by the Communist Party of India (Marxist) as an advanced outpost of revolutionary struggle. This struggle, however, has been waged primarily within the parliamentary system. With a coalition government headed by a Communist chief minister, the present Kerala government seeks to institutionalize fundamental social and economic change.[1]

The Origins of the Communist Party in Kerala
The origins of the Communist movement in Kerala are similar to those of Communist beginnings in other parts of India, since they can be traced directly to the pre-Independence nationalist struggle against the British. The undisputed leader of the early Communist Party in Kerala was P. Krishna Pillai, who received his early political training in the Indian National Congress. Until his death in 1949 (at the age of 42), Krishna

[1] Rather than the culmination of research, this article serves more as a preface. It represents some of the results of unsystematic study and four brief visits to Kerala over the past ten years. Conclusions are necessarily tentative. I should like to thank Donald S. Zagoria for allowing me to use biographical data on Kerala leaders he has collected in the course of his own research. Portions of this article appeared in earlier writings of mine: "Caste and the Kerala Elections," *Economic Weekly* (Bombay), 17 April 1965, pp. 669–672; and "The Marxist Dilemma in Kerala: Administration and/or Struggle," *Asian Survey* 10, (November 1970), pp. 993–1003.
   For detailed accounts of the political history of Kerala, see two recent volumes: Victor M. Fic, *Kerala: Yenan of India* (Bombay: Nachiketa, 1970) and Manfred Turlach, *Kerala: Politisch-Soziale Struktur und Entwicklung Eines Indischen Bundeslandes* (Weisbaden: Verlag Otto Harrassowitz, 1970).

Pillai exercised a formative influence in the early growth and development of the Kerala movement.[2] Krishna Pillai was reared in a poor Nair
family in a village near Alleppey in the state of Travancore. Too poor to
be given a formal primary school education, he was nevertheless able to
give himself sufficient self-education to become a Hindi school teacher.
In 1930 Krishna Pillai traveled from Travancore to Malabar, to make his
political commitment to the Congress salt *satyagraha* campaign, and in
Malabar he first came into contact with his early associates in the Communist Party of India (CPI).

In the years following World War I, a number of Malayalee professionals had become active in the Congress movement in the Malabar
region, then part of Madras Presidency. In addition, Home Rule Leagues,
under the leadership of Mrs. Annie Besant, had been established in
Malabar. The area had also been a center of peasant unrest, and the entry
of the middle classes into political activity in the period after the war had
provided badly needed new leadership for the Congress movement. In
this atmosphere it is little wonder that the Malabar District Political Conference, held in 1920, could be described as "the first example of peasants
being mobilized by the radical middle class in support of a militant political
line"—nonviolent noncooperation.[3] As the movement for noncooperation
gained momentum in Malabar after World War I, the region witnessed
the first Congress Provincial Conference in 1921 and a rapid increase in
political militancy.

The political volatility of the Malabar region after 1920 was further
accentuated by a number of other factors. The failure of the middle-class
leadership of the Congress during the Congress-Khilafat tenancy movement resulted in the 1921 "Moplah Rebellion," which ended with South
Malabar under Martial Law and 20,000 peasants in jail.[4] This rebellion
split the Congress communally, between Hindus and Muslims, with the
older leadership, discredited and burned by the rebellion, assuming the
role of "Sunday Congressmen" or withdrawing from politics altogether.
From this point on the Congress organization drifted, until the inauguration of civil disobedience in 1930. But a number of new movements—
exemplified by the campaign for temple-entry for untouchables and the

[2] T. V. Krishan, Kerala correspondent for *Link* magazine, has written a biography
of P. Krishna Pillai, in Malayalam, soon to be available in English translation
through the People's Publishing House of India. See *Sakhavu* (Trivandrum: Pra-
bath Book House, 1969).
[3] E. M. S. Namboodiripad, *Kerala: Yesterday, Today, and Tomorrow* (Calcutta:
National Book Agency, 1967), p. 129.
[4] Ibid., p. 142.

salt *satyagraha*—emerged under a new, young, predominantly Nair leadership in the 1930s.

In the 1930s Kerala was economically dependent on a plantation economy and was therefore especially vulnerable to the vagaries of international trade and the worldwide depression. Economic frustration combined with rapid social change, especially among the Nair community, to produce deep unrest. The matrilineal system of the Nairs, holding property intact through the female line, had long exerted pressure on young Nair men to seek their fortunes elsewhere, and the Nairs had always been quick to pursue opportunities for wealth, status, and education that were unavailable to the lower castes. Moreover, the civil bureaucracy of the British Raj in Madras had provided for the Nair, as it had for the Tamil Brahmin, access to power and a new modern status. All Nairs, needless to say, were not equally fortunate, and the dissolution of the matrilineal system, both through gradual social change and through explicit legislation providing for the partition of ancestral property and its equal division among sons, had brought many Nair families into decline. With the great depression, educated and economically insecure young Nairs began to find outlets in positions of political leadership in Malabar.

During the *satyagrahas* of 1930 to 1932, Krishna Pillai and many of his fellow Nairs were constantly in and out of jail. Here they encountered socialism for the first time in contacts with political terrorists from Bengal, imprisoned far from home in the Cannanore jail in Malabar.[5] Indeed, it was in the jails that Krishna Pillai met many of the young activists who later became the founding members of the Communist Party in Kerala.

K. P. R. Gopalan, a Nair from a prominent Malabar family, and C. H. Kanaran, an Ezhava, poor and with little education, were among those that the 1930 salt *satyagraha* had brought into the civil disobedience movement. K. Damodaran, of aristocratic Nair lineage, was the son of a petty landlord in Kozhikode District who had grown up in a joint household of two hundred members. Damodaran had become involved in the civil disobedience movement while acting as district secretary of the Kerala Students Federation (a Congress organization). After the completion of his studies at Zamorin's College, Calicut, in 1935, Damodaran went on to the Kashi Vidya Pith National College, at Benaras, where he joined the Communist Party. After two years in Benaras he returned to Malabar where he joined the Congress Socialists.

It was in this early period that A. K. Gopalan also became politically

5 Interview, P. T. Bhaskara Panikar, editor of *Vishwa Vidyana Kosh*, the Malayalam encyclopedia, and semiretired leader of the CPI, Trivandrum, 24 January 1969.

active. Gopalan was born in 1904 in Cannanore District of northern Malabar. His family, once aristocratic Nairs, had suffered a series of setbacks, as a result of which A. K. Gopalan had to settle for a career as a secondary school teacher after his matriculation from the Mission High School in Tellicherry. Gopalan joined the Congress movement in 1927, beginning a career of militant peasant leadership that eventually brought him to the heights of leadership in Kerala and in the Communist Party of India.

It was also in jail that Krishna Pillai first met E. M. S. Namboodiripad. EMS was born in 1909 of a wealthy and orthodox Namboodiri Brahmin family in Malabar.[6] As a student at St. Thomas College, Trichur, EMS became involved in politics and in 1932 abandoned his studies to join the civil disobedience movement. As a student he had read Laski and Fabian literature, and in jail in 1932–1933 he encountered works by Lenin and Stalin in stray pamphlets that had been smuggled into the prison. EMS describes his "education in socialism" as beginning with Jayaprakash Narayan's book, *Why Socialism?*, published in 1934. Although Marx was available in Malayalam, and the first biography of Marx to appear in any Indian language was written in Malayalam in 1912,[7] it was only in 1935 that EMS began his study of Marx, starting with the *Communist Manifesto*. It was not through socialist theory, says EMS, but in practical political work that he and others in Kerala were drawn toward socialism.[8] Another early Communist, N. E. Balaram, concurs: "The theoretical knowledge came only after the initial commitment." [9]

In 1934, after the organization of the Kerala Provincial Congress Committee (KPCC), the left-wing majority within the party joined the newly organized Congress Socialists. The first conference of the KPCC was held in Calicut in 1935 in coordination with the meeting of the newly formed All-Kerala Trade Union Congress. Through the organization of the Congress Socialist Party in Kerala, contact was made for the first time with various Communist groups, notably that of M. N. Roy. The national Communist Party of India (CPI) was only then recovering from the disaster of the 1928 *Meerut* conspiracy case, and its leaders were begin-

---

[6] See Autobiography, vol. 1 (Trivandrum: Deshabimani Book House, 1969), in Malayalam.
[7] By K. Ramakrishna Pillai, a radical journalist in Trivandrum. In 1968 a three-volume edition of *Das Kapital* was published in Malayalam, the first complete edition to appear in any Indian language.
[8] E. M. S. Namboodiripad, interview, Trivandrum, 27 January 1970.
[9] Interview, Trivandrum, 25 January 1970.

ning to come out of jail. It was at the conferences of the CSP that the Kerala Socialists met their first Communists. The Comintern made no approaches, but some of the CPI leaders—S. V. Ghate, then first secretary of the party and editor of the monthly *New Age*, and P. Sundarayya, now general secretary of the CPM, made contact with the Kerala Socialists.[10]

The left wing, while working within the Congress, also carried on independent activity in agitation and organization among workers, peasants, students, and teachers.[11] In 1935 the reorganization of the KPCC opened up a struggle for power between the Socialists and right-wing Congressmen. In this confrontation the left wing gained secure control of the committee, and under its leadership the KPCC built an organization of three thousand cadre members. Active work was begun among the Malabar peasants with the organization of Kisan Sabhas, much of the educational work being conducted by the party through drama. Traveling troupes presented revolutionary plays—the most celebrated of which were *Arrears in Rent* by K. Damodaran, depicting the agrarian struggle, and *Drinking of Blood*, dealing with the exploitation of the industrial working class. Folk songs were also adapted to the purposes of political mobilization.[12]

The Congress policy of "non-interference in the internal affairs of Indian states" had limited the development of an all-Kerala movement, but in Travancore and Cochin (both Princely states at the time) trade union and socialist groups had formed among the working classes as early as 1920. A Peasant and Worker Party had been formed in Cranganore in 1933, a Communist League in Trivandrum in 1931.[13] In 1938 the State Congress struggle for responsible government in Travancore brought in active Socialist leadership. In Alleppey, 20,000 coir workers, directed by P. Krishna Pillai, declared a general strike. Stirred by a rally of 100,000 people, workers offered militant resistance to the police in the face of firings and mass arrests. Not only was Krishna Pillai the organizer of the Alleppey strike, but he and the Socialist cadre of Malabar "were the brains behind the underground activities of the State Congress," and two jathas —one led by A. K. Gopalan—marched from Malabar to Travancore.[14] Within the "radical group" of the State Congress were K. C. George and

[10] Interviews, Bhaskara Panikar and N. E. Balaram, Trivandrum, 25 January 1970.
[11] Namboodiripad, *Kerala: Yesterday, Today, and Tomorrow*, p. 154.
[12] A. K. Gopalan, *Kerala Past and Present* (London: Lawrence and Wishart, 1959), p. 72.
[13] Namboodiripad, *Kerala: Yesterday, Today, and Tomorrow*, p. 159.
[14] Ibid., p. 162.

M. N. Govindan Nair, both of whom were to be among the early members of the CPI. M. N. Govindan Nair, educated at Arts College, Trivandrum, became involved in Harijan uplift, trade union activities, and, in 1938, in the State Congress movement, within which he became secretary of the radical party. When the CPI was organized in 1940, he joined and became an organizer among the cashew workers of Quilon District.[15] K. C. George, of a wealthy Syrian Christian family, was a leading lawyer of the Trivandrum bar and member of the Municipal Council before becoming involved with the State Congress. Quickly drawn into the center of the Socialist movement, George was one of the early leaders of the Communist Party in Kerala.

The trade union movement in Travancore and the Congress Socialist Party in Malabar provided the base for the emergence of the Communist movement in Kerala. Within the Congress in Kerala all effort was made to retain unity before the common enemy, the British. The bourgeois leadership of the national party, however, regarded the mass organizations as "vehicles through which the workers and peasants are mobilized behind that leadership," according to EMS. EMS later diagnosed the ideological roots of this position as "the failure to see the crucial role played by the peasantry in the national revolution; the failure to see that agrarian revolution is the axle around which the wheel of national revolution turns; that it is only the working class, headed by the Communist Party, that can successfully lead the agrarian revolution and hence the national revolution." [16]

In 1938 EMS was elected KPCC secretary and to membership in the All-India Congress Committee. In 1939 he was returned as a Congress Member of the Madras Legislative Assembly. At this same time, with the intensification of ideological struggle within the Congress Socialist Party, the Kerala Socialists sided with the pro-Soviet faction, and by 1937, according to EMS, "a definite Communist nucleus was formed." Their efforts "resulted in the wholesale transformation in 1940 of the Congress Socialist Party in Kerala into the Communist Party." [17] The decision was unanimous, and Krishna Pillai became party secretary. The CPI was then under ban throughout India, so the Congress Socialists had to operate clandestinely to set up the apparatus of the party in Kerala. "In the beginning of this activity," EMS describes, "the Communists were in a peculiar position: They were, on the one hand, an independent political party functioning illegally and fighting the official policy of the Congress; while, on the

---

15 Interview, M. N. Govindan Nair, Trivandrum, 25 January 1970.
16 Namboodiripad, *Kerala: Yesterday, Today, and Tomorrow*, p. 167.
17 Ibid., p. 168. Other reports date this decision to November or December 1939.

other hand, they were the leaders of the provincial, district and lower units of the Congress organization." [18]

In their dual role as Communists and Congressmen, they called for the observation of an Anti-Repression Day, 15 September 1940, and then organized militant resistance to the police. The violence that ensued enraged both the government and the national Congress leadership. The former brought down heavy repression in the areas of Communist strength; the latter dissolved the KPCC. For nearly two years, from October 1940 to July 1942, the CPI in Kerala operated underground.

During this period of underground activity, the character of the imperialist war changed: "With the entry of the Soviet Union as one of the contestants, the war had become a people's war." [19] The unity of the Left was broken as the CPI became isolated from the nationalist movement. Out of the conflict between international proletarian loyalty and the anti-imperialist movement emerged not only the Kerala Socialist Party and the Revolutionary Socialist Party but also a new generation of anti-Communist Socialists. EMS has identified the Communists' essential mistake of this period as "the under-estimation of the national factor in working out the tactics of the revolution, in the failure to realize that the Communists in a colonial country can fulfill their class tasks only if they take proper account of the national aspirations of the people. . . ." [20]

It was during the war period (1942–1945) that the CPI, operating legally, took on the character of a mass party. *Desabhimani* was established in 1942 as the weekly organ of the party, made possible by a gift to the party from EMS, derived from the sale of his ancestral properties. With Congressmen in jail in the wake of the 1942 Quit India Movement, Communists were able to move almost without resistance into the leadership of trade unions, kisan organizations, student congresses, and literary societies. The Communists exercised particular influence within the Progressive Writers Movement.

Recognizing the role of caste in political mobilization, Communists gained roles of leadership in various caste associations. Party cadres joined the Muslim League and the Pulaya Maha Sabha (an association of untouchables). One Communist leader became the organizing secretary of the SNDP in Cochin, the leading Ezhava caste association. [21] N. M. Govindan Nair became a leader in the Nair Service Society and played a major

[18] Ibid., p. 170.
[19] Ibid., p. 171.
[20] Ibid., p. 174.
[21] K. P. Pillai, *The Red Interlude in Kerala* (Trivandrum: Kerala Pradesh Congress Committee, 1959), p. 11.

role in mobilizing Nair caste support for the CPI.[22] EMS served as president of the Yogakshema Sabha, the Namboodiri Brahmin caste association.[23] It was also during the war period that the party advanced the goal of a United Kerala, to bring together the Princely states of Travancore and Cochin with the Malayalam-speaking areas of Madras Presidency into a single province.[24]

With the emergence of the party from underground, a new generation of members was recruited. C. Achutha Menon, of an aristocratic Nair family and an advocate in Trichur, joined the CPI in 1942, after seven years' activity in the Cochin Congress. T. V. Thomas, a Christian who had become involved in the Travancore State Congress movement as a student, later worked as a trade union organizer among the coir workers of Alleppey and joined the CPI in 1943.

Because of the tainted image that the CPI had acquired after cooperation with the British during the war, the party was severely defeated in the 1946 elections. In the five general constituencies of Malabar, however, the CPI secured 25 percent of the vote. It was here and among the organized workers of Alleppey that the Communists first engaged in militant struggle against the government. The police firings at Punnapra and Vayalar, in Alleppey District in 1946, became the symbol of resistance and martyrdom for a generation of Communists to follow, but this revolutionary upsurge only exposed the party's real lack of support among the working class and peasantry. Under ban from 1946 to 1951, the party's adventurism provoked a massive government response, when more than 3,000 Communists were imprisoned. "Mistakes were undoubtedly committed, both of a strategical and tactical nature," according to EMS. "The Party swung from the original mistake of over-estimating the role of the bourgeoisie in colonial revolutions to the new mistake of totally denying that role. . . . Mistakes were also committed in the direction of underestimating the role of parliamentary work [and in the advancement of] forms of struggle for which the masses were not yet ready." [25]

The sectarianism of the Ranadive thesis, emphasizing urban insurrection, did serve to purge the party of all but the most stalwart cadre members. Party membership fell disastrously, for the alternatives of prison and the underground were equally unattractive to the political opportunist.

[22] *Kerala Under Communism: A Report* (Bombay: Democratic Research Society, 1959), p. 21.
[23] Some informants suggest EMS's earlier involvement in the Namboodiri association.
[24] Namboodiripad, *Kerala: Yesterday, Today, and Tomorrow*, pp. 175–176.
[25] Ibid., p. 195.

Out of the disastrous Ranadive period came the series of turns that culminated in the Amritsar thesis and the "peaceful transition to socialism"
in India.

The Communist Party Split

Electoral participation and parliamentary activity have exposed the
Communist movement to serious problems. Since 1951, when the CPI
first began to contest elections seriously, the party has obviously had to
choose its candidates from among the more popular and articulate claimants to office. But revolutionary qualifications are not necessarily the same
as those required for a successful candidate for the assembly or the Lok
Sabha. While the major leaders might have little difficulty winning elections, effective cadre members at the district and local levels are often by-
passed in favor of more popular "vote getters." Elections have, therefore,
permitted opportunism at the same time that they have drawn into the
ranks of the Communist movement a number of political amateurs. As a
result, the "middle-class, intellectual B.A. Advocate" has become the
achetype of the Communist party member in Kerala.

While the use of popular "vote getters" and political amateurs has
served to broaden the base of Communist electoral appeal, it has also
promoted factionalism within the CPI. Some of the new entrants into the
party, through years of struggle in contact with the "basic classes," had
identified with the most militant party elements. Most became committed
to a parliamentary line opposed to "mass struggle." Indeed, the 1957
Communist victory in Kerala represented the fulfillment of the aspirations
of Communist electoralists, even though central government intervention
and the imposition of President's Rule 21 months later confirmed the
convictions of the militant left wing of the CPI. In the eyes of the militant
left wing, the Communist government in Kerala had existed only on the
sufferance of the central government. For the leftists, parliamentary democracy was essentially sham, and the participation of the CPI in electoral
politics in 1957–1958 had sapped the party's revolutionary fervor. E. M. S.
Namboodiripad, the pragmatic centrist in the CPI, walked the tightrope in
an effort to retain party unity, but after the Chinese invasion of India in
1962 and the deepening Sino-Soviet controversy, factional conflict within
the CPI deepened.[26]

Convinced that the party was moving toward alliance with the Congress,
and that a split was inevitable, the leader of the Left faction in Kerala,

[26] See Mohan Ram, *Indian Communism: Split Within a Split* (Delhi: Vikas Publications, 1969).

A. K. Gopalan, with the backing of EMS, began to organize support for the impending confrontation with the Right faction. By 1964, when the national split came about, the division between the CPI and CPM in Kerala was already complete. But CPI leaders were much less prepared for what happened. The CPI (Right faction) retained the intermediate, middle-class party leaders and a few upper echelon leaders (M. N. Govindan Nair, Achutha Menon, T. V. Thomas, and K. Damodaran), but the CPM (Left faction), with E. M. S. Namboodiripad, A. K. Gopalan, and a number of the early founding members of the CPI, held the party's local mass base.

The split in the Communist movement in Kerala in 1964 left the Right faction in possession of the formal party apparatus, the handsome new building that the party had constructed in Trivandrum, the offices in each district, and, at least initially, the party daily *Desabhimani*. Moreover, the CPI in Kerala remained convinced for some time that the split had left its support in Kerala basically unaffected. A party investigative commission reported to the central executive that the Marxists (CPM) would be able to carry away a maximum of only 20 percent of the rank and file, drawn largely from the personal followings of EMS and Gopalan.[27] The 1965 midterm elections proved otherwise. In 1965 the CPI won only 3 seats and 8.15 percent of the vote with 78 candidates, while the CPM won 40 seats with 19.99 percent of the vote with 73 candidates.[28] The decline of the CPI in terms of state influence and power was so severe that some CPI candidates (including two former ministers) lost their deposits, meaning that they secured less than one-sixth of the vote in their constituencies.

The National Council of the CPI, reviewing the 1965 elections, admitted that

by the time the split had actually taken place in 1964, the rival party [CPM] leaders had actually succeeded in politically bringing to their side the big majority of the traditional Communist mass. . . . We allowed a sense of complacency to take hold of us. We thought that since a big majority of the State Council was with us and they were all the traditional trusted leaders of the people and the leaders of the TU [trade union] movement in Kerala, the basic Communist masses would without much difficulty automatically follow our political line.[29]

The rival party leadership in Kerala had made the maximum possible use of our immobilization and lack of live personal mass contact, firstly to

---

[27] Interview, T. K. N. Menon, Marxist theoretician, Trivandrum, March 1970.
[28] Figures vary slightly among sources, depending on the manner of calculation. I have used the official figures published in India, Election Commission, *Report on the General Election to the Kerala Legislative Assembly, 1965.*
[29] *Resolutions of the National Council of the Communist Party of India*, New Delhi, 5–11 April 1965 (New Delhi: CPI, 1965), pp. 36–37.

strengthen their political hold and then to denounce the CPI and our leaders as the "tail of the Congress." [30]

The party split in 1964 also brought about a return by the Marxists to older Communist organizational forms. At the Amritsar Congress in 1958, the CPI had restructured itself into a mass party in order to more effectively participate in electoral and parliamentary activity. The new party constitution provided for new enlarged councils in place of the former committees, justified by the needs for more varied and balanced representation in decision making, to provide wider opportunities for promotion of capable cadre members, and, it was claimed, to more effectively enforce party discipline, especially on important members. [31] The party's primary unit, the branch or cell, ceased to function, and in its place general body meetings of both members and sympathizers of an entire village or neighborhood were held—making, Left critics argued, any real party discipline impossible. Smaller compact party committees were abandoned in favor of expanded taluk, district, state, and national councils, with membership from 50 to more than 100. [32]

After the 1957 elections, the CPI membership grew enormously, but its unstable and fluctuating character undermined coherent organization. In Kerala in 1958, there were 65,000 members, declining to 43,000 in 1961 and 23,000 in 1963–1964. These fluctuations were the result, in the Marxist assessment, of the failures of the new party organization, lack of political-ideological education, and the absence of class consciousness. [33]

The CPM thus sought to return to the old form, based on the cell, with a well-defined cadre policy.

A Communist party cannot pursue a correct proletarian political line, steadily and without serious deviations, if its class composition is defective, if the membership from petty bourgeois and middle class origin is predominant, if members from the urban and rural proletarian classes do not form the predominant force in the Party, if the leadership at different levels does not consciously and constantly strive to draw in increasing numbers of talented comrades of proletarian and semi-proletarian origin and if its Marxist-Leninist knowledge is not constantly improved and deepened. [34]

The split in Kerala gave the CPM a secure hold over a majority of the

[30] Ibid., p. 38.
[31] *Proceedings of the Seventh Congress of the Communist Party of India, Bombay, 13–23 December 1964, Vol. 1, Documents* (New Delhi: CPI, 1965), p. 122 (hereafter cited as *Proceedings*).
[32] *Our Tasks on Party Organization, adopted by the Central Committee of the CPI(M), Calicut, 28 October–2 November 1967* (Calcutta: CPM, 1967), p. 11 (hereafter cited as *Our Tasks*).
[33] Ibid., pp. 14–18.
[34] Ibid., p. 27.

party membership. In 1964, before the reality-testing experience of the midterm elections, the CPI claimed to have retained some 11,500 members while the Marxists were said to have retained 9,000, and another 4,000 remained undecided.[35] The CPM's figures for membership in 1964 correspond more closely to reality: 19,000 for the CPM, 3,000 for the CPI.[36]

The CPI had retained the allegiance of middle-class and middle peasant communities; the CPM held the support of the small peasant and landless laborer. The CPI held most trade union support, particularly in Alleppey, Quilon, and Ernakulam districts. Only in Cannanore and Kozhikode (Calicut) districts did the Marxists gain control of the trade unions, although in other areas they did retain considerable influence within the unions. In some cases, as in the cashew industry in Quilon and the coir industry in Alleppey, the CPM organized parallel and competitive unions.[37]

The student front has been neglected by both the CPI and CPM. Among the students, the Congress-affiliated Kerala Students Union is the dominant organization. The Marxists' Student Federation has a membership of 25,000.[38] In 1967, EMS held a school for 50 party cadre members working among students, and a summer camp was held for the Student Federation, but these efforts have not increased student membership significantly. While Naxalites have won considerable student support in West Bengal and Andhra, Kerala students have been less responsive to extremist appeals; within the CPM's Student Federation only the Palghat unit has aligned with the extremist faction.

The CPM is the dominant force among the poor peasants and agricultural workers, but the Kisan Sabha, for all its strength, is loosely organized in Kerala. Only among agricultural laborers in Kuttanad, Alleppey District, is there a genuinely effective organization. Although the CPM is beginning to develop the organization of plantation workers in Wynad, in most areas, like Palghat, where the Marxists have great influence among agricultural laborers, there is poor organization. One of the most serious problems they confront is in the contradiction within the Marxist rural

---

[35] *Proceedings*, p. 109.

[36] *Our Tasks*, p. 14.

[37] Interview, Bala Anandan, CPM assembly member and trade unionist, Trivandrum, February 1970.

[38] *Political-Organizational Report, Central Committee of the Eighth Congress of the CPI(M), Cochin, 23–29 December 1968* (Calcutta: CPM, 1969), p. 302 (hereafter cited as Political-Organisational Report).

base: the conflict between the landless laborer and the poor peasant with his meager portion of land.

Characteristics of the Party Split of 1964

The split in 1964 was in large part geographical, with CPI strength centered in Travancore, and especially in Alleppey District. At the leadership level, the geographic factor figured prominently—notably in the almost total collapse of the CPI in the Malabar region. The leaders staying with the Right Communists were also distinguished by their generally more middle-class character, with level of education being the most significant distinguishing variable.

While a number of prominent leaders in both the CPI and CPM do not hold elective office, an analysis of the membership of the 1967 Kerala Legislative Assembly provides some useful contrasts between the two parties. Of the 19 CPI members, 47.3 percent held a college degree, 42 percent law degrees. Of the 52 Marxists in the assembly, only 26.9 percent were degree-holders and only 13.5 percent in law. These educational differences were reflected also in the occupations returned by assembly members (see tables 2.1 and 2.2).

In terms of the number of members unmarried—a possible index of political dedication in Gandhian terms—there was little difference between the two parties, 21.1 percent for the CPI, 23.1 percent for the CPM. All

Table 2.1   Level of Education of Communist Assembly Members, Kerala, 1968

Education	CPI		CPM	
	Number	Percentage	Number	Percentage
Medical			1 ⎱	1.9 ⎱
M.A.	1 ⎱ 9	5.3 ⎱ 47.3	1 ⎰	1.9 ⎰
B.A./B.L.	8 ⎰	42.0 ⎰	7 ⎰ 14	13.5 ⎰ 26.9
B.A.			5 ⎰	9.6 ⎰
Some college	3	15.8	6	11.5
High school	6	31.6	13	25.0
Above 5th	1	5.3	7	13.5
Below 5th			5	9.6
Not mentioned			7	13.5
Totals	19	100.0	52	100.0

Source: Data for this table are calculated from biographical sketches in *Kerala Legislative Assembly Who's Who, 1968* (Trivandrum: Public Relations Department, Government of Kerala, 1968).

Table 2.2 Occupational Representation among Communist Assembly Members, Kerala, 1968

Profession	CPI		CPM	
	Number	Percentage	Number	Percentage
Full time pol. or social work	4	21.1	13	25.0
Trade union	3	15.8	13	25.0
Advocate	4	21.1	4	7.7
Agriculture	3	15.8	2	3.8
Others	5	26.3	20	38.5

Source: Data are calculated from biographical sketches in *Kerala Legislative Assembly Who's Who, 1968* (Trivandrum: Public Relations Department, Government of Kerala, 1968).

Communist MLAs are men, with the sole exception of one Marxist member—Mrs. Gouri, wife of CPI leader T. V. Thomas. The average age also varies only slightly, 46.8 years for the CPI, 47.9 years for the CPM. Far more significant is previous political background. Unfortunately the data are not systematic, as the biographical information available on assembly members does not always include the same items. There are, however, large differences between CPI and CPM members. Forty-two percent of the CPI members in the assembly mentioned previous Congress involvement, as against 26.9 percent for Marxists. Only 1 of the CPI's 19 members, however, had been among the Congress Socialists who constituted the founding members of the Communist Party in Kerala. Nine, or 17.3 percent, of the 52 Marxist members had joined the party with its formation in 1940.

Data on prison internment shows wide divergence: 15.8 percent of the CPI members specifically mentioned prison, as against 46.2 percent of the Marxists. Admittedly, many of the Marxists were detained in 1964–1965, but many as well had been imprisoned during periods of illegal party activity (1940 to 1942 and 1946 to 1951). That so few CPI members had served in jail would suggest that the larger number had entered after 1951. The biographical data on CPI and CPM members in the Lok Sabha from Kerala are roughly comparable in each variable considered, except for a higher educational standard among Marxist MPs than MLAs—a product of the demands of the English language at the national parliamentary level.

Assembly members from the CPI were more generally of high caste: 47.4 percent were Nairs or Brahmins, as against 26.9 percent of the Marxists. Indeed, caste representation among the Marxists in the assembly was

Table 2.3   Caste Representation among Communist Assembly Members, Kerala, 1968

	CPI		CPM	
Caste	Number	Percentage	Number	Percentage
Brahmin	3	15.8	3	5.7
Kshatriya (high caste)			3	5.7
Nair	6	31.6	11	21.2
Christian	3	15.8	3	5.7
Muslim	1	5.3	3	5.7
Ezhava	4	21.1	16	30.8
Harijan	—	—	8	15.4
Undetermined	2	10.5	5	9.6

rather evenly balanced, with a concentration among the lower castes, the Ezhava and Harijans, who together made up 46.2 percent (see table 2.3).

Over the years there has been within the Communist Party a gradual shift in the locus of power toward the lower castes, particularly the Ezhava community, from which the party has drawn substantial support. While the leadership of the CPI is relatively more high caste, middle class in origin than the CPM, Nair dominance has been challenged by the Ezhavas. Nairs still constitute the largest caste among CPI assembly members, but of the 7 members of the CPI secretariat, 4 are Ezhavas. In 1967, S. Kumaran was elected CPI secretary—the first time an Ezhava had been elected to the party's highest post. The position of lower castes within the CPM leadership is even more apparent. Of 11 top party leaders, 6 are from the depressed castes (5 Ezhavas and 1 Harijan), and the one Christian is of lower class origin.[39] At the district and local levels, CPM leadership resides predominantly within the hands of the lower-caste cadres. The Ezhavas, who had once constituted the dominant "social base" of the Communists in Kerala, have with time risen to a position of party leadership, displacing Nair dominance. But a process of "percolation" is now manifest with the emergence of new Harijan leadership at the lower levels of the party apparatus.

In Alleppey District and in Malabar particularly, agricultural labor has itself become a source of cadre recruitment, and as agricultural laborers have begun to rise in the party hierarchy, middle-class leaders—perhaps not yet fully "de-classed"—have often reacted against their less educated,

[39] Interview, P. Govinda Pillai, Cochin, 7 December 1969.

less theoretically sophisticated, and often less nationally conscious comrades. As mentioned previously, the Marxists had retained important leaders at the top level, but the middle levels of the once-united party leadership have gone with the CPI. This has left a gap within the CPM that has not yet effectively been filled, accentuated by the emergence of a rough-hewn parochial leadership that is beginning to make its presence felt. Without English, without the broadening experience of the nationalist movement, these new Marxist cadres are more nearly the reflection of the masses that the party seeks to mobilize and lead. They are, however, more separated in class and experience from the middle classes, and consequently, perhaps less capable than the older leadership of reaching beyond their immediate base of support to secure an electoral majority.

Caste and Communalism
Caste and communalism have been the catalysts of political consciousness in Kerala. Traditionally the elaboration of the ritual hierarchy reflected the economic position of the constituent castes, with each caste associated with a particular occupation and sharing a common economic status. The caste system historically, however, was not rigid, for as a caste gained economic power a commensurate ritual rank usually followed. Caste ranking in Kerala reflects such a process, but in the development of its linear elaboration a rigidity stifled the movement of castes in the hierarchy, freezing the lower castes in their positions of subservience. Only the Muslims and Christians, both being outside the hierarchy, were able to exploit new economic opportunities and in so doing to raise themselves in social status. The process of pauperization initiated by population growth and the divisions of lands accentuated the economic disparity between castes. Thus, in the high correlation between caste ranking and economic position, the socioeconomic structure of Kerala came to reflect the highly elaborate hierarchy of ritual purity.

The Hindus number about 61 percent of Kerala's population, and caste ranking places the Namboodiri Brahmins at the peak of the Hindu ritual hierarchy. Numbering less than 5 percent of the population, the Namboodiris remain primarily a landowning community. But despite the number of political leaders from this caste, such as the Left Communist E. M. S. Namboodiripad, the community has little political power. A far more potent political force is the Nair community, the traditional warriors of Kerala. As a landowning and mercantile community today, the Nairs, numbering 17 percent of the population, are a pivotal force in Kerala politics. They have traditionally held the balance, making or breaking a government by shifting sides. Economically subservient to the Nairs are the Ezhava, or Tiyyar as they are called in Malabar. Traditional toddy tappers, this community is considered ritually polluting but ranks higher in status than the untouchable castes. With about 25 percent of the population, however, the economically depressed Ezhavas are perhaps the single most powerful community in Kerala.

In addition to the mutually antagonistic Nairs and Ezhavas, the Christian community ranks as a major political power in Kerala. The Christians account for 21 percent of the population, divided among the Syrians (of whom there are two sects), the Protestants, and the Roman Catholics. It is the Catholic community that numerically dominates and that holds the locus of political power, largely through the organization of the church. The Muslims, with 18 percent of the population and represented by the Muslim League, are a major factor politically, particularly in the Malabar region of northern Kerala where Muslims are the dominant community.

As the Muslims are concentrated in certain areas of Malabar, so do each of the other communities dominate in particular regions of Kerala. The Christians are concentrated primarily in Ernakulam and Kottayam districts. The Nairs form the dominant community in the area of Trivandrum District, and the Ezhavas are particularly strong in Palghat. Each political party in Kerala must, therefore, seriously consider the dominant community, or as the Communists prefer, "the social base" in the selection of its candidate. That each party tends to choose its candidates from the dominant community, however, does not cancel out community as a factor. Although there are elements of each community in all parties (except for the Muslim League), the parties in Kerala have come to be associated with particular communities, and within each party, factionalism expresses the divisions of religion and caste. Indeed, the politics of caste form a fundamental reality of political life in Kerala.[40]

The Muslims of Kerala, known as Moplahs, were stirred to political consciousness through more than a century of peasant unrest. While some Muslims are in commerce and a few are feudal landowners, the vast majority are small peasants and landless laborers. During the nineteenth century, as a consequence of wholesale evictions and deepening impoverishment, the Muslim peasants participated in a series of uprisings, beginning in 1836. It was the tenancy movement among the Moplahs, EMS contends, "that gave our peasants the first elements of class consciousness."[41]

The political awakening of the Ezhavas, the largest community in

---

[40] Robert L. Hardgrave, Jr., "Caste and the Kerala Elections," *Economic Weekly* (Bombay), 17 April 1965, p. 669.
[41] Namboodiripad, *Kerala: Yesterday, Today, and Tomorrow*, p. 112.

Kerala, came later. In the late nineteenth century, more than 10,000 people signed the Malayalee Memorial to the Maharaja of Travancore, demanding greater rights for the Ezhavas and admission of Ezhavas into government schools. The official reply to the memorial stated that the vast majority of the Ezhavas were quite satisfied with their traditional occupations and that they were not interested in higher education and government, with the result that government action was not necessary at the time. But Ezhava leaders thought otherwise. One of the organizers of the memorial joined Sri Narayana Guruswamy, the representative of the Vivekananda movement in Kerala, in the formation in 1903 of the Sri Narayana Dharma Paripalana Yogam (SNDP) for the social and spiritual advancement of the Ezhava community.

Under the slogan "One Caste, one God, one Religion," Sri Guruswamy sought to bring about a social revolution among the Ezhavas, and his attacks on the caste system and traditional family relationships struck a responsive chord among many castes. The Nairs, and even the Namboodiri Brahmins, soon followed in the creation of caste associations, the first of these being the Nair Service Society, followed by the Uthana Kerala Nayar Samajam in Malabar and the Namboodiri's Yogakshema Sabha. It was the organization of the oppressed Ezhava and untouchable castes, however, as EMS argues, "that were, for the first time in the history of Kerala, mobilizing the overwhelming majority of the peasantry against the prevailing social order which was oppressive to the entire people of Kerala." Not unmindful that "the grip of these caste organizations on the peasantry has to be broken if they are to be organized as a class," EMS takes it as "a historical fact that the first form in which the peasant masses rose in struggle against feudalism was the caste association." [42] In the first stage of their development, the caste and communal associations infused the spirit of revolt among the downtrodden masses and organized them against the regime of oppression and injustice. "This is why," EMS writes, "Sri Narayana Guru, the saintly leader of the Ezhavas must be considered the first inspirer and organizer of the mass democratic movement of the cultivating and landless peasant masses of Kerala." [43]

Caste quickly became politicized when political parties began to form. In Malabar the lower castes (like the Ezhavas) opposed the Congress as being Nair-dominated. Their opposition may well have been strengthened also in defense of their traditional occupation (toddy tapping) against the Congress's advocacy of total prohibition. In the states of Travancore and

[42] Ibid., p. 115.
[43] Ibid., p. 120.

Cochin, the Congress policy of "noninterference" resulted in a political life revolving principally around caste in the contest for legislative representation and government jobs. It was in response to the 1932 constitutional reforms in Travancore, providing a system of representation favoring the Nairs, that the Christians, Ezhavas, and Muslims were brought into the common front that became the Travancore State Congress. After Independence, however, the Congress became increasingly a party of Christian domination, just as the Praja Socialist Party was regarded as a virtual Nair preserve. The Muslim League commands allegiance from most Muslims in Kerala, and the Communist Party has drawn its strength primarily from the Ezhava and untouchable communities.[44] The district in which the Communists have maintained their strongest hold, winning more than 40 percent of the vote in each election since 1957, is Palghat, the only district in Kerala with an Ezhava majority.[45]

Education and an accompanying high degree of political literacy, together with increasingly bad economic conditions, a restless youth frustrated in ambition, and the growing ranks of the unemployed, have generated an explosive political atmosphere in Kerala, in which each community seemingly tries to better itself at the expense of the other. But the coalitions and oppositions of the communities of Kerala in the years since Independence reflect not so much the politics of caste as the politics of class in the guise of caste. The unity of a community's political behavior has been tied closely to its homogeneity: To the degree that there is a fundamental economic disparity within the caste, the caste has been divided in its interests and dispersed in its political allegiance. In Kerala, the elaboration of caste ranking and the generally common economic position shared by members of a caste, together with the high correlation

[44] See Robert L. Hardgrave, Jr., "Caste in Kerala: A Preface to the Elections," *Economic Weekly*, 21 November 1964, pp. 1841–1847. In a survey conducted by the Department of Political Science, University of Kerala, castes broke along the following lines in the 1970 elections: Communists got support from 73 percent of Harijans and 53 percent of Ezhavas; the Congress–PSP–Muslim League alliance was supported by 72 percent of the Brahmins, 78 percent of Nairs, 93 percent of Catholics, 93 percent of non-Catholic Syrian Christians, 76 percent of other Christians, and 80 percent of the Muslims. *Times of India*, 2 September 1960, cited in K. P. Bhagat, *The Kerala Mid-Term Election of 1960*, (Bombay: Popular Book Depot, 1962), p. 137. One Congress leader and sensitive observer of the Kerala scene estimates community support for the two CPs as follows: Nairs—30 percent; Christians—10–15 percent; Muslims—15 percent; Ezhavas—60–70 percent; and Harijans—90 percent. Interview, Cochin, December 1969.
[45] Donald S. Zagoria, "The Social Bases of Indian Communism," in Richard Lowenthal, ed., *Issues in the Future of Asia: Communist and Non-Communist Alternatives* (New York: Praeger, 1969), p. 107.

between caste rank and economic position, have given rise to a political situation in which the most significant actors are castes and communities. While these communities are by no means wholly united, there is, nevertheless, a tendency toward an alignment of major communities with different parties. These sociopolitical constellations, reflecting a superimposition of ritual rank, social status, and economic position, represent essentially a class orientation.[46] This is particularly evident in the social base of the Communist parties in Kerala. The Communists draw support from the poorer classes of each community: Nairs, Christians, and Muslims. While the majority of the depressed Ezhavas may support the party,[47] the middle classes, and the SNDP itself, have tended toward Congress—especially during the period of Sankar's leadership in the early 1960s.

The 1965 election campaign, for example, was in large part fought by the Congress and the Communists to secure the affection of the Ezhavas. The failure of any party to secure a majority, however, only emphasized the fact that while the politics of Kerala may be caste-bound no party can rule with the support of one community alone. That the Congress eroded the political solidarity of the Ezhavas may reflect the initial stages of differentiation within the community. Under the impact of economic change, as each community becomes increasingly heterogeneous, their political interests will begin to differentiate and, as they do so, the polarity between communities in terms of party support may be expected to decline.[48]

Regional Diversity in Communist Support

In an analysis of regional diversities in Kerala in terms of the socioeconomic bases of Communist support, Lakshmana Rao and Seethalakshmi characterize the state's three distinct regions in capsule form. The region of Malabar (Palghat, Cannanore, and Kozhikode districts) is predominantly rural and characterized both by landlordism and a high ratio of agricultural laborers to owner-cultivators. Malabar is the least industrial and urbanized region in Kerala; its towns are middle-sized and dominated by unmechanized manufacturing pursuits. Malabar is also the poorest region of the state, with the highest unemployment and the lowest level of literacy. It is in Malabar that the Muslim community is dominant.

The region of Cochin (Trichur and Ernakulam) is highly urbanized and is the most industrialized of the state. Cochin also has the lowest level of

---

[46] Hardgrave, "Caste in Kerala," p. 1874.
[47] The general-secretary of the SNDP Yogam in 1958 said that of the 60,000 members of the CPI, half were Ezhavas, *Kerala Under Communism: A Report*, p. 20.
[48] Hardgrave, "Caste and the Kerala Elections," p. 672.

Table 2.4   Regional Diversities in Kerala

	Malabar	Cochin	Travancore	Kerala	India
Religion					
Hindus	62.65%	54.00%	61.18%	60.83%	83.51%
Christians	4.34%	34.42%	29.24%	21.22%	2.44%
Muslims	32.96%	11.50%	8.15%	17.91%	10.69%
Urban pop.	14.65%	16.60%	14.78%	15.11%	17.97%
Rural pop.	85.35%	83.40%	85.22%	84.89%	82.03%
Total literacy	38.93%	49.57%	52.29%	46.85%	24.02%
Agric. laborers per 1,000 cultivators	1,046	783	682	831	316
Unemployed (above age 15)	5.9%	3.6%*		4.2%	
Underemployed (casual labor)	12.1%	8.0%*		9.2%	

Source: Data compiled from Krishna Murthy and Lakshmana Rao, *Political Preferences in Kerala*, pp. 16–27.
*Figures in this column are for Travancore and Cochin combined.

unemployment and a high rate of literacy. Rural areas in Cochin are characterized largely by a peasantry of small owner-cultivators, and the Christian community exercises a major influence.

The region of Travancore (Trivandrum, Quilon, Kottayam, and Alleppey) is characterized by a pattern of fairly even land distribution and owner cultivation, with the lowest ratio of agricultural laborers in Kerala. Trivandrum, the largest town, is predominantly white-collar middle class in character, while the middle-sized towns are dominated by unmechanized manufacturing pursuits like cashew and coir. With the highest density rates, Travancore is also the most highly literate. Here the Nair community is dominant, with considerable Christian influence (see table 2.4).[49]

While Kerala is predominantly rural, its high density (1,126 per square mile in 1961 in comparison to the all-India average of 373) and the pattern of dispersed villages minimizes the urban-rural distinction, in both physical and in socioeconomic terms. Kerala's industrial proletariat is

[49] G. Lakshmana Rao and R. Seethalakshmi, "Socio-Economic Support Bases of Communists in Kerala," *The Indian Journal of Political Science* 29, (October–December 1968), 342–343. See also K. G. Krishna Murthy and G. Lakshmana Rao, *Political Preferences in Kerala* (New Delhi: Radha Krishna, 1968), pp. 16–27.

associated primarily with low productive, nonmechanical industries—
handloom, coir, dehusking, and cashew—and is concentrated in small
and middle-sized towns rather than in the larger towns. The big towns,
notably Trivandrum and Ernakalum, are associated more with the white-
collar middle class, both in private business and government service. In
1957 and 1960, reflecting the early trade union base of the party, the CPI
registered its highest turnout in the middle-sized and small towns. This
fell in 1965 and 1967, but with the split in 1964 the dominant Marxist wing
(CPM) emerged with a remarkable balance in its base of support along
the rural urban continuum (see table 2.5).

Table 2.5   Communist Voter Turnout in Kerala in Relation to Town Size (Percentage)

Election	Rural Area		Small Town Areas		Middle-Size Town Areas		Big Town Areas	
1957	33.59		34.74		38.68		29.28	
1960	38.14		40.93		40.23		35.37	
1965*	33.37		33.11		27.89		28.45	
1967*	36.38		26.64		28.00		30.93	
1967	CPI	CPM	CPI	CPM	CPI	CPM	CPI	CPM
	12.05	24.33	2.32	23.31	7.44	20.56	6.73	24.20

Sources: Compiled from Krishna Murthy and Lakshmana Rao, *Political Preferences in Kerala*, p. 65; and Lakshmana Rao and Seethalakshmi, "Socio-Economic Support Bases of Communists in Kerala," p. 356.
* Combined percentages for CPI and CPM.

Table 2.6   Communist Voter Turnout in Kerala in Relation to Laborer-Cultivator Ratio (Percentage)

Election	Heavy Labor Pressure Areas		Moderate Labor Pressure Areas		Low Labor Pressure Areas		Cultivator-Dominant Areas	
1957	42.84		37.61		32.99		34.91	
1960	50.00		42.34		37.26		38.57	
1965*	38.67		36.16		30.45		28.42	
1967*	39.65		37.49		31.16		24.64	
1967	CPI	CPM	CPI	CPM	CPI	CPM	CPI	CPM
	7.49	32.15	4.32	33.16	7.89	23.26	18.85	5.78

Sources: Compiled from Krishna Murthy and Lakshmana Rao, *Political Preferences in Kerala*, p. 65; and Lakshmana Rao and Seethalakshmi, "Socio-Economic Support Bases of Communists in Kerala," p. 356.
* Combined percentages for CPI and CPM.

The critical distinction within rural Kerala, where 85 percent of the population live, is between the peasant owner-cultivator and the landless agricultural laborer. The ratio of agricultural laborers to cultivators is a critical variable in distinguishing the areas of Communist support. The higher the ratio, the higher Communist support. After the party split in 1964, the Marxists retained predominant support in the areas of high labor pressure, while the CPI base remained strong in the regions where peasant-cultivators predominate (see table 2.6).

After the split in 1964, the CPI was left with its base of support in the areas of the Communists' weakest strength, the cultivator-dominant areas, whereas the Marxist base was concentrated in the traditional Communist stronghold, the areas of high agricultural labor. This distinction within Kerala reflects the all-India pattern, wherein the CPM retained dominance in the states with the heaviest Communist support (West Bengal and Kerala) while the CPI held the edge over the Marxists in the Hindi heartland, where the Communists had never gained an effective foothold.

One of the most significant characteristics of rural Kerala is the combination of the high ratio of agricultural laborers and sharecroppers with the existence of an enormous number of dwarf landholdings of one acre or less. What the statistics suggest, as Donald Zagoria argues (see table 2.7), "is that Kerala has an extraordinarily high concentration of agricultural laborers who are also sharecroppers and/or owners of dwarf holdings. Such 'propertied' or sharecropping laborers are more independent than are completely propertyless laborers, and, therefore, are more susceptible to radicalization." One possible reason for this, Zagoria contends, "may be the ambivalence of the position of this propertied proletariat; for the incongruity in status between owning land, sharecropping, and hiring out one's labor is perceived rather sharply by individuals who do all three, as opposed to individuals who are completely propertyless." [50] Kerala also has the heaviest concentration of plantation workers in India. In the factorylike conditions of the plantation, communications and organization are facilitated, making workers more immediately accessible to Communist mobilization. [51]

The differences in total voter turnout between urban and rural areas in Kerala are not pronounced. This is a product of the high level of literacy (92 percent of Kerala's children attend schools) and the highly developed communications infrastructure. There are, for example, 40 daily Malay-

[50] Zagoria, "Social Bases of Indian Communism," p. 111.
[51] Ibid.

Table 2.7   Landlessness in Kerala

Region	Agricultural Laborers[a] (as Percentage of All Cultivators)	Pure Tenancy (as Percentage of All Landholdings)	Dwarf Holdings[b] (as Percentage of All Landholdings)
India	19.7	5.1	5.0
Malabar			
Cannanore	71.1	77.9	37.4
Palghat	60.8	79.6	21.8
Kozhikode	46.9	75.3	35.0
Cochin			
Trichur	47.9	62.8	33.0
Ernakulam	40.6	29.8	45.4
Travancore			
Kottayam	43.1	2.9	50.4
Alleppey	51.6	12.1	61.4
Quilon	30.2	5.6	58.5
Trivandrum	40.5	8.2	60.7

Sources: Government of India, *Census of India, 1961,* vol. 1, Pt. 1-A(ii), Levels of Regional Development in India; table from Zagoria, "Social Bases of Indian Communism," *Issues in the Future of Asia,* p. 110, reprinted by permission of Praeger Publishers, Inc.
[a] The median for agricultural laborers is based on 296 districts; for pure tenancy, on 300 districts; and for dwarf holdings, on 299 districts. There are 336 districts in India, but data on some variables were not available from census publications.
[b] Those of one acre or less.

alam newspapers. Intense party competition and frequent campaigns have sustained a high level of political literacy throughout the state. Within the rural areas, the heaviest turnout is in the regions of cultivator dominance (77.61 percent turnout in 1967) and the lowest is in the regions containing a high agricultural labor ratio (64.67 percent).[52] Communist electoral fortunes in Kerala are in inverse ratio to voter turnout: The lower the turnout, the higher the percentage of Communist vote. Even in Malabar the Communist vote fails to rise in proportion to the increase in turnout, although the generally lower level of turnout might offer, with increasing mobilization of the agricultural laborers, a wider range for the expansion of Communist support than in other regions of the state. The inability of the Communists to enhance their support with larger voter turnout suggests a stabilized base or even a threshold in mobilization capacity (see table 2.8).

Although the Communists have deepened their hold among Kerala's poorest classes, particularly agricultural laborers, their support has re-

[52] Krishna Murthy and Lakshmana Rao, *Political Preferences in Kerala,* p. 56.

Table 2.8   CP Vote and Turnout Correlations, Kerala, 1957–1967

Election Year	Kerala Total Turn-out	Kerala CP Vote	Kerala Coeffi-cient	Malabar Total Turn-out	Malabar CP Vote	Cochin Total Turn-out	Cochin CP Vote	Travancore Total Turn-out	Travancore CP Vote
1957	65.69%	34.7%	0.53	58.6%	29.3%	69.9%	34.9%	70.0%	38.5%
1960	84.4	39.2	0.46	80.9	36.4	87.2	37.7	84.5	42.2
1965*	73.9	31.8	0.43	70.2	34.4	77.7	33.1	75.4	29.0
1967*	72.9	32.1	0.44	68.3	29.8	77.8	35.4	74.5	32.1

Sources: Derived from data in Krishna Murthy and Lakshmana Rao, *Political Preferences in Kerala*, p. 49; and Lakshmana Rao and Seethalakshmi, "Socio-Economic Support Bases of Communists in Kerala," pp. 344 and 347.
* Combined CPI and CPM vote. 1965 vote apparently includes independents. At official 28.1% CP vote, the coefficient is 0.38.

mained remarkably stable. Indeed, with a high degree of political literacy and participation, Kerala reflects a salience of party identity rare in India. In the five elections since 1957 in Kerala, the Communists have maintained approximately one-third of the vote, with fluctuations and a low of some 28 percent in 1965. The Congress, like the Communists, has maintained a fairly steady third of the vote, and an anti-Communist alliance would securely isolate the Communists from power—just as in 1970 the anti-Marxist coalition closed out the CPM's bid for power.

The 1965 election was the test of strength in determining relative support for the CPI and CPM in the immediate wake of the party split. The results proved the Marxists strongest in Malabar, in terms of winning seats and retaining security deposits, and weakest in Travancore. The CPI, in turn, was strongest in Travancore and weakest in Malabar. On the basis of this pattern of support, in the allocation of seats by the United Front alliance in 1967, the CPI was not allocated any constituencies to contest in Malabar. The CPI contested 7 and won 4 seats in Cochin, and in Travancore the party won all of the 15 seats contested. Marxist support confirmed the earlier 1965 distribution. In Malabar the CPM won 23 of 24 contested seats, while it contested and won 13 seats in Cochin and 16 of 22 seats in Travancore.[53]

Unlike the CPM, the CPI in 1965 had an inflated notion of its own strength. The CPI, therefore, contested a large number of seats, dissipated its capacity over far too wide an area, and forfeited deposits in nearly 70 percent of the constituencies in which it offered candidates. This is revealed dramatically in the comparison of the average valid votes per candidate

53 Lakshmana Rao and Seethalakshmi, "Socio-Economic Support Bases of Communists in Kerala," p. 351.

Table 2.9   Average Valid Votes per Candidate, CPI and CPM, Kerala Legislative Assembly Elections, 1965 and 1967

	CPI		CPM	
Region	1965	1967	1965	1967
Malabar	2,846	—	20,785	27,078
Cochin	7,538	24,055	20,969	25,037
Travancore	8,644	24,622	12,626	22,773
Kerala	6,580	24,446	17,231	25,023

Source: Adapted from Lakshmana Rao and Seethalakshmi, "Socio-Economic Support Bases of Communists in Kerala," p. 355.

between the two elections, for the CPI and CPM, respectively (see table 2.9).

While CPM voter turnout went up from 1965 to 1967 by 18.37 percent, the alchemy of the return does not reveal the degree of party strength as distinct from the effect of the United Front as an intervening factor. The CPI's increase was only 4.81 percent. In each case, however, with a smaller number of seats contested, a larger number of seats was secured. "Obviously," write Lakshmana Rao and Seethalakshmi, "the non-Congress parties had skillfully exchanged their scattered voting strength to maximize their seat winning capacity and the trick had paid unimaginable dividends." [54] The CPI, with a minimal increase in vote in 1967 was a major beneficiary of the UF alliance, moving from 3 to 19 seats. Without strength in Malabar and with widely dispersed support in Cochin and Travancore, the CPI's visibility as a party is closely dependent on a broad electoral alliance. In isolation it could well have been wiped out completely.

In terms of the total votes secured by each party in Kerala, the CPI in 1965 had less than half as many votes—for all the seats it contested—as the CPM. In 1967 the CPI secured an even smaller share, but with a smaller number of seats contested it made a far better showing in terms of candidates returned. The CPM secured a greater number of votes in both elections in all areas of Kerala, while the CPI did proportionately better in Cochin and Travancore (see table 2.10).

Communist Strategy and Tactics

During the period prior to the split in 1964, the CPI engaged in alternating strategies, reflecting the twists and turns of its ideological line between

[54] Ibid., p. 354.

Table 2.10   Relative Strength of CPI and CPM, Kerala Legislative Assembly Elections, 1965 and 1967

	1965			1967		
	CPM Vote	CPI Vote	CPI's % of CPM Vote	CPM Vote	CPI Vote	CPI's % of CPM Vote
Malabar	665,114	68,292	10.27	649,870	—	—
Cochin	188,721	133,690	70.84	325,487	168,384	51.73
Travancore	404,034	311,117	77.02	501,009	369,440	73.74
Kerala	1,257,869	513,159	40.80	1,476,366	537,824	36.43

Source: Adapted from Lakshmana Rao and Seethalakshmi, "Socio-Economic Support Bases of Communists in Kerala," p. 355.

"revisionism and dogmatism." [55] In the 1948 elections in Malabar and in Travancore, where the CPI formed a United Front with the Kerala Social-ist Party, the CPI failed to secure a single seat. Branded as "antinational" for its support of the British Raj in the war effort, the CPI had isolated itself from the people and abruptly switched to an adventurist strategy of terrorism, sabotage, and insurrection.[56] India, however, was not in a revolutionary situation: The bourgeois revolution itself was not yet com-pleted. This new understanding, with Soviet intervention, was formalized in 1951. The goal was to replace "the present anti-democratic and anti-popular government by a new government of People's Democracy created on the basis of a coalition of all democratic anti-feudal and anti-imperialist forces in the country." This was to be achieved by a four-class alliance of workers, peasants, intelligentsia, and the national democratic bourgeoisie in "a single democratic front." [57] Using the tactics of the "united front from above," the CPI contested the 1951–1952 elections in Travancore-Cochin under the banner of the United Front of Leftists, with the RSP and KSP, and in Malabar in alliance with the Kisan Mazdoor Praja Party and inde-pendents.

The 1951 line had cautioned against "premature uprisings and ad-venturist actions," but it by no means abandoned armed struggle.[58] The tensions between the left and right wings had only been papered over, but

[55] See E. M. S. Namboodiripad, *Revisionism and Dogmatism in the CPI* (New Delhi: CPI, 1963).
[56] See Mohan Ram, *Indian Communism*, p. 19.
[57] *Programme of the Communist Party of India* (Bombay: CPI, 1951), quoted in ibid., p. 51.
[58] Mohan Ram, *Indian Communism*, pp. 52–55.

as the Soviet attitude toward the Nehru government changed, so also the CPI softened its position toward the Congress party. The CPI, meeting in Palghat in 1956, carried the party more closely to "constitutional communism." At Palghat, the CPI proclaimed its willingness to support "all progressive policies and measures of the Government" against imperialism, feudalism, and monopoly capitalism, retaining "its absolute independence as well as its character as a Party of democratic opposition in relation to the government." [59] The magnitude and significance of this metamorphosis, writes Victor Fic,

> can best be gauged from the Election Manifesto, published in January, 1957, which presented the Indian people with a programme broadly identical with the aims of the government and the Congress Party. An important difference was, however, that the manifesto outlined a course of action promising a more thorough, earnest and swifter implementation of everything the Congress stood for. Above all, the CPI pledged itself to a swift and genuine implementation of the Preamble and the Directive Principles of the Constitution of India, calling for the establishment of a Socialist Pattern of Society.[60]

In 1956, after a period of instability, the president, under article 256 of the constitution, assumed the powers and functions of the government of Travancore-Cochin, abolishing the assembly until the General Elections of 1957 could give it a new lease on life. Before the 1957 elections, however, in 1956, the states of India were reorganized on a linguistic basis. The Malayalam districts of Malabar and South Kanara in Madras were added to the state of Travancore-Cochin to form the new state of Kerala, and the Tamil-speaking regions of southern Travancore were merged with Madras. Because of the heavy concentrations of Muslims in northern Malabar and Ezhava strength in the southern portions of the district, particularly in Palghat, the acquisition of Malabar deeply affected the communal balance in Kerala, and therefore the pattern of political power.

In preparation for the 1957 elections, the Communists in Kerala sought to achieve a united front of Left parties against the Congress. The RSP and KSP, with whom the Communists had united in 1952 and in 1954, decided to go it alone, however, and the major party of the non-Communist Left, the Praja Socialists, which had had an electoral understanding with the CPI in the 1954 Travancore-Cochin elections, now preferred the company

[59] *Report of the Central Committee to the Party Congress, Palghat, April 1956*, in V. B. Karnik, ed., *Indian Communist Party Documents, 1930–1956* (Bombay: Democratic Research Service, 1957), p. 297.
[60] Victor Fic, *Peaceful Transition to Communism* (Bombay: Nachiketa Publications, 1969), pp. 231–232.

of the Muslim League. The Communists stood alone, except for allied independents.

In the campaign, the All-Kerala Catholic Christian Convention called on all Catholics to oppose Communist candidates and to support the Congress. Kottayam District went heavily for the Congress, as did the predominantly Christian constituencies of Ernakulam, but the force of the church brought victory to only 43 Congress candidates for the assembly's 126 seats. The important position of the Christian community within the party, however, was reflected in the fact that 23 of the 43 Congress victors were Christian. The Nair-supported PSP fared even worse, securing only 9 seats. The strength of the Communist party rested with the Ezhavas and the scheduled castes and, to a lesser extent, with the Muslim laborers of Kozhikode and Palghat districts. The addition of the Malabar constituencies tipped the scales toward the CPI. Securing 60 seats, and 35 percent of the vote, the Communist Party, together with 5 Communist-supported independents, held a clear majority and was called upon to form a government. Party chief E. M. S. Namboodiripad became the chief minister of the first Communist government ever to come to power through free elections (see table 2.11).

The Communist victory in Kerala confirmed the new electoral strategy of the CPI as "correct." Some 12 months later, in 1958, the CPI held an Extraordinary Congress at Amritsar. The success of the Kerala Communists in peacefully transforming the democratic parliamentary system

Table 2.11   Election Results by Party, Kerala Legislative Assembly, 1957

Party	Seats Contested	Seats Won	Popular Votes Obtained	
			Number	Percentage
Congress	124	43	2,209,251	37.85
CPI	100	60	2,059,547	35.28
PSP	62	9	628,261	10.76
RSP	27	—	188,553	3.23
Muslim League*	17	8 ⎫	751,965	12.88
Independents	59	6 ⎭		
Total	389	126	5,837,577	100.00

Electorate   7,514,626
Turnout   65.49%

Source: India, Election Commission, *Report on the Second General Elections in India, 1957*, vol. 2.
* Contested as independents.

into a "people's regime"—even under the severe limitations imposed by the federal structure of the Indian constitution—set the mood of the Amritsar meeting. In euphoric confidence that Kerala was the prelude to the peaceful transition to communism in India, the CPI acclaimed the establishment of the Communist government in Kerala as "the single biggest event in our national-political life" and marked the high point of the "democratic movement" in India.[61]

The assumption of office by the CPI imposed considerable strain on the Kerala party and opened conflict as to whether the Namboodiripad government would be subordinate to party control—the classic conflict that had plagued Nehru in his first years as prime minister, as it had Attlee in dealing with Labour Party chairman Harold Laski. The central party executive intervened in favor of Namboodiripad and freed the state apparatus from control by the party.[62]

The Communists had come to power in Kerala on a tide of widespread opposition to Congress corruption and governmental instability. Analyzing the CPI victory, EMS underscored the broad class distribution of the vote. "This makes it all the more necessary for the Communist Party to see that its own ranks do not get 'dizzy with success'. . . . It is equally necessary for us to remember that even among those who have voted for the Communist Party, there are people who are apprehensive of what the Communists would do once they get into power." [63]

"We have to work within the frame of a system which includes several regulations and limitations which are not to our liking," EMS said after swearing allegiance to the constitution, "but we would work within the framework of the Constitution and would try to utilize the provisions of the Constitution to amend the Constitution itself." [64] One Communist minister said, "We are, if you want to put it that way, the true Congressmen." [65] CPI leader S. A. Dange, however, made it clear that "though the Communist Ministry in Kerala would function within the ambit of the Constitution . . ., (we) Communists have not changed." B. T. Ranadive declared that "the failure of the Ministry in Kerala would drive them once again to insurrectionary methods." [66] This was all opponents of the government

[61] *Resolutions of the Communist Party of India*, Amritsar, 1958, quoted in ibid., p. 344.

[62] See Fic, *Peaceful Transition to Communism*, pp. 379–387.

[63] E. M. S. Namboodiripad, "An Inspiring Experience," *New Age*, 24 March 1957.

[64] *Indian Express*, 6 April 1957, quoted in *Kerala Under Communism: A Report*, p. 27.

[65] *Statesman*, 4 June 1957, quoted in *Kerala Under Communism: A Report*, p. 28.

[66] Quoted in V. B. Sinha, *The Red Rebel in India* (New Delhi: Associated Publishing House, 1968), p. 102.

needed. Within days of EMS's assumption of office, the cry of "insecurity under Communist rule" was raised. The new police policy, neutralizing the police in labor-management and in peasant-landlord disputes, created considerable anxiety among the propertied classes; the agrarian reforms bill, attempting to secure the tenant from eviction, aroused the anger of landholding elements of the Christian and Nair communities; but it was the education bill that roused mass action against the government. In no sense could any of these government actions be termed revolutionary, but they were sufficient for Mannath Padmanabhan, the 83-year-old leader of the Nair Service Society, to proclaim a life and death struggle of direct action against the Communist regime. In the Vimochana Samara Samiti he welded a communal alliance of Nairs, Christians, and Muslims for the "Liberation Struggle" to free Kerala from Communist rule. In the six-week agitation by the Samiti and the allied Anti-Communist Front of Father Vadakkan, more than 80,000 arrests were made, some 10,000 persons were jailed, and 15 people were shot dead in police firings. In July 1959, the president of India, on advice of the cabinet, intervened in Kerala and imposed President's Rule after 28 months of Communist control.[67]

The front that had ousted the CPI from power now provided the base for an electoral alliance and the establishment of a coalition ministry of the Congress, the PSP, and the Muslim League. In the elections of 1960, following five months of President's Rule, the alliance secured 94 of the 126 seats. The Communists won 29. The CPI, however, substantially increased its portion of the vote, with 39.2 percent (see table 2.12).

The anti-Communist alliance soon foundered on communal rivalries. Within the Congress the factional maneuvers of R. Sankar succeeded in pushing the Muslim League out of the alliance and Chief Minister P. T.

[67] The details of those 28 months and the liberation struggle need not be elaborated here. An extensive literature describes the events, although systematic and first-hand field work has yet to be done. For a balanced analysis, based on secondary sources, see David L. Lemon, "The Communist Government of Kerala, 1957–1959," unpublished M. A. thesis, Department of Government, University of Texas, August 1970. See also Jitendra Singh, *Communist Rule in Kerala* (New Delhi: Diwan Chand Indian Information Centre, 1959); Ramakrishnan Nair, *How the Communists Came to Power in Kerala* (Trivandrum: Kerala Academy of Political Science, 1965); Carol Goldstein, "Kerala: A Unique Experiment," M. A. thesis, New York University, published privately in New Delhi, 1963; Ampat Koreth Baby, "Communist Rule in Kerala," unpublished Ph. D. dissertation, University of Indiana, 1964. For a favorable evaluation of the 1957–1959 ministry see: S. C. Joseph, *Kerala: The 'Communist' State* (Madras: The Madras Premier Company, 1959); H. Austin, *Anatomy of the Kerala Coup* (New Delhi: People's Publishing House, 1959); H. D. Malaviya, *Kerala: A Report to the Nation* (New Delhi: People's Publishing House, 1958). In opposition, see K. P. Pillai, *The Red Interlude in Kerala* and *Kerala Under Communism: A Report*.

Table 2.12   Election Results by Party, Kerala Legislative Assembly, 1960

Party	Seats Contested	Seats Won	Popular Vote	
			Number	Percentage
Alliance				
Congress	80	63	2,789,556	34.42
PSP	33	20	1,146,028	14.14
Muslim League	12	11	401,925	4.96
Alliance subtotal	125	94	4,337,509	53.52
CPI	108	29	3,171,732	39.14
Jana Sangh	3	—	5,277	0.07
RSP[a]	18	1⎫		
KSP[a]	12	—⎬ 589,559		7.27
Socialist Party[a]	4	—⎪		
Independents[b]	42	2⎭		
Total	312	126	8,104,077	100.00

Electrorate   8,038,268
Turnout   86.08 %

Source: India, Election Commission, *Report on the General Election to the Kerala Legislative Assembly, 1960.*
[a] The Election Commission Report on the 1960 election did not list RSP, KSP, and Socialist candidates by party label but grouped them in the "Independent" category. Popular votes (number and percentage) are listed for the total of all candidates from the three parties plus the 42 independents.
[b] Of the 42 independent candidates, 16 were known to have been supported by the CPI and 1 by the Congress.

Pillai (PSP), a Nair, out of Kerala into the governorship of the Punjab. Sankar, an Ezhava, took over as chief minister of an all Congress ministry. With the departure of Pillai from the arena of politics in Kerala, the Nair community felt its interests threatened by Ezhava ascendency, and the Christians were none too happy about prospects of the Ezhavas supplanting Christian influence in the Congress. Christians antagonistic to the ministry found a ready ally in the leader of the Nair Service Society, Mannath Padmanabhan, and with the defection of 15 Congress assembly members to the opposition the Sankar government fell in September 1964. President's Rule was again imposed.

In April of 1964 the Communist split had divided the CPI in Kerala into Left and Right parties, and soon after, in June, the elections to the Trivandrum city corporation served as a dress rehearsal for the assembly elections of the following year. The Left Communists, adopting the position they had taken within the CPI before the split, sought a united front on the basis of a common program with all left-wing parties. The Right

Communists were unwilling to join such an alliance, confident that they had retained the bulk of Communist support, and instead entered an electoral understanding with the PSP in opposition to the front of the Left Communists, the Revolutionary Socialist Party,[68] and independents. The Left CPI overwhelmed the Right CPI in the corporation election. The Right was now prepared to enter negotiation for a united front based on "firm policies and principles" and "directed as much against reactionary and communal parties as against the Congress." The Right tactic was to expose the Left Communists, who were then seeking an understanding with the Muslim League, as "unprincipled" and "opportunist." [69]

In the explorations for agreement, the Right CPI, the RSP, and allied independents proposed a united front of leftist parties based on a minimum program and an alliance that could carry on "equal and simultaneous struggle" against the Congress, the Muslim League, and the dissident "Kerala Congress." The Left Communists, however, were prepared to exploit the contradictions within the Congress, and to defeat Congress by reaching electoral understandings with both the Muslim League and the Kerala Congress. The Left was denounced as "hidden communalists." [70] It was the controversy over the allocation of seats, however, which finally broke negotiations. The Left argued that seats should be distributed in proportion to the political influence and organizational strength of the two rival Communist parties. Claiming 75 percent of the once united party, the Left was willing, nevertheless, to concede a 3 to 1 ratio to the Right. The Right, unwilling to accept the Left claims, demanded a "fair division" of seats on a 50:50 basis.

Unable to reach a compromise, the Communists faced each other in opposition. The Left, in an understanding with the Samyukta Socialist Party and the KTP,[71] attained an arrangement with the Muslim League

---

[68] Vaguely Trotskyite, and concentrated among the cashew workers of Quilon District.

[69] E. M. S. Namboodiripad, *What Really Happened in Kerala* (Calcutta: National Book Agency, 1966), p. 19.

[70] Ibid., pp. 23–24.

[71] The Karshaka Thozhilai Party (KTP), or "Workers and Peasants Party," was formed in 1962 under the leadership of Father Vadakkan, who had earlier founded the Anti-Communist Front. As a leader of poor Catholic peasants, Father Vadakkan championed the cause of the people in 1961 against the government's eviction policy in the High Ranges. In this he was joined by A. K. Gopalan, who made a fast of protest. While continuing opposition to Communist ideology, Father Vadakkan cast his lot with the Marxists. He organized the peasants of the High Ranges in the Malnad Karshaka Union and founded the KTP as a political ally of the CPM. Father Vadakkan's activity brought restriction by the church hierarchs. As a parish priest in Trichur, he remains the leader of the small party. Interview, B. Wellington, MLA (KTP), Trivandrum, February 1970.

Table 2.13   Election Results by Party, Kerala Legislative Assembly, 1965

Party	Seats Contested	Seats Won	Popular Votes Obtained	
			Number	Percentage
Congress	133	36	2,125,792	33.78
CPM	73	40	1,257,869	19.99
CPI	78	3	513,159	8.15
SSP	29	13	514,689	8.18
Muslim League	16	6	242,529	3.85
RSP	12	—	490,335	7.79
KTP	4	1	46,423	0.74
Kerala Congress	54	23	796,291	12.65
Jana Sangh	16		33,381	0.53
PSP	4	—	10,300	0.16
Swatantra Party	13	—	26,858	0.43
Republican Party	2	—	3,381	0.05
Independents	124	11	232,765	3.70
Total	558	133	6,293,772	100.00

Source: India, Election Commission, *Report on the General Election to the Kerala Legislative Assembly, 1965.*

involving the setting up of mutually acceptable independents where three-cornered contests were likely to lead to the victory of the Congress candidate. Elsewhere the League candidates, as well as those of the Kerala Congress, would be opposed.[72] In the campaign the Right Communists, in alliance with the RSP, opposed the Left Communists with as much, if not more, vigor as the Congress. The Left Communists—who had 40 candidates in jail as *détenus* under the Defence of India Rules—were denounced as "antinational" and "pro-China."

The Right strategy failed disastrously. Of the 78 seats contested, the Right won 3 and lost deposits in 67. The Left obtained 40 seats, with another 13 for the SSP and 5 for allied independents. The Left Communists were thus 11 seats short of an absolute majority—the exact number for which the Right Communists could be held responsible for defeat.[73] The actual percentage of the Communist vote, however, had declined some 10 percentage points since 1960—from 39.2 percent to a combined CPI-CPM vote of 28 percent in 1965 (see table 2.13). This is due in part

[72] Namboodiripad, *What Really Happened in Kerala*, pp. 33–34.
[73] Ibid., p. 59.

to the difference in the number of seats contested. It is not clear to what extent the decline represented the Congress's partial success in weaning away sections of the Ezhava community from the Communists. Despite the rise of Sankar in the Congress, the greater portion of the Ezhava community, as before, remained solidly behind the Communist Party. Indeed, in the very constituency Sankar had cultivated, the Congress leader was defeated by his Left Communist opponent. Although imprisoned throughout the campaign, Sankar's opponent, an Ezhava himself, commanded the support of the dominant Ezhava community.[74]

In examining its defeat in 1965, the CPI admitted that it had failed to "display enough flexibility in Kerala's concrete situation, for example, on the question of adjustment and alliance with the Muslim League. We overestimated our strength and underestimated the capacities of the rival party (the Left). . . ." [75] In a reversal of its adamant opposition to League communalism, the CPI now saw "that on account of its policy changes as well as change in Kerala's political situation, the Muslim League there has a positive role to play in advancing the democratic movement in that state." [76]

With the approach of the 1967 elections, the CPM (Left Communists) sought again to forge a united front. By September 1966, a common policy declaration had been reached by the seven components of the front—the CPM, CPI, RSP, SSP, KTP, KSP, and the Muslim League. The policy declaration applied only to state matters, leaving each party free to bring out its distinctive position on national and international questions. In addition, each party was free to carry out its own election propaganda on the basis of its election manifesto. All, however, would assume a common approach with respect to Kerala issues, and, in the course of the campaign, as all seven flags flew from a single pole, the UF minimum program was the focus of electoral concern. In securing the common policy declaration, the Marxists made a number of compromises, especially to the more conservative Muslim League. (All Muslims, however, were not open to the Marxist overtures. In forming a rival Samastha Kerala Muslim League, dissidents denounced communism and raised the issue of Muslim persecution in China's "cultural revolution.") In the allocation of seats among the UF partners, EMS argued for a formula based on 1965 electoral performance, and on this basis he allotted 65 seats to the CPM, 21 to the CPI, 20

[74] Hardgrave, "Caste and the Kerala Elections," p. 672.
[75] "Political Report," in *Documents, adopted by the Eighth Congress of the Communist Party of India*, Patna, 7–15 February 1968 (New Delhi: CPI, 1968), p. 77.
[76] Ibid., p. 78.

to the SSP, 12 to the Muslim League, 4 to the RSP, 3 to the KTP, and 1 to the KSP.[77] Remaining seats would be allocated by mutual adjustment. While the CPM operated from a position of overwhelming strength, its dominance raised a serious question. In order to make clear that the Marxists did not intend to capture office alone at the expense of their partners, the CPM agreed to contest only 59 seats, thus ensuring coalition government. The CPM also bolstered the Muslim League, and, as a gesture to the League's "secular" aspirations, the League was allotted a constituency in the Travancore region with a Muslim minority. The Marxists, however, were unwilling to meet the desire of the CPI for a constituency in Malabar, where the front was fundamentally a two-party alliance of the CPM and the Muslim League.[78]

The victory of the United Front alliance seemed assured from its inception. The Congress stood alone, this time with the support of the Catholic bishops and Mannath Padmanabhan of the Nair Service Society, but Sankar had fallen in favor and with him had gone Ezhava influence within the Congress. The Kerala Congress, with regional strength in the Travancore region, had entered an electoral understanding with the PSP, now little more than a clique without an electoral base, and the powerless Swatantra and DMK. The Jana Sangh had caste Hindu support in Malabar, and the Karnataka Samithi, supporting integration of Kannada-speaking pockets of Kerala with Mysore, held support in the border areas.

The election campaign was conducted in a period of economic difficulty. With rising prices and a shortage of food, attributed to the failure of the Congress at the center, the UF slogan for "basic changes" met wide support. Beyond this the UF seemed able to provide a stable government as a viable alternative to the succession of immobilized Congress ministries and Presidents' Rule. Communal factors, tempered by class differentiation, were again significant in the electoral calculus. The Muslim League fared best in the Muslim-dominant areas, and the Kerala Congress retained its hold among the Christians of Kottayam District. The Congress returned to its predominantly Nair-Christian character, and middle-class Ezhavas rejoined their poorer comrades in support of the Communists—this time

---

[77] Over the years, the Kerala Socialist Party had been reduced to the personal following of Mathi Manjooran and his brother. Its platform once called for an independent Socialist Republic of Kerala, but is now soft-pedaled as a demand for greater state autonomy. Its strength is in Ernakulam District and its support is primarily among Catholics, although the party is anticlerical. Manjooran died in January 1970.

[78] Horst Hartman, "Changing Political Behavior in Kerala," *Economic and Political Weekly*, Annual Number, January 1968, pp. 169–171.

Table 2.14   Election Results by Party, Kerala Legislative Assembly, 1967

Party	Seats Contested	Seats Won	Popular Vote Number	Percentage
United Front				
CPM	59	52	1,476,456	23.51
CPI	22	19	538,004	8.57
SSP	21	19	527,662	8.40
Muslim League	15	14	424,159	6.76
RSP	6	6	170,498	2.72
KTP	3	2	68,954	1.12
KSP	1	1	32,974	0.52
UF subtotal	127	113	3,238,707	51.60
Congress	133	9	2,225,026	35.43
Kerala Congress	61	5	475,172	7.56
Jana Sangh	24	—	55,584	0.88
PSP	7	—	13,991	0.22
Swatantra Party	6		13,105	0.21
Republican Party	3	—	2,176	0.05
Independents	62	6*	253,556	4.05
Total	423	133	6,280,942	100.00
Electorate 8,624,848				
Turnout 75.69%				

Source: India, Election Commission, *Report on the Fourth General Elections in India, 1967.*
* Four of the independents were supported by the United Front and in turn gave their support to the UF government. The 2 other winning independents were candidates of the Karnataka Samithi.

with the opportunity to distinguish between the more "respectable" CPI and the CPM.

The seven-party United Front, with 51.60 percent of the vote, gained 113 of the 133 assembly seats, plus support from 4 independents, and 17 of the 18 Lok Sabha seats. Congress was reduced to 9 seats in the assembly, despite its hold of 35.43 percent of the electorate (see table 2.14). For the second time E.M.S. Namboodiripad took over as chief minister of Kerala.

The United Front

In October 1969, the United Front government under E. M. S. Namboodiripad collapsed after 31 months in office—the longest tenure of

Kerala's 10 ministries and 5 periods of Presidential Rule. Hanging on after the resignation of 7 of the 12 ministers and the withdrawal of 4 parties from the coalition government, EMS finally resigned in the face of a majority motion in the assembly on the issue of corruption. Charges had been traded for weeks, and every man in the ministry had been accused of some form of corruption—less personal corruption than nepotism, political favor, and, for the Marxists, concessions and pressure to fill the party coffers. The issue provided a convenient smoke screen around which divergent parties, without regard to their class character and ideological incompatibility, might rally against the Marxists. The vote on the motion, 69–60, formalized what had been the deepening division among the constituent parties of the United Front. With the Marxist bloc of 50 votes were the Samyukta Socialist Party (6), Father Vadakkan's KTP (1), the Kerala Socialist Party (1) and 2 independents. Supporting the antigovernment motion were the CPI (21), the Muslim League (14), the Indian Socialist Party, a splinter from the SSP (11), the Revolutionary Socialist Party (6), the Jana Sangh–backed Karnatak Ekikaran Samithi (2), 1 KTP defector, the Kerala Congress (5), and the Congress (9). For all their disclaimers, the majority rested on the decisive nine-man Congress contingent.

A CPI member of Parliament Achutha Menon placed responsibility for the government's collapse on the big party bossism of the CPM, its disruptive behavior, and sectarian policies. To the surprise of all, in a bid to avert President's Rule, Menon succeeded in welding sufficient solidarity among the heterogeneous parties to form a government—united initially more in their opposition to the Marxists than in the promise to fulfill the promises of the 1967 election. But on the basis of this commitment, Menon claimed his government as successor to the United Front. The "minifront," as it was called by its opponents, became essentially an anti-Marxist front after supplanting the anti-Congress United Front. The new state government coalition, led by the CPI, included the Muslim League, the ISP, and the Kerala Congress, with the RSP in support outside the ministry. Unwilling to test his claim to a majority without Congress support by calling the assembly into session, Menon alluded to support from unnamed defectors from the Marxist camp. When they did not materialize, the 1969 Congress split conveniently opened the possibility of support from the "progressive" Indira Gandhi Congress faction.

The Marxists had been thrown out, ostensibly, on charges of corruption. Ministerial corruption, both for personal enrichment and party aggrandizement, had been an issue of increasing concern. In the Marxist view, however, some degrees of corruption, while not sanctioned, are perhaps inevitable—even in the most revolutionary parties—as they struggle in a corrupt society, to work in a dialectical process within the system in order to break the system.[79] Clearly, however, the real issues that brought down the state government were far more serious and lay in the nature of the United Front itself.

The UF had been forged as an electoral alliance of seven parties with a minimum program. Although less eclectic than Ram Manohar Lohia's "non-Congressism" (advocating a front of all opposition parties across the ideological spectrum to dislodge the Congress), the left-led United Front in Kerala came to power with serious internal contradictions. It was an electoral front with limited objectives, but the Marxists sought to establish their own hegemony within the front and to transform it into an instrument of struggle.

The Marxists conceived of the UF governments in Kerala and West Bengal as "*instruments of struggle* in the hands of the people, more than as Governments that actually possess adequate power, that can materially and substantially give relief to the people." "In clear class terms," the Central Committee stated in 1967, "our Party's participation in such Governments is one specific form of struggle to win more and more people, and more and more allies for the proletariat and its allies in the struggle for the cause of People's Democracy and at a later stage for socialism." [80] In an analysis of the breakup of the Kerala UF Government, B. T. Ranadive, leader of the leftist faction within the CPM Politburo, wrote, "The United Front is a sharp form of class struggle. Its edge is turned against the main class enemy. And yet at various stages of its development it includes elements which are close to the main enemy, which have the same ideology. . . . Therefore, inside the United Front a continuous struggle must go on—a struggle to isolate the line that wants to freeze the mass situation." [81] For the Marxists, then, the United Front is essentially a revolutionary concept. For the CPI and others such a stance was "big party chauvinism."

The CPI made much of a reported speech in London by Ranadive. The task of the UF government, he is reported to have said, was "to unleash discontent" of the people rather than "to give relief." [82] "Our objective," EMS and A. K. Gopalan said in a joint statement, "is to capture power

[79] Interview with Mathew Kurian, Trivandrum, January 1970. Also see M. Basava-punniah in *People's Democracy*, 19 October 1969, p. 7.
[80] *New Situation and Party's Tasks* (Calcutta: CPM, 1967), p. 70.
[81] *Right Communist Betrayal of Kerala U. F. and Government: A Collection of Documents* (Calcutta: CPM, 1969), p. 105.
[82] *Indian Express*, 22 June 1969.

making the fullest use of the constitutional machinery so that we can break the Constitution from within." [83] Achutha Menon, chief minister of the new "mini-front" government, in reviewing what had happened in Kerala, accused the Marxists of a "wrong and sectarian approach." "Of course," he wrote, "the power and resources of a state government functioning under our constitution are limited and we should certainly not be a party to foster unwarranted illusions among the people that everything they desire will be done for them. But within all these limitations, it is possible to give some relief to our much suffering people and give them a better administration than the Congress had given." [84] The Marxists were charged, on the one hand, with seeking to advance their own position at the expense of allied parties within the United Front and, on the other, with failure to implement the minimum program.

The Marxists were also alleged to have used the police and the administrative machinery of the state government as an adjunct of the party, their efforts being directed mainly against the CPI. And they were alleged to have interfered with the administrative spheres under the control of other parties, notably agriculture and industry, both under CPI ministers. In opposition to CPI agricultural minister M. N. Govindan Nair's program for agricultural mechanization, the CPM launched an "anti-tractor agitation" in support of a labor-intensive policy. Conflict then arose between EMS and CPI industries minister T. V. Thomas on the question of foreign aid for industrial development.[85] Thomas favored Soviet support, or, alternatively, collaboration with Japan, while EMS sought collaboration with Romania (with which the CPM has fraternal relations). Moreover, within the areas of their own administrative responsibility, the Marxists were alleged to have failed to provide any effective relief to the people—as in their handling of the food procurement program and in the two-year delay in passage of the land reform act.

The EMS state government does emerge with a relatively low performance record on a number of accounts, but ironically its failure to implement more of the minimum program was due in considerable measure to caution. In choosing to work within the system, the CPM was inevitably limited by it, conditioned by "the possible" *in the system's terms*. Indeed,

[83] *Hindu,* 8 July 1969.

[84] *What Happened in Kerala: Review of 30 Months of Namboodiripad Government* (New Delhi: CPI, 1969), p. 2. For E. M. S. Namboodiripad's response to Achutha Menon, see *Anti-Communist Gang-up in Kerala: Betrayers of U.F. Set Up Anti-People Government* (Calcutta: CPM, 1970).

[85] Thomas's wife, K. R. Gouri, is a member of the CPM and also served as revenue minister. The government allotted them separate, but adjacent, houses because of their incompatible political affiliations.

some six months after the UF government came to power in 1967, the Central Committee of the CPM was highly critical of the Marxist leadership in Kerala for its failure to "independently mobilize the people" and for putting forward "only such proposals as are likely to be immediately accepted by other partners." [86] A year later, the Central Committee again took note of the "serious shortcomings" of the Kerala leadership. It warned of the dangers inherent in the type of parliamentary struggle engaged in and of the "reformist and constitutional illusions it breeds." [87]

While the CPI attacked the Marxists for failure "to give relief," the Naxalite groups in Kerala, adhering to a Maoist line of revolutionary struggle, attacked the Marxists for their revisionist concern for incremental reform. Efforts to provide surplus land to the landless are regarded by the Naxalites, for example, as involving a danger of "en-bourgeoisification," thus creating a class of small peasants with little revolutionary potential. The Marxists, as Lenin earlier had done, reject the argument that only through intensification of poverty can a revolutionary situation emerge, that is, the worse it is the better it is. In rejecting the left sectarian thesis, however, the Marxists have not really answered the problem. There are indeed serious risks in a program of land reform when there is simply not enough land for those to whom it has been promised, and when the only viable economic answer is not land-to-the-tiller but collectivization.

Factionalism in the CPM

The Naxalite groups in Kerala have received wide publicity and have aroused much concern.[88] With most of its leadership now jailed or dead, the movement—never really larger than some 4,000 activists—has been severely set back, but from its inception the CPM in Kerala, as in India as a whole, has confronted the pressures of leftist factionalism of which the Naxalite movement has been the latest manifestation. At the national level, ideological debate had long been postponed, but the Naxalite revolt in West Bengal, coupled with the Nagi Reddy expulsion in Andhra, brought inner-party tension into unavoidable relief. Urging a more revolutionary stance, B. T. Ranadive and Pramode Das Gupta attacked the rigid centrism of General Secretary P. Sundarayya and M. Basavapunniah, while E. M. S. Namboodiripad and West Bengal's Jyoti Basu steered a "pragmatic" middle path. In Kerala, EMS had to contend with both latent revisionism and an increasingly manifest extremism.

---

[86] *Central Committee Resolutions, adopted at Madurai,* 18–27 August 1967, p. 33.
[87] *Political-Organisational Report,* p. 177.
[88] See Marcus F. Franda's analysis of the Maoist groups in India in "India's Third Communist Party," *Asian Survey* 9, no. 11 (November 1969), pp. 797–817.

The allocation of seats among the parties of the Left United Front and within the Marxist party in late 1966 opened intraparty conflict. Extremists, adhering to the Maoist line, gained control of the Trivandrum District Committee and sought to purge revisionist elements within the party unit. Designated for special attack was M. Anirudhan, who had openly attacked Chinese policy and had donated blood in the Indo-Pakistani war. EMS vigorously defended Anirudhan, an Ezhava who in the 1965 midterm elections had defeated Congress leader Sankar. Under the direction of Ranadive and the more militant national leadership, the Politburo directed the Kerala unit to bring into the open a report holding Anirudhan guilty of antiparty activity. The decision encouraged those critical of EMS, notably Joint Secretary C. H. Kanaran, to demand disciplinary action against a number of allegedly revisionist party members. Supported by the Politburo and following the recommendations of the Control Commission in Kerala, Anirudhan and two others were placed under one year suspension, and a dozen senior party members were officially reprimanded. With the threat of a split on the eve of the elections, Anirudhan, still under suspension, was given a place on the party ticket for the Lok Sabha. Facing Sankar, his old Congress rival, Anirudhan won the election with a secure majority.

Extremist animosity—or CIA provocation, as claimed by the Marxists —was reflected in wall posters appearing in Trivandrum during the elections. Signed by the "Kerala Red Guards," the posters denounced EMS as a "stooge" who, "spoiled by bourgeois acclaim, is running mad after crumbs of power in a stinking alliance with robbers and reactionaries." [89]

Under the new United Front ministry, EMS came under increasing criticism from those Marxists opposed to parliamentary participation and fearful of revisionist co-optation. In August 1967, the Central Committee of the CPM met in Madurai. While sensitive to the special problems of Kerala, the Marxist nationalist leadership criticized the state party for its "lack of vigilance." In its report the Central Committee stated that "it must be admitted that the Party in Kerala was not alive to its responsibilities to independently mobilize the people for correct solutions of problems. Our Party's representatives in the United Front have been putting forward from time to time only such proposals as are likely to be immediately accepted by other partners." [90]

Even before the Madurai meeting, Sundarayya sustained rumors that EMS might be replaced when he announced that he had successfully per-

[89] Joseph Lelyveld, "Communism, Kerala Style," *New York Times Magazine*, 30 April 1967, p. 59.
[90] Communist Party of India (Marxist), *Central Committee Resolutions, adopted, Madurai, 18–24 August 1967* (Calcutta: CPM, 1967), p. 33.

suaded EMS to continue in office in spite of criticism.[91] Kanaran later argued, however, that the rank and file wanted a more active party, and he did not rule out the possibility of a change in state leadership.[92]

Encouraged by official chastisement of the Kerala ministry at the Madurai conference, extremists captured the leadership of four district party committees: Trivandrum, Kottayam, Quilon, and Cannanore, the largest unit in the state with approximately one-third of the Marxist party membership in Kerala. In Trichur and Alleppey, the rival groups were evenly balanced, and only in Kozhikode, Palghat, and Ernakulam was the EMS group firmly in control. In January 1968, the Kerala CPM held a six-day plenum in Ernakulam. The national party leadership played an active role in seeking to avoid a factional confrontation in the organizational elections. Long before the plenum, they had begun to build support for A. K. Gopalan as party secretary. His leadership, it was believed, might correct the "lack of vigilance" and bring a greater militancy to the coalition government. Since he was acceptable to the extremists and thus might prevent open schism within the party, A. K. Gopalan was unanimously elected as general secretary of the State Committee. C. H. Kanaran was elected joint secretary.

The State Committee, on recommendation of the Politburo of the party's Central Committee, was reduced in size from 51 to 25 members. The list of members proposed by the Politburo was approved. There were some notable omissions in the constitution of the new committee, including K. P. R. Gopalan, a leader of the extremist faction, and P. Govinda Pillai, editor of the party daily *Desabhimani* and close associate of EMS. In the new committee, EMS managed to retain control. Of the 25 members, 11 were identified with the extremist group or as sympathizers.

With the decisions of the plenum, the district units fell into line. Scattered individuals, however, were less ready to accept party discipline. K. P. Kosalaramadas, advocate and former mayor of Trivandrum, had been mentioned among extremist circles before the plenum as a possible candidate for party secretary. Leader of the All Kerala Electrical Workers' Union and a member of the legislative assembly, Kosalaramadas broke with the party and subsequently resigned his membership in the assembly. In leaving the CPM, he joined another party rebel, N. C. Sekhar, who had been expelled just before the Ernakulam plenum. Sekhar, one of the founding members of the CPI in Kerala, had accused the Marxists of reverting to revisionism. They were soon followed in their break from the Marxists by K. K. Annan, a young MLA from North Wynad. The major

[91] *Hindu,* 7 August 1967.
[92] Ibid., 23 December 1967.

defector from the CPM, however, was K. P. R. Gopalan. Among the Congress Socialists who founded the Communist Party in Kerala in 1940, KPR was one of the movement's early heroes.[93] With the split in 1964, he went with the Marxists and "captured" from the CPI the offices of the party daily *Desabhimani*, of which he was then managing editor until 1967.

After the formation of the United Front government in 1967, K. P. R. Gopalan became increasingly critical of the Marxists' failure to transform the electoral minimum program into a genuine people's program. He urged the cooperation of the two Communist parties in bringing the United Front to a more radical path. The only alternative to the implementation of a radical program for the CPM, he believed, was withdrawal from the government coalition. "It is better for real Communists to stay out of the government." [94]

Within the CPM there remained many who shared with KPR and the expelled extremists the conviction that the United Front had sapped the revolutionary strength of the Communist movement. In Kottayam, extremists had established a parallel party district committee. They had captured trade union leadership in Palghat and claimed ascendancy within the party unit, and in Cannanore it was estimated that some 40 percent of the party had gone over to the extremist faction. Within the state as a whole, the extremists claimed support of 25 to 35 percent of the party membership, as against Sundarayya's "official" estimate of 15 percent.[95] The 1968 *Political-Organisational Report* put defections in Kerala at only 5 per-

[93] KPR, like most of the founding members of the Communist Party in Kerala, had been drawn into political activity through the Congress civil disobedience movement. In 1930, at the age of 21, KPR, a Nair from Cannanore District in Malabar, joined the salt *satyagraha*. He was a member of the Congress Socialist Party and was among the founders of the Communist Party in Kerala. Still formally within the Congress fold, the party called for an Anti-Repression Day, 15 September 1940. Implicated in the bloody clashes with police, KPR was among several party workers arrested. In what came to be known as the *Morazha* case, the sessions judge, ruling lack of intent to murder, handed down sentences of seven years' rigorous imprisonment. The government appealed to the High Court of Madras. The German and Japanese radio was proclaiming *Morazha* as the beginning of rebellion in India. Under enormous pressure, the court held that one of the defendants should hang—KPR. As preparations were made to take the case to the Privy Council, the Congress launched all-India agitation. On the eve of the Cripps Mission, Congress pressure was applied to set aside the capital sentence. With the intervention of the governor of Madras, the sentence was reduced to life. Because of his Communist affiliation, KPR was not freed with other political prisoners when the Congress came to power in 1946. Only with agitation in Malabar was his final release secured. Interview, K. P. R. Gopalan, Trivandrum, March 1970.
[94] Interview, K. P. R. Gopalan, Trivandrum, March 1970.
[95] *Hindu*, 25 July 1968.

cent.[96] Outside the party, a half dozen or more groups of Maoist inclination, inspired by Naxalbari, called for the establishment of base areas in the high ranges of Kerala and the beginning of protracted armed struggle. Radio Peking, in a series of broadcasts on the significance of Naxalbari, lauded the extremist defections from the CPM. Chinese papers attacked Namboodiripad as "firm against the peasant armed struggle," while the Kerala government was described as only part of the State machine "operating in the interests of the landlords and the bureaucratic-comprador bourgeoisie." [97] As for the Kerala Communists, they were, the Chinese proclaimed, enforcing "the fascist rule of the Central government." The center could at any time topple the Kerala government, as it had in 1959. "These facts prove that without a people's revolution, without a seizure of political power by violence, without smashing the old State apparatus there can be no change whatsoever in the social system nor in the nature of the real social reform." [98]

In late November 1968, two raids were conducted in Malabar as a prelude to revolution in Kerala. The abortive attacks were staged some fifty miles apart, at Tellicherry on the coast of Cannanore district and at Pulpalli in the mountainous forest of Wynad between Cannanore and Kozhikode districts.[99] At Tellicherry, just before dawn, a group of some three hundred men marched from the local stadium to the police station. Reportedly "armed with country-made axes, acid bulbs, grenades and chilly powder," they shouted slogans, threw some explosives, and fled the moment they met resistance, leaving behind some crude weapons and Maoist literature.[100] Forty-eight hours after the Tellicherry raid, the police outpost at Pulpalli was attacked. Here they murdered the radio operator and smashed equipment before they fled, frightened by the accidental detonation of the dynamite they carried.

Those implicated in the attacks included K. P. Narayanan, M.A., who ran a tutorial college at Tellicherry; Philip M. Prasad, former leader of the CPM Student Federation; K. Karunan, a peasant youth and former leader of the CPM Volunteer Corps, the "Gopala Sena"; and A. Varghese, the

---

[96] *Eighth Congress, Cochin, 23–29 December 1968* (Calcutta: CPM, 1969), p. 289.
[97] *Peking Review*, 8 September 1957, quoted in Mohan Ram, *Indian Communism*, p. 227.
[98] Radio Peking, 11 May 1957, quoted in Mohan Ram, *Indian Communism*, p. 226.
[99] E. M. S. Namboodiripad once noted that the terrain of the Kottayam and Wynad high ranges "are ideally suited for the tactics of guerilla warfare." See *Kerala: Yesterday, Today, and Tomorrow*, p. 109.
[100] *Hindu*, 23 November 1968.

young son of a poor Catholic peasant who had migrated from central Travancore to Wynad. The central figure, however, was Kunnikkal Narayanan. During the late 1940s, Kunnikkal had been active in the Indo-Soviet Friendship Society in Bombay and, in returning to his native Calicut with his Gujarati wife, he became actively involved in the Communist movement. He is alleged to have become involved in gold smuggling from Arabia—the profits going to the party as an important source of income—during this period. Within the Marxist party after the split, he launched a series of Maoist study groups and publications, opened a Maoist bookstore in Calicut, and staged various demonstrations. His group, the Marxist Forum, was the first to revolt against the state CPM leadership and was expelled from the party just before the 1967 election. He was accused of being on the CIA payroll. Kunnikkal soon became the self-appointed spokesman in Kerala for the All-India Coordination Committee of Communist Revolutionaries, the Naxalite organization that subsequently became India's third Communist party, the CPI (Marxist-Leninist). The national leadership of the committee soon found Kunnikkal too much to bear and expelled his group for "doubtful" contacts and "sectarian" conduct. In early November, just before the raids, Kunnikkal sold all of his property in Calicut; his wife resigned her post as a teacher in a Gujarati school; and their 23-year-old daughter Ajitha terminated her studies. The family disappeared from Calicut.

In the immediate wake of the raids, with rumors of scattered attacks throughout Kerala, it was reported that Naxalites under Kunnikkal had been training for five or six months in the Wynad forests at two main bases and a half dozen or so camps. The area (in which Pulpalli is situated) is predominantly tribal, with plantations of pepper, rubber, coffee, and tea. It is among the most isolated and neglected regions of Kerala and the insurgents were said to have befriended the tribals, promising them free land after the revolution. Reports of the size of the revolutionary force varied widely, from as little as two hundred[101] to two thousand.[102] According to the correspondent for the *Hindustan Standard*, Calcutta, in reports from Wynad, the Kunnikkalites were to have begun with attacks on isolated police stations in order both to create an atmosphere of terror and to seize arms and ammunition. The second phase was to involve blowing up bridges, the disruption of communications, and the strengthening of the revolutionary armed forces with more training camps. This would be

---

[101] *Hindu*, 28 November 1968.
[102] M. Sivaram, "Revolution in Kerala," *Hindustan Standard* (Calcutta), 6 December 1968.

followed by the liquidation of rich landlords in the areas of strength and the redistribution of land to the landless, while simultaneously rebel government councils would be established and recruitment intensified. The last phase, from insurgency to revolution, would bring the liberating forces out of the jungles into the towns, following the Maoist formula.[103]

The raids raised a severe problem for the Marxist leadership of the United Front government, just as had the earlier Naxalite rebellion in West Bengal for the UF government there. EMS said that newspaper reports were exaggerated—and, indeed, they surely were, for a revolutionary situation hardly existed even in Wynad—and that, in any case, the Naxalite problem should be tackled at the political level. In fact, with the raid on the police stations the Marxists could now treat the extremist challenge as a police problem. Neither the police nor the Marxists were very sure of what they were doing. The police were at first hesitant to move quickly against the extremists for fear of political criticism, and when they did they rounded up a number of Marxist activists and members of the "Gopala Sena." A. K. Gopalan denounced police brutalities and "anti-people" tendencies. Most of the principals in the raids, nevertheless, were soon apprehended. About one week after the Pulpalli attack, Kunnikkal's wife was arrested, and the following day, Ajitha, one of the leaders of the Pulpalli raid, was taken into custody. Ajitha, in her khaki slacks and bush shirt, had captured revolutionary imagination. Posters appearing in Trivandrum proclaimed, "Victory to the Revolutionaries: Ajitha Zindabad." Her statement to the police, however, was hardly calculated to strengthen revolutionary fervor. In describing their attempt to build a "Little Albania" in Malabar, Ajitha said that they had been told that the attackers, in launching the revolution, would be joined by eight thousand unemployed beedi workers from Cannanore District and by a large number of tribals to form the nucleus of a red army. In conclusion, she announced, "The revolution has failed." [104]

Kunnikkal, with his wife and daughter in jail and without money, surrendered to the police in Trichur. Under interrogation he admitted leading the Tellicherry attack. K. P. Narayanan was soon thereafter arrested in a Madras boarding house, and K. Karunan arrested at his home. Only 30-year-old Varghese remained at large. More than a year later, in February 1970, a new wave of Maoist terrorism in Wynad brought the joint action of the Kerala and Mysore police. In an exchange of fire with the police, Varghese, the last of Kunnikkal's followers, was killed.

[103] Ibid.
[104] *Hindu*, 6 December 1968.

Communist reactions to the Tellicherry and Pulpalli raids varied widely. Other extremist groups, under the name of "The Organizing Committee of the Communist Revolutionaries of Kerala," were meeting just as the attacks were staged. K. P. R. Gopalan, and others, denounced the activities of the Kunikkal group for seeking to wreck the attempt of the extremist groups to come together. Indeed, A. Achuthan, the convenor of the conference, was arrested as a suspect in the Tellicherry raid. Beyond this, the attacks and subsequent declaration that the revolution had "failed" seemed clearly to put back the cause of revolution in Kerala.

The CPM, ending a state conference on the day of the raid, denounced the adventurist activity as designed to embarrass the party. Marxist general secretary Sundarayya identified the raids as inspired by the Central Bureau of Intelligence and part of a conspiracy to unseat the United Front government through central intervention. T. Nagi Reddy, leader of the Andhra extremists, concurred but suggested CIA involvement as well. Others argued that the Chinese had played a role, referring to letters allegedly from the Chinese embassy in New Delhi to Kunnikkal Narayanan. In the Lok Sabha, a Praja Socialist reported that a Chinese submarine had been delivering arms and ammunition to places along the Kerala coast.

Kunnikkal himself denied any connection with the Chinese embassy, the CIA, the CBI, or the Congress party. The CPI, sensing sympathy in Kerala for the misdirected revolutionaries, refused to question the sincerity of those involved. A number of Right Communists—perhaps hoping to exacerbate Marxist tensions—joined the legal defense committee for the accused.

The fall of the Marxist-dominated United Front government in October 1969 deepened the problems of the Marxist leadership. Within the party, there were some who wanted reconciliation with the CPI. In the face of internal pressures toward greater militancy, two "revisionist" Marxist MLAs crossed the floor to join the CPI.[105] Extremists, especially in Alleppey, Kozhikode, and Cannanore were ready for armed insurrection. EMS and the party leadership were caught between, trying, in the words of a CPI leader, "to pacify both groups with a vacillating middle path." [106]

Some of the extremist groups outside the CPM, primarily those associated with K. P. R. Gopalan and A. Achuthan, had succeeded in early 1969 in organizing the Communist Revolutionary Party, claiming seven thousand active supporters. A year later, however, the new party split

[105] K. Sekharan Nair and M. K. George.
[106] Interview, N. E. Balaram, Trivandrum, March 1970.

over the decision of KPR and K. K. Annan to end their nine-month boy-
cott of the assembly and to resume their seats in support of the new
government, to become what one Marxist called the "tailist group of the
Mini-Front." The breakaway Achuthan group, the Communist Workers
Party, held the greater portion of the CRP following, including M. T.
Thomas's construction workers union. (Of all the Naxalite groups in
Kerala it is probably the strongest.)[107] In the 1970 elections, K. P. R.
Gopalan was defeated in his bid for an assembly seat. The number of
distinct extremist groups varies almost from day to day, but the six most
prominent are the following:

1. the Communist Revolutionary Party (K. P. R. Gopalan and K. K.
Annan);
2. the Communist Workers Party (A. Achuthan);
3. Kunnikkalites (led by Kunnikkal Narayanan, most are now in jail);
4. Kunnikkalite splinter (led by Philip Prasad and K. P. Narayanan, who
feel that Kunnikkal betrayed the revolution by surrendering to the police);
5. the Kosalaramadas group (limited primarily to the Trivandrum area);
6. the Communist Party of India (Marxist-Leninist)—the only Communist party in India officially recognized by China. The Kerala unit is
composed primarily of employees of the Indian Life Insurance Corporation in Trivandrum. Its advocacy of armed struggle is mostly verbal.

Party Conflict and Coalition Behavior
Within the CPM, the considerable sympathy for the extremist position and
a general feeling of unease with parliamentary—or at least governmental
—participation imposed an enormous strain on party leadership during
the period of the United Front. Criticized by the CPM Central Committee
and increasingly sensitive to the attack from the left, both within the
Kerala Marxist party and from the Naxalite splinter groups, the Marxists
assumed a more aggressive stance within the UF, particularly after the
Marxist success in the West Bengal midterm elections. The impetus to a
harder line with the coalition partners was closely linked to what seemed
an advance in their position vis-à-vis the Marxists. This was most apparent
in the case of the Muslim League. The League had, to begin with, come
into the United Front under very favorable conditions. With a geographic
stronghold, they elected 14 of their 15 candidates. Four of the 11 UF
ministers were Muslim, although Muslims form only 18 percent of the
population of Kerala. Under the UF government, the League won recogni-

107 Interview, K. R. S. Nair, correspondent for *Blitz*, Trivandrum, February 1970.

tion for Muslim private schools, and a Muslim majority district (Malappuram) was created in Malabar.[108] Moreover, middle-class positions in the bureaucracy were opened to Muslims and a Muslim was appointed to the High Court. With the electorate of the Malabar region divided in a three-way split between Congress, the Muslim League, and the Marxists, the ML holds the balance. In courting the League, however, the Marxists had contributed to the League's enhanced status among all Muslims, thus threatening the Marxist hold among the poor Muslim peasantry and agricultural labor. The benefits secured by the League were in fact largely for the middle-class, and the League leadership remained, as before, in the hands of a wealthy mercantile class. The League had, however, received a new respectability: Its communal and feudal character had been soft-pedaled by the Marxists themselves. It became imperative, then, that the Marxists recoup their position among the landless laborers of the Muslim community. The League, therefore, immediately became defensive.

The CPI seemed to be the other beneficiary of the United Front government. The split in 1964 had left the CPI with little more than its leadership, a hold on the trade union movement, and a pocket of support among the cashew workers of Quilon District. Using the industry and agriculture portfolios, the CPI sought to advance its position. Its policies, appealing to the middle peasant and the urban middle class, came into direct conflict with the Marxist position from the beginning. Within the early months of the ministry, the CPI had already begun the maneuvers that were to culminate in the isolation of the Marxists. The CPM reacted "from below" in more aggressive trade union activity, cutting at the already minimal base of CPI support through the creation of parallel and competitive unions in some cases or, in others, complete capture of the unions from within. "From above" the Marxists treated the CPI as the "main enemy" within the UF government and sought to undercut its ministerial position.

If the Marxist attitude toward its coalition partners became more "big brotherly," however, the fear of losing office by central intervention led, for all the talk of confrontation with the center, to ensnarlement in the bureaucratic imbroglio so much despised by the Marxists. Their experience did indeed demonstrate the difficulties of a state government under the Indian constitution, but this made little impression on the people.

---

[108] The new district, formed out of the Muslim-majority areas of Kozhikode and Palghat districts, was attacked as "Moplastan," a miniature Pakistan on Indian soil. Many Marxists were themselves uneasy about the new district. A. K. Gopalan feared that in the Muslim majority district, the Marxists would lose their position in the area, leaving the Muslim League undisputed master of the region. *Hindu,* 15 November 1968.

Moreover, the Marxists' ignominious departure lost the potential benefits of being cast from office because they had acted in the name of the people. Had the Marxists, once in power, simply begun to implement radical land reform measures, for example, rather than to placate their coalition partners and wait interminably for presidential approval, the government might well have been forced to resign, but the political capital accrued would have been enormous. Ranadive perhaps was suggesting such a tactic when he urged Marxist ministers "to press ahead with legislations which were likely to be vetoed by the center or the High Court. Such confrontations," he said, "were designed to tell masses of the impossibility of carrying through fundamental reforms under the present constitution." [109]

The Marxists under the UF government sought to combine administration and struggle, popular initiative plus utilization of the administrative machinery for the advancement of the "basic classes." The CPI sought "efficient administration." M. N. Govindan Nair, the Right Communist leader and agriculture minister under the UF, denounced the Marxist strategy: "Administration and struggle cannot go together: either give up administration and continue the struggle or give up the struggle and carry on the administration." [110]

For all their administrative failures, however, the Marxist government had not been without achievements. It was argued that whatever possible relief should be given, but that given "the extremely limited and curtailed powers and resources of the state Governments," only meager ameliorative relief measures can be provided. "The devastating effects of the deepening economic crisis . . . can only be redressed by a radical and revolutionary change in the entire social set-up." [111] With little potential for immediate economic growth and dependent almost wholly on the center for financial support, politics in Kerala approaches the character of a zero-sum game. The Marxists' achievements came at the expense of other parties; the relief of certain classes came at the expense of others.

With limited resources, the Marxists relied more on symbolic output than on a redistribution of wealth. The Marxist police policy is a case in point. The Kerala Home Ministry, as it did under the Communist government in 1957, specified that the police should not interfere in mass struggles except when there was an actual outbreak of violence. The police, as an instrument of the State, would no longer be used against the

---

[109] *Indian Express,* 22 June 1969.
[110] Quoted by E. M. S. Namboodiripad in *Right Communist Betrayal of Kerala U.F. and Government* (Calcutta: CPM, 1969), p. 7.
[111] *Political-Organisational Report,* p. 173.

people for the protection of vested interests. The *gherao* (coercive encircle-ment for "quick justice") was accepted as a form of peaceful demonstra-tion and therefore legitimate. The policy was attacked as being selectively enforced so as to advance Marxist struggles.[112] Local police were alleged to be willing to act only on the express instruction of Marxist cadres. The Marxists had also organized a Volunteer Corps popularly known as the "Gopala Sena" after A. K. Gopalan. Uniformed in khaki pants and red shirts, the corps of about 3,000 young men outnumbered the state police. The perceived threat to the propertied classes was equated with a "break-down of law and order." Like the mass upsurge of ten years before, the situation was highly colored by class perspective.

O. P. Sangal, in the *Citizen*, has written that

The very fact of the CPM emerging as the dominant political force in the State changed the psychology of the overwhelming majority of the down-trodden and oppressed masses. They felt as if they had themselves come into power. And this feeling was strengthened by their everyday experi-ence. For example, without any legislative or executive action on the part of the government, the wages of agricultural workers increased far above the normal market rate just because of the changed political atmosphere in the State. It became possible for ordinary worker and peasant leaders to get any oppressive government official transferred from his favorite area of operation.

"The greatest mistake that the CPI appears to have committed in Kerala," Sangal continues,

is its failure to make an objective assessment of the CPM's strength, its mass base and its place in the political life of the State. If the CPI leaders were not suffering from gross subjectivism, they would have seen that the CPM had become the chief vehicle and the main organizational expression of the communist movement in Kerala. Whatever mistakes the CPM might have committed in the past or may commit in the future, the CPI can never hope to replace it.[113]

During the period of "administration and struggle," the Marxists sought to extend their social base—particularly among agricultural labor. The reaction of the other parties in the UF was accelerated by the events within the Congress. The Congress split provided the ideological escape, for in the conception of the Indian situation held by the CPI, collaboration with

---

[112] The statement by Marxist ally and labor minister Mathai Manjooram of the Kerala Socialist Party that "it is only through lawlessness [that] order can be achieved," was given wide press coverage. *Hindu*, 30 September 1969.

[113] *Citizen*, 8 November 1969, p. 24. For an examination of the United Front, see Thelma Hunter, "Indian Communism and the Kerala Experience of Coalition Government, 1967–69," *Journal of Commonwealth Political Studies* 10, (March 1972), pp. 45–70.

"progressive" elements of the Congress is possible. Herein lies the narrow, yet crucial, ideological distinction between National Democracy, as held by the CPI, and People's Democracy, as held by the CPM. Both are regarded as transitional stages to socialism and involve the same class alliances—the antifeudal, anti-imperialist, and antimonopoly classes. People's Democracy, however, presupposes the hegemony of the working class, and such hegemony is only to be achieved by protracted struggle.

The Marxist assessment of the character of the Indian State is specified in the party program: "The present Indian state is the organ of the class rule of the bourgeoisie and landlord, led by the big bourgeoisie, who are increasingly collaborating with foreign finance capital in pursuit of the capitalistic path of development." [114] The CPI denies that Indian leadership is dominated by the monopoly bourgeoisie: "The State of India is the organ of the class rule of the national bourgeoisie as a whole, in which the big bourgeoisie holds powerful influence. This class has strong links with the landlords. These factors give rise to reactionary pulls on the State power." [115] The CPI takes the Congress split as opening "a new stage in the differentiation between the representatives of the monopoly and non-monopoly strata of the bourgeoisie in the Congress" and "a new alignment of political forces in the country." [116]

The various Maoist groups share the basic assessment of the CPI (Marxist-Leninist): "The Congress Government represents the interests of the Indian feudal princes, big landlords and bureaucratic-comprador capitalists." [117] There are no contradictions within the enemy camp, and the bourgeosie in its entirety must be fought together. The Marxists regard the Naxalite position as politically unrealistic, a form of political expressionism best characterized by Lenin's diagnosis, "an infantile disorder." However romantic the appeal of instant revolution, India is not, at this stage, in a revolutionary situation. The organization and consciousness of the working class remains "at a pitiably low level." [118] "Despite the intensifying economic-political crisis and the sharpening of class contradictions and the class struggle, moving the masses into action on an ever-increasing

[114] *Programme* (Calcutta: CPM, 1964), p. 25.

[115] "Programme of the Communist Party of India," in *Documents Adopted by the Eighth Congress of the Communist Party of India, Patna, 7–15 February 1968*, p. 297.

[116] Mohit Sen, "Differentiation Within the Indian Bourgeoisie," *Mainstream*, 13 December 1969, p. 28.

[117] Quoted from the CPML program by E. M. S. Namboodiripad in an interview in *Radical Review* (Madras) 1, no. 2 (January 1970), p. 17.

[118] *Present Political Situation, Report adopted by the Central Committee of the CPI (M), Calcutta, 20 February 1970* (Calcutta: CPM, 1970), p. 21.

scale, the political crisis is far from maturing into a revolutionary crisis or ripening into a revolutionary situation." [119] The raid on the police station or the assassination of a landlord may reap psychic benefits for those engaged in such furtive efforts, but they cannot substitute for political organization and protracted conflict guided by a sense of what can, in fact, be *achieved*. Going back to Lenin, Mathew Kurian, Marxist theorist and economist, argues that extremism is another form of opportunism. "Both revisionism and extremism are two forms of expression of the same middle-class petty bourgeois vacillation." [120]

In the path between the "revisionism" of the CPI and the "left sectarianism" of the CPML the Marxists have been willing to align with the nonmonopoly bourgeoisie for tactical purposes, "in the interests of the bigger battle." They regard the contradictions within the Indian bourgeoisie as real and seek to exploit them fully. Indeed, even the Indian monopoly bourgeoisie may come in conflict with foreign monopolists, and, in such instances, the Marxists are prepared to cooperate with the class enemy in anti-imperialist struggle. The Marxists, however, have regarded the CPI's stance as subservience to the national bourgeoisie. Their quarrel with the CPI, intensified by the internal conflicts of the UF governments, blinded the Marxists to the deepening strains within the Congress. After the Congress split, the Central Committee in February 1970 admitted underestimating "the inner contradictions in the Congress combine." In "utilizing the two UF state Governments of Kerala and West Bengal as the advanced outposts of the democratic revolutionary movement for unleashing big class and mass forces . . . we were, for the most part, emphasizing the intensification of the class and social contradictions and the consequent sharpening of the class struggle in the country and tended to underestimate the political impact of the differences and split on the ruling Congress party and Government." [121]

In seeking to combine administration and struggle, the Marxists have been unwilling to abandon the opportunities afforded by electoral democracy for the isolation of the underground, although they remain prepared to do so in the face of serious attempts to outlaw the party or to force it into political isolation. "Elections," says P. Govinda Pillai, editor of the Marxist Malayalam daily, "are a means to reach and mobilize large numbers of people." [122] The political campaign becomes a vehicle of the party's

---

[119] Ibid., p. 25.
[120] Interview, Trivandrum, January 1970.
[121] *Present Political Situation, Report adopted by the Central Committee of the CPI (M), Calcutta, 2–7 February 1970* (Calcutta: CPM, 1970), p. 21.
[122] Interview, Cochin, December 1969.

expanding social base. It reaches potential allies that violence and terrorism would only alienate and repel. While "the ruling classes allow the
luxury of parliamentary democracy only so long as their own class interests are not threatened," EMS, in so far as possible, would use the constitution as "an instrument of struggle." [123] "Our party is of the view that,
so long as this system continues, it is in the interest of the working class
. . . to so utilize the institutions as built up on the basis of this Constitution
as to further consolidate and strengthen the struggles of the working people
for basic social transformations." [124]

Any political party," Kurian states, "however revolutionary, if it understands real politics functioning within the bourgeois system, must play the
game of the system, but though sometimes compromise may be necessary,
a revolutionary party cannot build its program on bourgeois methods like
horse trading." [125] Thus, in addition to and inseparable from parliamentary tactics, the Marxists utilize extraparliamentary forms of struggle. Success is the criterion by which tactics are to be judged. "The only criterion
on which Marxism-Leninism bases itself when it selects a particular
method for bringing about social transformations," according to EMS, "is
whether it will serve the purpose." Namboodiripad does not reject or extol
any particular form of strategy, violent or nonviolent. "The form depends
on the mood of the people, their sentiments, their unity and cohesion." [126]

The "Mini-Front" and the 1970 Elections

When the "mini-front" government was formed, in 1970, the Marxists
denounced the ministry as a "betrayer" and vowed to begin agitation to
overthrow it. Marxist demonstrations brought down a heavily repressive
police reaction, with lathi charges and firings. The CPM attacked the
"police-goonda raj" as armed clashes between landlords and Marxist-led
laborers increased. Conflict intensified in January, when an ill-conceived
program of "direct action" was initiated by the Marxists to forcibly and
"non-bureaucratically" implement the land reform act. The "land grab"
brought more discredit than success and was abandoned, as was a later
and equally unpopular bus strike. Except for a deeply impressive kisan

---

[123] E. M. S. Namboodiripad, *The Republican Constitution in the Struggle for Socialism*, R. R. Kale Memorial Lecture (Poona: Gokhale Institute of Politics and Economics, 1968), p. 1. In this important statement, EMS spells out the Marxist stance
in relation to the constitution and introduces a program for overhauling the state
structure, with the "widest autonomy for the various states." Pp. 16–20.
[124] Ibid., p. 3.
[125] Interview, Trivandrum, January 1970.
[126] Ibid.

rally, the various strikes and demonstrations called by the Marxists largely fizzled out with little response.

The militant posture assumed by the Marxists immediately after the "mini-front" came to power served to cement what would have been an almost immediately unstable coalition. As it was, even the right wing Kerala Congress went along with land reform implementation. Frustration seemed more to dictate the Marxist tactic than a sensitivity to the situation. On all sides, however, it was admitted that the CPM had not lost any of its own support. The Marxists held the allegiance of the increasingly conscious and militant landless laborers, but their activities alienated them from the broader base of support required to secure an absolute majority in an election.[127]

The September 1970 elections in Kerala would seem to confirm this perspective and to underscore the basic stability of electoral behavior in the state. The call for elections had come as a surprise. The contradictions within the "mini-front" government were becoming increasingly evident with the demands for an expanded ministry. Buoyed by confidence of his own success, Chief Minister Achutha Menon dissolved the assembly in June and called for fresh elections in the early fall. The move was designed to strengthen the position of the CPI as well as to secure a decisive majority for the government. Under the impending strain of demands for the apportionment of seats, the tensions within the "mini-front" deepened. The Kerala Congress and the ISP withdrew, and an opposition "Democratic Front" was formed with an alliance between the Kerala Congress and the organization Congress[128] in electoral adjustment with the Jana Sangh, Swatantra, and the Kerala Karshaka Party, a splinter of the KTP. The Marxist bloc—the "People's Democratic Front"—remained intact, as the SSP, KTP, and KSP were joined by the ISP. The incumbent United Front, composed of the CPI, the Muslim League, and the RSP, added the Praja Socialist Party and, most significantly, entered into an "understanding" with Indira Gandhi's Congress (R).

The three-front election, attracting visits by national party leaders, including Prime Minister Indira Gandhi, brought a turnout of nearly 75 percent. The CPI United Front and the Congress (R) campaigned from virtually identical manifestos. The accomplishments of the Achutha Menon government were emphasized as the beginning of rapid progress toward a new social order: implementation of the Land Reforms Act, extension of

[127] Interview with K. P. Karunakaran, Trivandrum, January 1970.
[128] For a discussion of the Congress split, see Hardgrave, "The Congress in India: Crisis and Split," *Asian Survey*, March 1970, pp. 256–262.

the labor welfare gratuities scheme, government control of wholesale trade in food grains, steps to nationalize foreign-owned plantations, and financial assistance secured from the center. The main theme of the UF campaign was the promise of stability. The Marxists, on the other hand, denounced the police excesses of the Menon ministry, hammered at the impossibility of any real improvements, and argued for an intensification of Kerala's struggle against the center. Their main thrust was directed against the CPI and the Muslim League, and their strategy led them into cynical alignment with the right-wing organization Congress, the Kerala Congress, and the Jana Sangh in various constituencies to secure the defeat of their UF opponents.[129]

The election results gave the United Front–Congress (R) alliance a narrow majority of 68 seats in the 133-seat assembly. The CPI itself, while proclaiming victory, was reduced in its strength from 19 to 16 seats. The dramatic showing of the Congress (R), however, portending the results of the national parliamentary elections in March 1971, captured national headlines. After a virtual eclipse in the assembly, the Congress was again a force of considerable power, with 32 seats instead of its previous 5. Although initially choosing to remain outside the government, the Congress (R) provided Achutha Menon with the secure majority he sought. The Congress (R) received 18.29 percent of the vote, a sharp decline from that secured by the undivided Congress in 1967 (35.5 percent), but in 1970 the Congress (R) had contested only 56 seats instead of the full 133 of the previous election. The organization Congress, contesting 41 seats, was unable to secure even one seat and polled only 3.48 percent of the electorate. Despite the overall Congress decline in its share of the total vote, the victories of the Congress (R) brought into Kerala politics a powerful influence of youth and a renewed sense of stability and direction.[130]

The Congress (R) victory was clearly not the triumph over the Marxists so widely proclaimed in the Indian press, however. The Marxists were reduced from 49 to 28 seats, but retained the 23.45 percent of the vote that they had captured in 1967 (although contesting a greater number of

[129] *Link*, 27 September 1970.
[130] Much of the energy behind the party arises from the Youth Congress and from the Congress-affiliated Kerala Student Union, which controls some 70 percent of the college unions in the state. N. S. Jagannathan, in the *Hindustan Times*, 26 September 1970, p. 9. This source of energy soon proved a source of tension and generational conflict, however, as younger members of the party, particularly in the radical Youth Congress, have tried to take the party further to the left. *Hindu*, 24 February 1971.

Table 2.15   Election Results by Party, Kerala Legislative Assembly, 1970[a]

Party	Seats Contested	Seats Won	Popular Vote Number	Popular Vote Percentage
People's Democratic Front				
CPM	72	28	1,759,797	23.45
SSP	14	6	306,763	4.08
ISP	11	3	244,205	3.25
KSP	3	2	49,345	0.65
KTP	4	2	90,953	1.20
Totals	104	41	2,451,063	32.63
United Front–Congress (R)				
Congress (R)	56	32	1,372,346	18.29
CPI	31	16	701,558	9.34
Muslim League	20	11	579,320	7.72
RSP	14	6	330,983	4.40
PSP	7	3	182,760	2.42
Totals	128	68	3,167,467	42.17
Democratic Front				
Congress (O)	39	0	261,057	3.48
Jana Sangh	8	0	45,079	0.60
Swatantra	2	0	7,982	0.09
Kerala Congress	31	12	443,232	5.90
Totals	80	12	757,350	10.07
Independents and minor parties	193	12	1,133,115	15.13
Grand Totals	505	133	7,508,995	100.00

Electorate   10,170,038
Turnout   73.83%

[a] Unofficial results, with statistics, other than for seats won, varying slightly among sources. *Statesman*, 21 September 1970; *Times of India*, 19 September 1970; Ramakrishnan Nair and T. J. Nossiter, "The Rules of the Electoral Game: Kerala, 1970," *South Asian Review* 4, (April 1971), 204.
[b] The *Times of India* (19 September 1970) identifies 21 independents as aligned with the People's Democratic Front; 4 with the United Front–Congress (R); and 10 with the Democratic Front. Although there is variation with other sources on the election, the *Times of India* reports that among the 12 independents returned, 5 were supported by the Democratic Front, 3 by the People's Democratic Front.

seats). The CPM had, in fact, not only held its own in the percentage of votes, but emerged as the largest political party in Kerala, a position previously enjoyed by the undivided Congress. The impressive Congress (R) victories—like their defeats in 1967—were fundamentally the product of front tactics. This is especially clear in Malabar, where the Marxists suffered severe losses at the hands of the Congress (R). The Congress (R) understanding with the Muslim League tipped the balance against the Marxists, but the heralded defeat of the Marxist candidates did not cut into their percentage of the votes (see table 2.15).

The electoral strength of the CPM, however, could not obscure the fact that the party had been badly beaten. The Marxists confronted serious internal dissension in the wake of the Congress (R) victory. Despite the fact that the CPM had repeatedly called for fresh elections after the "mini-front" government took power, the Marxists were unprepared for the midterm election and had sought by various means to postpone it.[131] Opponents of EMS's electoral strategy leveled particular criticism at the Marxist attacks on the Muslim League, at CPM support of organization Congress candidates, at procedures by which Marxist candidates were selected, and at the party's lackluster campaign. The Politburo and the party's Central Committee reportedly admonished EMS for the "errors" of the midterm election. Securing his own position, EMS responded to the discontent through a series of purges directed both toward revisionists affected by the "bourgeois parliamentary mentality" of fighting for nominations and the spoils of office and toward those of the Left who would indulge in "self-seeking adventurism."

The elections had exposed the weakness of the Naxalites in electoral contests: All nine of the "revolutionary communists" who contested the election lost their deposits. EMS took the opportunity to dissolve the CPM Kottayam District Committee, which had been under the control of extremists for two years in consistent opposition to his leadership.[132] EMS sought to bring the party more effectively under his own control. The Marxists, however, had moved vigorously since their ouster in 1969 to establish their own militant credentials. Struggle had been the dominant theme of their campaign, and they were not going to set it aside in electoral defeat.

The people of Kerala again went to the polls in March 1971, as Prime Minister Indira Gandhi sought a mandate in national parliamentary elections. In assessment of the September 1970 midterm elections, the Kerala

[131] See Ramakrishnan Nair and T. J. Nossiter, "The Rules of the Electoral Game: Kerala 1970," *South Asian Review* 4, (April 1971).
[132] *Statesman Weekly*, 28 November 1970.

Table 2.16   Election Results by Party, Kerala Parliamentary Elections, 1971

Party	Seats Contested	Seats Won	Popular Vote Number	Popular Vote Percentage
United Front–Congress (R)				
Congress (R)	7	6	1,289,601	20.1
CPI	3	3	593,761	9.2
Kerala Congress	3	3	542,431	8.4
Muslim League	2	2	366,702	5.7
RSP	2	2	419,796	6.5
PSP	1	0	143,745	2.2
Totals	18	16	3,356,036	52.1
The Democratic Front				
Congress (O)	5	0	100,856	1.6
SSP	2	0	57,382	0.9
Jana Sangh	3	0	91,187	1.4
ISP	1	0	33,983	0.5
Swatantra	1	0	14,716	0.2
Totals	12	0	298,124	4.6
CPM	11	2	1,611,442	25.1
Independents	25	1	1,163,351	18.2
Grand Totals	66	19	6,428,953	100.0

Source: Unofficial results, *Times of India*, 15 March 1971.

coalitions shifted slightly. The ruling United Front–Congress (R) alliance drew into its fold the Kerala Congress for the contest for the 19 Lok Sabha seats. Allocating seats among the constituent parties of the alliance according to their 1970 strength, the alliance put up candidates in each parliamentary constituency except Palghat, where it supported an independent against CPM leader A. K. Gopalan. Gopalan had been shifted by the Marxists, as expected, from Sasargod to the safer Palghat seat.

In the 1971 elections the CPM stood alone. It had parted company with its former allies, the SSP, ISP, KSP, and KTP, regarding them now as liabilities that had stretched the party's revolutionary credibility.[133] The Marxists fielded 11 candidates and, in the remaining 8 constituencies, supported independents, including former defense minister and firebrand of the Left V. K. Krishna Menon in Trivandrum. The CPM political line was one of total opposition to the two fronts.

The Democratic Front of the Congress (O), the Jana Sangh, and Swatantra was expanded to include the SSP, the ISP, and assorted independents

[133] See Nair and Nossiter, "Rules of the Electoral Game."

in an electoral understanding in 15 constituencies. The United Front–Congress (R) alliance, repeating its earlier sweep of the polls, captured 16 of the 19 seats. The Democratic Front, led by the Congress (O), was wiped out. The combined vote of all five parties in the Front totaled less than 5 percent of the poll, and not one of the front's candidates could even retain his security deposit (see table 2.16).

In the 1971 elections the CPM was reduced to two seats from the nine it had won as a member of the undivided United Front in 1967. Marxist-supported independent Krishna Menon was returned, but the election was a major setback for the party, deepening the isolation of the CPM. The CPM's share of the vote, however, was roughly the same as it had been in the midterm elections (25.1 percent in 1971 compared with 23.45 percent in 1970).

Conclusions
The Marxists have retained their base of support among the poor and landless in Kerala, and, with effective social and political mobilization this base could expand. But the stability—or, perhaps more accurately, stagnation—of the CPM vote poses serious dilemmas for the party. In opposing the present United Front government, which has gone far to fulfill the progressive Minimum Program to which the CPM itself was committed, the Marxists risk remaining in ineffectual isolation, with possible erosion of their present support. An option, already closed by the CPM denunciation of the new government, would be a position of external support, from which they might be able to ensure the success of genuinely radical social legislation. The benefits of such a stance, however, would surely accrue more to the government than to the CPM. On the other hand, the Marxists could engage in cynical flirtation with those forces of the Right that could bring down the government and attempt in the wreckage of the United Front to form another ministry under their own tenuous suzerainty. They might also, and the alternatives are not mutually exclusive, assume a more militant leftist line. Under the present circumstances, their reduction of seats and isolation in the assembly could well serve as a catalyst to increasing extraparliamentary activity, agitation, and the revolutionary adventurism of frustration.

The CPI, heading the Kerala government, confronts its own dilemma. The results of the 1970 and 1971 elections imposed a new strain on the viability of the CPI, a strain deepened in September 1971 by the entrance of the Congress (R) into an expanded coalition cabinet. It was the first time in India that the Congress had shared power with the Communists.

The new ministry provided Achutha Menon with a more stable base for a legislative assault on the problems of unemployment, landless labor, agricultural production, and industrialization. At the same time, however, with 5 of the 13 ministers, the Congress became the largest single party in the ruling United Front cabinet.

The stability and, more significantly, the success that the United Front government has had in implementing its program is now threatened by renewed Congress strength—threatened not by resistance to democratic transformation but by an effort of young left-wing Congress leaders to lead that transformation in their own name. The Congress sweep in the March 1972 elections in other states has bolstered the Congress in Kerala, and there is a push within Congress ranks to withdraw support from the UF government and to force new elections, thus opening the way, in their estimation, for a Congress majority. Congress party leadership at the center may well oppose such a move because of its effect on the Congress relationship with the CPI nationally. But if this were to occur, unless it again allied with the Marxists, the CPI might well face eclipse. In sharp contrast to the CPM, the CPI simply has no secure electoral base. Even under the circumstances of the present United Front, the CPI faces increasing stress. In reaction to CPI dependence on Congress, the traditionally anti-Congress elements within the CPI may be drawn toward the Marxist fold. On the other hand, the far more serious threat is that the revitalized Congress might well succeed in weaning away the electoral base of the CPI.

The Kerala government today is committed to the economic and social transformation of society. The strength of the Communist movement in Kerala and the competing interaction between the CPI and the CPM have served to radicalize the state within a parliamentary framework. In a situation of scarcity, however, social transformation may bring little economic improvement, and the capacity of the government to respond may be lost in frustration and in the fratricidal battles of the Left.

West Bengal

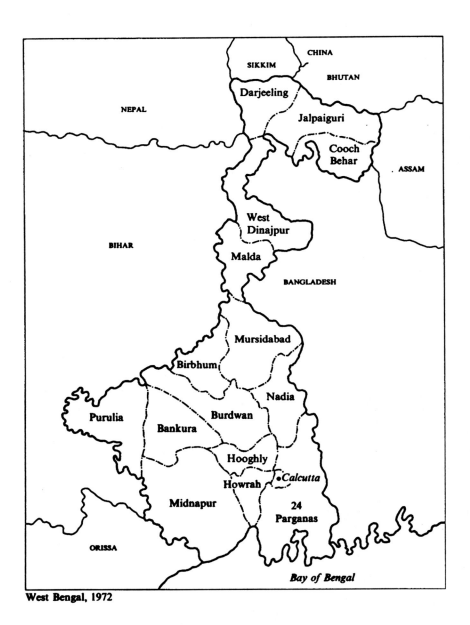

West Bengal, 1972

3
Radical Politics in West Bengal   Marcus F. Franda

Regardless of the index one uses, the Indian state of West Bengal seems to have been on a precipitous downward slope since the mid-1960s. In 1965–1966 West Bengal suffered a severe food shortage, which was aggravated by the famine in Bihar and accompanied by an industrial recession. To cope with its economic crisis, the state government imposed a series of levies on large landowners and rice mill owners in West Bengal, causing them to withdraw their support from the Congress party, on which the stability of the state government had depended since 1947. Congress also alienated a large number of its Muslim supporters in 1965–1966, when government arrests of Muslim leaders in the wake of the 1965 Indo-Pakistan war were resented by the sizable Muslim community in West Bengal. After Congress failed for the first time since Independence to gain a majority in the West Bengal Legislative Assembly in 1967, a series of three disparate state coalition governments (elected in 1967, 1969, and 1971) tried to govern the state, but none of them lasted for more than 13 months. President's Rule, which was operative in West Bengal for most of 1968, 1970, and 1971, failed to arrest the deterioration of both the political and economic situations, which were in turn complicated in 1971 by the Bangladesh crisis and the influx into West Bengal of more than seven million international refugees (three million refugees went to other Indian states as well).

West Bengal has always had a reputation for cultural unorthodoxy, social protest, and political radicalism, but that reputation has been considerably enhanced by the events of the past few years. Since February 1967, for example, West Bengal has witnessed a breakdown of law and order that is without parallel in other parts of India, accompanied by a massive land seizure movement, interparty rivalry that has resulted in an average of almost 500 political murders annually during the last four years, and the growth of an insurrectionist terrorist movement that has seriously challenged the possibility of orderly administration and economic development. In this atmosphere, the concern of the Indian government is reflected in the words of a minister in New Delhi, who told me recently: "We used to take pride in Gokhale's statement—'what Bengal thinks today, India thinks tomorrow'—but if anyone raised that same slogan now we would shudder at the thought of it."

West Bengal is an important part of India. Although it has relinquished its position as India's foremost industrial state (to Maharashtra), it still contains more than 15 percent of India's factories, which account for about 21 percent of India's total gross industrial output.[1] Calcutta, the capital of West Bengal, is also the principal administrative and commercial center for the whole of northeastern South Asia, stretching from the borders of China to the eastern districts of Uttar Pradesh, an area that has a population of almost a quarter billion people if one includes Bangladesh. Calcutta banks handle about 30 percent of India's bank clearances, and Calcutta port clears more than 40 percent of India's exports (it receives about 25 percent of India's imports). Despite its problems in recent years, West Bengal continues to sell products that account for a larger share of India's foreign exchange earnings than any other Indian state, including 90 percent of India's jute (still India's highest export earner) and 25 percent of India's tea. More than a quarter of India's steel, a third of India's coal, and almost half of India's railway equipment originate in West Bengal.

India is concerned about the recent trend of events in West Bengal, not only because of their consequences for the Indian economy but also because of the strategic political and military location of this border state. West Bengal borders on two foreign nations (Bangladesh and Nepal) and on two border kingdoms (Sikkim and Bhutan) that are nominally independent but are tied by treaties and subsidies to India. It is less than 30 miles from Tibetan China. At one point in Darjeeling district the "Siliguri corridor," only 14 miles wide, connects the main portions of India with its northeastern states and territories (Assam, Arunachal, Manipur, Meghalaya, Mizoram, Nagaland, and Tripura). The border with Bangladesh is 1,349 miles long, much of it consisting of mountainous and hilly terrain, covered with jungles and dotted with rivers, marshes, and swamps, an area particularly difficult to police or patrol in normal times, and almost impossible to control during the monsoons. If only to provide for its external security and regular intercourse with Bangladesh, India must give high priority to matters affecting the stability and well-being of West Bengal.

Politics and the Population Mix
Much of the difficulty in governing West Bengal stems from its high population density and peculiar migration patterns. West Bengal is India's second most crowded state (Kerala being a bit denser), with 1,307 people per square mile according to the 1971 Indian census. Almost a quarter of

---

[1] Figures on West Bengal's economic position relative to the rest of India are taken from A. K. Sen, *West Bengal: An Analytical Study* (Calcutta: Oxford Book Co., 1971), pp. v–vi.

the state's population lives in urban areas, and a little less than 16 percent of the state's population lives in the Calcutta urban area, now the seventh most populous metropolitan region in the world. The 1971 census estimates that there are approximately 14 million landed cultivators in West Bengal, competing for 13.4 million acres of cultivable land, which means that the average holding of cultivable land is less than one acre per farmer. Another 25.8 percent of those employed in West Bengal in 1971 were listed by the census as agricultural laborers, meaning that they owned no land but did work as agriculturalists for others on a day-wage basis.

Migration into West Bengal has come primarily from two sources, the first being a steady influx of refugees from East Bengal since 1947 and the second being internal migrants (primarily from non-Bengali rural areas) attracted by employment opportunities in West Bengal's cities. Table 3.1 lists the yearly total of migrants from East Bengal who registered as refugees during the period 1947 through 1970, a 24-year accumulation that adds up to more than four million. It is largely because of this accumulation that the population of West Bengal increased by 64.7 percent between 1951 and 1971, a figure considerably above the all-India average increase of 51.6 percent.

Exact figures for Indian migrants into West Bengal are not available, since Indian citizens are not required to register when they cross state

Table 3.1   Refugees from East Bengal, Registered in West Bengal, 1947–1970

Year	No. of Persons	Year	No. of Persons
1947	377,899	1960	8,629
1948	419,018	1961	10,095
1949	275,592	1962	12,804
1950	925,185	1963	14,601
1951 ⎫		1964	667,125
1952 ⎭ 477,186		1965	159,989
1953	60,647	1966	4,214
1954	105,850	1967	6,895
1955	211,573	1968	6,589
1956	246,840	1969	11,068
1957	9,133	1970	248,158
1958	4,285		
1959	5,539	Total	4,268,924

Source: Statistical Officer, Office of the Refugee Rehabilitation Commissioner, Government of West Bengal, quoted in A. K. Sen, *West Bengal: An Analytical Study* (Calcutta: Oxford Publishing Company, 1971), pp. 22–23.

Table 3.2 Non-Bengali Earners in Different Occupational Categories, West Bengal, 1961

Occupational Category	Percentage Non-Bengali
Executive	30
Technical/professional	21.5
Ministerial	15.0
Trading	59.0
Skilled manual labor	50.5
Unskilled manual labor	74.0

Source: Sen, *West Bengal: An Analytical Study*, p. vii.

boundaries, but some idea of the size of the migration into West Bengal can be gleaned from other sources. The 1961 census, for example, found that 79 percent of the jute textile workers in West Bengal came from other states and that 61 percent of total factory employment in West Bengal was non-Bengali, distributed between occupational categories according to the figures in table 3.2 (detailed 1971 census figures are not available). More recent estimates compiled by the Labour Directorate of the West Bengal government indicate the continued predominance of non-Bengali migrants in the West Bengal labor force.[2]

One reason for the massive presence of non-Bengalis in the West Bengal economy is the aversion of many Bengalis to occupations involving manual labor. This tradition is in turn a result of the predominance in the Bengali population of the Bengali *bhadralok*, an elite that is unique to the Bengali-speaking region. Neither a single class nor a single caste, the *bhadralok* (literally "respectable people" or "gentlemen," sometimes called just *borolok* or "big people") are a privileged minority, most often drawn from the three highest castes (Brahmins, Kayasthas, and Vaidyas), usually landed or employed in professional or clerical occupations, and extremely jealous of their social positions, which they have maintained by caste and ritual proscriptions and by the avoidance of manual labor. In the nineteenth century the *bhadralok* experienced a cultural renaissance that Bengali scholars frequently liken to the Italian Renaissance of the thirteenth and fourteenth centuries: a flurry of activities in literature, art, politics, and economics that placed Bengal firmly in the forefront of almost all Indian associational life. But in the twentieth century this elite has wit-

---

[2] Recent Labour Directorate statistics on migrants into West Bengal are summarized in Sankar Ghosh, *The Disinherited State: A Study of West Bengal, 1967–1970* (Calcutta: Orient Longmans, 1971), pp. 20–21.

nessed a series of dislocations that have seriously restricted the influence of its members outside of Bengal and have threatened its dominance within.

Although the Muslim community was in a majority in the larger province of Bengal at the turn of the century, the social position of the Muslims and their political and economic influence had never matched that of the predominantly Hindu *bhadralok*. Bengal's large Muslim population, unlike the Muslim population in other parts of India, was the result of local conversion rather than migration. Since Bengal had always been on the periphery of the great Brahmanic cultures, orthodox Hinduism had always been challenged among the lowly in Bengal—by Buddhism, Jainism, Vaishnavism, and finally by Islam—but the *bhadralok* had nevertheless maintained their dominant position for a number of centuries before the British invasion. By origin the Muslims of Bengal were low-caste Hindus, and in many ways they were indistinguishable from their former caste fellows throughout the nineteenth century, since their backwardness was less a consequence of the decline of Muslim power and the rise of the British than it was the "result of the poverty and lowly status of Bengali Muslims since time out of mind." [3] With the exception of a small clique of scholars in Persian, a few landlords who had adopted *bhadralok* customs, and a small scattering of educated Muslim elites, the Muslim community during the nineteenth century remained illiterate, unorganized, and poor.

In the twentieth century, however, the leadership of the Muslim community launched a series of successful political maneuvers that brought them into political power in the province of Bengal from 1926 until 1947, when Bengal was finally partitioned between two international states and most of the Muslim political leadership went over to East Pakistan. Before 1926 the Muslim community allied itself first with the British, in an elaborate system of patronage that lasted until 1911 and gained for the Muslims the extremely valuable institution of communal electorates in 1909. Then, under a new and younger leadership led by A. K. Fazlul Huq, the Muslims entered into an alliance with the Hindu *bhadralok* in the legislative councils and eventually outmaneuvered their new allies. Using their positions in the provincial government and forming coalitions after 1926 with the Europeans and the low-caste Hindu communities, the

[3] Muslims presently account for approximately 20 percent of West Bengal's population, and more than 85 percent of the population of East Bengal (Bangladesh). An excellent statistical account of the place of the Muslim community in Bengali society is given in Anil Seal, *The Emergence of Indian Nationalism: Competition and Collaboration in the Later Nineteenth Century* (Cambridge: Cambridge University Press, 1968), pp. 37–38, 300–315.

Muslims gained unquestioned control of Bengal's institutional life in the 1930s and 1940s.

In this atmosphere *bhadralok* political leaders had little alternative but to try to consolidate the members of their own community and to mobilize the *abhadra* (non-*bhadralok*) in order to gain a political base. In doing so they alternated among various strategies and eventually became divided among themselves. Some of the *bhadralok* sought to continue their dominance of the liberal institutions imported by the British raj—the bureaucracy, the educational establishments, the legal apparatus, and the legislatures—but they were outmaneuvered (until 1947) by the British government and the Muslim majority led by Fazlul Huq. As Broomfield points out, this turn of events was largely a result of the failure of the *bhadralok* to adapt to the mass electorates that were introduced in Bengal in the 1920s: "The problem the *bhadralok* faced . . . very crudely . . . was the problem of thoroughly literate men trying to make themselves understood by the unlettered, of a written tradition confronting an oral tradition." [4] Because they failed to gain legislative majorities in the 1920s and 1930s the *bhadralok* lost their control of institutional life in Bengal, and many of them became permanently disenchanted with electoral politics.

The effect of this disenchantment was that the majority of the *bhadralok* surrendered the liberal, secular, and parliamentary democratic movements to the Muslims and *abhadra* groups, and many of them took to Hindu revivalism in an effort to consolidate their positions. In the 1920s and 1930s Bengali high-caste communal associations grew in number and influence, lending their support to the terrorist movements and secret societies that flourished during these decades, and ultimately rallying behind Subhas Chandra Bose, the undisputed leader of the *bhadralok*. But this school was also unsuccessful in gaining a mass following, since the various Hindu revivalist movements only tended to create factionalism within the society, and since all of them made for greater and greater exclusiveness on the part of the high castes. Many of them even alienated the vast majority of the people living in Bengal, since most of the Hindu revivalist groups were based on the worship of the mother goddess (Durga) as the embodiment of strength, but only a few sections of the high castes in Bengal are Sakta (the Hindu sect in which worship of the mother goddess is prominent). In a society where most of the people were Muslims or Vaisnava Hindus, the myth of the mother goddess was "an exclusive myth," largely irrelevant even to most Hindus living in Bengal.[5] Thus, Hindu revivalism

---

[4] John H. Broomfield, *Elite Conflict in a Plural Society: Twentieth-Century Bengal* (Berkeley: University of California Press, 1968), pp. 321–322.
[5] Ibid., pp. 16–17.

in Bengal failed to serve as a rallying point for large-scale political organizations, and Bengali politicians abandoned strictly communal political organizations. Ever since Independence, the avowedly communalist parties that are so prominent in other parts of India have been all but extinct in West Bengal.

In addition to the loss of their dominant political position within Bengal, the *bhadralok* experienced a number of other dislocations. Earnings from land began to diminish throughout India in the late nineteenth and early twentieth centuries, and the landed gentry of Bengal were among the most severely affected by this development. Educated unemployment on a large scale began to be felt in and around Calcutta at the turn of the century, just as the leadership of the nationalist movement was shifting from Bengal to Gandhi and the Hindi-speaking Brahmanic heartland. The dominance of Bengalis in the Indian Civil Service receded as other areas gained in higher education, and business in Calcutta came increasingly to be dominated by non-Bengali Indians and British industrialists. All of these factors grew in intensity right up until the 1940s, when Bengal witnessed in rapid succession a major famine (in 1943), the activities of 200,000 Allied troops in and around Calcutta during World War II, the partition of 1947 and the communal riots that accompanied it, and finally a trade war between West and East Bengal that was accompanied by the influx into West Bengal of millions of Hindu refugees.[6]

By the late 1930s a number of Bengali *bhadralok* politicians were ready for Marxism. Marxism appealed to the *bhadralok* because it rejected electoral politics, which had led to the loss of *bhadralok* dominance; because it denigrated orthodox Hindu ideas and behavior at a time when Bengalis were becoming disenchanted with Hindu revivalism; because it promised the overthrow of the hated British and the anglicized ruling and commercial groups who were guided by their ideas (and who controlled Calcutta); because it promised a modern society in which the intellectual would have a more prominent position; because it legitimized the terrorist and conspiratorial activities on which the *bhadralok* had staked their reputations for three decades; and because it denied the usefulness of banyas (traders) and merchants, caste groups that had begun to rise in status in the twentieth century and that in Bengal were almost all *abhadra*.[7] In the

---

[6] These factors are explored in greater detail in my book *Radical Politics in West Bengal* (Cambridge, Mass.: M.I.T. Press, 1971), from which I have adapted much of the material in the earlier portion of the present article.

[7] An excellent description of the rise of these castes in Bengal before Independence is offered in a novel by Tarasankar Banerjee, *Panchagram* [Five Villages], translated by Marcus F. Franda and Suhrid K. Chatterjee (New Delhi: Manohar Publishers, 1973).

late 1930s, four Marxist-Left parties were founded by *bhadralok* leaders (the Revolutionary Communist Party of India, the Bolshevik Party, the Revolutionary Socialist Party, and the Forward Bloc), all of which are still in existence and allied in Communist-led coalitions against the Congress.

Radical Politics and the Bhadralok

The Communist movement in West Bengal can trace its origins back as far as 1921, when a number of Bengalis established working relations with the Comintern, but the growth of the Communist Party of India (CPI) as a significant factor in provincial and state politics dates from the late 1930s. As a result of a successful recruitment drive in the jails during the 1930s, the CPI was able to absorb a large number of the *bhadralok* terrorists who had been active in Bengal since the first partition of the province in 1905. These recruits were later joined by Bengali intellectuals returning from England, by graduates of the colleges and universities in Bengal during the 1940s, and eventually by a large section of the urban *bhadralok* living in and around Calcutta and the West Bengal industrial belt. The growth of the movement has been somewhat sporadic, with significant declines in membership taking place in 1948 and 1963, but despite these temporary setbacks it has on the whole grown fairly steadily. According to membership figures given by party leaders, the CPI in pre-Independence Bengal grew from 37 members in 1934 to more than 1,000 members in 1942 and to almost 20,000 members in 1947.[8] The partition of Bengal in 1947 divided the party between two international states, with more than half of the membership going over to East Bengal in Pakistan. From a membership of less than 10,000 in 1947 the party in West Bengal grew to more than 12,000 members in 1954 and to 17,600 in 1962. At present there are approximately 17,000 members in the Communist Party of India (Marxist), or CPM (which broke away from the CPI in 1964), and 8,000 members in the regular CPI.

The Communist movement is still led by educated, high-caste Bengalis from *bhadralok* families that are well established in the social structure, as the following figures show. Of the 33 members of the State Committee of the CPM in 1969, 24 (or 73 percent) belonged to the three highest

[8] These estimates of party membership are taken from Abdul Halim, *Where Are We Now?* (Calcutta: n.p., 1934), p. 6; from interviews with party leaders in 1969–1970, and especially with Muzaffar Ahmad in March 1969; and from estimates published in party newspapers. Most CPM leaders and members argue that the size of the party has increased somewhat since 1970, but precise figures were not available at the time of writing.

castes in Bengal (Brahmins, Kayasthas, and Vaidyas), and all but two
had been to college for at least a year.[9] Only 3 of the 33 members had ever
engaged in manual labor for their livelihood; most of them were sons or
relatives of landholders and professionals (lawyers, doctors, and teachers). Similarly, 8 of the 9 members of the CPI state secretariat in 1969
were from high-caste families (the other being a Muslim), all had been to
college or beyond, and all came from respectable and fairly wealthy
families.

Prior to 1967, the Communist and Marxist-Left parties of West Bengal
always provided the principal opposition to Congress party rule, but because of their elitism, and the almost constant factionalism among them,
they were never able to seriously challenge the electoral dominance of the
Congress. As is indicated in table 3.3, the Communist and Marxist-Left
parties in West Bengal were able to increase their combined portion of the
vote from 17.35 percent in 1952 to 24.92 percent in 1957 to 33.87 percent in 1962, while the combined number of seats increased from 39 to 61
to 72 over this same period. However, since these figures fell considerably
short of Congress totals and since the Communist and Marxist-Left vote
was so terribly divided, the position of the Congress in West Bengal remained secure.

This pattern of electoral distribution began to change in 1967, when the
Congress failed for the first time to gain a majority of the seats in the state
legislative assembly. In most party systems the Congress party might have
attempted to form a coalition government after the 1967 elections, since it
clearly had the largest number of seats in the new assembly (127 of 280,
the next largest party being the CPM with 43 seats), and since it was conceivable that some of the smaller parties and independent candidates might
have welcomed a Congress-led coalition. But Mrs. Gandhi, prime minister
of India for barely a year at the time, made a conscious decision to allow
the opposition an opportunity to form a government, and the non-Congress
parties were so jubilant over the failure of the Congress to secure a majority
that they quickly expressed their willingness to enter into a coalition
government. The first United Front government of 1967 was therefore
formed by a coalition of 14 parties and an independent, including the 2
Communist parties, all of the Marxist-Left parties, plus the Bangla Congress, Praja Socialist Party (PSP), Samyukta Socialist Party (SSP),
Gurkha League, and Lok Sevak Sangh (LSS).

[9] Data on the leadership of the Communist parties was collected by the author in
interviews with present and former members in 1962–1964 and 1968–1970, and
from biographical data furnished in *Who's Who*s, newspapers, and articles.

Table 3.3   West Bengal Legislative Assembly Results, 1952–1967

Political Party	1952		1957		1962		1967	
	% Votes	Seats	% Votes	Seats	% Votes	Seats	% Votes	Seats
Social Democratic								
Congress	38.93	150	46.14	152	47.29	157	41.14	127
Bangla Congress	founded in 1966						10.44	34
Praja Socialist	11.87	15	9.86	21	4.99	5	1.87	7
Samyukta Socialist	founded in 1964						2.13	7
Subtotals	50.80	165	56.00	173	52.28	162	55.58	175
Communist								
CPI	10.76	28	17.82	46	24.96	50	6.53	16
CPM	founded in 1964						18.11	43
Subtotals	10.76	28	17.82	46	24.96	50	24.64	59
Marxist-Left								
Forward Bloc	5.29	11	3.84	8	4.61	13	3.87	13
Forward Bloc (Marxist)	—	—	0.85	2	0.32	0	0.21	1
SUC	—	—	0.75	2	0.73	0	0.72	4
RSP	0.86	0	1.24	3	2.56	9	2.14	6
RCPI	0.43	0	0.42	0	0.42	0	0.31	0
Worker's Party	—	—	—	—	0.29	0	0.34	2
Subtotals	6.59	11	7.10	15	8.91	22	7.59	26
Others								
Jan Sangh	5.61	9	0.98	0	0.45	0	1.33	1
Hindu Mahasabha	2.37	4	2.04	0	0.80	0	—	—
Swatantra Party	founded in 1959			0	0.57	0	0.81	1
Lok Sevak Sangh	—	—	0.82	7	0.72	4	0.68	5
Gurkha League	0.46	3	0.43	0	0.40	2	0.45	2
Subtotals	8.44	16	4.27	7	2.94	6	3.27	9
Independents	23.41	18	14.81	11	10.88	11	8.92	11
Totals	100.00	238	100.00	252	100.00	252	100.00	280

Source: Figures are taken from the *Reports* on the elections published by the Election Commission, Government of India.

The failure of the Congress to secure a majority in the 1967 elections was largely a result of the defection of the Bangla Congress from the regular Congress and the subsequent decision of the Bangla Congress to join the Communist parties in a governmental coalition. But as subsequent election results indicate, the elections of 1967 were a significant turning point in the political life of West Bengal, if only because they enabled the Communist and Marxist-Left parties to gain access to governmental offices that could in turn be used to enhance their political power. After 1967, the Communist and Marxist-Left parties of West Bengal continued to grow in popularity and influence, to the point where they commanded a larger portion of the state electorate than the Congress in 1971 and were therefore able to win more seats than the Congress in the state legislative assembly. Moreover, the opposition to the Congress has increasingly been willing to ally behind one single political party—the CPM—which has now established itself as the leading opposition force in West Bengal.

The CPM

The Communist Party of India (Marxist) (CPM) came into being on 11 April 1964, when 32 of the 65 members of the CPI National Council walked out of a party meeting being held in New Delhi. The dissident 32 members eventually organized their own convention (at Tenali, in Andhra Pradesh) in July 1964 and their own National Congress (in Calcutta) in October and have continued to insist that they are the only genuine successors to the traditions of the Indian Communist movement. While they have been able to attract at least as large a membership and following (both in India and in West Bengal) as the parent Communist party, they continue to be described as dissidents from the regular CPI by most people in India, and they have now accepted the party label (Communist Party of India [Marxist], or CPM) that the Election Commission and Indian journalists have assigned to them.

The West Bengal unit of the CPM, which is larger than that of any other state, contains two quite distinct factional interests, now allied because of their mutual interests in opposing the pro-Soviet "revisionism" of the CPI. The organizational apparatus (frequently called "the cadre") of the CPM is headed by Pramode Das Gupta, traces its origins back to the older terrorist federations in Bengal, and is attempting to develop mass militant movements that can eventually be used to do away with electoral politics. The electoral wing of the CPM is headed by Jyoti Basu, derives its strength from a wide variety of Bengali occupational strata, and is intent on coming to power by electoral means. In a marriage of convenience, the electoralists in the CPM have chosen to ally with the cadre because of the ability of the cadre to mobilize large numbers of people for electoral (and nonelectoral) purposes. The cadre, on the other hand, has thus far been convinced that it can develop mass militancy within the electoral framework, even though it is hopeful that it will eventually be able to destroy that framework.[10]

The entry of the CPM into the ministries of the coalition government of West Bengal in 1967 posed innumerable difficulties for the CPM. Most Communist parties that have come to power have gained control of the entire apparatus of a nation-state, and if they have used political alliances to capture office, they have at least had open to them the possibility of reducing the effectiveness of their allies through party control of the government. In every part of Asia but India, communism has come to power through war and violence rather than through parliamentary means. But the CPM in West Bengal entered the minsitries in 1967 as part of one of two electoral coalitions, in alliance with 13 other political parties whose members cover the ideological spectrum, with two bitterly opposed Communist parties in minority positions in both coalitions, and with the coalitions in control of only 1 of 18 Indian states. By the time the coalition did gain control of the governmental machinery of West Bengal, the parliamentary system in India was already highly institutionalized, the Communists had failed to make significant gains outside of the two states of Kerala and West Bengal, and the Congress was still in power in the Union government. In adjusting to their position of partial power in a tenuous state coalition government and in confronting the responsibilities of power in a constitutional system with the complexities of Indian federalism, it is little wonder that the CPM in West Bengal has been seriously divided about the strategies it should pursue.

The nature of the election results in 1967 presented the CPM with three alternatives: (1) the party could enter into a coalition in opposition to the Congress if it were willing to ally with the "revisionist" CPI and the "vested interests" in the Bangla Congress; (2) it could enter into a coalition against the CPI and the Bangla Congress only if it were willing to ally with the "reactionary" Congress party; (3) it could go into opposition against all political parties in the state by refusing to join a coalition, but in this case it would have remained out of power entirely. For the electoralists in the CPM the first alternative was clearly the least of three evils. The electoralists had always been opposed to a nonelectoral strategy in West

---

[10] Factionalism in the CPM is traced out in great detail in *Radical Politics in West Bengal*, see especially pp. 45–81 and 242–269.

Bengal but had been willing to ally with the Left faction in the CPM in order to gain the benefits of the superior organizational apparatus controlled by Pramode Das Gupta. Moreover, many of the electoralists had been advocating a rapprochement with the CPI since the split in 1964, and cooperation in the ministries was seen as an excellent starting point.[11] Finally, the electoralists would undoubtedly gain most of the ministerial appointments as well as the patronage that accompanied entry into the state ministries, and this was appealing to them not only because of the personal gains involved but also because of the leverage that it would give them within the CPM.

For many of the same reasons, the vast majority of the leadership of the Left faction in West Bengal was initially opposed to the entry of the CPM into the state ministries. But the leadership of the Left faction was also divided and confused on this issue, since it was conceivable that the state party could use the ministries to enhance the militancy of its cadre. The leadership of the regular party organization, led by Pramode Das Gupta, was clearly faced with the cruelest dilemma. A decision to join in the ministries would alienate a large portion of Das Gupta's own Left faction, on which his regular party organization depended for support, but a decision to remain out of the ministries would either leave the electoralist faction in control of the Communist ministries (if the central leadership of the party supported Jyoti Basu) or, more likely, would split the party for a second time. In the final analysis Das Gupta himself voted against the decision to enter the ministries, but enough Left faction leaders deserted him in the state secretariat (and in the Central Committee) to push through the resolution announcing the entry of the CPM into the United Front government.[12]

Once the CPM decided to enter the ministries in 1967, Das Gupta agreed to obey party discipline and rally his organization behind the electoralists in a united-front strategy. But the result of Das Gupta's acquiescence was a revolt within the regular CPM party organization in West Bengal, which eventually resulted in the formation of a third Communist party (the Communist Party of India [Marxist-Leninist], or CPML). Unlike the CPI and CPM, the CPML believes that the present situation in

[11] The position of the electoralists regarding cooperation in the United Front governments is perhaps best stated in Jyoti Basu, "The Need for Unity," *Link* (New Delhi Weekly), 26 January 1968, pp. 21–22.

[12] For a description of the inner-party maneuvering that took place prior to the announcement that the CPM would enter the ministries see ibid., 26 February 1967, p. 15, and 5 March 1967, p. 12.

India is ripe for a violent one-stage revolution, based on Maoist ideology, and brought about by violent insurrectionist tactics. The party was officially launched in 1969 (on the birthday of Lenin) but it draws its inspiration from the "Naxalbari" movement of March–July 1967, when CPML leaders seized land by force and murdered landlords and policemen in the Naxalbari area of Darjeeling district in northern West Bengal.[13] In addition to the CPML, there have been a number of other "Naxalite" groups that have come into being in West Bengal since 1967, all of which are followers of Maoism, even though they have serious disagreements about the application of Maoism to Indian conditions.

The strategy of the CPM since 1967 has been conditioned by its defensive position relative to almost all other political forces in the state. On the one hand, CPM leaders fear that a lack of militancy might cost the party the support of its most dedicated cadre, many members of which are inclined toward the CPML. On the other hand, years of experience have convinced the CPM leadership that an insurrectionist posture would most likely expose the party to severe repression, without necessarily enhancing the organizational strength of the CPM. Leaders of the CPM argue that the CPI has made a serious tactical mistake by aligning itself with the Congress party, since this has strengthened the Congress without bringing recognizable gains to the Communist movement, and the unity of the CPM has therefore depended on the resolve of its leadership to maintain an independent Communist position.

The ability of the CPM to maintain an independent Communist position has in turn depended on the willingness of CPM leaders to concentrate on party organizational problems without constant reference to international Communist disputes. Following the split in the Indian Communist movement in 1964, the CPM has therefore sought selective support from external Communist parties but has refused to ally itself unequivocally with either the CPSU or the CPC. While the CPI has the unquestioned backing of the Soviets, and the CPML is now recognized by China as "the only Communist party in India," the CPM has attempted to establish itself as the *de facto* leader of the Indian Communist movement on the basis of its independent party activities and the strengthening of its organizational base.

In this sense too, the decision to enter the ministries in West Bengal in 1967 created problems for the CPM, since it immediately alienated China and gave rise to speculation about a reunification of the CPM and the CPI.

---

[13] An excellent description of the Naxalbari movement and its consequences appears in Ghosh, *Disinherited State*, pp. 97–114.

Less than six months after the inauguration of the first West Bengal United Front government, the Central Committee of the CPM therefore explained in great detail the differences between the CPM and the Chinese positions in the ideological debate[14] and made arrangements to conduct a long-delayed inner-party discussion of ideological questions. In order to facilitate the discussion, the Central Committee drafted a 54-page document describing a proposal by which disputed ideological questions could be resolved, which was circulated to all levels of the party.[15] Each party member was instructed "to express his or her views in his unit on the document frankly," and members of higher committees were forbidden to express their views in the lower committees. All units were instructed to send their opinions to the next higher unit in the party or to relay their criticisms directly to the Central Committee through their State Committees. This discussion, which was initially expected to last four months, was not completed until April 1968 (more than eight months later), and a central plenum of the CPM then passed a resolution embodying the results.[16]

Because of the revolt of the Left faction of the CPM in 1967, the party was unable to arrive at a resolution of the ideological debate that could be unanimously supported by all segments of the party. In the words of a CPM Politburo statement,

The inner-party discussions over the Central Committee's draft on ideological questions have clearly revealed that a section of our party members not only find themselves in fundamental disagreement with the ideological draft but also with the Party Programme and the Party's line on the current situation as enunciated in . . . resolutions of the Central Committee.
. . . some comrades, contrary to the instructions of the Central Committee, thought it necessary to force the discussion on questions that were sought to be kept outside the discussion on the ideological draft.[17]

Lacking ideological unity, and faced with the revolt of the Maoists in 1967, both the Politburo and the Central Committee of the CPM attempted to preserve some semblance of party unity by expunging the most extreme

[14] *Divergent Views Between Our Party and the CPC on Certain Fundamental Issues, Resolution Adopted by the Central Committee of the Communist Party of India (Marxist), Madurai, 18–27 August 1967* (Calcutta: CPM, 1967).
[15] *Central Committee's Draft for the Ideological Discussion, Adopted by the Central Committee of the Communist Party of India (Marxist), Madurai, 18–27 August 1967* (Calcutta: CPM, 1967). The procedure for conducting the inner-party discussion is detailed on pp. 1–2.
[16] *Ideological Resolution, Adopted by the Central Plenum, Burdwan, 5–12 April 1968* (Calcutta: CPM, 1968). Hereafter cited as *Ideological Resolution*.
[17] *Ideological Debate Summed Up by Politbureau* (Calcutta: CPM, 1968), pp. 1–2.

"left deviationists" from the party while seeking to maintain the organizational backing of the bulk of the Left faction leaders. In ideological terms this meant that the party had to "fight against revisionism, while guarding against left-sectarian deviation," a stance that subjected the CPML and CPI to a series of strategic and tactical machinations in self-defense.[18] In terms of the international ideological debate, the CPM found it necessary to depict "modern revisionism" as *the main danger* in the international Communist movement at the present juncture," while merely warning party members "against slipping into left opportunism and sectarian errors." [19]

The decision of the CPM leaders to label Soviet revisionism as the "main danger" was partly a response to the severe factional quarrels between the CPM and the CPI and to the necessity for some CPM leaders to soften party criticism of the Left faction. At the same time, however, it stemmed from the widespread feeling among CPM members that communism in India had for too long been dominated by foreign Communist parties, with a consequent loss of dynamism in the Indian movement. The April 1968 resolution of the central plenum, for example, emphasized the need for "independence and equality among fraternal Communist parties":

A working class party can play the role of a revolutionary party only if it is firmly based on Marxism-Leninism and proletarian internationalism; only if it can, as correctly put by the CPC, "use its brains to think for itself" ... [rather than] parrot the words of others, copy foreign experience without analysis, [and] run hither and thither in response to the baton of certain persons abroad....[20]

In the eyes of CPM leaders, "this sound proletarian internationalist principle" was frequently "violated by big Parties," the "glaring example" of such violations being the actions of "the CPSU after its 20th Congress," although "the CPC ... [was] also sometimes found to disregard this principle." [21] In order to stake out a more independent role for itself within India, the CPM found it necessary to criticize both the CPSU and the CPC for such violations.

Since April 1968 the CPM has maintained its independent position in the ideological debate, identifying most closely with Castro's Cuba, North Vietnam, North Korea, student protest groups in the United States, and

---

[18] These are detailed in *Radical Politics in West Bengal*, pp. 149–181 and pp. 215–241.
[19] *Ideological Resolution*, p. 54. (Italics in original.)
[20] Ibid., pp. 50–52.
[21] Ibid., p. 53.

the liberation movements in Africa, while calling on both the CPSU and the CPC to correct their "revisionist" and "sectarian" errors.[22] Party leaders and documents still praise the Chinese revolution of 1949 as "one of the biggest triumphs of the world working class and the imperishable doctrine of Marxism-Leninism" and emphasize Chinese achievements in industry, agriculture, science, technology, and education. According to CPM literature, China has far outstripped India in economic and technological development, has more ably prepared itself for defense against American "imperialism" by developing nuclear weapons, and has performed a great service to socialism in this century by "initiating the fight against modern revisionism." At the same time, the CPC is criticized for "its erroneous outlook," which "liquidates the existence of the socialist camp" and "rejects the necessity for united action of the socialist camp." [23] In a similar manner, the Soviet Union is praised for carrying out the first significant socialist revolution and for supporting world revolution during the first four decades of Soviet rule. However, the CPSU is criticized for its present "lop-sided emphasis on the peace struggle," for "underplaying the importance of all-sided direct struggle against imperialism," and for "minimising in particular the significant role of the worldwide national liberation struggles at the present stage." [24] The CPM's affinity with Cuba, North Korea, North Vietnam, Indonesia, and the African liberation movements is in fact based on a common sentiment that the Soviet Union has failed to give adequate support to liberation movements in these areas.[25]

For many party members this ideological stance provides enough satisfaction to maintain a high level of party involvement. As one observer has pointed out,

To the revolutionaries outside the socialist countries . . . and even to many communists of Asia, Africa and Latin America, the obsessive desire of the Soviet Union to establish a working relationship with the U.S.A. and the frenzied efforts by China to instigate armed struggle in every nook and corner of the world [seem] equally futile. The impression among many Asian Communists is that both the socialist giants—rival claimants to the leadership of world revolution—are acting more and more as national

---

[22] Based on a content analysis of articles appearing in *People's Democracy* (CPM weekly) and *Desh Hitaishi* (CPM daily) in 1968–1971, and on interviews conducted in 1969–1972.

[23] *People's Democracy*, 28 September 1969, p. 1. For other CPM statements on China and the CPC, see ibid., 4 August 1968, pp. 1, 12; ibid., 22 December 1968, pp. 1, 12; ibid., 29 December 1968, p. 1; and ibid., 23 February 1969, pp. 4, 10.

[24] *CPI(M) Central Committee Statement on Moscow Conference* (Calcutta: CPM, 1969), p. 5.

[25] Ibid., pp. 2, 10.

states, as cynically opportunist Big Powers, and not as the trusted vanguard of a worldwide revolutionary process.

Communism, of both the Soviet and Chinese varieties, appears to be turning into an Establishment, with hardly any message for . . . the socialist revolutionaries of the Third World.[26]

Among party *leaders* in the CPM, however, the ideological stance of the party is more closely tied to their own factional interests and their own contacts in the international Communist movement. The electoralists in the CPM, led by Jyoti Basu and E. M. S. Namboodiripad (of Kerala), are still critical of the party's unwillingness to seek the mediation of Moscow in Indian Communist disputes, but they have so far been reluctant to impose their views on the party. Basu and Namboodiripad did express a desire to be present at the meetings of the world Communist parties in 1967 (on the occasion of the fiftieth anniversary of the Russian Revolution), but the Central Committee of the CPM refused their request to travel to Moscow for fear that "the dazzling atmosphere of Moscow might lure them back to the pro-Soviet CPI." [27] Therefore, none of the meetings called by Moscow in 1967, 1968, and 1969 were attended by CPM delegates, and the CPM kept itself informed of the meetings only by means of visits by Left and electoral faction leaders to Romania and Great Britain, both countries whose parties have cooled toward, but not broken with, Moscow.

While the electoralists in the CPM have not been willing to press for closer relations with Moscow, they have insisted that pictures of Mao Tse-tung not be displayed at party conferences, that both China and the Soviet Union be equally blamed for Sino-Soviet border clashes, and that China be "corrected" for its open condemnation of the Soviet invasion of Czechoslovakia.[28] Moreover, electoral faction leaders have been able to include themselves in delegations selected by the CPM to travel to Europe and Vietnam and have been responsible for strong party statements criticizing Chinese support of Indian Naxalites. Factional struggles over control of the domestic stance of the CPM therefore find parallels in the approach of various party leaders to international ideological disputes, leaving open the possibility that either international or domestic events might at some point in the future disrupt the balance that has been achieved in recent years.

[26] O. P. Sangal, "Moscow Meet Saw a Fractured Globe," *Citizen and Weekend Review*, 28 June 1969, p. 23.
[27] *Citizen and Weekend Review*, 4 November 1967, p. 14.
[28] See the *Hindusthan Standard* (Calcutta daily), 24 December 1968; *Amrita Bazaar Patrika* (Calcutta daily), 17 March 1969; and *People's Democracy*, 25 August 1968, pp. 1, 2, 10.

Thus the independence and flexibility of the CPM in matters of state and national politics must be viewed as the consequence of a precarious balance of competing forces within the party rather than as a consensus based on the firm commitment of major factional interests. Each of the resolutions adopted by the CPM since February 1967, whether on ideological or tactical issues, has created great strains and tensions among factions, and each has been passed only after inner-party accommodation on a host of amendments and alterations. Both Left and electoral faction leaders have differed publicly with the party on a number of occasions, both have been disciplined by the Central Committee, and both factions have resorted to threats and cajolery. The success of CPM leaders in reconciling diverse factional interests both on political and on ideological matters since 1967 suggests that continued unity depends on organizational and electoral success, while the persistence of long-standing factional interests points to the fragile nature of party unity, which might shatter in the event of reverses.

The United Front Governments and Other Radical Parties

During the period of the United Front governments (1967–1970), the CPM attempted to maintain its independence in West Bengal by pursuing what it called a "modified Right" strategy and "united front from below" tactics.[29] Like the classical Right Communist strategy, the modified Right strategy calls for a two-stage revolution, with the Communists coming to complete power only in the second stage and only after preconditions have been established in the first stage. During the first stage the Communists seek to ally with the broadest strata of the population (particularly peasants and workers, but also the petty bourgeoisie and the anti-imperialist sections of the bourgeoisie) by outbidding the nationalist and reformist parties (such as the Congress and the Bangla Congress) for their support. However, like the classical Left Communist strategy, the modified Right strategy insists on leadership of the alliance by the "true" Communist party and a power base that is separate from that of the nationalist parties and the other parties in the alliance. This last requirement stems from the need to exert constant pressure on the nationalist parties and to prevent parties allied with the "true" Communist party from "backsliding" on the way to the second stage of the revolution. In short, the insistence on CPM

[29] For an analysis of the "modified Right" Communist strategy and "united front from below" tactics, see Donald S. Zagoria, "Communist Policy and the Struggle for the Developing Countries," *Proceedings of the Academy of Political Science* 28 (April 1965), 69 ff.

leadership of the United Front governments in West Bengal stemmed from the need for a "united front from below."

In order to pursue its "united front from below" strategy during the period of the two United Front (UF) governments, the CPM insisted that it have control of the police, land revenue, and labor ministries, all three of which were instructed to work in conjunction with mass organizations and political parties. CPM land revenue minister Hare Krishna Konar, for example, argued that the police in West Bengal were "in the habit of readily going into action on the complaints of big *jotedars* (landholders)," and he therefore instructed police officials (through the CPM minister of police, Jyoti Basu) that policemen were "to consult officers of the Land Revenue Department before they decided to act on the basis of *jotedars*' complaints."[30] At the same time Konar stated that the government would make every effort to enlist the cooperation of rural mass organizations behind a program of land reforms, in order to ensure "prompt action, instead of allowing time to *jotedars* to go for court injunctions which delay distribution of vested land."[31]

As a result of this policy a large number of rural political leaders in West Bengal began to organize peasants to take possession of lands held by *jotedars* in excess of the 25-acre statutory ceiling—particularly benami lands (i.e., lands held by relatives), fisheries, and land held in the names of tenants and the state government—and the CPM state secretariat even issued a directive to party workers to "recover benami lands and distribute them among the landless peasants."[32] During the first UF government, in 1967, the front claimed that it had redistributed 248,000 acres of land, largely land that had been earmarked for transfer by the previous Congress government but had not yet been redistributed because of court cases, bureaucratic delay, and political favoritism. During the second UF government, in 1969–1970, the UF claimed redistribution of another 200,000 acres. Since the total acreage under cultivation in West Bengal is estimated at 13,400,000, the land involved in the UF's redistribution programs amounted to only a little more than 3 percent of the total arable land, but the transfers that did take place had a considerable impact at least on the style of politics conducted in the state.

During the United Front ministries, the CPM was not the only party that took part in the land redistribution movement. Almost every party in the UF sought to use the policy of the Land Revenue Ministry to its own advantage, either by expanding its peasant organizations by the adoption

[30] *Statesman* (Calcutta), 18 March 1969.
[31] Ibid.
[32] *Hindusthan Standard*, 27 March 1969.

of strategies like the CPM's or by resisting the CPM in the hope of discrediting the new tactic. Land Revenue Minister Konar did issue a warning to the other parties in the front that they should be wary of "indiscriminate acts of seizure" if they had "no mass base and little idea about land records," [33] but his warnings did not deter the larger UF partners (CPI, Forward Bloc, SUC, RSP, and Bangla Congress) from active participation in the land redistribution program. The result was a flurry of political activity in the West Bengal countryside, with units of at least five major parties in the United Front organizing peasants to seize lands and fisheries, with a larger and larger volume of court cases and countercases being filed back and forth by landholders, tenants, government, and political parties, and with the administrative and police services remaining generally inactive as violence became the order of the day.

On the trade union front the strategy and tactics of the CPM during the two UF governments were devised in a similar manner. In the words of the Central Committee, "The effort for united front from below includes constant appeals to all sections of workers. . . . It consists of joint actions at the base, in factories, *under our initiative*." [34] The tactics of the CPM, according to the Central Committee, were aimed "at organizing a disciplined working class with revolutionary socialist consciousness, drawing it nearer the Party, with its best elements joining the Party in hundreds, enabling the class as a whole to play its historic political role in the revolutionary struggle." [35]

However, the position of the CPM in the trade union movement in West Bengal differs significantly from its position in the peasant organizations. In contrast to the mass peasant organizations in West Bengal, which have never been well established, trade unions have effectively engaged in mass agitational activities and have played an important role in the politics of the state since the 1920s. By 1967 the CPM was clearly on the defensive in the all-India trade union front despite its control of large numbers of trade unions in the state, and a number of the other parties in the UF governments (and even the Congress) could boast of larger membership figures for affiliated trade unions. This was in sharp contrast to the peasant front, where the CPM was the only party that had attempted to form mass organizations on a large scale. The position of the party in the trade union

[33] *Amrita Bazaar Patrika*, 14 April 1969. For the reaction of the regular CPI to this challenge, see Ajoy Dasgupta, "West Bengal: Peasants' Initiative," *New Age* (CPI weekly), 4 May 1969, p. 4.
[34] *Tasks on the Trade Union Front, Resolution of the Central Committee of the Communist Party of India—Marxist* (Calcutta: CPM, 1967), p. 33. Italics in the original.
[35] Ibid., pp. 3–4.

Table 3.4   Indices of Trade Union Activity in West Bengal

	1964	1965	1966	1967
Number of disputes raised during the year	6,187	6,444	6,720	10,331
Number of work stoppages	215	228	244	447
Number of men involved in work stoppages	113,695	123,654	154,354	169,259
Number of man-days lost	1,556,185	1,362,568	2,754,447	6,118,816
Number of unions	269	257	274	897
Membership (claimed by unions)	42,469	42,990	33,274	128,794

Source: *Labour in West Bengal, 1967*, compiled by Government of West Bengal, Statistics, Research and Publications Branch of the Labour Directorate (Calcutta: West Bengal Director of Information, 1967), pp. 1, 2, 14.

front was acknowledged by the CPM Central Committee in a 1967 report to party members:

> We must constantly bear in mind that . . . we ourselves form a far from dominating and leading force in the organised trade unions, the other sections being stronger than us in many industries and equal to us in some industries.[36]

Because of its minority position in the trade union movement in 1967, the CPM pursued what the Central Committee called "the real bolshevik method of mobilising the masses" during the UF governments. This consisted of militant and aggressive tactics toward employers and other trade unions but "supplemented by offers of united front from the top which at times is a pre-condition of united front from below." [37]

The environment in which the CPM pursued this strategy and tactical line was one of great ferment and upheaval. The increased activities of all the trade unions in West Bengal after the UF's assumption of political power in 1967 is indicated by a number of factors, some of which are listed in table 3.4. The table makes it quite clear that the activities of the trade unions in 1967 were far greater than in any previous year, regardless of the index that is being used. While complete figures are not available for 1968 and 1969, those that have been published show that the activities of trade unions in the state have continued to increase at an extremely rapid rate. Figures published by the Labour Department during the period of President's Rule in 1968, for example, showed that the number of men involved in work stoppages in 1968 was "nearly double the number in the previous

[36] Ibid., p. 30.
[37] Ibid., p. 31.

year," while man-days lost in 1968 "surpassed all previous records, not only of West Bengal but of any other State of India." [38]

The reasons for this growth in trade union activity obviously stemmed from the two UF governments' approach to labor. Immediately upon assuming office, the first UF labour minister (Subodh Banerjee of the SUC), supported by all of the parties in the United Front, announced "a break with the past, with the anti-people and bureaucratic policies and approach of the Congress." [39] The essential feature of Banerjee's "new approach" was the attempt "to enlist the people's cooperation for the implementation of policies rather than depend on the administrative machinery." Through a series of devices the Labour Ministry sought to create machinery that would "solve industrial disputes as expeditiously as possible and prohibit police interference in normal trade union disputes": All committees and boards of the Labour Department were completely reorganized "on a more democratic basis"; the police were instructed not to interfere in "the legitimate democratic trade union movement"; and layoff or retrenchment without the sanction of the government was "discouraged." Especially important for the style of trade union politics in the state was the decision by the first UF Labour Ministry to legalize the tactic of *gherao*.

A *gherao* consists essentially of a blockade, imposed by a number of trade union workers on the office of a manager or group of managers for a considerable period of time. The employees who are "*gheraoing*" the manager usually squat around him, shout slogans, and sometimes take turns abusing him. In many cases food or water is not allowed to reach the person being *gheraoed*, and electricity, telephones, and bathroom facilities are frequently rendered inaccessible. *Gheraos* have varied in length from a few hours to several days, and the goal of those who stage *gheraos* is usually the extraction of signatures on documents that would not be signed under normal circumstances. The tactic had been in use in West Bengal for at least a decade prior to the assumption of political power by the United Front, but it had always been considered illegal and improper by the Congress governments. When it was declared legal by the state Labour Ministry in 1967, the number of *gheraos* throughout the state mushroomed disconcertingly. According to the most authoritative estimates available, there were 1,018 *gheraos* in 583 establishments in West Bengal during the

[38] Manindra Bhattacharjee, "1968: A Bad Year for Labour," *Hindusthan Standard Weekly Supplement*, 31 December 1968, p. iv.
[39] The labor policy of the first UF government is described in Ajoy Dasgupta, "Bengal: A New Approach to People's Problems," *New Age*, 16 April 1967, p. 4. The quotations that follow are taken from this article.

six-month period March–August 1967,[40] and only one party in the United Front (the Bangla Congress) ceased to support *gheraos* after they were declared illegal by the Calcutta High Court.[41] Because of their support by the other UF parties, *gheraos* became a regular feature of life in West Bengal after 1967, despite the ruling of the judiciary.

The new approach of the state Labour Ministry, which did not change appreciably when the ministry was assumed by the CPM in February 1969, provided an impetus to the organization of trade unions in West Bengal during the United Front period. From March–September 1967, for example, 591 new trade unions were registered in West Bengal, by far the largest short-run increase that had ever taken place.[42] Moreover, the vast majority of these unions were affiliated with political parties, and their origins were unquestionably a result of the feeling on the part of workers that trade union organizations might be more effective under the UF than they had been under the Congress regime. In this scramble to increase the unionization of workers, the CPM and the CPI were by far the largest gainers, with the CPM adding 170 new trade unions between March and September 1967 and the CPI 140 during the same period, a combined total that accounts for more than half of the new trade unions founded in this period. That both the CPM and the CPI used the tactic of *gherao* to gain support among trade union workers is shown by the fact that 397 of the 1,018 cases of *gherao* in March–August 1967 were instigated by CPM or CPI trade unions. The success of the CPM in expanding its trade union base was strikingly demonstrated by its increased support among labor unions in the Calcutta industrial belt in the 1969 and 1971 election campaigns.

In addition to their acquisition of new affiliates, both the CPM and CPI made concerted efforts to infiltrate and capture trade unions of other parties during the United Front governments. A survey carried out by the CPI in May 1969, for example, indicated that the CPM had been able to capture the registered trade unions of other parties in 10 establishments during the months of February, March, and April 1969, while in another 60 industrial concerns it was still waging protracted fights with trade unions

[40] Nitish R. De and Suresh Srivastava, "Gheraos in West Bengal–I," *Economic and Political Weekly* (Bombay), 18 November 1967, p. 2015.
[41] Relevant rulings of the Calcutta High Court on cases of *gherao* are reprinted in Arjun P. Aggarwal, *Gheraos and Industrial Relations* (Bombay: N. M. Tripathi Private Ltd., 1968), pp. 172–175.
[42] Nitish R. De and Suresh Srivastava, "Gheraos in West Bengal–III," *Economic and Political Weekly*, 2 December 1967, p. 2099.

controlled by non-Communist parties.[43] According to the same survey, the CPM was gaining considerable ground among jute and textile industry unions in West Bengal, though it was perhaps losing some of its affiliates in the engineering industry. Of particular concern to the CPI was the fact that the CPM had either formed new trade unions or captured existing organizations in more than 200 establishments where there were unions affiilated with the CPI. As a result of the aggressiveness of CPM trade union organizers during the UF period, a number of the Marxist-Left parties repeatedly threatened to quit the UF government, and many of them fought back with arms and assassination. The most serious clashes between the UF parties were those that involved the CPM, with the RSP, SUC, SSP, Forward Bloc, and CPI providing the opposition.[44]

Electoral Politics after the United Front
Because the CPM was clearly the most aggressive of the state parties in seeking to cement its relationships with peasants and trade union members, the other parties in the UF became increasingly willing to unite against it, with the result that the second UF government fell from power in March 1970. But in spite of its relative isolation during the next state elections (in February 1971) the CPM was able to emerge as the leading political party in the state, in an electoral situation that was even more highly factionalized than it had been before. In the 1971 state assembly elections in West Bengal, the CPM was allied with four of the smallest Marxist-Left parties (the Revolutionary Communist Party of India, the Worker's Party, the Forward Bloc [Marxist], and the Biplabi Bangla Congress) in an electoral coalition known as the United Left Front (ULF), which succeeded in capturing a total of 123 of 277 seats (see table 3.5). Allied against the CPM was a four-party electoral coalition led by the CPI, known as the United Left Democratic Front (ULDF) as well as nine other parties that succeeded in capturing at least 1 seat each. While the ULDF could win only 25 seats in the state assembly, Indira Gandhi's New Congress garnered a total of 105 seats, and these two totals, when combined with the totals of other parties running independently of electoral coalitions, were enough to keep the CPM from assuming power in 1971. After the 1971 elections, a Congress-led coalition government was formed in West Bengal, with

---

[43] The results of the survey are detailed in *Amrita Bazaar Patrika*, 14 May 1969.
[44] For an analysis of trade union feuds between rival parties in the UF, see Amitava Das Gupta, "Inter-Party Rivalries: A Real Danger to the United Front," *Hindusthan Standard*, 27 May 1969.

nine political parties tenuously allied with the New Congress in the ministries, but this government fell within a month.[45]

A major turning point for the CPM came in the 1972 elections when the CPM was absolutely routed by Mrs. Gandhi's New Congress, which has since formed the government in West Bengal. As is indicated in table 3.5, the CPM in 1972 suffered one of the worst defeats that has befallen any electoral party anywhere in the world, winning only 14 of 280 seats and 27.53 percent of the vote (compared with 111 seats and 33.8 percent of the vote in 1971). Not only was the CPM bested in virtually every district of West Bengal, but so were its Marxist-Left allies (the RCPI, Worker's Party, Forward Bloc, Forward Bloc [Marxist], Revolutionary Socialist Party, and Socialist Unity Centre), which had hesitatingly rejoined the CPM in an electoral alliance against the resurgent Congress. Representative of the crushing defeat of the CPM was the party's loss in Baranagar constituency, where Jyoti Basu secured only 30.4 percent of the votes, thereby losing an election for the first time in his life (Basu had held elective office in West Bengal since 1946).

The 1972 elections in West Bengal were significant from a number of different perspectives, but perhaps their most important aspect for the future of electoral politics in West Bengal was the allegation by the CPM and its allies that the elections were not free and fair. From the very beginning of the election campaign in 1972, the CPM charged that the state Congress party youth and student wings (the Yuvak Congress and the Chhatra Parishad) had collaborated with hired goondas (thugs) to "let loose a reign of unbridled terror and physical attacks" against CPM candidates and supporters, which made it impossible for the CPM to conduct a normal election campaign. Moreover, the CPM state committee issued a statement in which it alleged that the Election Commission had "removed thousands of names of genuine voters from the electoral rolls with the specific objective of helping the ruling party," while "thousands of fake names were added to pad the electoral rolls." [46] In a memorandum to Mrs. Gandhi in late January, the leader of the West Bengal CPM electoral organization, Mr. Jyoti Basu, listed 34 West Bengal assembly constituencies where "free and fair elections had been seriously endangered"

45 Six of the nine parties in the 1971 state coalition government were represented in the ministries: the New Congress, Bangla Congress, Gurkha League, Muslim League, PSP, and SSP. Three of the nine parties supporting the ministry chose not to be represented in the ministries: the CPI, the Forward Bloc, and the Old Congress. The combined number of seats for the nine parties in the coalition was 141, one more than a majority if all 280 members of the state legislative assembly had been elected, and two more than a majority in a 277-member assembly.
46 Statesman (New Delhi), 17 and 19 January 1972.

Table 3.5   West Bengal Legislative Assembly Results, 1967–1972

Parties	1967 % Votes	Seats	1969 % Votes	Seats	1971 % Votes	Seats	1972 % Votes	Seats
Social-Democratic								
Congress	41.1	127	40.4	55	29.8	105	49.1	216
Congress (O)	Founded in late 1969				5.9	2	1.4	2
Bangla Congress	10.4	34	8.0	33	5.5	5	(joined Congress)	
Socialists[a]	4.0	14	3.1	14	2.4	4	1.2	0
Subtotals	55.5	175	51.5	102	43.6	116	51.7	218
Communist								
CPI	6.5	16	6.8	30	8.6	13	8.4	35
CPM	18.1	43	19.6	80	33.8	111	27.5	14
Subtotals	24.6	59	26.4	110	42.4	124	35.9	49
Marxist-Left								
Forward Bloc	3.9	13	5.4	21	3.7	3	2.7	0
Forward Bloc (Marxist)	0.2	1	0.2	1	0.2	2	0.2	0
SUC	0.7	4	1.5	7	1.5	7	1.4	1
RSP	2.1	6	2.8	12	2.3	3	2.0	3
RCPI	0.3	0	0.4	2	0.4	3	0.2	0
Worker's Party	0.3	2	0.4	2	0.4	2	0.2	1
Subtotals	7.5	26	10.7	45	8.5	20	6.6	5
Other parties								
Lok Sevak Sangh	0.7	5	0.7	4	0.5	0	0.4	0
Gurkha League	0.5	2	0.5	4	0.5	2	0.5	2
Muslim League	—	—	1.5	3	1.7	7	1.0	1
Subtotals	1.2	7	2.7	11	2.7	9	1.9	3
Independents	11.2	13	8.7	12	3.4	8	3.9	5
Totals	100.0	280	100.0	280	100.0	277[b]	100.0	280

Source: Figures for 1967 are taken from the *Report* of the Election Commission. Figures for 1969, 1971, and 1972 are from the cyclostyled sheets distributed after each election by the Press Information Bureau of India.
[a] Figures for 1967, 1968, and 1969 are the combined totals for the Praja Socialist Party (PSP) and Samyukta Socialist Party (SSP), which merged to form the Socialist Party in 1972.
[b] Elections were not held in three constituencies in 1971 because of the deaths of candidates.

as a result of "violent operations by Congress hoodlums and the police." Continuing further, the memorandum stated:

... hoodlums operate almost in all cases with the knowledge of the local police and with their active help. In every case where rowdies are confronted by the local people, the police actively intervene to beat up and arrest those who defend themselves. There are cases where Congress hoodlums dragged people out of their homes, beat them and then handed them over to the police. But the police, instead of apprehending the Congress supporters for taking law into their hands, arrest their victims.[47]

In its last issue before the 1972 elections, the CPM party weekly (*People's Democracy*) stated that 487 CPM organizers and supporters had been killed in West Bengal since the downfall of the last United Front government on 16 March 1970, the names of which had all been listed in previous issues of the newspaper.[48] Moreover, the party called for an 11-point program to "restore social and political peace to West Bengal," which included demands for freedom of assembly, assurances against indiscriminate arrests, release of political prisoners detained without trial, and withdrawal of the Central Reserve Police from West Bengal. At the same time, however, CPM leaders indicated that they did not expect their demands to be met, nor did they expect the campaign of violence against the CPM to stop, since, in Jyoti Basu's words, the CPM had become the object of a "conspiracy at the top." [49]

In response to these charges, Mrs. Gandhi stated that Basu's January memorandum was filled with "blatant lies," and pointed to statistics to show that the incidence of violence in West Bengal had actually declined after the imposition of President's Rule in 1970. Moreover, a number of central government leaders undertook tours of West Bengal to investigate the allegations of the CPM, and all issued positive (if qualified) statements attesting to the fairness of the elections and the decrease in violent activities. The central election commissioner, Mr. S. P. Sen-Verma, for example, found after his tour of the state that the elections were "undoubtedly fair," although he also admitted that "there are pockets of dissidence where normal campaigning has been somewhat circumscribed." [50] At present the Election Commission is investigating charges that the electoral rolls were tampered with by political parties. Similarly, Mr. K. C. Pant, union minister of state for home affairs, found that there

[47] *Times of India* (New Delhi), 1 February 1972.
[48] *People's Democracy*, 5 March 1972, p. 4.
[49] *Hindustan Times* (New Delhi daily), 1 February 1972.
[50] *Statesman* (New Delhi), 3 March 1972.

had been a "striking improvement in the law and order situation in West Bengal," but with the significant exception of "inter-party clashes," which Mr. Pant described as follows: "very often the case is the CPM's resistance in its strongholds to the entry of Congressmen, or the CPM's bid to dislodge Congress members." [51] The union home secretary (Mr. Govind Narain) also found that violent political incidents in West Bengal had declined—from 646 in the month of July 1971 to only 92 in January 1972—while political murders had declined from 125 in July 1971 to only 17 in January 1972. [52]

From the point of view of the central government, no one was willing to argue that the 1972 elections in West Bengal were held in an atmosphere of complete calm, but granted the recent political history of West Bengal, many observers were surprised that the elections could be held without greater violence and disruption than that which undoubtedly took place. Much of the credit for the degree of order that did exist should go to the governor of West Bengal under President's Rule, Mr. A. L. Dias, who did not hesitate to use the Indian army and the police services to maintain law and order during the election campaign and polling. This aspect of the 1972 election was supervised by a special election "cell" that was established in the West Bengal Home Department, under the direct authority of the West Bengal home secretary, Mr. M. M. Kusari, which was instructed "to deal with law and order problems that may arise in connection with the holding of the elections [and] to create a climate of confidence for the holding of a free and fair election." [53]

In order to promote the possibility that elections would be free and fair, more than 56,000 police and security personnel were detailed to guard candidates, party installations, and polling stations throughout the state, while all district police headquarters were provided with special radio transmission vans to patrol polling areas. [54] Prior to the elections over 6,000 "anti-social elements" were arrested in West Bengal under preventive detention legislation, and 800 political prisoners being held under the Maintenance of Internal Security Act were transferred from West Bengal to jails in Tamil Nadu to relieve jails in West Bengal that were described by West Bengal chief secretary N. C. Sengupta as being "too overcrowded." [55] In addition to the West Bengal police, other police units (the Central Reserve Police and the Border Security Forces) were called

[51] Ibid., 11 March 1972.
[52] *Hindustan Times*, 6 February 1972.
[53] *Statesman* (New Delhi), 29 February 1972.
[54] *Hindusthan Standard*, 11 March 1972.
[55] Ibid., 27 February 1972.

in to assist with the maintenance of law and order, while Indian army contingents were dispatched to every district headquarters and special army camps were set up in "sensitive areas." [56]

Under these circumstances, most observers and politicians in West Bengal were ready to admit (privately if not publicly) that some Congress youth may have ganged up on the CPM, with the assistance of "anti-social elements" and the police.[57] But those opposed to the CPM were quick to point out that the situation in 1972 was much better than in 1971, when elections in three West Bengal constituencies had to be postponed because of the deaths of *candidates*. In the words of a *Statesman* editorial,

> The claim by West Bengal's Inspector-General of Police that the law and order situation in the State is 'normal' . . . tends to confirm the Chief Election Commissioner's view, expressed late last month, that the State is in this respect 'definitely' in a better condition than it was last year. Much would of course depend on what is conceived to be 'normal' and too strict an application of this concept would almost certainly be misleading in West Bengal's conditions. . . .[58]

Moreover, most observers in India could muster little sympathy for the CPM in West Bengal, since it was patently clear to everyone that the CPM itself had been more responsible than any other party for the rapid increase in violent activities after 1967. To quote Mr. N. C. Menon, a correspondent for the *Hindustan Times* (New Delhi),

> If the CPM now complains that they are unable even to enter some of the constituencies, there is undeniably some truth in the charge, but the party is only reaping the whirlwind of violence they themselves have sown.[59]

In short, the allegations of the CPM, that the 1972 elections in West Bengal were not free and fair, throw into bold relief the dilemma that all democratic societies face when trying to allow normal freedoms to a political party that is committed to the use of violence. To refuse to use the

[56] *Hindustan Times*, 25 February 1972.
[57] As N. C. Menon has pointed out, "[West Bengal] as a whole, and Calcutta in particular, has always had a large brigade of mercenary activists, available to the highest bidder for whatever dirty work was afoot—political, industrial or to do with violent trade unionism. In the shameful history of political patronage to such anti-social elements, no single party has its hands clean. It has also been normal practice for anti-social elements to take on the political or ideological hues of whichever party or group seemed to be more powerful, only to defect and change colour when the balance of power changes. With the increasing power and influence of the Congress in the State, large sections of such mercenaries gravitated towards it." See N. C. Menon, "West Bengal Elections: Role of Anti-Social Elements," *Hindustan Times*, 15 March 1972.
[58] *Statesman*, 3 March 1972.
[59] *Hindustan Times*, 26 February 1972.

police and the army to control organized violence is to invite greater and greater disruption, to the point where a democratic process becomes impossible. But by using the police and the army against those who claim to use violence legitimately, a democratic party government always leaves itself open to the charge that it is using its near-monopoly of the use of force to destroy competitive opposition parties. What was striking about the 1972 elections in this context was the willingness and ability of the Congress party in West Bengal to effectively counter the violent tactics that had been initiated by the CPM, in sharp contrast to the previous lack of effectiveness on the part of Congress organizations.

Much of the effectiveness of the Congress was in turn related to the feeling among Congress workers that the Bangladesh crisis had seriously crippled the CPM and the Naxalites—the two principal political forces in West Bengal capable of promoting widespread organized violence. For the Naxalites, the failure of China to support the Bangladesh liberation struggle proved disastrous, since it shattered the small factional Naxalite units that were already in disarray prior to 1971. One section of the Naxalite CPML, led by Charu Majumdar, argued consistently that the Bangladesh movement of Sheikh Mujibur Rahman and his Awami League was the result of an "anti-China conspiracy contrived by U.S. imperialists, Soviet revisionists, and Indian reactionaries," but this position lost its force when the United States failed to support the Bangladesh Awami League, and China gave its support to the Pakistani military regime of Yahya Khan. Another section of the CPML, led by Ashim Chatterjee, alienated itself from the Charu Majumdar faction of the party, when it gave full support to the Yahya Khan regime, which, according to Ashim Chatterjee, "belonged to the anti-imperialist camp by virtue of its alliance with China." [60]

After Ashim Chatterjee was arrested by the police in early November 1971 and Charu Majumdar was subsequently expelled by the Central Committee of the CPML, clashes between Naxalites (in the jails as well as outside) intensified, and a number of Naxalite activists immediately began to switch their political loyalties. Somewhat suprisingly, most of the Naxalites who did defect to other political parties in West Bengal in late 1971 chose to join with the Congress, since this action enabled them to maintain their personal factional stance against both the CPI and CPM. The result is that the Congress ranks in West Bengal in 1972—particularly the student and youth wings of the Congress—received a significant boost. Not only

[60] A summary of Naxalite factionalism in response to the Bangladesh crisis appears in Hiranmay Karlekar, "The Bangladesh Liberation: Impact on West Bengal Politics," *Statesman* (Delhi), 1 January 1972.

did the Congress acquire a large number of idealistic youth who had previously been engaged in Naxalite militant political activities, it also found that it could resist the cadre of the CPM without having to fear the large-scale attacks from Naxalites that had been characteristic of past electoral campaigns.

Moreover, the CPM had also alienated a large portion of the West Bengal electorate in 1971 by seriously miscalculating the effectiveness of Mrs. Gandhi's policies toward Bangladesh. In mid-1971, for example, the CPM argued that the Indian government had failed to give adequate relief to the Bangladesh refugees (in the words of the CPM Bengali daily, *Desh Hitaishi* "[the refugees] are presented with death and the agony of hell on crossing the border and setting foot on the territory of the Congress-League Government led by Indiraji . . . there is not the slightest arrangement for relief"),[61] an assessment that lost its credibility when the Indian government carried out one of the most successful relief operations ever witnessed in South Asia. To take another example, the CPM throughout 1971 constantly accused Mrs. Gandhi of "uttering brave words and doing very little [for Bangladesh]," [62] but this position failed to gain public support when Mrs. Gandhi was able to fight a quick and successful war against Pakistan for the liberation of Bangladesh.

Encouraged by the success of Mrs. Gandhi's diplomatic moves during the Bangladesh crisis and buoyed by the addition to their ranks of young, bright Naxalite activists, a number of Congress youth and student organizations came to life in 1972, and it was these organizations that aggressively fought against the CPM during the election campaign. Moreover, Mrs. Gandhi encouraged the youth and student wings of the Congress by personally intervening in the state nomination process to grant 125 party tickets to members of Congress youth and student organizations, a larger number by far than in any other Indian state. Mrs. Gandhi was also instrumental in bringing about an electoral alliance with the CPI in West Bengal, which had gained considerable prestige in the state as a result of the Indo-Soviet Treaty and the support exhibited by the Soviet Union during the Bangladesh liberation movement. While an electoral alliance with the CPI (Congress supported the CPI in 41 of 280 West Bengal constituencies) did create strains and tensions among the older Congress leaders, it was extremely popular with the more leftist-oriented youth and student wings of the Congress.

Mrs. Gandhi also aided the Congress campaign against the CPM in West Bengal in 1972 by addressing 26 political meetings scattered

---

[61] *Desh Hitaishi*, 11 June 1971.
[62] *People's Democracy*, 14 November 1971.

throughout the state during three separate campaign trips from New Delhi. During her campaign appearances, Mrs. Gandhi articulated a "pledge to the people of West Bengal" that there would be "rapid economic advance if the Congress was returned in sufficient strength to form a stable government in the state." [63] Mrs. Gandhi spoke of "special programmes" being set up for "*harijans* [untouchables], *adivasis* [tribals], and minority communities who have fallen behind"; she talked of massive flood control schemes and a large-scale expansion of trade to be carried out in cooperation with the Bangladesh government; she stated that she would work to "frame a law for curbing the arbitrary powers of industrial owners to dismiss workers"; she promised that the central government would invest considerably more resources in Calcutta and West Bengal than it had in the past; and she repeatedly assured the electorate that Congress policies (including new land reform legislation) would be implemented with "the good of the people in mind" rather than for "private interests." [64]

In a more concrete manner, Mrs. Gandhi could point to specific programs and actions that she and the Dias administration in West Bengal had undertaken in 1971, which were designed both to develop the state and to blunt the growing popularity of the Marxists. In August 1971, Mrs. Gandhi announced a 16-point program for the development of the West Bengal economy, which included plans for a new bridge across the Hooghly river in Calcutta, more rapid development of a new port city at Haldia (complete with a large fertilizer factory and other industries), and a number of schemes (including an underground railway) designed to make the city of Calcutta a more livable metropolitan area. On a smaller but no less important scale, the 16-point program included a promise to release substantial orders of India's railway wagon-building industry to factories in West Bengal, a target of 2,000 small industrial units to be set up in West Bengal each year, assurances of timely and sufficient supply of credit and raw materials to West Bengal industry, permission to work multiple shifts, and provision of concessional finance for industries to be set up in "backward areas" of the state. The 16-point program also contained a promise that the Indian government would review its scheme of incentives in order to make them more attractive to West Bengal businessmen. [65]

In November 1971, the Indian government released its promised

---

[63] *Times of India*, 1 March 1972.

[64] *Statesman* (New Delhi), 9 March 1972.

[65] A review of Mrs. Gandhi's economic initiatives in West Bengal during 1971 is "Economy of West Bengal—and Bangladesh," *Eastern Economist* 58, (7 January 1972), 12–13.

scheme for incentives, which were more or less patterned after those granted previously (with considerable success) to Maharashtra and other Indian states. The incentives that were granted relate primarily to preferences in state purchases, fiscal relief for new units and for the substantial expansion of existing units, availability of land on long-term lease at industrial "growth centers," contributions towards the cost of feasibility studies of development projects, subsidies for power generation, long-term loans and working capital for industries, and industrial exemption from the payment of water rates. Simultaneously with these new incentives to businessmen have come experiments in patterns of industrial administration, highlighted by the appointment of a labor leader as the new general manager of the giant Durgapur steel plant and the invitation by Governor Dias to a group of experts from Poland to help find ways to improve production in Durgapur.

Central to India's new economic initiatives in West Bengal is the assumption that the "green revolution" in agriculture will eventually spread to West Bengal, as a result of new gains being made in rice technology. If the new technology does take root in Bengal and if Bengal follows the patterns that have been exhibited in other states where the new technology has caught on, there is likely to be a surplus of agricultural labor, along with an increase in food supplies, and this will mean increasing pressure on the already overcrowded lands of West Bengal.[66] Increasing pressure on land will in turn release large numbers of peasants from the land, either for migration to less densely populated areas (such as India's northeastern states and territories) or for absorption in the industrial sector.[67] In the eyes of Indian planners, therefore, one of the most compelling reasons for the development of industry in West Bengal is the need to absorb larger and larger numbers of surplus rural peasants as industrial laborers, in order to prevent both large-scale future migration and political upheaval.

Radical Politics after Bangladesh

As a result of Mrs. Gandhi's development initiatives, her skillful handling of the Bangladesh crisis, and her overwhelming victory in the 1972 elections, the CPM and its allies have suffered a serious setback in West

[66] For an excellent discussion of the political and social problems associated with the "green revolution" in one district of West Bengal (Burdwan) see Francine R. Frankel, *India's Green Revolution* (Princeton, N.J.: Princeton University Press, 1971), pp. 157–190.

[67] A discussion of migration patterns in northeastern India and Bangladesh appears in my monograph, *Refugees and Migration Patterns in Northeastern India and Bangladesh* (Hanover, N.H.: American Universities Field Staff, 1972).

Bengal. The party has been embarrassed at the polls for the first time since Independence, its organizational cadre is under serious attack by youthful members of the Congress, it has completely lost whatever control of the state police and administrative networks it gained during the period of the United Front governments, and it is at least temporarily without issues that can be used to attack a Congress government that now has a two-thirds majority in the legislative assembly. Perhaps most important, it now faces a serious financial crisis, since many of its previous sources of funds—from Moscow or from the patronage of state governments, for example—have been cut off. Under these circumstances, one could write a number of future scenarios for West Bengal, but the two that are most frequently being talked about at present (shortly after the 1972 elections) have to do with a massive split in the CPM and the possibility of an insurrectionist strategy by the CPM cadre.

The possibility of another split in the CPM is enhanced by the recent actions of the Soviet Union during the Bangladesh crisis, which drew warm praise from a number of CPM leaders despite the party's anti-Soviet stance. In the words of an editorial in *People's Democracy,*

It was the Soviet Union which came to India's help. It was the Soviet Union which pledged all support to India through the Friendship Treaty. It was the Soviet Union which foiled the imperialist moves in the United Nations Security Council, it was the Soviet Union which warned other powers not to interfere in the situation in the sub-continent. It was the Soviet Union which sent its fleet to the Indian Ocean to counter the threat posed by the presence of the Seventh Fleet.

The Indian people saw clearly who India's enemy is; they saw who India's friend is.[68]

For those members of the CPM who value the actions of the Soviet Union, there may well be a possibility of alignment with the CPI, some portions of which were disappointed that the CPI was not included in Congress coalition governments in the states after the Congress-CPI electoral alliance in 1972. As correspondent Dilip Mukherjee has pointed out,

. . the objective situation [after Indira Gandhi's electoral victory and Bangladesh] may compel both the CPI and the CPM to put out cautious feelers to each other for tactical alliances . . . as the CPI's honeymoon with the ruling Congress comes to an end. This will not happen overnight, but the direction events are likely to take can be discerned in the CPI's increasingly vocal criticism, especially in its language press, of the style of Congress politics.[69]

[68] *People's Democracy*, 20 February 1972.
[69] Dilip Mukerjee, "Communist Infighting: The Possibility of a Truce," *Times of India*, 4 March 1972.

Should some of the electoralists in the CPM move toward a rapprochement with the CPI, the issue that is likely to divide the CPM will be the
party's posture on the question of India's unity and integrity, which has
frequently created factional problems for the party. In its original formulation in 1951, the united Communist Party of India argued that India's
various "nationalities" were united by their "voluntary consent to the
creation of a common state," a position that admittedly implies the right
of secession.[70] After the split in the Communist movement in 1964, a
number of CPM cadre leaders argued that the party should make this
right explicit, but formal party action was postponed by the intervention
of CPM electoralists. When the CPM Central Committee met in Calcutta
in November 1971, Pramode Das Gupta again voiced his support for an
explicit CPM policy enunciating the right of secession, but again he was
voted down. The result was that the CPM fought the 1972 elections on a
party platform that called for greater powers and finances to the states,
while the question of the right of secession was ambiguously stated in party
documents.

In this atmosphere, the possibility of a split in the CPM arises in the
event that some of the CPM electoralists move closer to the pro-Soviet
CPI, since the CPI is unreservedly committed to the unity of India while
the CPM cadre is not. Both the CPI and CPM electoralists can agree that
West Bengal has been disadvantaged by an Indian government policy that
has favored the development of non-Bengali areas, and both seek amendments to the constitution that would give more powers to the states for
development purposes, but neither the CPI nor CPM electoralists have
shown any willingness to talk about secession. The attitude of the CPM
cadre in West Bengal, however, is reflected in statements like the following, by Hare Krishna Konar at a party meeting in Calcutta on 4 June:

> Preparations are afoot here for a repeat of what happened in Dacca. So
> we should be prepared, we should learn from Bangladesh. . . . No one can
> suppress a person once he is aroused. Yahya has not been able to do it; the
> Americans have not been able to do it in Vietnam; the people of West
> Bengal too have never bowed their heads.[71]

Whether or not the CPM splits in the future, it is clear that a fairly large
section of the CPM cadre in West Bengal has for a long time advocated a
nonelectoral party strategy and that pressure within the party for enhance-

---

[70] The history of the Indian communist experience with the "nationality thesis" is
recounted in Selig S. Harrison, "Communism in India: The Dilemma of the CPI,"
Problems of Communism 8, (March–April 1959), 27–35. See also *Radical Politics
in West Bengal*, pp. 265 ff.

[71] *Desh Hitaishi*, 11 June 1971.

ment of the guerrilla capability of the cadre will now increase. Indeed, in this sense the 1972 elections have come as a relief to many CPM leaders, since the results of the election have at least for the present united the party behind a stance of unequivocal opposition to electoral democracy. Even Jyoti Basu, for example, has stated that he will not recognize the results of the "farcical election" of 1972, and Basu has supported a move that would call for the 14 members of the CPM who did win assembly seats to refuse to take their oath of office when the West Bengal assembly convenes. So long as the CPM remains outside of the assembly, there will be increasing pressure on CPM members to either defect from the party or to become more militantly attached to a nonelectoral political style.

In this sense, the CPM now faces a greater challenge than any that it has confronted in the past. If it should ever want to regain the imposing electoral position that it achieved during the United Front governments, it must somehow preserve its option to reenter the state ministries and the legislative assembly. To simply go off into the wilderness could conceivably gain for party members nothing more than police repression, dwindling support, and a violent more often than a peaceful death (unless, of course, Mrs. Gandhi's development efforts completely fail). To quote one CPM member, "the specter of Bangladesh is haunting us, but so is the specter of Indonesia." [72]

[72] Based on an interview in Calcutta in February 1972. The obvious reference is to the quick and brutal decimation of a strong Communist Party in Indonesia in 1965.

Bangladesh

Bangladesh

4
Radical Politics and   Talukder Maniruzzaman
the Emergence of Bangladesh

Bangladesh (formerly East Pakistan) emerged as an independent and sovereign state in December 1971, after having witnessed one of the most tragic and brutal bloodbaths in modern history. During an eight-month period that lasted from 25 March 1971 until mid-December, fanatic West Pakistani troops perpetrated a massive genocide directed against key segments of the East Bengal population, resulting in the extermination of approximately 3 million unarmed Bengali civilians. In these eight months the Pakistani military and their supporters violated about 200,000 women, burned more than 6 million homes, left almost 1,500,000 peasants without farm implements or animals, and forced nearly 10 million people to flee to India.[1] The Bangladesh liberation movement that developed in response to Pakistani repression and atrocities was led by the Awami League (AL), the largest political party in Bangladesh.

The Awami League captured the leadership of the Bangladesh liberation movement in the late 1960s, when its principal leader (Sheikh Mujibur Rahman) formulated a six-point demand for near-independence from Pakistan that quickly captured the imagination of the Bengali population. Indicative of the popularity of "Sheikh Mujib" in East Bengal was the victory of the Awami League in the December 1970 elections, when the AL secured 76.5 percent of the vote and 288 of 300 seats in the East Bengal Provincial Assembly and 72.6 percent of the vote and 160 of 162 seats in the national (Pakistan) assembly. When the Pakistan government refused to recognize the results of these elections and instead responded with repression and brutality, the majority of the leaders and activists of the Awami League took shelter in India, where they quickly formed a government-in-exile in Calcutta. With the help of the Indian government, the Awami League trained more than 100,000 guerrilla fighters during 1971, and it was this guerrilla force that was instrumental in immobilizing the Pakistan army in Bangladesh. In alliance with the Indian army, Bangladesh guerrillas steadily secured large portions of Bangladesh territory and finally (on 22 December 1971) returned the Bangladesh government-in-exile to Dacca.

When the Awami League, under the leadership of Sheikh Mujibur Rahman, first launched its movement for "full autonomy" in early 1966,

---

[1] These figures are given in Vladimir Simonov, "Bangladesh: From Ashes to Republic," *Morning News* (Dacca), 5 March 1972. The figure for numbers of people killed (about 3 million) is also given by Sheikh Mujibur Rahman, the prime minister of Bangladesh, who based his calculation on reports supplied by local units of the Awami League.

it was primarily a movement of the Bengali national bourgeoisie and middle classes, who found their road to rapid advancement blocked by their counterparts in West Pakistan. As the movement gained momentum and the masses became involved in it, however, its character quickly changed. During a period of mass upheaval against the Ayub Khan regime in East Bengal (November 1968–March 1969), radical students, laborers, and other lower-class people filled the streets of the urban centers in East Bengal, demanding not only the emancipation of Bengal but also the establishment of *Krishak-Sramik Raj* (rule of peasants and workers). The Awami League leaders, fearful of losing the leadership of the movement, soon added a program of radical economic reforms to their plank of "full autonomy" for East Bengal, and this program subsequently became even more radical during the liberation war.

This turn of events was primarily a result of the fact that the majority of the guerrillas recruited to the Bangladesh liberation army (the Mukti Bahini) were idealistic students of schools, colleges, and universities in East Bengal, who had already been deeply influenced by the leftist literature that is so widely read in Bengali intellectual circles. If only to maintain their control over the guerrillas, the AL leadership found it increasingly necessary to link their liberation movement with revolutionary and socialist ideologies. Moreover, after the liberation of Bangladesh, the Awami League government has continued to insist that nationalism, democracy, secularism, and socialism are the main pillars on which the new state of Bangladesh is to be founded.

If the emergence of Bangladesh as an independent and sovereign state has brought about a transition to secularism, socialism, and linguistic nationalism, it has also supplanted the Islamic ideology and Islamic nationalism that led to the founding of Pakistan. How could this ideological revolution take place? How could ideas of secularism take hold so quickly in an area where the majority Muslim population had been intensely swayed by a powerful religious fervor as recently as 1947?

In order to answer questions of this kind it is necessary to examine both the Awami League and the background of leftist politics in Bangladesh, for it was clearly the leftists of East Bengal who took the lead in bringing about the ideological revolution that has recently occurred.[2] By using the

---

[2] The term "leftists" in this paper is consciously defined quite loosely, primarily because that was the way one had to define the term in Bangladesh before liberation. Since Communist membership was illegal in Pakistan from 1954 up to the liberation of Bangladesh, most Communists preferred to be called simply "leftists," which meant that it was extremely difficult to distinguish degrees of "leftism" in public discourse. As is pointed out below, however, the "leftist movement" in Bangladesh had its roots in the Communist movement.

tactics of cultural subversion through front organizations, infiltration of popular parties, and incorporation of secular, anti-imperialist and socialist planks into their programs, while creating resentment among the masses by exploiting the delicate and sensitive issues of language, autonomy, and economic distress, the leftists first created an atmosphere for socialist and secular nationalist appeals. The leftists in East Bengal were also the only politicians that had given some prior thought to (and raised public discussion about) the possibility of guerrilla warfare and other revolutionary tactics before the armed liberation struggle began in early 1971. In the late 1960s, however, the leftist leadership in East Bengal was almost completely immobilized, largely because it was so divided among mutually hostile and warring factions. It was this lack of doctrinal and tactical unity that made it possible for the leadership of the Bengali nationalist movement to pass to the hands of the Awami League.

In this context, a study of the radicalization of East Bengal politics and the emergence of East Bengal as a socialist-oriented independent state should appropriately begin with a discussion of the leftist movement. How did the leftist movement grow in East Bengal? What were the main bases of support for the leftists? Who were the most prominent leftist leaders? What was the nature of factionalism in the leftist movement that immobilized it in the late 1960s? How significant were the differences between political generations and changing channels of political recruitment among the Left parties? How did the leftist movement relate to the Bengali nationalist movement initiated by the Awami League? Who were the Awami League leaders and what were the main channels of their recruitment? What are the bases of support for the Awami League? How did the constitutional movement of the Awami League turn into an armed liberation struggle? What was the nature of the genocide perpetrated by the West Pakistan military during March–December 1971 in Bangladesh? What was the relationship between the Mukti Bahini and the Awami League and leftist cadres? To what extent has the political balance between the Awami League and the leftist parties in Bangladesh been altered by the liberation movement? The following paper attempts to provide at least tentative answers to such questions by placing the leftist movement in Bangladesh in historical perspective.

The Early Years of Leftism in East Pakistan

When independence came to Pakistan in 1947 there was only one leftist ideological platform in the entire country. This was provided by the former members and sympathizers of the Communist Party of India (CPI) who had chosen to remain in the Pakistan areas. Since most of these people were Hindus, and since large numbers of Hindus left Pakistan in the aftermath of partition, the size of the Communist Party in Pakistan declined rapidly in the years immediately following Independence. Indian CP leaders estimate that more than 10,000 members of the CPI were initially resident in East Bengal after the partition of 1947, but by the 1950s the number of Communists in East Bengal did not exceed a few hundred (in West Pakistan there were never more than a handful of Communist Party members).[3]

For the first few months after partition (August 1947–April 1948), the Communists in East Bengal tried to operate through the secretariat of the CPI of India. This method of operation was not only conducive to the CPI policy of "responsive cooperation" with the Indian National Congress and the Muslim League at the time of Independence, it also made sense because of the lack of leaders with stature and roots in Pakistan. However, tensions between India and Pakistan made this arrangement increasingly difficult, with the result that the second Calcutta Congress of the CPI (February–March 1948) established a separate Communist Party in Pakistan. Sajjad Zaheer, a member of the CPI Central Committee and general secretary of the All-India Progressive Writers Association (a literary front organization of the CPI) was named the first secretary-general of the Communist Party of Pakistan (CPP) and sent to Lahore to organize the party.[4] The Calcutta Congress of 1948 also discarded the policy of "responsive cooperation" and adopted the Ranadive line of violent socialist revolution for South Asia.[5]

Ranadive's tactical line, which called for revolutionary violence and terrorism against both the bourgeoisie in the cities and the rich peasantry in the countryside, proved to be as disastrous for the CPP as it was for the CPI. In West Pakistan the Communists had previously gained significant influence in the Punjab Railway Workers Union, primarily through the organizational efforts of Mirza Ibrahim Beg and C. R. Aslam, but the policy of strikes and violence that was undertaken by the Railway Workers Union after the adoption of the Ranadive line soon led to a head-on collision with the Pakistan government. Similarly, Sajjad Zaheer had combined with two very effective poets of the Urdu language (Faiz

---

[3] For a more detailed study of CP membership in East and West Pakistan see Marcus F. Franda, "Communism and Regional Politics in East Pakistan," *Asian Survey* 10, no. 8 (August 1970), 588–606.

[4] Hafeez Malik, "The Marxist Literary Movement in India and Pakistan," *The Journal of Asian Studies* 26, no. 4 (August 1967), 649 ff.

[5] John H. Kautsky, "Indian Communist Party Strategy Since 1947," *Pacific Affairs* 28, no. 3 (Fall 1955), 147.

Ahmad Faiz and Ahmad Nadim Qasmi) to draw a large number of young and idealistic writers and poets to the All-Pakistan Progressive Writers Association (APPWA), but when the Lahore Conference of the APPWA issued an outright condemnation of the Pakistan government in November 1949, the influence of the APPWA began to wane. By March 1951, Pakistan prime minister Liaquat Ali Khan had accused a group of Pakistan army officers of conspiring with the CPP to establish a "communist-model dictatorship under military domination," and a legal case (the *Rawalpindi* conspiracy case) had been started against the "conspirators."[6] Sajjad Zaheer and Faiz Ahmad Faiz, along with Major General Akbar Khan (the chief of staff of the Pakistan army) and his wife and 11 officers of the army were tried and convicted of "conspiracy to overthrow the government."[7]

In East Bengal the CPP followed the "hit and hit" policy of Ranadive for a few years after the Calcutta Congress of 1948, attempting to paralyze communication systems by organizing strikes among railway workers while fomenting peasant revolts among the Hazong peasants in certain areas of the district of Mymensingh and among the Santal tribals at Nachol in Rajshahi district. Some indication of the limited ability of the CPP to mobilize followers behind it can be gained from the fact that the poorly established East Pakistan government was able to effectively thwart the Communist-led uprising by simply arresting 150 Communist leaders.[8] By 1954 the CPP had been banned throughout Pakistan, and most of its leadership had either been jailed or had fled to India. Moreover, the effectiveness of the CPP had virtually been eliminated by the heightened factionalism within the party, largely a result of charges and countercharges by party members that someone in the party had betrayed CPP secrets to the government.

While the *Rawalpindi* conspiracy case marked the demise of the Communist movement in West Pakistan, the Communist Party in East Pakistan (EPCP) did manage a continued existence as an underground party after the Communists were officially banned in July 1954. In 1951 the

[6] Prime Minister Liaquat Ali Khan's statement, along with a statement on the *Rawalpindi* conspiracy case appears in the *Debates of the Constituent Assembly of Pakistan* 1, no. 2 (21 March 1951), 34 ff.

[7] All of the people convicted in the *Rawalpindi* conspiracy case were released in 1955, when H. S. Suhrawardy joined the central cabinet as law minister. Upon his release from prison, Sajjad Zaheer left for India, where he has remained permanently.

[8] A government account of the 1948–1951 Communist insurrection in East Pakistan is contained in the *Proceedings of the East Pakistan Assembly* 16, no. 3 (1957), 155–160.

CPI had rejected the Ranadive policy and had called for the replacement of the "present anti-democratic and anti-people government by a Peoples' Democracy, created on the basis of a coalition of all democratic anti-feudal and anti-imperialist forces in the country." Following the CPI line, the Communist Party in East Pakistan had also rejected the hard line. But the Communists in East Pakistan were faced with a number of tactical dilemmas, since they now found their ideology totally unwelcome among people who had been swayed by Islamic nationalism. Unlike the situation in West Pakistan, most EPCP members were Hindus, and they were therefore viewed as "enemy (Indian) agents" by the government. Because of this factor serious inner-party controversies arose in East Pakistan over the alternatives of working as an open party in a hostile environment or infiltrating other popular parties in an attempt to incorporate noncommunal, secular, antifeudal, and anti-imperialist planks into their programs.

In 1951 a number of leading Communist prisoners in Rajshahi jail formulated a thesis (the "Rajshahi jail thesis") that called for the EPCP to work openly. The Rajshahi jail thesis argued that if the Communists worked through other bourgeois or petty-bourgeois organizations and adopted their ideas and methods the Communists would gradually lose their revolutionary fervor. However, the Cominform, in early 1951 (in a political note published in its organ, *For a Lasting Peace, For a People's Democracy*), praised the role of the Awami League for "unleashing a struggle against feudalism and colonial domination," and the EPCP took this as a hint by the Cominform that the party should work through the Awami League and other popular front organizations.[9]

The first front organization started by the Communists in East Pakistan was the Youth League, formed in 1951. Its policy was to "mobilize maximum numbers of people of all classes on the minimum programme of secularism, anti-imperialism, anti-feudalism, world peace, unfettered democracy and employment opportunities for all people within the country."[10] Most of the Youth Leaguers came from middle-class families, and ten of them are now the top leaders of the various Communist parties. The Youth League initially tried merely to counteract the government policy of keeping alive Muslim religious fervor through the obser-

[9] This incident is analyzed in K. G. Mustafa, "Awami League Manifesto: Hopes and Realities," *Holiday* (Dacca Weekly), 14 June 1970, p. 2.

[10] Information on the Youth League was gathered from interviews and is especially dependent on an interview with Ali Ashraf, one of the founder members of the Youth League and a former publicity secretary of the Ganatantri Dal. Ali Ashraf has also served as chief reporter for the *Danik Pakistan*.

vance of Islamic cultural festivals by organizing cultural shows and literary functions on occasions like Bengali New Year's Day, the death anniversary of Sukanta (a Communist poet of Calcutta), and the birth and death anniversaries of Rabindranath Tagore (a Hindu Bengali poet of international reputation). Later the Youth League also fomented or actively supported various movements against the Muslim League government, the most important of which was the movement for the adoption of Bengali as one of the state languages of Pakistan. Indeed, the Action Committee of the state language movement of 1952 had 4 Youth Leaguers out of a total of 12 members, and a Calcutta newspaper (*Swadhinata*) claimed in its issue of 11 March 1952 that the state language movement in East Pakistan was being led primarily by the Communists.

Charges concerning Communist influence in the state language movement gave the Muslim League government of Pakistan an excuse to arrest the members of the Action Committee and the Youth League in early 1952, and by March 1952 more than three-quarters of the members of the Executive Committee of the Youth League had been arrested.[11] The remaining Youth League leaders then organized a student front, the East Pakistan Students Union (EPSU) in April 1952, with noncommunalism, secularism, and anti-imperialism as the main planks.[12] This again gradually became one of the largest student organizations in East Pakistan and has since functioned as the main channel of recruitment for leftist cadres.

In the meantime, the EPCP had adopted a policy of working through the East Pakistan Awami Muslim League (formed in 1949), which as stated below was fast acquiring mass popularity. Some of the CP leaders defied this official decision of the EPCP on the ground that the Awami Muslim League was a Muslim communal party and that the Communists could not work through it. These dissidents formed a noncommunal Ganatantri Dal in January 1953, under the presidentship of Haji Mohammad Danesh, a former member of the CPI. The Dal adopted a fairly radical manifesto. It mentioned imperialism and feudalism as the main enemies of the masses of Pakistan; it advocated the confiscation of all foreign capital invested in Pakistan and the nationalization of foreign

[11] These are the figures quoted by Chief Minister Nurul Amin in the East Bengal Legislative Assembly on 24 March 1952. See the *Proceedings of the East Bengal Legislative Assembly* 8, no. 3 (March 1952), 6–14.
[12] The formation of the EPSU is described in *Annual Report of General Secretary in the Provincial Convention of the EPSU held on 2, 3, 4 June 1966* (Dacca: Shafiqur Rahman, Joint Secretary, EPSU, 1966), pp. 6–7.

banks and insurance companies; it resented the Muslim League government's decision to abolish the zamindari system with compensation, demanding that the zamindari system be abolished without compensation and that excess land held by zamindars and other big landholders be distributed freely among the landless peasants; and it urged the people to destroy imperialism and feudalism and its agent (the Muslim League).[13]

Those Communists who joined the Awami League in 1952 began to consolidate their positions by "exploiting" its president, Maulana Abdul Hamid Khan Bhashani. Maulana Bhashani, now over 80, had for a long time been a prominent Muslim peasant leader in Bengal and Assam. Born of an obscure peasant family, and having only madrasah (Islamic religious school) education, Maulana Bhashani acquired fame for leading peasant agitations against the oppressive Hindu zamindars in the districts of Mymensingh, Pabna and Rajshahi in the early 1920s. Bengali Hindu landlords had managed to get Maulana Bhashani banished from Bengal on the pretext of preserving peace in the province, but the Maulana had then moved to Assam and settled in the char (silted islet of a river) named Bhashan.[14] Here again he had made headlines by disobeying the orders of the Hindu zamindar of the locality prohibiting the slaughter of cows. He soon took up the case of Bengali immigrants flocking to Assam, who had been refused entry by the Assam government, and started an agitation against the Assam government on that issue. When the Assam government finally amended its legislation and allowed about 350,000 Bengali peasants to settle in Assam, Bhashani became a folk hero. Although Bhashani had never read Marxist literature before Pakistan's independence, his lifelong work among the peasants had given him an insight into the nature of both class struggle and the forces of imperialism. During the time of the Pakistan movement he had tried to give the movement a revolutionary character in his own way by propagating the view that the Pakistan movement was the movement of the oppressed people for independence from British imperialism and its agents (zamindars, Raja Moharajas, the capitalist class, and moneylenders). Since the Congress had become an organization of the above-mentioned agents of British imperialism, according to Bhashani, the exploited Muslim could find his salvation only through the more revolutionary Pakistan movement.

[13] The program of the Ganatantri Dal is detailed in *Pakistan Ganatantri Dal: Aims and Programme* (Feni: Hamida Press, 1953).
[14] It was from the name of the char, Bhashan, that Maulana Abdul Hamid Khan received his popular name, Bhashani.

Bhashani further argued that Islam enjoined everyone to the view that all properties belonged to God. He firmly believed that when Pakistan was achieved all of the properties of landlords and other exploiters would be taken over by the state and distributed freely among poor peasants and workers.[15] When Maulana Bhashani moved to East Pakistan from Assam after partition and became the president of the East Pakistan Awami Muslim League, the Communists and their fellow travelers found him a natural sympathizer to their cause and a "trojan horse in which to take shelter." Members of the EPCP therefore joined the Awami Muslim League in large numbers, and slowly worked to win over Maulana Bhashani to their side by incorporating more and more leftist planks into Awami League programs. They also pressed for the adoption of a secular approach by the Awami Muslim League, with the result that the Awami Muslim League (through a resolution of its Council) dropped the word "Muslim" from its name in 1953.

The new post-1953 Awami League then began to advocate a joint electorate system in place of the separate electorate system that had been the program of the Muslim League since its birth in 1906. Separate electorates, it was argued, had been responsible for the widening chasm between Muslims and Hindus that ultimately led to the partition of India. Through the nominating power of Bhashani as president of the AL, the leftists gained 9 out of 37 members in the executive committee of the EPAL and continued to exert considerable influence in the overall policy decisions of the party.

In May 1954, when the Pakistan government signed the Mutual Defence Assistance Agreement with the United States, and later joined American-sponsored defense pacts (SEATO and the Baghdad Pact), Maulana Bhashani and his leftist associates became the most vocal opponents of these arrangements. In late 1954 they were able to get official resolutions passed by the executive committee of the EPAL condemning the Defence Assistance Agreement and the defense pacts, while anti-imperialism and autonomy for the various linguistic nationalities of Pakistan quickly became the dominant themes of the political speeches of Maulana Bhashani.[16]

[15] See, for example, Bhashani's speeches just prior to Independence, which were published in the *Azad* (Calcutta), 27 January–15 March 1946.
[16] See, for example, *Presidential Address of Maulana Bhashani in the Convention of North Bengal Awami League Workers held on 9 and 10 October 1955* (Dacca: Bengal Printing Works, 1955). See also *Presidential Address of Maulana Bhashani at the Special Council Session of East Pakistan National Awami Party held at Rangpur, 30 November 1967* (Dacca: Mohammad Sultan, Kaptan Bazar, 1968), p. 17.

Before the general elections of 1954 the leftists in the Ganatantri Dal and Awami League began to propagate the idea of forming a united front of all opposition political parties against the ruling Muslim League. The Communists of Mymensingh district, having infiltrated the district AL council, were able to push through a resolution favoring the formation of the united front. When the front (consisting of the AL, the Krishak Sramik Party of A. K. Fazlul Huq, a former prime minister of united Bengal, and the Ganatantri Dal) was finally formed, it promptly succeeded in routing the Muslim League in the 1954 elections.[17] In these elections Communist candidates fought openly in 10 seats, 6 of the Communist nominees being Muslim and 4 Hindu. Paradoxically, the 4 Hindu nominees won their elections (in Hindu constituencies), while the Muslim nominees were all defeated (all ran in Muslim constituencies). The Communists, however, obtained another 18 seats through the United Front, in contests where they did not openly reveal their affiliations. When the United Front split a few months after the 1954 elections, all of these Communist legislators went with the Awami League.

NAP: The Anti-Imperialist Popular Front

The leftists in the AL became dissatisfied when AL-led coalitions formed the government in East Pakistan as well as at the center in 1956. Soon after his elevation to the post of prime minister of Pakistan, H. S. Suhrawardy (the national convener of the Awami League) began to defend vigorously Pakistan's alliances with the United States, and to oppose the granting of "full autonomy" to East Pakistan (full autonomy had been demanded in the manifesto of the AL as well as in the 21-point program issued by the United Front at the time of the 1954 elections). Goaded by the leftists, Maulana Bhashani took the issue to the East Pakistan Awami League Council, and the council approved Suhrawardy's prowestern foreign policy by a vote of 800–60.[18] At this point Maulana Bhashani together with nine leftist members of the Executive Committee, resigned from the Awami League.

After his resignation from the AL, Maulana Bhashani called a convention of all the "anti-imperialist democratic forces" in Pakistan that took place in Dacca in September 1957. In West Pakistan a millionaire landlord and fellow traveler of the Punjabi Communist movement (Main

---

[17] In the 1954 elections the Muslim League secured only 9 seats out of 237 Muslim seats in East Bengal. The rest were captured by the United Front.

[18] See the analysis in the *Times* (London), 15 June 1957, p. 2.

Iftekharuddin) together with landlord politicians like Khan Abdul Ghaffer Khan, a Pakhtoon nationalist, G. M. Syed, a Sindhi nationalist, Prince Abdul Karim Khan, a Baluch nationalist, and different leftist factions in the various regions of West Pakistan had already formed the National Party. These men all responded to Maulana Bhashani's call for a convention. In East Pakistan both the leftists in the AL and the Ganatantri Dal members joined the convention. A national "anti-imperialist front" —the National Awami Party (NAP)—was formed, with the three main planks in the NAP platform being anti-imperialism, antifeudalism, and right of self-determination for the various linguistic nationalities of Pakistan. Maulana Bhashani was made the president of both the national and East Pakistan units of the new party.

During the course of the next decade some of the top leaders of the EPCP became members of the Executive Committee of the East Pakistan National Awami Party (EPNAP), and EPNAP became the exclusive popular front of the EPCP. However, the CP members in the assembly formed a separate parliamentary party of NAP, and this gave them considerable strength. Since the AL and Krishak Sramik–led coalitions were almost equally divided in the East Pakistan assembly, the 22 CP members of NAP held the balance, and they were eventually able to discredit the parliamentary system by bringing about the downfall of a number of ministries in quick succession in 1957.

In addition to their parliamentary activities, the Communist members of NAP who had been working among the peasants formed the East Pakistan Peasants Association (with Maulana Bhashani as president) at a peasants' conference held in north Bengal in December 1957. Abdul Huq, a first class honors graduate in economics from Calcutta University and a former member of the CPI, was elected secretary. The association began to organize peasant rallies where immediate issues concerning the peasantry (such as lack of land reform legislation, high taxation, high prices of daily necessities, low prices for farmers' products, oppression by landlords, high rates of interest charged by village moneylenders, and oppressive methods of land revenue collection by petty revenue officers) were highlighted. It was hoped that this would create the "subjective conditions" for a peasant revolution.

In a similar manner, leftist trade union leaders who had infiltrated a variety of East Pakistan trade unions formed the East Pakistan Mazdoor Federation in February 1958, with Mohammad Toaha, a former Youth League leader and an M. A. in political science from Dacca University, as president. The influence of the Mazdoor Federation soon began to grow, particularly among those unions where leftist trade union leaders had been working, and it became especially strong during the next year among the workers of navigation companies, the Adamjee jute mills, textile mills, bidi (crude cigarettes) factories, and in the Sylhet tea gardens. As was the case in the parliamentary and peasant fields, federation leaders were less interested in building up a healthy trade union movement than they were in issues that were likely to create class consciousness among the workers.

The Split in EPCP and the Breakup of EPNAP

The Martial Law regime that was imposed on Pakistan in October 1958, brought about a new wave of repression for the leftists. All political parties were banned, Maulana Bhashani was arrested, and warrants of arrest were issued against a large number of leftist leaders and workers. Some were eventually arrested and some went underground. Maulana Bhashani was released from detention after the inauguration of the 1962 constitution, but many others remained under detention or underground for years after 1962. It was not until January 1964, when the ban on political parties had gradually been lifted, that NAP and all other leftist front organizations could be revived.

During the intervening years, however, the unity of the leftists had been strained by several factors. One was the split in the international Communist movement; others were related to the foreign policy of the Pakistan government and the internal political movement of East Pakistan for full provincial autonomy. These conflicts came to a head in 1963–64, when two members of the Central Committee of the EPCP presented a thesis on the "Two Principles of the Communist Movement." In that thesis they argued that the four major decisions of the Twentieth Congress of the Soviet Communist Party were wrong. The "two principles thesis" argued vehemently against: (1) peaceful coexistence of the two world systems (capitalism and socialism); (2) the practical possibility of prevention of war; (3) the possibility of adopting different roads to socialism in different countries and the possibility of peaceful transition to socialism in certain countries; and (4) the denunciation of Stalin. In addition, the "two principles thesis" contended that the decisions of the 12-party congress in 1957 and the 81-party congress in 1960 (both of which were based on the thesis of the Twentieth Congress of the CPSU) were also unacceptable to true Marxists. At the same Conference, nine other members of the Central Committee of the EPCP presented a 70-page counterthesis, justifying the decisions of the CPSU in the context of present realities in the world, while charging that the other two members were echoing the "non-creative" line adopted recently by the CPC.[19]

Following the Chinese formula of 1963, on the internal struggle of each CP ("unity-struggle or even split—a new unity on a new basis"), the pro-Chinese CP leaders in 1963–1964 were attempting to split the EPCP by forming a separate group of pro-Chinese cadres and sympathizers. This conflict, between pro-Soviet and pro-Chinese Communists, was soon reflected in the deliberations of Communist front organizations. The pro-Chinese Communists finally left the EPCP and formed the East Pakistan Communist Party (Marxist-Leninist) (EPCPML) in 1966, while the student front of the leftists—EPSU—soon split into two separate organizations and EPNAP thereafter broke into two separate parties. The pro-Chinese faction held its party council session at Rangpur in November 1967, under the chairmanship of Maulana Bhashani, while the pro-Soviet faction boycotted the Rangpur session and held a separate session at Dacca in December 1967.[20]

The Rangpur address of Maulana Bhashani, when compared with the addresses of the pro-Moscow Communist leaders at the Dacca session, delineate the main differences between the pro-Peking and pro-Moscow factions with regard to their varying analyses of the Pakistan political situation and the tactical lines to be used for bringing about socialism in Pakistan.[21] The pro-Peking group's analysis was based on the orthodox interpretation of Lenin's theory of imperialism and the Maoist tactic of using the fight against imperialism as a means to establish people's democracy. The pro-Peking group argued that, although the British had formally granted independence to Pakistan, Pakistan could not be really free because of the financial hold that imperialism and its agents had on the economy of Pakistan. Colonialism, they argued, had simply been replaced by a more subtle form of imperialism. Through the Defence Assistance Agreement, and because of defense pacts like the Baghdad Pact and SEATO, the American imperialists had tightened their grip on

[19] The "two principles" thesis (formally titled "Two Principles of the World Communist Movement") was written by Sukhendu Dastidar and Mohammad Toaha, writing under the aliases "Khaled" and "Bashir." A copy of the thesis (publisher and date not mentioned) is available from the author.

[20] Both factions of NAP claimed the original name of the party, so journalists and politicians simply referred to the two factions as pro-Peking and pro-Moscow. These are the names that are used below to distinguish the two parties from one another.

[21] The Rangpur address of Maulana Bhashani was reportedly written by Abdul Huq, one of the principal theoreticians of the pro-Peking EPCPML.

Pakistan and had turned independence into a farce. By granting aid through interest-laden loans, the American imperialists were further exploiting the masses of Pakistan. To maintain their hegemony the U.S. imperialists had been preventing the establishment of a people's democracy that alone could take measures for creating a self-reliant, independent country following an independent foreign policy. This in turn had prevented a government that could force the imperialists to forfeit foreign capital and liquidate big business and feudalism.[22] According to this line, American imperialism was the number one enemy of the masses of Pakistan. Or, as Maulana Bhashani put it,

> In our country the American imperial interests and the interests of the big business and feudal elements are woven together by a common thread. The fight against one of these enemies involves the fight against all of them. So the struggle for people's democracy and the anti-imperialist fight are one and indivisible.[23]

If imperialism was the main enemy, what would be the tactics and methods to bring the anti-imperialist fight and struggle for people's democracy to fruition? The questions involved were: (1) What should be the attitude of the leftists toward the Ayub Khan government? (2) Should the leftists form a united front with the other opposition parties and start a mass movement against the government? and (3) What attitudes should the leftists take towards the movement started by the EPAL (for "full autonomy") in early 1966?

Since imperialism had been named as the number one enemy, foreign policy became the key factor in determining the attitude of the pro-Peking NAP toward the Ayub government. After the Sino-Indian conflict of 1962, the governments of the United States and the United Kingdom began to supply huge amounts of arms and ammunition to India. This created great concern in Pakistan as it upset the power balance in the subcontinent. President Ayub then sought closer alliance with the Chinese government and began to woo the pro-Peking faction of NAP, formally led by Maulana Bhashani.[24] In return the pro-Peking leftist workers of Pakistan began to extol Zulfikar Ali Bhutto, Ayub's foreign minister and the architect of the new "anti-imperialist pro-Chinese"

[22] This description of the pro-Peking NAP tactical line is based on the *Presidential Address of Maulana Bhashani at the Special EPNAP Council Session at Rangpur on 30 November 1967*, pp. 11–20.

[23] Ibid., p. 21.

[24] Ayub's own version of his foreign policy during this period is traced out in his autobiography, *Friends Not Masters* (Karachi: Oxford University Press, 1967), pp. 133 ff.

foreign policy. Maulana Bhashani even led a semi-official goodwill mission to China in September 1963 and, upon his return from China, began to eulogize the Chinese system and advocate openly the establishment of a socialist system for Pakistan.

In the years that followed, the pro-Peking NAP showed an attitude of increasing cooperation with the Ayub Khan government. During the Indo-Pakistan war in September 1965, the pro-Peking leftists argued that the war was the result of the machinations of the American imperialists who wanted to topple the pro-Peking Ayub government and put in its place an absolutely pro-American regime. The weekly paper *Janata*, which at the time was the spokesman of the pro-Peking leftists, described the 1965 war as an "anti-imperialist, people's war" and urged the people to rally around the Ayub government. Willingly or unwillingly, the Ayub Khan government had assumed "the leadership of the anti-imperialist struggle."

The attitudes of the pro-Peking leftists to united movements forged successively by the other opposition parties were also determined by considerations of the "anti-imperialist struggle." In 1964 all of the opposition parties (including NAP) had formed an electoral alliance—the Combined Opposition Parties (COP)—and the alliance had in turn nominated Miss Fatima Jinnah as the one presidential candidate to oppose Ayub Khan. However, as the election campaign developed, the pro-Peking leftists gradually withdrew from Miss Jinnah's side and began to work for President Ayub, on the grounds that if the COP included such rightist parties as the Jamaat-i-Islami, the AL, and the Council Muslim League, then any government it would control would again be under the hegemony of the American imperialists. Again, when the rightist parties formed the Pakistan Democratic Movement (PDM) in 1967 and launched a campaign for the restoration of the system of parliamentary democracy, the pro-Peking leftists refrained from joining the movement on the grounds that the PDM program did not include the plank of "anti-imperialism, anti-monopoly capitalism, and anti-feudalism." In the words of Maulana Bhashani again,

Today the leadership of the anti-imperialist democratic struggle can be provided by no other class excepting the proletariat. NAP is the only party which has adopted the programme of the workers and peasants—that is, the proletariat of our country. NAP, thus, cannot follow the programme of any other class forgetting its own programme.[25]

[25] *Presidential Address of Maulana Bhashani at the Special EPNAP Council Session at Rangpur on 30 November 1967*, p. 31.

The principal leader of the opposition in East Pakistan after the 1965 Indo-Pakistan war was, of course, Sheikh Mujibur Rahman, the leader of the EPAL. As stated in detail below, Sheikh Mujib quickly captured the center of the East Pakistan political stage by launching a movement for the autonomy of East Pakistan, on the basis of his six-point program. But the pro-Peking leftists again stayed away from this "six-point revolution." They argued that the six-point program did not reflect the aspirations of the East Pakistani workers, peasants, and lower-middle classes, who constituted the overwhelming majority of the population. According to NAP, Mujib's six-point program merely aimed at the creation of a new class of monopolists in East Pakistan, and the vacillating leadership of the AL, coming as it did from the bourgeois and petty-bourgeois classes, was seen by NAP as an ultimate compromise with the international imperialist forces led by the United States. The struggle for autonomy, according to NAP, could not be separated from the overall fight against imperialism. The NAP, therefore, could not join the movement of Sheikh Mujib on the basis of a six-point program that did not include an anti-imperialist plank.

In short, following the Chinese model of Communist revolution, the pro-Peking leftists tried to bring about a program for waging a resolute anti-imperialist struggle with the help of workers and peasants, under the leadership of the underground EPCP. They found it tactically necessary to protect the Ayub government so long as it maintained an anti-imperialist posture, and through cultural agreements with the Chinese government this opened the way for the younger generations of Maoists in East Pakistan to imbibe Maoist literature. The dilemma for NAP at this point was to keep the Ayub government in good humor as NAP cadres went on creating the "subjective conditions" for a Chinese-type revolution in East Pakistan (by agitating on issues like the Vietnam War, the food problem, agrarian reforms, and the like).

While pro-Moscow leftists did not disagree with the view that American imperialism was the main enemy of the masses of Pakistan, they argued that the pro-Peking leftists were reading anti-imperialism into Ayub Khan's foreign policy. The Ayub government did not quit the American sponsored SEATO and CENTO pacts; Pakistan's Defence Assistance Agreement with America was still in effect; government development plans were still dependent on American economic aid; and monopoly capitalism and feudalism—the main agents of the international imperialists—continued to thrive under the patronage of the Ayub government. The pro-Moscow leftists argued further that the composition of the eco-

nomic classes, the degree of class consciousness, the nature of anti-
autocracy groups and parties were such that a direct socialist revolution
(as advocated by the pro-Peking leftists) could not be successful in
Pakistan. To talk of a socialist revolution under such conditions, the pro-
Moscow leftists argued, was to condemn the leftists to a prolonged period
of inactivity. What was first necessary was the replacement of the Ayub
government by an anti-imperialist, anti-monopoly capitalist and antifeudal
democratic government. Only a "national democratic government" could
ultimately pave the way for socialism in Pakistan, according to the pro-
Moscow left.[26]

In order to obtain a "national democratic government" the pro-
Moscow theoreticians argued, it was first necessary to establish a united
movement of various democratic parties on a minimum program of restoration of parliamentary democracy and provincial autonomy. The pro-
Moscow leftists therefore advocated a mass movement against the Ayub
government on the basis of cooperation with the EPAL. When mass
agitation against the Ayub government was initiated by students in November 1968, the pro-Moscow NAP joined the Democratic Action
Committee formed by all of the opposition political parties to continue
the movement. This "bourgeois revolution" almost came to a halt when
President Ayub called a Round Table Conference of the opposition
leaders and agreed to restore parliamentary government and universal
adult franchise, at which time the pro-Peking leftists tried to turn the
"bourgeois revolution" into a proletarian one by denouncing the Round
Table Conference as a betrayal of the cause of the proletariat and by
exciting the workers and peasants to arson, looting, and killing of the
"imperial agents." But the pro-Peking forces were too weak organizationally to usher in an "uninterrupted revolution," and their provocative
slogans only helped the bourgeois parties to close ranks and accelerate
the army take-over and the proclamation of Martial Law.

Leadership of the Pro-Moscow and Pro-Peking Parties, 1967–1968

Until the time of the split in 1966 the underground EPCP was led by
Moni Singh. Now nearing 70, Moni Singh is the descendant of a Hindu

---

[26] For more detailed descriptions of the pro-Moscow NAP tactical line see the
speeches of Professor Muzzaffar Ahmad and Mohiuddin Ahmad in NAP Council
sessions, as reported in the *Sangbad* (Dacca), 17 December 1967, pp. 1, 4, 7, 16.
The thesis of these pro-Moscow leaders obviously follows the concept of "national
democratic revolution" as advocated by the Soviet Union since 1956. See *World
Revolutionary Movement and the Working Class* (Moscow: Progress Publishers,
1967), pp. 331–372.

zamindar family from Mymensingh district in East Pakistan. Quite early in his life he left the family property and joined the CPI. He first worked in the labor movement in Calcutta in the 1930s, but after a ten-year period of imprisonment in the late 1930s and early 1940s he started peasant movements in his own zamindari that soon spread to the entire district of Mymensingh. In 1946 he held an All-India Kisan (Peasants) Conference in Mymensingh, which was reportedly attended by about 200,000 peasants. After 1951 he was the secretary-general of the EPCP and worked underground for 16 years, until he was arrested on 10 November 1967. Moni Singh, together with a number of other comrades of his age group (all former members of the CPI) have continued to publish a journal called *Flame* under the most trying of circumstances.[27] Through this journal and within party meetings, Moni Singh and his comrades tried at first to persuade the pro-Peking Communists not to split the EPCP and its front organizations. When the split did finally occur (in 1966) most of the senior Hindu, as well as Muslim, Communists remained with the pro-Moscow group. Among the cadres the majority of the Hindu Communists also sided with Moni Singh.

While Sukhendu Dastidar, a senior Hindu Communist, did become the secretary-general of the pro-Chinese underground Communist Party (EPCPML), the majority of the other top leaders, as well as the cadres of the EPCPML, were Muslims from comparatively younger age groups.[28] More precise information is available about the leaders of those leftist groups that worked openly through the two NAPs (see table 4.1). A comparison between the figures for the two EPNAPs would indicate that the number of Hindu leftists was higher among the pro-Moscow party leadership than among the pro-Peking group. In addition, pro-Moscow party leaders were generally older, while leaders of the pro-Peking party were better educated. The professional backgrounds of the two groups of leaders, however, indicate that the majority of the leadership of both groups comes from middle-class backgrounds.

Factionalism among the Pro-Peking Leftists

After their split with the pro-Peking leftists, the pro-Moscow leftists began working on the thesis that because of the international influence of the socialist countries and possibility of the growth of a national democratic

---

[27] *Flame* was the official underground journal of the EPCP until the split in 1966.

[28] Dastidar is the descendant of a prominent middle-class Hindu family of Chittagong District. He was connected with the famous Chittagong Armoury Raid in 1930 and was given the sentence of transportation for life by the British for his participation in the raid. However, his sentence was commuted in 1946 by the Suhrawardy ministry of the united Bengal Province.

Table 4.1 Demographic Characteristics of the Executive Committees of the Pro-Moscow and Pro-Peking EPNAP (January 1968)

	Pro-Moscow EPNAP		Pro-Peking EPNAP	
	Number	% of Total	Number	% of Total
Age:				
Over 60	6	15	1	3
50–60	5	13	2	6
40–50	17	43	16	54
Under 40	12	30	11	37
Totals	40	100	30	100
Education:				
At least a B.A. degree	28	70	25	84
Entered college but did not graduate	5	13	3	10
No college	7	17	2	6
Totals	40	100	30	100
Religion:				
Muslim	36	90	29	97
Hindu	4	10	1	3
Totals	40	100	30	100
Profession:				
Lawyer	11	28	10	33
Businessman	6	15	3	10
Journalism and literature	3	8	4	14
Pir (religious man)	—	—	1	3
Trade union work	3	8	4	14
Peasant leader	5	12	5	17
Doctor	1	3	1	3
Professors and teachers	9	23	2	6
Service in private firm	2	5	—	—
Totals	40	100	30	100

Sources: Biographical data on the party elite of the pro-Moscow EPNAP was supplied to the author by Fazlur Rahman, publicity secretary, pro-Moscow EPNAP and assistant editor of the *Sanqbad* (Dacca), a pro-Moscow daily. Biographical data on the party elite of the pro-Peking EPNAP was supplied to the author by K. G. Mustafa, sub-editor of the *Pakistan Observer* (Dacca) and a member of EPCPML. Assistance was also rendered by Abdul Karim, member of the Executive Committee of the pro-Peking EPNAP.

system, socialism could be achieved peacefully through the parliamentary road in East Pakistan. They believed that the real strength of the leftists "springs not from the barrels of guns but from the revolutionary consciousness and unity of the working people." [29] This revolutionary awareness of the suffering people could be aroused through electioneering and parliamentary politics. The pro-Moscow leftists, therefore, took part in the elections held on 7 December 1970. On the basis of their tactical line of forming an "anti-imperialist national democratic government" as a prelude to transition to the socialist system, they advocated ceaselessly for an electoral alliance of all leftist forces and secular democratic parties, even though neither the pro-Peking leftists nor the AL paid any heed to them. They advocated this alliance on the basis of the 11-point program which, as stated below, was drawn up by the East Pakistan Student Action Committee (SAC) in November 1969 when they launched a massive public agitation against the Ayub government. The pro-Moscow leftists argued that the 11-point program had the "germ of socialist consciousness," and, since it aroused wide support it could well be the basis of unity among all of the democratic forces in East Pakistan.[30]

The pro-Peking leftists were meanwhile faced with an almost interminable factionalism, which revolved around varying analyses of the objective revolutionary tactics to be adopted by the leftist forces. Since the differences between each of these groups involved rather complicated ideological notions, it might be best to spell out the differences in some detail rather than attempt to summarize their positions in short cursory statements. In what was generally regarded as their relative order of strength, these five groups could be listed as follows (1) the East Pakistan Communist Party (Marxist-Leninist) (EPCPML); (2) the East Bengal Communist Party (EBCP); (3) the Coordination Committee of Communist Revolutionaries (CCCR); (4) the East Bengal Workers Movement (EBWM); and (5) the Mythi Group.

The EPCPML

According to the EPCPML, the principal feature of the economic system of East Pakistan was its semifeudal and semicolonial character. In the view of EPCPML theoreticians, the "bourgeois revolution" remained incomplete in Pakistan after 1947, since British rule failed to destroy the feudal elements on the Indo-Pakistan subcontinent. Indeed, the British

---

[29] A discussion of the secession issue, as viewed by various Communist factions in East Bengal in 1969, appeared in *Hatiar* [Weapon] 1, no. 23 (19 September 1969). *Hatiar* was the official weekly underground organ of the EPCP.
[30] *Hatiar*, 2 December 1970, p. 1.

had strengthened both the position of Pakistani feudal elements and an indigenous capitalist class, since both were props of British imperialist rule. Some indications of revolutionary consciousness had indeed been indicated toward the end of British rule, when an anti-imperialist rebellion had taken place in the Indian navy (1946) and when this later was coupled with strikes by industrial workers and peasant revolts in Bengal and Bihar. But the British had been able to quash these revolts by collaborating first with Hindu and Muslim bureaucrat-comprador capitalists and later with American imperialists through various AID programs. As a result, the EPCPML argued, East Pakistan had remained a semifeudal and semicolonial country.[31]

According to the EPCPML, the only way to supplant Pakistan's semifeudal and semicolonial system was through a "people's democratic revolution," to be led by an alliance of landless peasants (33 percent of the agricultural population) and small landholders (37 percent of the agricultural population). The conflict between these two large sectors of the populace on the one hand and the big landholders and moneylenders on the other was highlighted in EPCPML literature as the main contradiction of the society, and revolution under the EPCPML was depicted as the only means for bringing an end to the contradiction. Because of the practical impossibility of organizing peasant revolutions simultaneously in both East and West Pakistan, under the direction of a clandestine Communist Party, the EPCPML argued that revolution would have to be planned in one wing at a time, beginning with East Pakistan.[32]

The East Bengal Communist Party (EBCP)
The EBCP viewed its program as a direct counterthesis to the EPCPML, since it argued that Pakistan was a bourgeois state with a capitalist economy. Indeed, in contrast to the EPCPML, the EBCP argued that the main impact of British rule had been the decay of Indian feudalism rather than its preservation. The EBCP acknowledged that the British had created a permanent class of landlords through the Permanent Settlement of 1793, but in the eyes of EBCP theoreticians this class of landlords had become mere rent collectors, while the British had protected the rights of some peasants through a series of legislative enactments.

The EBCP emphasized in its formulations that East Bengal peasants were not land slaves, as was the case with the serfs under European

---

[31] The principal theoretical statement of the EPCPML is Abdul Huq, *East Bengal. Semi-Feudal and Semi-Colonial* (Dacca: Syed Zafar, Kaptan Bazar, 1968).
[32] See Abdul Huq, "Colonial Theory and Democratic Movement," *Ganashakti* (Dacca Weekly), 29 March 1970.

feudalism. Besides, through the introduction of modern means of communication the British had brought the commodities produced by the peasants into international capitalist markets, and peasants had begun to grow commodities for the purpose of securing higher profits. Side by side with the decay of the feudalistic system and a gradual change from the earlier system of agricultural production into a sort of capitalistic method of production, an indigenous bourgeois class had grown up in India. This class had found it difficult to flourish quickly because of the restrictions imposed upon it by the British; so it had spearheaded the independence movement.

According to EBCP theoreticians, the larger and stronger part of the Indian bourgeoisie during the independence movement had been Hindu, while the smaller and weaker part was Muslim. When the British left India in 1947 the Muslim bourgeoisie was therefore fearful of being absorbed by the Hindu bourgeoisie; so it had carved out a separate state (Pakistan). Thus, the establishment of Pakistan was itself a bourgeois revolution. However, soon after the establishment of Pakistan, contradictions arose between the larger and stronger bourgeoisie of West Pakistan and the smaller and weaker bourgeoisie of East Pakistan. The East Pakistan bourgeoisie was now working to separate East Pakistan from West Pakistan by using the resentment of the masses in East Pakistan. If the East Pakistan bourgeoisie could secure independence from West Pakistan under its own leadership, it could obviously come to a compromise with the United States, and East Pakistan would then continue to be under the domination of the international imperialist forces. The only course of salvation for East Pakistan, therefore, was to secure East Pakistan's independence under the leadership of the workers (Communist) party, with the active assistance of the peasant proletariat (that 33 percent of the agricultural population that sold its labor to the richer landlords), through a "people's democratic revolution." This could prevent the future growth of capitalism and liquidate the remnants of feudalism, both prerequisites for the establishment of a complete socialist system.[33]

It should be pointed out that the leaders of the EPCPML rejected this analysis of the EBCP on the grounds that it highlighted the conflict between the East Pakistan and West Pakistan bourgeoisie, thereby diverting the attention of the urban and rural proletariat from launching a struggle

[33] EBCP theoretical positions are spelled out in *The Character of the National Economy: Capitalistic,* by Abdul Samad, Hasan Ali Mollah, Alauddin Ahmad, and Abdul Matin (Sirajganj: Tamizul Islam, 1967). The four authors of this book are all prominent leaders in the EBCP.

against their class enemies. Moreover, the EPCPML argued that this
EBCP platform would help the East Pakistan bourgeoisie and their
political ally (the EPAL) to bring about the secession of East Pakistan
under bourgeois leadership.

Ideological differences between the EPCPML and EBCP were paralleled by socioeconomic differences in their leadership cadres, with the
EPCPML leadership coming from well-educated professional backgrounds and the EBCP coming from peasants and workers. Of the nine
top leaders of the EPCPML in early 1970, eight were university educated
men from upper middle-class families, while the majority of the cadres of
the EPCPML also came from the educated upper classes, At the same
time, only three of the nine top leaders of the EBCP were college graduates, and the other six leaders were from the ranks of the labor and
peasant movements. All of the top leaders of the EBCP were known to
have worked directly with peasants, while their cadre members were
drawn almost exclusively from among the workers of the peasant and
labor movements. Perhaps because of their socioeconomic backgrounds,
there was intense personal enmity between the two rival groups of leaders.
The leaders of the EBCP generally argued that the leaders of the
EPCPML were merely armchair theoreticians who preached peasant
revolution while sitting in their offices in Dacca, and the EPCPML leaders were also accused by the EBCP of acting as the agents of the monopoly
capitalists of West Pakistan by presenting the conflict between the peasants and feudal elements as the main contradiction of East Pakistan
society. The EPCPML leaders, on the other hand, dismissed the leaders
of the EBCP as "uneducated adventurists passing off as Maoists." [34]

The CCCR

Partly as a result of their dissatisfaction with the personal bickerings of
the leaders of the EPCPML and the EBCP, partly as a consequence of
their frustration in securing positions of leadership in those parties, and
partly because of subtle theoretical differences, some of the younger leftist cadres (mostly in their early thirties and late twenties) had revolted
against both of the aforementioned older leadership groups and formed
separate CPs in the late 1960s. One such group—the Coordination Committee of Communist Revolutionaries (CCCR)—was led by university

[34] Debates between the EPCPML and EBCP were filled with personal attacks and
charges back and forth. Some of the debates were aired publicly, particularly in the
editorial columns of *Ganasakti* [People's Strength] and *Swadhikar* [Self-Right], the
official organs of the EPCPML and EBCP, respectively. See, for example, *Ganasakti*, 24 May and 24 June 1970; and *Swadhikar*, 22 June, 6 July and 20 July 1970.

educated pro-Chinese students in their early thirties, almost all from upper middle-class family backgrounds. As a result of a variety of activities the CCCR had come to control the majority of the labor force in Tongi industrial area, near the capital city of Dacca, and from this base they had tried to lead an unsuccessful revolt against both the EPCPML and the EBCP in late 1969.

In their debate with the EPCPML and the EBCP, CCCR theoreticians argued that Pakistan as a whole was a "semi-capitalist, semi-feudal, and semi-colonial country," but that indigenous monopoly-capitalism was mainly based in West Pakistan. According to the CCCR, this accounted for the exploitation of the masses of East Pakistan, since that exploitation had taken the shape of exploitation of one nation by the monopoly representatives of another nation, in collaboration with international imperialist forces. In East Pakistan itself, the CCCR argued, the main contradiction was between the landless and lower class peasants on the one hand and feudal elements on the other. For the CCCR, revolution in East Pakistan would take the shape of a peasant revolution, but it would also include the program of separating East Pakistan from West Pakistan.[35]

The EBWM

A second group of young Communists, led by a 30-year-old engineer, first became established in the late 1960s around the "Mao Research Centre" in Dacca, eventually becoming an underground political party (the EBWM). EBWM theoreticians argued that the main contradiction in Pakistan was the conflict between the ruling clique of West Pakistan and the colonially exploited masses of East Pakistan. Other external contradictions—the conflicts of the people of East Pakistan with American-Soviet imperialism and Indian expansionism, conflicts between workers and capitalists, and conflicts of the landless and lower class peasants with feudal elements and moneylenders—all of these were of secondary importance. According to the EBWM the revolution in East Pakistan had to take the shape of a revolution for national independence, and, by presenting various theses about whether the country was semifeudal and

[35] For the CCCR program in 1969–1971 see Hyder Akbar Khan (also known as "Rono"), *The Main Features of Imperialism* (Dacca: Jagrati Prakshani, n.d.). "Rono" holds a B.Sc. and LL.B. degree from Dacca University and is the son of the former chief engineer, Road Division, Department of Construction and Building, Government of East Pakistan. "Rono" was an active labor organizer in the period just prior to his founding of the CCCR. For a description of the activities of the student front of the CCCR see *Political Report Adopted in the Annual Meeting of East Bengal Revolutionary Students Union* (Dacca: East Bengal Revolutionary Students Union, 1970).

semicolonial or capitalistic or semicapitalistic, the other "so-called" pro-Peking Communist groups were denying the fundamental contradiction in Pakistan. According to the EBWM the other Communist groups were acting willingly or unwillingly as the agents of West Pakistani imperialists and giving over the leadership of the independence struggle to Bengali bourgeois elements. Their first program, therefore, was to bring about the secession of East Pakistan through an armed rebellion by the people's militia, and to continue the revolution further to establish a "people's democracy" in a sovereign East Bengal." [36]

The Mythi Group

A similar but more sophisticated argument was put forward by another group of young Communists, almost all of whom were in their thirties in 1970, all of whom were university educated, and all of whom were from middle-class backgrounds. These people, who called themselves the Mythi Group, agreed with the analysis of the EBCP that Pakistan as a whole was essentially a capitalist country.[37] According to the Mythi Group the monopoly capitalists of West Pakistan had needed the help of American imperialism at the early stage of its growth and had accepted American aid in order to grow bigger at a very fast rate, all the while concentrating on light consumer industries. This monopoly capitalist system had now reached a stage when it itself had become an imperialist force, exporting goods and capital to other countries, while East Pakistan had become the largest direct colony of the monopoly capitalists. Since the West Pakistan government—the agent of the monopoly capitalists of West Pakistan—kept East Pakistan under its domination through sheer military might, the revolution in East Pakistan (according to the Mythi Group) necessarily had to take on the character of a "national liberation struggle." [38]

While it is clear that there were significant differences between the five major Maoist factions in 1969–1970, it is also clear that there were some similarities. All of the above-mentioned groups were against participation in the elections of December 1970, and all propagated armed rebellion in East Pakistan.[39] Indeed, the EPCPML had even drawn up a four-point

[36] "The Party Thesis of the Revolutionary Council," 3d impression, cyclostyled (Dacca: East Pakistan Workers Movement, 1969).

[37] The Mythi Group takes its name from its leader Agni Provo Mythi (probably a pseudonym).

[38] *Lal Pub* ["The Red East"] 1, no. 1 (January 1970). *Lal Pub* was the organ of the Marxist Writers' Association of Chittagong, which was the literary front organization of the Mythi Group.

[39] The elections of December 1970 had originally been scheduled for October 1970. They were postponed until December because of the devastating floods in East Bengal in August, which affected more than half of the people of East Bengal.

program of revolution: (1) to develop a strong and secret revolutionary party, armed with Marxist-Leninist-Maoist doctrines, in order to destroy opportunist, rightist, and revisionist forces; (2) to form a revolutionary united front of anti-imperialist, antifeudal, and anti-bureaucrat-capitalist classes under the leadership of the above party; (3) to form units of revolutionaries in the villages (as the villages are the weakest parts of the enemies of the revolution), in order to emancipate the villages and encircle the urban areas; and (4) ultimately to usher in a revolution all over the province to free East Bengal from the centralized State dominated by the agents of imperialism, with a view to establishing a sovereign People's Democratic Republic in East Bengal.[40] Similar programs were circulated by both the EBCP and CCCR in late 1970.[41]

While both the EPCPML and CCCR did recruit members of the party for guerrilla units during the year preceding the secessionist movement of March 1971, none of these units attempted to emancipate any village areas during this period for fear of severe reprisals by the Martial Law authorities of the Yahya Khan regime. In contrast, the EBCP, which was able to win over the largest number of pro-Peking workers, had adopted a militant pose not only in their literature but also in their actions. "Petty guerrilla units" of the EBCP attempted a number of "land grabs" in certain pockets in the districts of Rajshahi, Kushtia, Rangpur, Bogra, Jessore, Khulna, and Sylhet in 1969,[42] as a result of which many of the workers of the EBCP were jailed. In response to these movements the other pro-Peking factions repeatedly accused the EBCP of "ultra-revolutionary adventurism" and "Trotskyite and Che Guevarian deviationism."

The Maoist faction that was most critical of the EBCP was the EBWM, under the direction of the Mao Research Centre. The EBWM argued that the EPCPML, EBCP, and CCCR were blindly following the Naxalite tactics of Charu Mazumdar and Kanu Sanyal of West Bengal, without taking into consideration the fact that tactics of emancipating village areas

[40] "Programme of the East Pakistan Communist Party (Marxist-Leninist): People's Democratic Revolution," cyclostyled, publisher and date not mentioned.
[41] See the *Eleven-Point Programme for Establishing a Sovereign, People's Democratic Republic in East Bengal* (Dacca: Mahbubullah, 1970). Mahbubullah was the president of the student front of EBCP and was arrested and convicted under Martial Law regulations for reading out his program in a public meeting at Dacca on 22 February 1970. For the program of the CCCR see *Political Report of East Bengal Revolutionary Students Union Adopted at its Provincial Conference on 1 May 1970* (Dacca: East Bengal Revolutionary Students' Union, 1970), pp. 40–42. This union was the student front of the CCCR.
[42] For a description of these movements see *Purba Bangla* [East Bengal] 1, no. 1 (April 1969). *Purba Bangla* was the underground paper of the EBCP.

and encircling cities are not suitable for a terrain covered by a network of modern systems of communication and administered by a highly central- ized State apparatus backed by an efficient army. Since almost all of the villages of East Pakistan are readily accessible to the army, the EBWM argued that any given village would only be "emancipated" for a short time. The EBWM, therefore, advocated the formation of a people's militia that could free East Bengal at a moment of severe political crisis, and similar views were also held by the Mythi Group.[43]

It should be mentioned that a few pro-Peking Communists, unorganized and without a following among the cadres, did advocate participation in the December 1970 elections. These men also advocated a "people's dem- ocratic revolution" with the help of landless and lower class peasants and also wanted to free East Pakistan from West Pakistan. However, they were convinced that the fight to establish a people's democracy should be launched on all fronts, both inside and outside Parliament, and therefore desired to contest elections.[44]

[43] The EBWM thesis was published in *Programme for Establishing a Sovereign, Democratic Progressive Republic of East Bengal* (Dacca: EBWM, n. d.), pp. 15–16. On 6 May 1970, two handmade bombs were thrown into the offices of the Pakistan Council in Dacca, and the Mao Research Centre of the EBWM immediately issued a leaflet in which they claimed credit for the bombings. Bombing incidents were repeated during the next few days in Dacca and Khulna, but they stopped shortly afterwards when they were denounced in East Pakistan by Peking Radio.

[44] The similarities between the splits and factions among the Communists in East Pakistan and those in West Bengal (in India) are striking. The split of the Commu- nists in West Bengal into Soviet and Chinese tactical lines was followed by the division of the Communists in East Pakistan into pro-Moscow and pro-Peking parties. The EPCPML, following the CPML in West Bengal, highlighted the feudal characteristics of the East Pakistan economy to justify a peasant revolution. When the faction of the CPML of West Bengal, led by Kanu Sanyal and Charu Mazum- dar, fomented a peasant revolt in Naxalbari in West Bengal, the EPCPML (follow- ing the Jyoti Basu faction) disapproved of it. The EBCP, on the other hand, quickly supported it as the correct revolutionary line for East Pakistan. When Peking Radio and the *Peking Review* dubbed the Naxalbari tactic the correct line of revolution, the EPCPML as well as the CCCR began to advocate the Naxalbari line.

The nature and degree of cooperation between the various CPs in East Bengal and doctrinally similar counterparts in West Bengal before the liberation struggle could not be ascertained. The senior leaders of the pro-Moscow Communists, who were co-workers of the pro-Moscow leaders of West Bengal in the CPI before partition, certainly had close relations with one another. The EPCP, before its split in 1966, even used to hold its annual congress in Calcutta. According to a report in the *Times of India* (3 June 1970), the EPCPML appealed to the CPML in West Bengal for cooperation in launching a joint guerrilla movement in both East and West Bengal. Moreover, the Naxalbari faction of the CPML in West Bengal was reported to have commented favorably on the activities of the EPCPML in one of its position papers [see *Swadhikar* (Khulna Weekly), 6 July 1970].

The formation of so many CPs by the pro-Chinese leftists, and their mutual recriminations and vilifications made it impossible for them to maintain one popular front in 1970. Maulana Bhashani, who had for so long been the non-Marxist leader of the revolutionary Marxists, had neither the intellectual sophistication to weave together the divergent views of the various leftist groups into a coherent doctrine nor the training to lead a truly revolutionary party. In 1970 he therefore revived the doctrine of "Islamic socialism" that he had propagated at the time of Independence and began to organize peasant conferences to press the peasants' demand for food, exemption from taxes, protection against floods, ending of the corrupt practices of officials, and so forth.

Leaders of the EPCPML who had been the closest associates of Maulana Bhashani since 1956 then began to resign from NAP on the ground that Maulana Bhashani was harming leftist politics by reviving communalism. They continued to insist that the people's democratic revolution could be brought about only by a disciplined and well-organized Communist party. Instead of working through mass or class organizations, however, the EPCPML leadership argued that Communist revolutionaries should concentrate on spreading a secret revolutionary Communist party organization among workers and peasants. For this reason they also resigned from the Bhashani-led Peasants Association.

The Mao Research group and the Mythi Group had from the start of the formation of their parties disassociated themselves from the NAP. The EBCP and CCCR leaders for some time remained associated with NAP and the Peasants Association on the ground that the activities of these front organizations were helpful in intensifying class consciousness among the poorer and landless peasant proletariat and that the clandestine Communist parties and the front organizations would have to work in complementary ways to hasten the process of people's democratic revolution. But they also disassociated themselves from NAP and the Peasants Association when Maulana Bhashani sided with the proelection faction of the pro-Peking Communists and decided on NAP's participation in the December 1970 elections. Bhashani later fell out with even the proelection faction of the pro-Peking Communists and just a few days before the election (held on 7 December 1970) started demanding an "independent and sovereign East Pakistan." By this time, of course, Bhashani had outlived his usefulness for the Communist revolutionaries. Abandoned by the leftists, Bhashani sought political survival by trying to ride the wave of Bengali nationalism that ultimately brought a massive victory to the EPAL.

To sum up our discussion so far, by 1969–1970 the leftist movement in

East Pakistan had moved a long way from its poor start in 1947–1948. Through the techniques used by the leftists in all underdeveloped countries—cultural subversion, infiltration of popular political organizations, manipulation of sensitive issues like language, autonomy, and economic distress, and anti-imperialist agitation—the leftists in East Bengal had created an atmosphere favorable to a secular and radical politics. The leftists had also gained full advantage of the shift in foreign policy by the Ayub Khan government toward the socialist countries, and particularly toward Communist China. Under the patronage of the Ayub government, the leftists stepped up their anti-imperialist propaganda and circulated Maoist literature widely among the impressionable younger generation. All of these activities helped to radicalize East Bengal politics.

By 1970 the number of leftist cadres in East Bengal had also increased considerably. While in 1947–1948 the number of EPCP members was only a few hundred, membership reportedly rose to about 3,000 in 1966, just before the first split in the EPCP. Moreover, while the overwhelming majority of the cadres in the early years were from the minority Hindu community, the Muslim cadres were reported to account for more than 90 percent of the membership of the CPs in Pakistan in 1970.[45]

The leftists in East Bengal, however, were faced with new problems and fresh dilemmas. The split in the international Communist movement and problems of finding correct revolutionary theory and consequent tactical methods severely affected the unity of the leftist movement. The cohesion of the leftist cadres was further strained by the gap between political generations, and demands by the younger cadres for positions of leadership. The result was the splitting of the EPCP into several CPs—one pro-Moscow and several pro-Peking. While the pro-Moscow group upheld the theory of peaceful transition to socialism through the parliamentary path, all the pro-Chinese groups advocated armed revolution for bringing about a "people's democracy in a sovereign and independent East Bengal." Each of the parties claimed several hundred full members and a steady increase in support. Believing in the Leninist dictum that a correct revolutionary theory was a prerequisite for a successful revolution, each of them adopted its party thesis, outlining a "correct" analysis of the objective conditions in East Pakistan and the consequent strategies of bringing the "people's democratic revolution" to successful fruition. Each of them was also trying to build up the party on the Marxist-Leninist-Maoist principle of strict "democratic centralism" while playing down the role of front organizations. Each of them upheld the view that, since the

---

[45] These approximate figures were cited to the author by a leader of the EPCPML in October 1970.

objective and subjective conditions were favorable, the revolution might be sparked off at any time and once the revolution started the dynamics of the revolution would sweep away the other "wrong" parties.

The greatest factor hindering the faster spread of the influence of the Communist revolutionaries was the upsurge of Bengali nationalism that rapidly advanced in East Pakistan during the last decade of the rule of Ayub Khan. One of the major doctrinal lapses of Marxist international communism has been the nonrecognition of the force of nationalism as a factor in the change of history. Engaged in theoretical hair splitting on the division of the international Communist movement, East Pakistan Communist revolutionaries, while thrashing out their tactical moves, failed at the beginning to take into consideration the force of East Pakistan nationalism. In the mid-1960s, the pro-Peking Communists, by siding with the Ayub Khan government on the ground of Ayub's pro-Chinese stand in foreign policy, even found it necessary to oppose the six-point autonomy movement, which ultimately gave the leadership of East Pakistan's liberation struggle to the Awami League. The pro-Moscow leftists, after their break with the pro-Peking leftists, did lend their support to the six-point program of the EPAL, but by this time they could not snatch away the leadership of the Bengali nationalist movement from the Awami League.

The Awami League and the Demand for Autonomy

The origins of the Awami League can be traced to the factionalism that developed in the Bengal Muslim League at the time of the partition of India in 1947. In the late 1940s Bengali Muslim youth joined the Muslim League in large numbers and quickly took control of the organization in Bengal, under the progressive leadership of H. S. Suhrawardy and Abul Hashim. When the older conservative faction of the Muslim League, led by Khwaja Nazimuddin, failed to get its nominees elected to the Bengal Muslim League Parliamentary Board in 1945, largely because of the dominance of the younger generation in the Muslim League Council, Nazimuddin went into voluntary retirement from politics and the influence of the conservatives was considerably weakened.[46] Suhrawardy and Hashim then led the Muslim League campaign during the 1945–1946 elections to the Bengal Provincial Legislature, as a result of which the Muslim League captured 113 out of 119 Muslim seats and 87 percent of the Muslim votes.

[46] See the *Azad* (Calcutta), 1, 7 October 1945.

During the period March 1946–August 1947 Suhrawardy was the prime minister of the undivided British Indian province of Bengal, but in early 1947 Suhrawardy and Hashim (in cooperation with Sarat Bose, the brother of Subhas) advanced their proposal for a "united sovereign Bengal," to be separated from both India and Pakistan. Despite the fact that the Suhrawardy-Hashim proposal was advanced primarily to avoid the partition of Bengal, and despite Jinnah's tacit support for the proposal, it ultimately failed. After Pakistan was created in 1947, Suhrawardy's opponents in the Muslim League quickly seized on the Suhrawardy-Hashim proposal as a means of discrediting Suhrawardy himself, arguing that Suhrawardy had not supported the idea of Pakistan. The landlord and orthodox sections of the Bengal Muslim League, led by Khwaja Nazimuddin and Maulana Akram Khan and supported by the non-Bengali speaking Muslim businessmen of Calcutta, immediately launched a propaganda campaign against Suhrawardy (he was described as an "anti-Pakistan element"), with the tacit approval of the central leadership of the All-India Muslim League.[47] Perhaps more important, the Nazimuddin group secured the allegiance of 20 key Muslim legislators of Sylhet district of Assam (whose people joined East Bengal through a referendum in July 1947) by promising them two seats in the new East Bengal cabinet. Finally, at a meeting of the Muslim League Parliamentary Party held on 5 August 1947, Nazimuddin was elected leader of the party in place of Suhrawardy.[48]

The election of Nazimuddin as the leader of the Muslim League Parliamentary Party, and his consequent assumption of the office of chief minister of East Bengal, created a deep sense of frustration among the youthful architects of the Muslim League victory in the 1945–1946 elections. But they were even more resentful when the central Muslim League leadership appointed the aging and conservative Maulana Akram Khan (71 in 1948) as chief organizer of the East Bengal Muslim League. When Maulana Akram Khan and his associates systematically excluded Suhrawardy followers from membership in the East Bengal Muslim League during the new membership drive in 1948–1949,[49] resentment turned into open revolt.

The frustration of the younger generation in the Muslim League immediately after partition was further enhanced by the policies pursued by

---

[47] Ibid., 8, 10, 23, 31 July 1947.
[48] Ibid., 6 August 1947.
[49] Ataur Rahman Khan, *Ojarotir Dhui Basar* [Two Years of Ministership] (Dacca: Standard Publishers 1961), pp. 26–29.

the Muslim League government of Pakistan. All of the key officers appointed in the subdivisions, districts and the secretariat in East Bengal were non-Bengali Muslims drawn from West Punjab and the provinces of former British India, to the exclusion of Bengali freedom fighters. Moreover, the chief secretary (a Punjabi) not only dominated the East Bengal cabinet but also sent secret reports about the activities of East Bengal ministers to the central government. As a result, a feeling began to grow among East Bengalis, as was stated by Begum Shaista Ikramullah in the Pakistan Constituent Assembly early in February 1948, that East Bengal was being neglected and treated merely as a "colony" of West Pakistan.[50] This feeling of being colonized was further heightened when central Muslim League leaders began to suggest that Urdu—a language that was not understood by even 1 percent of the East Bengalis—would be the only state language of Pakistan.

On 4 January 1948 a pro-Suhrawardy group of students formed the East Bengal Students League (EBSL), with Sheikh Mujibur Rahman (a former student worker of Suhrawardy's group in Calcutta and at that time a student at Dacca University) as the organizing secretary. By the beginning of February 1948 the Students League had launched a movement for recognition of Bengali as one of the state languages of Pakistan, and in June 1949 this movement gave birth to a new political party, the East Bengal Awami League. With Maulana Bhashani as president[51] and Suhrawardy as convener, the Awami League resurrected the Lahore Resolution of the All-India Muslim League (1940), which demanded that "the areas in which Muslims were numerically in a majority—as in the North-Western and Eastern Zones of India—should be grouped *to constitute Independent States in which the constituent units shall be autonomous and sovereign.*"[52]

Shortly after its formation, the Awami League issued a 42-point manifesto, the main points of which were as follows: (1) regional autonomy for East Bengal in the context of the Lahore Resolution of 1940, with only three powers—defense, foreign affairs, and currency and coinage— left with the central government; (2) recognition of Bengali as one of the state languages of Pakistan; (3) abolition of all rent-receiving interests in

50 *Constituent Assembly of Pakistan Debates* 2, no. 1 (24 February 1948), p. 7.

51 Bhashani's role in the AL is discussed in detail in Abul Mansur Ahmad, *Amar Dhekha Rajnitir Panchas Basar* [Fifty Years of Politics as I Saw It] (Dacca: Nowroj Kitabistan, 1968), pp. 244–245.

52 For the text of the Lahore Resolution see G. Allana, ed., *Pakistan Movement: Historic Documents* (Karachi: Paradise Book Subscription Agency, 1968), pp. 226–227.

land without compensation and distribution of the surplus land among the landless cultivators; (4) nationalization of the jute trade; (5) introduction of cooperative farming; (6) guarantees for the economic and social rights of industrial labor according to the ILO conventions; and (7) introduction of free and compulsory primary education.[53]

In January 1952, Khwaja Nazimuddin, then prime minister of all of Pakistan, provoked a series of public demonstrations in East Bengal when he declared that Urdu alone would be the state language in Pakistan. Nazimuddin's declaration was in clear violation of an agreement that he, as chief minister of East Bengal earlier, had made with student leaders in March 1948, and a Committee of Action (with representatives from the Awami League, Youth League and Students League) quickly called for observance of a protest day on 21 February 1952. On that day, the students of Dacca University brought out a procession despite a police order against it, and the police opened fire on the students' procession and killed several students.

The killing of these students in 1952 provided the Awami League leaders with the names of martyrs that could be invoked to rouse public passions. Throughout 1952 and 1953 Awami League leaders like Suhrawardy, Bhashani, Ataur Rahman Khan, Abdul Mansur Ahmad, and Sheikh Mujibur Rahman, together with a host of leaders from the Students League, toured the length and breadth of East Bengal, addressing mass meetings and arousing nationalistic sentiments on the basis of their demands for adoption of Bengali as a state language and for regional autonomy. Finally, in 1954, the Awami League formed a United Front with the Krishak Sramik Party of A. K. Fazlul Huq, the mover of the Lahore Resolution of 1940, and the United Front subsequently won 223 out of 237 Muslim seats (with 57 percent of the votes) in the 1954 elections.[54]

Despite its victory in 1954, the United Front was unable to bring about radical change in Pakistan's political life, largely because of its own internal factional rivalries. Indeed, by 1956 it was generally acknowledged that the Bengali nationalist movement had lost its momentum, and this became even more evident after 1956 when the persuasive Suhrawardy assumed the office of prime minister of Pakistan (in October 1956). As I have pointed out elsewhere, Suhrawardy after 1956 increasingly began

[53] Interview with Abul Mansur Ahmad, who had been a vice-president and ideologue of the Awami League during the period 1950–1956, on 3 June 1970.
[54] The percentage of the votes received by the United Front was tabulated from the constituencywide results of the 1954 elections published in the *Azad* (Dacca), 16, 17, 18, 19, 20, 21, 22 March 1954.

to think more in terms of building a national consensus in Pakistan, and less about the concerns of East Bengal.[55]

The Six-Point Revolution

The complete domination of East Bengal by West Pakistan throughout the period of Ayub Khan's naked military rule (1958–1962) and his constitutionally veiled dictatorship (1962–1969) not only revived Bengali nationalist sentiment, it also added a new militancy to the Awami League and other political parties. The "ruling class" of Pakistan during the Ayub decade was composed primarily of President Ayub and his advisors, drawn almost exclusively from the top echelons of the bureaucracy and the armed forces. In this ruling class, East Bengal was hardly represented. Moreover, Ayub Khan added insult to injury by recruiting his ministers from among those politicians who were rejected by the Bengalis in the 1954 elections, the only elections held on the basis of adult franchise before the last general elections of December 1970. Of the 16 East Bengalis who served as Ayub's ministers, 4 were drawn from the services and 1 was a journalist. The remaining 11 members were Muslim League leaders, 8 of whom had contested and lost the elections of 1954. Of the 4 governors of East Bengal during the Ayub decade, the first was an East Bengal police officer, the second a Pathan general, and the third a Pathan civil servant. The last governor, who held office for seven years, was an East Bengali, but he had been defeated so badly in the 1954 elections that he had been required to forfeit his electoral deposit.

Aside from the political domination by West Pakistan over East Bengal, the economic system of Pakistan developed in a manner reminiscent of the exploitation of East Bengal on the classical nineteenth-century colonial pattern. For example, from 1955–1956 until 1964, the Pakistan central government spent 18,847 million rupees, of which 10,107 (about 54 percent) was for defense, almost all of which was spent in West Pakistan. During the same period, 3,678 million rupees (about 19 percent) supported civil administration, and nearly 70 percent of this was expended in West Pakistan.[56] To take another example, foreign trade balances for the 19 years from 1948 to 1967 show that East Bengal's cumulative surplus amounted to 4,878 million rupees, yet during this

[55] Talukder Maniruzzaman, *The Politics of Development: The Case of Pakistan (1947–1958)* (Dacca: Green Book House, 1972), pp. 53–54, 62–63.
[56] Pakistan Ministry of Finance, *Pakistan Economic Survey* (Rawalpindi: Government of Pakistan, 1965), p. 124.

period East Bengal had deficit trade balances of 5,712 million rupees with West Pakistan.[57] Moreover, according to government policy, East Bengal had to buy West Pakistan's consumer goods in a protected market, at much higher prices than it would have paid for equivalent foreign products.

During the years 1958–1962, when political parties were banned, the two student organizations—the Students League (affiliated with the Awami League) and the Students Union (affiliated with the NAP)— became the main vehicles for the expression of Bengali nationalist feelings. Students continued to observe 21 February each year as Martyrs' Day, and they staunchly resisted an attempt by the Ayub government to destroy the cultural distinctiveness of East Bengal through the introduction of Roman script for the Bengali language. Students also prevented the implementation of the Report of the Commission on National Education (1959), which recommended a series of regimented proposals for an educational system on Islamic ideological lines. When Ayub promulgated his constitution on 1 March 1962, to give a constitutional cover to his dictatorship, the students, especially those of Dacca University, went on strike for most of the 1962–1963 academic session.[58]

The removal of the ban on Pakistan's political parties in 1964 coincided with the revival of the Awami League. By this time, Suhrawardy— the moderating influence within the Awami League during his later years —was dead, and the control of the organization had passed to a more militant group of Awami Leaguers, led by Sheikh Mujibur Rahman. The failure of Miss Jinnah (who promised the restoration of parliamentary democracy and evoked tremendous popular enthusiasm in East Bengal in the stilted elections of January 1965) convinced these younger Awami League leaders that President Ayub could not be dislodged through the electoral system devised by him.[59] The Awami League, therefore, began to prepare for a mass movement in support of their demand for "full autonomy."

Awami League plans for a mass movement were accelerated by the

---

[57] Anisur Rahman, "Who Pays Debts to Whom?" *Pakistan Observer*, 21 March 1968. The figures are from annual trade reports published by the Pakistan government.

[58] In the 1962–1963 academic session at Dacca University students attended classes for only 32 days.

[59] Under the Ayub system the president was elected by an electoral college of 80,000 "basic democrats" who were elected members of the Union Council, the base tier of the Basic Democracies Scheme and the main beneficiaries of government patronage.

Indo-Pakistan war in September 1965, when East Bengal was completely cut off from West Pakistan and the people of East Bengal felt completely helpless.[60] After the cessation of hostilities, Sheikh Mujibur Rahman—a political entrepreneur par excellence—thought that East Bengal's sense of isolation could be manipulated to spark a nationalist explosion among the politically discontented and economically frustrated Bengalis. At a press conference, he stated: "The question of autonomy appears to be more important after the War. Time has come for making East Pakistan self-sufficient in all respects." [61] And he then announced a six-point "charter of survival" program for East Bengal, which included: (1) reintroduction of a parliamentary form of government and universal adult franchise; (2) a federal form of government with only two departments—defense and foreign affairs—to be lodged with the central government and all residual powers to reside in the two states (East and West Pakistan); (3) separate currencies and state banks for the two states; (4) all heads of taxation under the states, with the central government dependent on a fixed levy from the states; (5) the independence of the two states in international trade; and (6) the development of a militia or paramilitary force in East Pakistan.[62]

To say that Sheikh Mujib's six-point program evoked tremendous enthusiasm among the people of East Bengal would be an understatement. Encouraged by overwhelming popular support, Sheikh Mujib convened a meeting of the Council of the EPAL, at which his program was enthusiastically approved and he was elected president of the party (before this he had been the general secretary). With a phalanx of organizers from the Students League, Sheikh Mujib then launched a vigorous mass campaign. For about three months after this (from mid-February to mid-May 1966) the urban centers of East Bengal seemed to be in the grip of a "mass revolution," prompting the government to arrest Sheikh Mujib and his chief lieutenants under the Defence of Pakistan Rules and to put down a complete general strike in Dacca (7 June 1966) by killing 13 participating strikers. The government later charged Sheikh Mujib, along with three East Bengal members of the Civil Service and 24 junior officers in the armed forces, with "conspiracy to bring about the secession of East Pakistan with Indian help."

60 The headquarters of the army, navy, and air force were in West Pakistan. About 90 percent of the armed forces personnel were recruited from West Pakistan and were also stationed there.
61 *Daily Ittefaq* (Dacca), 15 February 1966.
62 Summarized from Sheikh Mujibur Rahman, *Six-Point Formula: Our Right to Live* (Dacca: EPAL, 1966).

As one might have expected, Sheikh Mujib's arrest in 1966 only served to enhance his popularity, to the point where he became the veritable symbol of Bengali nationalism. But at this point most of the support for his six-point program in East Bengal still came from a section of the rising East Bengal entrepreneurial class (lawyers, students, government officers, and teachers). Indeed, the "six-point revolution" was in essence the revolution of the petty bourgeoisie of East Bengal, who found their road to advancement blocked by their counterparts in West Pakistan that were patronized by the military-based dictatorship of General Ayub Khan.

The 11-Point Program

With the detention of Sheikh Mujibur Rahman and other prominent leaders of the Awami League in 1966 the leadership of the Bengali nationalist movement again fell upon the students. Toward the end of 1968, the leaders of the Students League and the Students Union formed the East Bengal Students Action Committee (SAC), with Tofael Ahmad, the fire-spitting vice-president of the Dacca University Central Students Union as chairman. Under Tofael Ahmad's leadership, SAC drew up an 11-point program and launched a movement against the Ayub government. The 11 points of the SAC were: (1) repeal of the National Education Commission Report, the Hamoodur Rahman Commission Report and the University Ordinances; (2) restoration of democracy and universal adult franchise; (3) autonomy for East Bengal along the lines of the six points; (4) establishment of a subfederation in West Pakistan, giving full autonomy to Baluchistan, the Northwest Frontier Provinces, and Sindh; (5) nationalization of banks, insurance companies, and big industrial units; (6) reduction of taxes upon agriculturalists; (7) payment of proper wages to laborers; (8) introduction of a flood control plan in East Bengal; (9) lifting of the state of emergency, public safety acts, and other repressive measures; (10) formulation of an independent foreign policy, including withdrawal from the CENTO and SEATO pacts; and (11) release of all political prisoners and students and the dropping of all political cases, including the *Argatala* "conspiracy case" against Sheikh Mujibur Rahman.[63]

The 11-point program radicalized the politics of East Bengal in a way that had never happened before. By subsuming the AL's six-point program with the leftists' planks of socialist reforms and an anti-imperialist foreign

[63] Summarized from the text of the 11-point program published in the *Azad* (Dacca), 6 February 1969.

policy stance, the SAC aroused massive popular support among all classes of people. For about five months—from November 1968 to March 1969—virtually the whole mass of East Bengal revolted against the Ayub government. Surging crowds filled the streets of the cities, towns, and thana (police station) headquarters, defying police orders that were intended to prohibit the assembly of more than four persons. The imposition of army curfews designed to prevent the spread of the slogans for *Swadhikar* (emancipation) of East Bengal and establishment of *Krishak-Sramik Raj* (rule by peasants and workers) seemed almost naive. The preponderance of laborers, radical students, and members of the lower classes in mass demonstrations during this period was indicated by the fact that of 76 persons killed by the police and the army during November 1968–March 1969, 34 were laborers, 20 were students, 7 were lower-class government employees, 5 were small businessmen, 1 was a school teacher, and another a university professor.[64] To appease the masses, General Ayub withdrew the "conspiracy case" against Sheikh Mujib and others and released them on 22 February 1969. But at a reception held on 23 February 1969 at Dacca's Raman Race Course, more than half a million people welcomed Sheikh Mujib, chanting the new slogans of *Joi Bangla* (long live Bengal) and *Krishak-Sramik Raj*. Sensing the mood of the people, Sheikh Mujib declared that his party would work for the realization of both the six-point and 11-point programs.[65]

The Awami League and the 1970 Elections

In the short run, the effect of the 1969 mass upheaval in Bengal was the fall from power of General Ayub Khan and a declaration of Martial Law throughout Pakistan by Ayub's successor, General Yahya Khan, on 25 March 1969.[66] According to knowledgeable political circles in West Pakistan, there was at that time considerable debate within the Pakistan military as to the wisdom of holding future elections, with the "hawks" (led by General Tikka Khan) reportedly of the view that East Bengal had to be "cleared" of the "secessionists" before any elections could take place. General Yahya, supported by General Abdul Hamid, advocated a more subtle strategy, which was eventually adopted. According to the Yahya strategy, elections would be held under a Martial Law Order, but this

---

[64] The profession of the other eight persons are not known. The names and professions of the persons killed during the anti-Ayub movement in November 1968–March 1969 were published in the *Ittefaq* (Dacca), 21 January 1970.

[65] See the *Pakistan Observer* (Dacca), 24 February 1969.

[66] See Talukder Maniruzzaman, "Crisis in Political Development and the Collapse of the Ayub Regime in Pakistan," *The Journal of Developing Areas* 5, no. 2 (January 1971), 236.

order would also preclude the possibility of enacting the new constitution by the elected National Assembly on the basis of the six-point program.[67] This, the Legal Framework Order, issued by General Yahya as the chief Martial Law Administrator, and binding on the proposed National Assembly, provided that ". . . the Federal Government shall also have adequate powers, including legislative, administrative and financial powers to discharge its responsibilities in relation to external and internal affairs and to preserve the independence and territorial integrity of the country." [68]

Sheikh Mujib simply ignored the Legal Framework Order. During the election campaign of 1970 Sheikh Mujib declared that elections were a referendum on the AL's six-point and 11-point programs, and the election manifesto focused primarily on a detailed explication of its plank for autonomy.[69] For the better part of two years—from March 1969 to December 1970—Sheikh Mujib had toured the length and breadth of East Bengal, repeating the AL demands to party workers, while addressing innumerable mass rallies. Finally, when elections were called for December 1970, the Parliamentary Board of the Awami League carefully drew up a slate of party nominees that included within it the leaders of the dominant interests and age groups of East Bengal, in an attempt to promote a broad-based "national coalition" (the demographic characteristics of the 162 nominees are provided in table 4.2).

As is shown in table 4.2, the vast majority (78 percent of the total) of the nominees of the AL belonged to the age group 40–50 and below, a generation that constituted the majority of the voters in 1970 and had fewer emotional ties with the Pakistan movement. Moreover, this generation had never experienced the economic exploitation of Bengali Muslims by the Hindu *Mahajans* (moneylenders), businessmen, and zamindars, with the result that they were less adverse than their forefathers to an alliance with India and the destruction of Pakistan. Eight of the AL nominees in 1970 were in their 20s, and three were prominent leaders of SAC, while the majority were recruited to the AL initially through their participation in either the Students League or the Students Union.

With regard to the professional background of the nominees, it is striking that 19 percent of the total were drawn from business and industrial

[67] Interview with Dr. Javed Iqbal, a Council Muslim League leader in the Punjab, on 19 November 1969.
[68] See the text of the Legal Framework Order published in *Dawn* (Karachi), 30 March 1970.
[69] See the *Manifesto of All Pakistan Awami League* (Dacca: Abdul Mannan, Publicity Secretary, All Pakistan Awami League, 1970).

Table 4.2 Demographic Characteristics of the Awami League Nominees for the National Assembly in 1970 General Elections

Demographic Characteristics	Number	% of Total
Age:		
60 and over	9	5
50–60	24	15
40–50	77	47
30–40	42	26
20–30	8	5
Not known	2	2
Totals	162	100
Education:		
At least a B.A. degree	132[a]	81
Graduate of secondary school	6	3
Matriculation or less	12	8
Madrasah (traditional Islamic) education	2	2
Not known	10	6
Totals	162	100
Profession:		
Lawyers	77[b]	47
Doctors	7	4
Businessmen	31	19
Former government servants	3	2
School teachers	6	4
University and college teachers	10	6
Trade union leaders	1	1
Student leaders	3	2
Journalists	5	3
Former military service	3	2
Not known	9	6
Totals	162	100
Religion:		
Muslim	160	98.8
Hindu	1	0.6
Buddhist	1	0.6
Totals	162	100.0

[a] Ten of the 132 nominees having graduate and postgraduate degrees (6 percent of the total) had higher education in foreign countries (8 in Great Britain, one in Europe, and one in the United States).
[b] Three lawyers also had business concerns and one lawyer was also a landholder.
Sources: Part of the information about the nominees was supplied to the author by Obaidur Rahman, social service secretary of the Awami League (1969–1970) and an Awami League candidate himself in the 1970 elections; the rest of the data was collected from the life sketches of the AL nominees published in the *Banglar Bani* (Awami League Weekly, Dacca) in its various issues in November–December 1970.

groups. Like the national bourgeoisie in most former colonial countries, the majority of the Bengali businessmen and industrialists backed the liberation movement launched by the Awami League and ultimately financed its election campaign. Since the one trade union leader that was nominated in 1970 was the general secretary of the Jatio Sramik League (National Labor League), which in 1969–1970 was the largest labor organization in East Bengal, this meant that the AL had large-scale support from both business and labor. Finally, 7 percent of the AL nominees were landholders, with the rest being drawn from among Western-educated lawyers, doctors, school, college, and university teachers, retired men of the services, and journalists.

The AL won as complete a victory in the elections of 1970 as has been witnessed anywhere in the world, capturing 160 of 162 seats in the East Bengal assembly, with 72.57 percent of the votes cast. Neither the pro-Moscow leftists nor the proelection faction of the pro-Peking NAP were able to win a single seat, securing only 1.83 and 0.3 percent of the votes, respectively. The Jamaat-i-Islami, various factions of the Muslim League, the Pakistan Democratic Party, the Nizam-e-Islam—all political groupings that advocated a strong and viable central government for the whole of Pakistan while propagating Islamic nationalism—secured a total of 16.93 percent of the votes.[70] In West Pakistan, the Pakistan People's Party, led by Zulfikar Ali Bhutto (which also supported the notion of a strong and viable government, based on Islamic socialism and a policy of confrontation with India) won 81 of a total of 138 National Assembly seats allotted to West Pakistan.[71]

Military Action and Genocide in East Bengal
The Awami League's massive victory, followed by repeated declarations by Sheikh Mujibur Rahman that the constitution would be enacted in strict conformity with the six-point and 11-point programs, alarmed both the army generals and Bhutto. For at that point it was clear that if the elected National Assembly was called into being, the AL would easily be able to enact a constitution based on its autonomy programs, and this

---

[70] Of the registered voters in East Bengal in 1970, 57.69 percent cast their votes in the National Assembly election in December. The percentage figures for votes cast and votes obtained by different political parties were released to the press by the Election Commission. See the *Ittefaq* (Dacca), 23 January 1971.

[71] In the elections for provincial assemblies the Pakistan People's party secured 113 of 180 seats in the Punjab assembly, 34 of 60 seats in the Sindh assembly, 4 of 40 seats in the NWFP assembly, and none of 20 seats in Baluchistan.

would in turn convert Pakistan into nothing more than a loose confederation. As an elite group with high salaries and entrenched privileges,
spending more than half of the country's yearly budget, the armed forces
had a material stake in keeping East Bengal as an integral part of
Pakistan.

For Bhutto, the acceptance of a constitution based on the AL programs
would mean the loss of his massive popularity in the Punjab, where he
had all along promised a strong central government, a powerful army, and
"a thousand year war with India." For these reasons, both General Yahya
and Bhutto attempted to postpone the opening session of the assembly,
while Bhutto launched a campaign to rouse the feelings of West Pakistanis
against East Bengal. Bhutto declared that Sindh and Punjab were "the
bastions of power" in Pakistan,[72] and since his party had emerged with a
sweeping electoral victory in these two provinces in 1970, his party would
not accept any constitution that was thrust upon West Pakistan by the
"brute majority" of the Awami League.[73] A series of meetings between
General Yahya and Sheikh Mujib, between Bhutto and Yahya, and
finally between Sheikh Mujib and Bhutto in January 1971 ultimately
produced a promise from Yahya Khan that a session of the National
Assembly would be convened at Dacca on 3 March. But the real intentions of the Yahya regime were betrayed when, on 17 February, the
airport at Dacca was fortified with antiaircraft guns, and a few days later
a ship with a heavy load of arms and ammunition left Karachi for
Chittagong.

On 23 February the civilian Council of Ministers of Pakistan was dissolved, "in view of the political situation obtaining in the country," and
Bhutto then declared that he would not attend the session of the National
Assembly "to sign a dictated constitution." Bhutto also insinuated that
India had played a large role in Sheikh Mujib's future plan of action, and
stated that his partymen could not become "double hostages" by going
to Dacca to attend the assembly session.[74] In Bhutto's words, "Under the
circumstances the Assembly would be a slaughter house."[75] Finally, before a mammoth public meeting at Lahore on 28 February, Bhutto
declared that his party would organize a large-scale hartal (strike)—
"from the Khyber Pass down to Karachi"—in protest against the sum-

[72] *Pakistan Observer* (Dacca), 21 December 1970.
[73] *Holiday* (Dacca), 27 December 1970.
[74] *Morning News* (Dacca), 16 February 1971.
[75] Ibid., 18 February 1971.

moning of the National Assembly, and he promised to "liquidate" any member of his party that attended the opening session.[76]

The threatening tactics of General Yahya Khan, when coupled with the inflamatory speeches of Bhutto, elevated the passions of the Bengalis. When on 1 March it was announced over Radio Pakistan that General Yahya had postponed the forthcoming session of the National Assembly, people in Dacca and other cities and towns spontaneously came out into the streets and demanded an outright declaration of independence for East Bengal. The Students League held a mammoth rally on 2 March at Dacca and hoisted the flag of Bangladesh in the presence of Sheikh Mujib, and a number of Students League leaders—Nur-e-Alam Siddiqui, A. S. M. Abdur Rab, Sahjahan Siraj, and Abdul Quddus Makhan— banded together a few days later to form a Swadhin Bangladesh Kendrio Chattra Sangram Parishad (Central Students Action Committee of Independent Bangladesh).

In response to these events, Mujib called for a "non-violent non-cooperation movement" against the central government of Pakistan for an indefinite period. In an impressive display of unity, all of the employees in the government offices, including the judges of the High Court, absented themselves from their offices, and promised to continue to do so for as long a period as Mujib demanded. But General Yahya Khan showed an utter lack of empathy with the feelings aroused among the Bengalis, and ultimately he reacted in a desperate manner. First he recalled the governor of East Bengal, S. M. Ahsan, as well as the Martial Law administrator of East Bengal, General Yakub, since neither of these men were willing to take military action to suppress the noncooperation movement. As replacements he sent the hawkish General Tikka Khan as both governor and Martial Law administrator of East Bengal. In a radio broadcast, General Yahya then warned that "the armed forces would ensure the integrity, solidarity, and security of Pakistan, a duty in which they never failed."

Sheikh Mujibur Rahman still stood fast. On 7 March he addressed a mammoth gathering of about a million people in the Raman Race Course, demanding the immediate abolition of Martial Law and transfer of power to the people's elected representatives. He urged the people to continue their nonviolent noncooperation movement until these demands were realized and declared that the struggle this time was for complete

---

[76] Ibid., 1 March 1971.

"emancipation and independence." [77] At the behest of the Central Students Action Committee of Independent Bangladesh, people all over Bangladesh observed a Resistance Day on 23 March (a day that had for 24 years been observed as Republic Day in Pakistan) by raising from their rooftops the flag of Bangladesh.

When General Yahya Khan flew into Dacca from Islamabad to make a belated personal appearance, on 15 March, it was already clear that he had only two alternatives before him—either to accept a confederal solution with Bangladesh or to engage his army in a massive genocide to crush the movement. But from every available piece of evidence it is certain that Yahya himself had already decided on the second alternative. While the AL leaders continued discussions with Yahya for several days, his advisors, army officers, and political leaders were busily engaged in making preparations for a military crackdown. Troops were dispatched to district towns, the non-Bengali people in the Mohammadpur and Mirpur areas of Dacca were armed, and, according to AL sources, one of the West Pakistani leaders even leaked word to Sheikh Mujib on 24 March that the army had prepared a systematic plan for the suppression of the independence movement. In this atmosphere, Sheikh Mujib decided that he himself would remain in his home in Dacca—taking the chance that he would be arrested rather than killed—but he urged his AL colleagues to either hide themselves or flee.

Facts are often stranger than fiction. The author himself could not have believed the extent and the intensity of the atrocities committed by West Pakistani troops after 24 March 1971 if he had not been present in Bangladesh during the entire eight-month period of occupation. At midnight on 25 March, the Pakistan army launched a virtual slaughter on the unarmed people of Dacca and other cities and towns of Bangladesh. In Dacca the first targets of the military were the student residences and teachers' quarters of Dacca University, the police headquarters at Rajarbagh, the East Pakistan Rifles (EPR) headquarters at Pilkhanas, and the Hindu populated areas of old Dacca. Some of the more politicized students had already fled from the student residences by the time of the crackdown on 25 March, but a number of innocent students (particularly those living at Iqbal Hall, where the Central Students Action Committee of Independent Bangladesh had opened an office, and Jagannath Hall, the residence of Hindu students) were killed on the night of 25 March. Along with nine teachers from the University, who were also killed, the

---

[77] *Pakistan Observer* (Dacca), 8 March 1971.

students were put into a mass grave in the football grounds in front of Jagannath Hall. In addition, the entire Tanti Bazaar and Shakhari Bazaar areas of old Dacca were set on fire and most of their residents killed, while many of the rootless people of Dacca—who spend their nights on streets and in bustees (slums) or in huts along the railway lines—were exterminated. The police force at Rajarbagh and the EPR men at Pilkhana managed to put up some resistance, but the army soon overpowered them with their use of sophisticated weapons (including tanks).

The initial army operations in Dacca continued without interruption from midnight of the 25th until the morning of the 27th, and similar mass killings were perpetrated by West Pakistani troops in Chittagong during this same two-day period. In other district towns, the West Pakistani soldiers, assisted by non-Bengalis, searched the homes of prominent Hindus for AL leaders and workers, killing all of those who were found.[78] At the same time, however, the news of mass killings had stirred almost every single Bengali to rebellion, including those Bengalis in the EPR and the East Bengal Regiment (EBR). In the Comilla and Jessore cantonments the EBR and EPR had been caught by surprise on 25 March, with the result that they were massacred by West Pakistani soldiers. But in Chittagong, Brahmanbaria, Kushtia, Dinajpur, Bogra, and Rajshahi the Bengalis in both the EBR and EPR took up arms and began to organize resistance.

Some of the Bengali district and subdivisional officers in the towns opened their police stations to the public and began to distribute rifles among the students and workers of the AL, as well as the various factions of NAP. The masses joined these resistance groups spontaneously and began to cut roads, destroy bridges, and build barricades. In the district towns where the number of West Pakistan soldiers was small, the EBR/EPR-led police, students, and political workers exterminated West Pakistan forces, but in places like Sylhet and Rajshahi, where the number of West Pakistani soldiers was large, the EBR/EPR-led men could only force the Pakistanis into restricted defensive enclaves. Up until the middle of April, the troops of West Pakistan had virtually no control over the

[78] The author himself was in Dacca from 24 March to 29 March 1971, whereafter he fled from the city to the rural areas. For some details of the genocide committed by the West Pakistan troops in Bangladesh see Jaffar Sadeq, "Bangladeshe Gonohatya" [Genocide in Bangladesh], in *Raktakta Bangla* [Blood-Stained Bengal] (Calcutta: Swadhin Bangla Sahitya Parishad, 1971), pp. 374–422; and *Jallat Yahyar Bangali Hatya* [Genocide of Bengalis by Bloodthirsty Yahya], ed. Vwabesh Roy (Dacca: Sulekha Prakashani, 1972).

bulk of Bangladesh, the principal exceptions being the city of Dacca and the cantonment areas of Chittagong, Comilla, Jessore, Saidpur and Rangpur.[79]

But by mid-April reinforcements from West Pakistan had begun to pour in. For several days a stream of PIA commercial jets with West Pakistan soldiers on board landed at Dacca airport via Colombo. A convoy of ships carrying soldiers, arms, and ammunition also reached Chittagong port, which had been secured by the guns of the Pakistan navy. With these two operations, the Pakistan military managed to move two full divisions into Bangladesh, and these divisions then began to move out in separate columns toward the district towns, burning roadside houses and killing people indiscriminately. Since there was no coordination among the different EBR/EPR-led resistance groups, and since the West Pakistan army had superior weapons, the EBR/EPR officers thought it prudent to cross over to India without offering much resistance to the advancing columns of the Pakistan army. By the end of April the army was able to reestablish its control over all district and subdivisional towns.

After these operations in April, the Pakistan army then tried to seal the borders between Bangladesh and India, killing in the process thousands of unarmed men and women who tried to flee to India during May and June. By July the killings inside Bangladesh had become systematized. People belonging to the Jamaat-i-Islami, various factions of the Muslim League, the Nizam-i-Islam, and the Jamiat-e-Ulema-Pakistan formed Peace Committees in the districts, subdivisions, thanas, and at the village level, being joined by adventurers who sought only plunder and loot. Some of the members of the Peace Committees and the adventurers provided the intelligence networks for the army, by identifying Hindus, AL workers, and educated youth who were sympathizers with the Bangladesh liberation movement.

By August, however, guerrillas began to pour back into Bangladesh from India, and they immediately set to work to destroy bridges, railway lines, and other communications facilities while ambushing army patrol parties. In an attempt to counter the guerrillas, the Pakistan army recruited more than 100,000 Razakars whose names were recommended by the Peace Committees, and gave them training and arms to protect the bridges and railway lines. Moreover, indiscriminate killings again became the order of the day. Indeed, Pakistani soldiers were now *instructed* to

[79] For some details of the early resistance to the West Pakistan army in March–April 1971 see Rehman Sobhan, "Bangladesh's Liberation War: An Analysis," *Morning News* (Dacca), 9 January 1972.

loot and burn everything in sight wherever the guerrillas were active.

In September–October two other groups—the Al Badr and the Al Shams—were armed by the Pakistan army. These two groups were manned by the members of the Islamic Chattra Sanga (Islamic Students Organization), the fanatical student wing of the Jamaat-i-Islami, and they launched a campaign to burn the "anti-Pakistani" books and journals of Bangladesh supporters. In addition, they began to exterminate leading left-wing professors, journalists, litterateurs, and even doctors.[80]

The Exile Government and the Liberation War
Sheikh Mujibur Rahman was arrested on the night of 25 March 1971 and taken to West Pakistan, where he remained in prison until mid-December. However, most of the AL leaders who were elected members of the National Assembly (MNAs) and the Provincial Assembly of East Bengal (MPAs) managed to flee to India. On 17 April these elected representatives were finally able to meet together in Calcutta, where they formed the Constituent Assembly of Bangladesh in exile. Through a Declaration of Independence, the Constituent Assembly of Bangladesh then proclaimed the sovereignty of Bangladesh, electing Sheikh Mujibur Rahman president, and Syed Nazrul Islam vice-president of the new nation. According to the terms of this declaration, the vice-president was empowered to act as president of Bangladesh in the absence of Sheikh Mujib.[81] After Syed Nazrul Islam's elevation to the position of acting president, a ministry (headed by Tajuddin Ahmad and consisting of Khondokher Mustaq Ahmad, Mansoor Ali, and A. H. M. Kamruzzaman) was quickly formed.[82]

With the assistance of the Indian government, the exile government then began to prepare for the armed liberation of Bangladesh. Colonel Ataul Ghani Usmani (52), a former officer in the Pakistan army, was appointed commander-in-chief of the liberation armed forces, and several thousand men from the EBR and EPR who had fled to India were placed in charge of the regular units of the Mukti Bahini (Liberation Army).

[80] The Al Badr killed 10 professors of Dacca University, 5 leading journalists (including the BBC correspondent), 2 litterateurs and 26 doctors in Dacca alone. The names and professions of these victims were published in *Dainik Bangla* (Dacca), 22 December 1971.
[81] For the text of the Declaration of Independence see *Raktakta Bangla*, pp. 20–22.
[82] Syed Nazrul Islam, Khondokher Mustaq Ahmad, and Mansoor Ali were the vice-presidents of the EPAL. Tajuddin Ahmad was the general secretary of the EPAL. A. H. M. Kamruzzaman was the general secretary of the All-Pakistan Awami League.

Youth reception camps were set up along the border areas to recruit young men from Bangladesh, and eventually more than 250,000 volunteers came forth to fight for the liberation of their motherland. The best material among them were recruited for the regular units of the Mukti Bahini, and these were given rigorous training. Most of the others were recruited as Freedom Fighters and were given training in the use of light automatic weapons, mortars and explosives, in an attempt to build a guerrilla force. By the end of November some 100,000 guerrillas had been equipped with sten guns, rifles, mortars, and explosives, and sent back into Bangladesh territory, while another 100,000 were still being trained in Indian camps. In addition, a naval wing of the Mukti Bahini was being trained in the use of gunboats, underwater sabotage, and limpid mines.[83]

As far as possible the guerrillas were sent to their home areas, charged initially with the liquidation of the Peace Committees and the Razakars. By the end of October an estimated 20,000 collaborators and their families had been liquidated,[84] with the result that many areas now became secure enough that they could be used by the guerrillas as areas for concealment or retreat. From these liberated areas, the guerrillas subsequently launched commando raids on the convoys and isolated posts of the Pakistan military, capturing weapons and creating perpetual tension for the Pakistan forces. Besides these attacks, the main aim of the guerrillas was to disrupt the communications system so that West Pakistan forces could not feed, regroup and reinforce their ranks. By the end of November, the guerrillas were able to completely paralyze the communication lines by destroying bridges and causing extensive damage to embankments, roads, and railway lines.

This disruption of the Bangladesh communications system by the guerrillas, when coupled with the activities of the Mukti Bahini frogmen and gunboats in Chittagong and Chalna ports, brought exports of jute, jute goods, and tea—the commodities that had previously earned valuable foreign exchange and sustained the West Pakistan economy—to a standstill. Therefore, when 100,000 guerrillas became fully active inside Bangladesh, and the infantry divisions of the regular units of the Mukti Bahini intensified their activities in the border areas toward the end of November, the generals of Pakistan, in sheer desperation, launched a war with India. During the war, which began on 3 December and lasted less than

[83] See Rehman Sobhan, "Bangladesh's Liberation War: An Analysis-II," *Morning News* (Dacca), 10 January 1972.
[84] Ibid.

two weeks, Indian forces cooperated with the Mukti Bahini to bring about the liberation of Bangladesh.

Political Commandos and the Role of the Left

The vast majority of the guerrillas that were recruited to the Mukti Bahini were students of schools, colleges, and universities, drawn largely from peasant, lower middle-class and middle-class families. But a fair portion of the guerrillas came from the laboring class,[85] and there also were some small businessmen and cultivators among the guerrillas. The overwhelming majority of the guerrillas were below 25 years of age. In order to impose some semblance of orderly selection on such a diverse group, all prospective recruits to the liberation forces were first scrutinized in youth reception centers by the Awami League MPAs of the area from which the prospective recruits came, and those with pronounced affiliations to political parties other than the AL were screened from the list. But in spite of this screening process, the class composition of the guerrillas and the sufferings that they had to undergo during 1971 led them to a political orientation that was left of the regular Awami League. Indeed, the guerrilla commanders and their rank-and-file were frequently critical of the more moderate AL leadership throughout 1971.

Because of the massive popular support that the guerrillas received, the new recruits to the Mukti Bahini often emerged as exceedingly popular heroes in Bangladesh, with considerable political influence in local areas. This led a number of observers to fear an eventual take-over from the older AL leadership by the Liberation Armed Forces, especially in the event that Sheikh Mujibur Rahman should not return from prison. With this in mind, four chiefs of the political commandos (Tofael Ahmad, Sheikh Fazlul Huq, Serajul Anam Khan, and Abdur Razzak), who had reportedly been close confidants of Sheikh Mujib, formed an organization called the Mujib Bahini, to preserve the interests of Sheikh Mujib and his closest supporters. College and university students belonging exclusively to the Students League were recruited secretly to the Mujib Bahini from youth reception camps throughout 1971, until its total strength was reported to have reached 7,000–8,000 in November. These units were reported to have been given special training by an elite branch of the Indian army in Dehradun (in Uttar Pradesh) and Haphlong (in Assam) in India. Besides being trained in guerrilla warfare, these men

---

[85] Abdul Mannan, general secretary of the Jatio Sramik League, claimed that 30,000 workers belonging to the Sramik League fought as Freedom Fighters. See *Dainik Bangla* (Dacca), 1 January 1972.

were also given political courses on "Mujibism"—Sheikh Mujibur Rahman's ideas on nationalism, secularism, socialism, and democracy. So effectively was this operation carried out that the existence of the Mujib Bahini was not even known to most other sections of the Mukti Bahini until the late summer, when occasional clashes between the Mukti Bahini and the Mujib Bahini erupted.[86]

Not only did the Indian government recognize the AL as representative of popular opinion in Bangladesh, it also channeled its aid and support for the liberation struggle exclusively through the Bangladesh government-in-exile in Calcutta. The result was that the leftist party leaders and cadres who had sought shelter in India could play only a secondary role in the liberation struggle. The pro-Moscow CP of Bangladesh and their front organizations—the pro-Moscow NAP, Students Union, Krishak Samity, and the Trade Union Centre—lent full support and cooperation to the Bangladesh exile-government in the liberation struggle, and approximately 6,000 of their workers were reportedly recruited to the Liberation Army despite the AL's policy of excluding the other party cadres.[87] But the formation of the Mujib Bahini as a special force of political commandos distinct from the Mukti Bahini led the leaders of the pro-Moscow CP to organize a separate guerrilla unit of their own. With the assistance of the CPI in India, the pro-Moscow CP opened separate youth reception camps and arranged for the training of over 20,000 guerrillas, who later became active in the Dacca and Comilla areas.

In a party thesis dated 21 May 1971, the central committee of the pro-Moscow CP of Bangladesh argued for the formation of a National Liberation Front, consisting of the AL, the pro-Moscow CP, the pro-Moscow NAP and other parties participating in the liberation struggle. In this party thesis it was argued that the formation of such a National Liberation Front would be helpful in securing the support of the progressive forces of the world, and especially the socialist bloc. On the insistence of the pro-Moscow CP and the pro-Moscow NAP and, possibly, to ensure greater help from Soviet Russia, the AL government finally agreed in September to form a Consultative Committee, consisting of (1) Maulana Bhashani; (2) comrade Moni Singh (president of the pro-Moscow Bangladesh CP); (3) Professor Muzzaffar Ahmad (pro-Moscow NAP); (4) Monoranjan Dhar (Bangladesh Congress); (5) Tajuddin Ahmad

---

[86] This paragraph is based on interviews with several members of the Mujib Bahini in March 1972.
[87] See the statement of Muzzaffar Ahmad in the *Dainik Bangla*, 22 December 1971.

(prime minister of the Bangladesh government-in-exile); and (6) Mushtaq Ahmad (foreign minister of the Bangladesh government-in-exile).

According to its original agreement, the Consultative Committee was formed to conduct the liberation struggle of Bangladesh, accepting no solution other than complete independence.[88] In September–October, however, a section of the AL had reportedly tried to arrive at some sort of compromise with General Yahya Khan on the basis of an agreement that would ensure the release of Sheikh Mujibur Rahman and the autonomy of Bangladesh in the context of one Pakistan, such agreement to be brought about through the good offices of the government of the United States. In response to this rumor the pro-Moscow weeklies *Nutun Bangla* (New Bengal) and *Mukti Judho* (Liberation War) immediately launched a campaign against these alleged "CIA-sponsored moves to foil the liberation struggle of Bangladesh," [89] and both the acting president and acting prime minister of the Bangladesh government-in-exile quickly issued a series of statements affirming that no solution except the complete independence of Bangladesh would be acceptable to the people.[90] In this atmosphere, the cooperation of the leaders of the pro-Moscow camp was important in maintaining unity, and in securing international support for the liberation struggle. Professor Muzzaffar Ahmad, president of the pro-Moscow NAP, was included in the delegation that was sent to the UN General Assembly, and before that Dewan Mahboob Ali (another leader of the pro-Moscow NAP) was sent to the World Peace Conference in Budapest (in April 1971). In addition, comrade Abdus Salam, secretary of the pro-Moscow CP, was reported to have visited the Soviet Union.[91]

The pro-Peking leftists, who had already split into several factions prior to the liberation struggle, became totally confused when Peking chose to support the Yahya regime in its brutal suppression of the liberation movement. Some sections of the EPCPML, EBCP, and CCCR did flee to India, where they formed the Bangladesh Mukti Sangram Samonnoy Committee (the Coordination Committee of the Bangladesh Liberation Struggle), and Maulana Bhashani eventually became known as

[88] See the party thesis, *Bangla Desher Swadhinata Sangramer Mullayon* [Evaluation of the Liberation Struggle of Bangladesh] (Calcutta: Bangladesh Communist Party, 1971).

[89] See the leaflet issued by the pro-Moscow NAP on the formation and resolution of the Consultative Committee, dated 9 September 1971.

[90] See *Nutun Bangla*, 16 September, 18 October 1971; *Mukti Judho*, 3, 17 October 1971.

[91] *Mukti Judho*, 17 October 1971.

chairman of this committee. But Bhashani himself disowned his connections with this committee, opting instead for a position of full support to the Bangladesh government and its Liberation Army. According to a number of press reports, the Samonnoy Committee was backed and financed by the Communist Party of India (Marxist) (CPM) in Calcutta, which disapproved of the Chinese attitude towards Bangladesh and supported the liberation movement, but also resented the dominance of the Indian government and the AL.[92] As later events indicated, this position had little appeal among the guerrillas who were fighting for the liberation of the country.

Other sections of the pro-Chinese Left remained inside Bangladesh during the period of the liberation war, where they continued to engage in factional polemics. One section of the EPCPML (led by Toaha) considered the Chinese attitude toward Bangladesh wrong, but also argued that the AL-led movement was part of a "conspiracy of Indian expansionism and Russian social imperialism." This group collected more than 10,000 "red guerrillas" at Ramgati in Noakhali district and planned to liberate a part of Bangladesh under pure Communist leadership. However, since they were distrusted and unaided by the guerrillas of the Mukti Bahini, the poorly equipped "red guerrillas" of the Toaha group were hardly any match for West Pakistani troops, with the result that most of them were eventually killed.

The Matin-Alauddin group of the EBCP, on the other hand, took the lead in the liberation of Pabna district town in the early phase of the resistance in March–April. Their cadres, along with the police and AL volunteers, were equipped with rifles supplied by the East Bengal police, which they used to kill more than 100 West Pakistan soldiers posted in Pabna. At that time they issued a pamphlet supporting the armed liberation movement, advocating an alliance of all nationalist classes including the national bourgeoisie, but later on they were reported to have changed their views to conform with the Chinese line. Another section of the EBCP (led by Ohidul) collected about 1,000 guerrillas and cooperated fully with the guerrillas of the Liberation Army throughout 1971, ignoring the Chinese attitude towards Bangladesh. This group was active in the Attrai areas in Rajshahi district.

The young militant cadres of the EBWM were the first to have declared a national war of liberation against the West Pakistan military junta, on 2 March 1971, and their leaflet (urging a national liberation war) was quoted in the "White Paper" issued by the Yahya regime as "proof" of

92 *Nutun Bangla*, 28 October 1971.

the Awami League's revolt against the Pakistan government. In the early phase of resistance the cadres of the EBWM were active in several thanas of Barisal, Dacca and Munshiganj, and they chose to stay inside Bangladesh throughout the eight months of terror. As a result, they lost most of their cadres at the hands of the Pakistani troops. The last of the Maoist groups—the Mythi Group—disintegrated during the period of liberation struggle, with most of their cadres joining the guerrilla wing of the Mukti Bahini out of sheer determination to liberate their motherland and with scant attention being paid to doctrinal justifications.

Conclusions

The ideological revolution that established secularism and socialism as dominant themes of the Bangladesh liberation movement was initiated by the leftists of East Bengal, but the autonomy movement that was spearheaded by the EPAL in the late 1960s represented a confluence of both radical and secular Bengali nationalism. The refusal of the West Pakistan military dictatorship to come to terms with militant nationalism led to a national resistance movement in March 1971, in the shape of a massive noncooperation movement led by Sheikh Mujibur Rahman, whose sacrifices and qualities of leadership had already made him the veritable symbol of the spirit of the emergent Bangladesh. In the crucible of brutal military oppression, the national resistance movement burst forth, until it finally became a true people's liberation war. Despite its high price—in both blood and gold—Bangladesh did emerge as an independent and sovereign state, with the proclaimed goals of secularism, socialism, and democracy.

The possibility of a bitter struggle for power among the guerrilla leaders and the civilian Awami League leadership, between senior and junior cadres of the AL, or between the AL and the pro-Moscow Communists in the wake of the liberation war was considerably diminished with the return of Sheikh Mujibur Rahman—now called Bangabandhu, or "Father of the Nation"—to Bangladesh on 11 January 1972.[93] In an impressive

[93] Sheikh Mujibur Rahman was taken to West Pakistan and kept in detention in a solitary prison cell in a district town. Later he was tried by a special military court for "waging war against the Pakistan Government and other treasonable activities" and given the death sentence. The sentence was approved by General Yahya as chief Martial Law administrator, but before the sentence could be carried out General Yahya was replaced by Zulfikar Ali Bhutto as president and chief Martial Law administrator of Pakistan. Bhutto released Sheikh Mujib and sent him to London by a special plane; from there he flew to Bangladesh via India. See the proceedings of the press conference of Sheikh Mujib in London on 8 January 1972, published in *Morning News* (Dacca), 9 January 1972.

display of unity, the various guerrilla units of the Mukti Bahini, the Mujib Bahini, and the guerrilla units of the pro-Moscow Communists, as well as those of the Samonnoy Committee, surrendered their arms at ceremonial occasions throughout Bangladesh in early 1972. It is, of course, widely suspected that a fairly large portion of their arms and ammunition have been retained by various groups of guerrillas. But the equation of authority and support from the nation is clearly in favor of the Awami League government led by Sheikh Mujib.

As a first step toward establishing a regular army, the erstwhile units of the Mukti Bahini have now been transformed into the Armed Forces of Bangladesh, under the command of Colonel Usmani.[94] Most of the popular guerrilla leaders are also personally loyal to Sheikh Mujib, and the Mujib Bahini has been acting as Mujib's personal military force since his return to Bangladesh in January 1972. Moreover, the legend of Sheikh Mujib, his charismatic appeal, and his hypnotic spell over the masses, are enormous assets for the present Awami League government. The rival forces, on the other hand, are far too weak. The Islamic right was more or less completely wiped out during the liberation war, and Maulana Bhashani has lost much of his prestige despite his break with the pro-Peking leftists on the eve of the liberation movement. The pro-Peking NAP has hardly any cadre strength to be an effective force again.

The Maoists in Bangladesh continue to be split into numerous factions and subfactions, having lost most of their cadres and also much of their goodwill among the people because of China's support for the West Pakistan military regime. It will take time and dedicated effort on their part if they are ever again to be a force of consequence. The only opposition that is of some importance at present is the pro-Moscow Communist camp. The appeal of this group among the masses was considerably heightened by their active participation in the liberation war and by the valuable support of the Soviet Union during the Bangladesh liberation struggle. The pro-Moscow Bangladesh CP, under experienced leaders, is now working openly. The front organizations of the party—the pro-Moscow NAP, the Students Union, the Krishak Samity (Peasants Organization), and the Trade Union Centre—have also stepped up their activities. This camp, however, is still committed to "national democratic revolution" through parliamentary politics and is not likely to attempt the dislodgement of the present government through armed rebellion.

[94] Colonel Usmani was promoted to the rank of a full general by the government of Bangladesh soon after liberation. Later he resigned his job in the army and became a minister in the cabinet of Bangladesh.

Nevertheless, the triumphant beginnings of Bangladesh are only a door to massive problems for Sheikh Mujibur Rahman and his government. The enormous tasks of development and reconstruction in one of the poorest countries of the world, with about 70 million people in an area of only 55,126 square miles, are likely to prove more difficult than the leadership of a liberation struggle with millenarian appeal. Given the best of efforts and intentions, it will be a massive task to alleviate to any appreciable degree the economic distress of the people of Bangladesh, who have now been ravaged by West Pakistani troops. Under these circumstances, the buoyant optimism at the birth of the nation could soon become pessimism, and the vast army of the educated unemployed, many of whom participated in the liberation war, may feel particularly frustrated. Given the proclivity to oppositional politics, and the extreme politicization of the Bengali masses, the reassertion of strong radical opposition movements can be expected to develop rather quickly.

Andhra Pradesh

MAHARASHTRA

Adilabad

Nizamabad   Karimnagar

ORISSA

Srikakulam

MADHYA
PRADESH

Medak   Warangal

Visakhapatnam

Hyderabad

Khammam

East
Godavari

Nalgonda

West
Godavari

Mahbubnagar

Krishna

Guntur

Kurnool

Bay
of
Bengal

Anantapur   Cuddapah

Nellore

MYSORE

Chittoor

Miles

50   0   50   100

MADRAS

Andhra Pradesh

5
The Communist Movement in Andhra Pradesh

Mohan Ram

Although the Communist movement in Andhra Pradesh has maintained a variety of national and international organizational affiliations over the course of the last half-century, it has always had an intensely regional character.[1] During the many dialectical zigzags and vicissitudes of the Indian Communist movement prior to Indian Independence, the Andhra Pradesh Communists frequently played the role of trend setters or daring nonconformists, primarily because of their willingness to challenge both the established structure of the Communist Party of India (CPI) and international Communist authority. After 1947 the independent nature of the Andhra movement led to the discovery of a new political idiom for India. In the pages that follow I shall attempt to assess both the degree of creativity and the regional moorings of the Andhra movement, in an effort to better understand the relationship between communism in Andhra Pradesh and communism elsewhere.

The Andhra Communists first gained national and international prominence in the early 1940s, when the leadership of the Andhra CPI identified with the demands of the Telugu-speaking people for a separate Telugu-speaking state.[2] In early 1947 the Andhra CPI escalated this demand—to the point of secession—thereby unnerving the leadership of the CPI at the all-India level. After India's Independence was achieved (in August 1947), the Andhra Communists pitted their regional revolutionary strategy against the Zhdanov line of the Cominform, again causing serious rifts between the CPI in Andhra and the national CPI (now heavily supported by Moscow).

[1] Andhra Pradesh is the fifth largest state in the Indian Union in terms of area and the fourth largest with regard to population. It was initially created in 1953 by carving the Rayalaseema region and the Circars region out of the old Madras Presidency. In 1956 the Telengana region of the old Hyderabad state was added to Andhra state to constitute Andhra Pradesh. Andhra Pradesh now has an area of 106,052 square miles and its population according to the 1961 census is 35,977,999.
[2] The fight for a Telugu-speaking state first began inside the Congress party, at its Bombay plenary session in 1915, and continued through the Nagpur session in 1920, where the principle of redistribution of the provinces on the basis of language was accepted as a political goal. The Congress leadership could not ignore the growing sentiment among several language groups for states based on language. Following the appointment of the Indian Statutory Commission in 1927, the Congress formed a committee of the All Parties Conference that met at Allahabad in 1928 (known as the Nehru Committee), and this committee subsequently reinforced the demand for linguistic states in India. See Mohan Ram, *Hindi Against India* (New Delhi: Rachna Prakashan, 1968), pp. 16–19.

The Zhdanov line, adopted by the Cominform in September 1947, was intended primarily for European Communists who were attempting to find some means of adjustment to a postwar world. Throughout Southeast Asia the application of the Zhdanov line took the form of abortive insurrections, as was the case within India, where the national CPI swung from "right reformism" to "left sectarianism" at its Second Congress in early 1948. While the Second Congress of 1948 appeared at the time to be an application of the Zhdanov line to India, later events were to prove to the CPI that the Second Congress was a "weird Titoite deviation" that sought to combine two stages of the Indian revolution in one.

The Andhra Communists were the first to recognise the Second Congress of 1948 as "a Titoite deviation." The Andhra CPI had already launched (in 1946) a peasant armed struggle against the feudal tyranny in the Telugu-speaking region of the former Hyderabad State, invoking Mao Tse-tung's "New Democracy" in support of its own revolutionary strategy. In defiance of the Second Congress of 1948 and in defiance of Moscow as well, the Andhra CPI called for a four-class alliance with people's war as the principal form of struggle.

As a result of these events perhaps the first recorded debate about the legitimacy of Mao Tse-tung's teachings and their place in Marxism-Leninism took place in India.[3] This basic Communist confrontation, which generated considerable heat in India in the late 1940s and early 1950s, found the peasant leadership of the Andhra Communist movement pitted against the sophisticated urban leadership of the CPI at the national level. Moreover, during the course of this debate the Communist Party of the Soviet Union (CPSU) was unreservedly opposed to the Andhra leadership. This is indicated by the fact that the general secretary of the CPI, during the course of his polemic against the Andhra Communists, virtually denounced Mao Tse-tung as a charlatan, and the Soviets continually countenanced this attack on Mao. Yet this brief Maoist interlude continued for more than three years, because of the persistence and success of the Andhra Communists, until international intervention forced the abandonment of the Telengana peasant war in 1951.

After 1951, when the Cominform jettisoned the disastrous Zhdanov line and Soviet foreign policy interests gained precedence over class struggle, the Andhra CPI found itself increasingly at odds with the rest of the party and with the Cominform. In 1953 Soviet national interests demanded a "peace front" in India against the United States, and the CPSU called for

[3] A detailed account of this debate can be found in Mohan Ram, *Indian Communism: Split Within a Split* (New Delhi: Vikas Publications, 1969), pp. 12–18.

the subordination of the CPI's domestic goals (to fight for complete independence of the country from the British stranglehold on the economy) to its international obligations. Identification of the "main enemy" was the issue at the CPI's Third Congress in 1953–1954. At the Third Congress the Andhra Communists regarded British imperialism as the main enemy of India, placing the CPI's national obligations above the needs of international communism and the interests of Soviet foreign policy, while the national CPI sided with the CPSU. The differences that manifested themselves at the Third Congress continued for a decade, leading to a split in the party in 1964.

Although the 1964 split in the CPI coincided in many respects with the major schism in the international Communist movement, the rift in India was not a simple break between pro-Moscow and pro-Peking Communists. A major portion of the CPI leadership did seek verbal support from Mao Tse-tung in 1964, when they were in the process of withdrawing from the CPI to form the Communist Party of India (Marxist) (CPM), but this rebel leadership did not remain loyal to Mao after 1964. For a number of years after the split in 1964 the CPM leadership refused to take a stance on ideological issues, and when it did state its position on the world ideological debate in 1968 it was immediately faced with a second split. As I have explained elsewhere, the split in India was a "split within a split," and its most significant outcome was the reassertion of the Maoist trend in India, after nearly two decades from its first appearance and suppression.[4] It was Andhra Communists who were in the forefront of the revolt against the "revisionism" of the CPM after the first (1964) split, and it is now Andhra Communists who are upholding Maoist ideological positions in India.

At present the Indian Maoist movement is divided into two streams. One of these is led by the Communist Party of India (Marxist-Leninist) (CPML), which was formed in 1969 and is now recognized by Peking.[5] The second is led by the Andhra Maoists, who have not yet formed a political party, and who have neither been recognized nor disowned by Peking.[6] In the pages that follow I shall attempt to analyze the differences between these two streams of Indian Maoism, but first it is necessary to trace the development of the Communist movement in India as it relates to Andhra Pradesh.

[4] See ibid., pp. 159 ff.
[5] The formation of the CPML is traced out in Marcus F. Franda, "India's Third Communist Party," *Asian Survey* 9, no. 11 (November 1969), 797–817.
[6] The Andhra and West Bengal Maoist movements are compared in great detail in Mohan Ram, *Maoism in India* (New Delhi: Vikas Publications, 1971).

The CPI and the Andhra Communists

The CPI, formally launched in 1925, grew out of a number of nebulous groups of romantic Indian expatriates—students, intellectuals, and political exiles and émigrés—who tried to build a Communist movement in India from abroad. These people sought the assistance of the Comintern throughout the 1920s and 1930s, and they directed their appeal to those middle-class intellectuals in India's freedom movement who had been inspired by the Bolshevik revolution. M. N. Roy, an Indian revolutionary who was a member of the Comintern executive in the early 1920s, was Moscow's first link with the Indian Communists. But Roy's influence on the CPI began to decline in the mid-1920s, when leaders of the Communist Party of Great Britain (CPGB)—especially R. Palme Dutt—began guiding the movement in India. The CPGB sent several functionaries to India in the late 1920s to assist indigenous leaders in building a movement.

By 1929, 31 CPI leaders found themselves in jail, as a result of the *Meerut* conspiracy case, and the Indian movement suffered a severe setback. This disruption of party activities was then accentuated in the 1930s by the decision of the Comintern at its tenth plenum (July 1929) to adopt a sectarian line, which isolated the CPI from the freedom movement. The *Meerut* prisoners sought to change the Comintern's line throughout the succeeding years, and some changes were made in 1932, but mistakes were not fully corrected. Only when fascism gained ascendancy in Europe, menacing communism, did the Comintern line change significantly (in 1935). By the mid-thirties, however, the Indian Communists had come under severe criticism within India because of their sectarianism, and the corrective they then prescribed was a soft line towards the bourgeois nationalist Congress party. In short, the CPI in 1935 decided to work for an anti-imperialist united front, the colonial version of Front Populaire, requiring Communist identification with bourgeois nationalism. In practice this became a "united front from below," with the CPI in alliance with the Congress Socialist Party (CSP), a Socialist democratic formation inside the Congress. Although the CPI was technically illegal throughout the 1930s the CSP agreed to admit individual Communists to its fold. Following charges of Communist attempts to disrupt and capture it, the CSP did stop admitting Communists in 1938, but by this time the Communists had successfully infiltrated and captured entire regional units of the CSP.[7]

The regional movement in Andhra was not deeply involved in national

[7] For an account of Communist infiltration and subversion of the Congress Socialist Party see Minoo R. Masani, *The Communist Party of India: A Short History* (London: Derek Verschoyle, 1954), chaps. 3 and 4.

party affairs in the 1920s. For the most part, the Communist movement in India during these early years had gained a foothold only in cities and working class centers, but not in predominantly rural areas like Andhra. When the movement did gain momentum in the agricultural Telugu areas in the 1930s, the activities of the Communists in these areas were considerably different from those of the CPI in other parts of India.

The disruptive nature of the Communist movement in Andhra can only be understood in terms of the unusual socioeconomic patterns obtaining in the Telugu areas, which differ considerably from other parts of India. The Andhras, who trace their origins in South India back more than 3,000 years, were located in three distinct regions and two contiguous administrative units during the latter part of British rule. For administrative purposes the British had combined the perenially irrigated and fertile coastal districts (known as the Circars) with the chronically famine-stricken Rayalaseema districts within a sprawling multilingual Madras Presidency. The backward Telengana districts were part of Hyderabad state, ruled by the Nizam of Hyderabad under the tutelage of the British. The three distinct natural regions—the Circars, Rayalaseema, and Telengana—differ from one another with regard to levels of socioeconomic development, spread of education, living standards, and cultural and political awareness. These differences are also reflected in the variegated and uneven growth of the Communist movement in Telugu country.

The Circars (which now include the districts of Krishna, Guntur, East Godavary and West Godavary) have been the cradle of all political and cultural movements in Andhra since the turn of the century. The Circars provided the leadership for the so-called non-Brahmin movement, which was a reaction to the Brahmin domination of the political and cultural life of the Telugu people; the language renaissance movement, to replace the pedantic and archaic Telugu used by the elite with simple, spoken Telugu; the movement for a Telugu-speaking province; the movement for a Greater Andhra or Vishalandhra; the successive waves of the freedom struggle in the 1920s, 1930s, and 1940s; the social democratic movement in Andhra; and later the Communist movement.

The dominance of the people of the Circars can only be explained in terms of the socioeconomic factors and class relations determined by them. The Circars, except for a few zamindari pockets,[8] have had the benefit of

---

[8] The zamindars were intermediaries in the land tenure system first created by the British (the permanent revenue system). Under this system land revenue was fixed permanently, according to a contract drawn up between the British government in India and the first zamindar. From that point on the zamindar collected rents from his tenants, paid the contracted amount to the British, and retained the surplus.

the ryotwari system of land tenure,[9] making for the emergence of a class of sturdy, independent middle and rich peasant proprietors. This, together with well-developed irrigation facilities under the major river projects and high land fertility, has contributed to a measure of capitalist land relations. Even before post-Independence land reforms and massive state aid created a new kulak class in the rest of India, the Circars had a significant middle and rich peasant class, a sizable urban petit bourgeoisie, and a politically conscious rural intelligentsia. After Independence the size of the middle and rich peasant class increased, until it now accounts for almost 50 percent of the rural population of Andhra, juxtaposed between a small (about 5 percent) landlord class and a large (40 to 50 percent) rural proletariat.[10] In other regions of Andhra many more vestiges of feudal exploitation predominate.

Before the Communist movement struck roots in Telugu country, the freedom movement (led by Mahatma Gandhi) had met with tremendous response in the Circars. Gandhi's noncooperation movement of the late 1920s took the form of a sprightly no-tax campaign in Andhra, which continued to maintain a high level of militancy even after Gandhi issued directives to call it off. In some of the tribal tracts in the Circars the no-tax campaign grew into guerrilla action, in defiance of the Gandhian dictum of nonviolence. In early 1929, when the British administration in Madras Presidency raised land revenue in the ryotwari areas, there was strong opposition to the decision from the peasants of the Circars. These were the earliest precedents for the peasant movement in the Circars area of Telugu country, which later was to provide a powerful base for the Communists.

Peasant discontent in all of Andhra was considerably heightened in late 1929, when the depression brought commodity prices down, seriously affecting agricultural incomes. The depression roughly synchronized with a new phase in the freedom movement in the early 1930s, but the lack of militancy on the part of Gandhi, following the Gandhi-Irwin pact in 1931, disillusioned the Andhras, and particularly the young nationalists in the Congress party. One of the early Andhra Communists (Jonnalagadda

---

[9] Under the ryotwari system of land tenure—which was tried after the zamindari system—the government contracted with landholders periodically, rather than contract at one specific time on a permanent basis. Theoretically this prevented the growth of intermediaries in the land revenue system, although in practice some intermediaries did exist (but far fewer than in zamindari areas).

[10] Figures are taken from Indian Communist sources. See *Why the Ultra-Left Deviation?* (Calcutta: CPM Central Committee, 1968), p. 22; and "Agrarian Programme of the Andhra Committee on the Communist Party of India," *New Age* (Monthly) 3, no. 12 (December 1954), 61.

Ramalingiah) states that he was first attracted to Communism during this period, when he came into contact with Bengali terrorists who were critical of Gandhi during a term in jail in 1932.[11] Ramalingiah had previously been a Gandhian, but like other young men he reacted strongly to the 1931 pact, in which he saw signs of capitulation by the bourgeois-nationalist leadership of the freedom struggle. Ramalingiah and others were especially influenced by a widely read class analysis of Gandhism (*Swaraj or Surrender*) written under the signature of "Mascarenhas," believed to be the pseudonym of M. N. Roy.

Throughout the 1930s a number of disillusioned young nationalists from Telugu country, like Ramalingiah, joined the Congress Socialist Party, and it was from the CSP that the Andhra Communist movement drew its early cadre members. Puchalapalli Sundarayya (who was later a Politburo member of the CPI, and is now general secretary of the CPM), Chalasani Vasudeva Rao, Uddaraju Ramam, and the late Katragadda Narayana Rao were among the first Andhra Communists. All of these men were from the Circars, and all had participated in the freedom struggle under Gandhi. Each of them joined the CPI in the 1930s, after a period of disillusionment with the leadership of the Congress.

It was an idealistic beginning. Hundreds of middle-class intellectuals and educated children of aristocratic landlords joined the CPI in the 1930s and fanned out to work among agricultural laborers and the sparse industrial working class in Andhra.[12] Their puritan living, spartan discipline, personal integrity, and supreme sacrifice helped them integrate themselves with the peasant masses. The statement of a former general secretary of the CPI, recorded during his conversation with an Andhra Communist leader in 1946, is representative of the idealism and conviction of this older cadre:

[11] Jonnalagadda Ramalingiah, "Andhra Pradeshamlo Sapagrasthamaina Communist Udyamam Pai Sameeksha," *Jwala* (Telugu Weekly), 13 December 1968.

[12] While Andhra Pradesh is known for its relatively low rates of urbanization, a large number of the intellectuals from peasant families are engaged in liberal professions in small towns or are still farmers of one kind or the other. These are the people whom I have called "middle-class intellectuals." Indian Communists have generally used the term "rural intelligentsia" to denote this class. But whatever term is used, it should be pointed out that this is a class that is quite distinct in Andhra. In the words of Mrs. Aruna Asaf Ali, "A distinguishing feature of the Andhra Communist Party is its social content. It was a party not only of the peasant masses but the rural proletariat and rural poor of every category. The rural intelligentsia, numerically stronger and politically a great deal more mature than elsewhere in India, has provided the party with a leadership that knows its mind and is unmistakably competent." "Communist Party is a New Reality in Andhra," *New Age Weekly* 2, no. 20 (13 February 1955), 7.

It is we who built the Congress organization in the villages, and becoming Communists did not make us any less Congressmen in the eyes of the masses, simply because the party taught us to become organisers.[13]

The first major struggle of the Andhra Communists came in 1931, when they organized a 1,500-mile march to Madras city, the Presidency headquarters, to rouse the peasants against the land system. The march, which drew participants from 525 villages has since been the subject of considerable debate among Indian politicians. Communist writers argue that the march was devised to create a new consciousness among the peasants in the backward Rayalaseema tracts,[14] while Professor N. G. Ranga, a nationalist leader from Andhra who pioneered the Congress party's work among the peasantry, has spoken of the 1931 movement as "a Communist plan to drive a wedge between the landholding peasants and landless agricultural labour." [15] Whatever their motives, it is clear that the Andhra Communists were the first Indian party organizers to seek the support of agricultural laborers by organizing them into rural unions,[16] and this is hardly surprising since the Andhra region has no industrial proletariat worth the name.

In contrast to other parts of Andhra Pradesh, the Communist movement came to the Telengana region (which now comprises nine districts with about 10 million people) rather slowly. Although the CPI began functioning in the Telengana area as early as 1933–1934, it could not set up even an illegal nucleus until 1941. The first Telengana Communists, who were recruited from among petit bourgeois intellectuals and radical young men of landlord origins, therefore functioned through the state people's movement, led by the Andhra Mahasabha, a literary-cultural organization that articulated the demand for a Telugu homeland. The Mahasabha was important to the Andhra movement because it was the only mass platform in a system that denied civil liberties. The Telengana Communists, under the guidance of the Andhra CPI, were also important to the Mahasabha, since they radicalized the Mahasabha by gaining accep-

[13] P. C. Joshi, *Among Kisan Patriots* (Bombay: People's Publishing House, 1946), p. 4.
[14] A. S. Rao, "Andhras Struggle for Their Own State," *New Age* (Monthly) 2, no. 11 (November 1953), 106.
[15] N. G. Ranga, *Fight for Freedom* (New Delhi: S. Chand, 1968), p. 231.
[16] Because of the early work of the CPI among agricultural laborers, the strength of organized labor among agriculturalists has always been greater in Andhra than elsewhere. According to Ranga, the principal CPI organizers of agricultural labor in the 1930s were P. Sundarayya and J. Ramalingiah, and they were most active at that time in the districts of Nellore, Guntur, Krishna, and the two Godavary districts (East and West). See ibid., pp. 208 ff.

tance for Communist agrarian demands in the Mahasabha program. By 1944 the Communists had managed to elect a party member president of the Mahasabha, and in later years both Ravi Narayan Reddy and Baddam Yella Reddy (two prominent leaders of the Mahasabha) were to emerge as important leaders of the CPI.[17]

The war years (1939–1945) witnessed a phenomenal growth of the Communist movement in Telugu country. The CPI denounced the war as "imperialist" in 1939, but effected a neat volte-face when the Soviet Union joined the allies. From February 1942 until the end of the war the CPI described the conflict as a "people's war." The CPI's proffered support to the British war effort did isolate the party from the mainstream of the freedom struggle once the Congress party launched the Quit India movement in August 1942. But, despite this, the CPI stood to gain, primarily because of the British decisions to allow CPI legality and to enlist CPI leaders in support of the National War Front. After August 1942 Communists rushed in to fill the vacuum in the All-India Trade Union Congress, the All-India Kisan Sabha, the All-India Students Federation, and other Congress-led mass organizations.

In the Andhra area, the Communists increased their strength and influence during the war years despite their isolation from the freedom struggle. But, according to Ramalingiah, most of the members of the pre-1942 CPI cadre in Andhra were idealists and selfless workers while those who entered the party after 1942 were of a different genre.[18] The CPI membership in the Circars and Rayalaseema districts rose from 1,000 in 1942 to 8,000 in 1946,[19] and it is possible that the quality of membership suffered during this period. Certainly the leadership of the movement passed to the rural elite. Ramalingiah says that the rich peasant leaders of the CPI and its front organizations became virtual "fund clubs" during this period,[20] meaning that they financed the party and its organizations in return for leadership status. However, the dedicated old-time cadre members generally retained control of CPI mass organizations, if only because of their links with the people. Its members having parted with almost all of their

---

[17] The Reddis (also spelled Reddy) are one of the most prominent landed peasant castes in Andhra, and many of the members of this caste take the name Reddi (or Reddy) as a last name. This accounts for the frequency of the name Reddi (or Reddy) in this article.

[18] Ramalingiah, "Andhra Pradeshamlo Sapagrasthamaina Communist Udyamam Pai Sameeksha," p. 6.

[19] Puchalapalli Sundarayya, *Visaalandralo Praja Rajyam* (Vijayawada: Publisher Unknown, 1946), chap. 6.

[20] Ramalingiah, "Andhra Pradeshamlo Sapagrasthamaina Communist Udyamam Pai Sameeksha," p. 6.

property and having demonstrated its integrity in a number of campaigns, the older cadre was able to maintain itself by receiving donations from the people.

During World War II the Andhra Communists articulated the grievances of the people with remarkable effectiveness and intervened on their behalf on a number of occasions to secure administrative justice from the British government. Oppressed by wartime shortages all around, the urban people looked to the Communists for the satisfaction of their demands— for everything from the obtaining of ration cards to the regulation of queues in front of food depots. However, the Communists continued to direct their principal appeal to the poor peasantry and the landless agricultural laborers in the countryside.[21] When the government tried to realize its Grow More Food campaign with the help of an uncommitted bureaucracy, the CPI's front organizations intervened to help the government. The Grow More Food campaign was in fact the central task of the Andhra Communists on the peasant front, and this was linked with the campaign to bring waste land under the plough and to allot fallow land to the landless and poor peasants (the waste land issue was to become a major campaign plank in the postwar years).[22]

By 1946 the Communists had succeeded in providing an alternative to the Congress movement in the Andhra area. The CPI leadership was still essentially elitist, belonging to the middle and rich landlord upper castes, but hard-core support was increasingly being obtained from the poor peasantry and lower caste agricultural laborers. A strange interaction of caste politics and Communist articulation of the linguistic regionalism of the Telugu people undoubtedly contributed to the growth of the party during the war years, even though writers like Selig Harrison have exaggerated the importance of the caste factor since Independence.[23] Caste was a prominent factor in the Telugu areas during the war and has continued to

---

[21] Selig S. Harrison devotes an entire section of a chapter to the role of agricultural labor in Andhra politics and establishes that even in 1946 Communist electoral performance in the Andhra area was good in centers of farm labor concentration. The same was true for the 1951 elections. See Selig S. Harrison, *India: The Most Dangerous Decades* (Princeton, N.J.: Princeton University Press, 1960), pp. 213–216. See also "The Struggle for People's Democracy and Socialism: Some Strategy and Tactics," *Communist* (Monthly) 2, no. 4 (June–July 1949), 35; and "The Andhra Elections and the Communist Party," *New Age Weekly* 2, no. 23 (6 March 1955), 1.

[22] N. Prasada Rao, "Struggle of the Andhra Peasantry for Cultivable Waste Land," *New Age* (Monthly) 3, no. 4 (April 1954), 56–59.

[23] Harrison's thesis on the Andhra Communists is spelled out in detail in *India: The Most Dangerous Decades*, see especially pp. 204–245.

be a salient feature of political life in independent Andhra, but a discussion of caste must be placed in the perspective of Telugu regionalism.

Throughout the pre-Independence period the nationalist movement in Andhra was the preserve of the Brahmin caste, while the economically strategic Kammas in the Circars, and the Reddys in Rayalaseema, were fighting Brahmin domination. To be sure, some Kammas found in the Communist movement a vehicle for the advancement of their political ends, and most of the CPI leaders in the Circars happened to be Kammas (the Rayalaseema Communist leaders were Reddys). At the same time, however, N. G. Ranga, a Kamma, advanced amorphous peasant Socialist slogans from an anti-Communist platform within the Congress party. Perhaps a more important factor in attempting to understand the CPI's growth in Andhra—and its unique character as well—is the party's identification with the regional nationalism of the Telugu people, which took the form of a demand for a linguistic state. This is what gave the CPI the character of a regional nationalist movement and a broad independent mass base as well.

The demand for a linguistic Telugu state is much older than the CPI itself and even predates the 1916 resolution of the Congress party, which first accepted the linguistic reorganization of India as a Congress principle. The 1916 resolution was in fact passed under pressure from Andhra delegates, and Andhras were also instrumental in getting a similar resolution passed by the Congress in 1921. In 1927, when the Congress threatened to boycott the Simon Commission's visit to India, the possibility of a Telugu province (comprising the Madras portion of the Telugu-speaking tracts) was held out by the British as bait for Congress cooperation, but the Andhra leaders of the Congress movement rejected the offer under these conditions. In 1929 the all-party conference in Lucknow (a nationalist blast at the Simon Commission) demanded linguistic provinces for the entire country.

While the early Telugu demand covered only the Andhra area (that is, the Telugu-speaking areas in Madras Presidency) and was directed at the British, the Communists claim that they were responsible for the formulation of the demand for a Greater Andhra (Vishalandhra), an area that includes the Telengana region. "Vishalandhra" was the slogan adopted by the Andhra CPI during the 1946 elections to provincial legislatures, a slogan that proved to be the major campaign issue in that year. While it was not clear that the CPI was bent on secession, P. Sundarayya's famous tract, *Visaalandhralo Praja Rajyam* [People's Government in Vishalandhra], could be read as a manifesto for secession because of the manner in which it charged "betrayal" on the part of the Andhra Congress leadership. In Sundarayya's words:

> One question to Andhra Congress leaders: we are three crores of Telugu people; living in the same or only one area; our history is very ancient; we have our own language, culture, and traditions. Our political and economic future will be bright if all our Telugu people formed one political unit or state. Do you agree that all of us, Telugu people, belong to one race, have a right to decide freely and independently whether to join an Indian federation or not?[24]

As the freedom struggle entered its final phase, and the last round of negotiations for the transfer of power was in process, Sundarayya found it expedient to moderate his secession demand into one for fullest autonomy and voluntary participation in the union: "A united Telugu nation should exist in the independent Indian federation, as an independent Telugu state." [25] But this was perhaps a mere tactical move to gain the support of all-India leaders who placed the unity of India high on their list of post-Independence priorities. Throughout the pre-Independence period it is clear that Sundarayya wanted a voluntary union of Indian states when the country became free: "We believe that a free Indian Union can come into being only by the sovereign nationalities freely and voluntarily coming together and not by denying them the right of self-determination." [26] At any rate, by making the Vishalandhra demand an election issue, the Andhra Communists took the 1946 elections out of the drawing rooms of the elite nationalist leadership and from the debating chambers of legislatures, thrusting it into the streets. The distinctive character of this demand can be seen from the fact that no other state unit of the CPI conducted its election campaign in 1946 with a linguistic demand as its main plank.

As is indicated in the previous discussion, the Communist movement in Andhra was in an unusually strong position relative to other parts of India by the end of World War II, despite the fact that the movement in Andhra had started at a later date than the Communist movement elsewhere. By 1946 the Andhra Communists had outlived the stigma of being an antinational force with extraterritorial loyalties. Members of the CPI in Andhra had effectively allied themselves with Telugu regional aspirations and were not as closely identified with Moscow as CPI members in

24 Sundarayya, *Visaalandhralo Praja Rajyam*, p. 103.
25 A discussion of the Telugu demand in the context of the CPI's pre-Independence "nationality thesis" appears in Gene D. Overstreet and Marshall Windmiller, *Communism in India* (Bombay: Perennial Press, 1960), pp. 233–234.
26 Sundarayya, *Visaalandhralo Praja Rajyam*, pp. 86–87.

other Indian states. Despite their decision to remain apart from the Quit India agitation of the Congress, the Andhra Communists had made a number of gains during the war.

In addition to their political activities, the Andhra Communists had also taken the lead in a number of other respects during the period preceding India's Independence. Andhra Communists were in the forefront of the fight against untouchability in Telugu country, being the first to organize untouchable agricultural laborers into unions (on issues like land reform and better wages). The Andhra Communists also campaigned for equal rights for women and a number of other social reforms, to such an extent that N. G. Ranga was once prompted to charge the Communists with claiming that all social reformers in Andhra history were "Communists in the embryonic stage." [27] Moreover, the Andhra Communists were quick to identify with a variety of social reform movements in Telugu country, as is indicated by their frequent description of the late Veerasalingam Pantulu as "Comrade Veerasalingam." [28]

In journalism and literature the Communists were the first to promote simple, clear, and crisp modern prose, in place of the archaic style preserved by generations of establishment Telugu writers. Young Telugu writers today draw considerable inspiration from committed Communist writers and poets, who over the years have constituted an avant-garde in Telugu letters. Sri Sri, the idol of two generations of aspiring Telugu writers, was a revolutionary poet leading a writers' movement a full decade before the CPI organized its literary front in the form of the All-India Progressive Writers Association (1943). Even the Telugu stage and screen owe several of their modern trends to Communist stage and screen artists, scriptwriters, lyricists, and film photographers. The interest of the Communist Party in education and other diverse fields is reflected in the publications of the party, which include extremely popular works on such diverse subjects as maternity and child welfare and economic geography, all written in simple Telugu. In no other region of India has the Communist Party given so much attention to the cultural and social development of the people.[29]

[27] See Ranga, *Fight for Freedom*, p. 235.
[28] Veerasalingam Pantulu was a non-Communist scholar–social reformer in Andhra who was especially prominent in campaigns for women's rights (including widow remarriage) around the turn of the century. See ibid.
[29] The Communists in Andhra have been particularly important in the revival of *burrakatha*, a distinctly Telugu folk form of ballad singing. Nazar, the most famous *burrakatha* troupe leader has been a party man, and lesser Communist *burrakatha* performers have propagated the politics of class struggle and armed resistance among the peasantry of Andhra for years.

The strength of the Communist movement in Andhra at the time of Independence is palely reflected in the figures for the 1946 elections. The electoral system that was devised by the British for the1946 elections did not provide for proportional representation (which would have aided the Communists), and it was limited to a small segment (13 percent) of the adult population on the basis of property and educational qualifications. This meant that the poor peasants and agricultural laborers, who provided the hard-core support for the CPI, did not have the vote. The CPI, therefore, could win only one seat (a factory labor constituency), but their showing was nonetheless surprising. In an election that did not provide for adult franchise the CPI vote in the Circars (where 24 of its 29 candidates were concentrated) ranged from 11.5 percent in some constituencies to 31.9 percent in others, with the median just above 20 percent of the vote. Even more significant was the large number of candidates the CPI could field in the Andhra region in 1946 (24 candidates out of a total of 110 CPI candidates in all of India).[30]

Because of the links between the CPI and a host of groups within Andhra, most observers saw the Communists as the only alternative to the Congress in the Andhra region on the eve of India's Independence. The CPI's Andhra unit not only represented a broad interest aggregation that was intertwined with major caste interests—the Kamma and Reddy upper caste and middle and rich peasants—it also had hard-core support from among poor peasants and agricultural laborers. In addition, the party represented the hopes and aspirations of a large portion of urban middle-class intellectuals, many of them Brahmins, and it had cultivated Telugu regional aspirations with fanatical zeal. In short, the CPI in newly independent Andhra was a dynamic radical movement with a strong regional base.

The Telengana Movement

Since 1947 the Communist movement in Andhra has not lived up to the expectations of its leadership, nor has it moved in directions that could be anticipated in 1947. In the 1955 elections the Andhra CPI suffered a drastic setback in terms of electoral support, after a series of steady gains, and the movement is now seriously divided among a number of different groups. The one major factor that has influenced the course of the Andhra movement since Independence is the Telengana movement (1946–1951), which must be analyzed in some detail.

[30] *Returns Showing the Results of Elections to the Central Legislative Assembly and Provincial Legislatures, 1945–46* (New Delhi: Government of India Press, 1946), 80–96.

It was in Telengana that the contradiction between the mass of the peasantry and the feudal nature of British India was most advanced in 1945–1946; so it was not surprising that the Communists there should have been swept up by an upsurge of peasant discontent. The movement was initially centered around simple demands against eviction and oppressive feudal extortions, but it quickly escalated when it met with the combined repression of the landlords and the Nizam's governmental machinery. Peasant resistance to the attacks of organized hoodlums, police, and the Nizam's military took the form of armed clashes, which eventually swelled into a movement to overthrow the Nizam himself. By mid-1946 the Telengana movement had acquired the characteristics of a national liberation struggle—to free the people from the rule of the Nizam and the feudal order—and the CPI leadership was as surprised as anyone else to meet with a series of unanticipated successful attempts at organization. In the Circar and Rayalaseema regions the CPI had a more efficient organization and a well-trained cadre, but in these two areas it was still struggling to get widespread support. In contrast, the party in Telengana was not nearly as well-established, and the people of Telengana did not have a tradition of political participation, yet the CPI found itself leading an armed struggle in Telengana that was to last for five years.

This apparent paradox can be explained by a number of factors. First, the Telengana region had been under a medieval feudal monarchy during the years of British rule, even though it was formally under the ryotwari system, while the other parts of Andhra were in fact under the ryotwari system. This meant that the contradictions between the peasantry and the landlords had become very sharp in Telengana, while they had been blunted elsewhere. Second, the nationalist movement in British India had been led by the national bourgeoisie, whereas in Telengana the Communists were in effective control of the small nationalist movement that had developed under the Nizam's autocracy (the Congress pursued a consistent policy throughout India, which dictated that no attempt be made to organize in the Princely states). Finally, the decision by the Nizam of Hyderabad to refuse accession to India after Independence placed him in direct contradiction to the new Indian government. This last factor made it possible for the Communist-led movement in Hyderabad to take on the character of a national liberation struggle, with the support of national bourgeois leadership in the rest of Telugu country, and this in turn blunted the edge of anti-Communist feelings. Indeed, the Communists of the Circars and Rayalaseema gained considerably from the agitation in Telengana, and they in turn offered a great deal of organizational, material, and moral support, to the young movement.

During the initial stages of the Telengana movement the struggle was confined to 150 villages, but within the short space of a year it had spread to hundreds and thousands more.[31] Throughout the Telengana region Communist guerrillas were locked in combat with the Nizam's police and army, and with a small private army known as the Razakars.[32] In early 1948 the CPI began to establish liberated zones—with people's governments, people's courts, and people's militia—and by 1950 the whole of Nalgonda and Warangal districts were claimed as a large contiguous liberated zone by the CPI.[33]

As the Telengana movement progressed, the Andhra CPI began to link the war of liberation with the thought of Mao Tse-tung. Telengana was widely considered the Yenan of India. Agrarian programs were undertaken in the liberated zones through CPI peasant committees. More than a million acres of land were distributed in 3,000 villages under Communist control, according to CPI sources, and approximately 4,000 Communists and supporters died in encounters or in prison camps. CPI sources also estimate that more than 5,000 women were raped by the police and military during the conflagration, while 1,000 villages were burned to the ground and 15,000 villages throughout Andhra were raided by the police. CPI figures would also indicate that approximately 10,000 people died of starvation and epidemic disease in concentration camps.[34]

The entire Telengana operation was directed from the Munagala jungle on the Madras-Hyderabad border, a fairly large territory that comprises more than 40 villages. Communist guerrilla squads spread themselves throughout the Telengana area from this jungle base, with some guerrilla units moving as far as the Circars region. The leaders of the movement were almost exclusively from the Circars, appearing in the role of fellow countrymen across an artificial border, fighting in battle on the side of their Telengana brethren. When the Indian army marched into Hyderabad in March 1948 and forced the Nizam to accede to India, the situation changed qualitatively, since the Nizam's autocracy was then formally at an end and the Communists were now confronted with Indian army units.

[31] "Telengana Peasants Fight for Freedom," *People's Age* 6, no. 30 (25 January 1948), 1, 13.
[32] "Free People's Governments Being Set Up All Over Liberated Area of Hyderabad," *People's Age* 6, no. 35 (21 March 1948), 3.
[33] The people's militia—as well as the people's courts and people's governments—in the Telengana "liberated zones" are discussed in "On Telengana," CPI Information Document No. 7 (2), October 1950. This is a confidential and unpublished party document.
[34] P. Sundarayya, "Communists Emerge as the National Party of the Telugu People," *Crossroads* 3, no. 45 (21 March 1952), 5, 14.

Nevertheless, the CPI decided to fight a protracted war with the Indian army, and the struggle was not called off until late 1951.

The Communist Party in Andhra has been very much influenced by the Telengana movement, from the time of the movement itself right up until the present. Indeed, the origins of the Indian Communist split in 1964 can be traced back to the confused understanding of the Mountbatten Award (under which power was transferred to Indians in 1947), which accompanied both the Telengana agitation and Independence. In June 1947, the CPI thought that the bourgeois-nationalist government of Jawaharlal Nehru could be pressured into following leftist policies or at least accommodating leftist elements, but by December 1947, the party had denounced its own earlier assessment as "opportunist," when it found that big business in India had become "a reactionary force opposed to the anti-imperialist national front." Arguing along with the Zhdanov thesis of September 1947, the CPI saw in the Mountbatten Award the capitulation of the bourgeois-nationalist leadership, to the point of collaboration with Anglo-American imperialism. For this reason India's Independence was branded by the CPI (in late 1947) as "fake." [35]

At its Second Congress, in early 1948, the CPI called for a "united front from below," a new class alliance of the working class, peasantry, and revolutionary intelligentsia, to be welded together in a one-stage people's democratic revolution through violent means. The obvious inspiration for this was the Titoite theory of the "intertwining" of the two stages of revolution, propounded by Edvard Kardelj at the Cominform's inaugural meeting in September 1947. It was a logical step for the CPI to move from the left sectarian oversimplification of the Second Congress thesis to a sectarian deviation that led to terrorist adventurism in practice.

For the Andhra Communists who were leading the Telengana peasant struggle the ideological debates of 1947 and 1948 were especially disheartening. The strategy that the Andhra Communists would use in Telengana depended on the outcome of the ideological debate, and yet the preferences of the Andhra unit were rarely taken into consideration by either the CPI or by Moscow. The Andhra Communists were at the time invoking Mao Tse-tung's "New Democracy" as an alternative to the Second Congress thesis. "New Democracy" called for two-stage revolution with a four-class alliance to realize the party's program. This "Andhra thesis" (as it came to be called) identified both feudalism and imperialism as the main enemies, and it identified a "new democratic stage" (as distinct from the "proletarian stage") as the stage of imminent revolution.

[35] See Overstreet and Windmiller, *Communism in India*, pp. 266–270.

The Andhra Communists sought to unite the entire peasantry (the middle peasant was regarded as a stable ally), including the rich peasantry, under working class leadership. The alliance was also to include the middle bourgeoisie and the petit bourgeoisie, and the form of struggle was to be guerrilla warfare.[36] While the Andhra Communists were for guerrilla warfare, relying on the peasantry, the Second Congress thesis emphasized urban insurrection and the general strike as weapons for a proletarian revolution. By applying the Chinese experience to the Indian reality, of course, the Andhra Communists were challenging the tactical line of the national CPI.

CPI general secretary B. T. Ranadive quickly attacked the source of the heresy in his polemics against the "Andhra thesis." The "Andhra thesis" said that Mao Tse-tung's "New Democracy" was "a new form of revolutionary struggle to advance towards socialism in colonies and semicolonies," and that new democracy was "distinct from the dictatorship of the proletariat." [37] In reaction to this, Ranadive joined issue immediately, denouncing both Mao and his "New Democracy":

Firstly, we must state emphatically that the Communist Party of India has accepted Marx, Engels, Lenin and Stalin as the authoritative sources of Marxism. It has not discovered new sources of Marxism beyond these. Nor for that matter is there any Communist Party which declares adherence to the so-called theory of new democracy alleged to be propounded by Mao and declares it a new addition to Marxism.

It must be admitted that some of Mao's formulations are such that no Communist Party can accept them; they are in contradiction to the world understanding of the Communist parties.[38]

For the first time in the history of the international Communist movement the bona fides of Mao's theories as part of Marxism-Leninism were being debated in public. There was no evidence to suggest that the Andhra leadership had any communications with the Communist Party of China (CPC), but it is certain that Ranadive was denouncing Mao in the belief that he had the support of the Soviet party leadership, which was then the sole legitimizing authority in the world Communist movement. Nor was the CPSU willing to discipline Ranadive so long as the Cominform still subscribed to the Zhdanov line. It was not until early 1950, when the Soviet Union decided to replace class struggle with the Cold War, that the

[36] "Andhra Letter" (Unpublished CPI inner-party document), June 1948.
[37] Ibid.
[38] B. T. Ranadive, "Struggle for People's Democracy and Socialism: Some Questions of Strategy and Tactics," *Communist* (Monthly) 2, no. 4 (June–July 1949), 77.

Cominform was willing to drop the Zhdanov line, and it was only at this time that Ranadive was debunked by the Soviets. It was at this time too that the Cominform journal first endorsed Liu Shao-chi's famous speech at the Peking conference of Asian and Australasian trade unions (November 1949), prescribing the "road of Mao Tse-tung" as the path for other colonial countries "wherever and whenever possible." [39]

The stand of the Cominform journal in early 1950 was an endorsement of the four-class alliance and two-stage revolution advocated by the Andhra Communists, and a rejection of Ranadive's "one-stage" theory of revolution, even though it played down the role of armed struggle in the Indian revolution. Thus, the Andhra Communists received the blessings of Moscow in 1950 and shortly thereafter found themselves leading the CPI. Andhra leader C. Rajeswara Rao replaced Ranadive as general secretary in 1951, and several other Andhras were placed in prominent party posts, giving the Andhra unit of the CPI a brief period of hegemony over other party units in India. Prior to this time the leadership and the intellectual capabilities of the Andhra Communists had never been acknowledged by the all-India party despite the strength of the Andhra movement relative to other parts of India. The Cambridge and Oxford-educated leaders who packed the CPI's central committees during the war years (and in the postwar years as well) looked at the unsophisticated Andhra leaders as interlopers and agrarian reformers who were invoking Mao's teachings. They did not recognize the Andhrans as worthy of holding leading positions in the party. Moreover, the Andhra leaders—notably Sundarayya and Rajeswara Rao—were mass leaders and not intellectual leaders, and it is significant that no Andhra leader had written a theoretical article in the party press during this period.

During the brief Maoist interlude in 1950–1951, the Telengana line of peasant partisan warfare prevailed over Ranadive's line of urban insurrection, which had already degenerated into mere terrorism in other parts of India. But Moscow, which had been waging a cold war against Nehru, felt compelled to intervene when the Andhra leadership of the CPI persisted in armed struggle in Telengana after that period when the Soviets began to court Nehru. An initial attempt at intervention from Moscow came in the form of a letter from the British party in late 1950, but when the Andhra leadership ignored this letter the British party's ideologue—R.

---

[39] "Mighty Advance of the National Liberation Movement in the Colonial and Dependent Countries," *For a Lasting Peace, For a People's Democracy* (Cominform Journal), 27 January 1950, p. 1. This article refers specifically to India at a number of crucial points.

Palme Dutt—laid down a series of directives with greater clarity. In Dutt's words, India needed "a broad democratic front from above on the basis of a common action programme for peace and for independence." According to Dutt's analysis, armed struggle was not the correct path for India for the present.[40] In 1951 the CPI was therefore directed to launch a peace offensive, to pressure Nehru into supporting the Soviet bloc, and to relegate class struggle to a lower order of priority.

Rightist elements in the CPI, who had consistently opposed the Andhra line, now launched a campaign against the Rajeswara Rao leadership and the Telengana peasant struggle, and international intervention helped these elements in their efforts to oust the Andhras from their positions in the party. Amidst serious differences, a delegation of the CPI (comprising two Andhra Maoists, Rajeswara Rao, and the young theoretician M. Basavapunniah, and two rightists opposed to armed struggle, S. A. Dange and Ajoy Ghosh) clandestinely visited Moscow for consultations with the Soviet party.[41] The Soviet commission at these talks included J. V. Stalin, V. M. Molotov, and G. M. Malenkov, among others. The result was a new program and tactical line for the party and the replacement of Rajeswara Rao by Ajoy Ghosh as general secretary. Finally, in late 1951, the CPI declared the Telengana armed struggle at an end.

The 1951 program did not represent a fundamental departure from the Andhra thesis of 1948, since it accepted the need for a four-class alliance and a two-stage revolution. But the new tactical line rationalized the rejection of armed struggle as the immediate tactic of the Indian revolution. During the next 13 years the major controversies in the CPI were related to the program and tactics of the party, but the party split into two parts in 1964, before it could devise a new program. Throughout these years the CPI participated in India's bourgeois parliamentary system, based on adult franchise, beginning with the General Elections in 1952.

Electoral Communism in Andhra

By the end of 1951 the CPI could agree to settle for peaceful constitutionalism, at the behest of Moscow. This was understandable within India, since the party had suffered so heavily during the years of insurrectionist

---

[40] "Palme Dutt Answers Questions on India," *Crossroads* 2, no. 27 (19 January 1951), 3. See also *Indian Communist Party Documents, 1930–1956*, ed. V. B. Karnik (Bombay: Democratic Research Service, 1957), 63–69.
[41] This was revealed by S. A. Dange, chairman of the present CPI, in S. A. Dange, "Can a Country Have More than One Communist Party?" *Mainstream* 6, no. 46 (3 August 1968), 33.

struggle. In 1952, when the first elections were held in India, the party was still illegal in Hyderabad and Travancore-Cochin and only formally legal in the rest of the country. Its organizational machinery was all but smashed; its leading cadres were either in jail or still underground or in some cases had just been freed on conditional bail. The loss in terms of cadres was heaviest in the Telugu country, where thousands had died in guerilla encounters or had been executed.

The CPI's Andhra Committee, in its 1952 election manifesto, promised to campaign for Vishalandhra, abolition of zamindari,[42] struggle in alliance with the rich peasantry against zamindari and other forms of exploitation, and minimum wages for agricultural labor.[43] In practice, however, the CPI election strategy in 1952 was designed to exploit the Kamma-Reddy caste rivalry inside the Congress. Following his defeat at the hands of Sanjiva Reddy, the Kamma leader N. G. Ranga had left the Congress to form the splinter Krishikar Lok Party (KLP) in 1951, and the KLP came to represent the small and middle peasant interests, particularly of Kamma caste members. The Brahmin leadership of the Congress had formed its own splinter party—the Andhra regional unit of the all-India Kisan Mazdoor Praja Party (KMPP), while the faction-ridden and corrupt Congress faced its main challenge in the Communists. In the 1952 elections the CPI in Andhra found itself campaigning in the midst of strong anti-Congress feelings throughout the Andhra area.

The performance of the CPI in the Andhra area in 1952 can only be termed spectacular, since the CPI won more seats than any other party, despite its severe handicaps. Of the 140 seats in the Andhra area (which were then part of the Madras state assembly), the CPI bagged 41, while the party also helped to secure victory for 8 independent candidates that it supported. Moreover, of the 20 KMPP winners, 10 had the backing of the CPI. The Congress gained only 40 seats in this same area. In the elections the CPI polled 20 percent of the vote, even though it contested in only 75 of the 140 constituencies, while the Congress could poll only 30 percent of the vote while running candidates in all of the 140 constituencies. CPI gains in the Andhra area were concentrated in five districts that make up the Circars: The CPI won 10 of the 12 seats in Krishna, 10 of the

[42] Zamindari was officially abolished in 1948 (see the Zamindari Abolition Act, 1948, of the Madras Presidency), but follow-up measures remain to be taken. While statutory landlordism was abolished by the 1948 act, no "basic changes" in the land relationship had taken place by 1954. See "Agrarian Programme of the Andhra Committee of the Communist Party of India," *New Age* (Monthly) 3, no. 12 (December 1954), 66–67.

[43] "Communist Programme for Happy Vishal Andhra," *Crossroads* 3, no. 24 (19 October 1951), 6–7.

18 seats in Guntur, 5 of the 12 seats in West Godavary, 6 of the 12 in East Godavary, and 3 of the 13 in Nellore.[44]

In the Telengana region, the electoral situation was extremely complex, but the CPI did as well (or better) in Telengana as it did in the Circars. More than 2,000 members of the CPI cadre were still in jail in 1952, and more than a thousand others were still underground when the elections took place. Moreover, the CPI was still illegal in Telengana, which meant that CPI candidates had to run under various guises. Under these circumstances the CPI encountered great difficulty in finding candidates who could file nominations, and the People's Democratic Front (PDF) (the party's legal front for purposes of elections) could therefore run candidates in only 45 of the 98 constituencies in Telengana. In order to provide opportunities for a wide variety of electoral experiences for its cadre, a number of CPI members contested in two constituencies at the same time, and, in addition, the PDF supported independent candidates in another 10 constituencies.

The extent of the Communist victory can be seen from the fact that 36 of the 45 candidates that ran under the banner of the PDF were elected. In addition, 10 Socialist candidates that had contested in alliance with the front were victorious. The Congress won 41 seats in Telengana in 1952, but 25 of these were located in Mahboobnagar and Hyderabad districts, the two districts where the front did not offer candidates. In the "red" district of Nalgonda, the front made a clean sweep of all 14 seats; in Warangal, another "red" district, the front won 11 of 14 seats; in Karimnagar the front won 10 of the 15 constituencies. Thus, 35 of the 45 PDF seats in 1952 were located in those three districts where the Communists had led the Telengana movement. Of the 2.5 million votes polled, the front captured approximately a third, while the Congress (which again contested every one of the 98 seats) could only poll the same approximate percentage.[45]

After the elections it was unmistakably clear that Communist gains in Telugu country were most spectacular precisely in those areas where the party had led peasant partisan warfare or guerrilla squad actions, inviting massive police and military repression. If the vote meant anything at all, it was the vindication of the Andhra Communist line of Maoist armed struggle. At the end of the poll the CPI could claim that it was the party of the Telugu people's "national unification." And the party could also

---

[44] Selig Harrison, *India: The Most Dangerous Decades*, pp. 214 ff.

[45] P. Sundarayya, "Communists Emerge as the National Party of the Telugu People," pp. 5, 14.

identify three key factors that were responsible for their electoral success: (1) the party's leadership on the Vishalandhra issue, (2) its hard work among the people, and (3) the party's image among the people as the party that secured land for them.[46]

Agricultural labor and the poor peasantry continued to account for the hard-core following of the CPI in Andhra in the 1952 elections, but the party had also come to represent an aggregation of other interests. Not only had it allied successfully with a number of middle and rich peasant interests, it had developed a tremendous hold over the important rural intelligentsia in the process. The untouchable and depressed castes that comprised the bulk of the agricultural laborers voted with the CPI, as did the poor peasants who belonged to the depressed castes. As mentioned above, the CPI also picked up a considerable number of votes from the dominant Kamma and Reddy castes, the mainstay of its leadership.

The pattern of Communist support that was demonstrated in Andhra in 1952 has not changed much over the years since then, although the extent of CPI support has dwindled considerably. In fact, in a very ironic way the decline of the fortunes of the CPI can be explained by the very success of the party in the 1952 elections. But to understand the irony of the CPI electoral decline since 1952 it is necessary to analyze in some detail each of the elections in which the CPI has contested.

As a result of the 1952 elections the Andhra Communists were highly confident that they could wrest power from the Congress, if only they could bring into being a separate Andhra state. The CPI therefore stepped up its campaign for a separate Telugu-speaking Vishalandhra, leading the people of Telugu country to a crescendo of activity shortly after the 1952 poll. When the Nehru government partially conceded the demand for Vishalandhra in 1953 by carving out the Telugu-speaking areas from Madras state into a new Andhra state, the CPI proclaimed this a first logical step, but continued with the demand that the Telugu-speaking areas of Hyderabad be included in the new state. This demand was also met in 1956 when, on the basis of the States Reorganization Report, the entire country, with a few exceptions, was reorganized into unilingual states. Andhra Pradesh came into being as part of this reorganization and this was the fulfillment of the Vishalandhra demand.

However, the growing strength and confidence of the Communist movement in Andhra had led the non-Communist parties to band together against the CPI, as was evident in the first Andhra state assembly (formed in October 1953). To be sure, the Congress party was in a minority in the

46 Ibid.

140-member state assembly, but because of the threat of the Communists the Congress had found it possible to forge a coalition ministry with the smaller KMPP and KLP. The CPI, with its 41 members and supporting independents, was forced to play the role of the loyal opposition, trying to embarrass the government inside the assembly while leading mass movements outside.

Nevertheless, the Communists in Andhra remained confident that they could wrest power in the state if they could manage to force a midterm election to the state legislative assembly. The CPI therefore stepped up its campaign for the distribution of wastelands to the landless and poor peasants of Andhra and was successful in pushing through the state legislative assembly a resolution embodying most of the CPI land program. In addition, the CPI launched campaigns on a number of smaller issues: a larger allocation of central government funds for the state; central government endorsement of irrigation schemes; and opposition to Congress dry laws. On these minor issues the CPI was not successful in the state legislature, but it was one of these minor issues (the dry laws) that finally split the Congress-dominated coalition ministry. When the ministry failed to gain a majority in the state legislative assembly, the assembly was dissolved, and fresh elections were called for in 1955.

It should be explained that the decision of the Andhra CPI to force a fresh election in Andhra was a result of conscious policy. The CPI's Third Congress (in 1953) had argued that India was soon going to encounter a serious economic crisis, which would mature into a political crisis, and that this would work to the electoral advantage of the Communists. Following this line of thinking the CPI in Andhra argued that the Congress ministry had indeed brought about an economic crisis by its policies, and the party therefore judged the sentiment of the voters as one of extreme distaste for Congress rule. By forcing the state ministry to call for fresh elections in 1955, the CPI was convinced that it alone would benefit.

But the all-India leadership of the Congress, unnerved at the prospect of losing the new Andhra state to the Communists, moved quickly to forge an election front against the CPI. Using the skills of a number of Congress leaders throughout India the Congress welded together the Reddy-dominated Congress, the Kamma-dominated Krishikar Lok Party, and the Brahmin-led KMPP, all cooperating with one another in a series of electoral agreements.[47] As the election campaign proceeded it became increas-

[47] A description of Congress coalition building in Andhra Pradesh is available in Hugh Gray, "Andhra Pradesh," in *State Politics in India*, ed. Myron Weiner (Princeton, N.J.: Princeton University Press, 1968), pp. 408 ff.

ingly clear that the CPI, by proclaiming its intention to capture power, had only managed to unite all of the major parties against itself. But by the time the CPI realized this, it had lost its maneuverability, and the new Congress alliance had precluded the possibility of exploiting Andhra caste rivalries.

In the 1955 elections the Congress-led alliance won 146 of the 196 seats in the assembly, with the CPI gaining only 15 seats and the Socialist Party 13 (nonaligned independent candidates obtained another 13 seats, with the remainder being scattered among smaller parties). The 1955 alignment of seats hardly reflects the relative strength of the political parties in Andhra at that time, but it does indicate the skillfulness of Congress coalition builders. The Congress-led electoral front polled only 51 percent of the recorded vote, while the Communists polled 31 percent. In almost every district the Communists made considerable gains in terms of the percentage of the vote received by their candidates, but because of its isolation the party suffered disastrously in terms of seats (see table 5.1).

Because of the importance of the 1955 poll in Andhra, the election results must be analyzed in some detail. As is indicated in table 5.1, the CPI continued to draw its greatest support in the Circars, although the party managed to increase its support in almost every district in the state. The factors that contributed to the decline of the CPI in terms of seats

Table 5.1 Communist Performance in the 1952 and 1955 Elections to the Andhra Legislative Assembly (Excluding the Hyderabad Regions), by District

District	% CPI Vote		CPI Seats	
	1952	1955	1952	1955
Srikakulam	4.9	12.7	—	—
Visākhapatnam	6.7	19.0	2	
East Godavary	22.3	37.8	6	6
West Godavary	28 7	41.1	5	—
Krishna	46.3	43.3	10	3
Guntur	30.2	40.8	10	2
Nellore	13.7	37.1	3	4
Chittoor	4.7	15.0	1	
Cuddapah	16.7	19.1	2	—
Kurnool	5.9	21.8	1	—
Anantapur	9.4	28.0	1	—

Source: Craig Baxter, *District Voting Trends in India: A Research Tool* (New York: Southern Asian Institute, School of International Affairs, Columbia University, 1969), pp. 3–25.

are numerous. First, as the Central Committee of the CPI admitted in its postmortem on the elections, the Andhra unit had failed to assess the political situation objectively, and it had therefore underestimated the importance of forging a united front of non-Congress parties. In the words of the Central Committee:

> The anti-Congress sentiment of the mass of the people was a reflection of their desire to have an alternative government of the Communist Party and other [non-Congress] parties, groups and individuals—*but not a Communist bloc government.*[48]

To the voters in Andhra it was clear that the CPI slogan calling for "a government of democratic unity" would in practice mean a Communist government, since the CPI was contesting 169 of the 196 seats without adjustments or alliances.

Second, the Congress-led alliance had seized upon the CPI slogan of alternative government to raise the red bogey and conjure up visions of totalitarianism in Andhra, sidetracking all of the campaign issues into the broad issue of communism versus democracy. Third, the CPI demand for Vishalandhra had lost its appeal by 1952, since the Congress leadership in Delhi had partially granted the demand by carving out the new Andhra state, and the Congress leadership in Andhra said very little about the issue in elections (the Congress election manifesto did not so much as mention the demand). Fourth, development spending by the Congress government, along with more remunerative prices for agricultural commodities following decontrol of food-grain prices, had resulted in renewed prosperity for many farmers and better wages for agricultural labor. Fifth, the caste factor was no longer in the CPI's favor, since the Congress electoral alliance had handcuffed the CPI in its attempts to exploit Kamma-Reddy-Brahmin rivalries. Sixth, the Congress party had launched a new ideological offensive on the eve of the Andhra elections, accepting a "socialist pattern of society," as its goal, and this had blunted the edge of the Communist platform.[49]

Finally, however, there was a seventh factor that played an important part in the outcome of the elections in Andhra in 1955, and this had to do with the role of Moscow and the international Communist movement in the elections. As I have indicated above, Moscow had been pursuing a

[48] "Resolution on Andhra Elections," unpublished resolution of the CPI Central Committee, March 1955. This document is reproduced in *Indian Communist Party Documents*, 1930–1956, pp. 216–223.

[49] The electoral struggle between the Congress and the CPI in Andhra in the 1950s is traced out in Myron Weiner, *Party Building in a New Nation* (Chicago: University of Chicago Press, 1967), pp. 141 ff.

policy designed to court Nehru since the failure of the Zhdanov line in the early 1950s, and as part of this policy the CPSU had encouraged the CPI to lend its support to Nehru's group within the Congress. As part of this policy a *Pravda* editorial on India's Republic Day (a few days before the Andhra poll) warmly praised the achievements of the Nehru government when it said that India was "a peace-loving state upholding its national independence . . . [a state which had] set itself the grim task of gradually eliminating colonialism." [50] The *Pravda* editorial not only marked the end of seven years of Soviet attacks on Nehru, it also blighted the chances of the Andhra Communists at the polls. Paradoxically, it had been the CPI's crash campaign in support of socialist policy measures that had forced Nehru to take an anticapitalist orientation in his domestic programs; but by 1955, when Nehru's new orientation brought him electoral gains, this worked to the greatest disadvantage of the CPI.

As the Central Committee of the CPI ruefully noted after the 1955 elections in Andhra, Indo-Soviet amity had had an "enormous effect" precisely on those classes that the party was trying to befriend—middle class intellectuals and the national bourgeoisie. After reviewing in some detail the results of the 1955 elections, the Central Committee was dismayed at the inability of the party to exploit this situation. Since the elections had revealed a swing of "large sections of the middle class elements in towns, the majority of rich and middle peasants and the rural intelligentsia" toward the Congress, the CPI Central Committee feared that the Congress might now attempt to exploit the CPI debacle in Andhra by working for the elimination of the CPI cadre. As a result of these fears the Central Committee decided that it should continue to fight for the demands of poor peasants and agricultural laborers but that it should also take upon itself a more zealous defense of the interests of middle and rich peasants, the rural and urban middle classes, traders, and industrialists. In short, the party was now determined to expand its class base, directing its principal appeal to sections outside of its previous hard-core following.[51]

The elections of 1955 were the closest that the Communists have ever come to capturing political power through the ballot box in Andhra. Since 1955 the percentage of the vote received by the Communists has declined in almost every Andhra district (see table 5.2), and the split in the CPI in 1964 has seriously impaired the chances of a united electoral effort on the part of the Communists in the near future. The failure of electoral communism in the state is underlined forcefully by developments since the

[50] Quoted in the *Times of India*, 1 February 1955.
[51] This section is dependent throughout on the unpublished Resolutions of the Central Committee of the CPI, 1955.

Table 5.2   Percentage of the Vote Polled by Communist Parties in Andhra Pradesh (1952–1967), by District

District	1952	1955/1957[a]	1962	1967[b] CPI	CPM
Andhra Area: Circars					
Srikakulam	4.9	12.7	5.6	1.2	3.2
Visakhapatnam	6.7	19.0	13.2	6.6	2.8
East Godavary	22.3	37.8	14.7	11.6	3.4
West Godavary	28.7	41.1	25.3	9.4	13.6
Krishna	46.3	43.3	38.0	13.9	12.5
Guntur	30.2	40.8	27.2	8.1	12.4
Nellore	13.7	37.1	21.3	9.2	7.9
Andhra Area: Rayalaseema					
Chittoor	4.7	15.0	13.9	4.1	2.8
Cuddapah	16.7	19.1	7.3	—	—
Anantapur	9.4	28.0	11.5	6.5	8.9
Kurnool	5.9	21.8	9.9	3.5	4.5
Telengana Area					
Telengana	26.1	25.7	21.4	8.9	8.6
Mahboobnagar	1.8	10.5	9.7	2.0	1.1
Hyderabad	13.8	6.3	2.9	2.1	1.7
Medak	16.2	17.6	18.3	11.8	2.1
Nizamabad	—	12.5	2.3	0.9	—
Adilabad	8.7	16.0	13.0	13.0	—
Karimnagar	26.5	29.2	11.2	12.6	—
Warangal	33.3	31.4	27.2	11.9	11.6
Khammam	51.2	44.8	42.9	7.2	26.1
Nalgonda	67.5	50.2	51.2	16.7	27.6
Andhra Pradesh	21.8	29.5	19.5	7.8	7.6

Source: Compiled from Craig Baxter, *District Voting Trends in India: A Research Tool* (New York: Southern Asian Institute, School of International Affairs, Columbia University, 1969), pp. 3–25.
[a] Those districts formerly in Madras Presidency witnessed elections in 1955; those districts formerly in Hyderabad state witnessed elections in 1957.
[b] In 1964 the united CPI split, and in the 1967 elections the two postsplit parties contested against one another without any kind of electoral understanding between them.

1964 split in the Indian Communist movement. In the 1967 elections to the state legislature, the CPI and the CPM (which came into being as a result of the split) opposed each other in a good number of constituencies. Together they polled 15.4 percent of the vote as against 19.5 percent by the undivided CPI in 1962 and 29.5 percent in 1955–1957). Between 1967 and the latest elections (March 1972), the CPM was again rocked by a schism, with a majority of its members turning Maoist and opting out of the parliamentary system in 1968. The truncated CPM's poor showing in 1972 is largely explained by this. Its vote slumped from 7.6 percent in 1967 to 3.1 percent in 1972. In contrast, the CPI's vote did not decline so sharply, though it fell marginally, from 7.8 percent in 1967 to 6.1 percent in 1972.

Back to Maoism
In the mid-1950s, when the Soviet attitude toward Nehru changed drastically, the CPI committed itself to open support of Nehru's foreign policy with little difficulty. But there were great differences within the CPI when it came to the question of supporting Nehru's domestic programs. The Right faction within the CPI—following the lead of the CPSU—began to advocate a united front with Nehru's government, but the Left faction continued to insist on the formulations of the obsolete 1951 program. A compromise was then effected between Right and Left at the Fourth Congress of the CPI in 1956, when the party rejected united front with the Congress for the time being, while taking care to stress that future democratic fronts might not be anti-Congress. However, when the CPI won partial power in Kerala in the 1957 elections, the national leadership of the party saw this as vindication of the peaceful transition thesis expounded at the Twentieth Congress of the CPSU, and it was therefore possible for the party to adopt the thesis of peaceful transition to socialism at its Fifth Congress (in 1958).

The Fifth Congress thesis exacerbated the factionalism between Right and Left, although an open split was narrowly averted at the Sixth Congress of the CPI in 1961. In the meantime, the Sino-Soviet ideological dispute had reached the point of no return and had exploded into the open, creating enormous difficulties for the Indian Communists, particularly after the eruption of the military conflict between India and China in late 1962. The combination of a Sino-Soviet rift and a Sino-Indian border dispute was too difficult to be contained by India's faction-ridden CPI, with the result that the party split in 1964. The dominant Right faction leadership had committed the presplit CPI to support of the Soviet ideological position without so much as a party discussion, and it was this faction that was recognized by the CPSU as India's only legitimate Communist Party after the split. The breakaway faction, which eventually became the CPM, did not declare its support for either the Soviet or Chinese positions, but instead called for widespread discussion of all sides of the ideological dispute.

By 1967 the CPM had maneuvered itself into a position where it was leading elected coalition state ministries in Kerala and West Bengal, and these events coincided with Peking's vigorous assertion that the Maoist model of people's war was applicable to the entire Third World. A peasant revolt in the Naxalbari area of West Bengal, led by extremists within the CPM in West Bengal, provided Peking with an occasion for spelling out its strategy for the Indian revolution, and this in turn had an enormous impact on a number of CPI members throughout India. On 10 June 1967, a Peking Radio commentary (credited to "a Red Guard") stated that the extremists within the CPM in West Bengal were leading a movement that "represented the general orientation of the Indian revolution at the present time." At the same time, Peking Radio called for "relentless armed struggle to overthrow the Indian government and seize power." [52]

The peasant revolt that had prompted the Peking broadcast was centered in the subdivision of Naxalbari, which is located at precisely that point where India's narrowest corridor joins the main body of India with its northeastern territories. By hailing the Naxalbari revolt, Peking was forcing the CPM in West Bengal into a severe dilemma, since it was CPM extremists that had launched the peasant agitation during a period when the CPM was participating in a bourgeois state coalition ministry. If the CPM supported the Naxalbari agitation it would invite dismissal by the Indian government, thus damaging its tactical position relative to the bourgeois parties with which it was allied. If it suppressed the agitation, the CPM stood to lose some of its best cadre members, discrediting itself in the eyes of many Communists in the process.

In reaction to the Naxalbari agitation—and to Peking's support of the "Naxalites"—the CPM leadership in West Bengal continued to hedge, although its Central Committee did draft a statement on ideological issues in keeping with a long-standing promise to its ranks. This draft document examined the Soviet position on all of the issues then in dispute and found them wanting, but it did not examine the Chinese position except on the issue of unity of action in Vietnam. On this one issue the CPM leadership

[52] *Times of India,* 11 June 1967.

differed with the Chinese. In short, the CPM was attempting to clarify its anti-Soviet stance without identifying the party with the Chinese.

While all of the other state plenums of the CPM approved of this draft document, the Andhra Pradesh plenum rejected it by a wide margin (158 to 52, with 8 neutral votes).[53] Moreover, after rejecting the draft document the Andhra plenum demanded that the Central Committee of the CPM prepare a new draft on the basis of the general line proposed by the Communist Party of China in its letter of 14 June 1963 and its nine comments on the CPSU's open letter of 14 July 1963. Finally, the Andhra plenum forwarded to the Central Committee two resolutions that had been placed before the Andhra plenum by three Andhra Maoists (T. Nagi Reddy, C. Pulla Reddy, and Kolla Venkiah). These two resolutions severely criticized the original draft document of the Central Committee and endorsed the Chinese assessment of the Indian situation.[54]

The resolutions that were forwarded by the Andhra plenum to the Central Committee in 1967 argued that the CPM's post-1967 election-document (*New Situation and Party's Tasks*) was a "revisionist compromise with bourgeois parliamentarism," and they attacked the participation of CPM leaders in the United Front ministries in West Bengal and Kerala. Both resolutions argued that the state ministries in West Bengal and Kerala were alliances with "reactionary elements," which had resulted in an increasing failure to unleash struggles out of fear that these coalitions might break up or might be dismissed. One of the resolutions also stated (in part):

We feel the party has to seriously think whether our work in the united front ministries with bourgeois sections and revisionist sections has not resulted in blunting the edge of the people's struggle against the policies of the bourgeois-landlord government.[55]

The conclusion of those who moved the resolutions was that people's war was essential in India: "We categorically say that in all backward countries, winning the majority of the people, building mass organisation and party-building is closely linked with armed struggle." [56]

In late 1967, when Peking found that it had failed to force the CPM out of the bourgeois parliamentary system and into the path of armed

[53] *Andhra Plenum Rejects Neo-Revisionist Draft* (Vijayawada: Janasakthi Publishers, 1968), p. 1.
[54] *Divergent Views between Our Party and the CPC on Certain Fundamental Issues of Programme and Policy* (Calcutta: CPM Central Committee, 1967).
[55] *Andhra Plenum Rejects Neo-Revisionist Draft*, p. 58.
[56] Ibid., p. 60.

struggle, it called upon the CPM party members to repudiate their leadership and form a Maoist party. To the leaders of the Naxalbari movement in West Bengal this idea was appealing, and the Bengali Naxalites therefore set about the task of creating a new party based on Mao's thought. However, Maoist leadership in Andhra assessed the situation in India quite differently, and now began to argue that India was not ready for immediate armed struggle. In the words of the Andhra plenum,

Of course we do not mean to say that such a struggle could be started tomorrow. The whole point is, the party has no perspective on this and no conscious preparation toward this direction—political, organisational, or ideological—which is being undertaken.[57]

At the same time, the most significant contribution of the Andhra leadership to the ideological debate was the formulation that the contradiction with revisionism was an antagonistic one, and therefore unity of action between the Soviet and Chinese parties (and between the CPM and CPI at home) was impermissible.

At the all-India plenum of the CPM in Burdwan (in April 1968) the Andhra unit pressed its resolutions to a vote, losing on almost every issue. The only effect that the Andhra unit had on the plenum was to sharpen the anti-Soviet tone of the draft of the Central Committee. In the wake of the all-India plenum the Andhra leadership of the CPM was therefore expelled from the party, and they eventually took with them a majority of the CPM membership in the state. The wheel had now turned full circle. The same Telugu-speaking areas that had thrown up the first Maoist movement in India in the late 1940s now witnessed the return of Maoism in a changed context. The Andhra Maoists had galvanized the second split in the Indian Communist movement and proved that the first split had little to do with ideology. On the very first occasion when the CPM attempted to take a position on the ideological dispute, it too had suffered a split.

After the Burdwan plenum the dissidents in the CPM began holding regular meetings of the All-India Coordination Committee of the Communist Revolutionaries (AICCCR), which had been formed shortly after the Naxalbari uprising and called for the building of a true Communist party through Naxalbari-type struggles. Viewing Naxalbari as the turning point of the Indian revolution, the AICCCR called for a boycott of all elections in India, to be followed by positive action to draw the people into revolutionary class struggles "under the banner of Chairman Mao's thought."

[57] Ibid., p. 61.

At the next meeting of the AICCCR (in October 1968) the committee found that Naxalbari-type struggles had moved into their second stage—"the stage of guerrilla warfare"—in various parts of India. The committee therefore called on the revolutionary forces of India to plunge into work in the countryside in order to set up revolutionary bases. Throughout this period the AICCCR had remained silent on the question of forming a new party, and it had refused to take a stand on the question of establishing mass organizations.

The unwillingness of the AICCCR to take a stand on the question of establishing new organizations was the result of a dispute that was raging within the committee, with the Andhra Pradesh Coordination Committee pitted against leadership from other parts of India. The Andhra group was at that time heavily involved in a massive movement among the tribal population (the Girijans) in Srikakulam district in Andhra Pradesh, a movement that had been initiated well before the 1967 agitation in Naxalbari. Beginning in early 1959, the Andhra Communists had made serious attempts to build a broad-based organization among the tribals (the Girijana Sangham), using the organization to carry on struggles against the feudal exploitation of the Girijans. By 1967 the movement had reached a new stage with the implementation of the CPM agrarian program among the tribals, and in early 1968 this resulted in a number of clashes and police raids of Sangham households. To the dismay of the Maoist leadership in Andhra, the CPM found itself organizationally unprepared to resist police attacks, and at this point differences cropped up between the CPM state committee and the Srikakulam District Committee regarding the specifics of armed struggle to be used in the tribal areas. It was at precisely this same time too that the revolt of the Andhra Pradesh unit of the CPM against the CPM Central Committee was in full swing, with the result that the Srikakulam struggle became one of the first questions to be dealt with by the new Andhra Coordination Committee.

The Andhra Pradesh Coordination Committee of Communist Revolutionaries (APCCCR) had serious reservations about joining the AICCCR, because of the differences within the all-India Committee over the question of immediate armed struggle. The APCCCR therefore remained temporarily aloof from formal membership in the AICCCR, although it clearly favored unification of all revolutionaries through some committee device. At the same time, however, some members of the Srikakulam District Committee, instead of concentrating on preparations for armed struggle, were establishing direct links with the AICCCR, and carrying on a campaign against the state leadership of the APCCCR on the issue of armed struggle. In fact the district committee was able to pass a resolution (in September 1968) in which the committee asked permission of the APCCCR to both initiate armed struggle and to join the AICCCR directly.

The Srikakulam District Committee (SDC) had been informed by the APCCCR in June that a regular guerrilla struggle could be initiated in Srikakulam if there were signs of a mass upsurge, but the SDC was now talking of a guerrilla struggle when no such signs were evident. In fact the SDC had most likely already secured affiliation with the AICCCR directly, bypassing the APCCCR, and this in turn led to a great deal of confusion when the APCCCR decided to join the AICCCR on its own initiative. In the eyes of SDC leaders they were faced with the choice of joining either the APCCCR or the AICCCR, even though these two parent organizations had reached substantial agreement on a number of points.[58] The APCCCR therefore informed the SDC that it (the APCCCR) would assist in preparations for armed struggle in Srikakulam if the SDC would agree to function under the leadership of the APCCCR. Because of its confused understanding the SDC rejected this offer (in November 1968), and began functioning as a rival party center, later to be encouraged by the AICCCR.

By the time the armed struggle in Srikakulam was about to begin, the AICCCR had met again (in February 1969), only to decide that it had "basic differences" with the APCCCR. In the eyes of AICCCR leaders, their differences with the APCCCR related to such questions as loyalty to the Communist Party of China, divergent attitudes toward the Srikakulam struggle, and attitudes toward participation in India's parliamentary system.[59] The AICCCR argued that its relations with the APCCCR would be nonantagonistic, but that the needs of a fast-developing revolutionary situation could no longer be met by a coordination committee that was unwilling to transform itself into a revolutionary party. The AICCCR therefore converted itself into the Communist Party of India (Marxist-Leninist) (CPML) on 22 April 1969. India now had its first Maoist party, formed from above, and excluding the Andhra Maoists, the largest Maoist formation in the country. Even though several other state coordi-

---

[58] At a meeting of the AICCCR in October 1968, both the APCCCR and AICCCR found that there was no basic difference between them with regard to the following: (1) allegiance to Mao's thought, (2) character of Soviet leadership, (3) rejection of the parliamentary path, and (4) recognition of armed struggle as the immediate form of struggle. See "On Srikakulam Girijan Armed Struggle," mimeographed report of the Andhra Pradesh RCC, 1969.

[59] "Resolution on Andhra State Coordination Committee, AICCCR, 7 February 1969," *Liberation* (CPML Monthly, Calcutta) 2, no. 5 (March 1969), 8–9.

nation committees chose to remain out of the new party, Peking was quick to confer recognition on the CPML by publishing its political resolution in the *People's Daily*.[60]

The tactical line of the AICCCR, and later the CPML, has undergone several twists since its uncertain beginning in 1968 and now has little Maoist content. Shortly after the Naxalbari failure, Charu Majumdar (now chairman of the CPML), the principal ideologue of the Peking-backed Maoists, argued that the CPML cadre working in peasant areas, while propagating the politics of seizure of power through armed struggle, should pay attention to economic struggles in order to attract backward peasants to the movement.[61] Without mass struggles, Majumdar argued, peasants could not be drawn into armed struggle. However, this line of open mass struggles on economic demands did not fit easily with the CPML tactic of secret politicization by underground and armed party units. In mid-1969 Majumdar resolved the dilemma when he said, "the revolutionary initiative of the wide sections of the peasant masses can be released through annihilation of class enemies by guerrilla methods, and neither mass organisation nor mass movement is indispensible for starting guerrilla war." [62]

According to Majumdar, mass struggle for economic gains is to follow guerrilla action, but not precede or accompany it. In Majumdar's theoretical formulations CPML party units, after some preliminary propaganda for seizure of power, were instructed to form small guerrilla bands in a conspiratorial manner to annihilate some of the most hated class enemies in the countryside. After the first such action, CPML political cadres were to start a series of whisper campaigns, speaking of the advantages that would accrue if other class enemies were annihilated or forced to flee the countryside. After a few offensive actions and after the "annihilation line" had been well-established in an area, the political cadres of the CPML were to then publicize their general economic slogans, calling for seizure of the crops of class enemies.

Since 1969 the CPML has applied this line in Srikakulam district in Andhra, and in the Gopiballavpur-Debra area in West Bengal. But annihilation of the class enemy has in practice turned out to be nothing more than the murder of landlords through conspiratorial squad actions, unrelated to mass movements or mass struggle. The line has placed reliance

[60] *People's Daily* (Peking), 2 July 1969.
[61] *Deshabrati* (Bengali Weekly of the CPML), 1 August 1968. Quoted in Abhijnan Sen, "The Naxalite Tactical Line," *Frontier* (Calcutta Weekly) 3, nos. 13–15 (4 July 1970), 21.
[62] *Deshabrati*, 23 June 1969.

on a few petit bourgeois cadres functioning in the countryside, expecting them to liquidate individual landlords as a shortcut to revolution. In Srikaklulam the party could claim some initial success for its line because there was already a mass movement present. But in the long run the tactics of the CPML can hardly achieve anything, even where there is a mass movement. In Srikakulam in fact the CPML has managed to liquidate the mass movement that was present, and in Gopiballavpur-Debra (where there was no mass movement to begin with) the party has fared even worse. By mid-1970 all of the frontline leaders of the CPML, both in Srikakulam and in Gopiballavpur-Debra, had been killed in clashes or arrested, while the remaining guerrilla cadre members in these areas had fled the "liberated zones" where red power was supposed to have been established. The people of these areas have been left to bear the brunt of the police raids.

The CPML, a party that wanted its cadre to fan out into the countryside, abandoning the cities because they were regarded as areas of "white terror," has now returned to the cities. When the party held its first conference a year after its formation, the Srikakulam movement had already petered out and the Gopiballavpur-Debra movement was nearly crushed. The student and youth cadre, which had gone into the West Bengal countryside during the previous year, had already returned to Calcutta city, where it has been staging an urban guerrilla operation since May 1970. The annihilation line has now been extended to include the cities, and the party's main activities are limited to its campaigns of "red terror," taking the form of hit and run raids, murder of policemen, and assassination of political rivals.[63]

In contrast, the Andhra movement (now functioning under the Andhra Pradesh Revolutionary Communist Committee or RCC) represents a different shade of Maoism, and the differences between the CPML and the RCC relate both to tactical line and methodology of struggle. As early as April 1969 the RCC welcomed the beginning of the armed struggle in Srikakulam, but expressed doubts about its methodology. At that time the CPML was trying to establish the legitimacy of its "annihilation" line as the precondition for organizing the peasants on a mass scale. But paradoxically enough, the CPML was implementing the annihilation line in Srikakulam, where there already was a mass movement among the peasantry. General mass participation in some of the annihilation raids in Srikakulam was cited by the CPML as vindication of its tactical line, while in fact such participation was the result of the mass movement al-

63 *Statesman* (Calcutta), 1–3 January 1971.

ready present in the area. In this confused situation the RCC remained aloof from the struggle as much as it could.[64]

When the RCC reviewed the question of armed struggle in Andhra in mid-1969, it found that the Srikakulam movement still had a mass character but was now clashing with state governmental machinery. In other districts, where there was no mass movement, the RCC found that the CPML had embarked on a series of terrorist squad actions, killing landlords and rich peasants. The RCC was meanwhile conducting limited armed struggles in those areas where there were genuine mass movements —in Warangal, Khammam, Karimnagar, Nalgonda, and East Godavary —while lending tacit support to the struggle in Srikakulam.

For the RCC, armed struggle is defined as a form of resistance, not as a form of offensive. The people's army can be built only through resistance related to people's demands and people's struggle. But the CPML does not believe in any form of struggle other than armed struggle, irrespective of strength and mass following. In the RCC's view this has not helped the CPML to build a mass movement in those areas where annihilation squads have been active. According to RCC theoreticians, the CPML's form of struggle cannot lead to protracted armed struggle, for two reasons: (1) if the people are not organized on the basis of their demands, mere squad action will only divert their attention from the issues on which they eventually have to fight; and (2) the people will be their own liberators (under the party's leadership), which means that they must be part and parcel of squads. From the point of view of the RCC, the CPML has operated in such a manner as to make the people feel that someone else, and not they themselves, will be their liberators.[65]

The tactical line of the RCC is based on the inseparable relationship between the party, armed struggle, and the united front. Moreover, it is assumed by the RCC that the beginning, development, consolidation, and extension of all peasant movements will be based on an agrarian program. Peasant struggles to implement an agrarian program will develop into armed struggles only if the masses are trained and tempered to resist the attacks that such struggles invite. The program of the agrarian revolution must therefore be coordinated with intensive propaganda for people's war, so that the masses understand the relationship between agrarian revolution and seizure of power.

[64] *On Srikakulam Girijan Armed Struggle* (Vijayawada: Andhra Pradesh RCC, 1969).

[65] T. Nagi Reddy, quoted in Nayaranamurti, "Srikakulam Story-II," *Frontier* (Calcutta Weekly), 20 September 1969.

The CPML line, which calls for the creation of base areas through annihilation of landlords (or by forcing landlords to flee the countryside) is at variance with Mao's concept of liberated areas, as understood by the RCC. Mao laid down three conditions for developing an area into a liberated or base area—building the armed forces, defeat of the enemy, and mobilization of the broad masses of the people. As the RCC understands Mao, building the armed forces means the building of the people's armed forces; defeating the enemy does not mean annihilation of class enemies, but rather the defeat of the class enemy along with its armed forces; and mobilizing the masses means mobilizing and arming them against the class enemy and its armed forces, in complete coordination with the people's armed forces.[66]

Conclusions

The Indian Communist movement of today presents a complex picture. The non-Maoist stream comprises the pro-Moscow CPI and the independent CPM. Both of these parties are participating in the Indian parliamentary system, and both believe in peaceful transition to socialism. The Maoist stream comprises the CPML and the RCC in Andhra Pradesh, as well as a number of groups outside Andhra Pradesh that are presently supporting the RCC.

The Communist movement in Telugu country reached its crescendo at the time of the Telengana armed struggle, during the early Maoist phase, as is evident from the impressive electoral performance of the CPI prior to 1955. But its influence and strength declined in direct proportion to its participation and involvement in the parliamentary system, after its abandonment of armed struggle. As the CPM noted in 1968, the "sweeping electoral victories" of 1952, both in the Andhra and Telengana regions, in no small way influenced party leadership at several different levels. The thought and actions of Communists throughout India were then "permeated with parliamentary illusions," subordinating sustained work among the basic classes and masses to different types of electioneering at various levels.[67]

The presplit CPI, once it lost itself in parliamentary politics, was obliged to choose issues that did not disturb its electoral alliances, its ministerial fronts, and its tactical line of class harmony. The struggle for the distribution of wastelands, for example, did not affect the landlords

[66] "Problems of People's War," unpublished document circulated among members of the Andhra Pradesh Revolutionary Communist Committee, 1970.
[67] *Why the Ultra-Left Deviation?*, pp. 26–27.

directly because it was aimed at the State. Other issues, like the Vishal-andhra demand, location of the state capital in Kurnool, and sanctioning of federal funds and plan projects for the state, were multiclass or non-class issues. By the mid 1950s the party had gradually begun to represent a multiclass interest aggregation, becoming less and less militant in the process. Preoccupation with the parliamentary system and electoral fronts ruled out any mass movement, and premiums were placed on typically non-Communist methods like signature campaigns, deputations to the government, and speeches in the legislatures. Often the CPI took part in clandestine local arrangements with caste lobbies. The 1955 election in Andhra underscored all of these weaknesses (as well as the strong points) of the CPI.

After the 1955 debacle, the Communist movement in Andhra Pradesh lost its edge. The CPI settled for peaceful transition, and Soviet interests demanded total identification of the party with the Nehru government in the name of fighting the growing Right reaction in the country. The CPI in Andhra Pradesh became a pressure group for those who stood to bene-fit from trade with Soviet bloc countries. The beneficiaries of these events were the party's patrons and then only because the CPI's help was neces-sary to get Soviet bloc export orders for cash crops (like tobacco) and minerals (like mica).

Between 1957 and 1962 the rightist forces in India effected a major breakthrough, menacing the Left. In Andhra Pradesh the Swatantra Party, representing landlord interests, emerged in some strength in 1959, cutting into Communist strength among landlords, and especially among the small, middle, and rich peasants.[68] Later, with massive state aid to farming and with the benefits of major irrigation projects, the rich peas-ants emerged as a strategic force in Indian politics, especially in Andhra. The new kulaks are the result of these benefits, and every political party in India's parliamentary system has to look to this strategic class for sup-port at the elections. As the two "establishment" Communist parties are

[68] When the Congress decided on cooperative farms to solve the country's food prob-lem at the Nagpur plenary session in 1958, the right wing of the Congress broke to form the Swatantra Party. "Farm and family in danger" was the slogan of the Swatantra Party at its inception, and this slogan gained for the new party some strength among a small base of peasants in the Andhra area. The only possible ex-planation for the shift of some pro-Communist landlords (who previously had not seen the Communists as threats to property) to Swatantra is the anti-Congressism of landlords in general after the threat to property became real. It should also be pointed out that common interests among landlords made possible a number of deals between the Swatantra Party and the CPM in Andhra Pradesh at the time of the 1967 elections.

getting more and more involved in the parliamentary system, they too have become reluctant to alienate the new kulak class.

In Andhra Pradesh the Maoist movement has immense potentialities, primarily because Andhra already has a high degree of capitalist land relations in some pockets. Indian state policies now seek to create capitalist land relations all over the country. These policies are not aimed at solving India's agrarian problems. There is a new polarization of property relations in the countryside, eliminating the middle peasant as a category and reducing small peasants to the status of landless laborers who cannot be absorbed immediately in the secondary tertiary sectors. New tensions are already surfacing in the countryside as a result of the distribution of new seeds and fertilizers.

The return of Maoism in India might well mark the rebirth of the Communist movement in Andhra Pradesh. Leaders of the CPML and the RCC are facing mass trials (separately) for conspiracy and sedition, trials which are strongly reminiscent of the *Meerut* conspiracy trials of Indian Communist leaders forty years ago. To the idealistic young man from the rural intelligentsia in Andhra Pradesh, neither of the two Communist parties participating in the parliamentary system hold any attraction, since a fragmented electoral system has so little to offer by way of a solution to basic problems. In Andhra Pradesh there is no non-Communist Left worth the name, and the electoral fortunes of the two establishment Communist parties have been constantly declining.

The CPML, to which many young men looked during the last two years, has left many disillusioned. The CPML has been a West Bengal–centered party, let by petit bourgeois intellectuals, while the Andhra Pradesh RCC is led by peasants who are neither mass leaders nor intellectuals. The CPML today has a strong urban character. Its cadre in West Bengal is drawn from the urban middle classes, to be sent out to the countryside and withdrawn to the cities as the situation demands. In contrast, the cadre of the CPML in Andhra Pradesh (particularly Srikakulam) came largely from peasant families and intellectuals of peasant origin. This means that the CPML in Andhra Pradesh has more in common with the RCC than with the West Bengal–centered leadership of the CPML. The serious differences reported between Charu Majumdar and his aides on the one hand, and the Srikakulam leadership of the CPML on the other, underlines this fact.

The Andhra Maoists, organized under the RCC, have the benefit of both the positive and negative experiences of India's Maoist movements

—in Telengana two decades ago and in Srikakulam in recent years. More-over, the RCC has proved its ability to apply Maoism creatively to the situation in Andhra Pradesh, while the CPML has applied Maoism to India in a mechanical fashion. A powerful Maoist movement might yet emerge in India, and unity of the two Maoist formations (or perhaps co-ordination between them) is not impossible, especially after the serious setbacks the CPML has suffered in Srikakulam. Whatever the relationship between the two formations, however, Andhra Pradesh is likely to pro-vide a strong base for Indian Maoism in the future. When and if it does, this much is certain: The Andhra Maoist movement will retain its distinc-tive regional character, regardless of its national and international moorings.

Bihar

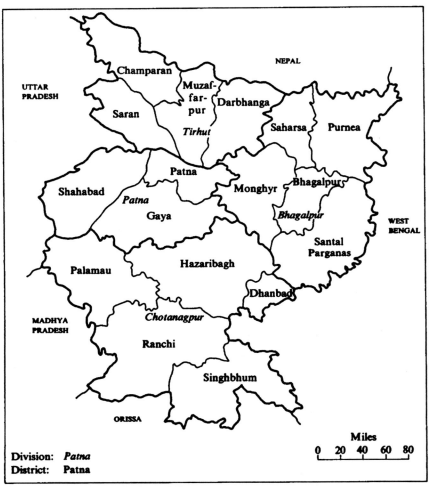

Divisions and Districts of Bihar, 1967

Source: Harry W. Blair, "Caste, Politics and Democracy in Bihar State, India: The Elections of 1967," unpublished Ph.D. dissertation, Duke University, 1969.

6
Radical Parties of the Left in Bihar: A Comparison of the SSP and the CPI

Paul R. Brass

Bihar is not one of the more renowned radical states in India. Its politics are not dominated, as politics are in Kerala and West Bengal, by the parties of the Marxist and Communist Left. If Bihar has a predominant political image, it is one of a state in which caste is the most important symbol, providing the preeminent basis for political mobilization and a good portion of the political dialogue. Most scholarly analyses of politics in Bihar have stressed their caste bases.[1] Harry Blair has argued, in the most systematic analysis of caste and politics in Bihar to date, that Bihar can be distinguished from all other Indian states in the preeminent importance of caste. Although caste politics have been important in other states, Blair argues that, in Bihar, caste has been both the chief "organizing principle" in politics and nearly the exclusive organizing principle.[2] It has flourished in the absence of strong competition from other kinds of loyalties, such as language, religion, and class, and has more often than not taken precedence over party loyalties. Caste was the "organizing principle" in Bihar politics in voting and in factional recruitment and conflict

The research for and the writing of this chapter were carried out with grants provided by the Center for International Studies at M.I.T. from Ford Foundation funds in 1969–1970 and from a grant by the South Asia Committee of the Far Eastern and Russian Institute, University of Washington, in the summer of 1970. I have also drawn upon interviews carried out in previous field trips to India for some of the information provided here.

I have benefited from the advice of Professor Chetakar Jha of Patna University during my visits to Bihar. Mr. Ganganath Thakur traveled and worked with me indefatigably on field trips in Bihar. My debt to him is very great. Dr. Ram Rajya Prasad Singh provided me hospitality and good humor, as always, during my days in Patna. My greatest debt, however, is to my wife Linda and to my children David Michael and Leah Sarah, who had to stay home in Seattle while I went off alone for field research in India.

I am grateful for the assistance and encouragement of all those named above and of all those unnamed who have given me their time and hospitality in India. The responsibility for all statements, conclusions, and opinions expressed herein, however, is entirely mine.

[1] See especially Ramashray Roy, "Politics of Fragmentation: The Case of the Congress Party in Bihar" and Chetakar Jha, "Caste in Bihar Congress Politics," both in Iqbal Narain, ed., *State Politics in India* (Meerut: Meenakshi Prakashan, [1968]), and Ramashray Roy, "Dynamics of One-Party Dominance in an Indian State," *Asian Survey* 8, no. 7 (July 1968), 553–575.

[2] Harry Wallace Blair, "Caste, Politics and Democracy in Bihar State, India: The Elections of 1967," unpublished Ph.D. dissertation, Duke University, 1969, esp. chaps. 2, 4, and 5.

in the Congress before 1967. It has continued to play a role also in influencing the formation and the breakup of coalition governments in the post-1967 multiparty politics of Bihar.[3]

There are several aspects of politics in Bihar and of caste politics in particular, however, which suggest that the preeminence of caste as the "organizing principle" of politics may not prevail in the future. First, whereas the history of political mobilization during the past half century in Bihar has been characterized by the "successive recruitment of newer caste groups into the Bihar Congress,"[4] the opportunities for further recruitment in this way are severely limited. Nearly all the caste groups in Bihar that, either because of their elite status, economic power, or numerical concentration, could be mobilized as groups in the political system have already been mobilized. These include particularly the elite Kayastha, Bhumihar, Rajput, and Brahman caste groups and the larger backward caste groups of Yadav, Kurmi, and Koiri. Second, the process of caste mobilization has resulted in a considerable degree of inequality of representation in the Bihar political system, such that the elite castes and the three large backward castes are overrepresented and the scheduled castes are represented by law in proportion to their population, but the smaller backward castes and the Muslims are underrepresented. In some cases, the underrepresentation is extreme. Thus, Blair has shown that, in 1962, some 30 percent of the population of the state (by caste) had no MLAs in the Bihar Legislative Assembly and that 26 percent of the population went unrepresented in 1967. Moreover, some caste groups achieved minimal representation in the Bihar assembly in the election of only one MLA from the entire state.[5] Most important is the fact that, for nearly all the unrepresented and underrepresented caste groups, the old process of caste mobilization is not relevant because these groups lack the status, economic power, political consciousness, and numerical concentration in compact geographical areas that have provided the bases for the entry of the other caste groups into the system. Third, the process of caste mobilization has so far not produced a high degree of political participation in Bihar as compared to other Indian states. In 1967, Bihar had the second lowest rate of electoral turnout in the country after Orissa.[6] Fourth, although caste has been the chief "organizing principle" of Bihar politics,

[3] Ibid., pp. 322–347 and *Economic and Political Weekly* 4, no. 24 (12 June 1971), 1170–1171.

[4] Blair, "Caste, Politics and Democracy in Bihar State, India," p. 85.

[5] Ibid., p. 355.

[6] See Paul R. Brass, "Political Participation, Institutionalization and Stability in India," *Government and Opposition* 4, no. 1 (Winter 1969), 26.

paradoxically, caste solidarity has not been pronounced at the state level and has not taken organized form. Caste associations have not been significant political forces at the state level. Moreover, all the caste groups have been divided and fragmented among and within the leading political parties of Bihar, so that all the main parties are multicaste in composition. Caste has not produced a segmented, compartmentalized political system in Bihar. Fifth, the old system of Congress dominance of Bihar politics, which provided the basic framework of caste politics, was broken and replaced by a more competitive multiparty system between 1967 and 1972.[7] Although the Congress (R) was returned to power again after the 1972 elections in Bihar, it was returned with the smallest popular vote percentage achieved by the Congress in a major Indian state (34.12 percent) and with only a bare majority of the seats in the legislative assembly.

These five aspects and consequences of caste mobilization and of politics in Bihar suggest that politics in that state are ripe for reorganization and further mobilization on alternative bases. I have explored elsewhere the prospects for a reorganization of Bihar politics along the lines of linguistic and religious differentiation.[8] In this contribution, I propose to examine the prospects for the leading radical political parties of Bihar of their playing a major role in that reorganization and mobilization.

The Place of the Radical Parties in Bihar Politics
If caste has been the major theme of Bihar politics in modern times, the ideological appeals of the parties of the radical Left have provided an important minor theme. In fact, Bihar has been a center of some importance in the history of radical politics in north India. The foundation conference of the Congress Socialist Party (CSP) was held in Patna, the capital of Bihar, in May 1934. The first general secretary of the party, Jayaprakash Narayan, was born in a Bihar village and has spent most of his public life in Bihar. Bihar also spawned one of the more vigorous organized peasant movements against the zamindars in north India, the Bihar Kisan Sabha, which frequently came into conflict with the more conservative elements in the Bihar Congress.[9] Bihar was also one of the leading provinces in the participation of its politically active people in the August 1942 movement. During that movement in Bihar, between August

---

[7] Paul R. Brass, "Coalition Politics in North India," *The American Political Science Review* 62, no. 4 (December 1968), 1174–1191.
[8] See Paul R. Brass, *Language, Religion, and Politics in North India* (New York: Cambridge University Press, forthcoming).
[9] See Hari Kishore Singh, *A History of the Praja Socialist Party, 1934–59* (Lucknow: Narendra Prakashan, 1959), pp. 39–42.

Table 6.1   Percentage of Votes Polled by Political Parties in Bihar Legislative Assembly Elections, 1952–1972

Political Party	1952	1957	1962	1967	1969	1972
1. Congress	41.9	42.2	41.3	33.1	30.4	34.1
2. Congress (O)	Founded in 1969					13.9
3. Loktantric Congress Dal	Founded in 1968				3.9	—
4. JKD/BKD	Founded in 1967			3.3	2.1	—
Subtotal	41.9	42.2	41.3	36.4	36.4	N.A.
5. SSP	Founded in 1964			17.6	13.7	—
6. PSP		16.0	14.2	7.0	5.7	—
7. SP	18.8	—	5.2	—	—	16.1
8. KMPP	2.9	—	—	—	—	—
9. Forward Bloc (FB)	—	—	—	—	0.1	N.A.
10. FB (Marxist)	1.2	—	—	—	—	—
Subtotal	22.9	16.0	19.4	24.6	19.5	N.A.
11. CPI	1.1	4.9	6.2	6.9	10.1	7.0
12. CPM	Founded in 1964			1.3	1.2	1.6
Subtotal	1.1	4.9	6.2	8.2	11.3	8.6
13. Jan Sangh	1.2	1.2	2.8	10.4	15.7	12.0
14. RRP	0.6	—	0.2	—	—	—
15. Swatantra	Founded in 1959		17.3	2.3	0.9	0.8
Subtotal	1.8	1.2	20.3	12.7	16.6	12.8
16. Janata	3.1	7.9	—	—	3.1	—
17. Jharkhand	8.3	6.9	4.4	—	0.7	N.A.
18. Hul Jharkhand	Founded in 1969				0.9	N.A.
19. Shoshit Dal	Founded in 1968				3.6	N.A.
20. SCF/RPI	0.1	—	—	0.2	0.5	N.A.
21. Ganatantra Parishad	0.2	—	—	—	—	—
Subtotal	11.7	14.8	4.4	0.2	8.8	N.A.
22. Unsuccessful parties and independents	20.6	20.9	8.4	17.9	7.4	N.A.
Total	100.0	100.0	100.0	100.0	100.0	

Sources: 1952 to 1969 figures compiled from Craig Baxter, *District Voting Trends in India: A Research Tool* (New York: Columbia University Press, 1969), pp. 40–41; 1972 figures are preliminary from an American Embassy handout, "State Assembly Elections—1972 Final Party Position, Seats & Popular Votes (Prelim.), All-India & By State," mimeographed, 1972.

and November 1942, nearly 15,000 people were arrested, there were 83 police firings in different parts of the state, and 134 people were killed.[10]

In contrast to the situation in Kerala, Tamil Nadu, and Andhra where the Communists gained control over the Congress Socialist Party,[11] the non-Communist Left retained its dominance in the Bihar CSP. In the First General Elections in India in 1951, the Socialist Party emerged in Bihar as the major opposition party in the state, far ahead of the Communist Party (see table 6.1), and as the major state unit of the Socialist Party in the country, with 18.8 percent of the popular vote. After the merger of the Socialist Party and the Kisan Mazdoor Praja Party (KMPP) into the PSP, the Bihar PSP retained its preeminence as the leading Socialist party in India, polling 16.0 percent of the popular vote in the 1957 elections, and overshadowing the Lohia Socialist Party formed in 1954.[12] In 1962, the two Socialist parties, the PSP and the SP, polled 19.4 percent of the popular vote, with the PSP taking the larger share. When the two parties merged and split once again in 1964–1965, their positions were reversed and the new Samyukta Socialist Party (SSP) emerged from the 1967 elections as the predominant Socialist party in the state and once again as the largest non-Communist party of the Left in India. Finally, after the 1971 merger of the PSP and the SSP into the Socialist Party (SP), the SP emerged from the 1972 elections in Bihar as the second strongest party in the state in electoral support and as by far the leading non-Communist radical Left party in any Indian state.

However, during the past twenty years in Bihar, the Socialist parties have not succeeded in consolidating or significantly improving their popular support which, both in the 1969 midterm and 1972 General Elections, was below that acquired in 1952. In the meantime, the Communist Party of India (CPI), has steadily improved its popular support and its strength in the legislative assembly, although it will be argued below that the appearance of secular improvement in the CPI strength is deceptive. The narrowing of the gap in the strength of the SP and the CPI in the state makes Bihar an ideal state in which to compare these radical parties of the Left, whose organization, ideology, and tactics differ in important ways, and to ask why the radical Socialists have so far been stronger than

[10] See K. K. Datta, *History of the Freedom Movement in Bihar*, vol. 3, 1942–1947 (Patna: Government of Bihar, 1958), pp. 1–265 for a description of the August 1942 movement in Bihar and p. 231 for the figures cited.
[11] Hari Kishore Singh, *History of the PSP*, p. 64.
[12] Separate figures for the SP vote in Bihar in 1957 are not available because the party did not receive official recognition by the election commission. Its votes were counted with the independent vote in that year.

the Communists in Bihar and why both parties have failed to achieve for the Left a position of importance similar to that acquired by the leftist parties in Bengal and Kerala.

The PSP and the CPM have been deliberately excluded from the detailed analysis in this chapter. The CPM is not a significant force in Bihar politics and the PSP has been the weaker of the two democratic Socialist parties in the state. The decline of the PSP in relation to the SSP was a consequence of two factors: first, the impact of the merger with the SP in 1964, described below; second, the greater appeal of the SSP to Hindi regional sentiment. My purpose in this chapter is to confine the analysis as far as possible to a direct comparison of the more radical wing of the Socialist movement in India, represented by the SSP from 1964 until 1971, with its chief competitor in Bihar, the CPI.

At the most general level, the primary theoretical concern in this chapter is to explore the conditions for the success or failure of a radical party of the Left in a developing society, in a state characterized by a backward agricultural economy, the beginnings of an industrial economy in certain districts, religious and linguistic heterogeneity, and social fragmentation. Previous work on party politics in India leads one to believe that the success of any political party in India depends upon its ability to overcome the atomizing tendencies that exist in Indian society in the form of persistent personalism and factionalism; to find a basis of stable support in a socially fragmented society; and to relate to the strong forces of regional sentiment that exist. The radical Socialist Party (SSP) and the CPI in north India have adopted quite different techniques to deal with these forces. The SSP was a party of agitation and mobilization, whereas the CPI in the north is a party of organization. The SSP attempted to instill party loyalty through militant and personal leadership, whereas the CPI has emphasized ideology and discipline. The SSP tried to overcome social fragmentation by mobilizing a coalition of middle and low caste groups, whereas the CPI has refused to make such an open appeal to caste sentiments and has attempted to develop class allegiances and mass organizations. The SSP militantly supported regionalist demands for the spread of Hindi, whereas the CPI has tended to appeal to minority groups, such as the Muslims and tribals, that feel threatened by the rise of Hindu and Hindi regional-linguistic sentiment in the north. While the SSP and the SP have so far been more successful electorally than the CPI in the north, their support has tended to fluctuate more from time to time and place to place. The important question from the point of view of the relative balance between the two parties in the future is whether the more militant, agitational, and indigenous approach of the radical Socialists will continue to provide greater support for the radical Left or whether the CPI emphasis on discipline, organization, and a class appeal will ultimately prove more successful.

Radical Party Leadership In Bihar

The SSP and the CPI have represented two distinct kinds of approaches to radical politics in north India. They have differed in their history, in the characteristics and composition of their leadership, in their methods of organization, in their ideology and programs, and in their political success so far. In this section on the radical leadership of the SSP and the CPI in Bihar, the focus for comparison will be on the socioeconomic composition and political experiences of the state-level leadership of the two parties and on a more detailed comparison of the careers of their most prominent leaders.

The Sample

By combining information available in published *Who's Whos* and from personal interviews carried out by the author in 1966–1967 and in 1969,[13] it has been possible to compile a comparable sample of state political leaders of the SSP and the CPI from Bihar. The sample comprises 49 radical party leaders, of whom 29 were SSP and 20 CPI leaders. It includes all SSP and CPI members of the Bihar Legislative Assembly, 1962–1967, of whom 15 were SSP MLAs and 12 were CPI MLAs; all SSP and CPI MPs from Bihar in the Lok Sabha, 1967–1972, and the Rajya Sabha, 1966–1972, of whom 9 were SSP MPs and 6 were CPI MPs (including 1 CPI MLA from the 1962 legislative assembly); all SSP and CPI ministers of the first non-Congress government in Bihar (five SSP and three CPI); the SSP speaker of the 1967 Bihar Legislative Assembly; all SSP and CPI chairmen and general secretaries of the state party organizations between 1966 and 1970; and the chairman of the state control commission of the Bihar CPI. In addition to this sample of party leaders for whom fairly comprehensive biographical information is provided, data are also available on the caste distribution only of SSP and CPI MLAs elected in 1967 and on the caste composition of the members of the SSP

---

[13] Biographical data for this section have been derived from 20 personal interviews in Bihar and from the following published sources: Parliament of India, Fourth Lok Sabha, *Who's Who 1967*, 1st ed. (New Delhi: Lok Sabha Secretariat, 1967); Parliament of India, Rajya Sabha, *Who's Who 1968*, (New Delhi: Rajya Sabha Secretariat, 1968); *Bihar Vidhan-Sabha ke SadasyoN ka Sankshipt Jivan-Parichay* (1966), no other publication details given.

Table 6.2 Date of Birth of SSP and CPI Political Leaders from Bihar (by Percentage and Number)

Date of Birth	SSP	CPI	Total
1901–1910	17.2 (5)	— —	10.2 (5)
1911–1920	10.3 (3)	40.0 (8)	22.4 (11)
1921–1930	44.9 (13)	35.0 (7)	40.8 (20)
1931–1940	13.8 (4)	15.0 (3)	14.3 (7)
N.A.	13.8 (4)	10.0 (2)	12.2 (6)
Total*	100.0 (29)	100.0 (20)	99.9 (49)

* Totals in this and succeeding tables do not always add to 100.00 because of rounding.

state executive committee for 1969. The absence of full biographical data on radical party MLAs elected since 1967 or for the entire executive committees of the two parties limits the analysis to a small sample and, therefore, limits the extent to which the data can be broken up into subgroups. (For example, divisions cannot be made between the membership of the parliamentary and organizational wings of the two parties.) On the other hand, the sample does include all the most prominent legislative and organizational leaders of both parties from Bihar,[14] as well as some minor personalities. The most important leaders of both parties, therefore, can be selected out for more detailed comparisons.

Social Composition of SSP and CPI Leaders from Bihar
The vital statistics on the radical party leaders concerning sex and marital status reveal nothing of consequence. All 49 leaders are men and all but 2—1 SSP and 1 CPI man—are married. Figures on the date of birth of Bihar SSP and CPI political leaders reveal more interesting information both about radical party leaders in the state generally and about the differences between the two parties. Taking together the 49 radical party leaders, only 5 (all SSP men) or 10.2 percent were born in the first decade; 11, or 22.4 percent, were born in the second decade; 20, or 40.8 percent were born in the third decade; and 7, or 14.3 percent were born in the fourth decade of this century (table 6.2). The large majority, 31 or 63.2 percent, were born in the two decades from 1911 to 1930. Consequently, most radical party leaders from Bihar were either not born or were young children when Gandhi's first noncooperation movement was launched in 1921. Even the 10 percent born in the first decade reached

[14] For example, it includes the five highest-ranking members of the state executive of the CPI.

political maturity only in the 1920s. The political experiences of nearly all radical political leaders in Bihar have taken place entirely in the post-Gandhian, agitational period of the Indian nationalist movement.

There are some differences in the age-group distribution of the leadership of the two parties. The largest number of SSP political leaders were born in the 1920s, whereas the largest number of CPI leaders were born in the decade 1911–1920. Of the SSP leaders 58.7 percent were born after 1921, compared to 50.0 percent of the CPI leaders. In contrast, 40.0 percent of the CPI leaders were born before 1921 compared to only 27.5 percent of the SSP leaders. The differences in age group distribution are less pronounced when the median date of birth is considered—it is 1925 for the SSP and 1923 for the CPI leaders—but they have a political significance that will be discussed further below.

Bihar is one of the three most rural states in India, with a rural population percentage of 93.6 percent. Consequently, it is not surprising that the overwhelming majority of radical leaders from Bihar were born in villages and that they list their present residences in villages (tables 6.3 and 6.4). Only seven of the radical leaders for whom information is available were born in cities or towns and only eight listed their present residence in a city or town. There are no substantial differences between the two parties

Table 6.3 Birthplace of SSP and CPI Political Leaders from Bihar (by Percentage and Number)

Birthplace	SSP	CPI	Total
Village	75.9 (22)	70.0 (14)	73.5 (36)
Town	6.9 (2)	15.0 (3)	10.2 (5)
City	6.9 (2)	— —	4.1 (2)
N.A.	10.3 (3)	15.0 (3)	12.2 (6)
Total	100.0 (29)	100.0 (20)	100.0 (49)

Table 6.4 Present Residence of SSP and CPI Political Leaders from Bihar (by Percentage and Number)

Present Residence	SSP	CPI	Total
Village	75.9 (22)	70.0 (14)	73.5 (36)
Town	6.9 (2)	— —	4.1 (2)
City	3.4 (1)	25.0 (5)	12.2 (6)
N.A.	13.8 (4)	5.0 (1)	10.2 (5)
Total	100.0 (29)	100.0 (20)	100.0 (49)

with respect to birthplace, but there is a difference of some importance with regard to present residence. Only 10.3 percent of SSP leaders actually resided in a city or town, whereas 25 percent of the CPI leaders lived in a city—three in Patna and two in the industrial city of Jamshedpur.

Bihar can be conveniently divided into three relatively distinct geographical regions—north Bihar, consisting of the eight districts which lie mostly north of the Ganges; south Bihar, comprising five districts primarily south of the Ganges; and Chota Nagpur, comprising six hilly districts with large tribal populations and containing also the industrializing districts of Singhbum and Dhanbad. More than 40 percent of the population of the state lives in north Bihar, nearly a third in south Bihar, and somewhat more than a quarter in Chota Nagpur. The nationalist movement had its greatest strength in the heavily populated districts of north and south Bihar, where nearly all the larger parties in Bihar continue to have their main electoral strength. Chota Nagpur has been, traditionally, an area where regional and tribal parties have been strong.

The distribution of radical party leaders in Bihar according to region of birth and present residence (tables 6.5 and 6.6) reflects the historical development of nationalist consciousness and party development in the state. Nearly 80 percent of radical party leaders were born in north and south Bihar (19 in the north and 19 in the south) and more than 80 percent of the leaders listed their present residence in north and south Bihar (23 in the north and 17 in the south). The preeminent radical district of Bihar with respect to radical party leadership in the 1960s was Darbhanga district where 9 radical leaders were born and lived. There are no substantial differences between the two parties with regard to region of birth, but the greater interest and strength of the CPI in the industrial region of Chota Nagpur is reflected in the figures for present residence that show 4 CPI leaders living in Chota Nagpur. All SSP leaders in the 1960s for

Table 6.5 Geographical Region of Birth of SSP and CPI Political Leaders from Bihar (by Percentage and Number)

Region of Birth	SSP	CPI	Total
North Bihar	41.4 (12)	35.0 (7)	38.8 (19)
South Bihar	41.4 (12)	35.0 (7)	38.8 (19)
Chota Nagpur	— —	5.0 (1)	2.0 (1)
Outside Bihar	3.4 (1)	10.0 (2)	6.1 (3)
N.A.	13.8 (4)	15.0 (3)	14.3 (7)
Total	100.0 (29)	100.0 (20)	100.0 (49)

Table 6.6   Geographical Region of Present Residence of SSP and CPI Political Leaders from Bihar (by Percentage and Number)

Region of Present Residence	SSP	CPI	Total
North Bihar	51.7 (15)	40.0 (8)	46.9 (23)
South Bihar	34.5 (10)	35.0 (7)	34.7 (17)
Chota Nagpur	— —	20.0 (4)	8.2 (4)
Outside Bihar	— —	— —	— —
N.A.	13.8 (4)	5.0 (1)	10.2 (5)
Total	100.0 (29)	100.0 (20)	100.0 (49)

Table 6.7   Caste, Community, and Religion of SSP and CPI Political Leaders from Bihar (by Percentage and Number)

Caste, Community, or Religion	SSP	CPI	Total
Elite castes	44.9 (13)	35.0 (7)[a]	40.8 (20)
Backward castes	27.6 (8)	20.0 (4)	24.5 (12)
Scheduled castes	6.9 (1)	— —	4.1 (2)
Adivasis	3.4 (1)	5.0 (1)	4.1 (2)
Muslims	— —	5.0 (1)	2.0 (1)
N.A.	17.2 (5)	35.0 (7)	24.5 (12)
Total	100.0 (29)	100.0 (20)	100.0 (49)

[a] Includes three Bengalis of high caste.

whom information was available lived in north or south Bihar. Darbhanga was the leading district of birth for both CPI and SSP leaders and the leading district of residence for CPI leaders, but Saharsa was the leading district of residence for SSP leaders, with Darbhanga a close second. Four CPI and 5 SSP leaders were born in Darbhanga, and 4 CPI and 5 SSP leaders listed their present residence as Darbhanga.

The last ascriptive category on which information is available for a sufficient number of radical party leaders is caste. The castes of 37 radical party leaders from the sample were identified, of whom 20 or 40.8 percent of the total sample came from the elite caste categories of Brahman, Bhumihar, Rajput, Kayastha, and Bania;[15] 12 or 24.5 percent came from backward caste groups; 2 or 4.1 percent from scheduled castes; 2 from adivasis (tribals); and only 1 from the Muslim community (table 6.7).

[15] Including three Communist upper caste Bengalis.

The representation of elite caste categories among the radical party leadership is approximately three times the representation of those castes in the population as a whole (13.6 percent)[16] The one-quarter representation of the backward castes compares to a total population of such castes in Bihar of 50.7 percent. The 4.1 percent representation for scheduled castes and adivasis can be compared to their proportions of 14.1 and 9.1 percent, respectively, in the total population. Finally, the 1 Muslim in the group, representing 2.0 percent of the leadership stands for 12.5 percent of the population of his community in Bihar.

One of the most distinctive policies of the SSP, and a major point of difference between it and the CPI in theory, was its "60 percent policy" of reserving a minimum of 60 percent of all positions in the party for backward castes, scheduled castes, Harijans, Muslims, adivasis, and women. This policy has been a fundamental credo of the radical Socialists, which is proposed also as policy for the nation. Where it could control the results, the SSP adhered fairly closely to this policy. For example, on the SSP state executive committee of 21 in 1969, 14 of the 17 members whose caste could be identified were from backward castes, scheduled castes, adivasis, and Muslims.[17] However, nearly 45 percent of the SSP leaders in the sample came from elite castes. The breakup of CPI and SSP radical political leaders in the sample reveals a greater proportion of elite castes in the SSP leadership than in the CPI leadership, but the large number of unknowns in the CPI sample limits the usefulness of the comparison here. The representation of elite castes in the 1967 SSP and CPI legislative assembly parties was even greater than in the sample (see table 6.8). Moreover, the representation of nonelite castes in the SSP still fell short of 60 percent and also somewhat short of the representation of nonelite groups in the CPI. In practice, therefore, except in cases where deliberate selection was possible, the nonelite group composition of SSP political leaders in Bihar was not materially different from that of the CPI or, for that matter, of the Congress, 53.9 percent of whose MLAs in 1967 were from nonelite groups.[18]

Radical political leaders from Bihar tend to be well-educated (table 6.9). More than half the total sample have had a college or university education and more than three-quarters have had at least some secondary education. Only two (both SSP leaders) indicated they had had only a

[16] Caste population figures have been derived from the 1931 census and adjusted for boundary changes in Blair, "Caste, Politics and Democracy in Bihar State, India," p. 41.
[17] Information on the caste of members of the SSP state executive was provided to me in the SSP office, Patna.
[18] Blair, "Caste, Politics and Democracy in Bihar State, India," p. 327.

Table 6.8   Caste, Community, and Religion of SSP and CPI Members of the Bihar Legislative Assembly, 1967 (by Percentage and Number)

Caste, Community or Religion	SSP	CPI	Total
Elite castes	45.6 (31)	41.6 (10)	44.5 (41)
Backward castes	38.2 (26)	29.2 (7)	35.9 (33)
Scheduled castes	11.8 (8)	8.3 (2)	10.9 (10)
Adivasis	1.5 (1)	4.2 (1)	2.2 (2)
Muslims	1.5 (1)	16.7 (4)	5.4 (5)
N.A.	1.5 (1)	— —	1.1 (1)
Total	100.1 (68)	100.0 (24)	100.0 (92)

Source: Adapted from Harry N. Blair, "Caste, Politics, and Democracy in Bihar State, India: The Elections of 1967," unpublished Ph.D. dissertation, Duke University, 1969 p. 327, with corrections by personal communication.

Table 6.9   Education of SSP and CPI Political Leaders from Bihar (by Percentage and Number)

Education	SSP	CPI	Total
Primary	6.9 (2)	— —	4.1 (2)
Secondary	20.7 (6)	30.0 (6)	24.5 (12)
College or university	55.2 (16)	50.0 (10)	53.1 (26)
Private	3.4 (1)	— —	2.0 (1)
Not known	13.8 (4)	20.0 (4)	16.3 (8)
Total	100.0 (29)	100.0 (20)	100.0 (49)

primary education. The differences in educational attainments of SSP and CPI leaders do not appear to be substantial.

Information on the occupations of political leaders is often difficult to obtain. Many political leaders in India devote all their time to politics and social work. Some live off politics entirely. On the other hand, many own land, but either have left their lands in the hands of family members or are reluctant to reveal that they own much land because of land reform laws. For these and other reasons, there are a large number of unknowns in our sample. Nevertheless, some striking differences do emerge between the principal occupations of the leaders of the two radical parties. A far larger proportion of SSP leaders indicated continued connections with the land, and a much larger number also listed professional occupations. In contrast, the proportion of CPI leaders who listed politics or social work as their principal or sole occupation was nearly five times that of the SSP leaders (table 6.10).

Table 6.10 Main Occupation of SSP and CPI Political Leaders from Bihar (by Percentage and Number)

Occupation	SSP	CPI	Total
Agriculture	34.5 (10)	5.0 (1)	22.4 (11)
Politics or social work (whole-time)	10.3 (3)	50.0 (10)	26.6 (13)
Professions and government service	24.1 (7)	5.0 (1)	16.3 (8)
Not known	31.0 (9)	40.0 (8)	34.7 (17)
Total	99.9 (29)	100.0 (20)	100.0 (49)

These differences are maintained even when all occupations are counted, including secondary and former occupations. When all the known occupations, past and present, of SSP and CPI leaders are added up, there are 25 for the SSP, of which 11 or 44.0 percent are agricultural; 5 or 20 percent are political-social; and 9 or 36 percent are professional. In contrast, there are 18 known occupations for the CPI leaders, of which only 3 or 16.7 percent are agricultural; 10 or 55.5 percent are political-social and 5 or 27.8 percent are professional. It is very likely that these figures still underestimate the actual number of CPI leaders who have connections with the land; but the evidence does suggest a considerable difference between CPI leaders, who tend to be divorced from the land and more committed to full-time political activity, and SSP leaders, who tend more frequently to have retained their connections with the land and to have other occupations than politics. It deserves notice in passing that there were only two lawyers, both SSP men, in the entire sample.

Political Experiences and Activities of SSP and CPI Political Leaders from Bihar

The significance of the differences discovered above in the age-group distribution of SSP and CPI leaders becomes clear when the date of entry into politics of radical political leaders is considered. Of the 38 radical leaders for whom this information is available, 19 entered politics in the 1940s, 18 in the 1920s and 1930s, and only 1 since Independence (table 6.11). However, the overwhelming proportion of those who entered politics in the 1940s (15 of 19) were SSP people. More than half the SSP leaders had their first political experience in the 1940s. For nearly all of these, that first experience was in the August 1942 movement. In fact, it can be said without much exaggeration that the SSP or rather the radical

Table 6.11 Date of Entry into Politics of SSP and CPI Political Leaders from Bihar (by Percentage and Number)

Date of Entry	SSP	CPI	Total
1921–1930	13.8 (4)	10.0 (2)	12.2 (6)
1931–1940	13.8 (4)	40.0 (8)	24.5 (12)
1941–1947	51.8 (15)	20.0 (4)	38.8 (19)
After 1947	3.4 (1)	— —	2.0 (1)
N.A.	17.2 (5)	30.0 (6)	22.4 (11)
Total	100.0 (29)	100.0 (20)	99.9 (49)

Table 6.12 Jail Experience of SSP and CPI Political Leaders from Bihar (by Percentage and Number)

Jail Experience	SSP	CPI	Total
Jail before Independence	17.2 (5)	15.0 (3)	16.3 (8)
Jail after Independence	20.7 (6)	25.0 (5)	22.4 (11)
Both	24.1 (7)	25.0 (5)	24.5 (12)
Not known or not mentioned	37.9 (11)	35.0 (7)	36.7 (18)
Total	99.9 (29)	100.0 (20)	99.9 (49)

Socialist movement in Bihar is a product of the '42 movement. In contrast, and for quite obvious reasons, the '42 movement is of no consequence for most CPI leaders, since the party was cooperating with the British at the time. Half the CPI political leaders entered politics during the 1920s and 1930s, compared to only somewhat more than a quarter of the SSP leaders.

Although the SSP was the principal inheritor, therefore, of the most radical pre-Independence agitational movement, the history of the SSP and CPI political leaders is not significantly different with respect to participation in agitational movements generally. More than 60 percent of the leaders of both parties have been to jail in various movements one or more times (table 6.12). Moreover, both parties continued their agitational tactics into the post-Independence period. Twenty-three of the 30 radical leaders (including 13 of 18 SSP leaders and 10 of 13 CPI leaders) who have been to jail have achieved this agitational badge of merit at least once in the post-Independence period.

There have been five primary areas of political and social activity in

Table 6.13   Political and Social Activities and Memberships of SSP and CPI Political Leaders from Bihar (by Percentage and Number)[a]

Activity	SSP (29)[b]	CPI (20)[b]	Total (49)[b]
Education	34.5 (10)	15.0 (3)	26.5 (13)
Constructive work (shramdan, bhoodan, relief committees)	17.2 (5)	35.0 (7)	24.5 (12)
Trade union	20.7 (6)	35.0 (7)	26.5 (13)
Student and youth	24.1 (7)	40.0 (8)	30.6 (15)
Kisan movements	17.2 (5)	40.0 (8)	26.5 (13)
Professional	— —	5.0 (1)	2.0 (1)
Cultural	3.5 (1)	15.0 (3)	8.2 (4)
Backward caste and antiuntouchability	10.3 (3)	— —	6.1 (3)
Cooperatives	3.5 (1)	10.0 (2)	6.1 (3)
Rural local self-government	6.9 (2)	— —	4.1 (2)
Other	17.2 (5)	5.0 (1)	12.2 (6)

[a] In constructing this table, attention has been paid to the stated or listed activities of radical party leaders as well as to organizational memberships, but an attempt has been made to include only the individual work of party leaders and to exclude participation in all-party movements even when such movements are on behalf of particular groups.
[b] N is the number of party leaders. Multiple activities of individual leaders have been listed. Consequently, percentages do not add to 100.0. Six SSP and 4 CPI men listed no activities.

which radical leaders have participated—education (primarily helping to build or acting as a member of the managing committees of local schools); "constructive work" (shramdan, bhoodan, or membership on various famine and flood relief committees); trade unions; student and youth movements; and kisan organizations and movements (table 6.13). In all five areas, there are substantial differences between the extent of participation of SSP and CPI leaders. More SSP leaders were involved in local educational activities, but more CPI leaders have tended to do "constructive work" and to be involved in trade union, student and youth, and kisan activities. These contrasts reflect a basic difference in the organizational structure and orientations of the two parties. The SSP was based more on local constituency organization than the CPI. Consequently, its members tended to be involved more in local activities in their areas. The CPI places greater emphasis on mass organizations than the SSP, which is reflected in CPI-member participation in trade unions, student and youth organizations, and the CPI-dominated Bihar State Kisan Sabha.

The greater emphasis of the SSP on caste politics is suggested by the fact that three SSP leaders, but no CPI leaders, had been involved in backward caste and antiuntouchability activities. Only two CPI men and three SSP men were involved in institutions of local self-government and cooperatives. Such institutions tended everywhere to be dominated by the Congress in the 1950s, but rural local government institutions were less developed anyway and less important in Bihar than elsewhere in India.

At this point, it will be useful to summarize the data on the socioeconomic composition and political experiences of radical political leaders from Bihar by constructing profiles of what a typical radical leader of the SSP or CPI in the 1960s looked like. A radical leader from Bihar in the 1960s was likely to be a married man, born in the middle 1920s in a village in the Bihar plains, where he continued to reside. He was more likely than not to be a member of an elite caste group, but he may have been a member of a backward caste. He would almost certainly have had a secondary education at least and would probably also have attended college. If he was an SSP man, he may have maintained an interest in his land; but, if he was a CPI man, he was likely to be a whole-time political worker. If he was an SSP man, his first political experience was most likely in the 1942 movement, but if he was a CPI man, he probably entered politics in one of the earlier movements of the nationalist period. No matter what his party, he was likely to be a proudly inveterate jail-goer who had gone to jail under the Congress government more likely than under the British Raj. If he was an SSP man, his main fields of political and social activity were probably in education and in student and youth organizations, whereas the typical CPI man may have been involved in peasant organization, student and youth activities, trade unions, or constructive work.

The Prominent Men of the SSP and CPI in Bihar.

More than mere statistics and more even than the stated policies and programs, the character and the images of political parties in India are best seen through their most prominent leaders. Yet, parties in India differ in the degree to which individual leaders occupy positions of prominence and power. The SSP in India was associated in the public and rank-and-file party members' minds with the exuberant personality of the late Dr. Rammanohar Lohia. In fact, SSP members were frequently called "Lohia Socialists." The CPI has had no national leaders of similar prominence, though E. M. S. Namboodiripad may have a similar stature in Kerala. On the other hand, if the CPI leaders tend to be less conspicuous, there is often less doubt about who is most powerful.

In Bihar, the SSP has had two leaders who, in recent years, have occupied critical leadership positions in the party and who commanded wide respect from party members. They are Karpuri Thakur and Ramanand Tiwari.[19] They have been identified not so much by the positions they have held, though both have been state party chairmen and state ministers and Karpuri Thakur was the national chairman of the SSP, but by the esteem in which they have been held by their fellow party members and by the degree to which they have symbolized the party. Bhola Prasad Singh has been another influential SSP (and SP) leader in Bihar. The prominent men of the CPI in Bihar are less visible, but their preeminent positions in the party are more easily ascertained by their institutional positions and their rankings in the list of members of the state executive of the party.[20] They are the state secretary, Jagannath Sarkar; the previous state secretary, Indradip Sinha; and the first state secretary of the Bihar party, Sunil Mukherjee. A comparison of these six leaders can bring out what the statistics cannot show as well—the kinds of people who rise to power and prominence and the esteem of their party followers in the two parties.

Karpuri Thakur was born in 1921 in a village in Darbhanga District in a family belonging to a barber caste. He passed his intermediate examination in 1941 and began his studies for the B.A. degree, but never completed them. In his student days, he read the writings of the leading nationalist figures of the time, particularly Mahatma Gandhi, Jawaharlal Nehru, Jayaprakash Narayan, Acharya Narendra Dev, and Dr. Lohia. He was an active member of the All-India Students Federation and organized a youth organization in his own village. In 1942, he joined the Quit India movement in which he was arrested. He spent 26 months in jail, where he became associated with the Congress Socialist Party. Since his release from jail in 1945, he has been a whole-time worker of the Socialist Party. He left the Congress when the CSP split from the Congress in 1948, joined the PSP in 1952, where he remained until the formation of the SSP in 1964. In an interview, he stressed his political consistency in refus-

[19] These leaders have been selected on the basis of my impression, derived from interviews and other evidence available to me since 1967, that they were the most influential leaders in state-level Bihar SSP politics. They have continued to play influential roles in the present SP. They are not necessarily the men who have made the greatest contribution to the building of the party. If the criterion were long-standing contribution to the party as well as influence and esteem, Bhupendra Narain Mandal, MP, would also have to be included.

[20] *Bharatiya Kamyunist Parti ke AthveN Bihar Rajya Sammelan meN Svikrat Sangathanik Riport*, Katihar, 14–18 Aktubar 1968 (Patna: Bihar Rajya Parishad, Bharatiya Kamyunist Parti, 1968), p. 29.

ing to join splinter groups. He did not follow Dr. Lohia out of the PSP in 1955 nor did he go out of the SSP with the PSP splitters in 1965. He has risen steadily through the ranks of the Socialist movement in the party organization, in the Socialist peasant organization, and in the state legislature party. He has participated in many post-Independence Socialist agitations and has been jailed eight times since 1947. He has been a member of the Bihar Legislative Assembly since 1952 and is one of the very few members of the Bihar legislature to have been elected six times in succession from the same constituency. He has been leader of the SSP legislature party, deputy chief minister in the first United Front government of Bihar, chief minister of the United Front government in 1971, and chairman of the national SSP organization.

One cannot meet Karpuri Thakur or talk to his party colleagues in Bihar and fail to notice or hear of his humility, his sincerity, and his dedication to the party and to the Socialist movement. Every SSP member interviewed by the author in Bihar in 1969 listed Karpuri Thakur as one of the three most respected and admired leaders of the party in the state. He works and lives in the party office in Patna when he is in the capital and in the town of Samastipur when he is in Darbhanga District.

Ramanand Tiwari is an older man than Karpuri Thakur. He was born in 1909 in a poor Brahman family in a village in Shahabad District in south Bihar. His father, who plied a bullock cart for hire to make his living, died when Ramanand Tiwari was only six months old, leaving the family without sufficient resources for his son to go beyond primary school. Ramanand Tiwari began earning money at the age of nine, working first as a cook, then as a waterman in a railway station, as a newsboy in Calcutta, and finally as a police constable in Hazaribagh District in Bihar.

Ramanand Tiwari was drawn to politics because of his concern for the condition of poor people, which he began to feel would be improved if the British were removed from India. Although, being a government servant, he could not formally join the Congress, he was sympathetic to the Congress program, was inspired by Gandhi, and collected subscriptions from his fellow policemen for the Congress. In 1942, when the Quit India movement was launched, Ramanand Tiwari was stationed at Jamshedpur. There he organized a Revolutionary Police Force and led a strike by the policemen, for which he and 32 colleagues were arrested, sent to jail, and dismissed from service. After his release from jail in 1946, he formed the Bihar Police and Jailmen's Association, which organized a strike the following year. The 1947 policemen's strike ended in a series of violent confrontations with British troops, in which 6 policemen, 4 British soldiers, and 2 civilians were killed and approximately 900 policemen were arrested. At this point, Gandhi and Jayaprakash Narayan took a personal interest in the matter and advised Ramanand to surrender and submit to trial. He did so and, along with 71 colleagues, was put on trial and sentenced to transportation for life. He and his colleagues were, however, ultimately acquitted by the Patna High Court and released from jail in December 1950.

During his first period in jail in 1942, he met Jayaprakash Narayan, was greatly impressed by him, and joined the Congress Socialist Party. After Independence, he became a member of the Socialist Party and then the PSP. Like Karpuri Thakur, and for the same reasons, Ramanand Tiwari stayed with the PSP at the time of the Lohia split but joined the SSP in 1964 and remained with it after the PSP split from it. On different occasions, Ramanand Tiwari has been leader of the Bihar legislature party, chairman of the state party, a member of the national executive of the party, and, most poignantly, minister for police and jails in the first non-Congress government in Bihar. He was elected to the Bihar assembly from the same constituency from 1952 through 1969 but was defeated for the first time in the 1972 elections.

While both Karpuri Thakur and Ramanand Tiwari have many of the characteristics, discussed above, of the typical SSP leader, they have reached their positions of prominence and esteem at least as much because of their differences from other SSP leaders. Both have been whole-time party workers dedicated to the building of the party and the Socialist movement in Bihar. Both are self-made men from humble origins. Both distinguished themselves by their intense commitment to nationalist and socialist principles in the pre-Independence period. Both have had a stable political base in their constituencies. While there were other SSP leaders who shared some of these characteristics with Karpuri Thakur and Ramanand Tiwari, few shared all of them. Finally, their caste background deserves notice. Ramanand Tiwari comes from an elite caste, but he can also speak from personal experience for the poor and the downtrodden. He thus can command the respect equally of high caste men and men of backward and low caste status. Karpuri Thakur also occupies a conveniently ambiguous, though quite different, caste status from other SSP and SP members. Though he comes from a backward caste, he is not a member of any of the large and politically powerful backward castes in Bihar, that is, the Yadavs, Kurmis, and Koiris. Consequently, he really has no caste in a political sense but symbolizes the aspirations of backward castes generally and can consequently be an acceptable leader to competing backward and elite caste rivals in the party.

Bhola Prasad Singh comes from an entirely different kind of environment from that of Karpuri Thakur or Ramanand Tiwari. Bhola Prasad Singh was born in 1932 in Patna city. He belongs to the backward, traditionally agricultural caste of Kurmis. However, his entire life has been spent in the city. He has had much more formal education than either Karpuri Thakur or Ramanand Tiwari. He is a law graduate and a practicing advocate before the Patna High Court. He was attracted to political life as a young boy by the 1942 movement and began his participation in politics through the student movement in 1945. In contrast to Karpuri Thakur and Ramanand Tiwari, Bhola Prasad Singh has never been a member of the PSP. His primary sphere of political activity was in nonparty civic politics in Patna until 1955, when he joined the Socialist Party led by Dr. Lohia. He was elected to the upper house of the state legislature in 1962 and has since held various party and nonparty offices, including secretary and treasurer of the state SSP, membership on the state and national executive of the party, leader of the upper house, and minister for local self-government in the first non-Congress government in Bihar.

Bhola Prasad Singh represents the more flamboyant style of political leadership in the SSP and SP, associated in the past with Dr. Lohia and also with Raj Narain of Uttar Pradesh. Like both these men, Bhola Prasad has been inclined to make frequent public statements of a dramatic sort, hurling charges of corruption against Congressmen, of lying against Communists, of engaging in a hoax against Sarvodaya workers, and of lack of militancy against PSP men. His statements, because of their dramatic character, are frequently quoted in the Patna press. He represented a viewpoint in the SSP characterized by militant opposition to the ruling Congress party and disdain for the PSP as an alliance partner. These positions, particularly, placed him in the role of chief spokesman, if not the leader, of a bloc of SSP legislators who were discontented with the leadership of the former PSP cadres, particularly that of Ramanand Tiwari.

The prominent and powerful leaders of the CPI in Bihar are quite different kinds of men from the SSP leaders. The contrasting backgrounds and political careers of the two leaderships bring out more sharply than the statistics some of the differences between the two parties in Bihar. The *doyen* of the CPI in Bihar is Sunil Mukherjee, descendant of a Bengali Brahman family residing in Bihar. He was born in Bhagalpur town (in 1914). His father was a lawyer who became a Congress leader and a deputy minister in the Congress government in the post-Independence period. Sunil Mukherjee participated as a young boy in Congress movements in Bihar in the early 1930s. However, he soon came into contact with some important people connected with the Bengal terrorist movement and joined the Jugantar Party. He was jailed in 1932 for two months. In 1933, he was convicted in the *Arms Act* case in Monghyr and sentenced to five years in prison in Bengal jails. In jail in Bengal, he found time for study— he ultimately received his B.A. degree—and for discussion with political prisoners of various ideological persuasions. In 1934, he joined the Communist Consolidation inside the jail. Upon his release from prison in 1937, he was externed to Bihar where, along with 19 others, he founded the first Communist Party unit in Bihar in 1939 and became its first secretary, a position he continued to occupy until 1951. He continues to be a member of the secretariat of the state committee of the party and of the national council of the CPI. His primary field of political activity in recent years has been in the trade union movement in Jamshedpur, where he maintains his permanent address. In 1962, he was elected to the Bihar assembly from Jamshedpur and was the leader of the Communist Party in the assembly during the 1962–1967 period. He was defeated in the 1967 election but was returned again from Jamshedpur in the 1969 midterm election and from Patna West in the 1972 election.

The second of the three leading figures of the Bihar CPI, Indradip Sinha, was born in 1915 in a landed upper caste family in a village in Saran district. If Sunil Mukherjee represents one route to the Communist Party in the 1930s through the revolutionary terrorist movement, Indradip represents the more prosaic, intellectual route. Indradip Sinha's early political experiences were no different from those of countless others of his class, most of whom stayed with the Congress. His first political experience came in 1930 when he was only 15 years old and a student in school and was assaulted by the police during his participation in a *satyagraha*. He continued his studies and his politics in school, managing to excel in both. He took a first class first M.A. in economics in 1939. Politically, he organized the Patna University Students' Union in 1937 and became a member of the working committee of the All-India Students Federation from 1938 to 1940.

Dissatisfied with both the Congress and the CSP in the aftermath of the Haripura and Tripura sessions of the Indian National Congress,[21] he and Chandra Shekhar Singh (another prominent CPI leader of Bihar) joined the CPI in February 1940, four months after its foundation in Bihar. For a time, in order to disguise his Communist activity, he took a job as a lecturer in economics, but he has been a whole-time worker of the CPI

---

[21] These sessions were marked by open conflict between the conservative Congressmen and the CSP and radical Left over the election and reelection as Congress president of Subhas Chandra Bose, the famous Bengali radical leftist.

since 1942. He has been secretary of the Bihar CPI two or three times and a member of the central executive of the party. His work has been primarily organizational rather than in the electoral arena. He contested a parliamentary seat for the first time in 1967 but lost. He has been a member of the Bihar Legislative Council since 1964 and became revenue minister in the first non-Congress government. His intellectual attainments and organizational capacity stood him in good stead in the ministry where he acquired a reputation even outside his own party as one of the most competent ministers in the government.

The present (1972) state secretary of the party, Jagannath Sarkar, is of the same generation as Sunil Mukherjee and Indradip Sinha. He was born in 1919 in the town of Puri in Orissa, where his father was posted as a government doctor. He comes from a distinguished Kayastha family of East Bengal. Although his grandfather had been a zamindar, he and his closest family members had been removed from the land for 70 years. His uncle was the famous historian Jadunath Sarkar. All the other male members of his family were employed in liberal professions. He has lived in Patna most of his life. He received a B.A. degree from Patna University. Since his student days, he has been a political worker of the Communist Party and has had no other occupation. He joined the Communist Party in December 1939 out of "intellectual conviction." He found inspiration in Marxism and Marxist literature that he did not find in Gandhism and the Congress. He has never belonged to any other political party but the Communist Party. For a time, he was active in the trade union movement, but for the last ten to fifteen years he has devoted himself entirely to party organizational work. Like Indradip Sinha, he has been a member of the Bihar Legislative Council.

The differences between the top leadership of the Bihar CPI and that of the SSP in the 1960s were great. First, all three CPI leaders were members of elite castes from comfortable families. Two were townsmen, both Bengalis in origin. Second, the three top leaders of the CPI were colleagues of long standing. They belonged to the same age group, joined the Communist Party around the same time, and have remained in the leadership core of the party to the present. In contrast, Karpuri Thakur, Ramanand Tiwari and Bhola Prasad Singh reached their positions of leadership by separate routes and more because of their individual achievements or political styles than because of their contributions to the development of the party organization. One would look in vain among the SSP leaders for a leadership core comparable to that of the CPI. If the SSP did not have a leadership core comparable to the CPI, however, its leaders shared a central political experience, that of the 1942 movement. The CPI leaders, in contrast, have followed two different routes—the revolutionary terrorist route of Sunil Mukherjee and the radical intellectual route of Indradip Sinha and Jagannath Sarkar. Yet, all three CPI leaders, however different their political experiences, have in common an intellectual orientation that is not characteristic of the SSP leaders. If one were to try and sum up the differences in the leadership of the two parties in a few words, one would reserve the term populism for the SSP leaders and radical intellectualism for the CPI leaders. The SSP leaders were men who came from poor families, who felt a personal closeness to common people, and who thrived in agitational politics. The CPI leaders came from comfortable and cultured families, were cosmopolitan and sophisticated, took a radical intellectual approach to things political, and identified with party organizational work more than with mass politics.

Radical Party Organization in Bihar

Differences in the leadership of the two radical parties in Bihar have been paralleled by differences in organizational structure and style. The populist character of the SSP was reflected in loose membership qualifications, permitting a relatively larger and more fluctuating membership than the CPI; in a decentralized and imprecisely defined organizational structure; in its diverse appeals on issues of current popular concern; and in the vigor of its inner-party conflicts. The emphasis of the CPI on intellectualism and organization is reflected in somewhat tighter membership qualifications and a smaller membership, a centralized and more rigidly articulated organization structure,[22] and an emphasis on maintaining discipline and party cohesion. These contrasts are developed in this section.

Party Membership: Principal Areas of Organizational Strength
Table 6.14 gives the membership figures for the SSP and CPI in Bihar by district for the two most recent years for which figures were available.

[22] Maurice Duverger's discussion of articulation in party organizations is relevant here. The articulation of a political party refers to "the arrangements for linking and relating the primary groups of the party" and the definition of the relations between different levels in the party organization. In strongly articulated parties, the roles of each element in the party are prescribed in detail and all have a defined role to play. In weakly articulated parties, relations between levels and the composition and functions of bodies at different levels are imprecisely defined. The SSP tended toward weak articulation and the CPI toward strong articulation in Duverger's terms. See *Political Parties: Their Organization and Activity in the Modern State*, translated by Barbara and Robert North, 2d ed. (New York: Wiley, 1963), pp. 40–52.

Table 6.14   Membership Figures by District for the SSP and CPI in Bihar, 1965–1967

District	Party Membership			
	SSP 1967	SSP 1966	CPI 1966	CPI 1965
Patna	11,126	2,792	1,538	412
Gaya	9,725	5,064	2,050	880
Shahabad	19,226	5,806	1,451	841
Muzaffarpur	20,264	4,162	1,277	810
Darbhanga	18,256	5,635	5,000	2,226
Saran	5,005	2,749	1,200	820
Champaran	13,225	2,547	2,065	1,038
Bhagalpur	6,394	103	3,493	1,637
Monghyr	20,400	6,049	3,750	1,415
Saharsa	10,200	7,296	974	625
Purnea	8,146	1,311	1,046	313
Santal Parganas	1,795	113	350	8
Ranchi	2,043	25	140	10
Hazaribagh	5,960	2,721	338	220
Dhanbad	9,750	3,128	209	130
Singhbum	3,446	1,182	376	272
Palamau	2,465	873	34	—
Other	—	599	171	127
Bihar	163,426	51,596	25,462	11,784

Sources: *Bhāratīya Kamyunist Pārtī ke ĀthveN Bihār Rājya Sammelan meN Svīkrat Sāngathanik Riport,* Katihar, 14–18 *Aktubar* 1968 (Patna: Bihār Rājya Parishad, Bhāratiya Kamyunist Partī, 1968), p. 27 and *Samyukta Socialist Pārtī Sammelan, 8, 9, aur 10 March 1968, Rājya Mantrī kī Rapat,* by Chandradeo Prasad Varma (Patna: Samyukta Socialist Pārtī Rājya Kāryālay, n.d.), p. 59.

Comparable figures were available for the two parties for the year 1966, before the great increase in SSP membership caused by the electoral successes of the party in 1967. The SSP was the larger of the two parties in Bihar. Its membership of 51,596 in 1966 was almost exactly double that of the CPI.[23] Only in three districts in the entire state did CPI membership

[23] Membership qualifications are somewhat stricter in the CPI than in the SSP. Any adult "who accepts the aims and objects, means, policy, programme and discipline of the Party can become a member" of the SSP as long as he also agrees not to "observe caste or communal distinction" and not to join any opposed organization. The individual membership fee is 50 paise (6.5¢) per year. Samyukta Socialist Party, *Constitution,* as adopted at the Second National conference at Kota (Rajasthan), 3–6 April 1966 (New Delhi: SSP Central Office, 1966), pp. 3–4. Qualifications for membership in the CPI include recommendation from two members and a six months' candidate period. Moreover, there are special procedures for admission of "leading members" from other political parties. The annual membership fee is one rupee (13¢). "Constitution of Communist Party of India," in *Documents Adopted by Eighth Congress of the Communist Party of India,* Karyanandnagar, Patna, 7–15 February 1968 (New Delhi: CPI, 1968), pp. 333–335.

exceed that of the SSP—in Ranchi and Santal Parganas, where the membership of both parties was very low anyway, and in Bhagalpur, a major organizational stronghold of the CPI.

On the whole, in consonance with the similarities noted above in the birthplace and residence of SSP and CPI leaders, there was a close correspondence between the main areas of organizational strength of the two parties, whose memberships were concentrated in the districts of north and south Bihar. The major radical party districts of Bihar, where both parties had strength, are the four south Bihar districts of Monghyr, Shahabad, Gaya, and Patna and the two north Bihar districts of Darbhanga and Muzaffarpur. In addition, the SSP had relative strength in the north Bihar district of Saharsa and in the industrial district of Dhanbad (where a major organizational effort had been in progress in recent years) and the CPI has been relatively strong in Bhagalpur and Champaran. The close parallel between the geographical areas of organizational strength of the two parties can be seen by comparing the maps in figures 6.1 and 6.2, where the districts with the highest memberships, proportionate to population, for the two parties are shown.

Radical parties of the Left in industralized and industrializing societies have tended to be strong or to seek strength in urban industrial areas. In

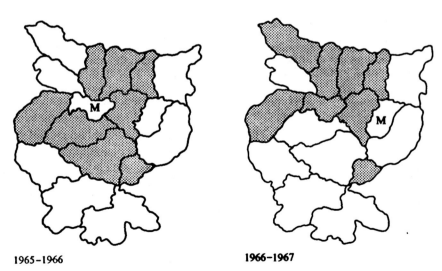

1965–1966   1966–1967

Figure 6.1   Districts with highest proportions of SSP membership to total population, Bihar, 1965–1966 and 1966–1967.

▓ — Districts above the median in percentage of SSP membership
M — Median district

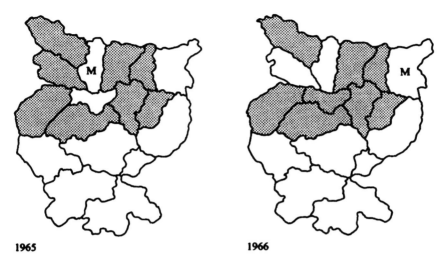

1965   1966

Figure 6.2   Districts with highest proportions of CPI membership to total population, Bihar, 1965 and 1966.

▦ — Districts above the median in percentage of CPI membership
M — Median district

eastern European countries, radical parties have been strongest traditionally in areas where ethnic and linguistic minorities have been concentrated.[24] The relationships between radical party strength and various socioeconomic and cultural groups in Bihar will be examined below. Here it is necessary to point out only that there are no self-evident associations geographically, at the district level, between radical party membership and such indices of modernization as literacy, urbanization, and industrialization or between radical party membership and the distribution of particular language groups. Figure 6.3 and table 6.15 show clearly that the more modernized districts of Bihar are in south Bihar and Chota Nagpur, rather than in north Bihar, where both the SSP and the CPI have had high membership districts. The SSP had only two high membership districts in Chota Nagpur (Dhanbad and Hazaribagh), but the CPI has had none in this industrial and tribal zone.[25] Six of the nine highest-membership SSP districts are predominantly Hindi-speaking, two are

[24] R. V. Burks, *The Dynamics of Communism in Eastern Europe* (Princeton, N.J.: Princeton University Press, 1961).
[25] Interestingly enough, the CPI organizational report for Bihar does not give separate membership figures for the big cities of Patna and Jamshedpur, whereas the SSP reports do.

Table 6.15 Comparison of Bihar SSP and CPI Membership by District in 1966, with Selected Indices of Modernization and Mother Tongue Distribution according to the 1961 Census (in Percentages)

Districts Ranked According to Highest SSP Membership	SSP 1966 %	Rank	CPI 1966 %	Rank	Literacy %	Rank	Urbanization %	Rank	Workers in Registered Factories %	Rank	Predominant Mother Tongue
Saharsa	0.423	1	0.057	5	14.0	15	3.9	17	0.13	17	Maithili
Dhanbad	0.269	2	0.018	13	25.5	2	25.0	1	4.77	2	Hindi
Shahabad	0.180	3	0.045	8	21.8	4	7.2	9	0.91	6	Bhojpuri
Monghyr	0.179	4	0.111	3	19.0	8	11.1	4	1.33	5	Hindi
Gaya	0.139	5	0.056	6	19.2	6	7.3	8	0.32	15	Hindi
Darbhanga	0.128	6	0.113	2	16.8	11	4.3	15	0.60	9	Maithili
Hazaribagh	0.114	7	0.014	14	14.5	14	8.4	7	1.94	3	Hindi
Muzaffarpur	0.101	8	0.031	11	17.2	10	4.6	14	0.36	14	Hindi
Patna	0.095	9	0.052	7	28.7	1	20.1	3	1.46	4	Hindi
Champaran	0.085	10	0.069	4	13.2	17	4.8	12	0.56	11	Bhojpuri
Saran	0.077	11	0.033	10	18.2	9	4.2	16	0.52	12	Bhojpuri
Palamau	0.073	12	0.003	17	13.6	16	4.7	13	0.67	8	Hindi
Singhbum	0.058	13	0.018	12	22.9	3	21.5	2	5.28	1	Tribal
Purnea	0.042	14	0.034	9	16.1	12	6.0	10	0.71	7	Hindi
Bhagalpur	0.006	15	0.204	1	20.3	5	10.9	5	0.59	10	Hindi
Santal Parganas	0.004	16	0.013	15	14.6	13	5.3	11	0.21	16	Tribal
Ranchi	0.001	17	0.007	16	19.1	7	9.5	6	0.50	13	Tribal
Bihar	0.111		0.055		18.40		8.43				

predominantly Maithili-speaking, and one is predominantly Bhojpuri-speaking. Thus, both parties have had high membership districts in the three largest language regions of the state, but neither has had high membership in the districts where tribals and tribal languages predominate.

The data on radical party membership reinforce the conclusions reached above in the discussion of place of birth and residence of radical party leaders. The leaders of both parties and the bulk of their memberships have come from the areas of the state where the nationalist movement was strongest and where political consciousness has been highest. The radical parties in Bihar are not only not confined to either the industrializing regions or minority language areas of the state but they do not have particular strength in such areas. In other words, both parties were not deviant political groups in the contemporary political and social structure of Bihar, but legitimate descendants of the central nationalist political tradition in the state.

Organizational Focus

There have been substantial differences in theory and practice in the organization of the SSP and CPI with regard to the locus of the strategic decision-making units and relations between units at different levels of the party. In general, the SSP organization was characterized within the state

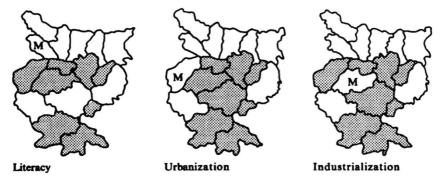

Literacy   Urbanization   Industrialization

Figure 6.3   Distribution of Bihar districts according to levels of literacy, urbanization, and industrialization, 1961.
M — Median district

▨ — Districts above the median in literacy, urbanization, industrialization

by an emphasis on local, constituency organizations; by close, frequent,
and informal interaction between different levels of the party organization, including the central level; and by a consequent diffusion and confusion of decision-making powers. The CPI organization is characterized
by emphasis within the state on the district and state units of the party
organization; by structured, formalized, and less frequent interaction between state and central units; and by a more precise demarcation of functions and decision-making powers.[26] These points can be illustrated by
comparing the different ways in which the two parties in Bihar made
decisions in recent years on selection of party candidates to contest the
elections and selection of ministers to join the United Front governments.

   In both areas of decision making, there was a striking contrast between
the relative weakness of the state organization of the SSP and the decisive
role played by the state organization of the CPI. A former chairman of the
Bihar SSP described the decision-making process of his party with regard
to selection of candidates in a way that brings out sharply the organizational differences between the SSP and the CPI.

The constituency party has the biggest say in the matter [of selection of
candidates]. If the constituency party unanimously selects a person, it is
hardly changed by the state party or the central party. But, if there [are]
serious differences of opinion, then we try to resolve [them] by talk and by
visit of state leaders. . . . And still if . . . there is any controversy, the

[26] In Duverger's terms, the SSP, though it was a mass and not a cadre party, tended
toward a caucus form of organization, weak articulation, and decentralization,
whereas the CPI has a branch form of organization and tends toward strong articulation and centralization. Duverger, *Political Parties*, pp. 40–52.

central party intervenes. And, generally, the decisions ultimately reached are correct. . . . But what happens [is] that all these things are done . . . at the last moment, in a great hurry. That shows that the organization is not very streamlined. . . . The PSP has got . . . very good . . . whole-time workers at Patna, who mostly devote their time at Patna and have their houses at Patna and . . . reside with their families and . . . attend to the office and to the requirements of the state party very much; whereas, in the SSP, everyone is attached to his constituency. And there is nobody to man the offices here. For instance, during the last general election, the whole state office was run by two clerks and there was nobody and so we had to call Mr. Badgaitkar [a central leader] from Maharashtra.

So, this is the main difference [from other parties] because everybody is constituency-bound, everybody is a field worker, nobody wants to reside . . . at Patna [whereas the] PSP have some . . . higher-level workers as well as the Communist Party. Mr. Indradip Sinha, Mr. Sunil Mukherjee, Mr. Jagannath Sarkar, they are always available at Patna. They attend the offices just like any [government] secretariat person. . . . We don't have a single person who can devote his time at Patna.[27]

This statement points to three characteristic features of SSP organization—the emphasis on the constituency unit of the party; the involvement of all levels of the party in decision making; and the weakness of the state organization. In contrast, compare the following statement of the state secretary of the Bihar CPI in response to the same question:

Selection of candidates we do . . . at three levels, one at the local level —they first send recommendations. Then, at the district level, they discuss it, and finalize at the state level. It is finalized at the state level, but it is difficult to say. In some cases perhaps, we go by the district decision. . . . In certain cases, but very few, we have to reverse the recommendation of the district at the state level. So generally I will say the district level is the crucial, district leadership of the party. That plays the most vital role in selecting the candidates, but state always makes some changes.

Asked if he considered the existing procedures satisfactory, the general secretary responded affirmatively and explicitly compared the CPI procedure with that of the PSP and SSP with regard to the roles played by the central leaders in those parties. He argued that there was "no sense" in the PSP and SSP practices of consulting the central leadership on candidate selection because the central leaders could not have the necessary knowledge—unless such consultation was for the purpose of taking "some unpleasant decisions."

For instance, the state leadership [of the PSP or SSP] doesn't want a particular person to be set up as a candidate, but if they say so, then the people will be very angry, so they just put the blame on the central leadership.[28]

In contrast, therefore, to the decision-making process in the SSP, the emphasis in the CPI is on the district rather than the local unit—there are no constituency organizations in the CPI. However, the state organization also plays a significant and decisive role, apparently without fear of taking "unpleasant decisions." The central leadership of the CPI is not at all involved. Unlike the SSP, where the decisions on candidate selection were announced by the central parliamentary board, the same decisions in the CPI are announced by the state council. Finally, there is no suggestion in the CPI secretary's statement of the kind of loose and informal bargaining and interlevel consultations that characterize candidate selection according to the SSP leader's statement.

Similar differences between the decision-making units and processes of the two parties were manifested in the selection of ministers for the first United Front government in Bihar. Asked how and at what level this decision was made in the CPI, the response of the state secretary and all other CPI persons interviewed on this point was that it was made in the state executive of the party, without consultation with the central leadership. Compare the CPI's approach with the following statement by the former SSP chairman on his party's procedure in the matter:

Selection of ministers . . . is generally done like this that the leader of the party [in the legislature] makes his choice and then he puts it before the various important leaders of the party and the whole thing is talked out. If there is any serious difference, it is put to the legislative party. Their advice is taken. And [if] still there is some difference, then the central parliamentary board is consulted.

[So, for example, how was it done last time?]

Last time Mr. Karpuri Thakur was elected the leader. He made certain choices. In fact, Bindeshwari Prasad Mandal's choice [discussed below] was his. And the general secretary of the [central] party, Mr. Ram Sevak Yadav, was there. He was informed. They generally agreed, except certain individuals, not concurring to certain names, but generally agreed. So it was accepted.[29]

The statement brings out again characteristic features of SSP decision making in contrast to that of the CPI—the involvement of central leaders in the process, the diffuseness of consultation among various units and

---

[28] Taped interview in Patna on 13 January 1969; citations from pp. 3–4 of interview document.
[29] Taped interview in Patna on 19 February 1969; citation from p. 11 of interview document.

levels of the party organization, and the informality implied in the consultation of "various important leaders." In contrast, in the CPI, there is one and only one locus of decision making on this matter—the state executive of the party. Finally, this aspect of decision making in the two parties reveals another major difference between them in the clear preeminence of the organizational wing of the CPI, which made the decision on ministers, in contrast to the SSP, where the process began in the legislature party and the state executive was never consulted.

Organizational Appeals

The radical Socialists and the CPI differ also in the appeals they make and the satisfactions they offer to party personnel. The appeal of the CPI tends to lie in its ideology, in its provision of a total approach to problems of social and political development. Consequently, commitment to the party tends to be all-encompassing. In contrast, the SSP and SP have different appeals to different people. A man may join the radical Socialists because he finds certain leaders or certain policies attractive. His commitment to the party is consequently a contingent one. If the leaders who attracted him disappoint him or the policies he approves are not satisfactorily implemented, then he may leave the party and join another political group.

Thus, SSP members, asked to give their most important reasons for joining the party and to state what they liked most about the party, tended to give a wide variety of responses. Some said they joined the Socialist movement in the pre-Independence period because it gave them a greater "sense of purpose" about the kind of society that would be created in the post-Independence period and because they admired the Socialist leaders more than the Gandhian Congress leaders. For many of those who remained in the original SP and joined the SSP in the post-Independence period, the leadership and policies of Dr. Lohia personally remained important influences in their attachment to the party. Others joined the party and continued to find satisfaction in it because of particular policies—on agriculture, on getting rid of English, and most prominently on caste. The SSP's "60 percent policy" had a touch of genius in it in the appeal it offered to low and high caste groups alike. In Bihar, low and middle caste men were attracted to this aspect of the party's policy because, as one SSP middle caste MLA put it, "I thought the Socialist Party was the best party for the downtrodden people and the backward community." [30] Yet,

[30] Interview in Patna on 16 February 1969; citation from p. 1 of interview document.

upper caste people in the party did not feel threatened by a policy that guarantees 60 percent of posts for women, backward castes, scheduled castes, Muslims, and tribals who, after all, comprise more than 90 percent of the population. Upper caste men could still occupy 40 percent of party and government posts and remain faithful to SSP policy.

The responses of CPI leaders and members to the same questions were quite different. The most important reasons given for joining the CPI stressed such broad factors as the "appeal to reason" of Marxism as opposed to Gandhism, the belief that Marxism showed the way not only to a particular kind of post-Independence society for India but to "the future of mankind," the belief that Marxism was the "only theory that will come into practice," and the like. This is not to say that some CPI members were not influenced by particular people or policies as were SSP men, but the emphasis was different among most CPI people interviewed. Moreover, when asked what they liked most about the party, the SSP people tended to give more specific answers, whereas CPI men spoke of broad principles, such as adherence to Marxist proletarian principles, or else insisted that they liked everything about the CPI. Similarly, it may be added here, most SSP men interviewed found something to criticize about their party when asked if there was anything they did not like about it, whereas CPI men either said there was nothing they did not like or else that they only wished for the strengthening of the party.[31]

Problems of Organizational Discipline, Factionalism, and Splits

Both major radical parties in Bihar have suffered organizationally from problems of factionalism, leading to party splits, but there have been great differences between the two parties in the general state of party discipline and in the causes of party splits. In the radical Socialist movement, the maintenance of discipline is a constant, continuing problem and acts of indiscipline are frequent and open to public view. Moreover, they tend to center upon issues relating to leadership, power, and specific party policies. In the CPI, outsiders rarely become aware of problems of discipline until a major party split is imminent. The issues then appear to be and frequently are in fact issues of broad party line on far-reaching principles.

Asked if there was anything about the party they did not like, only an

---

[31] It is, of course, possible that Communist leaders would be more reticent in speaking to an American interviewer on this point than SSP leaders, but I believe the differences in SSP and CPI responses on these points are consistent with other differences in their attitudes.

occasional SSP man found nothing to criticize about his party. One or two indicated only slight disagreements with party policies. Most, however, had something to say about the general state of party discipline. Most SSP members interviewed in Bihar felt that the party's policy of permitting complete freedom of speech for party members was abused—that there was too much inner-party debate and disagreement on issues both before and after decisions were taken, that personalities were discussed, and that such openness tended to lead "to bickerings, quarrels, sharp tongue, abuse, and ultimately indiscipline." [32] One respondent went so far as to suggest that the Socialist Party was born in an act of indiscipline when Madhu Limaye was expelled from the PSP and that indiscipline has literally been built into the party ever since.[33] Moreover, as in the Congress, factionalism and indiscipline exist at all levels of the party, and groups in the party are frequently connected at different levels. The organizational report of the SSP general secretary for 1968 openly referred to existing party factionalism in three districts and to the existence of two parallel organizations in the district of Shahabad.[34]

Although both parties have suffered from organizational splits in the recent past, the reasons have been different. As in the rest of India, the CPI in Bihar split into two parties in 1964. However, the split in Bihar was relatively mild. The Bihar CPI state secretary estimated that "only about 19 percent of the membership" left the party, of which only one member was on the state executive committee of the party.[35] The party secretariat was unaffected by the split. When asked to give specific reasons for the party split in Bihar, every CPI member insisted that there were no particular reasons affecting the party in Bihar. All members interviewed related the split to all-India and international considerations. Most CPI men in Bihar saw the issue as one of dogmatism and sectarianism in general terms, an unwillingness of the Left Communists to adjust Marxist doctrine to Indian conditions. A few suggested that personal considerations also influenced some people at the time of the split, but all agreed that there was no struggle for personal leadership in the

[32] Taped interview in Patna on 13 January 1969; citation from p. 2 of interview document.

[33] Taped interview in Patna on 13 February 1969; reference to p. 9 of interview document. On the expulsion of Madhu Limaye in 1955, see Hari Kishore Singh, *History of the PSP*, pp. 207–213.

[34] *Samyukta Socialist Pārtī: Bihār, Dwitīya Rājya Sammelan, 8, 9, aur 10 March 1968, Rājya Mantrī kī Rapat*, by Chandradeo Prasad Varma (Patna: Samyukta Socialist Pārtī Rājya Kāryālay, n.d.), pp. 38–51.

[35] Taped interview in Patna on 13 January 1969; citation from p. 7 of interview document.

Bihar CPI and that the lone state council splitter, now general secretary of the Bihar CPM, left for ideological reasons. Since the split of the CPM in 1964, there have been no open divisions in the Bihar CPI. Moreover, the party has been barely touched since 1967 by the problem of defections from the legislature parties, which has affected the other organized parties in Bihar.

In contrast, the SSP in Bihar suffered an organizational split in 1965 at the time of the national split in the party, a major defection of 10 members of the legislative wing of the party during its participation in the first United Front government in Bihar, and a continual open struggle in recent years among top leaders of the party. Up through the 1962 elections in Bihar, the PSP had been the major Socialist party in state politics, polling nearly three times the popular vote and winning four times the number of seats of the Socialist Party (SP). However, 12 of the 29 PSP MLAs elected in 1962 in Bihar joined the Congress, along with Ashok Mehta, in 1964. In the same year, in conjunction with all-India events, the PSP and the SP merged into the SSP in 1964. When the split at Varanasi occurred in 1965, 8 PSP MLAs came back to the old party while 9 remained in the SSP.[36] Thus, the first split in the Bihar SSP occurred, as elsewhere in the SSP in India, before the merger had become effective. In the process, however, the PSP was reduced to a fragment of its former strength, and the SSP emerged as the preeminent Socialist party in the state both in the legislature and in the district organizations.

There is widespread agreement among PSP and SSP leaders about the factors that led to the split, though individuals may emphasize some issues more than others. Four sets of factors were involved—an organizational dispute, disagreement over specific policies, disagreement over the leadership role in the SSP of Dr. Lohia, and temperamental differences between some of the old PSP people and the former SP people. In his pamphlet discussing the course of events leading to the split, S. M. Joshi emphasized three primary points of conflict—an organizational quarrel over the filling of vacancies among PSP delegates who had joined the Congress with Ashok Mehta, a dispute over the issue of allying with other parties in elections and extraparliamentary struggles, and the issue of extending an invitation to Dr. Lohia to join the SSP by a vote of the first SSP conference.[37] The twelve PSP leaders who led the withdrawal from the SSP at

[36] Interview in Patna on 7 April 1967; reference to p. 1 of interview document (BG 33).
[37] S. M. Joshi, *The Split at Varanasi: Some Notes* (Bombay: Lokamat Prakashan, n.d.).

Varanasi also emphasized these issues, as well as their feelings of being "disillusioned and disgusted with the Socialist Party's unscrupulous and uncivilised ways." [38] In fact, temperamental differences seem to have been decisive in bringing about the decision of the PSP leaders to break away. Agreement at the Varanasi conference frequently proved possible on even the most difficult issues, but the PSP men found the internal struggle, which frequently led to much verbal abuse and some fistfights at the conference, too unsavory to tolerate. After the split, however, PSP and SSP men in Bihar both stressed additional policy issues—particularly the 60 percent caste policy of the SSP, SSP militance on the language issue, what PSP men considered to be the excessive militance of the SSP generally and what SSP men considered to be PSP reluctance to participate in mass movements, and a feeling of mistrust on the part of SSP people that the PSP people, who had been considered soft towards Nehru, were still reluctant to oppose the Congress vigorously enough. The old Socialist Party leaders saw the PSP splitters as men lacking in the militancy and passion to put their principles into practice and do everything necessary to remove the Congress from power and bring about a realignment of political forces in the country. The PSP leaders who left the SSP saw themselves as maintaining ideological purity and political civility and avoiding an unscrupulous drive for power at all costs and in alliance with antidemocratic and antinational forces.

However much influenced by temperamental factors, there is little dispute that the 1965 split in Bihar of the PSP leaders was a principled split within both the organizational and legislative wings of the SSP and that it was intimately connected to all-India developments in the party. The defection of ten legislators from the SSP in 1968 was entirely different. The issues then were personal power and caste representation; they involved directly only the legislative wing of the party, and they arose out of specific developments in Bihar politics. In March 1967, the state SSP leaders selected as one of their ministers in the first United Front government Bindeshwari Prasad Mandal, who had been elected to Parliament on the SSP ticket. A prominent backward caste leader of the Yadav caste from Saharsa district, he had joined the party only two years before, after his resignation and simultaneous expulsion from the Congress party for indiscipline. Although the all-India general secretary of the party was present when the decision to include Mandal was made and he raised no objection, Dr. Lohia was enraged when he learned of it. He accused

[38] Praja Socialist Party, *The Merger Annulled* (New Delhi: PSP, n.d.), citation from p. 1.

Mandal of seeking personal aggrandizement at the expense of the party interest and expressed his displeasure with the Bihar SSP leadership. Under the law, Mandal was permitted to remain a minister for six months without being a member of the state legislature. The central leadership of the party had made it clear that they wanted Mandal to take his seat in Parliament. The state leadership of the party, however, possibly fearful of the consequences of a state directive for party cohesion and embarrassed by the whole course of events, simply waited for the six months to expire. For his part, Mandal remained in the cabinet until ten days before the expiration of the six months' deadline and built support primarily among discontented backward caste men, in the SSP and other parties, who coveted ministerial positions. Upon his resignation, Mandal criticized the failure of the SSP to follow its 60 percent policy in the appointment of ministers in the United Front government and announced the formation of a new legislature party, the Shoshit Dal (party of the exploited). He claimed a membership of 25, including 17 alleged defectors from the SSP, of whom one, Jagdeo Prasad, was at the time general secretary of the party organization as well as an MLA. In January, in alliance with the Congress, the Shoshit Dal succeeded in bringing down the United Front government, with the aid of 38 defecting legislators, of whom 10 in fact were from the SSP. The castes of the 10 defectors—4 Yadavs, 3 Koiris, 1 scheduled caste man, 1 Muslim, and only one upper caste man—shows how the defectors succeeded in turning the SSP's 60 percent policy against itself and in benefiting from the issue of backward and low caste representation.[39]

Although the Shoshit Dal succeeded in bringing down the United Front government and also formed a government that lasted for six weeks under Bindeshwari Prasad Mandal, it failed to establish an organizational base in the state. The Shoshit Dal damaged the SSP considerably, but it elected only 6 of its 123 candidates in the 1969 midterm elections and polled only 3.6 percent of the total vote. The SSP lost 16 seats in 1969 compared to 1967, dropping from 68 to 52 seats in the assembly, and polled only 13.7 percent of the vote in 1969 compared to 17.6 percent in 1967.

In the period since the 1969 midterm elections and especially since the split of the Indian National Congress into two separate parties, the SSP

[39] The Bindeshwari Prasad Mandal affair was fully covered in the press and is a recurrent theme in my personal interviews. Accounts of it have also appeared in secondary sources, among which, see Brass, "Coalition Politics," pp. 1183–1184; Blair, "Caste, Politics and Democracy in Bihar State, India," pp. 334–338; and Subhash C. Kashyap, *The Politics of Defection: A Study of State Politics in India* (Delhi: National Publishing House, 1969), pp. 195 ff.

was subject to continuing internal differences in which several lines of internal conflict were involved, particularly between the political strategies of the central and state SSP units, between those in the party at the center and in the state who disagreed on appropriate alliance partners for the SSP, and between SSP leaders in the state who differed on alliance strategy and on the implications of the party's caste policies. Even before the split in the Congress, a considerable segment of the Bihar party expressed its opposition to a continuation of the strategy of "non-Congressism," particularly if it meant alliance with parties of the Right and isolation from the PSP.[40] The Congress split intensified this division in the SSP. The split left the Congress party in Bihar divided into two large segments—the larger being the new Congress (R) allied with Mrs. Gandhi and holding 73 seats in the assembly and the smaller being the old Congress (O), allied with the "Syndicate" or organizational wing of the old party and holding 40 seats in the assembly.[41] In this situation, the SSP strength (then 53) appeared more formidable than before and the party became a favored alliance partner for both Congress parties. The problem for the SSP, then, was whether to ally with either Congress to form a government and, if so, with which Congress. The dominant central leadership of the party, led by the closest followers of Dr. Lohia—Raj Narain, Madhu Limaye, and others—favored continued opposition to Mrs. Gandhi's ruling Congress at the center and to her allies in the states.[42] The leading spokesman for this point of view in the Bihar SSP was Bhola Prasad Singh.[43] The continued pursuit of this strategy of "non-Congressism" in the face of Mrs. Gandhi's leftist posture and the support offered her by the CPI, however, would leave the SSP's possible alliance partners primarily among the Right. The former PSP leader and first chairman of the SSP S. M. Joshi and his supporters in Bihar, particularly Ramanand Tiwari and Karpuri Thakur, favored an alliance with the PSP and other parties of the Left.[44] Some SSP members in Bihar also favored joining a coalition with the Congress (R) itself in the state.[45]

[40] *Indian Nation*, 5 and 6 May 1969.
[41] *Economic and Political Weekly* 5, no. 10 (7 March 1970), 441.
[42] See the *Indian Recorder & Digest* 15, no. 9 (September 1969), 9; no. 10 (October 1969), 6; no. 11 (November 1969), 12; no. 12 (December 1969), 14; 16, no. 2 (February 1970), 8.
[43] See, for example, the *Indian Nation*, 11 and 17 December 1969 and the *Searchlight*, 22 December 1969.
[44] In fact, Joshi resigned the chairmanship of the SSP when a party conference rejected his line in May 1969; see the *Indian Recorder & Digest* 15, no. 6 (June 1969), 12. For the opposite view of Madhu Limaye at that time, see ibid. 15, no. 7 (July 1969), 10.
[45] See, for example, the *Indian Nation*, 5 December 1969.

At a national convention of the SSP in Bihar in January 1970, these issues were openly debated. The Bihar unit of the party was clearly divided into two blocs. One bloc, for which Bhola Prasad Singh was the chief spokesman, favored continued opposition to Congress (R) at the center and in Bihar and alliance with all its rivals, including Congress (O). The larger bloc, spoken for primarily by Ramanand Tiwari, argued for a more flexible strategy and was prepared to be more receptive to the Congress (R) if it should adopt "progressive" policies. Although the latter position had more supporters in Bihar, the old policy of "non-Congressism" had greater support among the predominant central leadership group and within the Uttar Pradesh wing of the party. The party convention failed to resolve the differences between the two groups and passed a political resolution that left the choice of alliance partners for the SSP open to all parties except Congress (R).[46]

As a consequence of the failure to resolve the issue of alliance strategy within the SSP, the Bihar party began to work at cross-purposes. The group led by Bhola Prasad Singh sought to form a united legislature party with Congress (O), Jan Sangh, Swatantra, and the Janata Party while the group led by Ramanand Tiwari sought alliance with the PSP, Loktantric Congress, CPI, BKD, and the Jharkhand Party.[47] In the meantime, a government led by the new Congress (R), headed by a backward caste chief minister, and supported by the CPI, the PSP, and other minor parties in Bihar, was formed on 16 February 1970.[48] The caste issue was now raised in a move by Bhola Prasad Singh, who, though he was allied with the faction that opposed the Congress (R) ministry, argued that it would not be proper to bring down this ministry led by a backward caste man if the SSP legislative leader Ramanand Tiwari, a Brahman, was to replace him as chief minister.[49] The party moved perilously close to an open split when 14 SSP legislators in the Bihar legislature, from the bloc opposed to the leadership of Ramanand Tiwari, deliberately abstained from voting on a no-confidence motion against the Congress (R) coalition ministry in June 1970.[50] A split was avoided through the mediating efforts of central party leaders who rushed to Patna and helped to resolve

[46] Ibid., 8, 10, 13, and 15 January 1970.

[47] The complete and counterproductive moves in which SSP party leaders engaged at this time are detailed in the 28 February 1970 *Letter of Ramanand Tewary (Leader, SSP Legislature Party, Bihar) to the Chairman, Central Parliamentary Board of SSP* (Patna: Baidyanath Press, 1970).

[48] *Indian Recorder & Digest* 15, no. 3 (March 1970), 21–22.

[49] *Economic and Political Weekly* 5, no. 25 (20 June 1970), 969; *Indian Nation*, 22 and 25 May 1970; *Searchlight*, 8, 10, 12, and 13 June 1970.

[50] *Searchlight*, 14, 15, and 21 June 1970; *Indian Nation*, 15, 16, and 22 June 1970.

the breach in the party by bringing about an agreement that Karpuri Thakur would replace Ramanand Tiwari as leader of the opposition united legislature party, although Ramanand Tiwari would remain as leader of the SSP legislature party. That is, Karpuri Thakur, a backward caste man, was to be the alternative chief minister if the Congress (R) government were brought down.[51] Although this compromise prevented a split, the Bihar SSP continued to be internally divided on the issues of alliance partners outside and leadership inside the party, which in turn were related to similar issues within the national executive of the party.

The SSP policy of "non-Congressism" received a mortal blow in the results of the 1971 elections to the Lok Sabha. In pursuit of its strategy of alliance with any parties opposed to the ruling Congress at the center, the SSP followed a policy of electoral adjustments with parties of the Center and Right—Congress (O) and Jan Sangh. The results were disastrous for the SSP. The party, which had won 7 seats from Bihar alone in 1967, won only 8 in the country as a whole in 1971 and only 2 from Bihar. The results turned the tide among the national SSP leaders against the old policy of "non-Congressism." With the exception of Raj Narain and his group, all the prominent central leaders of the party now favored a change in alliance policy.

By this time, the situation in the SSP was complicated by the fact that the SSP in Bihar had succeeded in bringing down the Congress (R) government on 18 December 1970 and had replaced it with an SVD government in which the SSP, with Karpuri Thakur as chief minister, was the dominant partner in alliance with Congress (O), Jan Sangh, Swatantra, and other minor parties.[52] SSP ministers in this government included both Ramanand Tiwari and Bhola Prasad Singh. At a special national convention of the SSP at the end of April and early May 1971, the party debated once again the entire policy of "non-Congressism" and alliance strategies.[53] Raj Narain from the central leadership and Bhola Prasad Singh from Bihar continued to defend the old policy, but sentiment in the party clearly favored a change. After heated debate, the party ultimately adopted a new compromise strategy that included the following points: the SSP would no longer form SVD governments unless it was the largest single opposition party in the legislature; the party would otherwise join with other parties in mass agitations, but not in forming governments; the

---

[51] *Searchlight*, 23 June 1970.
[52] The SVD government, led by Karpuri Thakur, was formed on 22 December 1970 and remained in power until its replacement by an alternative coalition on 2 June 1971.
[53] See the *Indian Nation*, 27 April through 2 May 1971.

SSP would continue to seek to remove the Congress (R) from power at the center, but would try to do so in cooperation with other leftist parties, particularly the PSP. The Bihar SVD government was treated as a special case and was given authorization to continue provided it worked to implement speedily certain specified programs.

The inner debate in the SSP on alliance policy weakened the SVD government in Bihar. Ramanand Tiwari and Bhola Prasad Singh intensified their criticisms of each other.[54] Dissident SSP MLAs announced their disaffection with their party's continued participation in the government. Defections from the SSP and from other parties in the SVD coalition began to occur until finally Karpuri Thakur resigned in June and was replaced by an alternative coalition with Bhola Paswan Shastri as chief minister in a government dominated by Congress (R). After the resignation of the Karpuri Thakur ministry, the deputy leader of the SSP announced the withdrawal of the SSP from the SVD coalition.[55]

Thus, in the years after the formation of the SSP in 1964, the party faced constant internal strains arising from a variety of sources and issues, which led to two major splits in the party and a continuing severe innerparty struggle. The first split, arising out of the resignation of a section of the old PSP, was both an organizational and legislative party division related to issues of principle and affected by temperamental factors. The second split was a legislative split, leading to the formation of the Shoshit Dal, and related to issues of personal power and caste representation. The recent inner-party struggle divided both organizational and legislative wings of the party in the state and central leadership and related to party alliance strategy. During this entire period, the Bihar CPI has shown no evidence of serious internal division and has lost only one member of its legislative party by defection (whom the party claims it had already expelled). Moreover, the CPI has been able to decide upon alliance strategies and act upon its decisions unitedly and reliably.

The differences in the organizational stability of the two parties have been related to the various aspects of party membership, organizational focus, and party appeals discussed above. The SSP was a less stable party than the CPI because it was a bigger party, with looser membership requirements; because the structure of the organization was more decentralized within the state; because decision making in the party was diffuse and informal, involving several levels of the party organization; and because its appeals were specific and the loyalties of its members were

[54] See, for example, ibid., 1 May 1971.
[55] *Indian Recorder & Digest* 17, nos. 7 and 8 (July–August 1971), 32.

consequently contingent. The CPI, in contrast, is smaller; it has a more centralized organizational structure within the state, with power concentrated in the state executive in the hands of a unified leadership core; its decision-making processes demarcate more clearly the units with authority to act; the party organization is supreme over the legislative wing; discipline is taken seriously; and party appeals are ideological and diffuse and the loyalties of members more all-encompassing. Clearly, the organizational structure and functioning of the two parties was entirely different. It is of considerable theoretical and practical interest, therefore, to explore the consequences of these basic differences by comparing the goals set by the two parties and their abilities to achieve them with the organizational structures and styles they possessed.

Radical Party Ideologies, Programs, and Tactics in Bihar
Long-Term Goals and Immediate Programs
The long-term goals of the SSP and the CPI, as stated in their party constitutions, were practically identical. The SSP sought "the creation of a socialist society by peaceful and democratic means so that the economic, social and political exploitation of man by man and of nation by another nation is ended." [56] The CPI "sets itself the goal of establishing a socialist society in India and ending all forms of exploitation of man by man." [57] Their agreement on ultimate aims frequently led both parties to adopt similar policies on particular issues, often in alliance with each other. However, there were also basic differences between the two parties in their definitions of short-term goals and in their entire approach to political life, which as often as not led the parties in different directions.

The SSP emphasized the indigenous content of its goals and tactics, deliberately distinguishing them from the historic goals of Soviet communism and European socialism.[58] The CPI openly declares its "unswerving adherence to the universal truths and revolutionary principles of Marxism-Leninism," which require only to be "correctly and creatively" applied to "Indian conditions." [59]

SSP ultimate goals, specific policies, and current tactics were closely related. Its party ideologists insisted that the concepts of "equality, social

[56] Samyukta Socialist Party, *Constitution*, p. 3.
[57] "Constitution of Communist Party of India," p. 331.
[58] See Madhu Limaye, *Why Samyukta Socialist?* (Bombay: Popular Prakashan, [1966]), pp. 19–20. This is the clearest statement available in English of SSP ideology, strategy, tactics, and recent policies by its leading ideologist.
[59] "Constitution of Communist Party of India," p. 331.

ownership, democracy and decentralization" must be given immediate, concrete meaning[60] and that the means used to achieve these goals must be consonant with the ends. The CPI has several sets of long-term goals. At the end of the road is communism, which is so distant a goal that its content is not defined in the party constitution. Before that lies socialism, the long-term goal of the party. Before socialism, there is "the immediate task" of completing the "anti-imperialist, antifeudal, democratic revolution." [61] The present policies and tactics of the CPI relate primarily to this goal, the completion of the democratic revolution, rather than the achievement of socialism.

The SSP, unfettered by Marxist dialectics relating policies and tactics to current definitions of existing social forces and the movement of history, seemed to believe that its goals could be achieved by pursuing them unswervingly and seeking power relentlessly. SSP leaders acted in recent years on the principle that the Congress was the main obstacle to the achievement of Socialist policies and that it must be removed from power at all costs in alliance with any parties that would accept certain SSP policies, such as abolition of land revenue or removal of English. The CPI attitude toward the Congress has been more ambiguous and has reflected both international considerations and the CPI's assessment of the role played by the Congress in completing the democratic revolution. Both the cordial relations between the Soviet Union and the central Congress government and the CPI belief that there are "progressive elements" in the Congress have frequently led the CPI to support the Congress and its policies. The tactical position of the CPI is that it supports political alliances with other "left and democratic parties" and that it seeks a broad "alliance of all anti-imperialist, anti-feudal and antimonopoly forces," which may or may not sometimes include the Congress.[62]

There were differences between the two parties also in practice in their means and their general militancy. Both parties have believed that parliamentary democracy will not produce social changes unless it is leavened by mass action. Both parties, therefore, have supported a combination of parliamentary and extraparliamentary tactics, including participation in elections, civil disobedience movements, *bandhs* or general strikes, fasts, and the rest. The only difference between the two parties in this regard

[60] For the concrete meanings, see Madhu Limaye, *Why Samyukta Socialist?*, pp. 15 ff.
[61] "Constitution of Communist Party of India," p. 332.
[62] Ibid. And S. G. Sardesai, *Why Communists?* (Bombay: Popular Prakashan, [1966]), p. 4.

was the institutionalization of extraparliamentary tactics in the SSP, the belief that such tactics must be used frequently in and out of the legislatures to achieve party goals and provide meaningful mass participation in politics. In fact, militancy was written into the party constitution, which declared that the "party will organise and provide leadership to peaceful and revolutionary class struggle, mass movements and civil disobedience." [63]

To summarize the differences between the two parties with regard to goals, strategy, and tactics, it can be said that the SSP emphasized the indigenous content of its policies and tactics, whereas the CPI openly declares its adherence to an alien ideology; the SSP emphasized concrete programs clearly related to ultimate goals, whereas CPI policies depend upon its assessment of international and national forces and the movement of history at the moment; the SSP believed that the Congress was the main political obstacle to the achievement of socialist policies, whereas the CPI believes that the Congress role has been sometimes progressive and deserving of support. The differences between the two parties on current issues have been in practice less common over issues of policy and program than over which issues to emphasize at a particular moment and over which parties are appropriate alliance partners.

Parliamentary and Extraparliamentary Tactics

The SSP and CPI arrived at their recent positions in Bihar politics as serious contestants for political power after nearly two decades of Congress rule, when the attainment of power by the smaller parties must have seemed remote. For long, the smaller parties themselves seemed to act as if the struggle for power was hopeless or even as if Congress rule was preferable to the available alternatives, refusing to form alliances with each other to remove the Congress from power. However, in the years after the Third General Elections in India, between 1962 and 1967, a combination of factors arose which led the leaders of many parties to rethink their roles in Indian politics. For one thing, the seat-winning capacity of the Congress in most states had been declining to a point where it became conceivable to think of the Congress losing its majority in many states. For example, in Bihar, although the Congress popular vote percentage remained stable over the three elections, its seat-winning capacity had declined by 25 seats in each election. A further drop of 25 seats in 1967 would give the Congress only the barest majority in the

---

[63] Samyukta Socialist Party, *Constitution*, p. 3.

legislative assembly.[64] Second, growing popular discontent over food shortages and high prices among urban middle classes, students, teachers, and government employees and increasing feelings of insecurity on the part of the large Muslim minority provided opposition parties with great popular issues with which to mobilize sentiment against the ruling party. Third, many opposition leaders had grown tired of tilting at windmills and wanted power and responsibility. Some, like Ashok Mehta, joined the Congress. Others, like Dr. Lohia, decided that the time was ripe to make a serious bid for power in the states in the 1967 elections in alliance with other parties.

As a result of this combination of factors, the period between 1962 and 1967 was characterized by increasing opposition militancy, the development of new agitational tactics, and movements for alliances between parties. In Bihar in this period, the pattern for opposition militancy and joint action was set in the August 1965 agitation.[65] August is a traditional month for mass demonstrations in Bihar. In August 1965, various discontented groups had planned demonstrations for different dates— government employees on 4 and 12 August, trade unions on 5 August, students on 9 August. The two major Left parties in Bihar also planned a series of demonstrations for the month of August. The SSP took the lead, with a call for a Patna Bandh on 9 August. The CPI responded favorably, agreeing to support the *bandh* and calling for Left opposition unity. The PSP refused to join the movement, but the CPM and the Revolutionary Socialist Party (RSP) formally supported the *bandh*, though they made little contribution to it. Although the students and the party leaders, therefore, planned their demonstrations for the same day, they agreed to hold their processions and demonstrations separately. The student protest was against increased tuition fees. The party movement was held to protest against food scarcity and high prices. The student demonstration, held before the legislative assembly and secretariat building, was supported by some discontented government employees. Angered by the refusal on the part of the chief minister to come and speak to the crowd, by his delay in agreeing to receive a student delegation, and by the presence of

---

[64] The Congress won 235 out of 310 seats in the Bihar Legislative Assembly in 1952, 210 out of 312 in 1957, 185 out of 318 in 1962, and 128 out of 318 in 1967. Figures from Craig Baxter, *District Voting Trends in India: A Research Tool* (New York: Columbia University Press, 1969), p. 40.

[65] Accounts sympathetic to the August movement are T. J. S. George, *Revolt in Bihar: A Study of the August 1965 Uprising* (New Delhi: Perspective Publications, 1965) and Secretary, Samyukta Socialist Party (Bihar), *Patna tatha Rajya ke Vibhinn SthanoN meN Goli Karan ke Jimmedar Kaun? Nyayik Janch Karao* [SSP (Bihar), 9 August 1965].

mounted policemen, the crowd was prepared for a confrontation. A bloody battle erupted between police and the students and government employees and violence spread over a broader area. Police firings occurred in which the government claims no one was killed, though others say many were. The political party leaders, when they learned of the violence, diverted their procession from the area of the assembly and secretariat and held a public meeting elsewhere in the town, which passed peacefully. However, violence spread from Patna to other towns in Bihar on succeeding days in August.[66] All prominent party leaders of the SSP and the CPI were arrested during the month, police firings were reported from 23 places, and the government announced on 27 August that 3,386 people had been arrested.

Several features of the events of August 1965 deserve stressing. First, the leaders of the SSP and the CPI in Bihar did not plan the violence that occurred. However, Herbert Heidenreich has shown that, at the local level in at least one area of north Bihar, individual party members from the SSP and from the Congress did incite and encourage acts of violence. In the same area, the CPI organization and its members remained aloof from violent actions, but the local CPM organizational cadre actively planned for and worked toward a violent result.[67] Second, the events of August 1965 were produced by the simultaneous, but not necessarily co-operative, action of a variety of discontented interest groups and political parties. There was little coordination of the various protest movements and only a partial party alliance. Third, the lead in organizing the party movement of 9 August was taken by the SSP. Fourth, among the major non-Congress parties, only the CPI responded to the SSP call for a *bandh* movement. The PSP at this stage, still rebuilding itself after the split from the SSP and still holding to its line of refusing to ally with the Communist Party, refused to join the movement. Finally, despite its partial character, a precedent was set for the operation of a united front of non-Congress parties.

In the months after the August 1965 movement, the SSP and the CPI took the lead in efforts both to broaden the base of the united front and to extend the range of its activities. In these efforts, the SSP line of alliance with all non-Congress parties prevailed over the CPI preference for alliance only with "left and democratic" parties. By December 1965, a United Front had been forged among the SSP, the CPI, the Revolutionary

---

[66] For a detailed account of the development of violence in the vicinity of a north Bihar industrial township at that time, see Herbert Heidenreich, "The Anatomy of a Riot: A Case Study from Bihar 1965," *Journal of Commonwealth Political Studies* 6, no. 2 (July 1968), 107–124.

[67] Ibid., pp. 120–123.

Socialist Party, the Socialist Unity Centre, the Jharkhand Party, and the right-wing, Raja-dominated Janata Party. The United Front parties agreed in principle to coordinate their activities in the legislatures, in public agitations, and in arranging electoral adjustments to oppose the Congress in the 1967 elections. The PSP and the Jan Sangh remained aloof from the United Front and the Janata Party later withdrew, but the CPM joined the front in February 1966.[68]

In the succeeding year up through the general elections, the United Front achieved only modest successes in coordinating party activities. No joint program or policy was prepared, nor was a full-scale electoral alliance achieved. However, the parties in the front did work together in carrying on a series of *bandhs* and agitations based on protest issues— opposing the Congress government, corruption, increases in taxes, grain procurement, and rising prices. Most notable was the joint action once again on 9 August 1966, on the Bihar Bandh, which acquired considerable popular support despite the fact that the government this time moved decisively to arrest all the state leaders of the parties and to detain and extern the all-India leaders who arrived at Patna on 9 August to join the movement.[69]

In the 1967 General Elections in Bihar, partial adjustment of seats among the parties in the United Front was arranged, but there were many constituencies in which members of the front contested against each other. Thus, although agreement was reached on 247 out of 318 legislative assembly constituencies, there remained 31 constituencies in which SSP and CPI candidates clashed, 9 in which CPI and CPM candidates opposed each other, and three in which candidates of all three parties contested.[70] Moreover, the Jharkhand Party ultimately remained out of the alliance. The predominance of the SSP and the CPI in the electoral adjustment is clear from the distribution of seats. Out of 247 adjusted seats, the SSP contested in 160, the CPI in 61, the CPM in 16, the RSP in 4, and independents supported by the front in 6.[71] Despite the best efforts of the SSP to bring into alliance all parties, irrespective of ideology, the United Front was clearly a Left front.

The Radical Left and Coalition Politics in the Post-1967 Period
In the period since the landmark 1967 elections in Bihar, which ended the Congress hegemony in that state and introduced a period of coalition

[68] On the formation of the front, see *Searchlight*, 16, 17 January; 5, 11, 12, 24 February; 27 April; 7, 9, 20, 21, 30 May; 6 July 1966.
[69] *Statesman*, 10, 13, 14 August 1966; *Indian Nation*, 27, 29, 30 August 1966.
[70] *Indian Nation*, 28 January 1967.
[71] Ibid., 15 December 1966.

Table 6.16 Alliance Patterns in Bihar Politics, March 1967–March 1972

Party[a]	First SVD Ministry of Mahamaya Prasad Sinha, as on 16 Mar. 1967	Expanded SVD Ministry of Mahamaya Prasad Sinha, as on 7 Sept. 1967	Shoshit Dal Ministry of Bindeshwari Prasad Mandal[b], as on 10 Feb. 1968	Second SVD Ministry of Bhola Paswan Shastri, as on 12 May 1968	Triple Election Alliance, 1969 Midterm Election Feb. 1969	Congress-Led Coalition of Sardar Harihar Singh, as on 7 Mar. 1969	United Front Ministry of Bhola Paswan Shastri, as on 24 June 1969
Congress						X	
Congress (R)							
Congress (O)							
Jan Sangh	X	X		X			
SSP	X	X			X		
CPI	X	X		X			
PSP	X	X		X	X		
Indian Socialist Party							
LCD (Loktantric Congress Dal)				X	X		X
Shoshit Dal			X			X	X
Second Shoshit Dal		X					
JKD/BKD	X						X
Janata				X		X	
Jharkhand (Horo)		X				X	X
Hul Jharkhand							
RPI		X					
Swatantra							
Forward Bloc							X

a List of parties includes only parties that participated in one of the alliances included in the table in this period.

politics,[72] alliance patterns have gone through two phases. The first phase began with the defeat of the Congress in the 1967 elections and ended with the all-India split of the Congress at the end of 1969. It is a period marked by alliance among the major organized parties against the Congress, in which the SSP and CPI worked in coalition with both the PSP and the Jan Sangh in Bihar. The second period is one in which the differences outlined earlier between the SSP and CPI strategy and tactics were manifested in the choice of different alliance partners from among the two wings of the Congress.

Even in the first phase, coordination between the SSP and the CPI was by no means perfect. Table 6.16 reveals that the SSP and the CPI joined together, along with all other organized parties in Bihar, only in the first United Front ministry of Mahamaya Prasad Sinha. In the second United Front ministry, the CPI joined, but the SSP delayed. By the time the SSP

[72] See Brass, "Coalition Politics," pp. 1174–1191.

Table 6.16 (continued)

Party[a]	Congress (R)-Led Coalition of Daroga Prasad Rai, as on 8 June 1970	SVD Ministry of Karpuri Thakur, as on 11 Jan. 1971	Lok Sabha Electoral Alliance, Feb. 1971	Lok Sabha Electoral Alliance, Feb. 1971	PVD Ministry of Bhola Paswan Shastri, as on 2 June 1971	General Election Alliance, March 1972
Congress						
Congress (R)	X			X	X	X
Congress (O)		X	X			
Jan Sangh		X	X			
SSP		X	X			
CPI				X		X
PSP				X		X
Indian Socialist Party		X				
LCD (Loktantric Congress Dal)	X					
Shoshit Dal	X	X				
Second Shoshit Dal						
JKD/BKD	X	X				
Janata		X				
Jharkhand (Horo)	X	X		X	X	
Hul Jharkhand	X				X	
RPI						
Swatantra		X				
Forward Bloc						

b Only members of the Shoshit Dal were included in the ministry, but the government was supported by the Congress.

agreed to join the ministry, the chief minister was on the point of resigning, which he did on 25 June 1968 before the SSP ministers could join the government. In the 1969 midterm elections, the SSP joined in an electoral alliance with the PSP and the splinter Loktantrik Congress Dal, from which the CPI was excluded. The CPI and the CPM reached an electoral adjustment between themselves. Thus, although the first phase of post-1967 coalition politics was marked predominantly by cooperation among the large organized parties, including the SSP and the CPI, the tendency toward the end of the period was for the two main radical parties to ally with their nearest competitors on the Left rather than with each other.

All previous alliance patterns were altered, however, when the split in the Congress occurred. Even before the Congress split, it was clear that the SSP and the CPI preferred different alliance strategies. The CPI reverted, after the fall of the second United Front ministry in Bihar and similar failures in other states, to emphasizing the line of Left-democratic alliance. In Bihar, before the Congress split, this meant the exclusion of the Congress, the Jan Sangh, and the Janata Party. At the all-India level, it meant increasing cooperation with Mrs. Gandhi's wing of the Congress in opposition to the CPM-dominated governments in Kerala and Bengal. By May 1970, the National Council of the CPI was clear that Left and democratic unity excluded the CPM.[73] When the split in the Congress occurred, the Congress (R) in Bihar became an acceptable alliance partner for the CPI. The SSP, however, adhered to its line of all-party coalition against the Congress. Madhu Limaye dismissed the notion of either Right consolidation or Left unity as irrelevant to Indian politics.[74] What mattered in Indian politics to the SSP was the removal of the Congress from power in the center. When the split in the Congress came, this line called for alliance with Congress (O) at the center and in the states. Thus, the second phase of post-1967 coalition politics found the two major radical parties in Bihar divided and in conflict with each other both at the center and in the state. Table 6.16 shows that, in Bihar, the SSP and the CPI participated only in opposed coalitions between 1968 and 1971.

However, the CPI was more comfortable with its alliance strategy in Bihar than the SSP, which was openly divided on the issue. As noted above, former PSP leaders in the SSP were uncomfortable in an alliance with Congress (O), Jan Sangh, Swatantra, and the Janata Party, and preferred an alliance with the PSP and Congress (R) in Bihar and even at the center. The preference for alliance with the PSP prevailed within the SSP with the merger of the two parties on 9 August 1971 into a unified Socialist Party.[75] However, a rump group within the PSP maintained its separate identity and contested the 1972 elections in alliance with Congress (R) and the CPI, winning 4 seats. Most important in terms of Left unity in Bihar politics was the continued divergence in alliance strategy between the radical Socialists and the CPI. The SP fought the 1972 elections without benefit of interparty alliances and won 33 seats, a considerable decrease in seats won from 1969 and 1967, whereas the CPI won 35 seats, its best performance in any Bihar election. The Congress (R), however, benefited most from the disunity of the Left and won a majority of seats in the Bihar assembly and a return to power.

---

[73] A resolution of the party council stated that Left and democratic unity could not be built through "an unprincipled compromise with the disruptive anti-unity line of the CPI(M)"; *Indian Recorder & Digest* 16, no. 6 (June 1970), 14.

[74] Ibid., 15, no. 7 (July 1969), 10.

[75] Ibid., 17, no. 9 (September 1971), 14.

The differences in SSP and CPI alliance strategy were not related to questions of ideology or specific policies. On the major issues that arose in the first phase of post-1967 coalition politics in the Bihar United Front governments, the two parties stood together, sometimes in opposition to the Jan Sangh. In the conflict over the status of Urdu, which arose during the first United Front government, both parties favored concessions to Urdu-speakers. The two parties also worked together on the *bataidari* issue that arose later and that called for protecting the rights of share-croppers. Current alliance strategies, which have placed the two parties on opposite sides, also have no ideological or policy significance. They concern only the strategy and tactics of achieving power in a federal system of government in which calculations of party interest must take account of the balance of forces at the center, in the state, and in other states in the Indian Union.

Radical Party Performance in Bihar
The Electoral Strength of the Parties: State Patterns
Bihar has had a highly fragmented multiparty system since the First General Elections in 1952 (see table 6.1). During the first three elections, one party, the Congress, was dominant. In the 1967 and 1969 elections, the Congress lost its dominant position and no other party was able to come close to the position previously held by the Congress. In 1972, Congress dominance was just barely restored. During the six elections, twenty-one parties have achieved representation in the Bihar Legislative Assembly by winning a seat in at least one election. Those parties can be conveniently divided into five groups—the Congress and those splinter groups from the Congress that have not been associated historically with the main socialist tradition in the state; the parties of the non-Communist Left; the Communist parties; the parties of the Right and of Hindu nationalism; and the parties representing regional, caste, and other special interests.[76]

The combined strength of all the parties of the Left in Bihar has ranged from a low of 20.9 percent in 1957 to a high of 32.8 percent in 1967. Over the six elections, the balance among the different parties of the Left and between the parties of the Left and other non-Congress parties has changed significantly. Among the Left parties, the relative strength of the

---

[76] Cf. the arrangement of West Bengal political parties in Marcus F. Franda, "Electoral Politics in West Bengal: The Growth of the United Front," *Pacific Affairs* 42, no. 3 (Fall 1969), p. 282.

Communist parties has improved. Among the non-Congress parties, the Jan Sangh emerged from the 1969 midterm elections with the highest popular vote (though it placed second after the SSP in seats won), but the SSP placed second in popular vote in 1972. It is clear, therefore, that the Left parties in Bihar are operating in multiparty systems in which no single Left party can hope to achieve power alone in the foreseeable future and in which the balance of party strength between parties of the Left and parties of the Center and Right is unstable. The immediate organizational issue for the two main radical parties is not, therefore, when and how they will achieve power alone or in combination long enough to introduce socialism or socialist policies in Bihar, but whether or not they can maintain a significant position of strength in state politics for the indefinite future.

How well institutionalized are the two radical parties in Bihar in general and in comparison with each other? Table 6.17 compares the SSP, the SP, and the CPI electoral performance in Bihar on several measures. On all measures, the SSP was the stronger of the two parties in Bihar, but SP predominance in relation to the CPI in 1972 is not so clear. Although the SSP both in 1967 and 1969 polled a higher percentage of popular votes and a much larger percentage of seats than the CPI, the CPI popular vote percentage increased steadily over the first five elections,

Table 6.17   Comparison of Electoral Performance of the SSP and the CPI in Bihar Legislative Assembly Elections, 1952–1972

Political Party	Votes Polled %	Seats Won No.	Seats Won %	Seats Contested No.	Seats Contested %	Seats Won to Seats Contested %	Deposits Lost to Seats Contested No.	Deposits Lost to Seats Contested %	Party Realism Index[a]
SSP and SP									
1967	17.6	68	21.38	199	62.58	34.2	89	44.7	−10.5
1969	13.7	52	16.35	191	60.06	27.2	87	45.6	−18.4
1972	16.1	33	10.38	255	80.12	12.9	N.A.	N.A.	N.A.
CPI									
1952	1.1	0	0.00	22	6.92	0.0	15	68.3	−68.3
1957	4.9	7	2.20	60	18.87	11.7	22	36.7	−25.0
1962	6.2	12	3.77	84	26.42	14.3	38	45.2	−30.9
1967	6.9	24	7.55	98	30.82	24.5	47	47.9	−23.4
1969	10.1	25	7.86	163	51.26	15.3	92	56.5	−41.2
1972	7.0	35	11.01	56	17.61	62.5	N.A.	N.A.	N.A.

Sources: 1952 to 1969 figures compiled from Craig Baxter, *District Voting Trends in India: A Research Tool* (New York: Columbia University Press, 1969), pp. 40–41; 1972 figures are preliminary from an American Embassy handout, "State Assembly Elections—1972 Final Party Position, Seats & Popular Votes (Prelim.), All-India & By State," mimeographed, 1972.
a Calculated by subtracting the smaller figure from the larger in the preceding two columns. The minus sign indicates that the percentage of deposits lost was greater than the percentage of seats won.
   The use of the term, "party realism index," poses some problems since a party may choose deliberately to contest a larger number of seats than it can hope to do well in for perfectly rational reasons, e.g., to test future prospects or to lay the groundwork for the future or even to draw support away from other parties rather than to win the seats. However, a party which did this often or did it even once and achieved an index of − 100.0 or close to it would not, in my view, be behaving realistically. Consequently, although the term does not describe perfectly what the index in fact measures, it comes closer than any other term I can think of.

while the position of the SSP declined between 1967 and 1969. Moreover, the gap in the popular vote percentage of the two parties narrowed to only 3.6 percent in 1969, although the SSP still won twice as many seats. In 1972, however, the gap in the popular vote percentages favored the SP over the CPI by 9.1 percent; but the CPI, benefiting from its alliance with Congress (R), won more seats than the SP. Figures on popular vote and seats won can be misleading, however. Any party that contests a large number of seats will win a certain percentage of votes. If the party has any organizational, financial, and membership resources at all, it is bound also to win a few seats. More important in comparing the performance and growth potential of parties are the figures on proportion of seats won to seats contested and the balance between the proportion of seats won and those lost by a wide margin. A part of the difference between the SSP and the CPI was simply that the SSP contested more seats than the CPI. However, it should also be noted that the CPI in 1969 overextended itself more than the SSP. That is, while the CPI showed a secular increase over five elections in percentage of votes polled, percentage of seats won, and percentage of seats contested, its percentage of seats won to seats contested declined between 1967 and 1969. Moreover, its peak success (up until 1969) of 24.5 percent of seats won to seats contested was lower than that for the SSP in both 1967 and 1969. In 1972, again, the positions of the SP and the CPI were reversed. This time, it was the SP which overextended itself, contesting 80 percent of the total seats and winning only 10 percent of the total and only 13 percent of the seats it contested. In contrast, the CPI contested only 18 percent of the total seats and won 11 percent of the total and 62.5 percent of the seats it contested.

Another indication of organizational overextension is the proportion of lost deposits to seats contested. That figure for the CPI increased in every election from 1957 through 1969, though the party position in this respect was somewhat better in 1969 than it was in 1952. Still, in well above half the seats the CPI contested in 1969, it was not a serious contender. Its proportion of lost deposits was also higher than that of the SSP both in 1967 and 1969.

The two measures of seats won and deposits lost to seats contested can be combined in a single measure of "party realism" [77] by subtracting one

[77] The index of "party realism" is a rough measure designed to assess the ability of a political party to judge its capacity to perform creditably in contested constituencies. A totally unrealistic party—and there are some—would lose its deposits in all seats contested and score — 100.0 in party realism. The Congress and well-institutionalized regional parties sometimes score as high as + 65.0 or more by winning a high proportion of seats contested and losing few or no deposits.

from the other. A party that wins more seats than it loses deposits is assigned a positive index, one which loses more deposits than it wins seats a negative index. By this measure, the weakness of both radical parties in Bihar becomes clear. Except for the CPI in 1972, in every other election in Bihar, both parties have lost more security deposits than they have won seats. Until 1972, the CPI overextended itself more than the SSP, but that situation was reversed as between the SP and CPI in the most recent election. It can be said with confidence, therefore, that neither the SSP nor the CPI in Bihar has the organizational potential in the foreseeable future, if past performance is a guide, to achieve power alone. More than that, the growth potential of both parties appears to be limited. It is possible that both parties have reached their peak achievement on the basis of their own resources. Any significant improvement in their state performance in the immediate future could come only through more extensive interparty alliances, mergers, or defections from one party to another.

The Electoral Strength of the Parties: District Patterns

An examination of the distribution of SSP and CPI popular vote percentages by district in 1967 and 1969 shows that the performance of the radical parties varies regionally, but it does not alter the preceding conclusions significantly. The district distributions in table 6.18 reveal a very great range in popular vote percentages for both parties from district to district but one that is much greater for the SSP than for the CPI. The range for the SSP was from 0.6 percent in Santal Parganas to 34.9 percent in Saharsa in 1967 and from 0.8 percent in Singhbum to 30.8 percent in Saharsa in 1969; that for the CPI was from 0.0 percent in Palamau to 20.3 percent in Bhagalpur in 1967, with a similar range in the same districts in 1969. The district distribution of votes also shows considerable fluctuation in some districts from one election to another, especially in the case of the SSP. The range in the case of the SSP covers 19.7 percentage points from a drop of 14.6 in Monghyr to an increase of 5.1 percentage points in Palamau. The CPI swing covers a smaller range of only 9.5 percentage points from a drop of 1.6 in Champaran to an increase of 7.9 percentage points in Monghyr.

Although the fluctuations in the case of the SSP were large, the direction of change for both radical parties between 1967 and 1969 was fairly uniform. The SSP popular vote declined in 12 out of 17 districts, whereas the CPI vote increased in 15 out of 17 districts. Moreover, there has been some consistency in the distribution of the main areas of strength of the two parties over time. SSP strength, though reduced in 1969, was

Table 6.18   Comparison of Valid Votes Polled (in Percentages) by the SSP and the CPI in Bihar Legislative Assembly Elections by District, 1967 and 1969

District	1967		1969		SSP Swing	CPI Swing
	SSP	CPI	SSP	CPI		
1. Patna	9.4	4.8	9.1	11.9	−0.3	+7.1
2. Gaya	15.4	9.3	12.0	14.0	−3.4	+4.7
3. Shahabad	24.6	4.2	14.8	9.3	−9.8	+5.1
4. Muzaffarpur	23.2	3.6	20.0	3.2	−3.2	−0.4
5. Saran	19.4	5.9	13.2	6.2	−6.2	+0.3
6. Champaran	6.5	12.2	5.3	10.6	−1.2	−1.6
7. Darbhanga	26.6	11.1	21.9	14.4	−4.7	+3.3
8. Bhagalpur	7.9	20.3	7.5	22.3	−0.4	+2.0
9. Monghyr	33.3	7.5	18.7	15.4	−14.6	+7.9
10. Purnea	7.9	2.3	6.5	6.4	−1.4	+4.1
11. Santal Parganas	0.6	8.1	4.5	10.0	+3.9	+1.9
12. Saharsa	34.9	3.3	30.8	4.5	−4.1	+1.2
13. Ranchi	1.1	1.5	1.5	3.0	+0.4	+1.5
14. Hazaribagh	6.9	5.7	8.8	10.4	+1.9	+4.7
15. Palamau	20.8	0.0	25.9	0.4	+5.1	+0.4
16. Singhbum	5.9	8.1	0.8	12.1	−5.1	+4.0
17. Dhanbad	3.1	7.9	5.7	9.1	+2.6	+1.2
Bihar	17.6	6.9	13.7	10.1	−3.9	+3.2

Source: Compiled from Baxter, *District Voting Trends in India*, pp. 42–62.

concentrated in the same districts as in 1967. For the CPI, 7 of its 9 highest-support districts in 1967 were among its 9 highest-support districts in 1969 also. In fact, there has been a fairly high degree of consistency in the distribution of CPI strength since 1952, despite the intervening split in the party. Figure 6.4 shows the distribution of the 9 highest CPI support districts over the five elections. There have been six districts that have been in that category in all five elections—Champaran, Darbhanga, Monghyr, Bhagalpur, and Singhbum; one, Gaya, that has been in the top nine four times; and, two—Santal Parganas and Dhanbad—that have been in the top nine three times.

The distribution of SSP and CPI high support districts reveals two important patterns. First, in contrast to the previous findings of similarity in the geographical distribution of party leadership and membership, there was some difference in the geographical distribution of electoral support for the two radical parties. SSP popular support was concentrated in

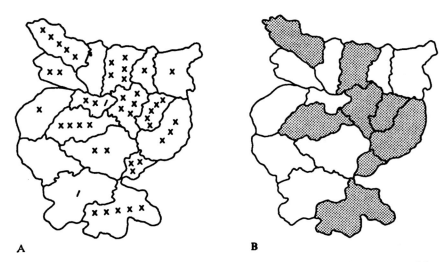

A   B

Figure 6.4   Distribution of the top nine support districts for the CPI, measured by percentage of valid votes polled, in the 1952, 1957, 1962, 1967, and 1969 elections for the Bihar Legislative Assembly. (Map A shows the distribution over the five elections. Map B identifies those districts that have been in the top nine at least three times. In map A, an ✕ indicates placement of a district in the top nine one time; a slash [/] indicates that two districts had identical CPI vote percentages in ninth position.)

the north and south Bihar districts and Palamau. The CPI has had strength in the north Bihar districts of Champaran and Darbhanga, but its main concentration of strength has been in south Bihar and Chota Nagpur (figure 6.5). In other words, the CPI has had greater success than the SSP in acquiring support in the southeastern tribal-industrial belt of Bihar state (compare figures 6.3 and 6.5). The second pattern of importance is that there is a stronger association between areas of high party membership and high popular vote for the CPI than there is for the SSP. The correlation coefficient for percentage of CPI membership in 1966 (table 6.14) with percentage of CPI electoral support in 1967 (table 6.18) by district is 0.79, whereas the correlation for the SSP between membership and electoral support in the same years is 0.59. Converting these figures into r^2 underlines the significance of the differences. In statistical terms, the distribution of CPI membership accounted for 62 percent of the variation in the CPI popular vote whereas the distribution of SSP membership accounted for only 35 percent of the variation in the SSP popular vote in the 1967 General Elections in Bihar. By this measure, then, in contrast to the "party realism index" based on electoral performance alone, the CPI appears as the stronger of the two parties in the sense that its electoral support is based more upon actual organizational strength and ought,

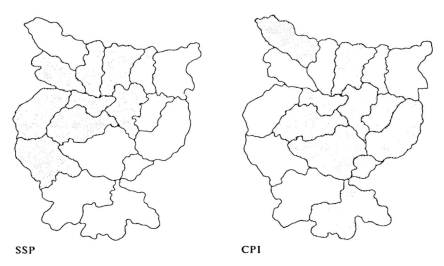

SSP   CPI

Figure 6.5   Districts with highest average SSP and CPI votes in the Bihar Legislative Assembly elections, 1967 and 1969.

therefore, to be less likely to be subject to a sudden negative fluctuation.

Other differences between the SSP and the CPI appear through a comparison of rural-urban vote distributions and through correlation analysis of selected socioeconomic variables for the 1967 election. There were only nine primarily urban constituencies in the 1967 elections in the major Bihar cities of Patna, Jamshedpur, Dhanbad, Gaya, Monghyr, Bhagalpur, and Ranchi. The SSP contested only three of these seats and polled only 1.1 percent of the total city vote compared to its poll of 18.2 percent in noncity constituencies. The CPI contested five city seats and did better in these seats than in its noncity constituencies. The party polled 12.8 percent of the total city vote compared to 6.8 percent of the total vote in the rest of the state.[78] The correlations in table 6.19 also show a difference between the SSP and the CPI in their strength in urbanized districts. Neither party showed a significant correlation with urbanization, but the SSP correlation was more strongly negative than that of the CPI.

The correlations in table 6.19 also suggest a different rural support base for the two parties. Existing literature on the Communist parties, previous correlation analyses, and personal interviews have indicated that they have sought strength both among the peasantry and among landless

[78] Figures on city and noncity voting come from Government of India, Ministry of Information and Broadcasting, *Fourth General Elections: An Analysis* (New Delhi: Registrar General, 1967), p. 137.

Table 6.19 Correlation Matrix of Socioeconomic Variables and Radical Party Votes (by District), Bihar Legislative Assembly Elections, 1967

Variables	SSP	CPI
1. Per capita income	−0.41	0.04
2. Literacy	−0.24	−0.11
3. Urbanization	−0.44	−0.00
4. Scheduled castes and tribes	−0.41	−0.01
5. Religious minority	−0.49[a]	−0.12
6. Cultivators	−0.41	0.10
7. Agricultural laborers	0.45	−0.07
8. Turnout	0.73[b]	0.16
9. Contestants per seat	−0.46	−0.04

Source: Provided by the courtesy of Professor W. H. Morris-Jones and B. Das Gupta.
[a] Significant at the .05 level.
[b] Significant at the .001 level.

laborers.[79] The SSP has also made broad appeals in the countryside to both "backward" agricultural castes and to the landless. The CPI strategy has been to seek support among the peasantry primarily, and it has had some success in peasant-dominated areas.[80] The matrix in table 6.19 does not show any statistically significant correlations for either party with cultivators or agricultural laborers, but it does suggest that there are differences between the two parties in their areas of support. The CPI did better than the SSP in areas where cultivators predominate, whereas the SSP did better than the CPI where there are larger numbers of agricultural laborers. The sense that the SSP has done better than the CPI in the poorer areas of Bihar is also reinforced by the difference between the two parties in their correlations with per capita income.

In its 1967 election manifesto, the CPI practically adopted in a paraphrased form the *People's Manifesto* of the Muslim interest organization, the Majlis-e-Mushawarat, and identified itself with every grievance of the Muslims in India.[81] The CPI has also made explicit appeals in the past to

[79] James Bjorkman and Elizabeth Kodama, "Chasing a Chimera or Perspectives on the Indian Communist Movement: A Jaded View," unpublished seminar paper done at Yale University in August 1968, pp. 35–46; Donald S. Zagoria, "The Ecology of Peasant Communism in India," *American Political Science Review* 65, no. 1 (March 1971), 1144–1160; *Economic and Political Weekly* 5, no. 34 (22 August, 1970), 1410; taped interview in Darbhanga on 23 January 1969, reference to p. 5 of interview document; taped interview in Patna on 17 February 1969, reference to p. 8 of interview document.
[80] Bjorkman and Kodama, "Chasing a Chimera," pp. 35–46.
[81] See R. Chandidas et. al., eds., *India Votes: A Source Book on Indian Elections* (New York: Humanities Press, 1968), pp. 51 and 116–120.

the Bihar adivasis.[82] Unfortunately, the correlations in table 6.19 do not distinguish between scheduled castes and scheduled tribes or between Muslims and other religious minorities. Moreover, the correlations for both radical parties are negative with both scheduled castes and tribes and percentage of religious minority in each district, although less strongly so for the CPI than the SSP. An assessment of the relative strength of the two parties in areas where various minority caste, religious, and language groups in Bihar are concentrated cannot be made until more data are available.[83]

The strongest correlation in table 6.19 is that for turnout for the SSP. The correlation for the SSP of .73 with turnout is higher than that reported for any other party in Bihar in 1967. This relationship, therefore, provides support for the hypothesis with which this chapter began that the SSP has been a party of mobilization in Bihar which, by its militancy and agitational tactics and by its appeal to caste and language sentiment, encouraged popular participation in voting. Moreover, the difference between the SSP and the CPI in this respect is greater than on any other variable in the matrix.

The available evidence on the distribution of SSP and CPI support by district indicates that both parties have had regional concentrations of strength and that there have been differences between the two parties in their areas of strength. The existence of consistent bases of support for the two parties means that both parties have been institutionalized forces in the politics of Bihar, but nothing in the district patterns suggests that their potential for growth in the immediate future is great. Both the SP and the CPI in the foreseeable future are likely to be no more than powerful contributors to the interparty coalitions that may be necessary for effective government in Bihar's multiparty system. Increases in their effectiveness will depend more on their ability to ally with each other and with other parties than on their ability to build new support.

The Performance of the Radical Parties in Government

In principle, one ought to be able to compare the performance of the two radical parties in office in terms of the abilities of their ministers, their success in implementing party policies, and their ability to provide effective support in the legislature from their own party members for the main-

---

[82] See especially Tarun Dutt, "The Problem of Bihar Tribals," *New Age* (monthly) 9, no. 6 (June 1960), 30–37.
[83] Data on minority language, religious, caste, and tribal groups in Bihar will be correlated with party votes at the census subdivision level in my computer project in progress.

tenance of the government. Since the first United Front government lasted only ten months, judgment on the first two aspects of party performance can only be highly qualified and somewhat impressionistic.

The SSP had six cabinet ministers and two ministers of state in the first United Front government. SSP members interviewed in 1969 singled out three ministers as having been particularly "good" ministers—Karpuri Thakur, who was the deputy chief minister and in control of education and finance; Ramanand Tiwari, the police minister; and Kapildeo Singh, minister for food supplies. Party men who commented on Karpuri Thakur's performance as a minister found it difficult to separate their estimate of his personal character and symbolic importance from his specific acts. One prominent SSP man saw Karpuri Thakur primarily as a symbol of "the common man, peasant, worker, simple man" who had risen to high office and from whom much was expected.[84] Another mentioned specifically his efforts to reform university education, particularly the examination system and casteism in the universities, and to encourage university teaching through the medium of the regional language.[85] Others spoke only of his honesty and ability to make decisions quickly. Ramanand Tiwari also had symbolic importance as a minister. He was seen as a formally uneducated man and a former police constable who had risen to become police minister. He was praised for his efforts to reform an outdated police code; for his efforts to check corruption, which included the suspension or retirement of 35 or 40 high police officers; and for his prompt personal action during the communal riot in Ranchi in August 1967.[86] Kapildeo Singh was seen as a courageous man who took over the portfolio of food supplies at a time of terrible food scarcity and who did his job well, preventing starvation deaths.[87] Such assessments, of course, are highly subjective and were not necessarily shared by non-SSP members, who sometimes gave entirely opposite evaluations of the performance of the SSP ministers. They are valuable, however, because they reveal something of the image that the SSP had of itself and its leaders. SSP men have had a populist image of their party and their leaders, whom they see as common men who have risen to high office to express the aspirations of the people and to protect them against hardship.

[84] Taped interview in Patna on 13 January 1969; citation from p. 5 of interview document.
[85] Taped interview in Patna on 13 February 1969; reference to p. 11 of interview document.
[86] Ibid., p. 12.
[87] Ibid., p. 11.

The CPI had two cabinet ministers and one minister of state in the United Front government. Most CPI men interviewed on the subject of ministerial performance singled out Indradip Sinha, the revenue minister, as having done an outstanding job. His personal style as a minister was quite different from that of most SSP ministers. He was seen by his party men as nondemonstrative, mild-mannered, and practical. He was praised especially for initiating measures of agrarian reform to protect the rights of sharecroppers and for his work in setting up consultative committees of nonofficials to work with the administrative officers at block, district, and state level to fight the famine.[88]

A somewhat less impressionistic judgment of the performance of the radical parties in office can be made by examining the success of the United Front government in implementing policies particularly associated with the SSP and the CPI. The United Front came to power in March 1967, with a 33-point program that it was pledged to implement. Many of these points were either highly specific or easily implemented—for example, withdrawal of the grain levy order, establishment of judicial enquiries into previous police firings, release of political prisoners, and the like. Others were in the category of vague promises—to provide famine relief, to give special help to students, to complete irrigation projects quickly, and the like. Most of the highly specific points were implemented, and much energy was devoted to famine relief. But, the SSP and the CPI had more fundamental policies that they wanted to implement to make an impact on the people. Three were particularly important in the first United Front government—abolition of land revenue, replacement of English by Hindi for official use in the Bihar government, and securing *bataidari* (sharecroppers') rights.

SSP strategy in the Bihar United Front government was, characteristically, very much influenced by pressure from the central leadership of the party. The official party strategy was that the SSP must justify its participation in any United Front government by implementing within six months "one or two basic policies," which would demonstrate "that it is the people's government as against the capitalist dominated, feudalistic, rich people's government of the Congress."[89] In an article highly critical of the Bihar SSP's performance published in *Mankind*, the chief party

[88] Taped interview in Patna on 13 January 1969, reference to pp. 11–12 of interview document.
[89] Kashinath Mishra, "The Programme of Non-Congress Coalition Government and SSP Election Manifesto," *Mankind* 11, no. 3 (May 1967), 23.

organ, in May 1967, Kashinath Mishra dismissed the entire 33-point program of the Bihar United Front as insubstantial, with the exception of the
proposal to abolish land revenue, which had not yet been done.[90] By July,
however, Dr. Lohia himself declared his satisfaction with the Bihar SSP,
which had by then committed the United Front government to abolition of
land revenue, steady elimination of English from public use, suspension of
a vagrancy law that had been allegedly misused by the Congress governments, and the exposure of a major corruption scandal involving the allot-
ment of house plots in Patna.[91] On these matters, it can be said that the
SSP did succeed in dramatizing, and identifying itself with, several important public issues and took decisions on them that were implemented,
at least during the period when the party was in power.

For its part, the CPI chose one dramatic issue during the United Front
government, enforcing and protecting the rights of the *bataidars* or sharecroppers, especially in the northeastern part of the state, where there
remain some big estates. It was the stated purpose of the CPI to ensure
that, according to existing law, the *bataidars* who had been occupying
their lands for three years or longer were given the statutory occupancy
rights due to them.[92] The Jan Sangh and other parties of the Right opposed the CPI on this issue, but, since the law was already on the books,
the CPI revenue minister could act to enforce it without the approval of
other parties. The SSP supported the CPI on this issue, but a prominent
SSP leader has argued that the *bataidari* drive in the United Front government actually worked to the disadvantage of the *bataidars*, who were
evicted in large numbers from their lands by landlords who anticipated
government attempts to enforce the rights of the *bataidars*.[93]

If it is difficult to judge the performance of the two radical parties in
office in Bihar, it is at least clear that both parties identified themselves
with dramatic issues that they pushed vigorously. The most dramatic
issues chosen by the two parties—abolition of land revenue and enforcement of *bataidari* rights—were both rural issues that would identify the
parties with the interests of poor cultivators. If nothing else was accom-
plished, the two radical parties succeeded in focusing the attention of
politicians, administrators, and the press on the need for reform of both
land revenue and land tenure arrangements in the Bihar countryside.

[90] Ibid., p. 24.
[91] Taped interview with Dr. Rammanohar Lohia in New Delhi on 31 July 1967;
citation from p. 1 of interview document.
[92] Taped interview in Patna on 13 January 1969; reference to pp. 10 and 12 of interview document.
[93] Taped interview in Patna on 19 February 1969; reference to p. 19 of interview
document.

Finally, it is possible to compare the performance of the SSP and the CPI directly with regard to their ability to maintain the inner-party cohesion necessary to provide support for government. On this point, the evidence is clear and has been discussed sufficiently above. The first United Front government fell because of defections from the SSP. The CPI maintained cohesion in its legislative party throughout.

The Radical Parties, Revolutionary Violence, and Agrarian Agitation in Bihar

Since the rise of the Naxalbari agitation in the spring and summer of 1967 and the spread of terrorist violence to other parts of India thereafter, the nonviolent and parliamentary-oriented radical parties have had to respond to the revolutionary activities of the extreme Left as well as to the electoral challenges of the parties of the Center and Right. In Bihar, Naxalite revolutionary activities have been limited to a few pockets in scattered areas of the state and to isolated acts of terrorism in a number of places. Naxalite activity was first reported in Bihar in July 1967 in an area called Thakurganj in Purnea District, which borders on the Naxalbari subdivision of West Bengal.[94] Like the Naxalbari area itself, Thakurganj contains a large tribal population. It is also an area where there has been conflict between big cultivators and their *bataidars*, especially on Marwari-owned jute-growing lands. Now and again, there have been reports of widespread Naxalite activity in this area, but the only major incident reported in the press between July 1967 and September 1970 was an alleged forcible occupation of 200 acres of land of the Thirani estate by some 500 persons in June 1969.

Another area of Bihar from which alleged Naxalite activity was reported is in the northwest corner of the state on the Uttar Pradesh–Nepal border.[95] In January 1968, it was reported that part of the Madanpur forest area in Bettiah subdivision of Champaran District had been cleared by a mob of 10,000 persons led by Communist activists. The activity had allegedly been going on for months before it was first noted in the press. A police firing was reported at the end of January in which one person was killed and three or four persons were injured. The general secretary of the CPM wrote a letter to the *Searchlight* in which he contradicted the press reports concerning unauthorized seizures of land in this area, but

---

[94] On Naxalite activities in Thakurganj, see the *Indian Nation*, 1 and 6 July 1967 and the *Searchlight*, 16 August 1967; 1 and 2 June and 9 July 1969; and 25 September 1970.

[95] This account of alleged Naxalite activities in the Madanpur forest area is derived from *Searchlight*, 20, 21, and 31 January and 1, 6, 8, and 14 February 1968.

the paper continued to consider the reports as authentic. It was reported on 14 February that 185 people had been arrested in these incidents, and that a press party that had visited the area had seen 150 newly erected but deserted huts.

A third area of reported Naxalite activity has been in the Surajgarh Police Station of Monghyr District.[96] Cases of loot, dacoity, and murder were reported from this area in November 1969 and were attributed to Naxalites "in association with hardened criminals." A number of arrests of alleged Naxalites were made at that time, but the "Naxalite menace" was reportedly developing again in this area in January 1970 when the situation was considered sufficiently serious by the authorities to establish a special police squad to deal with it. Shortly thereafter, some 42 persons were arrested, including one Kailash Mahton, who told police that an important Naxalite leader of Bihar had visited the area the year before and organized them for the purpose of murdering rich farmers and opposing mechanized farming.

A fourth major scene involving a confrontation between police and terrorist revolutionaries took place in the jungles of Singhbum District in the southeast corner of the state.[97] In this case, police chased a group of 54 persons through the jungle and captured all of them, including a British woman who was said to be a former member of the British Communist Party! Of the 54 arrested, 36 were said to be a gang of robbers, but a dozen were characterized as "hard core exponents of the cult of Naxalism," mostly young Bengali students from Calcutta. One of the arrested Bengalis reportedly told police that the group had wanted to establish a revolutionary base in Singhbum comparable to Srikakulam District in Andhra. He also said that, although group members did not belong formally to the CPML, they supported the party and its leader, Charu Majumdar.

The only other place in Bihar where sustained and major incidents have been reported is from the Musahari area of Muzaffarpur District.[98] This area acquired notoriety in June 1970, when certain Sarvodaya workers received written threats on their lives, allegedly from Naxalite terrorists. In response to this threat, Jayaprakash Narayan, the Sarvodaya leader,

[96] The Surajgarh incidents were reported in *ibid.*, 21, 22, and 26 November 1969 and 2 February 1970 and in the *Indian Nation*, 14 and 20 January and 2, 6, and 13 February 1970.
[97] See *Indian Nation*, 28, 30, and 31 May and 5 June 1970 and *Searchlight*, 6 June 1970.
[98] *Searchlight*, 3, 7, 10, and 21 June and 1 August 1970; *Indian Nation*, 5 and 12 June and 4 August 1970.

went to the area himself and took up his customary work of persuading landlords to distribute a portion of their lands voluntarily. While he was in the area, a rich farmer was killed. Later, in August, a Jan Sangh leader was also killed. Both incidents were attributed in the press to Naxalites. Moreover, the secretary of the Bihar CPML, Satyanarain Singh, issued a statement in which he described the incidents in Musahari as part of "a revolutionary people's war to achieve liberation from the oppressive rule of big landlords and bureaucrat capitalists." [99]

In addition to these five pockets from which either large-scale or prolonged incidents have been reported, there have been reports in the press from time to time of various activities attributed to Naxalite terrorists. There have been reports of a police firing and other incidents from the coal-mining and industrial area of Dhanbad;[100] crop lootings and unauthorized cultivation of lands in Muzaffarpur and Darbhanga districts;[101] bombings and attacks on educational institutions and other places in Muzaffarpur, Patna, and Jamshedpur;[102] an attempted assassination of the Bengal Communist leader, Jyoti Basu, at the Patna railway station;[103] and numerous other incidents, many only dubiously attributable to revolutionary activists.

For a time, the police authorities and state ministers did not attribute much significance to the alleged Naxalite actions.[104] Police officials said they did not consider the Naxalite movement as cause for concern, a state minister denied that incidents attributed in the press to Naxalites were actually committed by Naxalites, and the CPM general secretary argued that the police were using the "Naxalite bogey" as an excuse for unwarranted police actions. During 1970, a somewhat more serious view was being taken of Naxalite activities. In January, the state government announced that it estimated that there were some 900 Naxalites in Bihar, but that they were not established "in an organised way in any particular area." [105] However, it was acknowledged that there had been an increase in the incidence of agrarian violence in 1969 compared to 1968. It was reported that there had been "46 serious agrarian incidents" in 1969 compared to 21 in 1968 and that 20 people had been killed and 80 injured "in

[99] *Searchlight*, 21 June 1970.
[100] *Indian Nation*, 13, 17, and 27 July 1967 and *Searchlight*, 8 August 1968.
[101] *Indian Nation*, 6 April, 7 July, and 18 November 1969.
[102] *Searchlight*, 13 and 17 May, and 7 August 1970; *Indian Nation*, 17 November 1970.
[103] *Indian Nation*, 1 April 1970.
[104] See the *Searchlight*, 29 April, 10 June, and 11 November 1969 and the *Indian Nation*, 29 September, 9 October, and 21 December 1969.
[105] *Indian Nation*, 19 January 1970.

armed clashes" associated with these incidents in 1969 compared to 17 killed and 83 injured in 1968.[106] In May, it was reported that there were pockets of Naxalite activity in 12 out of the 17 Bihar districts and that 500 Naxalites had been arrested.[107] In October, Congress (R) Chief Minister Daroga Prasad Rai announced that "pockets of Naxalites existed at present mostly in the districts of Darbhanga, Monghyr, Muzaffarpur, Champaran, Purnea, and Singhbum" and that 826 Naxalites were in custody.[108] He claimed, however, that there was "no public support for the movement," that Naxalite "activities had been contained if not 'eradicated,'" and that such activities had anyway been "confined to the adventurism of some misguided youths" and to "criminals in the guise of extremists."[109] At the same time, the chief minister announced that, on the suggestion of the central government, a special deputy inspector general of police had been appointed to handle operations against Naxalites in Bihar.[110] In November, the chief minister said that 30 murders had been committed by Naxalites in Bihar from January to 30 October 1970; that Monghyr, Muzaffarpur, Darbhanga, and Singhbum continued to be the most affected areas; and that the Muzaffarpur group was being led by the famous Bengali Naxalite leader Kanu Sanyal.[111] In December, the central minister of state for home admitted in the Lok Sabha that Naxalite activities in Bihar had been increasing.[112] In June 1971, the Bihar home minister, Ramanand Tiwari at the time, announced that Naxalite murders in 1970 totaled 38 and that 24 people had already been killed in 1971. He also announced that 1,422 alleged Naxalites had been arrested between September 1969 and April 1971.[113]

From the press accounts of alleged Naxalite activities and the statements of the authorities in Bihar, the following general picture of the extent and character of revolutionary violence in Bihar emerges. Revolutionary violence in Bihar has been increasing, but it has been largely sporadic and has involved isolated acts of terrorism for the most part. There have been a few areas of Bihar in which there have been major clashes and prolonged situations of conflict, and there are certain districts in north Bihar and in the southeastern industrial belt where most of the

[106] Ibid., 19 January and 5 February 1970.
[107] Ibid., 11 May 1970.
[108] Ibid., 10 October 1970.
[109] *Searchlight*, 25 October 1970.
[110] *Indian Nation*, 25 October 1970.
[111] Ibid., 18 November 1970.
[112] Ibid., 17 December 1970.
[113] *Indian Recorder & Digest* 17, no. 6 (June 1971), 23.

incidents have occurred. However, there does not appear to be any stable revolutionary support base in the Bihar countryside. The press reports that refer to captured Naxalites suggest that most are young men and that many are from Bengal. There is an organization of the CPML in Bihar, whose general secretary is Satyanarain Singh. Virtually nothing is known about the Bihar CPML leadership and ideology. A press report concerning the CPML in December 1970 suggested that the Bihar party was opposed to Charu Majumdar, the Bengal CPML leader, on three points of ideology; namely, the Bihar CPML opposed the murder of rich peasants and favored such action only against landlords, it opposed guerrilla action in the cities, and it opposed self-sacrifice in revolutionary action and favored self-defense.[114]

The spread of Naxalite activities to Bihar since 1967 placed the established radical parties, particularly the SSP and the CPI, under some pressure to steal the revolutionary thunder from the Naxalite terrorists on the problems of land distribution. Opportunities for agrarian agitation exist particularly in north Bihar, where a number of very big estates have continued to survive either by exploitation of legal loopholes or by deliberate defiance of the major land reform measures passed in the state since Independence. The CPI-led *bataidari* movement was the first major effort by a radical Left party in Bihar to take steps to rectify this situation. The SSP was the next radical party in Bihar to make use of this situation to launch a nonviolent movement, well within traditional Gandhian techniques, involving the occupation and ploughing (by landless persons under the leadership of SSP workers) of the soil of lands held by large landlords and big estates and of fallow lands held by the state government itself.

The SSP movement was launched on 9 August 1969 in the north Bihar districts of Purnea, Saharsa, and Champaran in the form of conventional demonstrations before government offices. The land occupation aspect of the movement did not take place until October. By then, the PSP and the CPI had also made plans for similar agitations. The SSP spearheaded the agitation in Champaran district, focusing on fallow lands held by the government and by the Bettiah Raj estate, which under laws passed in 1950 (Bihar Land Reforms Act) and in 1955 (Bihar Emergency Cultivation and Irrigation Act) should have been distributed to landless and poor peasants.[115] The CPI expressed its support for the SSP-led agitation, but

---

[114] *Searchlight*, 26 December 1970.
[115] See the reports in the *Indian Nation*, 2, 6, and 7 October 1969, and the *Searchlight*, 22 October 1969.

the Left parties carried on their movements separately.[116] That the movement in Champaran District was primarily an SSP movement is revealed by the arrest figures in connection with the agitation; these were released on 12 October 1969 and showed that 287 persons had been arrested, 244 of them in the SSP agitation, 21 in the CPI agitation, and 22 in the CPM-led agitation.[117] The land movement in Champaran was not only non-violent but it was reported to have the sympathy of state and district officers. (At this time, Bihar was under administrative rule.) In fact, the movement was brought to a close at the end of October with assurances from the adviser to the governor and from the district magistrate of Champaran District that the government fallow lands in the district would be distributed among the landless and scheduled castes within two months.[118]

A second, much larger, and more competitive land occupation movement was launched in the summer of 1970 at a time when a coalition government was in power in the state, led by a Congress (R) chief minister, which the CPI supported, but the SSP did not. The CPI took the lead in the land movement this time, by occupying government waste lands from 1 July 1970, and privately held lands from 9 August. Not only was the CPI not deterred from its agitation by its support for the government, but it received the blessing of the Congress chief minister.[119] Moreover, the CPI leadership made it clear that the movement was not intended to disrupt law and order but was meant to speed up the implementation of land reform laws that already existed.[120] The SSP also announced its intention to launch its own "land to the landless" movement from 9 August.

Despite the announced desire of all participants to keep the land movement nonviolent, a violent confrontation occurred on 19 July during a CPI-led agitation in Champaran District in which two persons were killed during a police firing.[121] Several other violent clashes were reported later on in the movement, but no further bloodshed occurred. The agitations on private lands were directed against landlords and estates already identified by government and served with notices that they held lands that were in excess of legal ceilings.[122] Some news reports suggested that the parties, for the most part, concentrated their attention on government-held lands and avoided privately held lands where resistance could be

[116] *Searchlight*, 10 October 1969.
[117] Ibid., 13 October 1969.
[118] *Indian Nation*, 7 November 1969, and *Searchlight*, 11 November 1969.
[119] *Searchlight*, 26 June 1970.
[120] *Indian Nation*, 4 July 1970.
[121] Ibid., 20 July 1970.
[122] Ibid., 25 July 1970.

anticipated.[123] Competition between the parties of the radical Left during this movement emerged through press statements by SSP and CPI leaders attacking the sincerity that their rivals brought to the movement and by some isolated threats by SSP workers to occupy lands held by Communist landlords.[124] The CPI movement was suspended on 18 August. The SSP movement continued somewhat longer. The official arrest figures for the entire state, revealed on 25 August, suggest the relatively equal effort expended by the SSP and the CPI during the movement—and the relatively minor role of other Left parties. The arrest figures were: CPI members, 694; SSP, 641; PSP, 133; unspecified, 384; others, 9.[125]

Several aspects of the radical Left land agitations of 1969 and 1970 deserve note. First, the SSP and the CPI successfully captured the land reform issue from the revolutionary hands of Naxalite terrorists and turned it in nonviolent, essentially reformist directions. Second, the two major radical Left parties operated in this agitational arena competitively, as they have done in the electoral arena. In both spheres, the two parties have been relatively evenly matched. Moreover, the CPI and the SSP demonstrated that they were the leading radical Left parties in the agitational arena as well as the electoral arena and that their other competitors —the CPM, the CPML, and the PSP—did not have the same ability to launch mass movements. Third, the participation of the CPI in the *bataidari* movement in 1967 and in the land movement of 1970 demonstrate that, in India, a radical party need not give up its radical, agitational image because of its participation in or support for a government. Finally, the land movements of 1969 and 1970 achieved some successes in moving the government to implement more expeditiously land reform measures that had long ago been legislated and to pass amendments to previous legislation to close loopholes in the existing laws. For example, the Bihar assembly passed an amendment to the Bihar Privileged Persons Homestead Tenancy Act on 25 June 1970, granting full tenancy rights to certain categories of under tenants.[126] On 10 September 1970, the governor of Bihar issued a land reform ordinance that banned transfers of surplus land by landlords and empowered administrative officers in the districts to take immediate action to stop such land transfers.[127] In October 1970, the revenue minister claimed that 150,000 acres of land had been distributed during the previous two and one-half months to some 140,000

---

[123] See, e.g., the report on the movement in Purnea district in ibid., 14 August 1970.
[124] Ibid., 9 and 17 August 1970.
[125] Ibid., 26 August 1970.
[126] *Indian Recorder & Digest* 16, no. 7 (July 1970), 21.
[127] Ibid. 16, no. 10 (October 1970), 26.

landless families, primarily from the scheduled castes and scheduled tribes.[128] Thus, in 1969 and 1970, the SSP and the CPI were able to capture the rural revolutionary symbols of the Naxalite movement, turn them in nonviolent directions, and achieve some concrete results.

Conclusion

There are three salient features of radical politics in Bihar in comparison to the more radicalized states of Bengal and Kerala. First, the radical Socialists have been stronger than the Communists. Second, however, the CPI has succeeded in narrowing the gap between it and its strongest rival on the left, the SSP, now the SP. Third, the two major parties have not yet achieved the political strength of the Marxist and Communist Left in Bengal and Kerala.

The preceding analysis of radical party leadership, organization, and performance suggests why radical politics in Bihar have taken their present form. Both radical parties and their leaders are legitimate descendants from the central nationalist political tradition in Bihar. This fact has had its advantages and disadvantages for both parties. One advantage has been that the radical party leaders have shared some of the prestige of the independence movement. They have their jail credentials. One disadvantage has been that their strength has been concentrated primarily in the same areas where the Congress and the other large parties have had their strength. Consequently, the radical parties have not begun with pockets of strength in particular regions of the state but have had to challenge the dominant party in its strongholds without a secure base to fall back upon. Their rise to strength, therefore, had to await the crumbling of the Congress, which began in Bihar only in 1967 and was arrested in 1972.

Although both parties have shared in capturing legitimacy from the independence movement, the Socialist parties and the SSP in particular have taken a much larger share of it than the CPI. The CPI nationalist image was tarnished by Communist cooperation with the British during the war. The SSP nationalist image continued to shine because so many of its leaders were participants in the '42 movement. Moreover, the SSP continued to capitalize upon the revolutionary traditions of the '42 movement in its annual August demonstrations and in its generally militant approach to politics. The CPI has not been behind the SSP in the use of militant tactics, but it is the SSP that has been the symbol of militantly radical politics in Bihar.

---

[128] Ibid. 16, no. 11 (November 1970), 21.

If militancy was one side of the SSP coin, populism was the other. The differences in the socioeconomic composition of the SSP and CPI leadership were not very great, but the most prominent leaders of the SSP have tended to come from either a middle or low caste or an economically deprived background, whereas the most prominent CPI leaders have tended to come from landed or middle-class families and to have a radical intellectual approach to things political. The SSP leaders have seen themselves as risen from the common people and as protectors of the people against hardship and political-administrative injustice. The CPI leaders tend to be more "practical" in their approaches to political and economic issues and to have intellectually satisfying answers. They will go along when the radical Socialists raise the slogan to abolish land revenue, but it is not their idea. They are more likely to want to think out the economic implications of such a move and to have alternatives ready, whereas the radical Socialist leaders favor providing dramatic measures of relief for the common people, if necessary before the implications and alternatives have been exhaustively considered.

If the SSP has had a greater share of nationalist legitimacy and a more populist image, the CPI has had a more effective organization in Bihar. It is not at all a question of the mythic superiority of Communist organization, however. Neither party has been able to avoid inner-party factionalism and party splits, but the nature of the Communist appeal and the structure of the party organization have kept party cohesion more effectively and have made it possible for the CPI to act in a more unified manner at crucial times. The contingent character of SSP appeals and the weak articulation of its organization have kept the party in constant turmoil, faced by a continuing threat of indiscipline and defection. The more all-encompassing character of the CPI appeal and its strongly articulated organizational structure have confined factionalism within bounds, except when a major split is imminent, and have been instrumental in maintaining unity in the party organization and in the legislature whenever required.

Differences in party appeals and also in the immediate goals of the party have led in recent times to a divergence between the two parties in strategy and tactics for achieving power, to the detriment of both parties. The SSP concentration on removing the Congress from power at the center led it to oppose Congress (R) in the center and in the states, while the CPI was allying with Congress (R) in both. This divergence in the alliance strategies of the two parties in Bihar has made it easier for the parties of the Center and Right to take power in the Bihar government.

The SSP declined in electoral strength between 1967 and 1969. The SP in 1972 polled a smaller popular vote than the SSP in 1967. It has won less popular support than the old Socialist Party won in 1952. The CPI has improved its seat-winning capacity steadily. Neither party can, however, look forward soon to a significant increase in strength through its own efforts. The SSP did not succeed either in moving out from its traditional strongholds in north and south Bihar or in winning a stable base of support among particular social groups in its strongholds. The CPI has had greater success than the SSP in the tribal-industrial region of southeastern Bihar. However, its membership does not reflect its popular support in those areas. Moreover, the base itself is not a substantial one. Tribal support continues to go more to the explicitly tribal parties, whereas the industrial population of Bihar is relatively tiny in any case. The leaders of both parties in Bihar recognize explicitly that they must acquire more strength in the countryside, among the peasantry and agricultural laborers. Both parties used their positions in the first United Front government to promote policies favorable to the poor peasantry, but the time was too short for their policies to win them significant strength and the impact of those policies was questionable. Moreover, the SSP was unable to maintain the cohesion of its party in power, which raised questions about its reliability as a governing political party.

Thus, the answers suggested here to the questions posed above concerning the relative strength of radical Left parties in Bihar can be summarized as follows. The Socialist parties, particularly the SSP, have been traditionally stronger than the CPI in Bihar because the SSP captured more of nationalist respectability and succeeded in projecting a more militant, populist, and indigenous image. The CPI has been narrowing the gap between it and the SSP through patient organizational work and through gradual extension of its electoral base in each election. Radical parties in Bihar have failed so far to achieve the position of dominance acquired by Left parties in Bengal and Kerala because they have not been able to accomplish any of the three major tasks of a political party that seeks institutionalization in India. The SSP was never able to overcome personalism and factionalism. The CPI has succeeded better in this respect than the SSP, but even the CPI has split in the past. Neither party in the 1960s had developed stable support among major categories of the rural population. Despite SSP emphasis on Hindi and CPI support for Muslim and tribal interests, neither party had captured regional or minority cultural or linguistic sentiment. If the radical parties are to increase their strength in the immediate future, they are likely to be able to do so more through interparty alliances than through increasing their popular support or organizational strength. Neither the broad caste appeal of the SSP nor the class appeal of the CPI has yet provided the basis for overcoming the heterogeneity and fragmentation of Bihar society and for mobilizing the political population of Bihar on a new basis.

Ceylon

Ceylon

7
The Marxist Parties of Ceylon   Robert N. Kearney

Political radicalism in contemporary Ceylon is most readily identifiable
with a cluster of self-proclaimed Marxist parties and groups that with one
exception, trace a common origin to the founding of the Lanka Sama Samaja Party in 1935.[1] Ceylonese radicalism originated in the confluence of
nationalist and social-protest sentiments, directed toward Marxist ideology
by a group of young intellectuals, mostly graduates of British universities,
who returned to Ceylon in the early 1930s. A later group of young radicals educated at the Ceylon University College shortly before or during
the Second World War provided a second echelon of militants for the
Marxist parties in the years after 1940. The recent appearance of a new
radicalism rooted in different social strata and revealing a markedly different perspective and style confounded an otherwise orderly picture of a
highly sophisticated, intellectually inclined, increasingly domesticated
Ceylonese Left.

The Marxist movement has exhibited a tendency to splinter into many
separate and antagonistic groups. By 1968, no less than six separate parties claimed the mantle of Marx and Lenin in Ceylon. Since a 1940 split
between Trotskyists and Stalinists, the major division of the Ceylonese
Left has been between the Lanka Sama Samaja Party (LSSP), an affiliate
of the Fourth International from 1942 to 1964, and the Ceylon Communist Party (CP), a loyal devotee of Soviet communism. An LSSP split immediately after the Second World War, which produced momentarily a
Bolshevik Leninist Party (later called the Bolshevik Samasamaja Party),
was followed by a reunification in 1950. In protest against the reunification, the veteran Marxist Philip Gunawardena, often called the "father of
Marxism in Ceylon," left the LSSP and formed the Viplavakari Lanka
Sama Samaja Party (VLSSP), which since 1959 has styled itself the
Mahajana Eksath Peramuna (MEP). The LSSP was badly shaken by a
schism in 1953 that cost the party one-third of its members.[2] The dissidents
did not form a separate party, however. A number of them joined the CP
or the VLSSP, some returned to the LSSP, and others eventually entered
the non-Marxist Sri Lanka Freedom Party. The international Communist
cleavage between Moscow and Peking was reflected in a 1963 CP split that

[1] Lanka Sama Samaja Party can be translated as Ceylon Socialist Party. The Sinhalese term *sama samāja* or *samasamāja*, literally meaning "equal society," was
adopted by the early Ceylonese Marxists as the nearest equivalent for the term
"socialist." The members of the LSSP are known as Samasamajists, distinguishing
them from the Communists belonging to the Ceylon Communist Party.
[2] Leslie Goonewardene, *A Short History of the Lanka Sama Samaja Party* (Colombo: LSSP, 1960), p. 48.

produced two bitterly antagonistic parties, each claiming to be the Ceylon Communist Party.[3] The following year, the LSSP entered a coalition government with the SLFP. In opposition to the coalition, the orthodox Trotskyist wing of the party split away to form the Lanka Sama Samaja Party (Revolutionary), or LSSP(R). In 1968, the LSSP(R) itself experienced a splintering when a handful of dissidents formed the Revolutionary Samasamaja Party.

By 1970, a markedly different type of radical group, a semi-clandestine organization called the Janatha Vimukthi Peramuna (People's Liberation Front) or JVP, dubbed a "Che Guevarist" movement by the press, had surfaced among students and unemployed youths. Although professing to be Marxist, the JVP had few apparent personal or ideological links with the earlier radical movement. In April 1971, the island was deeply shaken by an armed insurrection attributed to the JVP, producing the most serious eruption of violence in recent history and posing an agonizing challenge to the established parties of the Left. Police and military action crushed the insurrection and apparently left most JVP activists dead or jailed. The prospects for a revival of the JVP or similar movements remain uncertain.

After the division in the radical movement between Samasamajists and Communists in 1940, the Marxist parties of the conventional Left that subsequently emerged have been little more than splinters, often vocal and combative, but able to mobilize little popular support and ordinarily exercising slight influence on political developments. Philip Gunawardena's party seemed in the late 1950s to be a growing and potentially powerful movement, but it has declined steadily through the past decade and in 1970 lost its last remaining seat in Parliament. It has been the LSSP and the regular CP that have been the major and durable Marxist parties, and it is with these two radical parties that this study is principally concerned. Particular attention is devoted here to the LSSP, as the largest, most influential, and most unique of the Ceylonese Marxist parties.[4]

The larger Marxist parties have been profoundly influenced by the style and character of Ceylon's open, pluralistic, and highly competitive political system, characterized by a multiplicity of political parties, energetic election contests, and repeated transfers of power between rival parties. In

3 Both parties continue to call themselves the Ceylon Communist Party. The smaller, pro-Peking party will be referred to here as the Left CP and the larger, pro-Moscow party simply as the CP or, if necessary for clarity, the regular CP.
4 I have elsewhere dealt in more detail with the two Communist parties. See Robert N. Kearney, "The Communist Parties of Ceylon: Rivalry and Alliance," in Robert A. Scalapino, ed., *The Communist Revolution in Asia*, 2d ed., (Englewood Cliffs, N.J.: Prentice-Hall, 1969), pp. 391–416.

each of the five parliamentary elections after 1952, the governing party or coalition has been driven from power and replaced by the principal opposition group. Since the introduction of universal suffrage in 1931, and particularly since the mid-1950s, mass political consciousness has spread throughout the Ceylonese electorate. Popular participation in elections is phenomenally high, topping 80 percent of eligible voters in the last two parliamentary elections.

The principal non-Marxist political parties of Ceylon are the generally conservative United National Party (UNP), formed shortly before Independence and identified by the Marxists as the party of the class enemy, and the Sri Lanka Freedom Party (SLFP), founded in 1951 as a democratic socialist party, which has combined agrarian populism with appeal to Sinhalese Buddhist linguistic and religious sentiments. The Federal Party and Tamil Congress represent the island's Tamil minority. The UNP governed the country from 1947 until it suffered a shattering election defeat in 1956 at the hands of an SLFP-led coalition. An election in March 1960 returned the UNP to power briefly, but in a second election the following July, resulting from the UNP government's defeat in Parliament, the SLFP won control of Parliament and formed the government. In June 1964, the SLFP entered into a coalition government with the LSSP. The coalition was defeated in an election in 1965, which brought to power a self-styled "national government" formed by the UNP, MEP, Federal Party, Tamil Congress, and a few other groups. Five years later, an SLFP, LSSP, and CP United Front scored an overwhelming election victory, capturing three-quarters of the seats in Parliament. The 1970 election seemed to represent the height of power and influence and the most promising prospects the Ceylonese Marxists had ever achieved. While retaining small memberships and commanding limited popular support, the LSSP and the CP had apparently succeeded in making effective use of the open, pluralistic, and competitive political process to come within sight of many of their long-standing political goals and to occupy an influential position in Ceylonese politics. Within a year, however, they were faced by an unprecedented armed uprising and the risk of estrangement from a new generation of radical youth.

Marxist Electoral and Parliamentary Strength

The voting strength of the Marxist parties has never been impressively large and had tended to stagnate until the recent coalescence of the United Front. The early years of Independence were times of enthusiasm and anticipation for the Marxists, who constituted the principal organized alternative to the UNP and who confidently expected to replace the UNP in power. The Marxists' opportunity, however, vanished with the rise of the SLFP, which quickly became the major alternative to the UNP and assumed leadership of the campaign that drove the UNP from power in 1956. The SLFP was able to mobilize sympathy and support from the numerous rural Sinhalese villagers, as the Marxists had never succeeded in doing, by combining appeals to the material interests of the rural under-privileged with symbolic appeals to linguistic and religious identification and solidarity. In the decade before 1964, the Marxists experienced frustration and discouragement as their electoral strength stagnated and they found themselves relegated to a role of minor allies of the SLFP against the UNP. The SLFP-LSSP coalition in 1964, which later included the CP and became the United Front of 1970, represented a new opportunity for the Marxists. While required to share power with the larger and more popular SLFP and adjust their objectives and actions to those of the SLFP, by joining in the United Front the Marxists were able to break out of the circle of stagnation and frustration, return to the center of the struggle for power, and renew in modified form the promising prospects of 1950.

Marxist Electoral Fortunes
In the 1947 election, the three Marxist parties then functioning captured one-fifth of the popular vote and nearly as large a proportion of the seats in Parliament (table 7.1). Thereafter, the electoral strength of the Marxists gradually declined, except in March 1960, when an unprecedented number of Marxist candidates entered the contest and the MEP momentarily showed considerable strength. While the total vote of the parties edged upward slightly, it failed to keep pace with the rapidly expanding electorate, except in March 1960. Following the enlargement of the House of Representatives, the lower house of Parliament, from 95 to 151 elected members in 1960,[5] the proportion of parliamentary seats held by the Marxist parties also tended downward until the 1970 election.

The LSSP has consistently been the dominant party of the Left, capturing between half and two-thirds of the total vote of the Marxist parties (table 7.2). Excluding the brief Parliament elected in March 1960, about two-thirds of all Marxist MPs have always been Samasamajists. The Samasamajist vote consistently hovered around 300,000 for 20 years, until the 1970 United Front landslide boosted it above 400,000. The CP record (table 7.3) indicates a similar relatively stable level of support of a little

[5] The feeble upper chamber, the Senate, was abolished in 1971. A new constitution adopted in 1972 provides for a single-chamber legislature called the National State Assembly.

Table 7.1   Performance of Marxist Parties of Ceylon in Parliamentary Elections

Election	Number of Marxist Parties Contesting Seats	Number of Candidates	Votes Received	Percentage of Popular Vote	Number of Seats Won	Percentage of Seats Won[a]
1947	3	51	387,544	20.5	18	18.9
1952	3	58	439,661	18.9	13	13.7
1956	2[b]	30	393,919	14.7	17	17.9
March 1960	3	243	790,041	25.7	23	15.2
July 1960	3	83	417,045	13.8	19	12.6
1965	6	103	528,663	13.1	15	10.0
1970	3	36	648,994	13.0	25	16.6

Sources: For 1947: Ceylon Daily News, *Parliament of Ceylon, 1947* (Colombo: Associated Newspapers of Ceylon, n.d.). For 1952: I. D. S. Weerawardana, "The General Elections in Ceylon, 1952," *Ceylon Historical Journal* 2, (July–October 1952), 111–178. For 1956: Ceylon Daily News, *Parliament of Ceylon, 1956* (Colombo: Associated Newspapers of Ceylon, n.d.). For March and July 1960: Ceylon Daily News, *Parliaments of Ceylon, 1960* (Colombo: Associated Newspapers of Ceylon, n.d.). For 1965: *Report on the Sixth Parliamentary General Election of Ceylon*, Sessional Paper XX—1966 (Colombo: Government Press, 1966); and Ceylon Daily News, *Parliament of Ceylon, 1965* (Colombo: Associated Newspapers of Ceylon, n.d.). For 1970: *Report on the Seventh Parliamentary General Election in Ceylon*, Sessional Paper VII—1971 (Colombo: Department of Government Printing, 1971).
[a] In the elections of 1947, 1952, and 1956, 95 seats and in the subsequent four elections 151 seats were at stake.
[b] The VLSSP, which contested as a part of the MEP coalition, is not included.

more than 100,000 votes. The performance of the two parties, at least until 1970, suggests that each possesses a core of dependable support that is neither growing nor diminishing significantly in size. With a rapidly expanding electorate and relatively static voting strength, both parties' proportion of the popular vote steadily slipped downward until the modest upturn of 1970. The election successes of the LSSP and the CP have been constricted by the two parties' electoral arrangements with the SLFP, which limited the number of candidates nominated by each of the parties, in four of the five elections since 1956. The two Marxist parties combined contest less than one-fourth of all constituencies (a few of which are regularly in the Tamil north, where they harbor slight expectation of victory). In the landslide of 1970, every LSSP and CP candidate outside of the Northern Province was elected.

The MEP, originally called the VLSSP, contested its first election in 1952 allied with the CP, and one of its members was returned to Parliament. The party fought the 1956 election in a coalition with the SLFP, and five of the successful coalition candidates were identified with the Marxist

Table 7.2 Lanka Sama Samaja Party Performance in Parliamentary Elections

Election	Number of Candidates	Votes Received	Percentage of Popular Vote	Number of Seats Won	Percentage of Seats Won[a]
1947[b]	38	317,213	16.8	15	15.8
1952	39	305,133	13.1	9	9.5
1956	21	274,204	10.2	14	14.7
March 1960	101	322,352	10.5	10	6.6
July 1960	21	223,993	7.4	12	7.9
1965	25	302,095	7.5	10	6.6
1970	23	433,224	8.7	19	12.6

Sources: Same as for Table 7.1.
[a] Ninety-five seats in the elections of 1947, 1952, and 1956, and 151 seats in the subsequent four elections were at stake.
[b] Includes the Bolshevik Leninist Party, which contested the 1947 election separately but was reunited with the LSSP in 1950.

Table 7.3 Ceylon Communist Party Performance in Parliamentary Elections

Election	Number of Candidates	Votes Received	Percentage of Popular Vote	Number of Seats Won	Percentage of Seats Won[a]
1947[b]	13	70,331	3.7	3	3.1
1952[c]	19	134,528	5.8	4	4.2
1956	9	119,715	4.5	3	3.1
March 1960	53	141,857	4.6	3	2.0
July 1960	7	90,219	3.0	4	2.6
1965	9	109,754	2.7	4	2.6
1970	9	169,199	3.4	6	4.0

Sources: Same as for Table 7.1.
[a] Ninety-five seats in the elections of 1947, 1952, and 1956, and 151 seats in the subsequent four elections were at stake.
[b] Does not include two candidates elected as independents who joined the CP immediately after the election.
[c] Results for the CP–VLSSP United Front.

contingent. The MEP made a strong showing in the first election of 1960, but its refusal to cooperate with the SLFP, LSSP, and CP against the UNP in that short-lived Parliament led to its isolation and precipitated a split in its ranks. The election a few months later reduced the MEP to three seats and cut its popular vote to one-third its level in March. Thereafter, the party declined steadily and became increasingly estranged from the other Marxist parties. The MEP entered the 1965 election contest informally allied with the UNP, the arch enemy of the Marxists, and presented 61 candidates, 55 of whom lost their deposits by failing to secure one-eighth of the votes cast in their constituencies. MEP leader Philip Gunawardena was the only member of his party to be elected. By 1970, the MEP seemed moribund. It failed to secure a single seat in Parliament, and its proportion of the popular vote fell below 1 percent. Gunawardena's death in early 1972 cast further doubt on the party's survival.

With the apparent demise of the MEP, the LSSP and CP remained the only Marxist parties able to achieve even modest electoral successes. The 1965 election resulted in a humiliating rout for the minor Marxist parties. Six Marxist parties presented 103 candidates—61 of whom were MEP candidates. The LSSP and CP together won 14 of the 15 seats and three-fourths of the total vote captured by the six parties. In addition to the 55 MEP candidates, all 4 LSSP(R) and all 3 Left CP candidates lost their deposits. The sixth Marxist group, an ephemeral organization called the United Left Front which had split from the MEP, offered a single candidate, who was defeated.[6] The election, the first following splits in the CP and LSSP in 1963 and 1964, dramatically demonstrated the dearth of popular support for the schismatic movements. In the three-member Colombo Central constituency, Left Communist leader N. Sanmugathasan secured less than 2,500 votes, while the regular Communist general secretary, Pieter Keuneman, won more than 40,000. The two other Left Communist candidates, both contesting in the Tamil-speaking north, obtained only a handful of votes. No less humiliating was the fate of the LSSP(R). Two LSSP(R) candidates were veteran MPs contesting the same constituencies they had won as LSSP candidates five years earlier. Both lost their deposits. One received about 1,000 votes while the regular LSSP candidate, in losing the contest, secured 16,000 votes. The second obtained

---

[6] The party, which was essentially the personal vehicle of Robert Gunawardena, brother of Philip Gunawardena, took its name from the United Left Front formed by the LSSP, CP, and MEP in 1963, which collapsed when the LSSP entered the coalition with the SLFP in 1964.

only 278 votes while the victorious LSSP candidate received 14,000 votes.[7]
By 1970, the United Left Front had vanished, and neither the LSSP(R)
nor the Left CP offered any candidates. One MP, elected in 1965 as an
SLFP candidate, had joined the Left Communists in 1968 but was expelled
from the party on the eve of the 1970 election. As an independent, he
contested the constituency he had represented in Parliament since 1952
and lost his deposit.

Sources of Electoral Support

Marxist electoral strength is heavily concentrated in the southwestern
corner of Ceylon, from Colombo on the southwest coast to Matara at the
island's southern tip. With a few scattered exceptions, the Marxists' successes in parliamentary elections have been limited to three of Ceylon's
nine provinces—the Western, Southern, and Sabaragamuwa provinces—
clustered at the southwestern extremity of the island. Both the LSSP and
CP have consistently displayed some strength in and around the city of
Colombo in the Western Province. Pieter Keuneman, CP general secretary, has represented the Colombo Central constituency in Parliament
since 1947. Bernard Soysa, who in 1970 became general secretary of the
LSSP, has represented the Colombo South constituency since 1956. Although Marxist strength in Colombo municipal elections has eroded over
the past decade, the Marxists, particularly the LSSP, remain the principal
opponents of the UNP in the greater Colombo area.

Strong and consistent LSSP electoral strength is confined to three adjacent areas, a narrow coastal belt extending south from Colombo and
stabbing into the western edge of the Southern Province, an inland pocket
in the Western Province to the southeast of Colombo, and a nearby group
of constituencies in neighboring Sabaragamuwa Province east of Colombo. Few LSSP victories have been scored outside of a triangle running
from Colombo eastward less than 50 miles to the Kandyan foothills in
Sabaragamuwa Province and from Colombo south along the coast nearly
to Galle in the Southern Province.

Of seven constituencies returning eight MPs (Colombo South is a two-
member constituency) stretching along the coastal strip south of Colombo, the LSSP won six in 1970, four in 1965, and five in July 1960. LSSP
strength along the coastal belt probably originated in part as an expression of caste protest and rivalry. The coastal fringe contains a heavy

[7] The 1965 election data are from *Report on the Sixth Parliamentary General Election of Ceylon*, Sessional Paper XX—1966 (Colombo: Government Press, 1966);
and Ceylon Daily News, *Parliament of Ceylon, 1965* (Columbo: Associated Newspapers of Ceylon, n.d.).

concentration of the Karāva (fishermen), Salāgama (cinnamon peeler), and Durāva (toddy tapper) castes, who for many decades have resented and rebelled against the pretentions of superiority of the Goyigama (cultivator) caste, which is both the largest Sinhalese caste—containing perhaps half the total Sinhalese population—and the highest in status. The Panadura, Moratuwa, and Kalutara constituencies immediately south of Colombo are centers of the Karāva caste and have also been LSSP strongholds. LSSP victories in the Colombo South constituency are often attributed in part to a sizable Durāva vote there. Goyigama domination of politics has always been marked, resting on the caste's numerical preponderance and even spread throughout the Sinhalese areas of the island. Early and persistent Marxist hostility toward the existing social order and pointed denunciations of caste distinctions, as well as inclusion of members of the coastal castes within the inner circle of party leadership, have unquestionably assisted the party in mobilizing support among the minority castes. Furthermore, particularly in the early years of Independence, the UNP was widely assumed to be Goyigama-dominated. As the Samasamajists were the main opponents of the UNP in the southwestern seaboard areas, the anti-UNP caste vote ordinarily went to the LSSP.[8] Partisan loyalties and voting habits have presumably persisted even when the direct influence of caste considerations has faded.

Away from the coast, the Western and Sabaragamuwa province constituencies won by the LSSP are primarily Goyigama in caste composition. Samasamajist strength there seems most readily attributable to intense organizational and agitational activities over nearly four decades. The Sabaragamuwa pocket includes the area that elected LSSP leader N. M. Perera to the State Council (the colonial legislature) in 1936. In this region, the Samasamajists built a reputation for selfless dedication to the common people through social welfare, trade union, and local government activities since the 1930s. The Marxist parties were the first coherent national organizations to involve themselves systematically in local government elections and institutions, and although virtually all other parties have moved into local politics over the past two decades, the Marxists continue to devote much attention and energy to local government bodies, both in the urban areas and in the villages.

[8] The caste element in the electoral strength of the Marxists along the coast shortly after Independence is discussed in Bryce Ryan, *Caste in Modern Ceylon* (New Brunswick, N.J.: Rutgers University Press, 1953), pp. 276–279. Although the approximate caste composition of an area is widely known, particularly by local politicians, there has not been a caste census of Ceylon in modern times, so that precise data on caste geography is unobtainable.

Samasamajists who have been elected to office generally have remained in close touch with their constituents and have energetically served individual and local interests of their constituencies. It is probable that many voters cast their ballots for Samasamajist candidates not because of the party's radical political and social doctrines but because they assume the Samasamajist candidate would be the most devoted, vigorous, and uncorruptible representative for the area. The important role of hard and sustained local organizational work in creating and maintaining LSSP support may help to explain the limitations as well as the extent of the party's strength. The party lacks both the numbers and the resources to carry on the same intense activities and services over broad areas of the island.

Communist electoral strength, other than in Colombo, is almost totally contained within a small pocket in the Southern Province, at the extreme southern tip of the island, hemmed in on the north and east by the southern extension of Samasamajist strength. At each election since 1947, the CP has won at least one and usually two Southern Province seats. In 1970, when the CP made its strongest showing, four of six Communist victories were in the Southern Province. The southern pocket contains the ancestral home of the CP president, Dr. S. A. Wickremasinghe. Both Dr. Wickremasinghe and his brother were repeatedly elected as Communist candidates from constituencies in the area until the latter abandoned the party in 1970. Communist strength in the south is commonly believed to have developed out of the local prestige of the Wickremasinghe family, paradoxically suggesting an element of deference voting for members of a family of high traditional status although representing a radical political party. Undoubtedly, CP strength in the Southern Province has been consolidated by a concentration of organizational efforts in the area and the habit of voting Communist. There is also probably an element of caste protest and competition in the CP support along the south coast. The CP has shown strength in the Matara constituency, containing a concentration of members of the Durāva caste, and other non-Goyigama coastal castes are numerous along the south coast. The only successful Communist penetration outside the south and the Colombo vicinity was a 1956 Communist victory on the Jaffna Peninsula at the extreme north of the island, the only Marxist parliamentary election victory in a Tamil constituency.

Marxists explain the concentration of their strength in the southwest as produced by the fact that this is the area of greatest exposure to and penetration by capitalism and, hence, is the most fully matured for the development of socialism. The southwest low country is the region of the longest and most intense impact of the West, dating from the arrival of the Portuguese in 1505. Since the late nineteenth century, it has experienced an accelerating pace of social, economic, and cultural change. It is the most developed region in terms of education, transportation, and communication, and is the most dependent on wage employment and production for the market. The population is highly literate and informed.[9] While it is one of the more affluent regions of Ceylon, population pressure is high, dependence on wage labor extensive, and unemployment widespread.

The Marxist parties have been primarily dependent for support on the majority Sinhalese ethnic community, particularly the low-country Buddhist Sinhalese.[10] They have won little backing from either the Muslim or Christian minorities. The Marxists, primarily the Samasamajists, are thought to have gained votes from the scattered members of the Tamil minority in the southwest, at least prior to 1964, because of their advocacy of Tamil language rights and general defense of minority interests. They have, however, had little success in the solidly Tamil-speaking north. Both the LSSP and the CP perfunctorily contest a few seats in the northern Tamil areas at each election, but only once has a Marxist candidate been elected to Parliament from a predominately Tamil constituency. In 1970, while the Marxists were scoring their greatest victory

[9] The five administrative districts from which the Marxists gain their principal electoral support (Colombo and Kalutara districts in the Western Province, Kegalle District in Sabaragamuwa Province, and Galle and Matara districts in the Southern Province) had literacy rates at the time of the 1963 census ranging from 84.6 to 69.3 percent of all persons five years of age and over. Only two (Matara with 69.4 and Kegalle with 69.3 percent) had literacy rates slightly below the island average of 71.6, and all five rank within the top half of the 22 administrative districts in rate of literacy. Department of Census and Statistics, *Census of Population, Ceylon, 1963* (Colombo: Government Press, 1967), table 14, pp. 52–53. A 1964 survey found a very high level of exposure to mass communications media among the urban working class and the rural villagers of the "wet zone" of the west and south. "Readership Survey, Ceylon, April–June 1964, Conducted for the Audit Bureau of Circulations Limited by the Market Research Department of Lever Brothers (Ceylon) Limited," mimeographed, Colombo, September 1964, table 5. A knowledgeable and well-informed village population in the southwest is described by Bryce Ryan, *Sinhalese Village* (Coral Gables, Fla.: University of Miami Press, 1958), esp. pp. 141–144.

[10] The Sinhalese ethnic community is divided into low-country and Kandyan branches, the former concentrated in the densely populated southern and western coastal plains and the latter inhabiting the interior hill country. The Kandyans, at least until recently, have remained closer to traditional customs and practices and have generally lagged behind the low-country Sinhalese in education, nonagricultural employment, and secularization. Both low-country and Kandyan Sinhalese are predominantly Buddhist, but the relatively small minority of Sinhalese Christians is composed almost entirely of low-country Sinhalese.

in the south, six of seven LSSP and CP candidates in the Northern Province lost their deposits. Of 21 contests involving LSSP and CP candidates in the north during the last three parliamentary elections, the Marxist candidate lost his deposit 12 times and succeeded in winning one-fourth or more of the votes only twice. The continued Marxist efforts in the north are clearly symbolic, intended to demonstrate the parties' continued concern for the Tamil minority. The Marxist leaders are predominately low-country Sinhalese, generally with Buddhist backgrounds,[11] and the Marxist parties obtain their support in Sinhalese, Buddhist areas. To the sensitive minorities, the Marxist parties presumably appear to be Sinhalese-dominated organizations. Furthermore, Tamil society tends to be more tightly woven, traditional, and resistant to change than Sinhalese society, and the Tamils appear generally to be politically and socially conservative, preoccupied with language and other minority problems, and disinterested in the Marxist calls for radical social and political innovation.

A major exception to the conservatism and traditionalism of the north is an eruption of caste protest among the "untouchable" castes of the Tamil Hindus, commencing in the mid-1960s. By 1967, Left Communist leader N. Sanmugathasan, himself a Tamil, began vigorously championing the discontents and may have gained some political support from the "untouchable" Tamil castes. The regular CP also began to publicize the plight of the disadvantaged Tamil castes, and following the 1970 victory of the SLFP-LSSP-CP United Front, a leader of the Tamil "untouchables" was named an appointed member of Parliament. The newly evident caste restiveness in the north may represent a potential source of support for the radical parties, but as yet its political consequences have been negligible.

Marxists in Parliament and Government

Always small in number and usually on the opposition benches, Marxist MPs nonetheless have succeeded in playing a surprisingly large and conspicuous role in Parliament. LSSP leader N. M. Perera was the first official leader of the opposition. For many years, Samasamajist Bernard Soysa has served as chairman of the Public Accounts Committee with a

11 There are a few significant exceptions. CP general secretary Pieter Keuneman is a member of the very small Burgher community of Dutch and Ceylonese extraction. N. Sanmugathasan, leader of the Left CP, and V. Karalasingham, a prominent Samasamajist theorist, are Ceylon Tamils. The LSSP(R) leader and trade unionist, Bala Tampoe, is of Tamil Christian background. Former LSSP Senator Doric de Souza is of Goan origin. Nonetheless, the 50-member LSSP Central Committee elected in 1969 included about 44 Sinhalese.

dedication and skill that has won virtually universal praise. Marxist leaders such as Pieter Keuneman, Colvin R. de Silva, and Leslie Goonewardene are undoubtedly among the most skillful and eloquent debaters to serve in Parliament. The educational level of the Marxist legislators is consistently well above the average of the chamber. Nine of 15, or 60 percent, of the Marxists elected to Parliament in 1965 were graduates of universities or professional schools, compared with 35 percent (47 of 136) of all other MPs.[12]

The first members of a Marxist party to serve in a Ceylonese cabinet were Philip Gunawardena and P. H. William de Silva, who represented the VLSSP in the coalition government formed in 1956. Gunawardena and de Silva were expelled from the cabinet in 1959, after a period of growing tension between them and the right wing of the SLFP, the VLSSP's much larger coalition partner. The two Marxist ministers had been isolated within the cabinet for some time and their accomplishments were presumably slight. Gunawardena again served as a minister from 1965 to 1970, in association with the UNP, by which time his party had become totally estranged from the other Marxist parties and appeared to have abandoned any clearly radical policies.

The first major opening to power for the Marxists came with the SLFP's invitation to the LSSP to form a coalition government in 1964. Three Samasamajists became cabinet ministers, with N. M. Perera holding the powerful Finance Ministry portfolio. The LSSP decision to enter the coalition represented a major turning point for the party, and generated both high expectations by Samasamajist supporters and severe criticism by the Samasamajist faction that broke away to form the LSSP(R) and others. A pro-LSSP trade union declared: "The formation of the Coalition Government was hailed by major sections of the working people as a progressive step. They saw some of their leaders sharing governmental power for the first time." [13] Within six months, however, the SLFP-LSSP government had suffered a defeat in Parliament, and it fell from power in the election of March 1965, about nine months after the Samasamajists assumed office. The Samasamajist judgment is that the period in office was insufficient for major achievements. The principal consequences of the experience were to bind the LSSP and SLFP together and reinforce the LSSP's commitment to the electoral and parliamentary path to power.

After five additional years in opposition, the overwhelming 1970 elec-

---

[12] Based primarily on data from Ceylon Daily News, *Parliament of Ceylon, 1965.*
[13] Government Clerical Service Union, *44th Annual Report (Part I), 1964–65* (Colombo: Government Clerical Service Union, 1965), p. 3.

tion triumph brought both the LSSP and CP, in alliance with the SLFP, their most serious and challenging prospect of exercising power. The 21-member cabinet headed by SLFP leader Sirimavo Bandaranaike included three Samasamajists and one Communist. N. M. Perera again became minister of finance, Leslie Goonewardene was named minister of communications, and Colvin R. de Silva was appointed minister of plantation industry, to which was added the post of minister of constitutional affairs. Communist leader Pieter Keuneman became minister of housing and construction. Other Samasamajists were brought into the administration as chairmen of public corporations or permanent secretaries to ministries. While the United Front government is heavily dominated by the SLFP, the LSSP and to a lesser extent the CP have obtained a share of power in an apparently strong and stable government. The long-run significance of the Marxist participation in power for Ceylonese government and society cannot, of course, be gauged for some time.

Party Structure, Operation, and Membership
Structurally, the Marxist parties follow the model of the Leninist party, organized according to the principles of democratic centralism. A hierarchy extends from the primary party units, called branches or locals, through periodic party conferences or congresses, to a Central Committee and a Politburo. The chief executive officer of each Marxist party is the general secretary. The party congress or conference is declared to be the supreme authority of the party. Although supposed to meet biennially, the CP has convened congresses only seven times since the party's founding in 1943. Between 1950 and 1969, the LSSP held 14 party conferences. LSSP conferences were open to the entire party membership until 1960, when provision was made for delegates' conferences. The Central Committee determines party policy between conferences. The LSSP Central Committee elected in 1969 contained 50 members and the CP Central Committee chosen at the last party congress in 1964 included 25 full and 12 candidate members. At the pinnacle of the party structure is the Politburo, the supreme directing organ of the party containing the inner circle of eight to ten top party leaders. Within similar organizational frameworks, however, the manner in which the parties function varies considerably.

Internal Democracy in the LSSP
The democratic internal functioning of the LSSP through vigorous discussion of alternative policies, open competition for party posts, and

adherence to majority decisions is a source of great pride for Samasamajists. The LSSP leadership appears to adhere meticulously to the rules and norms of the party in elections and policy making, and to follow the decisions reached by the party conference or Central Committee. Elections to the Central Committee at party conferences generate serious competition, with 70 or 80 candidates often vying for the 50 places on the body. The vote, frequently led by Leslie Goonewardene, who was LSSP general secretary for 20 years until he stepped down in 1970 to become a minister in the United Front government, is considered a significant indicator of prestige and influence within the party. The eight-member Politburo is regularly elected each year by the Central Committee on a written ballot. The Trotskyist outlook of the LSSP has produced strong emphasis on the evils of dictatorial control by a party bureaucracy, and the right of members to form factions and work within the party for the acceptance of their viewpoints is granted by the party constitution [14] and supported by the ethos of the party. As one LSSP leader asserted, in contrast with the Communist Party, which purged any member challenging the official line, in the LSSP, "every opportunity is provided for the expression and propagation within the party of divergent views. The final decision is taken democratically after full discussion by the membership." [15]

Party conferences have produced spirited battles and occasionally have adopted decisions on major questions in conflict with the desires of a majority of the leadership. Disagreement with the leadership on the question of LSSP cooperation with other parties appeared at a conference in 1952. A resolution presented by the dissidents was defeated, but the battle continued to rage within the party for an entire year. The dissident faction was allowed to argue its case in the party's *Internal Bulletin* and to send speakers to address local party units. A conference in 1953 rejected the dissidents' resolution in favor of one backed by the Politburo on a vote of 259 to 125. Following their defeat, the minority group left the party.[16] The issue of LSSP cooperation with the SLFP led to the convening of two party conferences within two months in 1960. A resolution calling for collaboration with the SLFP was approved although it was opposed by a majority of the members of the Politburo, Central Committee, and parliamentary delegation.[17] In 1964, the question of joining

[14] *Laṅkā Samasamāja Pakshayē Vyavasthāva* [Lanka Sama Samaja Party's Constitution] (Colombo: LSSP, n.d.), p. 11.
[15] Leslie Goonewardene, *The Differences Between Trotskyism and Stalinism* (Colombo: LSSP, 1954), p. 12.
[16] Goonewardene, *A Short History of the Lanka Sama Samaja Party*, pp. 46–48.
[17] Author's interviews with LSSP leaders in 1961 and 1962.

the SLFP in a coalition government led to a three-way division in the Central Committee and the presentation of three conflicting resolutions at a party conference called to decide the issue. One resolution, sponsored by 14 Central Committee members, categorically opposed a coalition. A second, backed by 8 members of the Central Committee including 3 leading Politburo members, called for a coalition only if the other Marxist parties were included. The third, supported by 20 Central Committee members, authorized the LSSP alone to join with the SLFP. Despite the opposition of a majority of the Central Committee and Politburo, the third position was adopted by the conference, receiving about 500 votes to about 160 for the anticoalition and 75 for the "centrist" resolution. Like the internal battle a decade earlier, the conflict produced a split in the party, with a small group of coalition opponents breaking away to form the LSSP(R). Most of the LSSP leaders, however, accepted the decision as an expression of intraparty democracy and remained within the party.[18]

The very vitality of internal democracy seems to have contributed to the schisms that have periodically ruptured the LSSP. Disagreement on a major issue occasionally causes factional cleavages to rigidify; the uninhibited clash of opinion tempts members without strong backing within the party to challenge the leadership or seek party endorsement of their viewpoint; and the enthusiastic advocacy of one position sometimes leads members to feel that they must leave the party if their opinion does not prevail. On the other hand, the existence of intraparty democracy has aided the party in maintaining its intellectual vigor and dynamism, in contrast with the CP, where a narrow leadership appears to maintain a firm grip on the party machinery and to determine party policy, which is proclaimed to the membership, producing an appearance of intellectual and ideological sterility, despite the brilliance of a few leaders. Without the possibility of effective participation in party decision making, it is unlikely that the more thoughtful, creative, and forceful members would remain in the LSSP.

Functioning of the Communist Party

Authority within the Communist Party seems to be firmly held by the Politburo, and two leaders, party president Dr. S. A. Wickremasinghe and general secretary Pieter Keuneman, appear to have dominated the

18 Based on the author's interviews with Samasamajists and ex-Samasamajists in 1965, 1967, and 1970.

party since its formation in 1943, except for the period in 1948–1950. There is no indication that the kind of lively debate and promotion of alternative policies found in the LSSP is tolerated, much less encouraged, by the leadership. Discipline is thought to rest in large part on the provision of relatively numerous salaried party posts. Rank-and-file dissatisfaction with party actions has led to individual resignations and expulsions, but only twice have internal conflicts come into public view. The first occurred in the early years of Independence, during the period of Communist-instigated insurrections across South and Southeast Asia. In 1948, proponents of insurrectionary struggle, later labeled "left sectarians," ousted the previous leadership, replacing Keuneman as general secretary and reportedly suspending many of their opponents from Central Committee membership in order to maintain their hold on the party machinery. Two years later, after abandonment of the insurrectionary strategy by the international Communist movement, the "left sectarians" were dislodged and the original leaders returned to power within the party.[19]

The most conspicuous battle within the CP erupted in 1963 and led to a party schism and formation of the Left CP. The battle was largely fought in the idiom of the Sino-Soviet dispute in international Communism. The CP Central Committee had taken a strongly pro-Moscow position, which was opposed within the party by a group led by N. Sanmugathasan, a Politburo member and general secretary of the Communists' Ceylon Trade Union Federation. In October 1963, Sanmugathasan and his supporters were expelled from the party, charged with forming a "Marxist Study Circle" as the "nucleus of a Party within the Party" and of seeking to use Sanmugathasan's position in the Communist labor federation to turn the trade unions against the party leadership.[20] Among those expelled were two members of the Politburo and eight other Central Committee members. In reply, the Left dissidents bitterly assailed the "temporary majority" of the Central Committee for forcing the pro-Moscow line on the party, expelling the pro-Peking members, and denying intraparty democracy by failing to call a party congress every two years as specified in the party constitution. They also charged that the regular CP leadership was excessively concerned with parliamentary affairs, leading to a disregard of revolutionary possibilities

---

[19] *25 Years of the Ceylon Communist Party* (Colombo: People's Publishing House, 1968), pp. 38–41.

[20] Pieter Keuneman, *Under the Banner of Unity: Report of Pieter Keuneman, General Secretary, on Behalf of the Central Committee* (Colombo: CCP, 1964), pp. 40–45.

and had failed to support the struggles of the party's trade unions.[21] Keuneman, however, claimed that the party split was instigated from abroad as a part of Chinese Communist strategy to challenge Moscow's leadership of world communism and had little immediate connection with the circumstances in Ceylon or within the local party.[22]

The minor Marxist parties are so small that the formal organizational structure seems in practice to be replaced by the personal control of one or two individuals. The Left CP has experienced considerable rivalry among leaders, resulting in expulsions and resignations and apparently leaving the party in the hands of N. Sanmugathasan. Soon after the Left CP was formed, its general secretary, Premalal Kumarasiri, broke with Sanmugathasan and left the party. The Left Communists gained their only voice in Parliament in 1968 when S. D. Bandaranaike, who had been elected as an SLFP candidate, joined the party. Two years later, however, he was expelled for recontesting his seat on the promise to cooperate with a United Front government.[23] The LSSP(R) initially attracted about 125 Samasamajists and remained a small band of dedicated militants, described by one LSSP(R) leader in 1967 as a "political group" rather than a party because of its small membership.[24] The following year, a split occurred between the doctrinaire Trotskyist wing, led by Edmund Samarakkody, and Bala Tampoe, head of the Ceylon Mercantile Union (CMU) and general secretary of the LSSP(R). The Samarakkody group walked out of the party charging Tampoe with using his trade union base to secure his control over the party and converting the LSSP(R) into "an appendage of the CMU." [25] Thereafter, Tampoe's control of the tiny organization appeared to be unrivalled.

Characteristics of Party Membership
The membership of the LSSP has been very small and highly selective. Soon after the schism of 1940, the party opted to limit membership to a small band of activists versed in Marxist and Trotskyist theory and willing to devote regular service to party activities. By the early 1960s, after

[21] The Left dissidents' accusations are contained in *Reply to the Central Committee of the Ceylon Communist Party* (Colombo: Worker Publication, n.d.); and *Statement of Ten Central Committee Members of the Ceylon Communist Party* (Peking: Foreign Languages Press, 1964).

[22] Author's interview with Pieter Keuneman, 3 August 1967.

[23] The acrimonious exchanges between Sanmugathasan and S. D. Bandaranaike appear in *Ceylon Daily News*, 8, 10, and 20 August 1970.

[24] Author's interview with Prins Rajasooriya, 27 June 1967.

[25] *Ceylon Daily News*, 1 May 1968, p. 13.

a quarter of a century of existence, the LSSP included fewer than 2,000 members.[26] The small, active, ideologically committed membership has made possible the vigorous rank-and-file involvement in party affairs and has given the LSSP an organizational coherence, discipline, and apparent sense of purpose and direction superior to those of most other Ceylonese parties. The party's elitist character, however, restricted the establishment of the multiple, widespread links with the general public that seem necessary for the effective mobilization of mass electoral support. It was not unusual for parliamentary constituencies contested by Samasamajist candidates, even in the principal areas of LSSP strength, to contain no more than 10 or 20 party members. One constituency in which the Samasamajist candidate has repeatedly been victorious and which was described as possessing a particularly strong local LSSP organization was said to contain 48 party members in 1965.[27] A solution to the problem of developing a mass base while sharply restricting party membership had been sought shortly after the Second World War by organizing a "youth league" for party sympathizers—irrespective of age. The party auxiliary was described as "composed of people who accept the leadership of the party but do not have to conform to the strict rules which apply to party membership." [28] The LSSP Youth League, and to some extent the party's trade unions, partially filled the need for broad mass organizations able to mobilize participants for demonstrations and rallies, canvass electoral support, and help to project the influence of the party through the general public.

Growing Samasamajist dissatisfaction with the size and structure of the party was reflected in a retreat from the idea of a tight, small, dedicated, and disciplined party and an expansion of the membership, commencing at about the time the 1964 coalition was formed. By 1970, the party membership had climbed to about 4,000.[29] Following the 1970 United Front triumph, applications for membership soared. Although the party viewed the new applicants with caution, it seemed likely that a further considerable expansion was in prospect. The relatively rapid growth of members inevitably has raised questions about the "dilution" of the party, with a possible decline in élan, cohesion, and dedication to traditional party objectives. The post-1964 recruits reportedly do not possess

[26] Author's interviews with Leslie Goonewardene in 1962.
[27] Author's interview in 1965 with the Samasamajist MP representing the constituency.
[28] Goonewardene, *A Short History of the Lanka Sama Samaja Party*. p. 36.
[29] Author's interview with LSSP assistant secretary J. Wanigatunga, 18 October 1970.

the same commitment to the long-standing LSSP perspectives, conventions, and leaders, and tend to be more concerned with immediate problems and objectives than the party veterans. The newer members are said to have generally been strong supporters of the coalition strategy prior to the 1970 election victory but following the election tended to be much more impatient for immediate results and to question the utility of the coalition, momentarily creating the appearance of greater revolutionary fervor among the new than among the veteran Samasamajists. The recent recruits tend to possess less education and to be less Westernized and cosmopolitan than the older members, suggesting the possibility of a widening generational cleavage within the party.[30]

The Communists have not been as highly selective and determined to maintain a tight, small cadre party as the Samasamajists. In 1960, they proclaimed the goal of creating a "mass" party.[31] Although CP membership appears to have fluctuated considerably with shifting party fortunes and probably has often exceeded that of the LSSP, in recent years it may have hovered around 2,000. Communist participation in the United Front government formed in 1970 probably produced a surge of fresh applications for party membership. The Federation of Communist and Progressive Youth Leagues has long served as a recruiting ground and mass organization for the party.

Little can be said with confidence concerning the social composition of the Marxist parties. It seems safe to assume that the members are primarily low-country Sinhalese, although some Tamils, Muslims, and Burghers can be identified. The LSSP and CP leaders are predominantly upper middle-class professionals and intellectuals, often from prominent and wealthy families. However, a number of party officers and functionaries are former clerks, school teachers, and other white-collar employees, and a few are industrial or nonclerical office workers. The CP newspaper claimed that 40 percent of the delegates to the party's 1964 congress were industrial or estate workers and 9 percent were clerical employees.[32] LSSP ex-senator and trade unionist D. G. William is one of the few persons of working-class origin who has risen to the top rungs of the party. Both the LSSP and the CP appear to enjoy considerable support at the lower levels of the public service. The LSSP has been

[30] Based on the author's interviews with Samasamajists during August 1969, May 1970, and October 1970.
[31] *Draft Thesis for the 6th National Congress of the Ceylon Communist Party* (Colombo: CCP, 1960), p. 49.
[32] *Forward* (Colombo), 5 July 1967, p. 3.

active in the government-operated railways for more than 30 years and reportedly has gained a substantial membership among the railway workers. It is widely believed that the LSSP has been particularly strong among the clerical employees in the government service, banks, and certain commercial firms. The Communists have occasionally identified and denounced the influence of an "English-speaking petty bourgeoisie" of clerks and other white-collar employees in their own ranks.[33] The CP has vocally extolled the necessity of recruiting party members from the working class, but there are indications that this objective has not been achieved to an impressive degree. After the 1963 schism, Keuneman complained of the small numbers of party members who had been recruited from the Communists' labor federation, and he charged Left Communist leader N. Sanmugathasan, who had headed the federation, with deliberately keeping workers from joining the party. Keuneman noted that among workers in the tea and rubber processing industry, where Communist trade unions had long been strong, there were less than 20 party members.[34] The membership of both major Marxist parties is almost certainly concentrated heavily in the Colombo vicinity, with most of the remaining members in the nearby areas of Marxist electoral strength.

The Marxists and the Labor Movement

The Ceylonese Marxists have been actively involved in trade unionism for nearly four decades, since before the formation of the first Marxist party, and the labor movement has long been identified politically with the Marxists despite the more recent entry of other parties into the trade union field.[35] The Marxists turned to trade unionism in an attempt to establish links with the working class and mobilize mass support for their political and social objectives. For the Marxists, trade union and party activities and interests are virtually inseparable. Both organizations are working toward the same broad socioeconomic goals, with the party providing leadership and guidance and the union providing a mass following. Over the decades, the Marxists have expended great energy in winning support in the labor movement and in championing the causes of their trade unions. As a Communist labor leader claimed for the Marxist

[33] E.g., Keuneman, *Under the Banner of Unity*, pp. 43–44.
[34] Ibid., p. 47.
[35] The Marxists' relations with trade unions are discussed at length in Robert N. Kearney, *Trade Unions and Politics in Ceylon* (Berkeley: University of California Press, 1971).

parties, "their service to the working class in organizing them [workers] into revolutionary trade unions and helping them to win their economic demands cannot be matched by any other party." [36]

The Ceylon Federation of Labor has been intimately connected with the LSSP and led by Samasamajists for more than two decades, and the Government Workers' Trade Union Federation has functioned in close and scarcely disguised association with the LSSP for a quarter of a century, despite the prohibitions against partisan attachments by public servants' organizations that existed until 1970. In addition, the LSSP has enjoyed the regular support and assistance of several other unions, among the more prominent of which is the Government Clerical Service Union. The small LSSP(R) has cooperated closely with the powerful Ceylon Mercantile Union, headed by Bala Tampoe, the LSSP(R) general secretary. The CMU had staunchly followed the LSSP on political questions until 1964, when Tampoe left the party to join in founding the LSSP(R). Since 1964, the union has often been in conflict with the LSSP on labor and political questions.

Unions under Communist leadership were grouped in the Ceylon Trade Union Federation (CTUF) in 1940, and the federation continued under close party control until the CP schism of 1963, when the labor federation was captured by the Left Communists, led by the federation's general secretary. The regular Communists promptly formed a rival Ceylon Federation of Trade Unions and launched a counterattack intended to split the CTUF unions and win over their members. The campaign is generally believed to have succeeded in recapturing a large proportion of the rank-and-file members, but the organization and many of its officers and activists remained with the Left Communists.

A Joint Committee of Trade Union Organizations (JCTUO) was formed by the labor organizations aligned with the LSSP, CP, and MEP and several influential unaligned unions in 1963. When the LSSP entered the government the following year, the JCTUO was asked to suspend agitation on a series of labor demands. The call for restraint was bitterly assailed by the ex-Samasamajists who had recently formed the LSSP(R), the Left Communists, and some other trade unionists, and the ensuing battle demolished the JCTUO, ending the Ceylonese labor movement's most serious attempt at unity. At the end of 1965, the JCTUO was reassembled as a labor grouping clearly aligned with the SLFP-LSSP-CP United Front and including only the labor following of the three United

[36] N. Sanmugathasan, *How Can the Working Class Achieve Power?* (Colombo: Worker Publication, [1963]), p. 57.

Front parties. The organization sponsored a political strike in January 1966 protesting official language regulations proposed by the UNP-led national government then in power.

The Marxists gained some political benefits from their position in Ceylon's large and aggressive labor movement. Trade unions have served as party recruiting grounds and as mass organizations providing participants for rallies and demonstrations. To some extent, trade unions contribute to the election campaigns of their associated parties. After the 1965 election, the general secretary of the Communists' labor federation boasted that the federation and other labor organizations had "played our full part in furthering the progressive cause and ensuring the return of a large number of progressive candidates to the new Parliament." [37] Occasionally, trade unions are called upon to dramatize a party demand or protest by staging a one-day political strike. Political protest strikes were called by the LSSP in 1959, by the Left parties in 1962, and by the LSSP, CP, and SLFP in 1964 and 1966. A Left-sponsored hartal in 1953, called in protest against an action of the UNP government, resulted in widespread disorder, serious disruption of transportation and communication, and the loss of at least 10 lives. Many other strikes, such as a major public servants' strike in 1968, although not avowedly political, have had strong political implications. Influence in the labor movement has undoubtedly enhanced Marxist strength in bargaining with other parties and has expanded the Marxists' ability to influence the course of political events. The SLFP decision to bring the LSSP into a coalition government in 1964 was motivated, at least in part, by the desire to stem rising labor militancy by associating a party with strong labor backing in the government.

As the emphasis of the major Marxist parties has shifted to electoral and parliamentary affairs, some tendency to question the utility of trade unions as political instruments has appeared. A few Marxists have begun to question whether the time and effort invested in trade unionism could not better be utilized in activities more directly promoting the party's fortunes at the polls. Particularly after the 1965 defeat, when many workers apparently voted for the Marxists' opponents, some feeling was evident that the workers had "exploited" the Marxist parties by accepting the assistance of the party and its activists without in turn providing reliable political support. The young party militant, who a few decades ago

---

[37] M. G. Mendis, *Ceylon Federation of Trade Unions: Report of the General Secretary to the 17th Sessions* (Colombo: Ceylon Federation of Trade Unions, 1966), p. 4.

commonly sought to participate in trade union activities, today is reported more frequently to wish to contest a seat on a village or town council. Nonetheless, the deep and long-standing Marxist commitment to and entanglement in trade unionism seems unlikely to decline appreciably in the immediate future.

Marxist Tactics, Strategies, and Goals

The Ceylonese Marxists have evidenced little difficulty in determining their ultimate objectives. The "fundamental aims" of the LSSP were defined in 1950 to include "the overthrow of the Capitalist state" and the "seizure of political power by the working class at the head of the toiling masses." [38] The first CP constitution, adopted in 1944, declared the party's basic purpose was "to achieve a Socialist Ceylon which will establish common ownership of the national economy, end the exploitation of man by man and nationality by nationality, [and] eliminate class divisions in society." [39] Seldom, however, have the Marxists harbored serious expectations that their ultimate objectives were attainable in the near future. Beneath the consensus on eventual goals, the Marxists have long struggled with a series of ideological and tactical problems related to the attainment of fundamental goals. These problems have been more readily apparent and more vigorously debated within the LSSP than within the CP because of the more open and flexible character of the former party and its greater intellectual vitality and tactical autonomy. The CP seems to have been preoccupied for 20 years with a presumably short-run united-front strategy and to have devoted relatively little creative thought to more distant party objectives. Two questions have repeatedly appeared, producing vigorous intraparty debate and occasionally leading to party schisms in the LSSP. Each has been viewed by some party members as a question of immediate tactics and by others as a matter of fundamental ideological principle. The first concerns the attitude of the party toward elections, legislatures, and legislation as instruments for achieving ultimate party goals, including the party's attitude toward the role of revolution. The second involves the question of cooperation or alliance with other parties, Marxist and non-Marxist. To a major extent, the second follows from the first. If the Marxist parties wish to maximize their electoral successes, they must cooperate with each other and with the SLFP because they lack the strength to seek power alone.

[38] Lanka Sama Samaja Party, *Programme of Action, Adopted at the Unity Conference, June 4th, 1950* (Colombo: LSSP, 1950), p. 3.
[39] Quoted in *25 Years of the Ceylon Communist Party*, p. 13.

The Parliamentary Path to Power

Among the most persistent and fundamental questions the Ceylonese Marxists have faced is the selection of a road to power. The ultimate social and economic goals of the movement were of slight consequence without a clear notion of how to obtain power to implement objectives. Formed in the days when colonial rule inhibited confidence in elections and constitutional processes and motivated by a doctrine skeptical of the attainment of power without the use of force, the Marxist movement has gradually, and at times grudgingly, adjusted to the open and competitive political process that unfolded after Independence. In 1960, a Communist Party congress asserted:

The C.P. seeks to establish full democracy and socialism in Ceylon by peaceful means. It considers that by developing a mass movement, by winning a majority in Parliament and by backing this majority with mass sanctions, the working class and its allies can overcome the resistance of reaction and ensure that Parliament becomes an instrument of the people's will for bringing about fundamental changes in the economic, social and state structure.[40]

The LSSP long displayed uncertainty regarding the possibilities of achieving party objectives through elections and legislation. In 1950, the party proclaimed that its "fundamental aims cannot be realized through bourgeois parliaments. The inevitable resistance of the bourgeoisie to their achievement necessarily calls for mass revolutionary action as the only means of realizing the will of the majority." [41] However, over the next two decades, the party appeared to devote its principal efforts to election contests and the activities of Parliament and local government bodies. The election of 1956, which saw the rout of the UNP, identified by the Samasamajists as the party of the capitalist class, unquestionably sharpened awareness of the possibilities of election contests and led to reconsideration of the most suitable path to the party's goals. The 1964 decision to enter the coalition government with the SLFP represented the triumph of the view that through elections and control of Parliament substantial and worthwhile gains could be achieved. The party schism that accompanied the decision removed the doctrinaire Trotskyist wing of the party and significantly reduced the doctrinal inhibitions on acceptance of the electoral and parliamentary path to the party's goals. Shortly before the 1970 election, which swept the United Front to power, an unofficial Samasamajist journal noted "many instances in recent history of crucial

[40] *Draft Thesis for the 6th National Congress of the Ceylon Communist Party,* p. 52.
[41] LSSP, *Programme of Action,* p. 4.

mass issues arising in the parliamentary context," and declared, "Where parliamentary democracy exists and political parties are permitted to represent class and mass interests, it is foolish for any revolutionary to refuse to plunge himself into parliamentary battles." [42]

The differing attitudes toward elections and Parliament represented, in part, a generational cleavage within the party. The LSSP was formed a dozen years before Independence, when the scope for political action and the potentialities of elections and legislative chambers were untested. During the Second World War the party was proscribed and its leaders arrested or driven into hiding. Many older party members who experienced this period of repression and a fettered political process tended, for some years at least, to remain skeptical of the efficacy of electoral and parliamentary politics. However, the younger Samasamajists were recruited to politics in a period when electoral campaigns were being vigorously conducted from the local to the national level and when the capacity of elections to alter decisively the personnel and policies of government had been conclusively demonstrated. The fateful decision to enter the 1964 coalition with the SLFP, at the cost of a party schism and LSSP expulsion from the Fourth International, was reportedly backed strongly by the younger party members as constituting a fresh approach to party goals and an escape from the impasse in which the party seemed to have found itself.

While the role of revolution as a means to power has withered, Samasamajists have continued to accord to revolutionary action an important psychological function. Some form of mass revolutionary action is considered essential to overcome the alienation and apathy of the masses produced by capitalist society, in order to make possible the new human relationships and attitudes required for the new socialist order. After the LSSP entered the coalition government in 1964, party leader N. M. Perera remarked:

There may be those who will say that we have not at one fell stroke taken over all foreign and local capitalist property lock, stock, and barrel, forgetful of the mass upsurge that must accompany it. Such a mass upsurge must be generated by the heightened class consciousness of the toilers, born of the social inequalities and wrongs of the capitalist system. [43]

Following the United Front victory in 1970, the public's parochialism, impatience, and indiscipline shocked some Samasamajists into expres-

[42] "Editorial Notes," *Young Socialist* (Colombo), no. 21 (April 1970), 3.
[43] N. M. Perera, *Budget Speech, 1964–65* (Colombo: Government Press, 1964), p. 74.

sions of regret that the party had accepted a share of power and responsibility without an accompanying mass resurgence producing a popular sense of purpose, self-discipline, and solidarity.[44] The pro-LSSP newspaper *Nation* lamented editorially, "We need a revolutionary spirit, but we have no revolution!" [45]

Both the CP and the LSSP have been subjected to bitter criticism from the Left CP and the LSSP(R) for their growing concentration on parliamentary politics and alleged abandonment of the revolutionary path to power. In 1967, Left Communist N. Sanmugathasan charged:

The basic reason for the present degeneration of the bulk of the left movement was their departure from Marxism-Leninism and their capitulation to parliamentarism and to the theory of peaceful transition to socialism through parliamentary means, particularly after 1956.[46]

Shortly after the 1970 election, a Left CP statement complained that "a considerable section of our people have been drugged by the modern revisionists, the Trotskyites and all manner of reformists with the opium of bourgeois parliamentary democracy," but conceded that in rejecting parliamentary elections the Left Communists were "painfully aware that we are swimming upstream at the present moment, against the current." [47] The LSSP(R) similarly declined to contest the 1970 election with the assertion that "there is no other road forward for the masses than the revolutionary road." [48] Earlier, the LSSP(R) leader and trade unionist Bala Tampoe had denounced "political parties which seek to subordinate the interests of the working-class to their sectarian interests in the arenas of Parliamentary and Local Government politics, and to foster in the working-class the illusion that its interests can best be served through Parliament, rather than by the building up of its own organized strength outside Parliament." [49]

---

[44] Author's interviews in October 1970.

[45] *Nation* (Colombo), 20 October 1970, p. 7.

[46] N. Sanmugathasan, "The Left Movement Must Adopt Revolutionary Perspectives," *Red Flag* (Colombo), 29 June 1967, p. 3. *Red Flag* commenced publication in 1967 as a weekly newspaper of the Left Communists but in 1969 was converted into a journal, issued somewhat irregularly.

[47] "Win the Masses to the Revolutionary Path," *Red Flag* (Colombo), no. 4 (1970), 3.

[48] *The Way Forward for the Masses: Manifesto of the Lanka Sama Samaja Party (Revolutionary)* (Colombo: LSSP [R], 1970), p. 7.

[49] Ceylon Mercantile Union, *Tenth Delegates' Conference, 17th & 18th March 1969, General Secretary's Report & Conference Resolution* (Colombo: CMU, 1969), p. 4.

The United-Front Strategy

Questions of relations among the LSSP, CP, and SLFP have reappeared repeatedly for two decades. Over the years, conflict and rivalry have gradually given way to cooperation, leading to the coalescence of the three parties in a United Front based on a common program after 1965 and the sharing of governmental power since 1970. Collaboration originated in the imperatives of the intensely competitive politics of Ceylon and a shared hostility toward a common enemy, the UNP. Increasingly, the alliance has been reinforced by a convergence of objectives and outlooks, as the LSSP and CP have become more pragmatic and the SLFP has become more radical.

Mutual antagonism toward the UNP provided the incentive for the first collaboration among the Marxist parties and the SLFP. In 1956, the SLFP, LSSP, and CP joined in a "no contest" electoral agreement intended to avoid contesting the same constituencies and splitting the anti-UNP vote. The arrangement was repeated in the July 1960 election. Both times, the alliance contributed to the defeat of the UNP and secured control of the government for the SLFP or an SLFP-dominated coalition. After initially offering qualified support to the SLFP government formed in 1960, the Marxists became increasingly estranged from the SLFP following a series of clashes between the Marxist-led trade unions and the government. In 1963, the LSSP, CP, and MEP combined to form a short-lived United Left Front. Early the following year, SLFP leader Sirimavo Bandaranaike, faced with sagging parliamentary support, opened negotiations with the United Left Front parties on the formation of a coalition. When the talks stalled, largely because of conditions imposed by the MEP, the LSSP abruptly agreed to enter the coalition without its United Left Front partners. Although excluded from the coalition, the CP nonetheless offered its support to the SLFP-LSSP government. In the 1965 election, the CP was allied to the coalition parties by a "no contest" pact and the three parties conducted a joint campaign. Following the coalition's election defeat, the Communists were admitted as recognized members in a three-party United Front, although the CP remained the junior partner in the alliance, in part because of its small size and limited influence and in part because of lingering LSSP and SLFP skepticism of its flexibility and autonomy. In opposition for five years, the United Front parties functioned in a common parliamentary group, established a joint committee of party leaders to coordinate activities, and formulated a common program, which became the basis for the 1970 United Front election manifesto and the policies of the United Front government.

For many years, the Samasamajists and the Communists were divided by deep ideological and tactical differences. A Samasamajist leader in 1950 charged: "The C.P. actually holds that its *first task* today is to destroy Trotskyism! . . . It claims a monopoly of Leftism." [50] Communist authoritarianism and subservience to the Soviet Union were perennial targets of scathing Samasamajist criticism. The Communists, in turn, accused the LSSP of serving as a tool of reaction by attempting to divide the Left and isolate the CP.[51] Intensive rivalry in the labor movement and in election contests sharpened the hostility and distrust separating the two parties. Both, however, had long realized that disunity and rivalry had weakened the Left. By the 1960s the emotional and ideological barriers between the LSSP and CP had begun to erode. In 1960, the CP claimed that mutual confidence built through the 1956 and 1960 electoral cooperation, together with changes in the international Communist movement following the Twentieth Congress of the Soviet Communist Party in 1956, had significantly reduced the obstacles to collaboration between the two parties.[52] The Samasamajist leadership felt that the changes in Soviet communism and relaxation of Moscow's control over foreign Communist parties since 1956 had allowed the Ceylon CP to be more flexible and capable of adjustment to local circumstances, consequently facilitating LSSP-CP cooperation.[53]

The Soviet suppression of Czechoslovakia in 1968 momentarily reopened Samasamajist-Communist conflict over democracy in a "workers' state." In a letter to the Czechoslovak Communist Party on the eve of the Soviet occupation, Leslie Goonewardene wrote on behalf of the LSSP: "It has been the consistent view of the Lanka Sama Samaja Party that socialism and human freedom go together, and that the rule of the proletariat is entirely consonant with the fullest democracy. It is therefore with the greatest pleasure that we have observed the steps taken in Czechoslovakia in the direction of democratisation." [54] The move against Czechoslovakia produced a joint LSSP-SLFP statement condemning the

---

[50] Colvin R. de Silva, *Left Disunity—A Reply to a Critic* (Colombo: LSSP, 1950), p. 3 (emphasis in original).
[51] *Lanka's Way Forward: Political Resolution of the 5th Congress of the Ceylon Communist Party* (Colombo: CCP, 1955), p. 28.
[52] *Draft Thesis for the 6th National Congress of the Ceylon Communist Party*, pp. 56–58.
[53] Author's interviews with Leslie Goonewardene, 29 June 1965, and 3 August 1965. Samasamajist attitudes toward the post-1956 changes in the Soviet Union appear in Leslie Goonewardene, *The 50th Anniversary of the October Revolution* (Colombo: Samasamaja Publications, 1967), pp. 17–20.
[54] The text of the message is contained in V. Karalashingham, *Czechoslovakia (1968)* (Colombo: International Publishers, 1968), pp. 71–74.

action of the Soviet Union and its East European allies.[55] The Ceylon Communist Party did not join in the statement, virtually the only instance since 1965 of an open breach between the United Front partners. To the LSSP Central Committee, the Soviet action in Czechoslovakia constituted a vindication of long-standing Trotskyist attitudes on the "bureaucratic deformation of socialist states." [56]

The CP had long displayed a fear of isolation and persistently sought cooperation with other parties. Almost as soon as the SLFP was founded in 1951, the Communists identified it as the party of the "national bourgeoisie" and a potential ally against the "reactionary" and "compradore bourgeois" UNP. For 20 years, with very few lapses, the CP tenaciously sought alliance with the much larger and more influential SLFP. The CP has repeatedly expressed a marked preference for the foreign policy of the SLFP, based on nonalignment and including cordial relations with the Communist states, over the relatively pro-Western and anti-Communist posture of the UNP. Presumably, the Ceylonese Communists concluded that their immediate objectives were most likely to be attained through supporting and cooperating with the SLFP. A recent CP history maintained: "The conclusion of the SLFP-LSSP-CP United Front and the signing of the Common Programme represented an important victory for the line of the Communist Party and a significant defeat for anticommunism, which had always sought to isolate and exclude the Communist Party from the mainstream of the anti-imperialist and progressive forces." [57]

The 1964 decision for coalition with the SLFP had deep repercussions for the LSSP. The more determined opponents of the coalition left the party to form the LSSP(R), which not only drained away a number of the LSSP's activists but weakened its influence in the trade union movement. Although most of the "centrists" who favored a coalition only if the other Marxist parties were included had remained within the LSSP, their enthusiasm for the coalition was slight. Veteran leaders Leslie Goonewardene and Colvin R. de Silva declined cabinet appointments in the coalition government and Goonewardene briefly relinquished the post of party general secretary. Bernard Soysa momentarily withdrew from the party. By the following year, however, altered political circumstances had essentially satisfied the objections of the "centrist" leaders who had

[55] Ibid., p. 75.
[56] Ibid., p. 80.
[57] 25 Years of the Ceylon Communist Party, p. 108.

been defeated at the 1964 conference. The Communists had been admitted to the coalition and the MEP had deserted the Left by associating with the UNP. The interval in opposition after 1965 provided an opportunity for the SLFP-LSSP-CP United Front to be consolidated and a common program to be drafted. Many dissidents who had joined the LSSP(R) drifted back to the main party. Consequently, by 1970 the party was again bound together and was able to accept office with apparently unanimous concurrence.

At the inception of the 1964 coalition many Samasamajists apparently felt that, although the LSSP was allying itself with a larger and more popular party, the Samasamajists would be able to exercise disproportionate, perhaps decisive, influence in the coalition because of the LSSP's superior cohesion, clarity of purpose, and leadership talent. Bala Tampoe, an opponent of the coalition, later wrote: "The SLFP leadership was considered to be not only politically immature but also so weak that once the LSSP entered into a coalition with the SLFP, the political relationship of forces within the Coalition would be transformed to the political advantage of the LSSP." [58] During the next half dozen years, however, the LSSP attitude toward the alliance with the SLFP appears to have shifted, largely as a result of the increasing "radicalization" of the SLFP. After 1960, the more conservative wing of the SLFP suffered a steady attrition. In December 1964, a group of MPs, commonly identified as the SLFP right wing, abandoned the party, producing the defeat of the coalition government in Parliament and precipitating the 1965 election. Other defections further reduced the party's right wing, so that by the 1970 election the SLFP's center of gravity had shifted perceptibly to the left. In the same period, significant numbers of one-time Marxists appeared in the SLFP leadership and parliamentary contingent. Many other SLFP activists were considered to share most of the immediate social and political objectives of the Samasamajists. The SLFP, which earlier had claimed to be a "center" party poised between the Marxists on the left and the UNP on the right, began to identify a polarization of politics between "progressives" and "reactionaries." SLFP leader Sirimavo Bandaranaike asserted in 1967: "Our country has been divided into two main camps ever since the General Election of 1956: The camp of the people fighting to . . . modernize our society along socialist lines and the camp of the foreign

[58] Bala Tampoe, "Open Letter to the Members of the Lanka Sama Samaja Party from the Lanka Sama Samaja Party (Revolutionary)," mimeographed, Colombo, 9 August 1969, p. 7.

and local vested interests seeking to restore and reinforce the old colonial order." [59] SLFP spokesmen increasingly stressed the party's commitment to socialism and tended to adopt the rhetoric of the Marxists in their political pronouncements. By 1970, Samasamajist hopes for the United Front seemed dependent less on the LSSP's ability to influence or dominate the SLFP than on a belief that the two parties shared common objectives and purposes, at least in the short run.

The strategy of alliance with the SLFP required a Marxist adjustment to the demands and aspirations of a Sinhalese national resurgence, expressed largely in linguistic and religious terms, with which the SLFP was firmly identified. The political impact of the Sinhalese resurgence had appeared a decade earlier with demands, pioneered by the SLFP, that Sinhalese be made the sole official language. The official language issue arose primarily as a protest against the exclusive privilege of the English-speaking middle and upper classes, but developed into a communal contest between the Sinhalese-speaking majority and the Tamil-speaking minority. The Marxists eventually retreated from their early advocacy of both Sinhalese and Tamil as official languages, the Communists by 1960 and the Samasamajists in the 1963 United Left Front program and more unequivocally in the 1964 coalition agreement with the SLFP. In the aftermath of the 1965 election, the Marxists joined with the SLFP in attacks on the UNP-led national government for reliance on support by the minorities and concessions to Tamil language demands. Samasamajist proponents of the united-front strategy argued that the Sinhalese resurgence had galvanized the masses and created the genuine mass movement of the contemporary period. The movement expressed deeply felt popular aspirations and contained "progressive" features, particularly as it represented the class revolt of the Sinhalese-educated rural masses against the English-educated classes, as well as containing "reactionary" divisive and obscurantist features. In the existing circumstances, the Samasamajists claimed, the strength of the movement was so great that opposition to it was futile and progress was possible only by associating with it and guiding it into progressive channels. [60]

The United Front program called for the nationalization of banks and the import trade but not for the nationalization of the large tea and rubber estates that produce most of Ceylon's foreign exchange earnings. Among the LSSP contributions was the promise of elected employees'

[59] *Tribune* (Colombo), 7 May 1967, p. 9.
[60] Author's interviews with LSSP leaders in 1965 and 1967.

councils in public agencies and nationalized enterprises.[61] Samasamajists had long argued that nationalized enterprises could succeed only with "a revolutionary change in the attitude of the workers to their work," and that the involvement of employees in the management of the enterprises through employees' councils was necessary to overcome the workers' alienation and apathy.[62] On assuming office, LSSP minister of communications Leslie Goonewardene quickly established elected employees' councils in the Ceylon Transport Board, the island's largest nationalized industry. The program was, nonetheless, a product of compromises among several tendencies within the SLFP, between the SLFP and the LSSP, and to a lesser extent between the former two parties and the CP. The predominant LSSP view was probably expressed in a reply to Communist demands for the nationalization of estates shortly after the United Front came to power: "The Common Programme as every militant will realize is not so much a milestone as a spring board. . . . The implementation of the common programme will create those conditions which will enable the socialist forces to go forward to their goal." [63]

Dangers and Opportunities

The overwhelming United Front election victory of 1970 seemed to open to the Marxists unparalleled opportunities and to represent the zenith of Marxist political fortunes. The United Front came to power with prior agreement on a number of specific plans and intentions, allowing the Marxists to hope that within the following five years many of their immediate programmatic goals could be achieved and perhaps the foundation could be laid for the more fundamental reconstruction of society they seek. The challenge to the major Marxist parties posed by the splits of the early 1960s had receded with the steady erosion of the strength and influence of the LSSP(R) and the Left CP. With a share of power, however, came responsibility for the performance of the United Front government. The very dimensions of the United Front victory magnified popular expectations and increased the pressures for swift accomplishments. The United Front came to power promising to solve acute prob-

[61] For a People's Government: The Common Programme of the Sri Lanka Freedom Party, the Lanka Samasamaja Party and the Ceylon Communist Party (Colombo: leaflet, n.d.).

[62] Leslie Goonewardene, What We Stand For (Colombo: LSSP, 1959), p. 16.

[63] V. Karalasingham, "What Should Be Today's Slogans?" Ceylon Daily News, 2 September 1970, p. 6. The article was originally published in the LSSP newspaper Samasamājaya.

lems of unemployment and rising living costs, while maintaining an extraordinarily high level of social services and subsidies provided to the public. The Ceylonese voter appears to possess high aspirations and expectations, encouraged by the vigorous partisan competition for office, but the economic and administrative resources available to any government are severely limited. Governing parties have fallen from power in five consecutive elections. Public dissatisfaction with the government's performance and a loss of popular support by the United Front could obliterate the recent gains of the Marxists. Furthermore, the Marxists' share of power in the coalition was sharply limited. The United Front's parliamentary group consisted of 6 Communists, 19 Samasamajists, and 90 members of the SLFP. Without its Marxist allies, the SLFP held almost 60 percent of the seats in Parliament. Despite prior policy agreements and an apparently growing similarity of ideological outlook, the alliance was not free of internal tensions. Even after the decimation of its right wing, the SLFP remained a heterogeneous party, embracing a wide range of attitudes and including some elements clearly unsympathetic or indifferent toward the social reforms sought by the SLFP radicals as well as the Marxists. A renewal of tensions between the Communists and the Samasamajists appeared within a few months of the election. The stresses of governing could easily produce conflict among the allied parties. Any failure of the united-front strategy, after the high expectations engendered, would almost certainly have serious repercussions within the Marxist parties.

The LSSP decision to join with the SLFP in the pursuit of parliamentary power undoubtedly constituted one of the major turning points of the party's 35-year history. A major risk of the united-front strategy was that the Samasamajists might lose their unique identity and be submerged or enveloped by their much larger United Front partner. LSSP(R) leader Bala Tampoe, in an open letter to his former comrades of the LSSP, warned that through subordination to the SLFP in the alliance "the LSSP has lost its own distinctive Samasamajist character, and has assumed more and more a political character that is hardly distinguishable from that of the SLFP." [64] The LSSP unquestionably faces a difficult task in maintaining a separate identity that is sufficiently distinctive and appealing to prevent its activists and supporters from gravitating toward the larger and more influential SLFP. Some former LSSP members and sympathizers have already shifted their loyalty to the senior partner of the United Front. Nonetheless, before the LSSP opted for the alliance, it

[64] Tampoe, "Open Letter to the Members of the Lanka Sama Samaja Party from the Lanka Sama Samaja Party (Revolutionary)," p. 7.

faced the equally debilitating problem of appearing to be a perpetual opposition party with no prospect of exercising governmental power. Its repeated frustrations and stagnating electoral fortunes created a crisis of loyalty and purpose for all but the most dedicated Samasamajist core. Through the united-front strategy, the party was able to rejuvenate itself, at least temporarily, with a new hope and sense of direction.

The Insurrectionary Challenge
The abrupt eruption of insurrectionary violence in April 1971 staggered the entire island and threw the Left movement into turmoil and confusion. The rebels were largely youths between 16 and 25 years of age, almost entirely Sinhalese, mostly of village backgrounds, and included a number of girls. Their arms consisted primarily of shotguns and homemade bombs. On the night of 5 April, the insurgents launched simultaneous raids on police stations across the island and reportedly planned an attempt to kidnap or assassinate the prime minister in what Sirimavo Bandaranaike described as "a carefully prepared plan to seize Governmental power in a single day." [65] The authorities had been alerted by a raid on the American Embassy a month earlier, the discovery of caches of explosives, and a premature attack on a police station a day before the general uprising. A state of emergency had been in force since 16 March. It seems unlikely that the insurgent plan, which appeared to rely heavily on surprise, had any reasonable prospect of success. When the attack failed on the first night it was almost certainly doomed. Nonetheless, heavy fighting occurred at scattered points for several weeks and mop-up operations in the heavily forested hill country continued for three months. About 14,000 persons had surrendered or been arrested by July. The prime minister's estimate in July put the death toll at about 1,200, of which 60 fatalities were suffered by the military and police.[66] Unofficial but informed estimates, however, generally placed the figure at 6,000 or more.

The Janatha Vimukthi Peramuna was credited with launching the insurrection. JVP spokesmen claimed the organization had existed since 1964, although it first appeared in public view in 1970, when JVP activists supported the United Front parties in the election campaign. Members of the youth leagues of most major parties were thought to have been

---

[65] "Text of Broadcast to the Nation by the Hon. Sirimavo Bandaranaike, Prime Minister, on April 24, 1971," mimeographed, Department of Information press release, 24 April 1971, p. 1.
[66] "The Statement on Insurgency Made in Parliament on 20.7.71 by the Honourable Prime Minister," mimeographed, Department of Information press release, n.d., p. 5.

involved, but a major portion of the insurgents could not be clearly identified with any of the established parties. The movement seems to have gained inspiration from Guevarist and Maoist ideas on the role of violent revolution and reliance on a rural base, but its ideological perspective did not appear to be clearly articulated or carefully developed. The self-professed head of the JVP, who was under detention at the time of the uprising, claimed to have been dropped from Lumumba University in Moscow, apparently for espousing Maoist positions. Combined with "ultrarevolutionary" slogans was a strand of narrow Sinhalese nationalism and hostility toward India, perhaps reflecting the parochial, Sinhalese village background of its members. A series of five indoctrination lectures given JVP recruits reportedly contained sharp criticism of the older Marxist parties, hostility and distrust toward India, and a reliance on small-scale agriculture to solve the nation's economic problems.

Much speculation centered on possible foreign instigation or involvement. Shortly after the uprising, the North Korean Embassy, which had been opened only after the 1970 United Front election victory, was closed and its entire staff was ordered from the country. According to Mrs. Bandaranaike, the North Koreans had been told "that the effect of certain activities carried on by them was giving strength and support to these terrorists" and when they persisted in these activities they were told to leave the country.[67] The objectionable activities were not specified but probably included the dissemination of revolutionary propaganda. The Ceylon government, nonetheless, persistently refused to accuse the North Koreans or any other foreign power of complicity in the insurrection. Various sections of the Ceylonese political spectrum held that North Korea, China, the Soviet Union, or the American CIA were behind the uprising. In response to its appeals, the Ceylon government received arms and supplies from India, Pakistan, the United States, the Soviet Union, Britain, Yugoslavia, and Egypt.

The insurgents presumably hoped to topple the government by a single swift stroke of violence. Their further expectations remain shrouded in uncertainty. Ceylon had evolved one of the most vigorous and widely accepted parliamentary democracies in Asia. The island had experienced a relatively low level of political violence and serious challenges to the constitutional order had been impressively few. The United Front government, the most radical government ever in power in Ceylon, had been installed less than a year earlier with an overwhelming popular endorse-

[67] "Text of Broadcast to the Nation by the Hon. Sirimavo Bandaranaike, Prime Minister, on April 24, 1971," p. 3.

ment and effectively controlled the police, the armed forces, and the civil administration. Possible explanations for the insurrection included claims that the insurgents expected substantial foreign assistance once they had thrown the island into confusion, that the rebels' outlook was essentially nihilistic and their objective was only to destroy the existing order in the expectation that a new social and political order would spontaneously emerge from the holocaust, and that the insurgents were so politically unsophisticated that they did not realize the obstacles to their seizure and retention of power. An additional hypothesis is that the insurgents expected a UNP victory in the 1970 election and they anticipated some support or at least acquiescence among opposition groups including the conventional Left parties and the trade unions. The United Front victory stifled this hope, but by the time of the election the insurrectionary movement had become the prisoner of the drama and excitement it had generated. The leaders had become hypnotized by their own dreams of destiny and power and were unwilling to abandon their plan simply because it had little prospect of success.

A legend of heroism and martyrdom quickly sprang up around the insurgency, enveloping many who were unsympathetic with the insurgents' goals and repelled by their tactics. It is possible that the perpetuation of the heroic legend, extolling the courage and daring of the insurgents, with uncertain implications for the political system, may be among the most important legacies of the April uprising.

The most commonly cited factor behind the insurgency was soaring unemployment among educated youths. An educational explosion had by 1971 produced a flood of young people with secondary or university educations, largely in the Sinhalese language and in the humanities, most of whom aspired to posts as school teachers or public servants. Between 1960 and 1970, the number of university degrees awarded annually increased more than sevenfold.[68] A similar explosion had occurred in secondary education. Employment opportunities, however, markedly failed to keep pace with the expanding output of the island's schools. In 1969–1970, unemployment among youths aged 15–24 with secondary education stood at 70 percent.[69] Restlessness and frustration leading to anomic protest had been increasingly evident among youths for several

[68] Ceylon, Department of Census and Statistics, *Statistical Abstract of Ceylon, 1964* (Colombo: Government Press, 1965), p. 340; Ceylon, Department of Census and Statistics, *Statistical Pocket Book of Ceylon, 1970* (Colombo: Department of Government Printing, 1970), p. 51.
[69] *Matching Employment Opportunities and Expectations: A Programme of Action for Ceylon* (Geneva: International Labour Office, 1971), vol. 1, pp. 3–4.

years. The insurgents seem commonly to have come from the educated village youth. Although government spokesmen have claimed that most of the captured insurgents were, in fact, employed, many may have held jobs they considered unsuitable, and the alienation and frustration of the army of unemployed youths may have been transmitted to their employed peers. The educational explosion also opened a wide generational gap between the educated village youths and their uneducated parents and elders, weakening family control and possibly undermining respect for authority and confidence in the existing social order. Yet, despite thwarted aspirations, the plight of youth did not approach despair. The village youth was not faced with privation or repression and indeed benefited from the high level of social services provided by the State. In certain districts, the insurgents were primarily youths from depressed castes of low traditional status, implying the compounding of frustrations among youths of low caste whose horizons had been widened and whose hopes had been stimulated by education but who remained trapped in the caste-conscious village, unable to obtain esteemed white-collar employment or to escape to an urban job. Across the island, however, no clear caste pattern was discernible. At least half of the suspected insurgents in detention were said to be members of the Goyigama caste.

The insurgency was a painful experience for the parties of the conventional Left. The Samasamajists and the Communists found themselves participating in a government that was required to rely on military force to crush a professed radical movement. The agony of the LSSP is suggested by the fact that one member of the party's parliamentary group was the only MP arrested in connection with the insurrection, and another was gravely wounded by rebel bullets while participating in a military expedition against the insurgents. Although the armed challenge failed and the JVP may have been obliterated, the insurrection highlighted the alienation of youth, which probably extends well beyond the ranks of the JVP, and the estrangement of a new generation of young radicals from the established Marxist parties. The Sinhalese-educated village youths are separated by stark differences in background, perspective, and style of living, as well as in age, from the urbane, Westernized intellectuals who have led the Marxist parties for three decades. Prior to the insurrection, the veteran Marxists tended to view the new radicalism as simply a temporary product of unemployment and a reflection of the worldwide restlessness and narcissism of youth. After years of sagging hopes and dwindling prospects, the major Marxist parties had accommodated themselves to parliamentary politics and had reached a peak of power and influence, only to collide with a new generation of alienated village youth. The future of the established parties of the Left may be determined by their capacity to contain the new restless radicalism of youth or to remove the frustrations behind it.

Over the past two decades, the major Ceylonese Marxist parties appear to have become progressively more domesticated and pragmatic. The growing commitment to the parliamentary path to power has forced them to adjust to the immediate practical realities of competitive election struggles and perhaps to dilute or abandon long-cherished dogma. The strategy of alliance with a non-Marxist party for electoral advantage and the capture of Parliament reflects the growing pragmatism and a realization that in the Ceylonese political environment the attainment of power means effective participation in election contests. With the domestication of the Marxists came a legitimization of the Marxist parties, programs, and perspectives, and a shift to the left of the entire Ceylonese political spectrum. Although they have never commanded massive popular backing, the Marxists have retained a core of support that has allowed them to participate vigorously in parliamentary and electoral maneuvers. The high intellectual level of its leadership and the energy and dedication of its activists have allowed the LSSP to wield an influence in politics far greater than would be suggested by the proportion of popular votes its candidates receive. The United Front victory of 1970 brought the Marxists a share of power, accompanied by both perils and opportunities. They could anticipate the realization of many of their social and political objectives, but they faced the risk of losing their distinctive political identity in the shadow of their larger coalition partner and the threat of increasing isolation from the new generation of village youth. There is little doubt but that the events of 1970–1971 will leave a deep imprint on the Marxist parties of Ceylon.

Name Index

Subject Index